NEUROPHYSIOLOGICAL AND NEUROPSYCHOLOGICAL ASPECTS OF SPATIAL NEGLECT

ADVANCES IN PSYCHOLOGY
45

Editors

G. E. STELMACH

P. A. VROON

NORTH-HOLLAND
AMSTERDAM · NEW YORK · OXFORD · TOKYO

NEUROPHYSIOLOGICAL AND NEUROPSYCHOLOGICAL ASPECTS OF SPATIAL NEGLECT

Edited by

Marc JEANNEROD
Laboratoire de Neuropsychologie Expérimentale
INSERM U 94
and
Université Claude Bernard
Lyon, France

1987

NORTH-HOLLAND
AMSTERDAM · NEW YORK · OXFORD · TOKYO

ISBN: 0 444 70193 1

Publishers:
ELSEVIER SCIENCE PUBLISHERS B.V.
P.O. Box 1991
1000 BZ Amsterdam
The Netherlands

Sole distributors for the U.S.A. and Canada:
ELSEVIER SCIENCE PUBLISHING COMPANY, INC.
52 Vanderbilt Avenue
New York, N.Y. 10017
U.S.A.

Library of Congress Cataloging-in-Publication Data

Neurophysiological and neuropsychological aspects
    of spatial neglect.

    (Advances in psychology ; 45)
    Bibliography: p.
    Includes index.
    1. Perception, Disorders of. 2. Space perception.
3. Spatial behavior. I. Jeannerod, Marc. II. Title:
Spatial neglect. III. Series: Advances in psychology
(Amsterdam, Netherlands) ; 45.
RC382.2.N48 1987   616.8   86-32994
ISBN 0-444-70193-1

PRINTED IN THE NETHERLANDS

To the memory of
Jeffrey D. Holtzman (1951–1985)

NEW ISSUES IN SPATIAL NEGLECT

Marc Jeannerod

Spatial neglect is one of the few areas in Neuropsychology where clinicians, psychologists and animal exprimenters have succeeded in adopting a common language, with the happy consequence of fruitful interactions between the three approaches of this striking phenomenon. Important new developments have resulted, which in turn justify the publication of the present book. To my knowledge, no monograph or multiauthored book fully devoted to this problem has appeared since Weinstein and Friedland (1977) and DeRenzi (1982).

Recent advances in Neuropsychology and Neurophysiology which have influenced the understanding of spatial neglect can be summarized under three main headings.

1. Space is a construct. The spatial field has long been considered as coextensive to the visual field, a misconception which originated in the clinical use of testing neglect by imposing fixation of patient's gaze on the observer while responses to stimuli presented in each half-field were explored.

The new experimental paradigms clearly dissociate the retinotopic map from the body-centered map of space, where object positions are encoded with respect to a body reference. Action-related signals, and not only sensory signals, are thought to participate in the construction of the spatial map.

The nature of these action-related signals, the brain areas where the spatial map might be elaborated, the way normal or brain-damaged subjects perceive their body coordinates are among the lines of research suggested by the phenomenon of spatial neglect.

2. Input-output transformation is not direct. Constraints on spatial behavior in higher vertebrates impose that a map or representation of extrapersonal space must be built before actions can be properly oriented. The notion of representation, once considered as a useful metaphor in cognitive psychology, is progressively gaining respectability among neuroscientists.

Simple psychological techniques, like the classical reaction time measurement, can be used for probing representations. Specific experimental situations, like those involving presentation of stimuli limited to one hemisphere, or those involving cueing of certain aspects of the stimuli, allow precise inference on the mental content.

Spatial neglect offers a paradigm for testing the relationship of spatial representation to brain function, and specially to hemispheric specialization.

3. Attention is a distributed function. Coupling between input and output is influenced by attentional mechanisms. The concept of attention, however, has evolued from that of a supraordinate function controlled by a single brain center, to that of a selective mechanism operating at the

sensorimotor level in each modality. This conceptual change owes much to animal experiments showing different neuronal responses to sensory stimuli when these responses are goals for action.

Human experiments have led to similar conclusions in showing that intention to orient is sufficient for shifting attention, hence dissociating the attentional component for the motor component of goal-directed responses. Spatial neglect may represent a critical condition for assessing hemispheric specialization for directing attention to various regions of space.

This book emphasizes these new issues in normal subjects, in patients with spatial neglect and in animal models.

References

DeRenzi, E. Disorders of space exploration and cognition. J. Wiley, New York, 1982.

Weinstein, E.A. & Friedland, R.P. (Eds.). Hemi-inattention and hemisphere specialization. <u>Advances in Neurology</u>, <u>vol. 18</u>, 1977, Raven Press, New York.

Acknowledgements

Most of the manuscript of this book was diligently typed by M. Rouvière.

TABLE OF CONTENTS

LIST OF CONTRIBUTORS

C.M. Butter

Department of Psychology
The University of Michigan
Neuroscience Laboratory Building
1103 East Huron
Ann Arbor, Michigan 48104-1687
U.S.A.

A. Berti

Università di Milano
Istituto di Clinica Neurologica
Via F. Sforza, N. 35
20122 Milano
ITALY

B. Biguer

Laboratoire de Neuropsychologie Expérimentale
INSERM Unité 94
16 avenue du Doyen Lépine
69500 Bron
FRANCE

E. Bisiach

Università di Milano
Istituto di Clinica Neurologica
Via F. Sforza, N. 35
20122 Milano
ITALY

D. Bowers

Department of Neurology
J. Hillis Miller Health Center
University of Florida
College of Medicine
Gainesville, 32610
U.S.A.

J.L. Bradshaw

Department of Psychology
Monash University
Clayton Victoria
Australia 3168
AUSTRALIA

R. Camarda

Istituto di Fisiologia Umana
Università di Parma
Facoltà di Medicina e Chirurgia
Via A. Gramsci, 14
43100 Parma
ITALY

S. Copland

Department of Psychology
Mount Sinaï Hospital
600 University Avenue
Toronto, Ontario M5G 1X5
CANADA

R.K. Deuel

Department of Pediatrics and Neurology
St. Louis Children's Hospital
400 South Kingshighway Building
Saint-Louis, Missouri 63110
U.S.A.

M.S. Gazzaniga

Division of Cognitive Neuroscience
Department of Neurology
Cornell University Medical College
New York, New York, 10021
U.S.A.

K.M. Heilman

Department of Neurology
J. Hillis Miller Health Center
University of Florida
College of Medicine
Gainesville, 32610
U.S.A.

G.W. Humphreys

Department of Psychology
University of London
Birkbeck College
Malet Street
London, WC1E 7HX
ENGLAND

M. Jeannerod

Laboratoire de Neuropsychologie Expérimentale
INSERM Unité 94
16 avenue du Doyen Lépine
69500 Bron
FRANCE

M. Kinsbourne

Department of Behavioral Neurology
Shriver Center
200 Trapelo Road
Waltham, Mass. 02554
U.S.A.

E. Ladavas

Department of Psychology
University of Bologna
Viale Berti Pichat 5
Bologna
ITALY

A.D. Milner

University of St. Andrews
Psychological Laboratory
St. Andrews, Fife KY16 9JU
SCOTLAND

M. Moscovitch

Department of Psychology
Erindale College
University of Toronto
Toronto, Ontario M5S 1A1
CANADA

G. Nathan

Department of Psychology
Monash University
Clayton Victoria
Australia 3168
AUSTRALIA

N.C. Nettleton

Department of Psychology
Monash University
Clayton Victoria
Australia 3168
AUSTRALIA

J.A. Ogden

Department of Psychology
University of Auckland
Private Bag
Auckland
NEW ZEALAND

D. Perani

Istituto di Clinica Neurologica
Università di Milano
Via F. Sforza, N.35
20122 MILANO
ITALY

J.M. Pierson

Department of Psychology
Monash University
Clayton Victoria
Australia 3168
AUSTRALIA

P. Reuter-Lorenz

Department of Psychology
University of Toronto
Toronto, Ontario M5S 1A1
CANADA

M.J. Riddoch

Department of Psychology
University of London
Birkbeck College
Malet Street
London, WC1E 7HX
ENGLAND

G. Rizzolatti

Istituto di Fisiologia Umana
Università di Parma
Facoltà di Medicina e Chirurgia
Via A. Gramsci, 14
43100 Parma
ITALY

E.A. Roy

Mount Sinaï Hospital
600 University Avenue
Toronto, Ontario M5G 1X5
CANADA

L.G. Roy   Department of Kinesiology
                        University of Waterloo
                        Waterloo, Ontario N2L 3G1
                        CANADA

G. Vallar   Istituto di Clinica Neurologica
                        Università di Milano
                        Via F. Sforza, N.35
                        20122 MILANO
                        ITALY

E. Valenstein   Department of Neurology
                        J. Hillis Miller Health Center
                        University of Florida
                        College of Medicine
                        Gainesville, 32610
                        U.S.A.

R.T. Watson   Department of Neurology
                        J. Hillis Miller Health Center
                        University of Florida
                        College of Medicine
                        Gainesville, 32610
                        U.S.A.

L.E. Wilson   Department of Psychology
                        Monash University
                        Clayton Victoria
                        Australia 3168
                        AUSTRALIA

Neurophysiological and Neuropsychological Aspects
of Spatial Neglect, M. Jeannerod (editor)
© Elsevier Science Publishers B.V. (North-Holland), 1987

VARIETIES OF ATTENTION AND DISTURBANCES OF ATTENTION:
A NEUROPSYCHOLOGICAL ANALYSIS

Charles M. Butter

It is proposed that an understanding of neglect as a disorder of attention may be facilitated by an analysis of the various ways in which attention is manifested, on the basis of which a model of various forms of attention can be formulated and related to brain processes. Following William James, reflex attention is distinguished from voluntary attention; the former is stimulus-controlled and involves primarily "bottom-up" processing, whereas the latter is controlled by the central activation of stored representations (James' "preparation from within") and thus involves "top-down" as well as "bottom-up" processing. Several forms of voluntary attention are distinguished on the basis of differences in the processes involved in central activation. A model that incorporates reflex and voluntary attention is presented; according to the model, mechanisms of voluntary attention are "added on" to those of reflex attention and control the latter in a hierarchical manner. It is proposed on the basis of various neurophysiological and neurobehavioral findings that different neural structures control different processes that are incorporated in the model. The implications of the model for the analysis of neglect and other disturbances of attention are discussed.

Introduction

In order to understand hemispatial neglect, it is necessary to identify the processes whose disturbance results in this disorder and to understand how these processes function in intact organisms. With regard to the first problem, it is generally, although not universally, agreed that hemispatial neglect is due to a disturbance of attention (e.g., Critchley, 1966; Heilman, Watson & Valenstein, 1985). Attention, according to these investigators and those who study it in intact animals and humans, is a central process that selectively facilitates particular sensory or motor processes (Kahneman, 1973). Attention by this view selects or amplifies sensory messages and/or motor commands for movement.

Admittedly, much of the evidence favoring the view that attentional disorders are responsible for hemispatial neglect is negative. Neglect in animals and humans can be dissociated from both sensory and motor deficits. Monkeys with unilateral neglect show cortical evoked potentials to external stimuli from the neglected side of space (Watson, Miller & Heilman, 1977; Nakamura and Mishkin, 1980). Furthermore, neglect appears after unilateral lesions of cortical polysensory areas far removed from primary sensory or motor areas of the cortex (Butter, in press). The finding that hemispatial neglect can be demonstrated when the ignored sensory input is lateralized not in physical space but in mental representational space (see Bisiach &

Berti, this volume) also underscores the nonsensory nature of the deficit. One might argue that a selective deficit in responding to a stimulus contralateral to a brain lesion when an ipsilateral stimulus is simultaneously presented, i.e., sensory extinction, constitutes positive evidence for an attentional loss, especially if there is no deficit in responding to the same contralateral stimulus when it is presented alone. However, findings that extinction can be demonstrated after sensory tract lesions (Bender, 1952) leads one to suspect that it may be a consequence of sensory as well as attentional disturbances.

The scarcity of positive evidence for an attentional loss underlying neglect is in part due to a paucity of studies in which patients or animals with neglect have been tested in situations where spatial attention has been manipulated independently of sensory and motor factors. An example of such a study is one in which patients with right parietal lesions (which are frequently accompanied by left hemispatial neglect) were impaired in disengaging their attention from a visual cue presented either centrally or in the right hemifield, in order to direct it to a stimulus presented in the left hemifield (Posner, Walker, Friedrich & Rafal, 1984).

It has been pointed out (e.g., De Renzi, 1982; Butter, in press) that whereas compensation for a restricted sensory loss is frequently observed in patients, these compensatory movements are strikingly absent in neglect. Thus, patients with neglect are severely deficient in exploring the affected half of space when they are instructed to search for a target (Chédru, Leblanc & Lhermitte, 1973; Chain, Chédru, Leblanc & Lhermitte, 1972). This failure to compensate for the deficit is the tell-tale sign that a system responsible not only for attending to one-half of space, but also for exploring and investigating it, is disturbed.

Whereas it is generally agreed that neglect is due to an attentional disorder, there have been few attempts to understand neglect in terms of the various ways in which attention is used in everyday life and in laboratory tasks. The goals of the present chapter are : (a) to describe several ways in which attention is used and to present simple models of the processes involved in each use ; (b) to present evidence concerning the neural structures that may control these processes ; and (c) to discuss the implications of these ideas for the analysis of neglect.

A Taxonomy of Selective Attentional Functions

Selective attention is manifested in several ways, each of which has a particular functional significance. A basic distinction in the taxonomy of attention - "reflex" vs. "voluntary" attention - was suggested by William James (1890). Reflex attention is triggered by stimuli with particular physical characteristics (described below); the recency and frequency with which the stimulus (or similar stimuli) has occurred also determine the degree to which it captures our attention. The term "reflex attention" underscores the involuntary and immediate character of this form of attention, which is controlled by stimuli that are sudden, intense, of high contrast or moving. James (1890) noted that reflex attention is also elicited by an "instinctive stimulus", one that "by reason of its nature...appeals to some one of our normal congenital impulses" (1890, p. 417). Another important characteristic of stimuli (other than "instinctive" ones) eliciting reflex attention is novelty: stimuli that are frequently repeated often fail to elicit attention, even if they have the appropriate physical characteristics. In addition, the degree to which attention is directed to a stimulus may also depend on stimulus complexity and incongruity (Berlyne, 1960). One important consequence of reflex attention directed toward stimuli with these properties is that the stimuli briefly acquire perceptual salience, or, in James' terms, "clearness" and "distinction from other things and subdivision".

Reflex attention is frequently accompanied by the orienting reflex (Sokoloff, 1963), which includes behaviors that orient the receptors to the stimulus source and thus enhance sensory information. Like reflex attention, orienting responses are triggered by novel stimuli and habituate to repeated presentation of the same stimuli. Overt orienting reactions to stimuli are temporarily linked to attentional shifts directed to the same stimuli, so that their salience is increased. Thus, programming the eyes to move to a target enhances the target's detection (Remington, 1980; Singer, Zihl and Pöppel, 1977) and its identification, if the target is a pattern (Crovitz and Daves, 1962; Bryden, 1961). Overt orienting to stimuli may also be accompanied by other exploratory-investigatory responses including reaching for, grasping and manipulating objects.

These characteristics of reflex attention to visual stimuli are diagrammatically illustrated in Figure 1. According to this model, stimuli are processed in two separate channels. One channel analyzes specific stimulus features, such as color and borders, that are necessary for recognition. The other channel conveys sensory responses to a mechanism that detects novel stimuli and increases their salience. This system also facilitates alerting systems so that the sensory representation of the stimulus is enhanced. By its connections with the alerting systems, the novelty-salience mechanism also activates the system that organizes exploratory-investigatory behaviors directed to the stimulus. The novelty-salience mechanism also commands orienting movements that direct the sense organs to the stimulus. Furthermore, as shown in Figure 1, it is assumed that a short-term central representation of the stimulus is responsible for both a decrement in stimulus salience and habituation of orienting responses with repeated stimulus presentations.

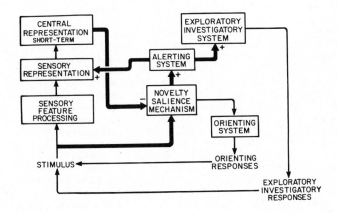

Figure 1
Processes involved in reflex attention to novel stimuli. Thick arrows refer to central effects of novel stimuli.

Whereas reflex attention is controlled primarily by the physical characteristics and novelty of the eliciting stimuli, it is suggested here that voluntary attention involves the central activation of stored representations of stimuli. Unlike reflex attention, which is primarily controlled by bottom-up processing of external stimuli, voluntary attention involves top-down as well as bottom-up processing. Here again, James' description of attentional states (James, 1890) provides clues to the underlying mental processes. As James observed, the effort to attend, for example, to the peripheral region of a picture is "nothing more or less than the effort to form as clear an idea as possible of what is there portrayed" (1890, p. 438). For James, voluntary attention to a peripheral stimulus is equivalent to "anticipatory preparation from within of the ideational centres concerned with the object to which attention is payed" (1890, p. 434). In keeping with James' analysis, it is proposed that voluntary attention involves both the peripheral and central (James' "preparation from within") activation of permanently stored representations of familiar objects (see Figure 2). These stored representations are activated peripherally by the appropriate (i.e., matching) sensory inputs. Recognition occurs when the appropriate matching sensory input activates its central representation to a critical level. Whereas input from the matching stimulus alone may be sufficient to activate the stored representation to its recognition threshold, it is assumed that central activation of the representation by an instruction (external or self-generated) or another stored representation increases the liklihood that the recognition threshold is attained. The model also assumes that activation of a stored representation to the recognition threshold enhances the perceptual salience of the stimulus by facilitating its sensory representation. Thus, voluntary attention in this model refers to the central facilitation of recognition and of perceptual salience. The assumption that central activation of a stored representation of a stimulus by an instruction (either to attend to or expect the stimulus) enhances its perceptual salience is supported by the finding that attention to a stimulus enhances sensitivity (d') for that stimulus (e.g., Broadbent and Gregory, 1963; Moray and O'Brien, 1967; Treisman and Geffen, 1967). Furthermore, it is assumed that centrally activated stored representations in turn activate the novelty-salience mechanisms that control orienting responses and facilitate the alerting system.

In one variety of selective attention, the central facilitation of the stored representation is provided by an instruction, either self-generated or from an external source, to detect the occurrence of a stimulus or to search for it. The instruction in turn may be controlled by or be part of a plan to carry out a sequence of goal-directed actions. In visual search, an increase in perceptual salience is manifested as the tendency of the target to "pop out", a phenomenon reported by well-practiced subjects in visual search tasks (e.g., Neisser, 1963). The model predicts that distractors sharing features of the target in a search task would be more likely than distractors not sharing the target's features to activate the target's central representation to its recognition threshold. This inappropriate activation would be expected to result not only in false recognition, but also in inappropriate activation of search mechanisms (e.g., those controlling head and eye movements), thus slowing down search. The predicted increase in search time in tasks where distractors share features with the target has been experimentally confirmed (Treisman & Gelade, 1980).

If central activation of the stored representation of stimulus by a search instruction enhances recongition of the stimulus, it should be

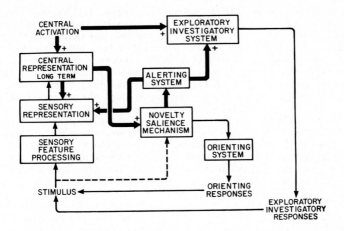

Figure 2
Processes involved in voluntary attention, involving "top-down", or central activation of a stored representation. Thick arrows refer to central activating effects; interrupted arrow refers to reduced effect or lack of effect of meaningful familiar stimuli on the novelty-salience mechanism.

possible to demonstrate an effect of searching for a particular target on its recognition. This prediction was tested in a situation where subjects searched for a visual target in an array of identical distractor items (Goodale & Butter, 1985). Interspersed among the search trials was a probe recognition task in which a pair of stimuli was briefly presented; on these probe trials, the subjects indicated whether the two stimuli were the same or different. When presented with a pair of stimuli both of which were the target item, the subjects made fewer recognition errors than they did when presented with a pair of distractor items. In addition, as predicted by the model, the subjects made more recognition errors when presented with stimulus pairs consisting of a "hybrid" (a stimulus containing all the features of the target and of the distractor) and the target than they did when presented with stimulus pairs consisting of the same hybrid and a distractor. Furthermore, these effects of the search task on recognition were also found when roles of target and distractor were reversed in a subsequent test: thus, they were independent of the particular features of the target and distractors.

Another way in which voluntary attention operates is by selecting a stimulus event for recognition (and perceptual salience) because it has intrinsic, permanent value in contrast to the example described above, in which selection occurs as the result of a transient instruction. Examples of stimuli of intrinsic value are the sound of one's name, which has attentional value in dichotic listening tasks (Moray, 1959). Treisman (1960) assumed that such stimuli are readily recognized and perceptually salient because the activation thresholds of their central representations are permanently lowered relative to those of other stimuli. A similar assumption may be made in the present model: As a consequence of its lowered recognition threshold, the stored representation of a stimulus with intrinsic value, compared to that of a stimulus without intrinsic value, is more likely to be recognized and produce the downstream facilitating effects shown in Figure 2 when the appropriate stimulus is presented.

The above example of attention directed to one's name is also an example of attention directed to stimuli of derived or "remote interest", to use James' term. A stimulus may acquire remote interest because it has been associated with a stimulus of intrinsic interest, which itself may be acquired or have an inherited component, as in the case of stimuli relevant to biological drives. The model presented here can accomodate this kind of voluntary attention by adding learned connections from the central representation of the stimulus of remote interest ("food's ready!") to the central representation of the stimulus with which it has been associated (food on the table), which in turn activates the novelty-salience mechanism. The resulting activation of the alerting systems then facilitates the sensory representation of the stimulus ("food's ready!") (see Figure 3). Thus, in this case, unlike the ones above, central activation of a central representation is indirectly provided by another central representation.

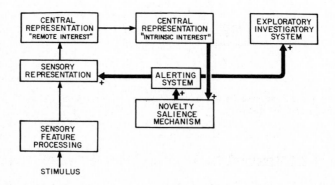

Figure 3
Processes involved in voluntary attention based upon a stimulus of "remote interest" that has become associated with a stimulus of intrinsic interest. Thick arrows refer to central activating effect. Effects of stimulus of remote interest on the novelty-salience mechanism, as in Figure 2, are assumed to be weak or absent. Orienting and exploratory-investigatory responses are assumed to be activated as in Figure 2.

A form of voluntary attention different from those described above involves attention directed to a representation in the stimulus domain in the absence of the appropriate stimulus – in other words, attention directed to a mental image of a familiar stimulus. In this case, an instruction, e.g., to form an image of an apple, facilitates the appropriate central representation which then activates the sensory representation of an apple (see Figure 4). Moreover, visual images can be not only passively inspected; they can also be mentally manipulated – that is, transformed with regard to egocentric viewpoint (e.g., rotated, brought up close and enlarged, or viewed from a long distance; Kosslyn, 1980).

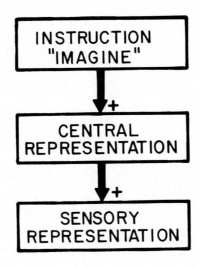

Figure 4
Processes involved in voluntary attention directed to a mental image in the absence of sensory input.

Functional and Structural Organization of Attentional Mechanisms : Reflex Attention

Anatomical and physiological findings point to the deeper layers of the superior colliculus (those below the <u>stratum opticum</u>) and the midbrain reticular formation as the crucial brain regions for novelty detection and salience. Furthermore, there is abundant evidence that the ascending and descending projections of these structures control reflex attention by facilitating sensory processing, exploratory-investigatory responses, and orienting responses (see Figure 5).

Sensory input from a variety of exteroceptive and proprioceptive sources converges on neurons in the deeper layers of the superior colliculus and the subajacent midbrain reticular formation (Huerta and Harting, 1984). Neurons in these two regions are morphologically indistinguishable

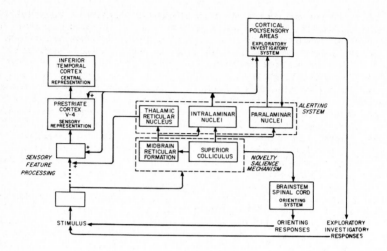

Figure 5
Neural mechanisms of reflex attention. See text for explanation.

(Edwards, 1980) and show similar discharge characteristics; they respond best to transient, moving stimuli, frequently in two or more modalities; they also lack specific trigger features and habituate to repeated presentations of the same stimulus (Chalupa, 1984). Within the deeper layers of the superior colliculus, receptive fields of stimuli from different exteroceptive modalities are topographically organized and in spatial register (Stein, 1984). The motor organization of the deeper tectal layers, as determined by electrical recordings and stimulation, is also topographic and in register with the sensory maps (Stein, 1984). Furthermore, the descending projections of the midbrain and deeper layers of the superior colliculus are similar: the deeper tectal layers send fibers to various brainstem and spinal regions controlling movements of the eyes, head, vibrissae, pinna and limbs (Huerta and Harting, 1984; Stein, 1984). These findings suggest that the tecto-tegmental region provides the sensory-motor integrative mechanism for commanding appropriate orienting movements to novel stimuli.

Whereas the sensory-motor organization and descending connections of the tectotegmental region provide information about the mechanisms controlling orienting movements elicited by novel stimuli, the ascending projections of these structures shed light on the mechanisms by which reflex attention produces alerting and attentional effects.

The midbrain reticular formation projects to a number of diencephalic regions including several groups of thalamic nuclei; it projects densely to the reticular nucleus and intralaminar nuclei, but only lightly to the paralaminar nuclei (Edwards & De Olmos, 1976; Graybiel, 1977; Robertson and Feiner, 1982), which are situated lateral to the internal medullary lamina (see Figure 5). Anatomical and physiological findings strongly suggest that reticular nucleus neurons are inhibited by excitation of the midbrain reticular formation, thus releasing sensory-specific thalamic neurons from the recurrent inhibition that reticular nucleus neurons exert on them. Consequently, excitation of the reticular formation enhances the flow of sensory information from thalamus to cortex (Singer, 1977; Skinner & Yingling, 1977; Yingling & Skinner, 1977).

The intralaminar nuclei have long been considered the thalamic component of an ascending "arousal" system which projects diffusely to all cortical areas (Lindsley, 1960). However, recent anatomical studies employing anterograde tracers have shown that only certain cortical areas receive moderate or dense intralaminar projections. In that cat, <u>n. centralis lateralis</u>, <u>paracentralis</u> and <u>centralis medialis</u> project to sensory-motor, premotor, parietal and anterior limbic cortex (Kaufman & Rosenquist, 1985) as well as to all visual cortical areas except for area 17. The centre median nucleus and <u>n. parafascicularis</u> also project to sensory-motor, premotor and anterior limbic structures (Royce & Mourey, 1985). Steriade & Glen (1982) reported that 13% of units in <u>n. centralis lateralis</u> and <u>paracentralis</u> of cats project to areas 4, 6, 8 and 5. Whereas anterograde tracers have not been used to study intralaminar projections in monkeys, pathways from intralaminar nuclei to motor and premotor cortex, frontal eye fields, areas 5 and 7, and cingulate cortex have been described by the retrograde HRP method in monkeys (Herkenham, 1986). The intralaminar projection to motor, limbic, polysensory and visual association cortex of cat and monkey suggests that via this route the midbrain reticular formation activates cortical areas beyond the primary sensory areas and thus may facilitate processing in higher cortical areas.

Whereas the midbrain reticular formation projects only lightly to the paralaminar nuclei, the deeper collicular layers project heavily to both the intralaminar <u>and</u> paralaminar portion of <u>n. medialis dorsalis</u> as well as to other paralaminar nuclei - the medial pulvinar, <u>n. lateralis posterior</u> and <u>n. lateralis dorsalis</u> (Harting, Huerta, Frankfurter, Strominger & Royce, 1980) (see Figure 5). In the monkey, the cortical projections of the paralaminar nuclei, unlike those of the intralaminar nuclei, may be limited to certain cortical polysensory and limbic areas implicated in neglect. Proline injections into medial pulvinar in the monkey result in labelled terminals in cingulate cortex, frontal eye fields, the dorsal bank of the superior temporal sulcus and area 7 (Baleydier & Mauguière, 1985), all of which are directly interconnected (Butter, in press). These cortical projections of the medial pulvinar have also been reported in studies employing retrograde transport of HRP (e.g., Burton & Jones, 1976; Kasdon & Jacobson, 1978; Barbas & Mesulam, 1981). Furthermore, the frontal eye fields and area 7 also receive projections from two other paralaminar nuclei - <u>n. medialis dorsalis</u>, <u>pars multiformis</u> and the magnocellular division of <u>n. ventralis anterior</u> (Barbas & Mesulam, 1981). In addition, another cortical polysensory area implicated in spatial attention, the premotor cortex, also receives an input from the medial pulvinar and the magnocellular division of <u>n. medialis dorsalis</u> (Kievit & Kuypers, 1977). Furthermore, all the cortical projections from the medial pulvinar described by Baleydier and Mauguière (1985) include terminals in layer I. Likewise, in cat and rat, all paralaminar thalamic projections investigated include terminals in this layer (Herkenham, 1986). These paralaminar inputs could depolarize apical dendrites of pyramidal cells, increasing excitability and thus could facilitate processing in cortical areas far removed from primary sensory input. As Baleydier and Mauguière (1985) note, the reciprocal connections they described between the medial pulvinar and several cortical polysensory areas provide cortico-thalamo-cortical pathways that mirror the direct cortico-cortical pathways between these polysensory areas; thus, they may facilitate inter-cortical processing of information.

Each of the above-described multiple ascending pathways arising from the midbrain may subserve different functions related to attentional processes. The midbrain tegmentum may play a role in generalized alerting functions by its inhibitory projection to the reticular nucleus and by its excitatory projections to the intralaminar nuclei. Moreover, the apparent preferential projection of the intralaminar nuclei to sensory-specific and polysensory association cortex may increase "synaptic security" and thus facilitate higher cortical processing in these areas, which are removed from primary sensory-specific input. Whereas these projections may subserve generalized alerting functions, the tectoparalaminar pathway to cortical polysensory areas may play a more specific role in spatially-directed attention (see below).

A number of physiological and behavioral findings suggest that the tecto-tegmental structures may subserve simple and crude orienting activity, whereas the cortical polysensory structures may mediate more specific and complex exploratory-investigatory behaviors and the shifts of attention that accompany them. Unilateral lesions of the superior colliculus in the monkey and other mammals produce contralateral hemispatial neglect of stimuli in several modalities (Butter, in press). Discrete unilateral lesions of the midbrain tegmentum also result in unilateral neglect (Watson, Heilman, Miller & King, 1974). Several findings suggest that the colliculus also participates in the control of eye movements and in spatial attentional processes related to eye movements. Units in the superficial layers of the colliculus in monkey show enhanced discharges to visual stimuli when these stimuli are the target of a saccade (Goldberg & Wurtz, 1972; Wurtz & Mohler, 1976). Furthermore, the enhanced sensory response is linked temporally with the discharges of eye movement-related neurons in the deeper collicular layers and is related to the intention to move the eyes rather than to the specific parameters of the eye movement (Wurtz & Mohler, 1976). Monkeys with colliculus lesions are impaired in performing discrimination tasks requiring gaze and attention shifts from the response sites to the stimuli (Butter, 1979); they are also impaired in shifting their gaze to peripheral visual targets (Kurtz & Butter, 1980) even when they are presented too briefly to be fixated (Kurtz, Leiby & Butter, 1982). The conclusion that the superior colliculus participates in spatial attention linked to eye movements is supported by the finding that patients with supranuclear palsy are impaired in spatially shifting their attention only in the direction in which their eye movements are impaired (Posner, Cohen & Rafal, 1982).

The sensory-motor coordinating mechanism provided by tectotegmental structures may contribute to orienting activity even in the absence of the forebrain. Decerebrate rats (Woods, 1964; Grill & Norgren, 1978) and cats (Bignall & Schramm, 1974) show orienting movements of the head to auditory and tactile stimuli. It has also been reported that a human anencephalic infant showed orienting responses to auditory stimuli (Brackbill, 1971).

Spatial attentional functions of the thalamus have not been studied as thoroughly as those of the tectum. However, two studies have reported disturbances in spatial attention following selective unilateral lesions of thalamic nuclei that provide links in the pathways described previously: n. parafascicularis in monkey (Watson, Miller & Heilman, 1978) and n. centralis lateralis in cats (Orem, Schlag-Rey & Schlag, 1973). Furthermore, injections of GABA-altering drugs into a region of the pulvinar bordering the medial pulvinar appear to alter spatial shifts of attention in monkeys

(Petersen, Morris & Robinson, 1984). Hemispatial neglect has been reported in patients with unilateral thalamic lesions (e.g., Watson & Heilman, 1979); in most of these reports, the lesions were extensive and involved a number of thalamic nuclei. However, Cambier, Elghozi and Strube (1980) described a patient with visual and tactile neglect contralateral to a discrete unilateral ischemic thalamic lesion that involved two tectorecipient nuclei – the pulvinar and dorsomedial nucleus – as well as n. ventralis posterior lateralis.

Hemispatial neglect in monkeys results from unilateral lesions of cortical areas to which the paralaminar nuclei project – frontal eye fields (Kennard, 1939; Welch & Stuteville, 1958; Latto & Cowey, 1971a & b; Schiller, True & Conway, 1980; Crowne, Yeo & Steele Russell, 1981), cingulate cortex (Watson, Heilman, Cauthen & King, 1974), inferior parietal lobule (Denny-Brown & Chambers, 1958; Bates & Ettlinger, 1960; Heilman, Pandya & Geschwind, 1970), the polysensory region of the superior temporal sulcus (Luh, Butter & Buchtel, 1986) and premotor cortex (Rizzolatti, Matelli & Pavesi, 1983). Significant proportions of single units responding to stimuli in more than one sensory modality have been reported in all these cortical areas with the exception of cingulate cortex, where unit polysensory properties have not been reported (Butter, in press). Electrophysiological and behavioral-ablation findings also indicate that the inferior parietal cortex[1], frontal eye field and superior temporal sulcus are involved in orienting movements and exploratory-manipulative manual movements (Butter, in press). Furthermore, all of these cortical areas are directly interconnected and project back to the deeper layers of the superior colliculus (Butter, in press) (See Heilman et al. and Rizzolatti and Camarda, this volume, for additional discussion of the role of cortical and thalamic structures in spatial attention).

These findings suggest that the deep tectal projections via the thalamus to cortical polysensory areas and their projections back to the deeper tectal layers may comprise a system controlling both spatial shifts of attention and orienting, exploratory-investigatory behaviors (Butter, in press). The findings reviewed above also suggest that structures at the brainstem and cortical levels of the system may make different contributions to these processes. Whereas the superior colliculus appears to control eye movements and spatial shifts of attention linked only with eye movements, the cortical areas in the system appear to control not only eye movements but complex spatially-directed manual movements involved in exploring and manipulating objects.

There is evidence that descending pathways from the forebrain may be crucial for habituation of investigatory responses. Monkeys with bilateral temporal lobectomies abnormally persist in investigating objects, a phenomenon referred to as "hypermetamorphosis" (Klüver & Bucy, 1939). This "release" of investigatory behavior appears to be due to removal of the amygdala (Weiskrantz, 1956), which also has been implicated in object recognition in monkeys (Mishkin, 1982). Thus, the amygdala may contribute to the habituation of investigatory responses by participating in a mechanism for labeling objects as familiar. The frontal lobe may also be crucial for habituation of orienting responses: removal of orbital frontal cortex, but not lateral frontal cortex, in monkeys interferes with habituation of the distracting effects of visual and auditory stimuli (Butter, 1964). Frontal lobe lesions have also been reported to interfere with the habituation of orienting reflexes in humans (Luria & Homskaya, 1970). Furthermore, electrophysiological evidence that frontal cortex provides excitatory inputs to the thalamic reticular nucleus (Yingling & Skinner, 1977) is consistent with the view that this cortical region suppresses sensory input to the cortex. The findings reviewed above, then, suggest that habituation of orienting and investigatory responses may require more than the building up of a short-term central representation, as shown in Figure 1; it may also require paralimbic and frontal regions which are anatomically linked with the highest visual cortical area (and those in other modalities) mediating object representations as described below (Jones and Powell, 1970).

Voluntary attention. It was proposed earlier that neural mechanisms of voluntary attention are added on to the mechanisms controlling reflex attention, a view consistent with prevailing ideas of the hierarchical organization of the central nervous system. According to the view presented here, a common feature of the neural mechanisms underlying the various manifestations of voluntary attention is the activation of central representations of stimuli to which attention is drawn, which in turn facilitate the same alerting systems involved in reflex attention. According to this view, one would expect that the highest levels of the sensory-specific association cortex play a crucial role in voluntary attention, for these cortical areas appear to be the storage sites of central representations of familiar objects, at least in the visual modality. There is a good deal of evidence from behavioral-ablation (Mishkin, 1982) and electrophysiological studies (Gross, Bruce, Desimone, Fleming & Gattass, 1981) that inferior temporal cortex (see Figure 6) is the highest cortical level at which visual information is processed in the primate visual system and is the site of central visual representations. It is likely that the other exteroceptive systems are also organized as a series of processing stages with representations of meaningful stimuli stored in circuits at the highest level of sensory-specific processing.

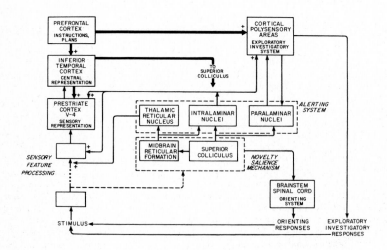

Figure 6
Neural mechanisms of voluntary attention. See text for explanation.

According to the model of voluntary attention presented earlier (see Figure 2), central representations receive peripheral inputs from sensory representations and are activated centrally by plans or instructions; in turn, central representations activate sensory representations (so as to enhance the perceptual salience of stimuli and produce mental images), as well as the novelty-salience mechanism. These features of the model of voluntary attention are consistent with the results of anatomical and neurobehavioral studies of the visual system. Inferior temporal cortex, the visual cortical area that is implicated in visual memory, is directly connected with several brain structures that mediate the functions included in the model (see Figure 6). Inferior temporal cortex receives projections from prefrontal cortex (Kuypers et al., 1965; Pandya & Kuypers, 1969; Jones & Powell, 1970; Umitsu & Iwai, 1981), which is implicated in the control of central sets (Mishkin, 1964) and planning of the temporal ordering of behavior (Pribram et al., 1964). Furthermore, Luria (1966) has presented evidence that patients with frontal lobe lesions are impaired in utilizing verbal instructions to control learned motor responses. Inferior temporal cortex also projects to V4 (Kuypers et al., 1965), a higher-level, retinotopically-organized visual cortical area that is part of the prestriate complex and from which it receives dense projections (Desimone, Fleming & Gross, 1980). Anatomical and physiological evidence suggest that V4, together with other prestriate visual areas with which it is interconnected, provide the structure for representations of visual inputs (Van Essen, Maunsell & Bixby, 1981). Thus, via its interconnections with V4 inferior temporal cortex receives visual inputs so that recognition can take place and so that it can modulate sensory representations in order to increase their perceptual salience or to provide visual mental images (see Figure 6). In addition, inferior temporal cortex also sends projections to the deeper layers of the superior colliculus (Whitlock & Nauta, 1956; Kuypers & Lawrence, 1967; Fries, 1984); via this route it can indirectly activate search mechanisms and the alerting systems with which the superior colliculus is connected.

Implications of the Present Analysis for Neglect and Other Cognitive Disorders

The available evidence with regard to associations and dissociations between neglect and other cognitive disorders will be examined in this section in order to determine whether they are consistent with the analysis presented here. In addition, predictions will be made of expected relationships between neglect and other cognitive disorders on the basis of the present analysis.

This analysis draws a fundamental distinction between reflex and voluntary attention. It assumes that voluntary attention involves stored representations and instructions mediated by neural structures that are located at higher cortical levels and that are superimposed on the mechanisms of reflex attention. Thus, according to this view, cortical lesions destroying structures contributing to voluntary attention may leave mechanisms of reflex attention intact or functioning at a reduced level, so that attention may be still directed to novel salient stimuli. Tests of hemispatial neglect that are commonly used, both in the clinic and experimentally, assess voluntary attention; that is, they all involve tasks including instructions to report a stimulus or perform some action, such as copying a drawing or bisecting a line. It is difficult to observe and quantify manifestation of reflex attention such as orienting responses, in part because they habituate rapidly. However, it might be possible to evaluate reflex attention in patients with neglect indirectly, by testing the distracting effects of novel stimuli on their performance in cognitive or sensory-motor tasks.

Whereas hemispatial neglect appears after unilateral lesions involving a variety of brain structures, its association with damage to the inferior parietal lobule (usually on the right side) is by far the one most frequently and consistently encountered (Heilman et al., 1985). As mentioned previously, damage to this cortical region is frequently associated with visuospatial disturbances and disorientation in space. Although the relationship between these impairments and hemispatial neglect is not obligatory (e.g., Ratcliff, 1979; Perenin and Vighetto, 1983), its frequent occurrence suggests a close linkage between spatial attention and spatial perception, perhaps analogous to the one posited earlier between object recognition and attention directed to objects. Furthermore, both spatially-directed attention and spatial perception are both functionally associated with exploratory and investigatory movements, which also depend upon the same cortical region. The anatomical findings reviewed previously also suggest a close relationship between brainstem mechanisms of spatially-directed attention and the cortical areas involved in visuospatial perception: The paralaminar thalamic nuclei, which receive a direct input from the deeper tectal layers, project selectively to the cortical polysensory areas, including those in the inferior parietal lobe.

The failure of some studies to find spatial attentional disorders accompanying visuospatial deficits or deficits in visually-guided reaching (optic ataxia) may be due, at least in part, to differences in test sensitivity. Whereas most tests of hemispatial neglect (such as line cancellation or copying a drawing) are designed to detect rather gross disturbances and present no problems for normal subjects, many tests of visuospatial disturbances are more difficult for normal subjects, who may commit errors in performing them. Furthermore, it is possible that lesions involving the inferior parietal lobule might initially disrupt the functions of other structures, such as other cortical polysensory areas or the superior colliculus, which are implicated in spatial attention and with which the inferior parietal region is interconnected. With the passage of time, however, spatial attention may return to normal, whereas visuospatial functions may not, because of their dependence on the integrity of the inferior parietal lobe.

On the basis of the present analysis of the voluntary attention, one would predict that disorders of different aspects of voluntary attention are dissociable by selective lesions. According to the model presented here, one set of disorders of voluntary attention could arise because stored representations of stimuli are no longer activated centrally by plans or instructions. Consequently, detection and search for these stimuli would be no longer under the control of plans or instructions. A breakdown in the central activation of a stored representation could be due either to a disconnection of the stored representation from neural structures generating plans or instructions or to direct damage to the latter neural structures. As mentioned previously, the frontal lobes appear to be crucial for planning and for executing task-related responses according to verbal instructions. Thus, one might expect that frontal lesions or lesions disconnecting the frontal and temporal lobes would disrupt search and instruction-based detection or imagery, without necessarily producing neglect. One would also expect that the perceptual phenomenon of target "pop-out" and the enhanced recognition of search targets, which according to the model are dependent upon central activation of stored representations, would also be impaired by the same lesions. The model also predicts that lesions resulting in a modality-specific recognition loss (i.e., an associative visual agnosia), which destroy the central representations of familiar objects, would also impair the perceptual phenomena (pop-out and enhanced target recognition, enhanced salience of stimuli with intrinsic or remote value) that accompany stimuli with "attention-value". One might also expect that subcortical lesions disconnecting the temporal lobes from tecto-tegmental structures would impair search for a target without necessarily altering spatial attention evaluated by standard tests of neglect.

The model also makes another and rather different kind of prediction, concerning the activity of neurons in inferior temporal cortex, the cortical region which in monkeys appears to be the site of stored visual representations. It would be expected that inferior temporal neurons selectively responding to complex stimuli (such as a particular object or a face) would also show enhanced discharges when the monkey searches for the stimulus, even when it is not in the visual field.

According to the model presented here, losses of imagery resulting from particular brain lesions would be associated in an obligatory manner with losses of some functions but not others. Thus, one would expect that modality-specific recognition losses for particular stimuli (e.g., faces, photographs of particular objects) would be accompanied by selective losses in the ability to report images of the same stimuli, or perform tasks that are assumed to require images of these stimuli (draw or describe verbally from memory). Two recent reviews of the literature on imagery impairments (Farah, 1984; Levine, Warach & Farah, 1985) have reported a high incidence of patients showing imagery loss for visually presented material who also are selectively impaired in recognizing the same material.

In contrast to this close association of imagery and recognition loss, there are many reports of brain damage resulting in imagery loss for familiar visual stimuli in the absence of obvious hemispatial neglect (e.g., Basso, Bisiach & Luzzatti, 1980). The model presented here is consistent with this kind of dissociation, for it distinguishes between mechanisms underlying visuospatial and spatial attention functions on the one hand and mechanisms of object recognition, imagery and object-directed attention on the other hand. In cases of imagery loss such as the patient reported by Basso et al. (1980), in whom neglect was absent, the investigators evaluated predominantly imagery of particular objects. In contrast, imagery based upon body-centered relations of objects or spatial relations between objects, would be expected to accompany neglect since it is assumed that visuospatial and spatial attentional functions are closely related. Evidence supporting this view has been provided by Bisiach, Capitani, Luzzatti & Perani (1981), who reported that patients with left hemineglect due to right-sided lesions, unlike those without neglect after right-sided lesions, were impaired in reporting the left side of mental images of familiar places. In this context, the "left side" is defined in reference to imagined body orientation. However, there are a number of reports of deficits in tasks requiring "dynamic imagery", that is, the mental manipulation of imagery, in the absence of clear hemispatial neglect. Patients with right posterior lesions are deficient in tasks demanding estimation of the position of cities on an imagined map (Morrow, Ratcliff & Johnston, 1985), "mental rotation" of imagined objects (Butters, Barton & Brody, 1970; Warrington & Taylor, 1973; Ratcliff, 1979), "mental displacement" of ego-centered viewpoint (Butters et al., 1970) and mental reconstruction of the spatial features of a visual display (Ogden, 1985); these deficits occurred in the absence of neglect in any or some of the patients tested. One way to resolve the discrepancy between the predictions of the model and these reports of dissociation between dynamic imagery and neglect is by appealing to the same factors previously suggested to explain the dissociation between neglect and visuospatial disorders - differences in task difficulty, and the possibly greater distribution of spatial attention mechanisms compared to that of visuospatial mechanisms. The argument based on differences in task difficulty appears to be even more cogent in this case, for in many of the imagery manipulation tasks employed in the studies cited above, control subjects achieve less than perfect scores. Alternatively, it is possible that a subtle form of internally-directed spatial attention required in imagery manipulation tasks is disturbed in patients who are impaired in imagery manipulation tasks and that this disturbance may be a factor in their deficient performance on these tasks. According to this view, then, one might expect that patients with right-sided lesions, who are impaired in imagery-manipulation tasks but who do not show overt neglect, would be more severely impaired if they were instructed to perform imagery manipulation on the left side of imagined space than on the right side.

Summary and Conclusions

The analysis of neglect presented here differs from others (e.g., Heilman et al., 1985; Kinsbourne, 1970; Bisiach, Luzzatti & Perani, 1979) in that it is based both upon a distinction between reflex and voluntary attention and upon distinctions between different forms of voluntary attention, in all of which, it is suggested, central activation of a stored representation is a common factor. The model based on these distinctions is consistent with structural, physiological and neurobehavioral findings. Furthermore, an initial test of one prediction made by the model (selective recognition enhancement of search targets) yielded results consistent with it.

The model deals with voluntary attention in terms of concepts, such as sensory representations, stored representations and plans, that are accepted concepts in cognitive psychology and may be mediated by distinct neural mechanisms. Thus, it has an advantage over models that attempt to explain attention in terms of hypothetical processes such as a "scanner", for which there is no known physiological mechanism. Furthermore, by making cerebral activation of representations the crucial factor in voluntary attention, higher-level influences acting on sensory and cognitive processes "from above" are restored to the position they formally had in earlier theoretical formulations in psychology, which used terms such as "determining tendency" and Aufgabe (the mentally represented task) to try to account for the selective, goal-directed aspect of cognitive task performance (Woodworth, 1938).

With regard to the puzzling phenomenon of neglect itself, the most general conclusions suggested by the present analysis are that neglect may take various forms and each may result from disturbance of a particular process. Thus, hemispatial neglect may be just one of several forms of neglect, including disturbances in directing attention to objects or images, that only become apparent when patients with particular selective lesions are tested under certain conditions. The question whether these predicted attentional deficits are demonstrable can only be answered by future neuropsychological investigations.

References

Baleydier, C. & Mauguière, F. Anatomical evidence for medial pulvinar connections with posterior cingulate cortex, the retrosplenial area and the posterior parahippocampal gyrus in monkeys. Journal of Comparative Neurology, 1985, 232, 219-228.

Barbas, H. & Mesulam, M.M. Organization of afferent input to subdivisions of area 8 in the rhesus monkey. Journal of Comparative Neurology, 1981, 200, 407-431.

Basso, A., Bisiach, E. & Luzzatti, C. Loss of mental imagery: a case study. Neuropsychologia, 1980, 18, 435-442.

Bates, J.A.V. & Ettlinger, G. Posterior biparietal ablations in the monkey. AMA Archives of Neurology, 1960, 3, 177-192.

Bender, M.B. Disorders in Perception. Springfield, Ill, Charles C.Thomas, 1952.

Berlyne, D. Conflict, arousal and curiosity. New York: McGraw-Hill, 1960.

Bignall, K. & Schramm, L. Behavior of chronically decerebrated kittens. Experimental Neurology, 1974, 42, 519-531.

Bisiach, E., Luzzatti, C. & Perani, D. Unilateral neglect, representational schema and consciousness. Brain, 1979, 102, 609-618.

Bisiach, E., Capitani, E., Luzzatti, C. & Perani, D. Brain and conscious representation of outside reality. Neuropsychologia, 1981, 19, 543-551.

Brackbill, Y. The role of the cortex in orienting: orienting reflex in an anencephalic human infant. Developmental Psychology, 1971, 5, 195-201.

Broadbent, D.E. & Gregory, M. Division of attention and the decision theory of signal detection. Trans. Proceedings of the Royal Society, 1963, B158, 222-231.

Bryden, M.P. The role of post-exposural eye movements in tachistoscopic perception. Canadian Journal of Psychology, 1961, 15, 220-225.

Burton, H. & Jones, E.G. The posterior thalamic region and its cortical projection in New World and Old World monkeys. Journal of Comparative Neurology, 1976, 168, 249-302.

Butter, C.M. Habituation of responses to novel stimuli in monkeys with selective frontal lesions. Science, 1964, 144, 313-314.

Butter, C.M. Contrasting effects of lateral striate and superior colliculus lesions on visual discrimination performance in monkeys. Journal of Comparative and Physiological Psychology, 1979, 93, 522-537.

Butter, C.M. The role of polysensory neuronal structures in spatially-directed attention and orienting responses to external stimuli. In D. Sheer (Ed.), Attention: Theory, Brain Function and Clinical Applications. New York: Academic Press, in press.

Butters, N., Barton, M. & Brody, B.A. Role of the right parietal lobe in the mediation of cross-modal associations and reversible operations in space. Cortex, 1970, 6, 174-190.

Cambier, J., Elghozi, D. & Strube, E. Lésions du thalamus droit avec syndrome de l'hémisphère mineur. Discussion du concept de négligence thalamique. Revue Neurologique (Paris), 1980, 136, 105-116.

Chain, F., Chèdru, F., Leblanc, M. & Lhermitte, F. Renseignements fournis par l'enregistrement du regard dans les pseudohémianopsias d'origine frontale chez l'homme. Revue d'EEG et de Neurophysiologie Clinique, 1972, 2, 223-231.

Chalupa, L. Visual physiology of the mammalian superior colliculus. In H. Vanegas (Ed.), Comparative Neurology of the Optic Tectum. New York: Plenum Press, 1984, pp 775-818.

Chèdru, F., Leblanc, M. & Lhermitte, F. Visual searching in normal and brain-damaged subjects (contribution to the study of unilateral attention). Cortex, 1973, 9, 94-111.

Critchley, M. The Parietal Lobes. New York: Hafner, 1966.

Crovitz, H.F. & Daves, W. Tendencies to eye movements and perceptual accuracy. Journal of Experimental Psychology, 1962, 63, 495-498.

Crowne, D.P., Yeo, C.H. & Steele-Russell, I. The effects of unilateral frontal eye field lesions in the monkey: visuo-motor guidance and avoidance behaviour. Behavioural Brain Research, 1981, 2, 165-188.

Denny-Brown, D. & Chambers, R.A. The parietal lobe and behavior. Proc. Association for Research in Nervous and Mental Diseases, 1958, 36, 35-117.

DeRenzi, E. Disorders of Space Exploration and Cognition. New York: Wiley, 1982.

Desimone, R., Fleming, J. & Gross, C.G. Prestriate afferents to inferior temporal cortex: an HRP study. Brain Research, 1980, 184, 41-55.

Edwards, S.B. Deep cell layers of the superior colliculus: their reticular characteristics and structural organization. In J.A. Hobson and J.A.B. Brazier (Eds.), The Reticular Formation Revisited. New York: Raven Press, 1980.

Edwards, S.B. & De Olmos, J.S. Autoradiographic studies of the midbrain reticular formation: Ascending projections of nucleus cuneiformis. Journal of Comparative Neurology, 1980, 165, 417-432.

Farah, M.J. The neurological basis of mental imagery: a componential analysis. Cognition, 1984, 18, 245-272.

Fries, W. Cortical projections to the superior colliculus in the macaque monkey: a retrograde study using horseradish peroxidase. Journal of Comparative Neurology, 1984, 230, 55-76.

Goldberg, M.E. & Wurtz, R.H. Activity of superior colliculus in behaving monkey. II. Effect of attention on neuronal responses. Journal of Neurophysiology, 1972, 35, 560-574.

Goodale, M.A. & Butter, C.M. Unpublished experiment. 1985.

Graybeil, A.M. Direct and indirect preoculomotor pathways of the brainstem: an autoradiographic study of the pontine reticular formation in the cat. Journal of Comparative Neurology, 1977, 175, 37-78.

Grill, H.J. & Norgren, R. Neurological tests and behavioral deficits in chronic thalamic and decerebrate rats. Brain Research, 1978, 143, 299-312.

Gross, C.G., Bruce, C.J., Desimone, R., Fleming, J. & Gattass, R. Cortical visual areas of the temporal lobe. In C.N. Woolsey (Ed.), Cortical Sensory Organization, Volume 2, Multiple Visual Areas. Clifton NJ: Humana Press, 1981, pp. 187-216.

Harting, J.K., Huerta, M.F., Frankfurter, A.J. & Royce, G.J. Ascending pathways from the monkey superior colliculus: an autoradiographic analysis. Journal of Comparative Neurology, 1980, 192, 853-882.

Heilman, K.M., Pandya, D.N. & Geschwind, N. Trimodal inattention following parietal lobe ablations. Trans. of the American Neurological Association, 1970, 95, 250-261.

Heilman, K.M., Watson, R.T. & Valenstein, E. Neglect and related disorders. In K.M. Heilman and E. Valenstein (Eds.), Clinical Neuropsychology (second edition). New York: Oxford University Press, 1985.

Herkenham, M. New perspectives on the organization and evolution of nonspecific thalamocortical projections. In E.G. Jones and A.A. Peters (Eds.), Cerebral Cortex, volume 5. New York: Plenum Press, 1986.

Huerta, M.F. & Harting, J.K. The mammalian superior colliculus: studies of its morphology and connections. In H. Vanegas (Ed.), Comparative Neurology of the Optic Tectum. New York: Plenum Press, 1984, pp 687-774.

Jones, E.G. & Powell, T.S. An anatomical study of converging sensory pathways within the cerebral cortex of the monkey. Brain, 1970, 93, 793-820.

James, W. Principles of Psychology, volume 1. New York: Henry Holt, 1890.

Kahneman, D. Attention and Effort. Englewood Cliffs, NJ, Prentice-Hall, 1973.

Kasdon, D.L. & Jacobson, S. The thalamic afferents to the inferior parietal lobule in the rhesus monkey. Journal of Comparative Neurology, 1978, 177, 685-706.

Kaufman, E.F.S. & Rosenquist, A.C. Efferent projections of the thalamic intralaminar nuclei in the cat. Brain Research, 1985, 335, 257-279.

Kennard, M.A. Alterations in response to visual stimuli following lesions of frontal lobe in monkey. Archives of Neurology and Psychiatry, 1939, 41, 1153-1165.

Kievit, J. & Kuypers, H.G.J.M. Organization of the thalamo-cortical connections to the frontal lobe in the rhesus monkey. Experimental Brain Research, 1977, 29, 299-322.

Klüver, H. & Bucy, P.C. Preliminary analysis of functions of the temporal lobe in monkeys. Archives of Neurology and Psychiatry, 1939, 42, 979-1000.

Kosslyn, S.M. Image and Mind. Cambridge, Mass: Harvard University Press, 1980.

Kurtz, D. & Butter, C.M. Impairments in visual discrimination performance and gaze shifts in monkeys with superior colliculus lesions. Brain Research, 1980, 196, 109-124.

Kurtz, D., Leiby, C.C. & Butter, C.M. Further analysis of S-R separation effects on visual discrimination performance of normal rhesus monkeys and monkeys with superior colliculus lesions. Journal of Comparative and Physiological Psychology, 1982, 96, 35-46.

Kuypers, H.G.J.M. & Lawrence, D.G. Cortical projections to the red nucleus and the brain stem in the rhesus monkey. Brain Research, 1967, 4, 151-188.

Kuypers, H.G.J.M., Szwarcbart, M.K., Mishkin, M. & Rosvold, H.E. Occipitotemporal cortico-cortical connections in the rhesus monkey. Experimental Neurology, 1965, 11, 245-262.

Latto, R. & Cowey, A. Visual field defects after frontal eye field lesions in monkeys. Brain Research, 1971a, 30, 1-24.

Latto, R. & Cowey, A. Fixation changes after frontal eye field lesions in monkeys. Brain Research, 1971b, 30, 25-36.

Levine, D.N., Warach, J. & Farah, M. Two visual systems in mental imagery: dissociation of "what" and "where" in imagery disorders due to bilateral posterior cerebral lesions . Neurology, 1985, 7, 1110-1118.

Lindsley, D. Attention, consciousness, sleep and waking. In Handbook of Physiology (Section 1), Neurophysiology, volume III. Washington: American Physiological Society, 1960, pp 1553-1594.

Luh, K., Butter, C.M. & Buchtel, H. Impairments in orienting to visual stimuli in monkeys following unilateral lesions of the superior sulcal polysensory cortex. Neuropsychologia, 1986, in press.

Luria, A.R. Higher Cortical Functions in Man, Second Edition. New York: Basic Books, 1966.

Luria, A.R. & Homskaya, E.D. Frontal lobes and the regulation of arousal processes. In D. Mostofsky (Ed.) Attention: Contemporary Theory and Analysis. New York: Appleton, Century, Croft, 1970, pp 303-330.

Lynch, J.C. & McLaren, J.W. A quantitative study of contralateral inattention in monkey following lesions of posterior parietal, prestriate and prefrontal cortex. Society for Neuroscience, 1984, 10, 59.

Mishkin, M. Perseveration of central sets after frontal lesions in monkeys.

In J.M. Warren and K. Akert (Eds.), The Frontal Granular Cortex and Behavior. New York: McGraw-Hill, 1964.

Mishkin, M. A memory system in the monkey. Philosophical Transactions of the Royal Society London, 1982, B298, 85-95.

Moray, N. Attention in dichotic listening : affective cues and influence of instructions. Quarterly Journal of experimental Psychology, 1959, 11, 56-60.

Moray, N. & O'Brien, T. Signal detection theory applied to selective listening. Journal of Acoustical Society of America, 1967, 42, 765-772.

Morrow, L., Ratcliff, G. & Johnston, S. Externalizing spatial knowledge in patients with right hemisphere lesions. Cognitive Neuropsychology, 1985, 2, 265-273.

Neisser, U. Decision time without reaction time: experiments in visual scanning. American Journal of Psychology, 1963, 76, 376-385.

Nakamura, R.K. & Mishkin, M. Blindness in monkeys following non-visual cortical lesions. Brain Research, 1980, 188, 572-577.

Ogden, J. Contralateral neglect of constructed visual images in right and left brain-damaged patients. Neuropsychologia, 1985, 23, 273-277.

Orem, J., Schlag-Rey, M. and Schlag, J. Unilateral visual neglect and thalamic intralaminar lesions in the cat. Experimental Neurology, 1973, 40, 784-797.

Pandya, D. & Kuypers, H.G.J.M. Corticocortical connections in the rhesus monkey. Brain Research, 1969, 13, 13-36.

Perenin, M.T. & Vighetto, A. Optic ataxia : a specific disorder in visuomotor coordination. In A. Hein and M. Jeannerod (Eds.), Spatially-oriented Behavior. New York: Springer-Verlag, 1983, 305-326.

Petersen, S.E., Morris, J.D. and Robinson, D.L. Modulation of attentional behaviors by injection of GABA-related drugs into the pulvinar of macaque. Society for Neuroscience, 1984, 10, 475.

Posner, M.I., Cohen, Y. & Rafal, R.D. Neural systems control of spatial orienting. Philosophical Transactions of the Royal Society London, 1982, B298, 187-198.

Posner, M., Walker, J., Friedrich, F. & Rafal, R. Effects of parietal injury on covert orienting of attention. Journal of Neuroscience, 1984, 4, 1863-1874.

Pribram, K.H., Ahumada, A., Hartog, J. & Roos, L. A progress report on the neurological processes disturbed by frontal lesions in primates. In J.M. Warren and K. Akert (Eds.), Frontal Granular Cortex and Behavior. New York: McGraw-Hill, 1964, pp 28-55.

Ratcliff, G. Spatial thought, mental rotation and the right cerebral hemisphere. Neuropsychologia, 1979, 17, 49-55.

Remington, R. Attention and saccadic eye movements. Journal of Experimental Psychology, 1980, 6, 726-744.

Rizzolatti, G., Matelli, M. & Pavesi, G. Deficits in attention and movement following the removal of postarcuate (area 6) and prearcuate (area 8) cortex in macaque monkeys. Brain, 1983, 106, 655-673.

Robertson, R.T. & Feiner, A.R. Diencephalic projections from the pontine reticular formation: autoradiographic studies in the cat. Brain Research, 1982, 239, 3-16.

Rondot, P. & deRecondo, J. Ataxie optique: Trouble de la coordination visuo-motrice. Brain Research, 1974, 71, 367-375.

Royce, G.J. & Mourey, R.J. Efferent connections of the centromedian and parafascicular nuclei: an autoradiographic investigation in the cat. Journal of comparative Neurology, 1985, 235, 277-300.

Schiller, P.H., True, S.D. & Conway, J.L. Deficits in eye movements following frontal eye field and superior colliculus ablations. Journal of Neurophysiology, 1980, 44, 1175–1189.

Seltzer, B. & Pandya, D.N. Afferent cortical connections and architectonics of the superior temporal sulcas and surrounding cortex in the rhesus monkey. Brain Research, 1978, 149, 1–24.

Singer, W. Control of thalamic transmission by corticofugal and ascending reticular pathways in the visual system. Physiological Reviews, 1977, 57, 386–420.

Singer, W., Zihl, J. & Pöppel, E. Subcortical control of visual thresholds in humans: Evidence for modality specific and retinotopically organized mechanisms of selective attention. Experimental Brain Research, 1977, 29, 173–190.

Skinner, J.E. & Yingling, C.D. Central gating mechanisms that regulate event-related potentials and behavior. Progress in Clinical Neurophysiology, 1977, 1, 30–69.

Stein, B.E. Multimodal representation in the superior colliculus and optic tectum. In H. Vanegas (Ed.), Comparative Neurology of the Optic Tectum. New York: Plenum Press, 1984, pp. 819–842.

Steriade, M. & Glen, L.L. Neocortical and caudate projections of intralaminar thalamic neurons. Journal of Neurophysiology, 1982, 48, 352–371.

Treisman, A. Contextual cues in selective listening. Quarterly Journal of Experimental Psychology, 1960, 12, 242–248.

Treisman, A. & Geffen, G. Selective attention and cerebral dominance in perceiving and responding to speech messages. Quarterly Journal of Experimental Psychology, 1967, 19, 1–17.

Treisman, A. & Gelade, G. A feature integration theory of attention. Cognitive Psychology, 1980, 12, 97–136.

Umitsu, Y. & Iwai, E. The posterior inferotemporal cortex in the monkey as an anatomically distinguishable area from adjacent cortical areas of the anterior inferotemporal cortex and the prestriate cortex. In M. Ito (Ed.), Integrative Control Functions of the Brain, volume 3. Tokyo: Kodansha Scientific, 1981.

vanEssen, D.C., Maunsell, J.H.R. & Bixby, J.L. Organization of extrastriate visual areas in the macaque monkey. In C.N. Woolsey (Ed.), Cortical Sensory Organization, volume 2. Clifton, N.J.: Humana Press, 1981.

Warrington, E. & Taylor, A.M. The contribution of the right parietal lobe to object recognition. Cortex, 1973, 9, 152–164.

Watson, R.T. & Heilman, K.M. Thalamic neglect. Neurology, 1979, 29, 690–694.

Watson, R.T., Heilman, K.M., Cauthen, J.C. & King, F.A. Neglect after cingulectomy. Neurology, 1974, 23, 1003–1007.

Watson, R.T., Heilman, K.M., Miller, B.D. & King, F.A. Neglect after mesencephalic reticular formation lesions. Neurology, 1974, 24, 294–298.

Watson, R.T., Miller, B. & Heilman, K.M. Evoked potential in neglect. Archives of Neurology, 1977, 34, 224–227.

Watson, R.T., Miller, B.D. & Heilman, K.M. Nonsensory neglect. Annals of Neurology, 1978, 3, 505–508.

Watson, R.T., Valenstein, E., Day, R. & Heilman, K.M. Ablation of area 7 or cortex around the superior temporal sulcus and neglect. Presented at American Academy of Neurology, Dallas, May, 1985.

Weiskrantz, L. Behavioral changes associated with ablation of the amygdaloid complex in monkeys. Journal of Comparative and Physiological Psychology, 1956, 49, 381–391.

Welch, K. & Stuteville, P. Experimental production of neglect in monkeys. Brain, 1958, 81, 341-347.

Whitlock, D.G. & Nauta, W.J.H. Subcortical projections from the temporal neocortex in Macaca mulatta. Journal of Comparative Neurology, 1956, 106, 183-212.

Woods, J.W. Behavior of chronic decerebrate rats. Journal of Neurophysiology, 1964, 27, 635-644.

Woodworth, R.S. Experimental Psychology. New York: Holt, 1938, chapter XXX.

Wurtz, R.H. & Mohler, C.W. Organization of monkey superior colliculus: enhanced visual response of superficial layer cells. Journal of Neurophysiology, 1976, 39, 745-762.

Yingling, C.D. & Skinner, J.E. Gating of thalamic input to cerebral cortex by nucleus reticularis thalami. Progress in clinical neurophysiology, 1977, 1, 70-96.

Footnote

1. Two recent experiments in which the cortex of the inferior parietal lobule was selectively lesioned in monkeys failed to find evidence of hemispatial neglect (Lynch & McLaren, 1984; Watson, Valenstein, Day & Heilman, 1985) reported in earlier studies. Thus, it is likely that the inferior parietal cortex, unlike other cortical areas receiving projections from the paralaminar nuclei, may not be involved in spatially directed attention.

Neurophysiological and Neuropsychological Aspects
of Spatial Neglect, M. Jeannerod (editor)
© Elsevier Science Publishers B.V. (North-Holland), 1987

UNILATERAL ATTENTION DEFICITS AND HEMISPHERIC ASYMMETRIES IN THE CONTROL OF ATTENTION

Eric A. Roy, Patricia Reuter-Lorenz,
Louise G. Roy, Sherrie Copland
and
Morris Moscovitch

Hemispheric differences in the control of attention are the focus of this chapter. Differential hemispheric involvement in the control of attention may be reflected in the increased incidence and severity of hemi-inattention associated with right hemisphere damage. Clues to the basis of hemispheric asymmetries in the control of attention are, then, sought through considering how components of attention may be affected in these hemi-attentional deficits. Alerting or arousal, orienting and capacity components of attention are each considered through reviewing work done in our laboratory and by others.

Deficits in attention have been a focus of study in neuropsychology for many years (e.g., Heilman, Watson & Valenstein, 1985; Mesulam, 1985). One of the more puzzling and well-known attention deficits is unilateral neglect or hemi-inattention, a disorder in which patients appear unaware of and fail to respond to stimulation occuring contralateral to the damaged hemisphere. Left neglect associated with right hemisphere damage tends to be more common and severe than right neglect associated with left hemisphere damage. This difference in the incidence of left versus right neglect may reflect differential hemispheric involvement in the control of attention. Clues to the basis of this difference between the hemispheres may emerge through considering how the components of attention contribute to the varied manifestations of hemi-attentional deficits: a deficit in alerting or arousal (Heilman & Watson, 1977), a deficit in orienting (Kinsbourne, 1977; Posner, Cohen & Rafal, 1982), or in directed attention (Mesulam, 1981).

This chapter will consider hemispheric differences in the control of attention in view of these different attentional processes. A brief overview of the distinctions between arousal/activation, capacity, and the selection aspects of attention begins the discussion. Evidence concerning possible hemispheric asymmetries in these processes is then considered through reviewing work done in our laboratory and by others. Studies on normal subjects and patients with lateralized brain damage, with and without neglect, are considered in an effort to understand the contributions of the right and left hemisphere to various attention processes and the role of these processes in neglect.

Components of Attention

It has long been recognized that attention comes in many varieties (James, 1890). Three basic aspects of attention have been described over the past two decades. These comprise arousal, capacity, and selection (Posner & Boies, 1971). Arousal or alertness is thought to be closely related to the

underlying level of physiological activation (Duffy, 1957). Arousal is
reflected in performance efficiency or the readiness to take in and respond
to information in the environment (Easterbrook, 1959; Kahneman, 1970).
Vigilance tasks which require periods of sustained attention have typically
been used to study the influence of alertness on information processing. The
effects of warning signals on reaction time and accuracy have also been
studied to determine the role of phasic changes in arousal on perceptual and
response readiness (Posner & Boies, 1971). A variation of these reaction
time experiments involves presenting warning signals to one or the other
visual hemifield (hemisphere) (e.g., Heilman & Van den Abell, 1979) or
presenting the reaction signal to one or the other visual hemifields (e.g.,
Berlucchi, 1978), and observing differences in reaction times between the
two hands or between signals presented to the two hemifields. These
comparisons enable a study of hemispheric asymmetries in response
preparation.

The notion of capacity or resources refers to the allocation of mental
energy to a task which, in turn, influences the quality of performance
(Navon & Gopher, 1979; Wickens, 1984). Since the pool of available resources
is finite, the ability to perform numerous tasks at once is limited. The
deficit in performance incurred by doing two tasks simultaneously rather
than separately may reflect the capacity requirements of a given task.
Capacity requirements can vary due to practice and as a result of the nature
and difficulty of a task.

The distinction between automatic and controlled, or effortful,
processing has been important in accounting for the decreased need for
attentional involvement that occurs with extended practice (Schneider &
Shiffrin, 1976; Schneider, Dumais & Shiffrin, 1984). The type of processing
associated with seemingly effortless, well-practiced behaviours has been
called automatic. These behaviours can occur involuntarily with little or
no conscious intervention and require minimal resources. On the other hand,
controlled   processing   is   effortful,   requires   resources   and   is
subject-regulated.

The selective property of attention is that which determines what
information will be processed relative to all the sources present.
Selective attention provides a means for choice to be exercised regarding
sensory experience. The selection of one stimulus from among many can be
done on the basis of any of a number of stimulus attributes, such as colour,
size, and location (Treisman, 1969; Duncan, 1980). In the study of
unilateral neglect, the process of selecting on the basis of spatial
location has been of most interest (Kinsbourne, 1970a,b, 1974; Posner et
al., 1982). Orienting towards the relevant location is central to spatial
selection. Orienting may involve overt movements of the eyes and head or
just a covert shift of attention (Posner, 1978).

In the following section, we consider evidence for hemispheric
asymmetries in each of these processes: arousal/activation, capacity, and
selection. We first discuss arousal/activation processes. Then we consider
capacity and the spatial allocation of attention in the context of visual
search. Finally, we examine work on the orienting of attention, a process
important in selective attention.

Arousal and Activation

Heilman and his colleagues (Bowers & Heilman, 1980; Heilman & Van den
Abell, 1979, 1980) have suggested that there may be differences between the
hemispheres in arousal/activation processes. They propose that the right
hemisphere is dominant for arousal/activation processes and is capable of
activating (preparing) responses for both hands. The left hemisphere,

however, is capable of activating responses for the contralateral right hand only. In studies by Heilman used to support this notion, subjects were required to release a response key upon the appearance of the reaction signal which was preceded by a visual warning signal presented to one hemisphere or the other. The main focus of these studies was on the relative effects of presenting the warning signal to the right or left hemisphere on reaction time. The prediction was that reaction time should be faster when the warning signal is directed to the right hemisphere than to the left hemisphere since the right hemisphere was thought to enjoy an advantage in arousal/activation processes.

The results from these studies generally supported this prediction in that faster reaction times were observed following warning signals presented to the right hemisphere. In addition, it was found that warning signals presented to the right hemisphere produced reductions in reaction time for both hands relative to a no warning signal condition, while those presented to the left hemisphere reduced reaction times only in the contralateral (right) hand.

Studies in our laboratory (Copland, Note 1) are further examining Heilman's predictions. All three experiments to be discussed below involved a task similar to Heilman's in which subjects were required to depress a response key upon the appearance of a reaction signal. Each trial began with the appearance of a fixation point followed 200 msec later by a warning signal lateralized to one visual field. As in Heilman's studies, the reaction signal followed the warning signal at varying time intervals. Also, as in Heilman's study, a no-warning signal condition was included. In experiment one, this no warning condition was embedded in the warned trials, while in the second experiment, the no-warning condition was run separately. A simple reaction time paradigm was used in which only one hand responded in any one block of trials.

Overall, the results of these first two experiments did not replicate Heilman's findings, that is, there was no advantage in reaction time for the right hemisphere. Possibly, this lack of support derives from the fact that a simple reaction time task was used in these experiments, a paradigm where the subject knows in advance the required response. Bowers and Heilman (1980) qualified their theory of right hemisphere dominance for activation by indicating that "a response-linked decisional process was necessary for inducing activation asymmetries". Therefore, a choice reaction time paradigm in which the subject does not know which hand will be used prior to the reaction signal might be more sensitive to activation asymmetries. The third experiment was designed to examine differences in reaction time between warning signal conditions, in a choice reaction time paradigm.

Results of this experiment basically replicated those of the first two experiments. There were no differences in reaction time between the lateralized warning conditions.

In considering the events on each trial, the lack of a right hemisphere effect of the lateralized warning signal may have related to the appearance of the fixation dot at the beginning of each trial. That is, on each trial, a fixation dot appeared 200 msec prior to the lateralized warning signal. The fixation dot may have acted as a warning signal, possibly washing out the predicted reduction in reaction time following warning signals directed to the right hemisphere. If the appearance of the fixation point was acting to alert the subject, then it would seem reasonable to remove its alerting characteristics thereby enabling the lateralized warning signals to be the sole source of activation. In a new series of experiments, then, several methodological changes are being made to reduce this alerting effect of the fixation point. These changes may permit a clearer examination of the activating effect of the lateralized warning signals on reaction time.

Visual Search

Kinsbourne (1970a,b) proposed a model of orienting in which a common regulatory principle governs hemispheric control of all directional orienting behaviours. He explained that like head and eye movements, attention shifts are directed to the right or left by the contralateral hemisphere. In neglect, the directional tendency of the intact hemisphere dominates when it can no longer be opposed by the damaged hemisphere. Therefore, left neglect is due to the unopposed rightward attentional bias of the intact left hemisphere, whereas right neglect is an expression of the right hemisphere's leftward bias. Kinsbourne (1974, 1977) has also proposed that the rightward orienting tendency of the left hemisphere is essentially stronger than the leftward tendency of the right hemisphere. The basic difference in strength is reflected in the asymmetry in overt orienting in the form of head turning found in infants ((Turkewitz, Gordon & Birch, 1965; Coryell, 1985) and in the differential incidence of right and left neglect.

Heilman's group has also offered an account of neglect which has considered the allocation of attention in space. Their multi-faceted theory addresses many aspects of neglect phenomena and centers on the idea that the right hemisphere is dominant for attention, although they do not refer specifically to spatial orienting in the sense used by Kinsbourne (1970a,b; 1974; 1977) and Posner (1980; see below). One aspect of this dominance is the ability of the right hemisphere to attend (orient) to both the right and left sides of space, whereas left hemisphere control is contralateral. This proposal is based primarily on the finding that electroencephalographic measures (EEG) in normal subjects indicated right hemisphere desynchrony to either right visual field (RVF) or left visual field (LVF) warning signals. Left hemisphere desynchrony followed only RVF warning events (Heilman and Van Den Abell, 1980).

Bilateral control could be operationalized as the ability to orient to the right and left sides of space. Alternatively, it could imply that the right hemisphere can attend to a broader region of space at a given point in time whereas the left hemisphere attends to a more restricted region. Heilman explains that bilateral attention of the right hemisphere enables it to compensate for the loss of attentional control when the left hemisphere is damaged. The left hemisphere cannot provide the same compensation after right hemisphere damage. Thus, left neglect is more common. Kinsbourne's idea of a stronger rightward than leftward orienting tendency predicts that right hemisphere damage would lead to a greater directional bias. In this section, research on hemispheric control of spatial attention will be considered in light of these hypotheses.

The role of hemispheric mechanisms in the spatial allocation of attention may be reflected in the search behaviour of patients with lateralized lesions. A number of studies have examined the ability of right hemisphere and left hemisphere patients to locate a target amidst an array of distractors. Search time and accuracy as a function of target location provide an index of search efficiency in the right and left sides of space.

DeRenzi, Faglioni and Scotti (1970) found that, on a visual search task, both right hemisphere and left hemisphere patients took slightly longer to find contralesional than ipsilesional targets. On a tactile search task, a similar but even stronger pattern emerged. Right hemisphere patients were more severely impaired, often failing to find the target within the alloted time period when it was in the contralesional field. The authors point out that search requires the integrated functioning of motoric, attentional, and representational processes. Although they conclude that the multimodal nature of the deficit argues for a disorder in space representation, their findings do not rule out the possibility of attentional impairment. It is conceivable that an orienting bias consequent to brain damage could constrain not only the spatial allocation of attention, but also the directional control of head and limb movements.

Although shifts in attention and eye movements can be dissociated, typically, the position of attention and gaze coincides. Thus, one way to study attentional orienting is to examine eye movements. Chédru, Leblanc and Lhermitte (1973) recorded the eye movements of right hemisphere and left hemisphere patients using a visual search task. Patients showed an overall increase in search time in relation to controls, and both right hemisphere and left hemisphere groups took longer to find a target positioned contralesionally. Therefore, disordered search behaviour was common to both groups. The measure which discriminated among patient groups was the percentage of time spent exploring the right versus left sides of the display. Eye movement records revealed that the right hemisphere patients spent a greater proportion of the search time in the right side of the display than in the left. Left hemisphere patients divided their time equally between the two halves.

Both Chédru et al. and DeRenzi et al. found increased search time for contralesional targets regardless of the laterality of the lesion. However, patients with right hemisphere damage seemed to have their attention anchored in the ipsilesional side of space more so than did left hemisphere patients. This suggests that while a spatially selective deficit in searching behaviour may occur after right or left hemisphere damage, the deficit associated with right hemisphere damage may be more severe and may reflect a different underlying disturbance than the left hemisphere deficit. These findings, however, do not distinguish between Kinsbourne's and Heilman's theories.

Some recent work in our laboratory (Roy, Note 2; Roy & Roy, Note 3) has utilized the visual search paradigm to evaluate further the proposal that the left hemisphere controls attention primarily in the right hemispace, while the right hemisphere directs attention to both fields. In this task, patients were required to indicate whether a target letter appeared on a television monitor by moving a small toggle switch. The target appeared with a probability of .75, was presented equally often in the left or right hemispace, and appeared alone or in concert with 17 or 35 distractors. According to Heilman's proposal, the prediction was that damage to the right hemisphere should be associated with increased search time and decreased accuracy in both fields, while damage to the left hemisphere should impair search time and accuracy in the right hemispace only.

The results for search time seemed to support these predictions. Right hemisphere patients demonstrated no significant differences between the hemispatial fields, while for the left hemisphere patients, search time was significantly longer in the contralesional hemispace. Both groups exhibited longer search times than the controls.

The finding that right hemisphere patients exhibited no difference in search time between hemispatial fields suggests that damage to this hemisphere depressed speed of visual search uniformly across both hemispatial fields. Such a pattern might be expected if the right hemisphere were involved in bilateral attentional control. The observation that left hemisphere patients exhibited increased search time only in the contralesional (right) hemispatial field is consistent with the idea that left hemisphere attentional control is primarily contralateral.

While our search time data seem to provide some support for the notion that the right hemisphere may direct attention to both hemispatial fields, a careful consideration of these data in conjunction with those for accuracy raises some concerns about the extent of support for this notion. One might predict that the pattern for accuracy data should conform to that for the search time data. Such a consistency in pattern was not observed, however. Right hemisphere patients were significantly less acurate in response to targets in the left hemispatial field while at the same time exhibiting a bilateral increase in search time. For left hemispheric patients, accuracy was equivalent across hemispatial fields, whereas search time was significantly longer for targets in the right hemispatial field.

The unexpected dissociation of search time and accuracy measures complicate the interpretation of these results and cautions against making attributions of hemispheric dominance or superiority in the control of search. The dissociation also underscores the importance of using several measures of task performance in order to determine how search is conducted. As in previous investigations of search, both patient groups show some spatially specific deficit. However, the styles or strategies of search used by the two patient groups seem to differ. Right hemisphere patients maintain a constant search time across hemispatial fields at the cost of more errors in the contralesional field. Left hemisphere patients, on the other hand, maintain accuracy scores across hemispatial fields at the cost of increased search time in the contralesional hemispatial field. Damage to one or the other hemisphere may cause different impairments in attentional control which in turn seem to influence the way the search task is carried out. These findings do not clearly support predictions from Heilman's or Kinsbourne's models.

To study the capacity demands of visual search, two search conditions were used, a single feature and a conjoined feature condition (see Treisman & Gelade, 1980). In the single feature condition, the target differed from the distractors on a single feature (colour or letter shape). In the conjoined feature condition, the target differed from the distractors on the two dimensions, sharing colour with some distractors and shape with the others.

Considering the notion of capacity demands in this type of visual search task, Treisman and Gelade (1980) have shown that the conjoined feature condition involves a serial search while the single feature condition involves a parallel search. This difference in the nature of search is reflected in the relationship between search time and number of distractors. In the single feature condition, they found that search time did not increase with number of distractors, while there was a significant increase in search time with the number of distractors in the conjoined feature condition. One could infer from these differences in the search time function, that the conjoined feature condition involved a more attention-demanding search process. To assess whether there was any difference in attention demands of visual search following left or right hemisphere damage, comparisons of the search time functions in the conjoined and single feature conditions were made between the two brain-damaged groups and the controls.

Examination of the data revealed a trend for left hemisphere patients to exhibit longer search times over both feature conditions. This finding may be due to the fact that verbal stimuli were used in this task. There were, however, no differences among the groups in the slopes of the search time functions in either feature condition. A closer examination of the search time functions in all three groups revealed a significant increase in search time with number of distractors in both the single and conjoined feature conditions, suggesting that a serial, attention-demanding search was involved in both conditions.

Taken together, our data suggest that there are no differences in the effects of varying attention demands on the manner in which search is carried out by left and right hemisphere patients. Damage to one or the other hemisphere, then, does not appear to alter selectively the resources available for processing information in this type of visual search task. Had damage to one hemisphere limited processing resources, one might have expected a greater slope to the search time function particularly in the conjoined feature condition in that brain-damaged group. This finding suggests that the difference between patient groups on search time and accuracy measures is not due to the effects of lateralized damage on resource availability. Other resource demanding tasks, however, need to be examined before one can accept this conclusion with confidence.

The unexpected evidence for serial search even in the single feature condition suggests that this type of attention-demanding search process was employed by all the patients, even the control, non-brain-damaged patients. Such was not the case in Treisman and Gelade's (1980) study in that serial search was found only in the conjoined condition. This discrepancy with Treisman's work could be due to the fact that all the subjects used in this study were at least forty to fifty years older than Treisman's subjects. Perhaps, the general slowing associated with advancing age (Salthouse & Somberg, 1982; Smith, 1984) places constraints on parallel processing which selectively affects automatic processing and forces the use of more controlled processing as reflected in the serial search patterns.

Orienting

Posner and his colleagues are pioneers in the investigation of the effects of lateralized brain damage on covert attentional shifts. Posner, Walker, Friedrich and Rafal (1984) had parietal patients perform a detection task in which an advance cue indicated which of two locations would most likely contain a target. Like normal subjects, parietal patients were faster at detecting a target at the expected location than at the unexpected location. This pattern emerged for both the ipsilesional and contralesional targets, although reaction time to contralesional targets was consistently slower. This finding indicates that these patients can voluntarily shift their attention in response to a cue.

The most striking deficits emerged when patients were misinformed about the subsequent target location (invalid trials). When they expected the target contralesionally and it occurred on the opposite side, they showed the normal increase in reaction time. However, when they moved their attention to the ipsilesional or "good" side and the target appeared on the opposite side, it took the patients significantly longer to respond to the target. This was true for both right and left parietal patients, but the effects were significantly greater for right parietal patients. Posner et al. proposed that the deficit on invalid trials when the target is presented contralesionally is due to the inability to disengage attention in order to shift contralesionally. According to Kinsbourne's account of unilateral neglect, the bias of the intact hemisphere dominates when it can no longer be opposed by the damaged hemisphere. Also, the rightward orienting bias of the left hemisphere is stronger than the leftward bias of the right hemisphere. Therefore, patients with right hemisphere damage should have more difficulty disengaging from the right than left hemisphere patients should have disengaging from the left. In fact, the findings of Posner et al. are consistent with this prediction. Moving attention either ipsilesionally or contralesionally did not seem to be the problem for these patients since attention shifts in either direction were evident on valid trials. Thus, any differences between right hemisphere and left hemisphere patients on this task cannot be readily accounted for by the hypothesis that the right hemisphere can direct attention to either side of space.

In a study of patients with right hemisphere damage, Riddoch and Humphrey (1983) found similar results using lateral cues on a line bisection task. Patients with lateralized damage typically draw the intersect towards the ipsilesional endpoint rather than at the midpoint, indicating their tendency to underestimate the contralesional extent of the line. Riddoch and Humphreys placed single letter cues at either the right or left endpoint or bilaterally. Patients with left neglect were asked to name any cue that they saw and then to bisect the line. It was found that a unilateral left cue was consistently named and significantly reduced the amount of neglect. When the cues were bilateral, subjects often failed to name the left cue and showed no significant decrease in neglect relative to the no cue condition. Neglect was the greatest when only the right cue was present.

Three important points are raised by Riddoch and Humphreys' and Posner's results. First, when cued, patients can deliberately orient their attention to both the ipsilesional and contralesional hemispaces. Second, in the presence of a competing ipsilesional stimulus, the tendency for contralesional orienting is minimized. Furthermore, Posner's findings suggest that there is greater difficulty in disengaging attention from the right hemispace for right hemisphere patients than disengaging from the left hemispace for left hemisphere patients.

A possible basis for the effects of lateralized brain damage on orienting has been suggested by our own work (Reuter-Lorenz, Note 4; Reuter-Lorenz, Moscovitch & Kinsbourne, Note 5) on the hemispheric control of orienting in normal subjects. A tachistoscopic line bisection task was used to assess the distribution of attention in space. Subjects viewed a series of briefly presented (less than 120 msec) horizontal lines each of which had an intersect positioned at midpoint or slightly to the left or right of center. The subject's task was to judge whether the intersect was located at the midpoint or to the left or right of center. The tendency to underestimate the left or right extents of the line was reflected in the pattern of errors associated with identifying the intersect's location.

When lines were presented unilaterally, subjects consistently underestimated the ipsilateral extent. That is, when the line was in the RVF, its left extent was underestimated, whereas, when in the LVF, the right extent was underestimated. This pattern suggests that the left hemisphere has rightward attentional bias and that the right hemisphere has a leftward bias.

The same pattern of results emerged in a further experiment in which the lines themselves were presented foveally. The line was flanked by a box which was slightly displaced from either the right or left endpoint. On half the trials, the box contained a dot and on half, it did not. In one condition, the subjects were told to ignore the boxes and simply to report where the intersects occurred. In a second condition, they had to attend to the unilateral boxes, report whether they were empty or full, and, then, indicate the intersect position. Subjects were instructed to keep their eyes fixated centrally. Conditions were blocked so that the box was presented in the same visual field for a series of trials. Regardless of whether the boxes were attended or ignored, they systematically biased attention. The RVF box produced a rightward bias or relative left neglect on the line bisection task, whereas the LVF box produced a leftward bias or right neglect. These biases were opposite in direction but equivalent in magnitude.

An interesting asymmetry emerged in further experiments when conflicting orienting demands were produced by the viewing conditions. In one set of conditions, stimuli were randomized so that subjects could not anticipate in which visual field the box would appear. In another, boxes were presented in both visual fields and subjects had to attend selectively to one or the other while making the bisection judgement.

In both types of conflict situation, there were no overall differences in bisection accuracy for RVF versus LVF conditions. However, the right bias associated with the RVF conditions proved to be robust, whereas the leftward bias associated with LVF conditions was significantly diminished in the presence of orienting conflict. In other words, in the presence of lateral orienting conflict, normal subjects showed a stronger tendency to orient to the right and neglect the left extent of the line than to orient to the left and neglect the right extent. This pattern is consistent with Kinsbourne's proposal that the rightward lateral orienting tendency is stronger than the leftward tendency. Furthermore, these findings may lend support to one interpretation of Heilman's notion of right hemisphere bilateral attention. Differential orienting strength may underlie hemispheric differences in the spatial allocation of attention. A strong directional bias in association with left hemisphere control may be related to a highly selective, focal allocation policy. A weaker directional orienting bias associated with the right hemisphere may allow attention to be allocated less selectively in space. A weaker directional bias may enable the right hemisphere to distribute attention over a broader spatial region.

Discussion

The evidence reviewed in this chapter suggests that there may be hemispheric differences in some aspects of attentional control. Our own work with normal subjects has indicated little support for the proposal that the right hemisphere has an advantage in arousal/activitation processes. Warning signals presented to the right hemisphere did not serve to decrease the time to react to the reaction signal relative to warning signals presented to the left hemisphere. The effect of the lateralized warning signals on reaction time may have been reduced due to the alerting effect associated with the appearance of the fixation point. Methodological changes are being made to remove this alerting effect so as to assess more clearly the effect of the lateralized warning signal on reaction time.

With regard to orienting and selection processes, work by Posner et al. (1982, 1984) suggests that damage to the parietal regions of either hemispheres leads to an impairment in disengaging attention from one location, particularly locations in the ipsilateral hemispace, in order to direct it to another location. This disengage component of orienting seems to be more affected by right parietal damage and is particularly exemplified in a tendency to maintain orientation toward the right.

The findings of Reuter-Lorenz et al. reviewed above, fit well with this pattern. Evidence that each hemisphere directs attention contralaterally was obtained in normal subjects. Furthermore, the rightward orienting tendency was found to be more robust than the leftward tendency. These findings suggest that the orienting behavior of patients with lateralized brain damage may reflect the bias of the intact hemisphere. As Kinsbourne has proposed, right hemisphere damage leaves the contralateral orienting bias of the left hemisphere unopposed, whereas left hemisphere damage leaves the right hemisphere unopposed. Thus, the inability to disengage attention from the ipsilesional focus may be due to the dominating influence of the intact hemisphere. Furthermore, a stronger rightward than leftward bias should lead to greater difficulty in the disengage operation for right than left hemisphere patients, which is the pattern found by Posner's group.

These findings suggest that the hemispheres may differ in their control of the spatial allocation of attention. A weaker lateral orienting bias in association with right hemisphere control may enable a broader spatial distribution of attention, whereas a stronger orienting bias may permit a focal, highly selective attentional mode in association with left hemisphere control.

The selection aspects of attention have also been examined in the context of search tasks in patients with lateralized brain damage. Generally, these studies have shown a greater impairment in terms of more errors and slower search time in right hemisphere patients, particularly those with visual field defects. A study in our laboratory (Roy & Roy, Note 3) examined both the selection and capacity aspects of attention in a visual search task. While there were no clear differences between the left and right-hemisphere patients in terms of overall accuracy or search time, somewhat different search patterns were observed in the two patient groups. Right hemisphere patients seemed to maintain search time constant across hemispatial fields at the cost of increased errors in the contralesional (left) hemispace, while the left hemisphere patients seemed to opt for maintaining accuracy across spatial fields at the cost of increased time to find targets in the contralesional (right) hemispace.

These differing search patterns may reflect different strategies. The right hemisphere patients may be focusing on search time, while the left hemisphere patients may be focusing on accuracy. The immediate implications of these apparently different strategies for understanding search performance is not clear. What is clear, however, is that we need to use tasks and measures of performance which afford the opportunity to identify different strategies in performance.

Considering the capacity aspect of attention, there were no clear differences between the hemispheric groups in the effects of varying capacity demands on visual search performance.

These findings that have been reviewed provide some initial clues to the neurobehavioural bases of attention, particularly as to hemispheric asymmetries. Many issues remain to be considered and examined, however. First, while we have viewed attention not as a unitary concept, but as one which involves a number of component processes, it is important to recognize that these components themselves may involve subprocesses of their own. Orientation, for example, seems to involve at least three aspects: disengaging attention from the current focus, moving attention, and engaging attention at a new location (Posner & Cohen, 1984). Arousal and activation, likewise, seem to involve at least two aspects, a sensory (input) and a motor (output) component. Given this idea of subprocesses, it behooves us to carefully study each of these with a view to understanding their neurobehavioural basis. Posner et al. (1982, 1984) have begun to show that the components of orienting may have different neural substrates. Disengaging attention, as we have seen, seems to depend on parietal areas. Moving attention, on the other hand, seems more dependent on midbrain and collicular structures. In the same vein, given that there appear to be both sensory and motor components to activation, it would be important to determine, for example, whether the right hemisphere advantage for activation proposed by Heilman is related to an advantage in processing input (sensory aspects) or preparing a response (motor aspects).

Another point here relates to the capacity component of attention. One study (Roy, Note 2; Roy & Roy, Note 3) carried out in our laboratory suggests there may not be differences between the hemispheres in the effects of varying capacity demands, at least as measured by search time functions in the context of visual search. Heilman's argument that the right hemisphere is capable of controlling attention in both hemispatial fields, however, suggests that the right hemisphere may engage in a processing mode which is less demanding of resources and, thus, enjoys the capacity of distributing those resources to both hemispatial fields. Using Schneider and Schiffrin's (1977) concepts of automatic versus controlled processing, the advantage conferred on the right hemisphere may then arise because this hemisphere is more capable of automatic processing than is the left hemisphere. Work with normals indeed suggests that the right hemisphere may be more capable of processing information in parallel (Bryden, 1982). This notion of capacity demand could be further examined using a dual task paradigm in which patients must perform a secondary task while engaging in visual search.

A second related issue concerns the interface between psychological and neural processes of attention. In this chapter, we have been particularly interested in hemispheric asymmetries in attentional processes. These hemispheric aspects form only a small part of a larger network of neural processes underlying attention. Attention like other aspects of human behaviour can be viewed as involving a complex system of functions, a so-called functional system. This idea of a functional system reflects the current view of brain-behaviour relations termed functional pluripotentialism (Luria, 1974) and has been applied to praxis (Roy, 1978, 1983) and to processes of attention (Mesulam, 1981). In this view, attention involves a number of functional components each of which is subserved by a particular brain area. These brain areas, comprised of reticular structures, cingulate cortex, and parietal and frontal cortical regions, form a neural network. Damage to any of these areas seems to disrupt attentional processes in a characteristic way depending on which component of attention has been compromised (see Mesulam, 1981). Given this view, a clearer understanding of attention would seem to depend on parallel advances in psychological and neurological perspectives of attention. Developing concepts of the psychological processes underlying attention may be mapped on to neural structures, thus fostering a description of attention based on an emerging interface between behavioural and neural processes. This approach is exemplified well in Posner's work (e.g., Posner, in press).

A final consideration deals with the relationship of the components of attention discussed here to an account of neglect. The evidence reviewed suggests that there may be hemispheric differences in certain aspects of attentional processes. Our own work on the effects of lateralized warning signals on reaction time provided no clear indication that the right hemisphere is dominant for activation in normal subjects. This result does not rule out the possibility that the right hemisphere has the ability to assume control of activational processes once the left hemisphere is damaged, whereas the left hemisphere cannot do so in the advent of right hemisphere damage. Such an ability may explain the bilateral impairment in search time found by Roy and Roy (Note 3) and, as others have suggested, could explain the greater increase in reaction time after right, as opposed to left, hemisphere damage. Yet, how could an activation problem of this kind produce the spatially selective (i.e., contralesional) disturbance found in neglect? The answer to this question is not likely to be a simple one because it involves the issue of the relationship among the different components of attention.

A deficit in directional orienting would provide a straightforward explanation of the spatial features of hemi-neglect. But can it alone fully account for the epidemiological fact of greater left than right neglect? According to Posner's results, parietal damage to either hemisphere impairs this disengage operation associated with orienting. The greater impairment on this task found in right than left hemisphere patients may be related to the stronger rightward bias in normal subjects (Reuter-Lorenz, Note 4) and may contribute to the greater incidence of left neglect (Kinsbourne, 1974, 1977). However, while the orienting deficit found by Posner's group was reliably associated with parietal damage, it was evident in patients with or without signs of neglect. It is possible that the magnitude of the orienting deficit on this task may correlate with other indices of hemi-inattention; however, this has yet to be established.

It seems reasonable to hypothesize that a directional orienting deficit could form the core of the neglect syndrome and, as such, provide the basis for the hemispatial or unilateral nature of the disorder. A stronger rightward than leftward attentional bias could contribute to the differential incidence of right and left neglect. If activation or arousal processes are also disturbed, the difficulties associated with an orienting impairment may be exacerbated. However, disturbances of activation/arousal alone may be insufficient to produce a unilateral impairment in spatial attention.

Decrements in resources may also be insufficient to produce unilateral attention impairment. As noted above, Roy and Roy (Note 3) found that the magnitude of contralesional search deficit was not influenced by the type or the number of distractors. If resource decrements underlie neglect, then increased capacity demands should have exacerbated the unilateral search deficit. Interactions between the capacity and selection aspects of attention may emerge if a heavier attentional load is imposed and/or the task uses materials (e.g., shapes) which the patient finds difficult to identify (cf. Leicester, Sitman, Stoddard & Mohr, 1969). Our findings suggest that decrements in attentional resources alone seem insufficient to produce unilateral attentional disturbance.

This analysis suggests that an impairment in lateral orienting may be a necessary condition for hemi-attentional disturbances of any kind. In cases where only orienting aspects of attention are affected, only subtle features of the neglect syndrome, such as extinction, may be evident. Increasingly severe forms of neglect may involve additional impairment in other components of attention (i.e., arousal/activation) in conjunction with an underlying deficit in orienting.

Our aim in this paper has been to move toward a more accurate characterization of the nature of the attentional impairments associated with lateralized cortical lesions in general and neglect in particular. It is our belief that this type of approach will help to define the nature of hemispheric differences in attention and will aid in the elaboration of neurobehavioral attention theory. Moreover, it may allow for the development of a taxonomy of hemiattentional disturbances which can guide patient classification and possibly patient treatment.

References

Berlucchi, G. Interhemispheric integration of simple visuomotor responses. In P.A. Buser and A. Rougeul-Buser (Eds.), Cerebral Correlates of Conscious Experience. Amsterdam: North Holland, 1978.

Bowers, D. & Heilman, K. Material specific hemispheric activation. Neuropsychologia, 1980, 18, 309-319.

Bryden, M.P. Laterality: Functional asymmetry in the intact brain. New York: Academic Press, 1982.

Chédru, F., Leblanc, M. & Lhermitte, F. Visual searching in normal and brain-damaged subjects (contribution to the study of unilateral inattention). Cortex, 1973, 9, 94-111.

Coryell, J. Infant rightward asymmetries predict right-handedness in childhood. Neuropsychologia, 1985, 23, 269-272.

De Renzi, E., Faglioni, P. & Scotti, G. Hemispheric contribution to exploration of space through the visual and tactile modality. Cortex, 1970, 6, 191-203.

Duffy, E. The psychological significance of the concept of "arousal" or "activation". Psychological Review, 1957, 64, 265-275.

Duncan, J. The focus of interference in the perception of simultaneous stimuli. Psychological Review, 1980, 87, 272-300.

Easterbrook, J.A. The effects of emotion on cue utilization and the organization of behavior. Psychological Review, 1959, 66, 183-201.

Heilman, K.M. & Van Den Abell, T. Right hemispheric dominance for mediating cerebral activation. Neuropsychologia, 1979, 17, 315-321.

Heilman, K.M. & Van Den Abell, T. Right hemispheric dominance for attention: The mechanism underlying hemispheric asymmetries of inattention (neglect). Neurology, 1980, 30, 327-330.

Heilman, K.M. & Watson, R.T. Mechanisms underlying unilateral neglect syndrome. In E.A. Weinstein and R.P. Friedland (Eds.), Advances in Neurology, Vol. 18, Hemi-Inattention and Hemispheric Specialization. New York, Raven Press, 1977.

Heilman, K., Watson, R. & Valenstein, E. Neglect and related disorders. In K. Heilman and E. Valenstein (Eds.), Clinical Neuropsychology. New York: Oxford University Press, 1985.

James, W. The Principles of Psychology. New York: Holt, 1890.

Kahneman, D. Remarks on attention control. Acta Psychologica, 1970, 33, 118-131.

Kinsbourne, M. A model for the mechanism of unilateral neglect of space. Transactions of the American Neurological Association, 1970a, 95, 143-145.

Kinsbourne, M. The cerebral basis of lateral asymmetries in attention. Acta Psychologica, 1970b, 33, 193-201.

Kinsbourne, M. Mechanisms of hemispheric interactions in man. In M. Kinsbourne and W.L. Smith (Eds.), Hemispheric Disconnection and Cerebral Function. Charles C. Thomas, Springfield, Illinois, 1974.

Kinsbourne, M. Hemi-neglect and hemisphere rivalry. In E.A. Weinstein and R.P. Friedland (Eds.), Advances in Neurology,Vol. 18, Hemi-Inattentional and Hemispheric specialization. New York: Raven Press, 1977.

Leicester, J., Sitman, M., Stoddard, L.T. & Mohr, F.P. Some determinants of visual neglect. Journal of Neurology, Neurosurgery and Psychiatry, 1969, 32, 580-587.

Luria, A. The Working Brain. London: Penguin, 1974.

Mesulam, M. A cortical network for directed attention and unilateral neglect. Annals of neurology, 1981, 10, 309-325.

Mesulam, M. Attention, confusional states and neglect. In M.M. Mesulam (Ed.), Principles of Behavioral Neurology. Philadelphia: F.A. Davis, 1985.

Navon, D. & Gopher, D. On the economy of the human processing system. Psychological Review, 1979, 86, 214-255.

Posner, M.I. Chronometric Explorations of Mind. Hillsdale, NJ: Lawrence Erlbaum, 1978.

Posner, M.I. Orienting attention. The VIIth Sir Frederic Barlett Lecture. Quaterly Journal of Experimental Psychology, 1980, 32, 3-25.

Posner, M.I. Hierarchical distributed networks in the neuropsychology of selective attention. In A. Caramazza (Ed.), Advances in Cognitive Neuropsychology, 1. Hillsdale, NJ: Erlbaum Associates, in press.

Posner, M.I. & Boies. Components of attention. Psychological Review, 1971, 78, 391–408.

Posner, M.I. & Cohen, Y. Components of visual orienting. In H. Bouma and D. Bowhuis (Eds.), Attention and Performance X. Hillsdale, NJ: Erlbaum Associates, 1984.

Posner, M.I., Cohen, Y. & Rafal, R.D. Neural systems control of spatial orienting. Philosophical Transactions of the Royal Society of London, 1982, B298, 187–198.

Posner, M.I., Walker, J.A., Friedrich, F.F. & Rafal, R.D. Effects of parietal injury on covert orienting of atention. Journal of Neuroscience, 1984, 4, 1863–74.

Riddoch, M.J. & Humphreys, G. The effect of cuing on unilateral neglect. Neuropsychologia, 1983, 21, 589–599.

Roy, E.A. Apraxia: A new look at an old syndrome. Journal of Human Movement Studies, 1978, 4, 191–210.

Roy, E.A. Neuropsychological perspectives on apraxia and related action disorders. In R.A. Magill (Ed.), Advances in Psychology, Volume 12, Memory and Control of Action. Amsterdam: North Holland, 1983.

Salthouse, T.A. & Somberg, B.L. Isolating the age deficit in speeded performance. Journal of Gerontology, 1982, 37, 59–63.

Schneider, W. & Shiffrin, R.M. Controlled and automatic human information processing: I. Detection, search, and attention. Psychological Review, 1977, 84, 1–66.

Schneider, W., Dumais, S.T. & Shiffrin, R.M. Automatic and control processing and attention. In R. Parasuraman, R. Davis and J. Beatty (Eds.), Varieties of Attention. New York: Academic Press, 1984.

Smith, C.B. Aging and changes in cerebral energy metabolism. Trends in Neurosciences, 1984, 7, 203–208.

Treisman, A.M. Strategies and models of selective attention. Psychological Review, 1969, 76, 282–299.

Treisman, A.M. & Gelade, G. A feature–integration theory of attention. Cognitive Psychology, 1980, 12, 97–136.

Turkewitz, G., Gordon, E.W. & Birch, H.G. Head turning in the human neonate: Spontaneous patterns. Journal of Genetic Psychology, 1965, 107, 143.

Wickens, C.D. Processing resources in attention. In R. Parasuraman and R. Davies (Eds.), Varieties of Attention. New York: Academic Press, 1984.

Acknowledgements : Preparation of this manuscript was funded through grants to E. Roy, from the Natural Sciences and Engineering Research Council and the National Health Research Development Program, Health & Welfare, Canada.

Footnotes

1. Copland, S. Hemispheric differences in attention and response preparation. Unpublished Master's thesis, Department of Psychology, University of Waterloo, May, 1985.

2. Roy, L. Attention deficits in patients with lateralized brain damage. Unpublished Master's thesis, Department of Kinesiology, University of Waterloo, May, 1985.

3. Roy, L. & Roy, E.A. Attention deficits in patients with lateralized brain damage. Poster presentation at annual meeting of North American Society for Psychology of Sport & Physical Activity, May, 1985.

4. Reuter-Lorenz, P.A. Hemispheric control of spatial attention. Unpublished Doctoral disseration, Department of Psychology, University of Toronto, 1986.

5. Reuter-Lorenz, P.A., Moscovitch, M., & Kinsbourne, M. Lateral attention bias in a visual line bisection task: Similarities between the performances of neglect patients and normal subjects. Paper read at North American Conference, International Neuropsychological Society, San Diego, California, February, 1985.

Neurophysiological and Neuropsychological Aspects
of Spatial Neglect, M. Jeannerod (editor)
© Elsevier Science Publishers B.V. (North-Holland), 1987

COORDINATES OF EXTRACORPOREAL SPACE

John L. Bradshaw, Norman C. Nettleton
Jane M. Pierson, Lyn E. Wilson
and
Gregory Nathan

Unilateral neglect may be considered with reference to several spatial-coordinate systems, e.g., those relating to the body midline, head and retina, and seems to involve alterations in the deployment of attention. Left hemineglect may be more frequent or, possibly, merely more salient than right hemineglect, perhaps because of asymmetries in the representation of extracorporeal space. In normal subjects we have reported a number of analogous phenomena. Visually presented lines or tactually/kinesthetically presented rods were typically transected slightly to the left of the true midpoint, an effect which could be manipulated by varying the salience of the two extremities. In a variety of tactuomotor tasks involving the fingers, the position in space to left or right of the body was found to be more important than the actual hand (left or right) employed, which was placed either on its own side of the body or across the midline to the opposite side. In vibrotactile reaction time experiments, performance was also found to be determined by the position of the responding hand, though <u>hand</u> asymmetries replaced <u>hemispace</u> asymmetries under conditions of stimulus uncertainty. In the auditory modality, it was the position, real or <u>perceived</u> (as under conditions of visual capture) of a sound source (loudspeaker) which determined performance asymmetries. In all these experiments asymmetries were lost by dissociating the head and body coordinate systems, through the maintenance of a 90° head turn to left or right, or by the dissociation of the gravitational and corporeal coordinate systems, when lying horizontallly upon the left or right side. The hemispheres may map both proximal sensory (and motor) events involving the body surface and more distal events occurring out in extracorporeal space. These two representations may be experimentally dissociated.

Hemineglect

Unilateral brain damage may lead to unawareness or neglect of stimuli or events in the side of space opposite to the lesion (De Renzi, 1982; Heilman, Bowers & Watson, 1984; Heilman & Valenstein, 1979; Mesulam, 1981, 1983). The syndrome is usually said to be more common after right hemisphere damage, though a minority find no differences in the frequency of the disorder after lesions on either side (Ogden, 1985, and see her review in this volume). Right hemisphere lesions, however, do usually lead to a more severe manifestation of the condition (Ogden,

1985). In severe cases it is as if the left half of the patient's world has ceased to exist, with failure to report, respond to or orient towards stimuli on the side contralateral to the lesion. The patient may shave, groom or dress only the right side, leave food untouched on the left side of the plate, read only words, letters or sentences written on the right side of a page, leave an unusually wide margin on the left, copy only the right side of a drawing, and bisect a visually-presented horizontal line to the right of the true midpoint, especially if the whole line lies to the left of the midline (Heilman & Valenstein, 1979). There may even be neglect of the left side of a scene which is currently being imagined (Bisiach & Luzzatti, 1978), such that the patient's inability to recall objects depends upon his or her imaginary standpoint. Thus we can delineate the affected "space" with respect to the actual observer (patient), i.e. extrapersonal space, or with respect to the vantage point of an imagined observer during topographical recall, or with respect to a particular component of a larger object (Halsband, Gruhn & Ettlinger, in preparation). The lesions causing the syndrome are usually large and either of sudden onset or are rapidly progressive, though the symptoms typically diminish over time. Nevertheless extinction, when all the other above symptoms have finally abated, may remain relatively intractable. Here, a patient capable of adequate response to unilaterally presented stimuli on either side, when given simultaneous bilateral stimulation (visual, auditory or tactual) may fail to report stimuli contralateral to the damaged hemisphere. (With normal subjects, the dichotic right-ear advantage with competing simultaneous stimulation of both ears may be an analogous phenomenon, see e.g. Bradshaw, Burden & Nettleton, 1986, for a review.) Hemineglect does not of course depend upon extinction, and unlike right hemineglect, right side extinction is by no means rare (Schwartz, Marchok, Kreinick & Flynn, 1979). Indeed hemineglect may reflect not just a deficit in directed attention, but also a deficit in how space is actually represented (De Renzi, 1982). Moreover unilateral neglect may be considered with reference to more than one spatial coordinate system, e.g. the body midline (the currently preferred viewpoint), head coordinates (e.g. when the head is turned with respect to the body), and even retinal coordinates, with respect to gaze direction (Bisiach, Capitani & Porta, 1985; Heilman et al., 1984); all three coordinate systems can be mutually dissociated by appropriate turn conditions. Bisiach et al. (1985, and see also Bradshaw and Pierson, 1985) have concluded that egocentric and extracorporeal space is organized topographically in the brain, in a projection system separate from that of the proximal receptor or body surface, and that there are circumscribed brain areas wherein lesions can result in representational loss limited to definite regions of space. Bisiach et al. found that the boundary of the neglected area of the tactile apparatus was influenced both by the sagittal midplane of the trunk, and by line of sight in terms of both head and gaze orientation. They also cite physiological and anatomical evidence of thalamic and premotor cells firing to visual stimuli in a definite region of peripersonal space irrespective of gaze direction, and independently of the retinal coordinates of the proximal stimulus. In man, the syndrome of hemineglect may involve damage to the frontal and cingulate cortex, the inferior parietal lobule, the basal ganglia, thalamus and mesencephalic reticular formation, all of which are richly interconnected and are involved with arousal and attention to meaningful stimuli (Bisiach, Comacchia, Sterzi & Vallar, 1984; Bisiach et al., 1985; Crowne,

1983; Heilman et al., 1983; Mesulam, 1981, 1983; Mishkin, Ungerleider & Macko, 1983; Ogden, 1985; Stuss & Benson, 1984). Animal studies (Meredith & Stein, 1985) emphasise the role of the superior colliculus, which receives polysensory information, in controlling orientation of the eyes, pinnae and head.

Left sided neglect after right hemisphere (RH) injury is generally held to be more common, severe and longer lasting than right hemineglect after left hemisphere (LH) injury (Mesulam, 1981; Ratcliff, 1982), though according to Ogden (1985) it may be severity rather than frequency of occurrence which characterizes the asymmetry. While right hemineglect may indeed be masked by incapacitating aphasia after LH trauma (De Renzi, 1982), left hemineglect is very often present in purely visual or copying tasks. The phenomenon cannot however be simply due to RH specialization for visuospatial processing, since if these mechanisms were damaged we would not expect the disability to be largely limited to left hemispace. Nor, probably, is hemineglect merely the consequence of the prevalence of the intact hemisphere's contraversive turning tendency, which can no longer be countered by the damaged hemisphere; disordered eye movements (Smith and Latto, 1982) may certainly play a role, though probably more as a consequence than as a cause of the syndrome (though cf. De Renzi, Colombo, Faglioni & Gilbertoni, 1982).

A traditional view (see e.g. De Renzi et al., 1982; Geschwind, 1981; Heilman, 1979; Mesulam, 1981) is that while the LH exclusively mediates attention for contralateral (right) hemispace, the intact RH can cope with both sides, even though its dominant tendency might be towards contralateral (left) hemispace. Thus LH damage is unlikely to produce hemineglect, as the intact RH can take over, while RH damage will lead to left hemineglect as the LH cannot compensate. Certainly RH injury is often associated with lowered affect, defective alerting, poorer arousal and reaction time decrements (with either hand), all indicating (Heilman, 1979) that the RH may mediate <u>bilateral</u> as well as <u>contralateral</u> arousal. Ogden (1985) found that right brain damage (leading to left hemineglect) was more often associated with posterior lesions, while left brain damage (leading to equally frequent but milder right hemineglect) usually stemmed from anterior damage. She speculates that a language invasion of posterior left hemisphere processing areas may bring about an impaired ipsilateral representation of (left) hemispace by the left hemisphere. However the LH must also have some residual ipsilateral capacity, since significant neglect is generally absent after right hemispherectomy and forebrain commissurotomy (Plourde & Sperry, 1984, though see below).

So can the LH operate in both halves of extrapersonal space, with, in the presence of intact commissures, differential suppression of left side awareness by a focally damaged RH? This model suggests that RH damage disrupts attentional functions of an entire integrated system, interfering with the expression of compensatory abilities in the intact as well as in the damaged hemisphere, since a damaged and nonfunctioning RH retains its dominant and suppressive role over the LH with respect to attentional functions - a mirror-image version of the conventional account of LH language dominance. Heilman et al. (1984) demonstrated the role of the commissures in integrating hemisphere-hand and hemisphere-hemispace mapping, which may be dissociated when the arms cross the midline. Thus when a commissurotomy patient tactually bisects a line with the right hand in left hemispace, because of the disconnection the right hand cannot be influenced by the RH which is

critical for mediating attentional-intentional functions in left
hemispace, but will instead be subject to the LH, which of course also
subserves sensory-motor processing of the right hand along the
conventional anatomical pathways. The attentional-intentional system of
the disconnected LH will direct the sensory-motor apparatus towards
contralateral right hemispace and so will generate errors to the right
of the true midpoint when the right hand tactually bisects in left
hemispace. This is exactly what was found, together with errors to the
left of the true midpoint whenever the left hand bisected lines in right
hemispace. In both cases such errors were far more pronounced when the
arms crossed the midline, each limb erring towards its own hemispace, a
consequence of the two (disconnected) hemispheres each mapping two
incongruent (because the arms were crossed) relationships, the
hemispatial and the sensory-motor. In normal subjects Heilman et al.
suggest that the tendency of each hemisphere to "intend" towards
contralateral hemispace may be counteracted by the other hemisphere, an
opposition which is lost when one hemisphere is damaged or the
commissures are severed.

Line Bisection by Normal Subjects

We have already seen that when left-hemineglect patients try to
bisect a line which lies across their midline, they tend to place the
transection to the right of the true center (Heilman & Valenstein, 1979)
as if a large extent to the left of center is seen as smaller than it
really is. Rosenberger (1974) investigated visual line bisection in
normal subjects. Here, rather than actually transecting the lines, the
subjects tried to discriminate between lines which were either
accurately bisected or asymmetrically transected. No asymmetries were
observed, but this could well have been due to the relative coarseness
of Rosenberger's difference scale, since when we required subjects
actually to bisect lines placed across the midline (Bradshaw, Nettleton,
Nathan & Wilson, 1985), we found that they consistently placed the
transection slightly to the left of center, a phenomenon which may be
labelled left side underestimation (LSU). It is as if such subjects see
the extent to the left of center as larger than it really is, possibly
because of the greater visuospatial processing power of the right
hemisphere (for review, see Bradshaw & Nettleton, 1981, 1983), and so in
compensation make the left side slightly smaller to seem equal to the
right. Thus when our subjects transected 10 lines, ranging in length
from 80 to 170 mm, they produced a highly significant (p < .001) LSU
averaging 1.6% of the true half length, an effect shown by 22 of the 24
dextral subjects. Interestingly when on another occasion (unpublished
data) we required 5 year old dextral and sinistral children to perform
the task, using both the preferred and the nonpreferred hand, dextral
children generally behaved like adults, showing a LSU which was slightly
larger with the left than the right hand. Sinistral children, however,
placed the transection far to the left with the left hand and far to the
right with the right hand, as if unwilling even to approach the midline
with either hand.

Visual Studies

Is it possible that the LSU depends upon subjects maintaining a
normal upright posture, with alignment of two possible sets of spatial
coordinates, those relating directly to the body midline itself
(whatever its posture) and those relating to left/right in terms of
normal gravitational coordinates, i.e. with respect to the gravitational
vertical and the direction in which a (possibly recumbent) subject may
happen to be looking? We therefore asked what are the roles of retinal

(corporeal) and gravitational coordinates (Bradshaw et al., 1985). These can be dissociated by getting subjects to recline horizontally on one or other side, with stimulus rods horizontal or vertical. Subjects performed a visual rod bisection task; they maintained fixation upon a central ring through which a rod passed, and adjusted the rod extremities (seen in peripheral vision) until they were judged equal. Such an arrangement of course also ensured that the two ends of the rods would project to opposite hemispheres, as scanning was not permitted. A LSU would now incorporate both a hemiretinal–hemispheric and a hemispatial–hemispheric component, and might therefore be larger than that which we had previously obtained (1.6%) when subjects freely scanned the lines before transecting them. We obtained a very large (3.75%) and significant (p < .001) LSU when subjects were upright, an effect which was significantly reduced when subjects lay horizontally, thus dissociating gravitational and retinal coordinates of space. The two systems of spatial coordinates must therefore be in alignment for hemispatial asymmetries to occur.

We can now ask whether the clinical phenomenon of left hemineglect is due to a reduced salience or "attention-getting quality" of events to the left of the midline. Conversely, with normal subjects, are extents to the left excessively salient, perhaps because of the relatively greater visuospatial information-processing capacity of the RH? We (Bradshaw, Nathan, Nettleton, Wilson & Pierson, in press) varied the salience of the test rods by manipulating the contrast with the background (left or right sides). Thus we had all black rods, or all white rods, on a horizontal background half of which (to the left or to the right of the subject's midline) was of contrasting tone (black background beneath a white rod, or vice versa); the other half was of noncontrasting (i.e. similar, low salience) tone, (white background beneath white rod, or black beneath black). For control purposes we also included a uniform background of high salience - i.e. an all white background beneath a black rod or vice versa. The midpoint of the uniform background, or the black-white juxtaposition of the two sharply demarcated and contrasting backgrounds, lay clearly marked exactly in front of the subject's midline. The subject adjusted the rods, by means of wires attached to their ends, so that the two extremities were judged equidistant from the marked midpoint. We included conditions of fixation upon the midpoint, and free scanning, to verify that LSUs are indeed greater under the former condition. We found this to be the case (p < .025, 2.65% versus 1.62%). The fact that the value for free scanning (where only hemispatial factors can operate) was considerably more than half that of the value for central fixation (where both hemispatial and hemiretinal factors would operate) suggests that hemispatial factors are more important than the traditional anatomical pathway variables (Kimura, 1961, 1967) associated with hemiretinal factors. However when we examined the effect of salience, LSUs proved to be biggest when salience was low on the left and high on the right, intermediate with a uniform background, and smallest when salience was low on the right and high on the left (p < .05). We must therefore conclude that while a manipulation of salience does affect the LSU in normal subjects, the phenomenon is not due to excessive salience of stimuli to the left of the midline, since a reduction in left-side salience only serves to increase the LSU. Indeed it is as if fainter stimuli are somehow seen as bigger, again perhaps because they require more processing resources. We addressed these issues by requiring (normal) subjects to bisect the space between two point sources of light, which were either both constantly illuminated (or both simultaneously flashing) with one light dim and the other bright, or one light on longer than another when simultaneously flashing, or both flashing alternately with same or different durations. We found (unpublished data) that faint, brief or flashing stimuli somehow attracted the subjective midpoint when either hand was used, and that the consistent effect of placing the subjective midpoint to the left of true centre was more pronounced when the left hand was used.

We next presented subjects with a single vertical target rod in left or right hemispace for 5 seconds. They then adjusted a vertical test rod located in the same or opposite hemispace to equal the remembered length of the target, under conditions of free scanning. We found that the configuration target-right/test-left produced a significantly greater (p < .01) LSU than the opposite configuration. Moreover while left and right target hemispace did not differ from each other, there was a very much greater (p < .001) underestimation for left (compared to right) test hemispace. This indicates that the phenomenon is not memory dependent (target based) but is related to the instantaneous perception of the test item. Furthermore this experiment suggested that it is truly a case of LSU rather than right side overestimation, as the configuration target-left/test-right did not produce overestimation, only a (nonsignificant) underestimation. We must then conclude that stimuli to the left of the midline are seen as 'bigger' (not more salient) than they 'really' are, again perhaps because the RH has more visuospatial processing capacity, so that compensation in matching tasks causes extents to the left to be made smaller, with the result that, for the subject, both extents appear equal.

Kinesthetic Studies

It has long been known that a right visual field (RVF) superiority, or a right ear advantage (REA), occurs with lateral presentations of verbal material (Bradshaw & Nettleton, 1983; Bryden, 1982); the opposite applies with certain classes of nonverbal or visuospatial stimuli. In the auditory (Kimura, 1961, 1967) and tactual modalities, laterality effects have traditionally been ascribed to the prepotency of the contralateral over the ipsilateral afferent pathways projecting to a hemisphere specialized for a particular mode of processing. However under these experimental circumstances receptor location and hemispace may as we have seen be systematically confounded; hemispace here refers of course to the position in extracorporeal space to left or right of the body midline, wherein stimuli may occur and towards which responses may be initiated, as distinct from ear of entry, hand or visual field. One way to unconfound the two factors is to place either hand in left or right hemispace, by making the arm cross the midline. Bowers and Heilman (1980) required their blindfolded subjects tactually to explore a rod which lay to the left or right of, or across the body midline. They were to point with the forefinger of the left or right hand, held either in its own hemispace, or across the midline, to the subjective center of the rod. The authors obtained a LSU (when the task was performed across the midline or in the right hemispace) which they termed a 'pseudoneglect', by analogy with the left hemineglect shown by patients suffering from RH trauma, though the direction of the two phenomena are of course opposite. We (Bradshaw, Nettleton, Nathan & Wilson, 1983) performed a version of this experiment with left or right hands in their own or opposite hemispaces; subjects tried to subdivide (into halves, quarters or fifths) a laterally located rod, using only

tactual and kinesthetic information. While we found no evidence of a
LSU, the left <u>hand</u> significantly (p < .05) underestimated relative to
the right hand. Moreover overall performance (i.e. irrespective of
directional effects) was slightly more accurate in left than in right
<u>hemispace</u>, though the effect just failed to reach statistical
significance. Interestingly, a significant left hand underestimation
relative to the right hand also emerged in another tactual experiment in
this series where subjects were required to bimanually bisect vertical
rods, positioned in left or right hemispace with one hand always
crossing the midline. (The rod passed vertically through a laterally
located horizontal baseplate and one hand kinesthetically measured and
adjusted the extent above the baseplate, while the other operated in the
same way beneath it.) Subjects wore goggles which occluded lateral
vision while allowing central fixation. Subjects next performed a
bimanual integration task, with the rod now lying across the midline and
the two arms either each occupying their respective hemispaces or
crossing the midline. One hand attempted to reproduce on one side an
extent, or ratio (1/2, 2/3 etc.) of an extent, perceived by the other
hand on the other side, by laterally moving the rod through a central
piece of short pipe. We found that the extent in left hemispace was
consistently (p < .01) underestimated by about 1%. Thus, overall, while
neither hand over- or under-estimated relative to its fellow, the extent
in left hemispace was consistently under-estimated. However, these
effects completely disappeared when the subject performed a version of
the task with the head turned 90° to left or right, thus dissociating
the coordinates of head and body hemispace. There was therefore no LSU,
either with respect to head or body hemispace, whether the rod ran from
side-to-side or front-to-back. (To achieve front-to-back passage of a
rod through the subject's midline, the whole experiment was performed
upon a specially constructed stool with the rod running directly beneath
the seated subject; a pipe extended out either between the subject's
legs and behind and beneath the coccyx, or on either side of and below
the hips. Subjects laterally adjusted the rod, which passed through and
was longer than the pipe, so that the protruding extents at either end
were felt to be equal in extent.) Thus just as in visual line
bisection, alignment of corporeal and gravitational coordinates may be
required for asymmetries to appear, so also in the kinesthetic modality
alignment of the coordinates of head and body hemispace may be necessary
for the development of asymmetries. Moreover early visual experience
may also be necessary for the development of a proper sense of
extracorporeal space, as LSUs proved to be absent in a group of
congenitally blind adults tested under normal orientation conditions
(unpublished data). Indeed it has long been claimed that "conventional"
asymmetries are reduced in the congenitally blind (Bradshaw, Nettleton &
Spehr, 1982; Harris, 1980; Hermelin & O'Connor, 1971a,b; Karavatos,
Kaprinis & Tzavaras, 1984; Larsen & Hakonsen, 1983) and the long-term
profoundly deaf (e.g. Bonvillian, Orlansky & Garland, 1982; Boshoven,
McNeil & Harvey, 1982; Cranney & Ashton, 1982; Gibson & Bryden,
1984; Neville, Kutas & Schmidt, 1982; Weston & Weinman, 1983).
    In conclusion, there may be underestimation of extents "perceived"
by the RH, either in terms of left <u>hand</u> or left <u>hemispace</u> performance,
the latter being easier to demonstrate when the <u>extents</u> symmetrically
cross the subject's midline, rather than exclusively occupying one or
other hemispace.

Finger Stimulation, Spacing and Sequencing Tasks

We have seen (above) that in our first kinesthetic experiment, a

magnitude estimation task was performed rather more accurately when it
took place entirely in left hemispace, as compared to right hemispace;
this effect was separate from the general phenomenon of a LSU, but, like
it, was probably a common manifestation of superior spatial processing
by the RH. Blindfolded dextral children (3.5 and 5 years of age) were
the subjects for an experiment in which textile patches were brushed
across the tip of the forefinger of the left or right hand, located in
left or right hemispace (Burden, Bradshaw, Nettleton & Wilson, 1985).
This target stimulus was followed by a test patch which was either
tactually identical to the target, or differed from it (the level of
difficulty of the difference discrimination being individually adjusted
for each child). The test patch was administered to the same or
opposite hand as the target, held in same or opposite hemispace as
before. We found no hand asymmetries whatsoever, but obtained a
significant (p < .025) left hemispace superiority for the initial target
presentation, though not for the subsequent test hemispace, suggesting
in this situation that memory rather than perceptual factors may
determine hemispace asymmetries. Either hand performed better when
located in its own hemispace than when it crossed the midline, an effect
which was much greater for young (p < .025) and female (p < .025) than
for older, male children, and may reflect otherwise established
differentials in the rates of commissural maturation (Hewitt, 1962;
Rakic & Yakovlev, 1968; Salamy, 1978; Yakovlev & Lecours, 1967). In
another task with an essentially similar hand-hemispace design,
blindfolded 5 year old boys and girls reproduced static configurations
of finger spacings which had been moulded on their hands by the
experimenter and then scrambled by clenching the fist. This time there
were both hand and hemispace asymmetries, again only at the level of the
initial (memory) target and not at the level of the subsequent
(perceptual) test. Thus performance was superior for left (compared to
right) target hemispace (p < .001), and for left (compared to right)
target hand (p < .01). The fact that both hand and hemispace effects
emerged may be due to the combination of spatial, kinesthetic and motor
components in this task. Once again, either hand was better (p < .05)
when operating in its own hemispace, rather than crossing the midline.
Finally, in a sequential finger-touching task designed to appeal to the
LH, 8 year old dextral and sinistral children were touched, serially, on
the fingers of the left or right hand, held in left or right
hemispace; they reproduced the target sequence with movements of the
fingers of the same or opposite hand held in same or opposite
hemispace. Dextrals showed no hemispace asymmetries, though both the
right target and the right test hand were superior to the left (in both
cases at p < .025), and again either hand performed better in its own
hemispace. With sinistrals there were no hand asymmetries, and either
(target) hand was better when in right than in left (target)
hemispace. We can conclude that hemisphere-hand connections predominate
in dextral children for this task, and hemisphere-hemispace connections
with sinistrals, who otherwise might have been subjected to a
dissociation between their preferred hand and the mediating
hemisphere. In either case a LH superiority emerged in this active
sequential task, with again effects appearing stronger at the level of
initial (memorized) target than for the subsequent (perceptual) test
stimulus.

Vibrotactile Experiments

So far we have measured performance accuracy rather than speed
while investigating hemispace asymmetries. Reaction times (RTs) to

vibrotactile stimuli are a convenient way of unconfounding the effects
of anatomical connectivity and hemispace while using a speed measure.
In our first such experiment (Bradshaw, Nathan, Nettleton, Pierson &
Wilson, 1983) subjects depressed a microswitch with the forefinger of
the left or right hand, held for a block of trials either in its own or
in contralateral (i.e. across the midline) hemispace, as soon as the
microswitch was felt to vibrate (250 Hz). Twenty-two out of 24 dextral
subjects gave a highly significant (p < .001) right hemispace
superiority of 9 msec, the hands not differing. When we repeated the
experiment (unpublished data) with 12 male and 12 female strongly
sinistral subjects, however, the RSAs became nonsignificant, only 17
subjects showing such an effect. Nevertheless the fact that the left
side was not favored with these subjects indicates that the phenomenon
of a RSA with dextrals was not simply due in some way to a preference
for performing manipulative or motor tasks on the same side of the body
as the preferred hand. When next we (Bradshaw et al, 1983, Experiment
2) unconfounded head and body hemispace by requiring subjects to turn
the head 90° to left or right, with the stimulated and responding limb
held out either in the midline, or to the side of the body, all
hemispace asymmetries were lost with respect to the body (hand held out
from side) and greatly reduced with respect to the head (hand held in
the midline). So just as 90° head turns earlier destroyed LSU's in a
rod bisection task, so also right-of-body hemispace superiorities were
lost and right-of-head hemispace superiorities greatly reduced under
similar circumstances in a vibrotactile RT task which dissociated the
head and body components.

What happens if instead we dissociate gravitational and corporeal
coordinates, as in the line bisection task, by getting subjects to
perform the task while recumbent on one or other side? By corporeal we
mean left and right with respect to the spinal axis irrespective of
posture; by gravitational left-right we mean with respect to the
gravitational vertical, while the subject is still facing in the
direction in which though now recumbent he or she is looking. Thus when
a recumbent subject lies on the left side, gravitational left extends
out beyond the top of the head, and gravitational right towards the
knees. These relationships reverse when the subject lies on the right
side. We repeated our first vibrotactile experiment with blocks of
trials for hand (left, right), posture (lie on left, right), arm (up,
down, or beyond head, between knees), and analyzed the data in terms
both of gravitational and corporeal coordinates (Bradshaw & Pierson,
1985). There were no significant hand or hemispace effects whatsoever,
indicating, as in the rod and line bisection tasks, that just as a 90°
head turn dissociates head and body hemispace and destroys hemispace
asymmetries, so also are hemispace asymmetries lost when gravitational
and corporeal hemispace are dissociated, when a subject reclines
horizontally on one or other side.

Are these right side advantages (RSAs) motor or sensory? If one
hand is stimulated and the other responds, we can separately assess the
independent contributions of left and right <u>sensory hand</u>, left and right
<u>motor hand</u>, left and right <u>sensory hemispace</u> and left and right <u>motor
hemispace</u>. Under these circumstances we found that only <u>motor hemispace</u>
gave a significant (p < .01) RSA (6 msec). So the locus of this effect
appears to reside in the preparation of a response, rather than the
discrimination of a signal. We investigated further the possible role
of stimulus uncertainty by including a low (as well as a high) signal
intensity condition. We found that while there was again a RSA (4 msec)

for motor hemispace (p < .01) with high intensity signals, just as before, this effect disappeared with low intensity stimulation, being replaced by an almost significant 4 msec sensory RSA. At the same time a hand asymmetry now appeared for the first time, the configuration left-hand-stimulated/right-hand-responding proving significantly (p < .025) faster (9 msec) than the reverse configuration. The responding (rather than the stimulated) hand was probably responsible, as the spatial-compatibility interaction Hand by Motor Hemispace (but not Hand by Sensory Hemispace) reached significance (p < .05). Thus left-hand-stimulated/right-hand-responding was faster in right as compared to left motor hemispace, and right-hand-stimulated/left-hand-responding was faster in left as compared to right motor hemispace.

Hitherto, we have obtained vibrotactile RSAs with trials to one or other side presented in blocks, rather than randomly. Does the phenomenon depend upon the establishment of position sets, subjects having a greater ability to hold attention to the right (compared to the left) rather than to shift attention to the right, as might occur with randomly alternating side of stimulation and/or response? If this is the case, then randomization of the side of stimulus and response should lead to a loss of effects. Subjects must now divide attention between the two sides of space to obtain maximal performance. If attention is therefore directed to both sides of space, then stimuli on the right cannot benefit from a greater ability to hold attention to this side for an extended period of time. We adopted just such a randomly-alternating paradigm, each hand having its own stimulus and response unit, the hand stimulated being the one to respond. Hands were held either in their own (uncrossed) or opposite (crossed) hemispace. This arrangement (which is of course also yet another approach to the question of stimulus-response uncertainty, as with the low-intensity threshold-level signals) is now in effect a choice RT task, though one of very high stimulus-response spatial compatibility. We found, as expected in an essentially choice task, that RTs considerably increased, and the crossed configuration was now for the first time considerably slower than the uncrossed (p < .001). Of course, this constitutes a hand/hemispace spatial compatibility effect, i.e. each hand is faster when located in its own hemispace. More importantly, however, all hemispace asymmetries were lost, as in the low stimulus intensity condition, and were replaced by a significant (p < .025) right hand superiority (13 msec). Spatial compatibility effects are of course traditionally absent from simple RT tasks, and present in choice RT situations (Bradshaw & Umilta, 1984); conversely, hemispace effects may be absent from choice tasks and present in simple RT tasks, where the spatial coding of limb position is unimportant. If so, we can ask whether hemispace asymmetries reappear, at the expense of hand asymmetries, if we employ blocks of trials for a given responding hand or side, but randomly alternate, as before, the stimulated hand or side. As the vibrotactile RSA has been shown to be motor rather than sensory, a RSA might be predicted when side of response is blocked. When we performed just such an experiment involving stimulus but not response uncertainty, once again there was no hemispace asymmetry, but the right hand was 8 msec faster (p = .05) than the left. Perhaps not surprisingly, when the same hand was stimulated and responded, performance was also faster (18 msec, p < .05) than when opposite hands were stimulated and responded. Moreover there was now no longer any advantage for the uncrossed configuration, so the need to select a response hand may determine whether or not there will be hand/hemispace spatial compatibility effects. Hemispace asymmetries may therefore only occur when there is no uncertainty about the spatial location of the stimulus, and attention can be wholly allocated to one or other side, both at the level of stimulation and of response.

We can conclude from the vibrotactile experiments that hemispace asymmetries will usually occur only when head and body coordinates and corporeal and gravitational coordinates are aligned. Moreover position of an event in extracorporeal space is at least as important as traditional anatomical connectivities (Kimura, 1961, 1967) in determining asymmetries. The cerebral hemispheres appear to code distal sensory-motor events occurring in contralateral hemispace, and not just events on the proximal receptor surfaces and the actions of the effector musculature. Hemispace RSAs occur with simple, not with choice RTs, i.e. where spatial position is unimportant in stimulus-response coding, and only in the absence of stimulus uncertainty, whether in terms of signal intensity, or uncertainty as to side. Thus they only occur when the subject can wholly allocate attention to one or other side, and they reflect a greater ability to hold attention to the right, rather than to shift it to the right. However these attentional aspects necessarily differ from Kinsbourne's (1973) attentional model; he invokes an activational component whereas our account implicates sustained attentional effects. He predicts that asymmetries should occur only when stimuli and responses occur randomly as to side, rather than when side of stimulation and response is blocked. We of course find that the hemispace asymmetries are absent with random side of stimulation and response, and present when lateral stimulation occurs in blocks. Even hand asymmetries, of course, may be attentional; thus with positional uncertainty (where we found hand asymmetries replaced hemispace effects), a good strategy may be to direct attention to the preferred hand. Indeed, we can ask what is the shape of the distribution of extracorporeal hemispace, as may be indexed by a vibrotactile RT map. Is there a privileged position with very short RTs, for processing incoming information? Is it at the true midline, with hemispace asymmetrically distributed about it? Is it offset therefrom perhaps slightly to the right, with hemispace symmetrically disposed about it? We measured vibrotactile RTs with the stimulated and responding limb (left, or right) placed out from the body either at the midline (0°), 15° to left or right of midline, or 45° or 90° to left or right of midline, i.e. at seven possible positions. Reaction times for the two hands were found to be identical, confirming the absence of hand asymmetries in the absence of positional uncertainty. There was a significant (p < .01) position effect; by Tukey test the only position which was significantly different from any other (and it was significantly different from all other positions) was 90° left (277 msec). All other positions varied between only 266 and 270 msec, the shortest in fact being 15° right, though none of these other values differed significantly from each other. We can conclude, therefore, that our RSAs should perhaps instead be characterized as a left side disadvantage (LSD), though perhaps only for positions well to the left (and possibly extending behind the body, though this remains to be determined). Indeed, if such hemispace effects can be extended right around the body, rather than characterizing them, at least in the vibrotactile RT paradigm, as a direct consequence of brain asymmetries, related e.g. to language lateralization, we should perhaps instead see them as reflecting differences in our abilities to attend to stimuli (or, perhaps more properly, to initiate responses) in different regions of circumcorporeal space.

Auditory Hemispace

     The most direct test between Kimura's anatomical-pathway model and the hemispace approach lies in the auditory modality. She specifically claims (1961, 1967) that the dichotic right ear advantage (REA) is due to the stronger, dominant, contralateral auditory pathways suppressing the weaker ipsilateral routes, so that the right ear has priviledged access to the verbal LH. We (Pierson, Bradshaw & Nettleton, 1983) replaced the traditional earphones (which separately stimulate each ear) with a single, laterally located, loudspeaker. Through this we played competing unilateral stimulation, sequences of aligned pairs of a digit (1, 8, 9 or 10) and a letter (g, v, k or z) which were not mutually confusable, one spoken by a male and one by a female as a further aid to discriminability. The stimuli, played from the single loudspeaker on one or other side of the subject, were loud enough to stimulate both ears. Subjects (dextral males, audiometrically screened to eliminate threshold differences between ears) shadowed (i.e. immediately repeated) each stimulus pair, and the vocal naming latencies were measured. Ten out of 12 subjects demonstrated a RSA of 38 msec (p < .005), the two reversals being very small. This finding conclusively demonstrates that competition at the two ears, as with dichotic stimulation, is unnecessary for demonstrating a verbal REA, and that Kimura's structural model is inadequate.

     We next asked whether it is the real or the perceived direction of a sound source which determines RSAs. We sought to generate "pseudo" RSAs via a ventriloquistic technique which relies upon the phenomenon of visual capture of the apparent direction of an ambiguously located auditory source. We placed two operating loud speakers one directly in front of, and one behind the subject's midline, one voice from the previous tape being channelled to one loudspeaker and the other voice to the other, thus creating positional uncertainty about the direction of a perceptually composite signal. An inactive dummy loudspeaker placed either on the left or the right of the subject, who believed it to be fully operational, effectively captured the sound source, creating a powerful directional illusion. Eleven out of 12 subjects were faster (p < .005) by 28 msec when the dummy loudspeaker was on the right than on the left side, indicating that it is the perceived, rather than the real, position of a sound source which determines hemispace asymmetries. We next, as in our rod bisection and vibrotactile RT tasks, sought to dissociate the two coordinates of (auditory) hemispace, head and body, by 90° head turns to left or right. When an (active) loudspeaker was placed before or behind the subject's midline, it lay to the left or right of the turned head. (We were careful to ensure that only subjects were used who were able to maintain the requisite 90° head turns.) Likewise when the loudspeaker was to left or right of the body, it lay exactly before or behind the head midline. Under both these circumstances all hemispace asymmetries again completely vanished, and RTs were identical for the averages of the head-turn-right and head-turn-left conditions, itself a finding which counts against Kinsbourne's (1973) activational-attentional account. According to him, performance in a verbal task should be superior when the subject orientates to the right. Indeed, we confirmed that the loss of a RSA with 90° head turns is a robust phenomenon by playing competing unilateral stimulation over a proximal earphone, rather than a distal loudspeaker source. We used the same stimulus tape as before, and as a control reincorporated a head-front (no turn) condition. We found that while the overall RTs for

head front, right and left did not differ significantly, with head front
there was a very large (64 msec) and significant (p < .001) REA, and no
significant ear asymmetries for either of the two turn conditions.
Subsequently we repeated the earphone version of the experiment
(unpublished data) with subjects lying horizontally on left or right
sides, to dissociate gravitational and corporeal coordinates of
extracorporeal space, as in our line bisection and vibrotactile tasks.
Again, ear asymmetries vanished, and it did not matter on which side
subjects lay.

General Discussion and Suggestions for Further Research

Over 70 years ago the first studies were reported concerning
magnitude estimation in the two halves of the visual field (see Ritter,
1917). Even the effects of body posture were investigated, but the
general conclusions, due probably to coarse measurements and inadequate
experimental control, were that individuals merely differed greatly.
Since then, the field has lain fallow. Some early workers even used
terms such as 'left side underestimation', though often in the opposite
sense to ours; where we mean that an adjustable extent on one side is
set smaller than it should be, perhaps in compensation for an apparent
phenomenological magnification at the perceptual level, others seem in
the past to have meant that an adjustable extent was presumably seen as
smaller than reality, and therefore was set larger in compensation.

From our own and other recent studies we can conclude that in rod
and line bisection tasks there is a LSU, especially when the extent
crosses the midline, and perhaps less so when it lies wholly in one or
other hemispace, or is vertically rather than horizontally oriented.
The LSU is immediate and perceptual, rather than somehow deriving from a
fading memory trace, unlike traditional asymmetries which tend to be
stronger with a memory component (Moscovitch, 1979; Nettleton &
Bradshaw, 1983). However, as we shall shortly argue, attentional as
well as sensory components contribute to the effect. The phenomenon,
moreover, is probably a true LSU, rather than one involving right side
overestimation. Any empirical attempt at dissociating the two possible
determinants, LSU or right side overestimation, however, has to
circumvent the procedural problem of a central standard or target
magnitude being perceived as lying to the left of a variable or
comparison extent on the right, or to the right of one on the left.

Moreover the LSU is not due to a greater salience of stimuli lying
on the left side, since it is greatest with salience low on the left and
high on the right. Increased underestimation with low salience
(background contrast) might be due to a required increase in directed
processing capacity (i.e. attention) to low salient, poorly contrasting
stimuli, which consequently appear larger. Generally, extents in the
two hemispaces may normally be asymmetrically matched because of
differences in visuospatial processing capacities of the two
hemispheres, itself perhaps a consequence of language pre-empting
visuospatial processing space in the LH.

However it is not then clear why such visuospatial asymmetries seem
to be so affected by choice of hand used for performing the perceptual
match. Ramos-Brieva, Olivan, Palomares and Vela (1984) and
Schenkenberg, Bradford and Ajax (1980) both incidentally observed that
line bisection LSUs were strongest when performed by the left hand. Our
5 year old dextral children performed similarly, while sinistrals of the
same age behaved in an even more extreme fashion, placing the
transection far to the left when using the left hand and far to the
right with the right hand, as if unwilling even to approach the midline

with either hand. Conversely, with dextral adults adjusting laterally-
located rods in the visual modality, LSUs tended to be stronger when the
right hand made the adjustment. The two kinds of task of course differ
in important ways; the former involves bisection of centrally located
stimuli, while the latter involves magnitude matching with peripherally
located stimuli. Otherwise in both cases hand used seemed to influence
performance; LeDoux, Wilson and Gazzaniga (1977) claim that asymmetries
are stronger at a manipulospatial than at a purely perceptual level. We
have found, informally, that when two visual extents equal in magnitude
appear side by side, they appear perceptually identical, i.e. there is
no LSU in a purely visual task.

To what extent may similar mechanisms determine the slight LSU
shown by normal subjects, and the typical left side overestimation shown
by hemineglect patients? One such dextral patient (NM) whom we examined
had two years previously experienced extensive RH damage; since then he
had undergone considerable rehabilitatory training. When tested on our
kinesthetic rod-bisection task, he gave a consistent LSU, like a normal
subject. However he seemed actively to be directing his attention to
the left, as shown both by his eye movements (which we monitored, even
though the task was purely kinesthetic), and by his performance in our
vibrotactile RT task; in the latter he gave a left side advantage rather
than the usual RSA. (Indeed, of 6 other hemineglect patients who had
undergone little or no rehabilitation training at the time of testing, 5
showed very large RSAs, and one gave a 1 msec LSA, the group as a whole
averaging 32 msec RSA, many times the normal magnitude.) However NM,
when given the rod bisection task with low salience (contrast) on the
right, overestimated the left extent and gave a typical left-
hemineglect response. It was as if he were forced by the low salience
on the right to direct attention away from the left to the right, thus
unmasking a latent left hemineglect. Consequently left hemineglect
patients probably do not find stimuli less salient on the left (i.e. a
low-level sensory explanation), but may indeed suffer from a leftwards
attentional deficit.

These hemispace asymmetries seem to be different from and stronger
than   anatomical   pathway   effects.   The   traditional   anatomical-
connectivity account of lateral asymmetries (Kimura, 1961, 1967) cannot
of course cope with our auditory, tactual or vibrotactile findings,
which indicate that it is the position in extracorporeal space (real, or
even as perceived) which often determines asymmetries, rather than just
the proximal locus of receptor stimulation. (For this reason the verbal
REA may not be just a special case of the RSA). Indeed our comparison
between the effects of free scanning and controlled fixation in the
visual rod tasks, and our observation that auditory asymmetries were
larger with a unilateral loudspeaker than with a unilateral earphone
(whose sound tends to be localized within the ear itself, rather than
"out" in space), indicates the major role of hemisphere-hemispace
connections.

We found left hemispace superiorities for kinesthetic judgments of
extent, texture matching and finger spacing, especially where memory
rather than perceptual factors predominated. There was a right
hemispace superiority for sequential finger-stimulation tasks (in
sinistrals, whose preferred hand and mediating hemisphere might
otherwise dissociate), for vibrotactile RTs (again, predominantly a
motor effect) in the absence of stimulus uncertainty, and for competing
auditory stimulation in a verbal shadowing task. The last effect
depended as much upon the perceived (but illusory) position of a sound

source as upon its real location.

Hemispace asymmetries were always lost or greatly reduced with 90° head turns which dissociate head and body coordinates, and with the adoption of a horizontal posture which dissociates corporeal and gravitational coordinates. Indeed recent physiological studies (see e.g. Jay & Sparks, 1984) of how the superior colliculus maps auditory space indicate that individual neurones are tuned to different sound source loci, and are arranged so that their anatomical position is systematically related to a preferred location in space, with the coordinates of the map shifting along the horizontal plane as the (monkey's) eye changes position. Thus the coordinates of the auditory map move systematically with the eyes. In a similar fashion, Bisiach et al. (1985) found with hemineglect patients that the boundary of neglect was influenced both by gaze direction and by the sagittal midplane of the trunk (trunk orientation). One might therefore speculate that the moment-to-moment symptoms of unilateral neglect might change as a function of head turn (90° left, right) and body posture (horizontally on one or other side). If so, there are obvious rehabilitative implications.

All this means, of course, that our own perceived position in space, and the locus of stimulation in extracorporeal space is the result of polysensory, multimodal integration, perhaps as mediated by posterior (parietal) association areas. Thus the brain probably maintains two simultaneous maps, one of the proximal receptor surface which mediates the traditional asymmetries, and the other one for events (sensory and motor) occurring out in extracorporeal space (see also Rizzolatti, Gentilucci & Matelli, 1985). Pit one sense against another, (e.g., as in our dummy-speaker ventriloquism experiment) and the apparent system of spatial coordinates changes. We should therefore be able to mislead subjects in other interesting ways. An upright subject in a tilted room might lose the auditory or vibrotactile RSA, or a tilted subject within a room tilted the same way may regain the RSA characteristic of an upright subject in a normal environment, such is the strength of visual capture. This phenomenon of course has been extensively explored in the context of interactions between vision and touch (Rock & Harris, 1967), and vision and vestibular input (Lee & Aaronson, 1974), and see also Pick, Warren and Hay (1969) for proprioceptive capture of nonveridical auditory information where the sound source is systematically misperceived through the use of pseudophones. Indeed a subject who has worn laterally – displacing prisms (see e.g. Weiner, Hallet & Funkenstein, 1983) until adaptation is complete, may on their removal sense that a laterally displaced limb is central to the midline, or vice versa, all of which should affect vibrotactile RT asymmetries, or pointing accuracy. There is in fact a suggestion (Heilman, Bowers & Watson, 1983) that normal subjects (with their eyes closed) may tend to deviate slightly to the left when asked to point out with the right hand directly in front of their midline. This may be somewhat analogous to the normal LSU in line bisection. In an incomplete study, we have found the opposite : 12 out of 14 subjects (with their eyes open) deviated to the right, when using their right hand, and very slightly to the left with the left hand. Hartmann (1983) found that subjects trying to locate ambiguous sound sources were biased to the left from the correct azimuth in their errors by about 0.75°. (He also reviewed evidence of superior localization accuracy in left rather than right space, analogous to some of our own findings in the tactual modality reviewed above). Finally, Hartmann found that bias effects increased enormously if subjects shifted their gaze, suggesting, to us, once again that the auditory map of space is linked to eye position. Again a wealth of possible research is revealed in terms of accuracy of manual pointing to visual targets as a function of head and/or gaze direction with respect to each other and/or to the body. Gaze and head directionality could also be fruitfully varied in the vibrotactile and the competing monaural auditory paradigms. While not strictly involving the technique of pitting one sense against another, the old observations (see Krueger, 1982, for historical review) that skilled machinists employing screwdrivers, seamstresses using needles, and the blind relying upon their canes all project their sensation of pressure or touch to the very tip of the tool, suggest an interesting experiment. If a subject holds one end of a cane, rod or pipe, with either hand, on one side of the body, and the implement crosses the body to the other hemispace for discriminating e.g. texture, in which hemispace is the discrimination better mediated -- the "proximal" one where the hand holding the cane receives the stimulation, or the "distal" one to which the sensations are apparently projected? Is active exploration rather than passive stimulation necessary for sensations to be so projected? Thus White, Saunders, Scadden, Bach-y-Rita and Collins (1970) developed a tactual prosthesis for the blind, a two-dimensional array of vibrators on the back of the subject, which was driven by a television camera attached to the wearer's head, and which responded to simple "visual" contours to which it was directed by exploratory head turns. Subjects reported that if they actively explored, they rapidly got the feeling that events were outside and even in front of the body, rather than merely proximal sensations received on the back.

We have described how hand rather than hemispace asymmetries may appear during kinesthetic judgments of extent when stimuli lie wholly in one or other hemispace, or in vibrotactile RT tasks when there is stimulus uncertainty in terms either of low signal intensity, or random (left-right) location of the next stimulus or response event. Hemispace asymmetries only occur when the subject can wholly allocate attention in advance to one or other side, reflecting a greater ability to hold it to one or other side than to shift it, since they disappear with random stimulus alternation from side to side. Does this mean that we have then to revert to the traditional anatomical-connectivity account of e.g. hemisphere-hand connections to explain these hand asymmetries? Not necessarily, if hand asymmetries may sometimes reflect a strategy of deployment of attention to the preferred hand e.g. under conditions of spatial uncertainty, instead of to a particular hemispace; in the absence of such uncertainty, hand differences typically disappear in our vibrotactile RT tasks, and are once again replaced by hemispace asymmetries. Does this mean that an account invoking hemisphere – hemispace mapping should itself be replaced by one invoking differential attentional biases, towards stimuli, responses or both, just as the hemispace model seems partly to have replaced the anatomical pathway account of e.g. hemisphere-hand connectivities? In the vibrotactile modality, it is as if the (dextral) subject is more ready to initiate a response everywhere to the right of the midline, and perhaps as far to the left as the hands usually operate in normal psychomotor activity, as long as all sensory and motor aspects of the RT task are predictable and free of uncertainty; the disadvantaged region lies far to the left. In the auditory modality, where the RSA seems to reflect LH language lateralization, it is as if the subject is more ready to respond to

stimuli tagged as (really or apparently) coming from the right side.
While attentional factors may be responsible for the loss of the
vibrotactile RSA when side of presentation is random, such findings
could also perhaps be at least partly explained in terms of hemisphere-
hemispace relationships. Sensory-motor events successfully tagged ahead
of time as coming from the right or left side of space are processed by
the contralateral hemisphere. In the case of auditory-verbal and
vibrotactile tasks, stimuli tagged as coming from the right are
therefore processed by the left hemisphere which may be relatively
specialized for these tasks. However when position information is not
available ahead of time, there is no division of labour between the
hemispheres. Both hemispheres now begin stimulus processing, but
sensory-motor events regardless of their spatial location are now
mediated by the specialized hemisphere which is always first to complete
the required processing. We should of course be wary of assuming that
similar mechanisms underlie the vibrotactile and the auditory RSA. In a
preliminary study we have failed to find a significant correlation
between the magnitudes of the auditory and the vibrotactile RSAs across
a sample of left and right handed subjects. The auditory phenomenon may
reflect both language lateralization (a true RSA) and attentional
processes (a left side disadvantage?), while the vibrotactile phenomenon
may only reflect the latter, a differential ability to allocate
attentional processes (perhaps predominantly motor) around the azimuth
of extracorporeal space. Nevertheless it is certainly true that we
cannot simply replace traditional anatomical-pathway maps of the
proximal receptor surfaces, in explaining all manifestations of lateral
asymmetry, by alternative hemisphere-hemispatial representations,
without including attention somehow in the scheme of things. This does
not however mean that we can equate our view of attention with that
proposed by Kinsbourne (1970, 1975).
    According to Kinsbourne, the levels of activation in the two
hemispheres are normally in a reciprocal balance, and this state is
associated with a straight-ahead orientation of receptors and
attentional tendencies. Eccentric stimulation or, conversely,
endogenously generated activation in the contralateral hemisphere, both
of which disturb this balanced equilibrium, will lead to an
orientational response in that direction, to inhibition of orienting
responses in the other hemisphere, and to a biased readiness to accept
stimulation and emit responses in a direction contralateral to the
activated hemisphere. Verbal processes activate the LH; visuospatial
processes activate the RH and bias attention and the orientation of
receptors in the opposite direction. Asymmetries are not therefore seen
as directly due to structural determinants but as a consequence of
attentional and activational biases. However many studies (see Bradshaw
& Nettleton, 1983) have failed to support Kinsbourne's hypothesis. The
hemispatial account we propose here though superficially similar to
Kinsbourne's approach, argues that all sensory stimuli come position-
tagged, real or apparent, and the hemisphere contralateral to its real
or apparent origin is biased towards its processing. However our
account does not require Kinsbourne's activational component; he
predicts larger verbal RSAs with rightwards head turns, while according
to our account, and on the empirical evidence, asymmetries disappear
with head turns. Kinsbourne predicts asymmetries should be largest:
1. When the subject knows in advance the verbal (or nonverbal) nature
    of the next stimulus (yet Geffen, Bradshaw & Nettleton, 1972, found
    that such advance knowledge made no difference to the size or

direction of asymmetries)

2. when subjects <u>cannot</u> predict which side will next be stimulated, since such advance knowledge permits the appropriate hemisphere (left or right) to build up activation, thus washing out asymmetries; however we found that hemispace asymmetries were <u>lost</u> under these circumstances.

Indeed the fact that the traditional procedure of randomly presenting visual stimuli to the left or right of fixation (to forestall fixational eyemovements) did <u>not</u> destroy visual field asymmetries is itself further evidence that anatomical pathway asymmetries (cf. Kimura, 1961, 1967) are qualitatively different from hemispatial asymmetries.

Why did we not find a vibrotactile RT RSA when stimuli occurred randomly on either side, but nevertheless one limb responded on the same side for a block of trials? If the general vibrotactile RSA is motor rather than sensory, as we have argued earlier, then a constant side of motor responding should lead to a RSA, rather than to a right hand advantage. Conversely, when dissociating vibrotactile sensory and motor hemispace, subjects had to remember to respond with the limb <u>opposite</u> to that receiving stimulation; why did we not lose any (hemispatial) RSAs and instead gain a hand asymmetry? We would argue that in the latter instance there was no uncertainty since subjects knew where the stimuli would occur and were practised at always responding with the limb opposite to the one stimulated. (It is in fact noteworthy that the hemispace asymmetries were small in this experiment.) However with respect to the former case, any uncertainty, about the position of the stimulus or in terms of (low) intensity, may be enough to destroy motor asymmetries. Thus even though it does not help to know the side on which a stimulus will occur, as in a Stroop task it may not be possible to prevent the encoding of such unwanted information, and here its absence, or its unpredictability, may somehow be disruptive. Alternatively, with stimulus unpredictability processing resources may be borrowed from the motor end (cf. Friedman & Polson's, 1981, limited-resource-allocation model). This reallocation of resources may therefore lead to the elimination of these motor hemispace asymmetries. Indeed the distinction (Norman & Bobrow, 1975) between data limitation and resource limitation is useful in this context; data-limited stimuli (low intensity) do not lead to increased asymmetries. Asymmetries, which probably occur more at a level beyond the stage of immediate input, may increase as a function of competition for resources. Hence competing monaural presentations (e.g. with male and female speakers), rather than monaural presentations with a single speaker, may be needed to generate asymmetries. If so, will the asymmetries increase as a function of an increasing number of additional to-be-ignored speakers? In the visual modality, bilateral presentations generate greatly increased asymmetries (Seitz & McKeever, 1984). Conversely, if the locus of the vibrotactile RSA is motor rather than sensory, do other motor tasks generate large asymmetries? We have already seen that our finger-sequencing task did so (Burden et al., 1985). What happens if <u>movement</u> time (MT) rather than RT is measured in a vibrotactile-hemispace context (cf. Jeannerod, 1984)? Thus instead of a simple unitary response, a complex ballistic sequence of elements may be timed to completion. A concurrent-task paradigm might also be employed, where the effect of a verbal or a visuospatial secondary task is measured upon a primary (tapping) task taking place in one or other hemispace (though cf. McFarland, 1982). Another form of concurrent task where both tasks are hemispatially located would be to combine the auditory and the vibrotactile paradigms.

Several other experiments remain to be done in the auditory and vibrotactile modalities. Can we generate a LSA in the auditory modality, with e.g. discriminations based on speaker's emotionality (Bryden & Ley, 1983; Scherer, Ladd & Silverman, 1984) or on voice recognition (Landis, Buttet, Assal & Graves, 1982), or, perhaps best of all, on a speech-perception task which appeals to the right hemisphere such as voice onset time (VOT) discriminations (Molfese & Molfese, 1979a,b)? Thus if two tasks, respectively appealing to the left and right hemispheres, can be given to the same subjects, we can avoid the problem (Bradshaw, et al., 1986) of a single test underestimating the true incidence of language lateralization (Lauter, 1982; Sidtis, 1982), as the results of the two tests can be expressed relative to each other rather than merely to an absolute (zero) midpoint. In the vibrotactile and auditory modalities, what is the effect on hemispace asymmetries of manipulating the predictability of side to be stimulated next? This can be achieved in either of two ways. Either stimuli can be presented in blocks to one or other side, with occasional "intrusive" items occurring on the unexpected side, or subjects can be precued (before each trial) as to side next to be stimulated, with occasionally the precue (deliberately) misinforming the subject. While in either case the hemispace asymmetries of interest are those (if any) occurring with the minority (misleading) stimuli, in the former paradigm the ability to hold attention is paramount, in the latter paradigm what is more of interest is the ability to shift attention. In the vibrotactile modality under these circumstances are hemispace asymmetries again replaced by hand asymmetries? Moving on from this issue, what happens if a go/no-go response is employed (i.e. a nonspatial choice of giving or withholding a response) for discriminating high from low (or vice versa) intensity (or frequency) stimuli? Such an experiment should permit us to ascertain whether it is choice RT per se, or spatial uncertainty, which destroys hemispace asymmetries. What happens if spatial choice is now made between the two adjacent fingers on a single limb, or even between two limbs (crossed or uncrossed with respect to each other) but now both on the same side of the midline - is there a superiority for the rightmost of the two (cf. Nicoletti, Umilta & Ladavas, 1984)? Indeed we note that according to MacKenzie and Martenuik (1985), in a choice RT task between pairs (all possible pairs) of fingers, the finger that happened to be on the right always proved faster. Can we measure anterior (motor) and posterior (sensory) evoked potentials, simultaneously with vibrotactile RTs, over left and right cortices, in the contexts of:

(i)   anatomical connectivities (contralateral pathways between limb, sensory or motor, and hemisphere), and

(ii) hemisphere-hemispace relationships (i.e. contralateral hemispace, irrespective of whichever limb currently occupies it)?

Thus it might be possible, electrophysiologically, to separate out the two brain 'maps', the traditional anatomical-pathway map, and the map of extracorporeal space. It is, of course, likely that the two representations are fairly tightly coupled, since as we have seen, not only can a hemispace (left or right) within which a hand operates determine (hand) performance (Burden et al., 1985), but a hand (left or right) which operates within a given hemispace can itself influence hemispace asymmetries (e.g. LSUs etc. in line and rod bisection).

While our findings cannot yet allow us to determine the exact

mechanisms of the hemineglect syndrome, with our new procedures we can
now for the first time try to quantify the syndrome in all its stages,
and (e.g. with the vibrotactile technique) determine the relative
contributions of (sensory) posterior and motor (anterior) processes, and
maybe demonstrate the hitherto-elusive right-hemineglect syndrome.
Indeed one subject with minimal left paresis was able to perform the
bimanual version (which permits separate evaluation of sensory and motor
components); he demonstrated an 89 msec sensory RSA and only a 15 msec
motor RSA. Another patient, late in the recovery phase, showed a near
normal vibrotactile RSA until he was required to perform with eyes
closed; the RSA then increased enormously. (Chedru, 1976, also found
that hemineglect patients without visual field defects demonstrated left
neglect on a tactual space-exploration task only when their eyes were
closed). Properly designed experiments should permit us to separate out
sensory, motor and memory components, attentional deficits, stimulus
salience, extinction, failures to acknowledge events or objects on one
side of the body, or of a display (wherever positioned), or one side of
each of a group of objects in a display, together with midline shifts
and unilateral distortions of apparent size - all of which may
differentially characterize different manifestations of a nonunitary
syndrome. Thus a patient may be asked to adjust a rod laterally so that
its two ends are equidistant from a central loop or ring through which
it passes; the loop or ring may be placed either objectively on the
patient's midline, or where he/she says it is (e.g. to the right of the
true midline). In the former case do we find a right side
underestimation, with objective equality in the latter case? If so a
midline shift would appear to be the underlying mechanism. Otherwise,
we would have to appeal to perceptual neglect. With the dummy
loudspeaker (ventriloquism) paradigm, do patients perform badly when the
dummy loudspeaker is to the left and the sound appears to come from the
neglected side, or do they do well because the dummy loudspeaker simply
is not noticed, and the sound therefore seems to come from the right?
If, in nonverbal tasks, the RH normally pays attention to both sides of
space, while the left can only cope with contralateral hemispace, in the
auditory-verbal paradigm does the LH now pay attention to both sides of
space, and the RH only to the contralateral side?
    Finally, we can ask what is the possible role of vision in these
tasks? We have already seen that 90° head turns may destroy
asymmetries; conversely evidence is emerging that deviation of gaze
(necessarily limited to a few tens of degrees) towards a given hemispace
may favor stimulus processing in the contralateral hemisphere (Gross,
Franko & Lewin, 1978; Honore, 1982; La Torre & La Torre, 1981;
Lempert & Kinsbourne, 1982). Tressoldi (personal communication) found
that lateral asymmetries may appear in visual tasks even when stimuli
are presented in right or left hemispace, with foveal presentations, the
head facing forward but with fixation deviated to left or right. With
respect to long term visual experience, Kinsbourne and Lempert (1980)
claimed that tactile-kinesthetic information cannot fully compensate for
visual experience in the formation of an internalized representation of
the human body, when they compared congenitally blind children with
normally sighted but blindfolded controls. Brown (cited in Pick, 1980)
found that vision (eyes open) may be necessary for an adequate
conception of gravitationally defined coordinates. Attneave and Benson
(1969) found that subjects, judging the directionality of vibratory
stimulation delivered to the hands held in various orientations with
respect to the body, used a gravitational frame of reference when their

eyes were open, and an egocentric (i.e. corporeal) reference frame with eyes closed. Hermelin and O'Connor (1971c) found that sighted children with eyes open performed a tactual task by relying upon gravitational coordinates, while blind and blindfolded children relied upon a corporeal frame of reference. Pick (1980) wonders whether the immediate availability of a concept of visual space encourages the use of gravitational over egocentric (corporeal) coordinate systems. Earlier the same author (Rieser & Pick, 1976) had found that subjects made to adopt a horizontal posture used an egocentric frame of reference for stimuli traced directly upon the proximal body surface, but adopted a gravitational reference frame for more distal objects palpated by the hands in extracorporeal space. As previously noted, we have already seen that blindfolding appeared to reinstate the acute phase of the syndrome in an apparently recovered hemineglect patient. What happens with normals, as well as hemineglect patients, when blindfolded while performing kinesthetic rod bisections, vibrotactile RT tasks, and auditory hemispace tasks? What happens with the congenitally blind? We have already found (see above) that tactual LSUs are not shown by such subjects, and we earlier noted (Bradshaw et al., 1982) with such a group that neither hand nor hemispace asymmetries emerged in a Braille reading task. Do they appear if an "Optacon" transducer is instead employed, presenting vibrotactile patterns of real letter shapes to the forefinger? Does it depend on the (tactual or phonological) similarity of the stimuli (cf. Mousty, Bertelson & Kurrels, 1982)? We have noted an unusually high incidence of nondextrals in our samples of congenitally blind subjects. (Bonvillian et al., 1982, noted the same in the congenitally deaf.) Karavatos et al., (1984) found that the congenitally blind fail to exhibit the usual ear asymmetries, and Gibson and Bryden (1984) review similar effects in the congenitally deaf. We have found (unpublished data) that the congenitally blind fail to give the usual LSU in kinesthetic rod bisection. Finally, if the blind, or normally sighted but blindfolded subjects, are asked to walk in a straight line, are there consistent turning biases or deviations, perhaps to the left, due perhaps to asymmetries in the extrapyramidal motor system (cf. Glick & Ross, 1981)?

In conclusion, the conventional picture of lateral asymmetries reflecting differences in the way information is processed when presented to receptors found on one or other side of the body, and which project via fixed anatomical pathways largely to one or other cerebral hemisphere, needs a radical reappraisal. At the very least this picture cannot take into account the dynamic changeable nature of empirically determined asymmetries. The other approach, which should perhaps be seen as complementary and additional to, rather than alternative to the traditional anatomical-connectivity account, appeals to the concept of hemispace. Thus the brain may map both the distribution of stimuli upon the proximal receptor surfaces, and also the occurrence of relatively distal sensory and motor events which occur out beyond the immediate body in extracorporeal space. These two maps may be dissociated by such strategies as crossing the arms across the body midline, turning the head relative to the body and possibly the eyes relative to the head's orientation), and adopting a horizontal posture upon one or other side, to dissociate corporeal and gravitational coordinates. Gardner and Ward (1979) concluded that information about the spatial position (to left or right of the body) is probably more important than which hand actually felt a stimulus. In this context we find curiously prescient the words of Attneave and Benson (1969):

"Behaviour is much more simply predictable from the external
situation, i.e. from 'distal stimuli', than from events at
the receptor surface, or 'proximal stimuli'" (p.216).
Indeed their very techniques foreshadowed our own -- the effects of head
tilt and rotation on judgments of line orientation, and judgments of
orientation relative to an internal reference system, whose vertical may
or may not correspond to the objective vertical. They even examined the
effects of blindfolding, concluding that spatial location is represented
primarily in visual terms, even when another modality is under
investigation. Other strategies available to us for dissociating the
two hypothesized brain maps, strategies whose effects are not predicted
by the traditional anatomical-connectivity account, include pitting one
sensory modality against the other (e.g. vision and audition, vision and
kinesthesis, and, possibly, kinesthesis and audition), and manipulating
the effects of uncertainty and attention. Indeed it seems that
vibrotactile hemispace effect (and perhaps auditory effects as well) may
also reflect attentional biases towards certain regions of space, rather
than just being the simple consequence of hemisphere-hemispace
relationships.It is within these contexts that we believe future
research, both pure and applied (e.g. with respect to the clinical
syndrome of unilateral spatial neglect, and to congenital blindness)
needs to be directed.

References

Attneave, F. & Benson, B. Spatial coding of tactual stimuli. Journal
    of Experimental Psychology, 1969, 81, 216-222.
Bisiach, E., Capitani, E. & Porta, E. Two basic properties of space
    representation in the brain : Evidence from unilateral neglect.
    Journal of Neurology, Neurosurgery and Psychiatry, 1985, 48, 141-
    144.
Bisiach, E., Comacchia, L., Sterzi, R. & Vallar, G. Disorders of
    perceived auditory lateralization after lesions of the right
    hemisphere. Brain, 1984, 107, 37-52.
Bisiach, E. & Luzzatti, C. Unilateral neglect of representational
    space. Cortex, 1978, 14, 129-133.
Bonvillian, J. D., Orlansky, M. D. & Garland, J. B. Handedness patterns
    in deaf persons. Brain and Cognition, 1982, 1, 141-157.
Boshoven, M. M., McNeil, M. R. & Harvey, L. O. Hemispheric
    specialization for the processing of linguistic and nonlingusitic
    stimuli in congenitally deaf and hearing adults: A review and
    contribution. Audiology, 1982, 21, 509-530
Bowers, D. & Heilman, K. M. Pseudoneglect: Effects of hemispace on a
    tactile line bisection task. Neuropsychologia, 1980, 18, 491-498.
Bradshaw, J. L., Burden, V. & Nettleton, N. C. Dichotic and dichhaptic
    techniques. Neuropsychologia, 1986,
Bradshaw, J. L., Nathan, G. Nettleton, N. C., Pierson, J. M. &
    Wilson, L. E. Head and body hemispace to left and right III:
    Vibrotactile stimulation and sensory and motor components.
    Perception, 1983, 12, 651-661.
Bradshaw, J. L., Nathan, G., Nettleton, N. C. Wilson, L. E. & Pierson,
    J. M. Why there is a left side underestimation in rod bisection.
    Neuropsychologia, 1986,
Bradshaw, J. L. & Nettleton, N. C. The nature of hemispheric
    specialization in man. Behavioral and Brain Sciences, 1981, 4, 51-
    63.

Bradshaw, J. L. & Nettleton, N. C. Human Cerebral Asymmetry. Englewood Cliffs, N.J.: Prentice Hall, 1983.

Bradshaw, J. L., Nettleton, N. C., Nathan, G. & Wilson, L. E. Head and body space to left and right, front and rear II: Visuotactual and kinesthetic studies and left side underestimation. Neuropsychologia, 1983, 21, 475-486.

Bradshaw, J. L., Nettleton, N. C., Nathan, G. & Wilson, L. E. Bisecting rods and lines: Effects of horizontal and vertical posture on left-side underestimation by normal subjects. Neuropsychologia, 1985, 23, 421-426.

Bradshaw, J. L., Nettleton, N. C. and Spehr, K. Braille reading and left and right hemispace. Neuropsychologia, 1982, 20, 493-500.

Bradshaw, J. L. & Pierson, J. M. Vibrotactile reaction times in left and right hemispace: Stimulus and response uncertainty and gravitational and corporeal coordinates. In M. I. Posner & O. S. M. Marin (Eds.), Mechanisms of Attention: Attention and Performance XI. Hillsdale, N.J.: Erlbaum, 1985, pp. 221-237.

Bradshaw, J. L. & Umilta, C. A reaction time paradigm can simultaneously index spatial compatibility and neural pathway effects: A reply to Levy. Neuropsychologia, 1984, 22, 99-101.

Bryden, M. P. Laterality: Functional Asymmetry in the Intact Brain. New York: Academic press, 1982.

Bryden, M. P. & Ley, R. G. Right hemisphere involvement in the perception and expression of emotion in normal humans. In K. Heilman & P. Satz (Eds.), Neuropsychology of Human Emotion. New York : Guilford Press, 1983, pp. 6-44.

Burden, V., Bradshaw, J. L., Nettleton, N. C. & Wilson, L. Hand and hemispace effects in tactual tasks involving interhemispheric integration in children. Neuropsychologia, 1985, 23, 515-525.

Chedru, F. Space representation in unilateral spatial neglect. Journal of Neurology, Neurosurgery and Psychiatry, 1976, 39, 1057-1061.

Cranney, T. & Ashton, R. Tactile spatial ability : Lateral performance of deaf and hearing age groups. Journal of Experimental Child Psychology, 1982, 34, 123-134.

Crowne, D. P. The frontal eyefield and attention. Psychological Bulletin, 1983, 93, 232-260.

De Renzi, E. Disorders of space exploration and cognition. New York: Wiley, 1982.

De Renzi, E., Colombo, A., Faglioni, P. & Gilbertoni, M. Conjugate gaze paresis in stroke patients with unilateral damage. Archives of Neurology, 1982, 39, 482-486.

Friedman, A. & Polson, M. C. Hemispheres as independent resource systems : Limited capacity processing and cerebral specialization. Journal of Experimental Psychology : Human Perception and Performance, 1981, 7, 1031-1058.

Gardner, E. B. & Ward, A. W. Spatial compatibilities in tactile-visual discrimination. Neuropsychologia, 1979, 17, 421-425.

Geffen, G. Bradshaw, J. L. & Nettleton, N. C. Hemispheric asymmetry: Verbal and spatial encoding of visual stimuli. Journal of Experimental Psychology, 1972, 95, 25-31.

Geschwind, N. The perverseness of the right hemisphere. Behavioral and Brain Sciences, 1981, 4, 106-107.

Gibson, C. J. & Bryden, M. P. Cerebral lateralization in deaf and hearing children. Brain and Language, 1984, 23, 1-12.

Glick, S. D. & Ross, D. A. Lateralization of function in the rat brain. Trends in the Neurosciences, 1981, 4, 196-199.

J.L. Bradshaw et al.

Gross, Y., Franko, R. & Lewin, I. Effects of voluntary eye movements on hemispheric activity and choice of cognitive mode. Neuropsychologia, 1978, 16, 653–657.

Halsband, U., Gruhn, S. & Ettlinger, G. Unilateral spatial neglect : A neuropsychological investigation. In preparation.

Harris, L. J. Which hand is the eye of the blind? A new look at an old question. In J. Herron (Ed.), Neuropsychology of Left Handedness. New York: Academic Press, 1980, pp. 303–329.

Hartmann, W. M. Localization of sound in rooms. Journal of the Acoustical Society of America, 1983, 74, 1380–1389.

Heilman, K. M. Neglect and related disorders. In K. M. Heilman and E. Valenstein (Eds.), Clinical Neuropsychology. Oxford: Oxford University press, 1979, pp. 268–307.

Heilman, K. M., Bowers, D. & Watson, R. T. Performance on hemispatial pointing task by patients with neglect syndrome. Neurology, 1983, 33, 661–664.

Heilman, K. M., Bowers, D. & Watson, R. T. Pseudoneglect in a patient with partial callosal disconnection. Brain, 1984, 107, 519–532.

Heilman, K. M. & Valenstein, E. Mechanisms underlying hemispatial neglect. Archives of Neurology, 1979, 5, 166–170.

Hermelin, B. & O'Connor, N. Functional asymmetry in the reading of Braille. Neuropsychologia, 1971, 9, 431–435(a).

Hermelin, B. & O'Connor, N. Right and left handed reading of Braille. Nature, 1971, 231, 470(b).

Hermelin, B. & O'Connor, N. Spatial coding in normal, autistic and blind children. Perceptual and Motor Skills, 1971, 33, 227–132(c).

Hewitt, W. The development of the human corpus callosum. Journal of Anatomy, 1962, 96, 355–358.

Honore, J. Posture oculaire et attention selective a des stimuli cutanes. Neuropsychologia, 1982, 20, 727–730.

Jay, M. F. & Sparks, D. C. Auditory receptive fields in primate superior colliculus shift with changes in eye position. Nature, 1984, 309, 345–347.

Jeannerod, M. The timing of natural prehension movements. Journal of Motor Behavior, 1984, 16, 235–254.

Karavatos, A., Kaprinis, G. & Tzavaras, A. Hemispheric specialization for language in the congenitally blind : The influence of the Braille system. Neuropsychologia, 1984, 22, 521–525.

Kimura, D. Cerebral dominance and the perception of verbal stimuli. Canadian Journal of Psychology, 1961, 15, 166–171.

Kimura, D. Functional asymmetry of the brain in dichotic listening. Cortex, 1967, 3, 163–178.

Kinsbourne, M. A model for the mechanism of unilateral neglect of space. Transactions of the American Neurological Association, 1970, 95, 143–146.

Kinsbourne, M. The control of attention by interaction between the cerebral hemispheres. In S. Kornblum (Ed.), Attention and Performance IV, New York: Academic Press, 1973, pp. 239–255.

Kinsbourne, M. The mechanism of hemispheric control of the lateral gradient of attention. In P. M. A. Rabbit and S. Dornic (Eds.), Attention and Performance V. New York : Academic press, 1975, pp. 81–97.

Kinsbourne, M. & Lempert, H. Human figure representation by blind children. The Journal of General Psychology, 1980, 102, 33–37.

Krueger, L. E. Tactual perception in historical perspective : David
Katz's world of touch. In W. Schiff and E. Foulke (Eds.), Tactual
Perception : A sourcebook. Cambridge, Cambridge University Press,
1982, pp. 1-54.

Landis, T., Buttet, J., Assal, G. & Graves, R. Dissociation of ear
preference in monaural word and voice recognition.
Neuropsychologia, 1982, 20, 501-504.

Larsen, S. & Hakonsen, K. Absence of ear asymmetry in blind children on
a dichotic listening task compared to sighted controls. Brain and
Language, 1983, 18, 192-198.

La Torre, R. A. & La Torre, A. M. Effect of lateral eye fixation on
cognitive processes. Perceptual and Motor Skills, 1981, 52, 487-
490.

Lauter, J. Dichotic identification of complex sounds : Absolute and
relative ear advantages. Journal of the Acoustical Society of
America, 1982, 71, 701-707.

LeDoux, J. E. Wilson, D. H. & Gazzaniga, M. S. Manipulo-spatial aspects
of cerebral lateralization : Clues to the origin of
lateralization. Neuropsychologia, 1977, 15, 743-750.

Lee, D. N. & Aaronson, E. Visual proprioceptive control of standing in
human infants. Perception and Psychophysics, 1974, 15, 529-532.

Lempert, H. & Kinsbourne, M. Effect of laterality of orientation on
verbal memory. Neuropsychologia, 1982, 20, 211-214.

McFarland, K. Effects of hemispace on concurrent task performance.
Neuropsychologia, 1982, 20, 365-367.

MacKenzie, C. L. & Martenuik, R. G. Motor skill : Feedback, knowledge
and structural issues. Canadian Journal of Psychology, 1985, 39,
313-317.

Meredith, M. A. & Stein, B. E. Descending efferents from the superior
colliculus relay integrated multisensory information. Science,
1985, 227, 657-659.

Mesulam, M. M. A cortical network for directed attention and unilateral
neglect. Annals of Neurology, 1981, 10, 309-325.

Mesulam, M. M. The functional anatomy and hemispheric specialization
for directed attention. Trends in the Neurosciences, 1983, 6, 384-
387.

Mishkin, M., Ungerleider, L. & Macko, K. A. Object vision and spatial
vision : Two cortical pathways. Trends in the Neurosciences, 1983,
6, 414-417.

Molfese, D. L. & Molfese, V. J. Hemisphere and stimulus differences as
reflected in the cortical responses of newborn infants to speech
stimuli. Developmental Psychology, 1979, 15, 501-511(a).

Molfese, D. L. & Molfese, V. J. VOT distinctions in infants : Learned
or innate? In H. Whitaker and H. A. Whitaker (Eds.), Studies in
Neurolinguistics, Vol. IV. New York : Academic press, 1979, pp.
225-240(b).

Moscovitch, M. Information processing and the cerebral hemispheres. In
M. S. Gazzaniga (Ed.), Handbook of Behavioral Neurobiology, Vol. 2 :
Neuropsychology. New York : Plenum Press, 1979, pp. 379-446.

Mousty, P., Bertelson, P. & Kurrels, V. Effect of reading number in one
handed apprehension of Braille. Paper read at the Fifth European
Conference of the International Neuropsychological Society,
Deauville, June 15-18, 1982.

Nettleton, N. C. & Bradshaw, J. L. The effects of task, practice and
sequencing upon the lateralization of semantic decisions.
International Journal of Neuroscience, 1983, 20, 265-282.

Neville, H. J., Kutas, M. & Schmidt, A. Event related potential studies of cerebral specialization during reading II : Studies of congenitally deaf adults. Brain and Language, 1982, 16, 316-337.

Nicoletti, R., Umilta, C. & Ladavas, E. Compatibility due to the coding of the relative position of the effectors. Acta Psychologica, 1984, 57, 133-143.

Norman, D. A. & Bobrow, D. G. On data-limited and resource-limited processes. Cognitive Psychology, 1975, 7, 44-64.

Ogden, J. A. Anterior-posterior interhemispheric differences in the loci of lesions producing visual hemineglect. Brain and Cognition, 1985, 4, 59-75.

Pick, H. L. Perception, locomotion and orientation. In R. L. Welsh and B. B. Blasch (Eds.), Foundations of Orientation and Mobility. New York : American Foundation for the Blind, 1980.

Pick, H. L., Warren, D. H. & Hay, J. C. The resolution of sensory conflict between vision, proprioception and audition. Perception and Psychophysics, 1969, 6, 203-206.

Pierson, J. M., Bradshaw, J. L. & Nettleton, N. C. Head and body space to left and right, front and rear 1: Unidirectional competitive auditory stimulation. Neuropsychologia, 1983, 21, 463-473.

Plourde, G. & Sperry, R. W. Left hemisphere involvement in left spatial neglect from right-sided lesions. Brain, 1984, 107, 95-106.

Rakic, P. & Yakovlev, P. I. Development of the corpus callosum and cavum septi in Man. Journal of Comparative Neurology, 1968, 132, 45-72.

Ramos-Brieva, J. A., Olivan, J., Palomares, A. & Vela, A. Is there a right hemisphere dysfunction in major depression? International Journal of Neuroscience, 1984, 23, 103-110.

Ratcliff, G. Disturbances of spatial orientation associated with cerebral lesions. In M. Potegal (Ed.), Spatial Abilities : Development and Physiological Functions. New York : Academic Press, 1982, pp. 301-33.

Ritter, S. M. The vertical-horizontal illusion. Psychological Review Monograph Supplement, 1917, 23(4), 1-99.

Rizzolatti, G., Gentilucci, M. & Matelli, M. Selective spatial attention : One center, one circuit or many circuits. In M. Posner & O. S. M. Marin (Eds.), Mechanisms of Attention : Attention and Performance XI. Hillsdale, N.J. : Erlbaum, 1985, pp. 251-265.

Rock, I. & Harris, C. S. Vision and touch. Scientific American, 1967, 216, 96-104.

Rosenberger, P. B. Discriminative aspects of visual hemi-inattention. Neurology, 1974, 24, 17-23.

Salamy, A. Commissural transmission: Maturational changes in humans. Science, 1978, 200, 1409-1411.

Schenkenberg, T., Bradford, D. C. & Ajax, E. T. Line bisection and unilateral visual neglect in patients with neurologic impairment. Neurology, 1980, 30, 509-517.

Scherer, K. R., Ladd, D. R. & Silverman, K. E. A. Vocal cues to speaker affect : Testing two models. Journal of the Acoustical Society of America, 1984, 76, 1346-1356.

Schwartz, A. S., Marchok, P. L., Kreinick, C. & Flynn, R. E. The asymmetrical lateralization of tactile extinction in patients with unilateral cerebral dysfunction. Brain, 1979, 102, 669-684.

Seitz, K. S. & McKeever, W. F. Unilateral versus bilateral presentation methods in the reaction time paradigm. Brain and Cognition, 1984, 3, 413-425.

Sidtis, J. J. Predicting brain organization from dichotic listening performance : Cortical and subcortical functional asymmetries contribute to perceptual asymmetries. <u>Brain and Language</u>, 1982, <u>17</u>, 287-300.

Smith Y. M. & Latto, R. An investigation of visual neglect following parietal lobe lesions in man. <u>Behavior and Brain Research</u>, 1982, <u>5</u>, 120-121.

Stuss, D. T. & Benson, D. F. Neuropsychological studies of the frontal lobes. <u>Psychological Bulletin</u>, 1984, <u>95</u>, 3-28.

Weiner, M. J., Hallet, M. & Funkenstein, H. H. Adaptation to lateral displacement of vision in patients with lesions of the central nervous system. <u>Neurology</u>, 1983, <u>33</u>, 766-772.

Weston, P. & Weinman, J. The effects of auditory and linguistic deprivation on lateral preferences of deaf children. <u>Developmental Medicine and Child Neurology</u>, 1983, <u>25</u>, 207-213.

White, B. W., Saunders, F. A., Scadden, L., Bach-y-Rita, P. & Collins, C. Seeing with the skin. <u>Perception and Psychophysics</u>, 1970, <u>7</u>, 23-27.

Yakovlev, P. I. & Lecours, A. R. The myelogenetic cycles of regional maturation in the brain. In A. Minkowski (Ed.), <u>Regional development of the brain in early life</u>. Oxford: Blackwell, 1967, pp. 355-358.

Acknowledgments: This work was supported by the Australian Research Grants Scheme (to JLB and NCN). We gratefully acknowledge the continued assistance, in the design and construction of apparatus, of Bob Wood, John Dick, Geoff Mead, Bill Bramstedt and Noel Butson.

Neurophysiological and Neuropsychological Aspects
of Spatial Neglect, M. Jeannerod (editor)
© Elsevier Science Publishers B.V. (North-Holland), 1987

MECHANISMS OF UNILATERAL NEGLECT

Marcel Kinsbourne

Unilateral neglect of space is viewed as a bias in lateral
attention, due to imbalance in a brain stem opponent processor
control system for lateral orientation. Both percepts and images
are represented in laterally biased fashion. The preponderance of
left over right neglect syndromes is attributed to a more powerful
rightward than leftward orienting tendency in normals, revealed
in them by minor behavioral asymmetries, but resulting in major
inequalities when these tendencies are disinhibited due to
contralateral brain damage.

Introduction

Focal lesions in different areas of the human cerebral cortex induce
sharply distinctive behavioral deficits. The reasonable inference follows
that various parts of the cortical network are differentially specialized.
But a rush from behavior to brain courts circularity. Allotting to each area
of brain the function, in its undamaged state, of precluding the deficit
that characterized behavior when it is damaged does not explain, but merely
restates the finding. So it is with unilateral neglect. It is no explanation
of unilateral neglect of person that the lesion has compromised "the body
schema" or of unilateral neglect of space that it has damaged a center for
"attention". Nor will it do to write neglect off to the interaction of
sensory deficit and intellectual deterioration (Battersby, Bender, Pollack
& Kahn, 1956). In his pioneering paper, Babinski (1914) recognized in his
patient "in striking contrast to her apparent intellectual preservation,
her ignorance of her almost complete hemiplegia". Intellectually
unimpaired patients with severe neglect have often been documented. So have
neglect patients without sensory deficits (Chédru, Leblanc & Lhermitte,
1973). Neglect is a unilateral disorder of brain activation. The deficient
activation ipsilateral to the lesion has been amply demonstrated by
psychophysiological means in experimental animals, and non-specific
external stimulation, as well as stimulant drugs, counteract the behavioral
deficit (reviewed by Wolgin, 1982). So we proceed to inquire which cerebral
processors are insufficiently, and which are unduly, in control of behavior
in unilateral neglect? Which processor is released from control by which
other one, to generate the qualitatively abnormal and spectacularly
maladaptive phenomenology of the neglect syndrome? Which components of
neglect behavior represent deficit, which release, which compensation? I
shall argue (i) that unilateral neglect results not from attentional
deficit but from an attentional bias: imbalance in an opponent system that
controls lateral orientation and action; (ii) that the rightward directed
opponent processor is more potent, and when disinhibited generates more
extreme lateral orienting tendencies than the disinhibited leftward
directed facility; and (iii) that the attentional imbalance manifests at

various levels of abstraction from gross orienting to spatial representation, to generate the fully fledged syndrome of rightward bias in attention and evaluation of self and ambient space. The argument proceeds in the form of a series of propositions.

Neglect is a Directional, not a Hemispace, Phenomenon

A common consequence of lateral cerebral damage over a wide distribution on either hemisphere is the failure to detect a contralesional stimulus given a similar stimulus simultaneous with it or nearly so, to the intact side (Oppenheim, 1885). This double simultaneous stimulation (DSS) effect ("extinction" – Bender, 1952 ; Bender & Diamond, 1975) is commonly found even if there are no demonstrable sensory deficits in the modality in question (Kinsbourne & Warrington, 1961). Although customarily one infers extinction from the absence of verbal report or manual indication, a gaze shift toward the intact side also betrays the attentional bias. In DSS performed in the customary manner with one stimulus in each hemispace, the side of stimulation (left or right hemispace) is confounded with the relative location of the attended and inattended stimulus (one being to the right or the left of the other). They can be deconfounded by presenting the two stimuli in lateral relationship as before, but within a hemifield. When this is done extinction is still found (Kinsbourne, 1977) and so is the telltale gaze deviation (Weinstein & Friedland, 1977). Further, when the patient inspects a laterally extended display his attention wanders to its ipsilesional extreme regardless of the display's absolute location: "In looking at a picture, some patients neglect figures on one side even when – the picture is placed in the functioning visual field" (Weinstein & Kahn, 1959, p.974). Thus the dichotomizing term "hemispatial neglect" is misleading, as the attentional imbalance is not merely between one hemispace and the other.

Experimental observations confirm that relative rather absolute spatial location determines whether phenomena of neglect occur. Notably, patients with neglect are strikingly slow in shifting attention contralesionally, even when they initiate the shift within the intact visual half field and direct it to a more centrally located target that is still within the same intact visual half field (Posner, Walker, Friedrich & Rafal, 1984). Parietal patients with and without neglect oriented to briefly exposed targets laterally displaced from fixation. They were given advance notice of the side on which the target was to be expected. Control subjects could move their attention to the target (and respond to it with shorter latency) while their gaze remained centrally fixated (Posner, Nissen & Ogden, 1978). But if the directional cue was misleading, response latency was prolonged. The parietal patients behaved similarly, though latency of attention shift away from the lesion was relatively prolonged. But when although they were led to expect the target to appear ipsilateral to the lesion, it actually appeared contralaterally, parietal patients, and particularly those with neglect, exhibited by far the longest latencies of all. Posner et al. (1984) concluded that patients found it most difficult to disengage attention from its current focus when the direction of the intended shift was toward a target located further contralateral to the lesion. This happened within the right ("intact") as well as the left hemispace.

Gradients of attention within as well as between hemifields following lateralized lesions are readily demonstrable in patients with posterior hemisphere lesions by means of the tachistoscopic display of letter groups. Within the half field accuracy of identification is greatest in the extreme ipsilesional location (Kinsbourne, 1966). In letter cancellation tasks the probability of a target being missed increases the more contralesionally it is located.

When patients attempt to bisect horizontal lines their systematic errors betray the attentional imbalance. The transecting line is so placed that the segment on the "intact" side of space is shorter (Fuchs, 1920). The ipsilesional deviation from the physical center indicates how much the patient underestimates the contralesional side of the line and overestimates the ipsilesional side (It is not possible to measure those two effects separately). This bias is found even in the "intact" visual half field (Heilman & Valenstein, 1979). In line bisection one can also compare the degree of attentional bias when the subject orients (by head and eye turning) to one or the other side in order to fixate a bisection display displaced to one side. The degree of bias is greatest contralesionally (Heilman & Valenstein, 1979). Thus the more attention is constrained (by task demands) in the impaired direction, the greater is its tendency to rebound toward the dominant side.

Failure to attend contralesionally is complemented by exaggerated attention in the preserved direction. An ipsilesional stimulus is, as it were, a magnet for the patient (Barany, 1913; Silberpfennig, 1941). He has a predilection for events at the periphery of the intact field (Horenstein, 1969). Although instructed to maintain fixation, the patient's involuntary gaze shift toward an incidental stimulus on the intact periphery betrays the disinhibited directional orienting bias. Manual reaching errors also show a bias toward the lesioned side, in both half fields (Ratcliffe & Davies-Jones, 1972; Corin & Bender, 1972).

The difference between the hemispace and the directional concepts of unilateral neglect is illustrated by a comment made by Heilman and Watson (1977). They argue that attentional imbalance should generate not only defective performance with respect to the contralesional half field, but superior performance in the ipsilesional half field. This does not happen (Gainotti & Tiacci, 1971; Albert, 1973). The argument overlooks the gradient of attention effect. Even within the ipsilesional half field, performance is impaired for more central relative to more lateral locations. Whereas stimuli at the extreme periphery attract correct response, there can be much impairment even within the "intact" hemifield. This outcome is not predicted by a dichotomous hemispace model, according to which lateral differences can exist between, but not within, half fields.

Animal studies complement these observations (Lamotte & Acuna, 1978) and highlight them through the appearance of disinhibited unilateral turning tendencies. The laterally lesioned animal perpetually "circles" toward the lesion side (reviewed by Kinsbourne, 1974a), just as the patient with neglect turns ever to the lesioned side when negotiating his environment, even the familiar topography of his own home. Physiological studies in animals and man have amply demonstrated that opposing directional turning tendencies (of gaze, head and whole body) are in mutually inhibitory competition. The opponent processors in question are represented at brain stem level, but are under ipsilateral hemispheric control.

The hierarchical organization of the lateral orienting control systems generates specific predictions. If a lesion exists at a level at which facilitating influences on the ipsilateral activating control system are generated, or through which they are conducted, then the resulting unilateral neglect will be ameliorated by an additional lesion at the same level contralaterally. If the orienting processor itself is involved, then contralateral damage will not ameliorate the neglect, but generalize it to the other side. Thus, whereas a syndrome interpretable as bilateral neglect

does not result from bilateral cerebral disease (Welch & Stuteville, 1958),
it does occur after bilateral lesions of cingulate gyrus and of
mesencephalic reticular formation, in the form of akinetic mutism, and
after bilateral collicular excision (Denny-Brown, 1962).

Turning tendencies in humans are opposite but unequal

Babinski (1914) remarked that "perhaps anosagnosia is a feature of
right hemisphere lesions". Clinical series agree that neglect of the left
after right cerebral damage is perhaps more frequent, and certainly more
frequently severe, than neglect of the right after left lesions (although
the best documented series do show beyond question that the latter does also
occur - Ogden, 1985 and this volume). This is in sharp contrast to all animal
work, in which species-specific (as opposed to individual) left-right
asymmetry has not been documented. Any viable theory of the mechanism of
neglect in humans must explain the predominance of left neglect (De Renzi,
1982).

Whereas frank neglect symptomatology is far more common after right
hemisphere damage, extinction in isolation shows little or no lateral bias
in incidence (Weinstein & Friedland, 1977) (though Schwartz, Marchok,
Kreinick & Flynn, 1979, did report asymmetry of extinction in the tactile
modality). On these grounds, Weinstein and Friedland set it apart from
neglect. This position is hard to maintain. In neglect, extinction is
ubiquitous and most authors have regarded it as a minimal or residual
neglect manifestation (Denny-Brown & Banker, 1959). On this view, smaller
right than left lesions would set up extinction but smaller right than left
lesions would also generate more severe neglect. On balance, extinction
would be equally common with lesions on both sides, or nearly so.

Left neglect may be predominant because right and left directional
tendencies in humans, though opposite, are not equal. There is some
normative support for this view. Newborn infants turn spontaneously more to
the right (Gesell, 1938). They do so both for approach (to the right) and for
withdrawal (from a midline aversive stimulus) (Liederman & Kinsbourne,
1980) and even adults in an undifferentiated spatial field reputedly veer to
the right (Schilder, 1933). Adults prefer pictures in which the most
informative items are on the right (Swartz & Hewitt, 1970; Levy, 1976) or
draw attention rightward (Freimuth & Wapner, 1979), preferentially select
the rightermost of comparable commodities arranged in a line (Nisbett &
Wilson, 1977), and scan more to the right of center (Beaumont, 1985). The
question arises, what occurs when an opponent system with unequal opposing
forces is destabilized by change in one of the opponent processors? A
dramatic illustration derives from Altman, Balonov and Deglin's (1979)
study of auditory localization immediately after unilateral electro-
convulsive shock. When addressed from the left, the right-shocked patient
turned head and eyes to the right (allo-acousis). Left sided shock did not
induce a corresponding leftward orienting bias. Sound localization
similarly was biased by the right brain but not the left brain
electro-convulsive shock.

I propose that left brain activation powerfully generates rightward
turning. The right brain's opposing leftward bias is weak; mainly it holds
the left hemisphere's rightward bias in check. If the right hemisphere is
inactivated, attention swings sharply rightward. If the left hemisphere is
impaired the leftward attentional shift that results is quite mild. On this
view one would consider cases of extinction and of frank neglect as on a
qualitatively homogeneous continuum. Altogether, left inattention
(extinction through neglect) remains more common and more often more
severe.

Right Hemisphere Dominance for Attention Cannot Explain Neglect Phenomenology

A competing theory originated with Dorff, Mirsky and Mishkin (1965). Based on a tachistoscopic study of patients with unilateral temporal lobectomy, Dorff et al. (1965) postulated "a special role of the right temporal lobe in vision" (p.50). "While the left temporal lobe – facilitate(s) recognition in the right visual field, the right temporal lobe – facilitate(s) recognition in both visual fields" (p.69). This theory has recently been revived by Dimond (1979), Heilman and Van den Abell (1979) and Mesulam (1981) who attribute the predominance of right neglect to a specialization for "attention" of the right hemisphere. Whereas the left hemisphere controls attention only in right hemispace, the right hemisphere controls it bilaterally. A left hemisphere lesion would leave attention available for both sides whereas a right hemisphere lesion limits it to right hemispace.

The idea that the right hemisphere is dominant for attention will be considered first in its own right and then for its relevance to the phenomenology of neglect.

The impression that confusional states occur preferentially after right hemisphere infarction has been held to support a bilateral attentional function for neglect (Mesulam, Waxman, Geschwind & Sabin, 1976) on the assumption that confusion represents bilateral neglect. However, reports of confusional states following left sided infarction are not hard to find (Hyland, 1933; Aymes & Nielsen, 1955; Horenstein, Chamberlain & Comory, 1967; Medina, Rubins & Ross, 1974). They might be considered more prevalent still if aphasia did not mask the verbal expression of confusion which is its most obvious hallmark. In any case, confusion has little in common with neglect. Its characteristic features – disorientation for place and time, memory deficit and confabulation, illogicality, delusions and hallucinations – are precisely the type fo symptom that Weinstein and Friedland (1977) found not to be associated with severe unilateral neglect.

"The right hemisphere in man may be dominant for attention–arousal–activation response" (Heilman, Watson, Valenstein & Damasio, 1983, p.490). This claim is based on studies reporting greater right than left hemisphere arousal in terms of several psychophysiological indices, as well as the electroencephalographic hallmarks of right hemisphere underactivation in neglect patients with right parietal disease (Heilman, Schwartz & Watson, 1978). The idea that the right hemisphere has a special role in the individual's response to novel and emotional stimuli is well in line with current literature and theory on cerebral involvement in emotion (Kinsbourne & Bemporad, 1984). There is evidence that extensive left hemisphere stroke generates a depressive syndrome not to be found with disease of equal localization and extent on the right side (Robinson & Price, 1982). This could go far to explain the frequent finding of indifference among neglect patients (Weinstein & Friedland, 1977) in that adjacent and overlapping right hemisphere territories may be involved in both the indifference and the neglect state. But a special role of the right hemisphere in alerting does not in itself explain why rightsided lesions more than left cause a <u>directional</u> bias in attention. A mechanism for the relationship has to be suggested. Such a mechanism can be based on the notion of imbalance between opponent processors. A relationship between emotional indifference and diminished leftward attending does follow from what we know about how hemisphere specialization relates to the control of lateral orienting.

When subjects engage in mental processes that are largely based on the activities of one hemisphere they emit a selective orienting response observable behaviorally in terms of submotor attentional (Kinsbourne, 1970) and overt gaze (Kinsbourne, 1972) shifts toward contralateral space. When thinking about emotional material normal subjects have been shown to look to the left (Schwartz, Davidson & Maer, 1975; Krikorian & Rafales, 1982) indicating that the right hemisphere is activated. Thus emotional insensitivity due to right hemisphere damage should be associated with diminished leftward orienting, consistent with unilateral neglect of the left. But the right attentional dominance claim takes a different form – whereas the left hemisphere subserves the attentional needs of right hemispace the right hemisphere caters to both sides.

If right hemispace is served by both hemispheres, should their roles be considered additive or redundant? Presumably not additive, for that would imply substantially keener attention in right hemispace in the normal state, which is not the case. Also, the simple additive dichotomous model predicts that attention and performance across the visual field should be twice as decremented by right as by left hemisphere damage. A glance at pertinent data shows that this is not so. Different gradients of performance followed right as compared to left temporal lobectomy in Dorff et al.'s study. After left lobectomy the deficit in performance was more evenly distributed across both fields than after right, but overall, the performance deficit was comparable for both lobectomy groups.

If right hemispace were served redundantly by both hemispheres, this would not be a dominance phenomenon but one of selective compensation (the right hemisphere effectively assuming the role the left hemisphere relinquished after it was lesioned). But that conflicts with the fact that even mild leftsided lesions readily release rightsided extinction on DSS. Also, this dichotomizing approach misses the phenomenon of tradeoff between opposite attentional poles: the increased attention to the right that accompanies decreased attention to the left after rightsided damage. The previously discussed notion of differently sloping gradients of attention after right and left lesions captures more of neglect symptomatology.

The very data that Dorff et al. (1965) took to indicate rightsided dominance lend themselves to an interpretation in terms of orientational bias. They present data on the patterns of identification of bilaterally exposed letter sequences by right and left temporal lobectomy patients. In an unpublished experimental simulation that I performed on normal subjects, accomplished by presenting the right and left half field displays asynchronously so as to control the direction of scan, the differences in the error patterns of right as compared to left temporal patients were closely simulated in line with opponent process imbalance theory. Normals given left field displays a few milliseconds before right performed like left temporal patients and normals first presented with right field input like right temporal patients.

The greater turning tendency due to the disinhibited left hemisphere explains the exaggerated attention to the extreme right of a display as well as the impaired attention to its left. It explains "backward word completion" (Kinsbourne & Warrington, 1963). This is the tendency of right lesioned patients to infer a word from its terminal letters, as if only those were of importance in identifying the word. This was found even if the letters were presented well within the intact field. The attentional imbalance thus has evaluative as well as psychophysical consequences. At the cortical level turning tendencies are represented in abstract as well as sensorimotor form. The patient evaluates favorably whatever is rightward located but denigrates the same stimulus when located on the left. This is plentifully illustrated by clinical anecdotes of the patients' greatly different attitudes to observers approaching from the left as compared to the right side, and indeed their different attitudes to their own left and right body parts. They not only disdain to use left limbs, appearing not to regard them as useful, but refer to them with contempt or disgust, directly or in metaphor (Weinstein & Kahn, 1955). Turning to one side doubles for two activities: approaching that side or withdrawing from the other. The phenomenon of allesthesia, in which a subject attributes to the right a stimulus on the left, could represent the combination of detection of and withdrawal from a leftsided stimulus. An alternative possibility is that the leftsided stimulus has become assimilated into a "dominant focus" (Rusinov, 1973), a cortically generalized pattern of neuronal activity, based on the intact hemisphere.

The Process of Mentally Representing is Directional

The mental representation of remembered scenes and intended acts involves internal orienting. Current theorizing favors the view that intention involves representing the intended state, and that action is based on comparing the intended end point with the current state of affairs. Mental imagery shares brain mechanisms with direct perception (Farah, 1985). As one scans a scene so one scans a representation (Kosslyn, 1980). The prevalent dual-process view of imaging assumes that one first represents a display, then scans it for specifics. This is hard to prove, because one cannot establish whether something has been represented until one elicits the expected response. Did the subject scan an existing representation (for which there is no independent evidence)? While the subject represents one feature, is the rest of the display "present" (like the ground for a figure in direct perception)? Knowing of no evidence that it is, I prefer the simpler working hypothesis that, on demand, the subject represents the asked-for feature. The act of representing makes the information available, there being no need to hypothesize an additional "internal eye". In neglect, the act of representing is handicapped in proportion to the extent to which the asked-for detail is located toward the contralesional end of the display. Representing may be a "print out" process that is successive and subject to the same biases directional as are submotor attentional shifts across an external field. Kosslyn, Holtzman, Farah and Gazzaniga (1985) propose "that the same visual inspection mechanisms are used in perception and imagery" (p.313). But neglect can easily be demonstrated with visual exposure too brief to permit active inspection, and for imagery also the inspection ("internal eye") metaphor may be unnecessary. Bisiach and his colleagues ingeniously demonstrated that neglect extends to internal representations, both in terms of remembered scenes (Bisiach & Luzzatti, 1978) and of laterally extended information viewed successively through a slit (Bisiach, Luzzatti & Perani, 1979). Bisiach and Luzzatti explain that the damaged hemisphere has been rendered incapable of maintaining its half of a representation spread across both hemispheres. "The processes by which a visual image is conjured up by the mind may split between the two cerebral hemispheres, like the projection of a real scene onto the visual areas of the two sides of the brain" (p. 132). This dichotomizing formulation does not explain why, for instance in auditory localization, systematic directional error "to the right involves not only the contralateral, but also the ipsilateral half-space" (Bisiach, Cornacchia, Sterzi & Vallar, 1984, p.48). These findings could also be explained as due to a directional bias in the print-out of the representation. The critical experiment that determines whether neglect of a representation, like neglect of the external world, conforms to a gradient rather than a right-left dichotomy, remains to be done.

The disorder of intention emphasized by Valenstein and Heilman (1981) might also be a consequence of orientational imbalance at the level of representation. If one cannot represent the intended consequence of an act in one direction, one cannot intend, let alone act, in that direction.

Heilman and his colleagues (Watson, Miller & Heilman, 1978; Valenstein, Heilman, Watson & Van den Abell, 1982; Watson, Valenstein, Day & Heilman, 1986) attempted to deconfound sensory (attentional) and motor (intentional) neglect in an animal model in the following way: Monkeys were trained to respond to a lateral touch with contralateral limb movements. Regardless of whether they were then lesioned in the frontal or the parieto-temporal cortex, they continued to respond with ipsilesional movement to a contralesional stimulus, but made errors both of omission and commission when the touch was ipsilesional. They concluded that what was demonstrated here was a pure disorder of intention.

Heilman's design does not in fact pit the attentional against the intentional perspective on neglect. Whereas there was motor rivalry, there always being two limbs to choose from for response, there was only one sensory stimulus at a time, for which inattention would not be expected. The failure to respond contralesionally in a neglect preparation demonstrated experimentally has long been a familiar feature of neglect, and does not aid in deciding between rival explanations of the neglect syndrome.

Commissures at Cerebral and Brainstem Level Assume Different Roles in the Control of Laterally Directed Behavior

The basic blueprint of the central nervous system, vertebrate as well as invertebrate, features horizontal commissural interconnections at multiple levels between the paired structures of the neuraxis. These are known to mediate excitation-inhibition balance. Neglect experimentation teaches us that the functions of the forebrain commissure differ significantly from those of commissures at brainstem level, notably the intercollicular commissure.

The opponent relationship between right and left gaze and turning tendencies is not mediated by the corpus callosum (Kinsbourne, 1974a). Callosal section leaves conjugate gaze unimpaired (Pasik & Pasik, 1977). One would therefore not expect callosotomy to redress any existing imbalance between opposing turning tendencies induced by a lateral lesion, and indeed it does not (Eidelberg & Schwartz, 1971). Section of the intercollicular commissure does so however. Sprague (1966) induced hemianopia by occipital lesion in the cat and was able to reverse this by lesioning the contralateral superior colliculus. More significant yet, it sufficed to section the intercollicular commissure to restore vision in the affected half field. We infer that each hemisphere influences turning tendencies by downward projection onto the ipsilateral superior colliculus. Deuel and Collins (1984) have recently corroborated this by directly demonstrating hypometabolism of the superior colliculus ipsilateral to neglect- inducing hemisphere lesions in monkeys (an elegant demonstration of a remote effect of a brain lesion, named diaschisis by von Monakow, 1897). Reciprocal inhibition between colliculi mediates the balance of attention. The underactivated colliculus, if released from inhibition by its opponent, can reassume control of contralateral orienting even without the assistance of its ipsilateral hemisphere.

Sectioning the corpus callosum does influence lateral attention indirectly by virtue of the loss of hemispheric equilibration that results.

I have argued elsewhere (Kinsbourne, 1974b; 1982) that given unilateral hemisphere activation in support of a task for which that hemisphere is specialized, the corpus callosum mediates excitatory influences that hold the unused hemisphere in readiness for conjoint action, should it be required. In the split brain state activation readily accrues to the hemisphere in use, leaving the other underactivated and out of control of behavior. Thus when split-brain subjects searched for a target letter among two letters simultaneously exposed, one in each visual half field, the targets in the left visual field did not elicit the required discriminative response (Kinsbourne, 1974b). We further showed that each hemisphere, selectively aroused, exhibited the expected contralateral gradient of attention within its visual hemifield (Trevarthen, 1974). Gross neglect does not ensue (Plourde & Sperry, 1984) presumably because intact brainstem commissures preclude this.

Orienting imbalance does not necessarily imply gross hemisphere arousal differences. The disinhibited intact hemisphere is not expected to exhibit hypermetabolism. Cook (1984) has explained how hemispheric balance can be mediated by topographic inhibition, in the absence of diffuse changes in hemispheric excitation – inhibition balance. In fact it is probably an oversimplification to speak in terms of global hemisphere arousal differences as underlying neglect (Heilman & Watson, 1977). It is true that the electroencephalographic hallmarks of right hemisphere underarousal (high amplitude slow waves) are commonly to be found in cases of neglect (although a reciprocal electrophysiological overactivation on the intact side (high frequency rhythms) might also be found if looked for as it was by Reeves and Haganen (1971). Yet complete hemispherectomy fails to induce a substantial neglect syndrome (Smith, 1974). It follows that intrahemispheric imbalance must play a role. Release of parietal structures from control by the ipsilateral fronto-temporal system may be involved.

Modifying the Relative Activation of the Hemisphere Modifies Neglect.

Kinsbourne (1970a) suggested that neglect of the left would deepen if left hemisphere activation were to increase and that verbal activity might implement such an effect. Heilman and Watson (1978) tested this experimentally by comparing left neglect patients' cancellation performance for verbal and nonverbal shapes. As predicted, more left biased failures to cancel indicated that neglect was more severe when the stimuli were verbal. An observation by Silberpfennig (1941) may be similarly explained. Neglect could be transitorily relieved by caloric irrigation which induced nystagmus with fast component away from the lesion (that is, which stimulated the lesioned side of the brain). In contrast, if, in a split-brain monkey, one eye-hand combination only is consistently used, the other combination lapses into unresponsivity (Trevarthen, 1962). In this preparation, lateralized disuse induces neglect. In view of such observations, it is not surprising that reducing activation of the intact hemisphere has a similar mitigating effect on neglect. On account of the organization of the retino-collicular pathways, visual input through the right eye is more stimulating to the left hemisphere, and vice versa (Kaufman, 1974). Deuel (1985) occluded the eye ipsilateral to a neglect-inducing lesion in monkeys, and documented an accelerated recovery. Studies of split-brain man have indicated that when responding is confined to one hemisphere for an appreciable period of time, the other loses readiness for action (Trevarthen, 1972). There is therefore a rational basis for controlling the activity of the intact hemisphere in the remediation of attentional imbalance.

A simple way of manipulating the hemispheric balance of activation is by induced lateral orientation. Kinsbourne (1975) introduced the maneuver of having subjects turn head and eyes laterally prior to a cognitive judgement and demonstrated that the direction of turning influenced the efficiency of lateralized processing. Lempert and Kinsbourne (1982) manipulated verbal memory in this way. When subjects listened to sentences with head and eyes turned right they did better in cued recall than when they listened with head and eyes turned left. The effect on lateralized cognitive processes of induced lateral orientation have been confirmed and extended by others (Hines & Martindale, 1979; Gross, Franco & Lewin, 1978; Casey, 1981; Latorre & Latorre, 1981; Walker, Wade & Waldman, 1982). Inasmuch as neglect represents an extreme case of disease - induced lateral orientation, one might expect it to have effects analogous to those induced experimentally in normal subjects. Perhaps most relevant for neglect symptomatology are the studies of Drake. He found that normal subjects become more self engrossed, confirmed in their existing attitudes, optimistic about themselves and derogatory of others, during rightward than leftward orientation (Drake & Bingham, 1985). These characteristics presumably represent attributes of the individual during left brain activation dominance. If this work is confirmed, the method may hold promise for simulating in normal subjects, aspects of the personality characteristics that accompany the neglect syndrome in normal subjects.

Mood changes also might be influenced by lateral orientation. Grijalva (in press) found emotionally negative statements to have a depressing effect on normal subjects when presented through the left ear but not through the right. If this induced lateral orientation effect (while listening to right sided stimulation) is attributable to relatively greater activation of the left hemisphere, it could account for the indifference reaction (Gainotti, 1972) impaired emotional arousal and deficient emotional decoding and encoding (Heilman et al., 1983) that some patients with left neglect exhibit. This line of reasoning suggests an experimental test. Whatever aspect of a left neglector's behavior is attributable to left hemisphere overactivation, the reverse characteristics should obtain for patients whose left hemisphere lesions have generated neglect of the right side of space. They should show increased, not flattened, emotionality and sharpened sensitivity to external influences with emotional connotation. Conversely, personality attributes that right and left neglectors have in common can more plausibly be attributed to reactions secondary to the neglect disability.

If induced lateral orientation is a valid way of simulating aspects of neglect, it should simulate, to some extent the attentional distortion that characterizes the syndrome. This was accomplished by Reuter-Lorenz, Moscovitch and Kinsbourne (1985) with the use of tachistoscopic line bisection judgments. Normal subjects were presented with briefly exposed horizontal lines transected either centrally or to one or other side of center. They were asked to judge whether the transection divided the line into halves or not. When the line was exposed in the left half field there was a systematic bias toward overestimating the left end of the line and in the right half of the field the opposite was the case. A similar effect could be induced by exposing the lines in central vision but constraining attention to one end of the display. Thus left exposure simulated the bisection performance of subjects with right neglect of space and right exposure that of subjects with left neglect of space. The outcomes were predicted on the basis that leftward orientation will involve selective activation of the right hemisphere relative to left and vice versa. When perceptual rivalry was set up by placing line drawings of squares at one or the other end of the transected line, an asymmetry emerged. The square to the right of the line was more effective in attracting attention than the square to the left. The stronger orienting bias of the left hemisphere was thus revealed.

As an alternative to the then generally accepted "structural" model of perceptual asymmetry, Kinsbourne (1970b) presented the idea that behavioral asymmetries arise from imbalance in the level of hemisphere activation. On this view, neglect represents an extreme case of perceptual asymmetry, and is due to extreme asymmetry in activation of areas in the two hemispheres that control laterally directed behavior.

Similarities between Denial of Lateralized Disability and of Aphasia

Cortical sensory impairments are characterized by inattention to the affected modality. This is conspicuous in both acquired and developmental cortical deafness. The patient who is peripherally deaf strains to hear. He who is cortically deaf ignores sound (hence the characteristic variability of such a patient's audiometric thresholds). The analogous state has been demonstrated after excision of cat auditory cortex (Thompson & Welker, 1963). In the cat, audition is prepotent over vision. Given simultaneous auditory and visual stimuli, the auditory stimulus controls the cat's behavior. Post-operatively, auditory thresholds are unchanged, but in the bimodal condition the visual stimulus becomes prepotent. By this principle, ignoring a limb the cortical representation of which is damaged is not surprising. But there must be more to denial syndromes than that, because most cortical deficits are not accompanied by denial. Instead, flagrant denial is virtually limited to cases of unilateral neglect, cortical blindness, and to certain aphasics.

The hallmarks of denial are explicitly denying disability and even gratuitously asserting competence in the activity in question, and implicitly failing to modify one's actions and reorganize one's surroundings in view of the disability, and acting physically and metaphorically as if it did not exist. Both types of denial are common both in neglect (Weinstein & Kahn, 1955) and in jargon aphasia (Weinstein & Friedland, 1977).

No single pattern of linguistic deficit is invariably associated with the appearance of neologistic anosagnosic jargon. It is commonly superimposed on a receptive (Wernicke's) aphasia. But the fully elaborated syndrome can occur in the presence of intact speech comprehension (Kinsbourne & Warrington, 1963). The jargon aphasic emits fluent, even torrential, speech in disregard of its patently impaired nature and patent failure to communicate.

A speaker has at his disposal two ways of evaluating the success of his intention to communicate; he monitors his output, checking its lawfulness and intelligibility, and he monitors his listener's face, for the signs of comprehension. Speakers are highly skilled in inferring incomprehension from the expressions and actions of the listener even in the absence of the listener's statements to that effect. Indeed, the Broca's aphasia, painfully embarrassed by his truncated speech, prefers to withhold it altogether. In contrast the Wernicke's aphasic speaks freely at a normal rate, blithely unselfconscious about his grossly impaired speech and oblivious to the listener's obvious strained attempts to understand. The usual explanation, that his receptive difficulty includes an inability to monitor his own speech and judge it as abnormal, is unconvincing. When he fails to understand the speech of others he makes the fact known. Rather, his speech performance has escaped from the control of external cues. This obliviousness to the impaired quality of his speech is striking in the jargon aphasic. In addition he denies his disability. His ready flow of verbiage and evident glee in conversing imply verbal competence and he may explicitly assert this also. Kinsbourne and Warrington (1962) recorded the speech of two jargon aphasics, then played it back both as recorded, in the patient's own voice, and rerecorded in the voice of the experimenter. The patients judged the narrative in the experimenter's voice to be incomprehensible but the same text in their own voice to be "very good".

I speculatively attribute anosagnosia for aphasia to release of parietal mechanisms from temporal lobe control, on the view that the autonomous parietal lobe fosters the expression of the individual's thoughts and fantasies unqualified by external reality. The fronto-temporal system has the function of relating and adapting the state of the individual to external circumstances (Pribram & McGuinness, 1978). When it is ineffective the individual becomes self-engrossed and escapes from external stimulus control.

Interictal personality characteristics of temporal lobe epileptics illustrate this. The patients exaggerate their personal role in events and the relevance of events to their persons (Bear & Fedio, 1977). This I attribute to parietal release from temporal inhibition due to the temporal lobe damage that causes the seizures. In neglect dorsolateral frontal projections to posterior parietal lobe, both directly and through cingulate, are often disrupted. As Weinstein and Friedland (1977) have demonstrated, neglect patients, though by no means generally confused or disoriented, are apt to respond not with specifics or with reference to relevant data, but with emotive self-referential metaphor. Given the attentional and evaluative imbalance, there is thus great scope for colorful verbiage by neglectors when they refer to laterally located things and events.

The essential lesion in jargon aphasia involves the supramarginal gyrus and the parieto-temporal borderland (Kertesz, 1983). The parietal damage that causes severe left neglect is similarly localized on the right (Bisiach et al., 1979; Heilman, 1983; Vallar & Perani, in press). It makes sense therefore that, as in Weinstein and Friedland's (1977) experience, when aphasia and right neglect coincide, the aphasia is almost always of jargon type.

Goldstein (1939), Sandifer (1946) and Weinstein and Kahn (1955) have suggested that denial is a psychological mechanism compensating for the deficit. If so, there must be something highly distinctive about the nature of a cognitive deficit that elicits such a radical behavioral change. The scene would be set for secondary denial if the fact of flawed performance were excluded from attention, so that an illusion of competent performance persists. This could only occur if the performance is no longer appraised in terms of its instrumental success. Does the movement, or the proposition, secure the consequence in external space or in behavior of the listener that was intended and would be expected? Parietal release from temporal control, I have speculated, might release performance from such censorship. Though quite capable of observing the cues that would inform him that his perforamnce is defective, the patient fails to relate this information to the performance. Given that he feels that he is competent, he asserts this feeling in word and deed.

Multiple Dissociations within Neglect Symptomatology and Pathological Anatomy Offer Opportunity for Subtyping

Mesulam (1981) among others has listed the many central nervous system structures unilateral damage of which can generate neglect in animals and men. Indeed, it has long been known that lateral orienting is represented at multiple levels of the nervous system (see review by Kinsbourne, 1974a). But it should not be assumed that lesions at all these levels generate the neglect syndrome in identical expression. DeRenzi (1982) has criticized the proliferation of anatomical attributions for neglect inducing lesions, commenting that parietal lobe lesions (especially those involving the inferior parietal lobule) remain the only ones for which well elaborated neglect syndromes have been convincingly documented. Damage in the other reported locations generates neglect only infrequently (Vallar & Perani, in press). When subcortical lesions are associated with neglect, this may be mediated by secondary reduction in metabolic rate in ipsilateral parietal cortex (by a mechanism demonstrated by Olsen, Larsen, Hernig, Skriver & Lassen, 1983). Additionally there are multiple dissociations within neglect symptomatology. The partial syndromes that result offer as yet unexploited opportunity for clinico-anatomical correlation.

There are obvious failures of correlation between neglect of person and of space and within the latter between the several sensory modalities (DeRenzi, Gentilini & Pattacini, 1984). Neglect for input versus output is another promising dissociation. Valenstein and Heilman (1981) have presented evidence that dorsolateral frontal lesions emphasize the output disorder (of "intention"). But in its full elaboration, with anosagnosia, denial and self-referential behavior, neglect requires a posterior parieto-temporal lesion.

The multiplicity of neglect subtypes, and the wide dispersion of anatomical structures damage to which occasions neglect or related phenomena, suggest that multiple processors control lateral behavior of different kinds and under different stimulus control. That a basic functional propensity (lateral orientation) is adapted to a different purpose by each of a set of special purpose processors is not without precedent in neuropsychological theory. All the many overarching formulations of each hemisphere's specialization make this implicit assumption: that a general functional principle finds differential applications through the action of specialized processors in different parts of the hemisphere in question. The distinction between general and special purpose mechanisms somewhat misses the point. Instead, a set of special purpose processors enables a broad (general purpose) operational principle to find manifold application.

References

Albert, M.C. A simple test of visual neglect. Neurology, 1973, 23, 258–264.
Altman, J.A., Balonov, L.J. & & Deglin, V.L. Effects of unilateral disorder of the brain hemisphere function in man on directional hearing. Neuropsychologia, 1979, 17, 295–301.
Aymes, E.W. & Nielsen, J.M. Clinicopathologic study of vascular lesions of the anterior cingulate region. Bulletin of the Los Angeles Neurological Society, 1955, 20, 112–130.
Babinski, J. Contribution à l'étude des troubles mentaux dans l'hémiplégie organique cérébrale (anosagnosie). Revue Neurologique (Paris), 1914, 27, 365–367.
Barany, R. Latente Deviation der Augen und Vorbeizeigen des Kopfes bei Hemiplegie und Epilepsie. Wiener Klinische Wochenschrift, 1913, 26, 597–599.
Battersby, W.S., Bender, M.B., Pollack, M. & Kahn, R.L. Unilateral 'spatial agnosia' (inattention). Brain, 1956, 79, 68–93.
Bear, D. & Fedio, P. Quantitative analysis of interictal behavior in temporal lobe epilepsy. Archives of Neurology, 1977, 34, 454–467.
Beaumont, J.G. Lateral organization and aesthetic preference: The importance of peripheral visual asymmetries. Neuropsychologia, 1985, 23, 103–113.
Bender, M.B. Disorder in Perception (with particular reference to the phenomenon of extinction and displacement). Springfield, Ill. : Thomas, 1952.

Bender, M.B. & Diamond, S.P. Sensory interaction effects and their relation
    to the organization of perceptual space. In D.B. Tower (Ed.), The
    Nervous System, Vol. 3, Human Communication and its Disorders. New
    York: Raven Press, 1975.
Bisiach, E., Cornacchia, L., Sterzi, R. & Vallar, G. Disorders of perceived
    auditory lateralization after lesions of the right hemisphere. Brain,
    1984, 107, 37–52.
Bisiach, E. & Luzzatti, C. Unilateral neglect of representational space.
    Cortex, 1978, 14, 129–133.
Bisiach, E., Luzzatti, C. & Perani, D. Unilateral neglect, representational
    schema and consciousness. Brain, 1979, 102, 609–618.
Casey, S.M. The influence of lateral orientation on cerebral processing.
    Cortex, 1981, 17, 503–511.
Chédru, F., Leblanc, M. & Lhermitte. Visual searching in normal and
    brain-damaged subjects. Cortex, 1973, 9, 94–111.
Cook, N.D. Homotopic callosal inhibition. Brain and Language, 1984, 23,
    116–125.
Corin, M.S. & Bender, M.B. Mislocalization in visual space with reference to
    the midline at the boundary of a homonymous hemianopia. Archives of
    Neurology, 1972, 27, 252–262.
Denny-Brown, D. The mid-brain and motor integration. Proceedings of the
    Royal Society of Medicine, 1962, 55, 527–538.
Denny-Brown, D. & Banker, B.Q. Amorphosynthesis from left parietal lesions.
    Archives of Neurology and Psychiatry, 1959, 71, 302–313.
DeRenzi, E. Disorders of space exploration and cognition. Chichester:
    Wiley, 1982.
DeRenzi, E., Gentilini, M. & Patticini, F. Auditory extinction following
    hemisphere damage. Neuropsychologia, 1984, 22, 733–744.
Deuel, R. Salutory effects of binocular occlusion in hemineglect. Paper to
    the International Neuropsychological Society Meeting, Copenhagen,
    1985.
Deuel, R.K. & Collins, R.C. The functional anatomy of frontal lobe neglect
    in the monkey: Behavioral and quantitative 2-deoxyglucose studies.
    Annals of Neurology, 1984, 15, 521–529.
Dimond, S.J. Performance by split-brain humans on lateralized vigilance
    tasks. Cortex, 1979, 15, 43–50.
Dorff, J.E., Mirsky, A.F. & Mishkin, M. Effects of unilateral temporal lobe
    removals in man on tachistoscopic recognition in the left and right
    visual fields. Neuropsychologia, 1965, 3, 39–51.
Drake, R.A. & Bingham, B.R. Induced lateral orientation and persuasibility.
    Brain and Cognition, 1985, 4, 156–164.
Eidelberg, E. & Schwartz, A.S. Experimental analysis of the extinction
    phenomenon in monkeys. Brain, 1971, 94, 91–108.
Farah, M.J. Psychophysical evidence for a shared representational medium
    for mental images and percepts. Journal of Experimental Psychology:
    General, 1985, 114, 91–103.
Freimuth, M. & Wapner, S. The influence of lateral organization on the
    evaluation of paintings. British Journal of Psychology, 1979, 70,
    211–218.
Fuchs, W. Untersuchungen über das Sehen der Hemianopiker und
    Hemiamblyopiker, 1. Verlagerungserscheinungen. Zeitschrift für
    Psychologie, 1920, 84, 67–169.
Gainotti, G. Emotional behavior and hemispheric side of the lesion. Cortex,
    1972, 8, 41–55.
Gainotti, B. & Tiacci, C. The relationships between disorders of visual

perception and unilateral spatial neglect. Neuropsychologia, 1971, 9, 451-458.

Gesell, A. The tonic neck reflex in the human infant. Journal of Pediatrics, 1938, 13, 455-464.

Goldstein, K. The Organism, a Holistic Approach to Biology Derived from Pathological Data in Man. New York: American Book Company, 1939.

Grijalva, L.R. Emotional asymmetry elicited by dichotically presented depressive and neutral somatic statements. Acta Psychologica, in press.

Gross, Y., Franco, R. & Lewin, I. Effects of voluntary eye movements on hemispheric activity and choice of cognitive mode. Neuropsychologia, 1978, 16, 653-657.

Heilman, K.M., Schwartz, H.D. & Watson, K.T. Hypoarousal in patients with neglect syndrome and emotional indifference. Neurology, 1978, 28, 229-232.

Heilman, K.M. & Valenstein, E. Mechanisms underlying hemispatial neglect. Archives of Neurology, 1979, 5, 166-170.

Heilman, K.M. & Van der Abell, T. Right hemisphere dominance for mediating cerebral activities. Neuropsychologia, 1979, 17, 315-321.

Heilman, K.M. & Watson, R.T. The neglect syndrome - a unilateral defect of the orienting response. In S. Harnad, R.W. Doty, L. Goldstein, J. Jaynes & G. Krauthamer (Eds.)., Lateralization in the nervous system. New York: Academic Press, 1977.

Heilman, K.M. & Watson, R.T. Changes in the symptoms of neglect induced by changing task strategy. Archives of Neurology, 1978, 35, 47-49.

Heilman, K.M., Watson, R.T., Valenstein, E. & Damasio, A.R. In A. Kertesz (Ed.), Localization in Neuropsychology. New York: Academic Press, 1983.

Hines, D. & Martindale, C. Induced lateral eye movements and creative and intellectual performance. Perceptual and Motor Skills, 1974, 39, 153-154.

Horenstein, S. Sensorimotor concomitants of visual deficits in monkeys. In S. Locke (Ed.), Modern Neurology. Boston: Little Brown, 1969.

Horenstein, S., Chamberlain, W. & Comory, J. Infarction of the fusiform and calcarine regions: agitated delirium and hemianopia. Transactions of the American Neurological Association, 1967, 92, 85-89.

Hyland, H.H. Thrombosis of intracranial arteries. Archives of Neurology and Psychology, 1933, 30, 342-356.

Kaufman, L. Sight and Mind: an Introduction to Visual Perception. New York: Oxford University Press, 1974.

Kertesz, A. Localization in Neuropsychology. New York: Academic Press, 1983.

Kinsbourne, M. Limitations in visual capacity due to cerebral lesions. Proceedings of the 18th International Congress of Psychology. Moscow, 1966, 120-127.

Kinsbourne, M. A model for the mechanism of unilateral neglect of space. Transactions of the American Neurological Association, 1970a, 95, 143-146.

Kinsbourne, M. The cerebral basis of lateral asymmetries in attention. Acta Psychologica, 1970b, 33, 193-201.

Kinsbourne, M. Eye and head turning indicates cerebral lateralization. Science, 1972, 176, 539-541.

Kinsbourne, M. Lateral interactions in the brain. In M. Kinsbourne and W.L. Smith (Eds.), Hemispheric Disconnection and Cerebral Function. Springfield: Ill. : Thomas, 1974a.

Kinsbourne, M. Mechanisms of hemispheric interaction in man. In M.

Kinsbourne and W.L. Smith (Eds.), Hemispheric Disconnection and
    Cerebral Function, Ill. : Thomas, 1974b.
Kinsbourne, M. The mechanisms of hemispheric control of the lateral
    gradient of attention. In P.M.A. Rabbitt and S. Dornic (Eds.),
    Attention and Performance. London: Academic Press, 1975.
Kinsbourne, M. Hemi-neglect and hemispheric rivalry. In E.A. Weinstein and
    R.P. Friedland (Eds.), Hemi-inattention and Hemispheric
    Specialization. New York: Raven Press, 1977.
Kinsbourne, M. Hemispheric specialization and the growth of human
    understanding. American Psychologist, 1982, 37, 411-420.
Kinsbourne, M. & Warrington, E.K. A tachistoscopic study of visual
    inattention. Journal of Physiology, 1961, 156, 33-34.
Kinsbourne, M. & Warrington, E.K. Jargon Aphasia. Neuropsychologia, 1963,
    1, 27-38.
Kosslyn, S. Image and Mind. Cambridge, Ma : Harvard University Press, 1980.
Kosslyn, S., Holtzman, J.D., Farah, M.J. & Gazzaniga, M.S. A computational
    analysis of mental image generation: Evidence from functional
    dissociations in split brain patients. Journal of Experimental
    Psychology: General, 1985, 114, 311-341.
Krikorian, R. & Farales, L. Functional stimulation, defensive orientation
    and hemisphere activation. Brain and Cognition, 1982, 1, 371-380.
Lamotte, R.M. & Acuna, C. Defects in accuracy of reaching after removal of
    posterior parietal cortex in monkeys. Brain Research, 1978, 139,
    309-326.
LaTorre, R.A. & LaTorre, A.M. Effects of lateral eye fixation on cognitive
    processes. Perceptual and Motor Skills, 1981, 52, 487-490.
Lempert, H. & Kinsbourne, M. Effect of laterality of orientation on verbal
    memory. Neuropsychologia, 1982, 20, 211-214.
Levy, J. Lateral dominance and aesthetic preference. Neuropsychologia,
    1976, 14, 431-445.
Liederman, J. & Kinsbourne, M. The mechanisms of neonatal rightward turning
    bias: A sensory or motor asymmetry? Infant Behavior and Development,
    1980, 3, 223-238.
Medina, J.L., Rubins, F.A. & Ross, E. Agitated delirium caused by
    infarctions of the hippocampal formation and fusiform and lingual
    gyri: a case report. Neurology, 1974, 24, 1181-1183.
Mesulam, M.M. A cortical network for directed attention and unilateral
    neglect. Annals of Neurology, 1981, 10, 309-325.
Mesulam, M.M., Waxman, S.G., Geschwind, N. & Sabin, T.D. Acute confusional
    states with right middle cerebral artery infarctions. Journal of
    Neurology, Neurosurgery and Psychiatry, 1976, 39, 84-89.
Nisbett, R.E. & Wilson, T.D. Telling more than we can know: Verbal reports on
    mental processes. Psychological Review, 1977, 84, 231-259.
Ogden, J.A. Anterior-posterior interhemispheric differences in the loci of
    lesions producing visual hemineglect. Brain and Cognition, 1955, 4,
    59-75.
Olson, T.S., Larsen, B., Hernig, M., Skriver, E.B. & Lassen, N.A. Blood flow
    and vascular reactivity in collaterally perfused brain tissue. Stroke,
    1983, 14, 332-341.
Oppenheim, H. Ueber eine durch eine klinisch bisher nicht verwertete
    Untersuchungs-method ermittelte Form der Sensibilitatsstorung bei
    einseitigen Erkrankungen des Grosshirns (Kurze Mitteilung).
    Neurologisches Centralblatt, 1885, 23, 529-533.
Pasik, P. & Pasik, T. Ocular movements in split-brain monkeys. In E.A.
    Weinstein & R.A. Friedland (Ed.), Hemi-inattention and Hemisphere
    Specialization. New York: Raven Press, 1977.

Plourde, G. & Sperry, R.W. Left hemisphere involvement in left spatial neglect from right sided lesions. Brain, 1984, 107, 95–106.

Posner, M.I., Nissen, M.J. & Ogden, W.C. Attended and unattended processing modes: The role of set for spatial location. In M. Pickard and E. Saltzman (Eds.), Modes of Perceiving and Processing Information. Hillsdale, NJ: Erlbaum.

Posner, M.I., Walker, J., Friedrich, F.J. & Rafal, R.D. Effects of parietal lobe injury on covert orienting of visual attention. Journal of Neuroscience, 1984, 4, 1863–1874.

Pribram, K.M. & McGuiness, D. Arousal, activation and effort in the control of attention. Psychological Reviews, 1975, 82, 116–149.

Ratcliffe, G. & Davies–Jones, G.A.B. Defective visual localization in focal brain wounds. Brain, 1972, 95, 46–60.

Reeves, A.G. & Hagamen, W.D. Behavioral and EEG asymmetry following unilateral lesions of the forebrain and midbrain in cats. Electroencephalography and Clinical Neurophysiology, 1971, 30, 83–36.

Reuter–Lorenz, P.A., Moscovitch, M. & Kinsbourne, M. Lateral attention biases on a visual line bisection task: Similarities between the performances of neglect patients and normal subjects. Paper to the International Neuropsychological Society meeting, San Diego, CA, 1985.

Robinson, R.G. & Price, T.R. Post–stroke depressive disorder: A follow–up study of 103 outpatients. Stroke, 1982, 13, 635–641.

Rusinov, V.S. The Dominant Focus, translated by B. Haigh, New York, Consultant's Bureau, 1973.

Sandifer, P.H. Anosagnosia and disorders of body scheme. Brain, 1946, 69, 122–137.

Schilder, P. The Image and Appearance of the Human Body. London: Keegan, Paul, Trench, Trubner, 1935.

Schwartz, A.S., Marchock, P.L., Kreinick, C.J. & Flynn, R.E. The asymmetrical lateralization of tactile extinction in patients with unilateral cerebral dysfunction. Brain, 1979, 102, 669–684.

Schwartz, G.E., Davidson, R.J. & Maer, F. Right hemisphere lateralization for emotion in the human brain: Interactions with cognition. Science, 1975, 190, 286–288.

Silberpfennig, J. Contributions to the problem of eye movements. Disturbances of ocular movements with pseudohemianopia in frontal lobe tumors. Confinia Neurologica, 1941, 4, 1–13.

Smith, A. Dominant–nondominant hemispherectomy. In W.S. Smith (Ed.), Drugs, Development and Cerebral Function. Springfield, Il. : Thomas, 1974.

Sprague, J.M. Interaction of cortex and superior colliculus in mediation of visually guided behavior in the cat. Science, 1966, 153, 1544–1547.

Swartz, P. & Hewitt, D. Lateral organization in pictures and aesthetic preference. Perceptual and Motor Skills, 1970, 30, 991–1007.

Thompson, R.F. & Welker, W.I. Role of auditory cortex in reflex head orientation by cats to auditory stimulation. Journal of Comparative and Physiological Psychology, 1963, 56, 996–1002.

Trevarthen, C.B. Double visual learning in split–brain monkeys. Science, 1962, 136, 258–259.

Trevarthen, C.B. Functional relations of disconnected hemispheres with the brainstem, and with each other: Monkey and Man. In M. Kinsbourne and W.L. Smith (Eds.), Hemispheric Disconnection and Cerebral Function. Springfield, Il. : Thomas, 1974.

Valenstein, E. & Heilman, K.M. Unilateral hypokinesia and motor extinction. Neurology, 1981, 31, 445–448.

Valenstein, E., Heilman, K.M., Watson, R.T. & Van den Abell, T. Nonsensory neglect from parietotemporal lesions in monkeys. Neurology, 1982, 32, 1198-1201.

Vallar, G. & Perani, D. The anatomy of unilateral neglect after right hemisphere stroke lesions: A clinical ct-scan correlation study in man. Neuropsychologia, in press.

Von Monakow, C. Die Localization in Grosshirn. Wiesbaden: Bergmann, 1914.

Walker, E., Wade, S. & Waldman, I. The effects of lateral visual fixation on response latency to verbal and spatial questions. Brain and Cognition, 1982, 1, 399-404.

Watson, R.T., Miller, B.D. & Heilman, K.M. Nonsensory neglect. Annals of Neurology, 1978, 3, 505-508.

Watson, R.T., Valenstein, E., Day, A. & Heilman, K.M. Normal tactile threshold in monkeys with neglect. Neurology, 1986, 36, 636-640.

Weinstein, E.A., Friedland, R.P. Behavioral disorders associated with hemi-inattention. In E.A. Weinstein and R.P. Friedland (Eds.), Hemi-inattention and Hemisphere Specialization. New York: Raven Press, 1977.

Weinstein, E.A. & Kahn, R.L. Denial of Illness. Springfield, Il. : Thomas, 1955.

Weinstein, E.A. & Kahn, R.L. Symbolic reorganization in brain injuries. In S. Arieti (Ed.), American Handbook of Psychiatry, Vol. 1. New York: Basic Books, 1959.

Welch, K. & Stuteville, P. Experimental production of unilateral neglect in monkeys. Brain, 1958, 81, 341.

Wolgin, D.L. Motivation, activation and behavioral integration. In R.L. Isaacson and N.E. Spear (Eds.), The Expression of Knowledge. New York: Plenum, 1982.

Neurophysiological and Neuropsychological Aspects
of Spatial Neglect, M. Jeannerod (editor)
© Elsevier Science Publishers B.V. (North-Holland), 1987

THE DIRECTIONAL CODING OF REACHING MOVEMENTS.
A VISUOMOTOR CONCEPTION OF SPATIAL NEGLECT

Marc Jeannerod
and
Benjamin Biguer

The process of building up the spatial map for directing movements
toward extrapersonal space is examined. Respective contributions
of eye position signals and head position signals to the encoding
of position of objects are reviewed. The contribution of these and
other signals in documenting a central representation of the body
reference is also discussed. Spatial neglect is conceived as the
result of orienting bias created by unilateral lesion in areas
where the position of objects with respect to the body is encoded.

This chapter deals with integration of mechanisms for direction of
movements during reaching at visual objects. One of its basic postulates is
that direction of movements must be coded in a system of coordinates (a motor
"map" of space) referred to the body axis, different from the visual map on
which the retinal position of objects is specified. Therefore, the internal
representation of the visual world in which the subject behaves spatially
must include a body reference, if possible in coincidence with objective
body position.

The motor and the visual maps may be occasionnally superimposed when
the eyes are aligned with the head and the head with the trunk. In most
situations, however, the fact that the eyes move in the head, and the head
moves with respect to the trunk makes that a single locus in space may
correspond to a variety of retinal loci, according to the relative positions
of eye, head and body axes. Reconstruction of the position of objects in a
body-centered space should therefore integrate not only the retinal signal
documenting the position of the object images on the visual map, but also
extraretinal signals related to the position of the eyes in the orbit, the
position of the head with respect to the body, and the position of the
internal body reference with respect to the body itself.

The respective contributions of eye position and head position signals
to the construction of body-centered space will be reviewed first. A
subsequent section will address the problem of the representation of the
body reference and its neurophysiological bases. Analysis of visuomotor
behaviour during simple actions like pointing or looking will provide a
framework for understanding pathological aspects of visuomotor function.

The process of transforming the visual map into a motor map is likely to
involve largely distributed neural mechanisms and consequently to be
exposed to disruption by brain lesions. Lesions occuring in areas where
extraretinal signals are processed or monitored, or in areas in which they
converge with retinal signals to form the motor map should unavoidably
affect visuomotor behavior in producing spatial disorientation or
directional visuomotor bias. The hypothesis as to whether spatial neglect
might also be a consequence of mismatch between retinal and extraretinal

signals or between extraretinal signals from different sources is worth exploring in some detail.

1. Eye Position Signals

Evidence for the existence of extraretinal signals derived from eye position comes from experiments showing that goal-directed eye movements are in fact directed at the spatial, not the retinal, locus of the target (Robinson, 1975; Miles & Evarts, 1979). Hallet and Lightstone (1976), for example, took advantage of the fact that ocular saccades can accurately reach targets that are presented very briefly, that is, in a condition where they disappear before the saccade is initiated. In their experiment, subjects were instructed to fixate a target that jumped from its position on the central retina to a peripheral position, and then was flashed at another position immediately prior to the saccade intended at the first jump. They found that subjects indeed executed a saccade to the location of the first target, and from there directed their eyes at the location of the flash. The second saccade was therefore programmed to cover the distance between the location of the first target and the location of the flash and not the distance between the position of the eyes at the time the second target was flashed, and the location of that target. In other words the second saccade was not programmed according to the amplitude of the retinal signal, but according to the amplitude of the spatial difference. In other trials, the position of the flash was on the central retina itself, that is at the same position where the target was before the jump. A second saccade was nevertheless generated in order to bring the eyes back to their initial position, in spite of the fact that, because the eyes were still immobile when the flash was produced, no retinal signal actually ever existed for that saccade.

In animals, the dramatic results obtained by Sparks and his colleagues seem to have demonstrated unambiguously the contribution of extraretinal signals in reconstructing target position in space. In the experiment of Mays and Sparks (1980) monkeys were trained to look at small targets appearing in an otherwise dark room. The fixation target was extinguished and an eccentric target was illuminated for 100 ms. In this situation the animal normally makes a saccade after about 200 ms. On some of the trials, after the eccentric target was turned off but before the saccade began, the eyes were dirven at another position in the orbit by electrical stimulation of the superior colliculus. Nevertheless, the actual saccade was correctly directed at the position of the target in space. This finding supports the hypothesis that an accurate eye position signal is continuously combined with retinal signals to provide a representation of target position in space (see Sparks & Mays, 1983).

The need for a reconstruction of target position in space becomes particularly obvious when ones tries to understand the mechanisms for orienting toward targets which stimulate simultaneously the visual and the acoustic modalities. It is known that in many species, the superior colliculus contains superimposed representations of auditory and visual space, such that neurons in the deep collicular layers may respond to visual and auditory stimuli located within the same region of space. This property seems paradoxical: because coordinates of auditory space are defined with respect to the ears and hence the head, while coordinates of visual space are defined with respect to the retina, the two spaces should be disaligned each time the eyes deviate from the head axis. Studies of eye-head coordination in cats, however, have shown that saccadic eye movements are usually followed shortly by head movements in the same direction, so that the eyes rapidly return to the centre of the orbits after each saccade and the coordinates of visual and auditory space remain superimposed (Harris, Blakemore & Donaghy, 1980; Guitton, Douglas & Volle, 1984). This is not necessarily the case in primates, including man, where eye position may remain significantly deviated from head axis following orientation toward a peripheral stimulus (see below). In these species, the position of visual targets has to be reconstructed with respect to the head, so that visual and auditory signals from the same objects are matched. Jay and Sparks (1984) have studied the modalities of this reconstruction at the level of neurons of the intermediate layers of the superior colliculus in awake monkeys. Animals had their head fixed and were in the dark. Auditory targets were presented at a fixed position in space, while gaze position was changed by presenting visual fixation targets at different locations. It was found that neuronal responses to the same auditory stimulus varied as a function of gaze position, indicating that the auditory receptive fields of the neurons shifted with the position of the eyes in the orbit. According to Jay and Sparks (1984), these findings suggest that "an internal representation of eye position... has been subtracted from the head-centered spatial code of auditory targets...". "This translation allows the auditory and the visual maps in the intermediate and deep layers of the primate superior colliculus to share a common reference system..." (p. 347).

1.1. The Nature of Eye Position Signals

Arguments for the role of eye position signals in the reconstruction of target position in space, can be tracked in the literature as far as Charles Bell (1823, quoted by Wade, 1978). Bell had noticed that visual after-images seem to move with the eye in spite of being stationary on the retina. Hence, Bell thought that "... vision in its extended sense is a compound operation, the idea of position of an object having relation to the activity of the muscles". "If we move the eyes by the voluntary muscles... we shall have the notion of place or relation raised in the mind".

Thus, the first step for understanding how eye movements and/or positions can be monitored (and ultimately consciously perceived, as suggested by Bell) has been to determine the nature of the eye position signals. The hypothesis that has historical priority under this respect postulates that a subject can be aware of the "efforts of will" he directs to his eye muscles, and therefore can use these outflow signals to distinguish between displacement of objects across the retina arising within the external world, from displacement resulting from self-produced eye movements (Helmholtz, 1866).

A more elaborate theory, though using the same basic notion of a monitoring of the efforts of will, was put forward in 1950. According to this theory, the motor outflow responsible for self-produced movements was thought to be paralleled by neural discharges which represented a "copy" of the efferent activity sent to the muscles. This "efference copy" was thought to act on visual centers so as to cancel the interpretation of visual motion inflow to the sensory neurons each time this inflow was a direct product of behavior (Von Holst & Mittelstaedt, 1950).

Neuronal responses fulfilling the criterion for an efference-copy type of mechanism have been recorded from visual neurons, first from invertebrates species (Wiermsa & Yamagushi, 1967; Palka, 1969), and more recently in mammals. In the monkey superior colliculus, for instance, Robinson and Wurtz (1976) found neurons that responded when a visual stimulus rapidly crossed their receptive field, but did not when an eye movement swept their receptive field across the same but stationary stimulus. Neurons in other parts of the central visual system, including visual cortex, also have been shown to receive eye movement related

extraretinal signals (for review, see Jeannerod, Kennedy & Magnin, 1979).
These signals might originate either directly from the oculomotor neurons
themselves, or from other parts in the brainstem where neurons with tonic
firing rates proportional to eye position can be recorded.

In the behavioral context, the same mechanism might also account for
stabilization of the whole animal, particularly in those animal species
whose behavior is strongly driven by visual motion signals. Experiments
reported by Sperry seem to demonstrate the effects of efference copy on an
animal's behavior. Sperry (1943) first observed that fishes with inverted
vision caused by surgical 180° eye rotation tend to turn continuously in
circles, quite in the same way as a normal fish when stimulated by a visual
surround moving at constant velocity. In a later paper Sperry (1950)
interpreted this circling behavior due to inverted vision as the result of
disharmony between the retinal input generated by movement of the animal and
the compensatory mechanism for maintaining the stability of the visual
field. Surgical eye rotation, by making the compensatory mechanism in
diametric disharmony with the retinal input, "would therefore cause
accentuation rather than cancellation of the illusory outside movement".
The mechanism postulated by Sperry was a centrally arising discharge that
reached the visual centers as a corollary of any excitation pattern that
normally resulted in a movement and was specific for each movement with
regard to its direction and extent (see also Teuber, 1960).

"Efference copy" and "corollary discharge" are germane concepts that
both imply that outflow information (i.e., arising from efferent systems)
can be used at the central level to regulate sensory messages. These two
concepts, however, are included in, but do not completely overlap with, the
more general concept of extraretinal signals.

Another interpretation of the nature of these signals has been offered,
that was initially considered as mutually exclusive with the efference copy
hypothesis. By the end of the last century, authors such as W. James (1890)
rejected the "outflow" theory. James proposed that all incoming messages
had to proceed through sensory channels, and information flow within the
brain had to be directed in a sensory-to-motor, rather than in a
motor-to-sensory, direction. This idea was strenghtened by the Sherrington
(1897) finding that extrinsic ocular muscles are abundantly supplied with
neuromuscular sensory endings and therefore can signal their degree of
tension to the nervous system. In addition, Sherrington (1898) had noticed
that after the conjunctiva and the cornea on both sides were anesthetized,
the eyes could still be directed accurately to any given point in a
completely dark room. Based on this finding he deducted that proprioceptive
information as to eye position was not conveyed to the brain through the
trigeminal (sensory) nerve but took a retrograde pathway through the motor
nerves themselves. Later, however, Sherrington's belief was challenged,
and the ophtlamic branch of the trigeminal nerve was shown to be the main
pathway for extraocular proprioception (Batini & Buisseret, 1974). From
there, ocular proprioceptors largely project to the central nervous system.
In the cat, responses to eye muscle stretch are found in the cerebellum
(Fuchs & Kornhuber, 1969; Baker, Precht & Llinas, 1972; Schwartz & Tomlison,
1977), the superior colliculus (Rose & Abrahams, 1975; Donaldson & Long,
1980), the visual cortex (Buisseret & Maffei, 1977).

Experimental data demonstrating the contribution of ocular
proprioception in visuomotor behavior were recently reported in cats.
Fiorentini, Berardi and Maffei (1982) showed that adult cats with
unilateral section of the ophtlamic branch of the trigeminal nerve made
large systematic errors in jumping from a start box to a luminous target.
Typically, these errors were distributed to the side ipsilateral to the

section, but were observed when the animal was tested with either its deafferented or its normal eye. This result indicates that proprioceptive input from extrinsic eye muscles can be used for egocentric localization of targets. Localization errors observed after unilateral deafferentation would reflect the unbalance introduced into the proprioceptive system.

Hein and his colleagues, although they also stressed the proprioceptive contribution to target localization, showed that this function was limited to the period of maturation of visuomotor behavior. Their initial finding was that kittens with surgical eye immobilization fail to acquire visually guided behavior, as tested with placing responses and visually guided locomotion (Hein, Vital-Durand, Salinger & Diamond, 1979). Later, Hein and Diamond (1983) were able to directly demonstrate that this effect of eye immobilization was in fact due to lack of proprioceptive input from the eye muscles during attempts of the kittens to reach for visual targets. Kittens were first reared in the dark until they were 2-4 weeks of age, at which time one eye was enucleated and the kittens were returned in the dark. A few weeks later, the extrinsic ocular muscles of the remaining eye were deafferented by sectioning the ophtalmic branch of the trigeminal nerve. When the kittens were tested for the effects of deafferentation surgery on visuomotor behavior (after a few days spent in a normally lighted environment), they were shown to lack visual guidance. This result suggests that exclusion of proprioceptive input from the eye muscles precludes the acquisition of visually guided behavior.

Control experiments (A. Hein, personal communication, June, 1986) clearly showed that deafferentation must be complete in order to produce its effect. If, for example, one eye is made blind (by section of the optic nerve), and only muscles of the seing eye are deafferented, visuomotor behavior develops normally. Subsequent enucleation of the blind (but proprioceptively normal), eye, has no effect. This result is coherent with the fact that contribution of proprioceptive afferents was limited to the development period: eye immobilization in animals that had already acquired visuomotor behavior did not interfere with mediation of this behavior. Therefore, the logical conclusion to the whole set of experiments is that "without inflow from the eye muscles a mobile eye is not localizable in the orbit; without eye movement any proprioceptive input that remains available from the paralyzed eye seems insufficiently informative about eye posture" (Hein & Diamond, 1983, p. 132).

Even though extraocular proprioceptive mechanisms are not yet completely understood (eye muscles have no stretch reflex, Keller & Robinson, 1971, in the monkey), the above experiments demonstrate that proprioception does play a role in encoding eye position. It remains difficult, however, to sort out the respective contribution of these proprioceptive signals and of signals related to corollary discharge mechanisms for constructing a stable spatial representation and, by way of consequence, for initiating visuomotor behavior.

1.2. The Lack of Eye Position Sense

Position sense usually refers to the contribution of afferent mechanisms to subjective experience about respective positions of limb segments. In the case of eye position with respect to the head, experimenters have failed to demonstrate directly the existence of such sensations. Brindley and Merton (1960) reported the perceptual consequence of forced duction of the eye with a forceps (with an anaesthetized cornea and in the absence of vision with that eye). Passive rotation of the eyeball of 20° or more was undetected by the subject. When the eye was maintained immobile with the forceps, attempts by the subject to move it were accompanied by a feeling of movement. These results merely indicate lack of contribution of neuromuscular spindles to extraocular "muscle sense", although they do not exclude the possibility that other types of mechanoreceptors, blocked by anaesthesia of the cornea and the conjunctiva, might contribute to "position sense". Other experiments, however, demonstrate that this is not the case. Jeannerod, Gerin and Mouret (1965) recorded eye movements in subjects attempting to look in the dark at previously learned target positions. Subjects were unable to reproduce these target positions: although their saccades were directed in the proper direction they were of an exaggerated amplitude. This tendency to overshooting learned target positions was even increased when the attempts were made under lid closure. Poor performance of the subjects in reproducing target positions contrasted with their impression of being quite accurate. More recently, Allik, Rauk and Luuk (1981), using an electromagnetic eye movement recording technique (more accurate than the EOG technique used by previous investigators), showed that subjects were unable to reproduce simple eye movement trajectories behind closed eyelids. Rather, they tended to make highly hypermetric movements in poor topological correspondance to the previously observed visual pattern.

Position sense should also be involved in judging the direction of a point source of light in the dark. In the absence of a visual frame of reference the only way to determine the position of a target in space is to infer it from its position on the retina with respect to the eye axis, and from the position of the eye axis with respect to the head–body axis. Lack or paucity of information about eye position should therefore result in inaccurate judgements. This was confirmed in experiments where subjects were required to indicate the position of a briefly flashed target with respect to another, previously fixated, target. Matin and Kibler (1966) had their subjects fixating a small light monocularly for 4 s in an otherwise dark room. The fixation period was followed by a 3 s period of total darkness during which the subjects attempted to maintain the fixation position. This dark interval was followed by a 100 ms flash appearing either right or left of the previous fixation target. The subjects had to decide whether the flash appeared at the same position as the fixation target, or right or left to it. If the fixation target corresponded to a primary gaze position, subjects' judgements on flashed target direction with respect to the eye axis were accurate at the nearest 20 min of arc. If the fixation target was far from primary position (e.g., 35°), errors as large as one degree were made by the subjects. Matin and Kibler's conclusion was that accuracy in judging visual direction was relatively poor, especially if the judgement had to be made with respect to a position of gaze different from primary position. Their interpretation for such inaccuracy was that subjects were in fact unable to maintain their eyes in the previous fixation position during the dark interval. The same authors (Matin, Pearce, Matin & Kibler, 1966) were able to show by direct measurement of eye position that involuntary drifts of as much as one degree or more occured during the 3 s dark interval.

The Matin and Kibler interpretation was confirmed by Fiorentini and Ercoles (1966), who showed that the visual direction of the source could be reported with a small variance relative to its retinal location, but that the reports differed systematically from the expected values (those relative to the actual eye position) by an amount that increased with the duration of the dark interval. This result indicates that the spatial position of a target can be accurately detected based on its retinal "local sign", but that unnoticed and uncorrected drifting of the eye in the dark alters the relationship between the local sign of the target and its actual position with respect to eye axis.

Finally, another function where it seems reasonnable to assume that eye position signals should normally contribute is "direction constancy", whereby a stationary object is perceived at the same location in spite of changing eye position. Direction constancy holds in a natural, lighted, environment. In the dark, however, small luminous objects are commonly perceived to jump back and forth during saccadic eye movements, usually in the direction opposite to that of the saccade. This observation therefore demonstrates incomplete direction constancy in the dark, and points to relative inaccuracy of the eye position signals. Studies by Hill (1972) and LaVerne Morgan (1978) have confirmed a systematic underconstancy in the perception of visual direction. In the LaVerne Morgan study, subjects (with the head fixed) had to determine the position of test-flashes with respect to their subjective midline, while fixating stationary targets. Results of this experiment showed systematic departure from constancy of direction of the test-flash, which was perceived shifted in the direction of the eye fixation. The amount of the shift was proportional to the amplitude of the eye turn. LaVerne Morgan's conclusion was that the systematic error in perception of direction of the test-flash was due, at least in part, to misregistration of eye position.

Taken together, the above results suggest a relatively poor position sense in human eyes. This fact could reflect the absence of reliable encoding of eye position signals at the central level. The neurophysiological apparatus for detecting eye movements and/or positions is nevertheless present. It is likely that the signals it generates must be calibrated by vision before they can become truly informative. When retinal feedback is available, eye position remains stationary during gaze fixation, perceptual stability is achieved during saccades, and direction constancy is preserved during gaze displacements. But when retinal feedback is absent or degraded, eye position signals alone reveal insufficient for maintaining perceptual invariance of the environment.

1.3. The "Paralyzed-Eye Situation"

The situation where the eyes are pathologically or experimentally paralyzed has long been considered an ideal paradigm for demonstrating the monitoring of eye position in orbit by the central nervous system. As first described by Von Graefe (1870), pepole with paralysis of an extrinsic eye muscle display a striking behavioral impairment when they attempt to reach toward objects in their peripheral visual field viewed only with their paralyzed eye. Typically, they overreach in the direction of the attempted eye movement which is prevented by the paralysis, and miss the target ("past-pointing"). Attempts to move the eyes against the paralysis may produce an illusory displacement of the visual scene in the direction of the attempted movement. These phenomena have been documented by clinical cases (Jackson & Patton, 1909; Adler, 1943; Perenin, Jeannerod & Prablanc, 1977; von Noorden, Awaya & Romano, 1971), and by experiments that used reversible block of extraocular muscles in normal subjects (Kornmüller, 1931; Siebeck, 1954; Brindley, Goodwin, Kulikowski & Leighton, 1976; Stevens, Emerson, Gerstein, Kallos, Neufeld, Nichols & Rosenquist, 1976; Matin, Stevens & Picoult, 1983).

Pathological observations. Perenin et al. (1977) studied four patients with a complete paralysis of either the VIth or the IIId nerve serving one eye. Patients were tested for pointing by hand at visual targets appearing in their peripheral visual field. The normal eye was occluded, the head was fixed, and view of the arm used for pointing was prevented. In addition, movements of the normal eye under cover were recorded. When targets were presented to the affected eye in an area of the visual field that corresponded to non-paralyzed muscles, the patient pointed correctly at the target location. By contrast, when targets appeared in the area of the visual field corresponding to the paralysis, the hand was directed far more distal to the midline than the actual location of the targets. For example, target presentation corresponding to a retinal locus 30° from the fovea could yield a pointing movement directed 50° from the midline. Movements of the normal (covered) eye directed toward targets presented to the paralyzed eye were also exaggerated in amplitude, in such a way that they would have clearly overreached target position. Von Graefe's interpretation of the phenomena related to extraocular muscle paralysis was that, if one muscle is contracted more than normally required for a given result, the increase in effort makes the subject believe that his eye is displaced from its viridical position. The increased sensation of effort yields an overestimation of rotation angle made by the eye, together with the illusion of visual field displaced in the same direction. According to this account, past-pointing is a direct consequence of the perceived displacement. An observation made by Perenin et al. (1977) seems to confirm this view. They asked one of their subjects with extraocular paralysis to keep his gaze fixated at the midline during presentation of peripheral targets. His pointing movements were directed correctly to the location of the targets.

The notion of an exaggerated effort exerted against the paralyzed muscle, postulated by von Graefe for explaining past-pointing belongs to the same theory as the Helmholtz's notion of efforts of will, for which we have analyzed the possible neurophysiological substrates. Another plausible explanation for the increased oculomotor input might lie in the impossibility for the paralyzed eye to foveate the target. In that situation, the error between the retinal position of the target and the actual position of the eye cannot be nulled by a saccade, and the oculomotor system behaves as if it were constantly fed by the same error signal. A similar effect can be produced experimentally by feeding the output of the oculomotor system into target position with a positive feedback: the subject produces iterative saccades toward the target without being able to catch it (Young & Stark, 1963). This explanation preserves the possibility of an exaggerated oculomotor output which, if monitored centrally, can account for past-pointing. Alternatively, it could be argued that eye and arm movements tend to be coupled in the action of pointing, and that parametrization of the motor commands occur over the total coupled system. As a consequence, the increase in force required to move the paralyzed eye is also distributed to the system controlling the arm (Kelso, Holt, Kugler & Turvey, 1981). In the case where the subject fixates straight ahead while reaching for the target, thereby decoupling his eye and arm movements, past-pointing disappears.

Experiments in normal subjects. Results from other experiments in normal subjects question this explanation for past-pointing. In these experiments (Skavenski, 1972), subjects were required to maintain monocular fixation of a point source of light in the dark, while their eye was constantly loaded by mechanical traction. This situation of load involved neither change in retinal locus of the target image nor eye movement, since fixation was maintained actively. The only variable was the force exerted by the subjects to oppose ocular displacement by the traction. Subjects were requested to indicate the perceived direction of the fixation target by placing a second, movable, target in their subjective straight ahead position. The fixation target was perceived displaced contralaterally to the load direction and the amplitude of this displacement was roughly proportional to the load level. These results support the conclusion (Skavenski, 1976) that perceived target direction is determined by the magnitude of outflow signals related to eye position, and that this information is directly involved in subjective determination of spatial coordinates, therefore supporting the classical notion of a monitoring of the "efforts of will".

The effects, on spatial localization, of experimental paralysis of eye muscles in normal subjects, lead to the same conclusion. In the experiments reported by Matin et al. (1983), the subject was partially paralyzed by systemic injections of d-tubocurarine, which limited the range of ocular fixations that could be maintained. Within this limitation, however, maintenance of fixation in any given position was not accompanied by a greater sensation of effort than it is in the normal observer. During experiments the subjects lay with their head tilted backward with respect to the vertical. They were requested to fixate a target appearing in front of them at horizontal eye level. When all lights except for the fixation target were extinguished target appeared to move slowly downward. With reillumination of the room the target seemed to elevate immediately to its original height. Both magnitude and direction of the illusory target movement in the dark was dependent on the position of the head. When head tilt angle with respect to vertical was decreased, apparent movement of the target was reduced; if the head was tilted forward instead of backward, the target appeared to rise. Systematic variation of target height with respect to eye level revealed that illusory displacement was a function of eye position in orbit, and not head position with respect to the vertical. The more the target position deviated from eye level, the larger was the illusory displacement in the dark. When target position corresponded exactly to the position of gaze axis in space, no apparent displacement was noticed by the subjects.

These somewhat extreme experiments seem to provide a definitive clarification as to the role of eye position signals in determining spatial localization of targets. In the situation described by Matin et al. (1983), the tilt of the head backward or forward with respect to the vertical induced neural commands to the corresponding eye muscles (i.e., to muscles lowering the eye in case of backward tilting, and to muscles elevating the eye in the case of forward tilting), to maintain the gaze in its horizontal position and to achieve target fixation. Because of the paralysis these neural commands were inefficient in bringing the eyes to the required position, but the signals they provided to other neural structures involved in space perception were nevertheless monitored centrally. In the absence of a visual frame of reference (e.g., in darkness), they became an index of the gaze direction and, consequently, of the position of the target with respect to the body, hence accounting for mislocalization.

It has been shown, however, that past pointing and illusory displacement of targets occur only when the eye is partially paralyzed (as in the Matin et al. 1983 experiments), and not in the situation of total paralysis (Brindley et al., 1976). This fact indicates that the critical information for producing these effects may not be the extraretinal signal alone, but rather the discrepancy between the retinal and the extraretinal signals. When the two are correctly matched, space remains invariant, although mismatch between the two produces instability and mislocalization.

1.4. Experimental Deviation of Gaze Posture

The spatial consequences of ocular misalignment, whether the result of pathology or surgery, also provide arguments for understanding the contribution of eye position signals to visuomotor localization. Mann, Hein and Diamond (1979) examined eye-hand coordination in humans with monocular strabismus that had appeared early in childhood. For such subjects, only the visually aligned eye seems to be used in visuomotor localization. Vision with the deviated eye is constantly suppressed whenever both eyes are open. Tests which required the subjects to point a hand toward targets viewed by either eye, revealed constant errors that reflected the momentary orbital position of the dominant eye. Mann et al. (1979) proposed that during development these subjects had used only their dominant eye in constructing their spatial reference frame. Position signals from that eye became critical for localizing objects. Olson (1980) examined the effects on visuomotor localization of surgically induced monocular strabismus in cats. He measured the accuracy of jumps to a narrow platform. Jumps guided by the normal eye were accurate, those guided by the operated eye were systematically displaced in the direction opposite to the eye deviation. Olson (1980) concluded that the cats were "unaware" of the eye deviation and continued to use a "registered" eye position in conformity with their head axis (as cats normally do, see above), to guide their visuomotor behavior. Therefore, in jumping in the direction of their head axis, they systematically landed in the direction opposite to the target. Steinbach and Smith (1981) reported results along the same line in humans operated from strabismus. When some patients were tested shortly after surgery for hand pointing accuracy under control of the operated eye a large systematic error was observed. The direction of the error was consistent with the idea that the brain was unaware of the surgical eye rotation and still used eye position signals corresponding to the presurgical eye position to direct the pointings. This effect, however, was observed only in patients operated several times, and in whom extraocular muslce tendons had been damaged. In patients operated for the first time, pointings were not shifted because, according to the Steinbach and Smith interpretation, tendon organs were still intact and provided the central nervous system with afferent signals corresponding to the true eye position. This interpretation therefore implies that the eye position signal can originate from both inflow and outflow signals. A tentative conclusion could be that outflow information is used as the short-term indicator of eye position, whereas inflow informations allow for modification and recalibration of this fast system over longer periods of time (Steinbach & Smith, 1981).

1.5. The Role of Eye Position Signals in Pointing Accuracy

The above experiments have only provided indirect demonstration for the contribution of eye position signals to directional coding and accuracy of goal-directed movements. There are also studies in which a direct test of this problem has been attempted. These studies, however, have remained mostly inconclusive.

Prablanc, Echallier, Komilis and Jeannerod (1979) measured pointing accuracy in a condition where subjects could see their hand and in a condition where they could not (Visual-feedback and No-visual-feedback conditions, respectively). In addition, eye movements were not allowed during the pointing task, and subjects were instructed to keep their gaze fixated at the midline target while they pointed at other targets appearing in their peripheral visual field. In the Visual-feedback condition, pointing accuracy was little affected (the variable error was slightly increased) by the absence of eye movement toward the targets at which the hand pointed. In the No-visual- feedback-condition, no difference could be found with respect to the condition where eye movements are allowed, namely, in both conditions without visual feedback, an equally severe degradation of pointing accuracy was observed.

These results do not seem to favor a role of eye position signals in visuomotor control, because accuracy of pointing was not affected by whether these signals were used or excluded. However, other experiments which used pointing movements as an index, suggest different conclusions. In the Festinger and Canon's (1965) study, target lights were presented at different positions within the visual field. In each trial subjects had to point in the dark at the position of the target, after it had disappeared. If the target jumped from the central position to one of the peripheral positions, pointing was relatively accurate. If, however, the target moved slowly from central position to its final position before disappearing, large pointing errors were made. Interpretation of this result was based on the difference of mechanisms generating saccadic eye movements (which are present in the target jump condition) and smooth poursuit eye movements (which are present in the other condition). Saccadic eye movements are directed at stimuli located on the retina outside the fovea, although smooth poursuit relies on velocity signals across the fovea. Therefore, Festinger and Canon (1965) concluded that efferent command signals related to target position yield to better visuomotor localization than signals related to target velocity. Another study (Honda, 1984) also involved manipulation of the saccadic signal putatively used for target localization. Subjects had to point with their unseen hand at the location of a visual target after it had disappeared. Before stopping at its final position and disappearing, the target jumped at one or several other positions, at such a rate that a saccade was generated for each jump. The results showed that the pointing error increased with the number of jumps that occured before the target stopped. Honda's conclusion was that subjects were not able to use the sum of eye position signals generated for each saccade, but rather tended to use the signal corresponding to the largest saccade in the sequence.

Experiments such as those of Festinger and Canon (1965) and Honda (1984), where oculomotor signals related to target position in space could be more directly manipulated, give more positive indications concerning the role of these signals in visuomotor behavior. It remains, however, that these experimental situations only correspond to a limited number of situations in real life, i.e., those rare occasions where the head is fixed with respect to the body and only the eyes move. It seems reasonable to assume, that in situations with the head free, the eye-head system should behave as a unit in which the position signals generated by either component add to each other. The contribution of head position signals and of the eye-head-arm synergy in visuomotor behavior will be examined in the next section.

2. The Contribution of Head Position Signals

By contrast with the relative paucity of signals generated by eye position in orbit, signals related to head position with respect to the trunk seems to play an important role in encoding target position in space. In the monkey, Cohen (1961) showed that abolishing proprioceptive information from neck muscles (by sectionning the dorsal roots) rendered the animals unable to reach accurately for objects, even when their eyes were fixating these objects. In man, Marteniuk (1978) provided evidence that orienting the head toward a target consistently facilitated accurate localization of that target.

2.1. The Effects of Vibration of the Neck Muscles

Contribution of head position signals to visuomotor behavior seems to be best demonstrated by a simple experiment reported by Biguer, Donaldson, Hein and Jeannerod (1986). These authors took advantage of the distorsion of position sense produced by muscle vibration. It has been known since Goodwin, McCloskey and Matthews (1971) that vibrating a muscle can induce an illusory movement of the corresponding segment. If the vibrated limb is prevented from moving, it is nevertheless felt to move. In their experiment, Goodwin et al. (1971) vibrated the biceps brachii in one arm, in blindfolded subjects. Flexion of that arm was blocked, the other arm was used to "track" the illusory movement. With their tracking arm subjects consistently indicated that they felt their vibrated arm more extended than it actually was. The explanation to this finding was that, "the Ia discharges set up by the vibration are interpreted by the sensorium as due to a stretch of the biceps muscle, and thus taken to indicate that the joint is more fully extended than it actually is. This might perhaps be through some higher center recognizing a mismatch between the actual state of the muscle and that which was "intended by the controlling centers" (Goodwin et al., 1971, p 9P).

Biguer et al. applied vibrations at 100 Hz to the posterior neck muscles on one side. Their subjects were asked to maintain visual fixation on a dim luminous target which appeared directly ahead of them in an otherwise dark room. When vibration was applied, subjects reported apparent displacement of the fixation light. This illusory displacement was usually horizontal and to the side opposite to the stimulation but, by altering the exact location of the vibrator, illusions of vertical or diagonal movement could be produced. The target initially showed both motion and displacement. Displacement ceased within a second or two. Afterwards the target appeared to continue in motion without further change in position. Apparent movement persisted as long as vibratory stimulation was maintained. When vibration was discontinued, the light appeared to move in the reverse direction for a brief period of time.

Control experiments showed that this effect was not due to either eye or head movements during vibration. Indeed, the target motion was still perceived during vibration by subjects whose head was immobilized with the aid of a bite-plate. In addition, no eye movements could be detected on EOG recordings. Finally, in order to eliminate the possible role of very small eye movements (i.e., beyond the scope of the EOG technique), an opaque mask was placed in front of the subject's eye. A 0.5 mm vertical slit was made in the mask at the level of the subject's gaze axis, so that he could see the target. When vibration was applied to the neck at the proper location, the subject still experienced the illusion of motion of the target in the horizontal dimension. If the eye had moved during vibration, the subject would unavoidably have lost view of the target.

In accord with the explanation of Goodwin et al., vibration of the neck muscles on one side (e.g., the left) produces the same afferent spindle discharge as if the neck muscles were stretched by head rotation toward the opposite side (to the right in the example). This illusory change in head position is interpreted as apparent displacement of visual objects to the right. Therefore, if a subject were asked to point at a visual object under this condition of vibration, his pointing should err in the direction of the apparent displacement. This is exactly what Biguer et al. reported. When their subjects had their left neck muscles stimulated, they systematically pointed to the right of the actual target position. Figure 1 shows the mean location of pointings before, and during, vibration of the neck muslces on the left side. Vibration induced a shift of the trajectory of pointings to the right in all subjects. The loci of pointings before and during vibration did not overlap in five of the six subjects tested. For these five subjects, the mean displacement of the pointings was 5.0° (SD, 2.1°). The sixth subject reported that the visual illusion was present only for a short time

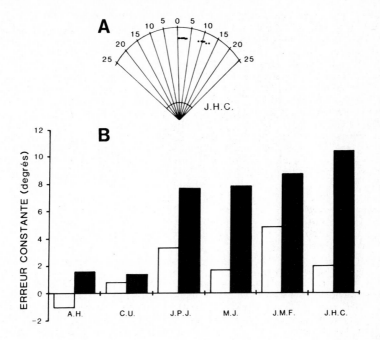

Figure 1
Systematic deviation to the right of pointings directed at a target
located at the mid-sagittal plane during vibration of left posterior
neck muscles, in six subjects. A: Position of pointings before and
during vibration in subject JHC. B: Mean values of pointing positions
before (white boxes) and during (black boxes) vibration in the six
subjects. Positive values, deviation to the right, negative to the left
(from Biguer et al., 1986).

after the vibration began. In fact, a detailed look at the individual
pointing movements performed by this subject revealed that the first
pointings were deviated to the right, as expected, but that this effect
disappeared during the course of the stimulation (Fig. 2). Displacement of
the pointings was therefore correlated with the intensity of the visual
illusion.

   This experiment not only confirms the contribution of spindle
afferents to position sense in general, it also demonstrates clearly that
perturbations in head position sense are directly translated into
mislocation of objects in space and misdirection of visuomotor behavior.

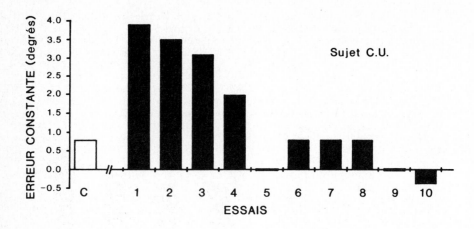

Figure 2
Effects of neck muscles vibration on pointing toward a mid-sagittal
target in subject CU. White boxes: mean position of the 10 pointings
executed before vibration. Black boxes: position of the 10 individual
pointings made under vibration (1-10). One can observe that vibration
effect was limited only at the beginning of experimental session as
reported by the subject (from Biguer et al., 1986).

2.2. Influence of Head Mobility on Pointing Accuracy

This point was examined specifically in an experiment where subjects
were tested for pointing accuracy, with their head either fixed or free to
move. The latency, duration and accuracy of eye, head and hand movements
were measured. Gaze position in space (i.e., the sum of eye and head
positions) was computed electronically. Subjects were instructed to point
as quickly and accurately as possible at randomly located peripheral
targets. Movements always started from the midline position. Experiments
were performed in the dark, so that no visual reafference from the hand
movement was available at any time (the previously described
No-visual-feedback condition). The target remained visible throughout the
duration of each trial. Two experimental sessions were run for each subject:
one in which the head was free to move (Head-free condition), and one in
which the head was fixed in the straight ahead position (Head-fixed
condition).

The latency data from this experiment confirmed those obtained by Biguer, Jeannerod and Prablanc (1982), i.e., eyes moved first, followed by the head (in the Head-free condition), and then the hand. In addition, eye and hand latencies were not affected by whether the head was fixed or free to move. Durations of eye, head and hand movements were significantly affected by target eccentricity, tending to increase with distance from midline. Experimental conditions (e.g., Head-fixed or Head-free) did not affect these durations. Latencies and durations of movements were such that head movement was always completed before hand movement, i.e., the time interval between the end of the head movement and that of the hand movement (TIHH) was always positive. The mean TIHH ranged between 110 ms for targets located at 10° from the midline and 160 ms for targets located at 40°. Similarly, the time interval between the end of the gaze movement and the end of the hand movement (TIGH) was also largely positive. It ranged between 243 ms and 375 ms on the average for targets located at 10° and 40°, respectively.

Pointing accuracy of hand movements was strongly affected by whether the head was fixed or free to move. In the Head-fixed condition, large constant and variable errors were observed, which tended to increase as a function of target distance from the midline. In the Head-free condition both constant and variable errors were consistently reduced with respect to the Head-fixed condition. In addition, the usual relationship of error size to target distance was no longer observed. Statistical analysis of errors in the two conditions (Biguer, Prablanc and Jeannerod, 1984) showed that improvement in pointing accuracy in the Head-free condition was significant mainly for targets located far from midline (40°). Similar results were obtained by Roll et al. (1981).

There are a number of possible explanations for the improvement in pointing accuracy in the condition where coordinated eye and head movement is allowed. First, the synergy of eyes, head and hand moving together may represent an advantage for terminal accuracy. These segmental movements during the action of reaching belong to the same motor ensemble, their commands are released synchronously and they are linked by a relatively strict temporal coordination. Artificial disruption of this ensemble, by head blocking for example, could introduce a mechanical limitation of its performance.

Alternatively, proprioceptive signals generated by the head movement itself (e.g., originating from neck joints, tendons or muscles) may facilitate the programming of target-directed hand movements and improve their directional coding. The interval between the end of the head movement and that of the hand movement (as measured by the TIHH, see above) is largely compatible with the time required for kinesthetic afferents to influence the course of a movement. However, it is likely that, in the Head-fixed condition, kinesthetic receptors in the neck adapt so much that the information they normally provide about head position becomes severely degraded. Paillard and Brouchon (1974) have shown in a different context that position of a limb can be accurately perceived immediately after it has been moved actively by the subject, but not when it has been moved passively by the experimenter or maintained in a fixed position for a long period of time.

Finally, it may be that the information used for encoding target position in the body centered space is not linearly related to eye and head positions. This hypothesis assumes that the pointing error is the sum of errors inherent in both the information about eye and head positions and the variability in programming and control of hand movements. It also assumes that the error in the estimation of eye position remains low up to a limiting angular displacement of the eye within the orbit. Thus, for targets within this limit, no head movement is required; beyond this limit, however, the error would increase sharply if no head movement occured. This hypothesis is consistent with the fact that head movements recorded during pointing do not cover the whole target distance. The residual distance, covered by the eye movement alone, seems to be maintained within about 15 degrees. This value might correspond to the limiting angular displacement of the eye, beyond which eye position signals are degraded. The same argument holds for the error in estimating the head position with respect to the trunk, that is, beyond a certain angular displacement of the head, the head position signals would become less accurate, and the trunk has to be rotated.

3. Signals Related to Body Axes

In this section we explore the hypothesis that there are mechanisms that encode the position of body axes. This process is posited as representing the sum of those visual, somatosensory, vestibular (and possibly other) mechanisms which provide an internal representation of the body itself. It is assumed therefore that "egocentric" body coordinates, such as body midline or sagittal axis, are represented as a reference for actions within personal space (like touching a part of one's own body), as well as for actions directed at objects within extrapersonal space.

Several concepts have been used to account for the fact that egocentric body coordinates can be perceived by the subject. Schilder (1935), for instance, included the body axis within the more general framework of the "body scheme". Similarly, Werner and Wapner (1952) postulated that perception of spatial coordinates reflected the innervation pattern of the whole organism during acquisition of targets within proximal space (the sensory-tonic-field theory). Observations of orienting and locomotory behaviour following unilateral lesions of the nervous system have provided experimental bases to these hypotheses.

3.1. Representation of Body Coordinates in Normal Subjects

The ability of normal subjects to perceive the position of their body coordinates has been studied in many experiments. Particular emphasis has been put on perception of the vertical (see Howard 1982). The present section, however, is restricted to perception of the position of body midline. Body midline can be considered as a functional sagittal axis segmenting body and space into left and right sectors, the perception of which being therefore directly relevant to the problem of spatial localization of objects in extrapersonal space. In fact, there are interactions between perception of the sagittal body axis and perception of the vertical. Subjects with different degrees of head and/or body tilt make errors in attempting to place a luminous line in conformity with the physical vertical: the error is in the direction of the head tilt, and increases with the amount of tilt (the so-called Aubert phenomenon). Mittelstaedt (1983) suggested that the subjective vertical is shifted toward the direction of the person's long axis as a result of competition between what he calls the "idiotropic vector" and the gravity system for dominance over a common reference. Because this idiotropic vector is not part of a specific sensory system (unlike the gravity system), it must be considered as a construct which would be part of an autonomous system of orientation.

One way to demonstrate the perception of the idiotropic vector is to ask subjects, in the absence of visual cues, to point their hand "straight ahead", that is, in the direction where they feel the middle of their body would project in front of them. By using this technique, Werner et al. (1953) were able to show that subjects could locate the projection of their body midline with relatively good accuracy, though they consistently deviated from the projection of objective midline. When the subjects pointed without vision (they had their eyes closed), the mean pointing position was deviated by 3.8 cm to the right of objective midline. When the subjects fixated a luminous target placed objectively straight ahead (although they could not see their hand during pointing), deviation of the mean pointing position was reduced to 1.4 cm to the right of objective midline. The larger deviation observed with the eyes closed might be explained by the fact that the subjects were standing upright during the experiment. In this situation, the absence of visual cues is known to increase the amplitude of body sway, which may reflect in inaccurate pointing.

The systematic pointing bias (to the right of objective midline in the Werner et al. experiment) is more interesting to consider. The fact that spatial orienting in normal subjects is biased toward one direction (in the absence of visual frame) seems to have been known for relatively long time. Schaeffer (1928) reported that blindfolded subjects walk in spiral paths when attempting to go straight away. Rightward spiralling was reported to be more frequent than leftward. Rightward bias was also reported in spontaneous position of gaze in newborn infants (Gesell, 1938; Liederman & Kinsbourne, 1980). Other studies, however, seem to have clearly demonstrated the existence of a leftward bias in manual exploration of space. This phenomenon was first described by Bowers and Heilman (1980) in a task involving tactual exploration of a rod. A leftward bias was found for both hands in estimating the midpoint of the line. The same was also true if the rod was placed in the subjects right hemispace, but not in their left hemispace. A similar effect, referred to as "left side underestimation (LSU)" was reported by Bradshaw, Nettelton, Nathan and Wilson (1983), using either the tactual or the visual modes. Bradshaw et al. (1983) attributed LSU to greater visuospatial processing power of the right hemisphere, which makes subjects see or feel the extent to the left of center as larger than it actually is and consequently to objectively underestimate the left half of the rod (for a review, see Heilman et al., this volume). In agreement with these studies showing a leftward bias in line-bisection tasks, Biguer and Jeannerod (in preparation) also found a consistent deviation to the left in pointing straight ahead. The study was conducted in 10 right-handed subjects. They had their heads rigidly fixed in alignement with sagittal body axis, by means of a bite-plate. They used their right hands for pointing. Mean deviation from objective midline was 1.89° to the left when pointing was made in the dark, and was reduced to 1.08° to the left when pointing was made toward a small light placed at objective midline (Fig. 3).

Demonstrating that the position of body midline can be perceived as a reference for spatially-oriented actions implies that it relies on signals independent from those generated by eye or head positions. Already in 1953, Werner, Wapner and Bruell had reported a study where subjects attempted to point straight ahead while fixating a target located 15° right or left of objective midline. They found that pointing positions were shifted in the direction of the fixated target. No difference was found whether fixation was made by the eyes alone or with the eyes and the head aligned on the target. By contrast, when the subjects eyes or head were deviated to the right or to the left but the eyes were closed while pointing straight ahead, the mean pointing position was shifted in the direction opposite to that of the eyes and/or head turn. In both conditions (fixation or eyes closed), the amplitude of the shift was much smaller than the actual eye or head turns.

The finding of opposite shifts of pointing positions whether a fixation target was available or not, is rather difficult to interprete. According to the authors, "Since ...when a fixated object is placed to the right the

M. Jeannerod and B. Biguer

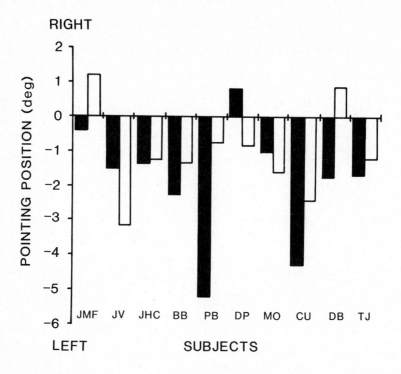

Figure 3
Leftward bias during pointing straight ahead in ten normal subjects.
- Black bars: pointing positions (in degrees of arc) during pointing straight ahead in the dark.
- White bars: pointing positions during pointing straight ahead while fixating a small luminous target at objective midline.
Subjects heads were rigidly fixed at a position corresponding to the sagittal plane.

position of the apparent median plane shifts to the right, we assume that the innervation pattern of the organism correlative with that position is similar to that under left head torsion (eyes closed)..." (p.298), where the apparent median plane is also shifted to the right. To explain this similarity, Werner et al. (1953) postulated that in the case of fixation to the right, the head or eyes are maintained on target by "active" forces which are exerted in the same direction as the turn. In the case of eye or head deviation without fixation, however, "counteractive" forces have to be exerted in the direction opposite to the turn, to counteract the normal tendency for the eyes and the head to remain aligned. Accordingly, keeping the head deviated to the left with the eyes looking straight ahead in the dark, would in fact require a force to maintain the eyes deviated to the right with respect to the head. If the force generated to maintain the eye or head positions is used centrally as a cue for directing pointing movements, it is not surprising to find that these movements are deviated to the right in both cases.

Further findings reported by Biguer and Jeannerod (in preparation) only partly confirmed the Werner et al. interpretation. The same right-handed subjects as in the above mentioned experiment, with their head fixed in the sagittal position, were requested to point straight ahead (with their right hand) while looking at targets located 5°, 10° or 15° right or left of their objective midline. Systematic pointing errors were found, such that subjects located the straight ahead direction too far in the direction opposite to the gaze deviation. For example, eye fixation at a target located 5° to the right of objective midline yielded to a -4° mean pointing error to the left. An error of a similar amplitude to the right occured in the case of eye fixation to the left. These errors did not change in sign but decreased significantly in amplitude when eye fixation was directed at more remote targets (e.g., 10° or 15°). (Fig. 4).

A possible interpretation to these findings is that deviations of the line of sight from the head-trunk axis remained unnoticed because of the weakness of the eye position signals. Therefore, when subjects were to indicate the straight ahead direction, they logically erred in the direction opposite to the eye turn because, if the eye deviation was not perceived the fixated target was perceived at midline, the head-trunk axis (the idiotropic vector) had to be perceived deviated from its viridical position by the same amount as the amplitude of the eye deviation and in the opposite direction. This interpretation accounts only for part of the results, however. If, according to the above reasonning, subjects actually ignored signals generated by the orbital position of their eyes, their perceived straight ahead (as indicated by pointing) should be negatively correlated to eye position. Figure 4 shows that this was not the case and that instead, pointing deviations were systematically smaller than eye deviations. This result indicates that both the eye position signals and signals generated by the idiotropic vector compete for the determination of the straight ahead direction. When the angle between the eyes and the head-trunk axis is small (e.g., ± 5°), eye position signals are too weak to be used as an index of the permanent eye deviation. When this angle increases, eye position signals become perceptible and can be used for detecting the deviation of the eyes with respect to the head-trunk axis, so that pointings get closer to the actual straight ahead. This hypothesis of a competition between two mechanisms for the determination of the straight ahead direction is quite distinct from that of Werner et al. (1953) which postulated the existence of counteractive forces to maintain eye-head-trunk postures in alignment.

3.2. Asymmetrical Behavior following Unilateral Lesion of the Nervous System

The notion of body (or egocentric, or idiotropic) reference seems therefore clearly needed for directing movements. This reference can be conceived as an equilibrium position between informations arising from both sides of space, and governing actions directed toward them. Pathological conditions where the equilibrium between the two sides is disrupted as a consequence of lesion of the peripheral or central nervous system has proved to be an interesting paradigm for studying this problem.

In invertebrates, the symmetry of orienting behavior seems to be related to tonic inflow from bilaterally represented sensory organs. In these species, asymmetrical visual stimulation results in asymmetrical locomotory behavior and postural abnormalities; unilateral lesion of these peripheral organs produces forced circling, such that animal's orienting or locomotion is constantly biased toward the intact side. These effects have been attributed to asymmetrical repartition of "visually induced tonus"

M. Jeannerod and B. Biguer

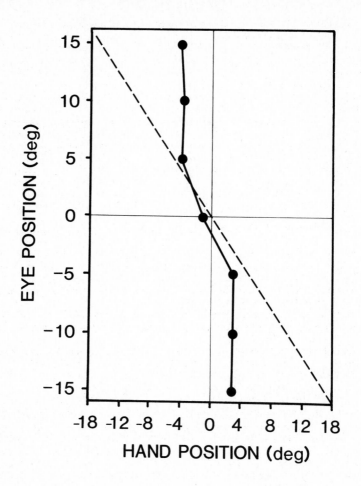

Figure 4

Pointing position (hand position, in degrees of arc) during pointing straight ahead, while fixating a small luminous target placed at objective midline (eye position = 0°) or at 5, 10, or 15 degrees from midline.

Positive values for hand or eye positions, deviation to the right. Negative values, deviation to the left.

The dashed line indicates theoretical hand positions if there were an inverse linear relationship to eye position.

Each dot represents a mean from the same 10 subjects as figure 3.

Subjects heads rigidly fixed at a position corresponding to the sagittal plane.

(for a historical account of the theory, see Meyer & Bullock, 1977).

In vertebrates, unilateral lesions of the central nervous system can produce similar effects. At the subcortical level unilateral lesion of the superior colliculus (Sprague & Meikle, 1965; Flandrin & Jeannerod, 1981), the thalamic intralaminar nuclei (Orem, Schlag-Rey & Schlag, 1973), the basal ganglia (Boussaoud & Joseph, 1985) produce strong, albeit transient, behavioral asymmetries: animals tend to walk in circles toward the side of the lesion, and ignore stimuli appearing on the other side. Spontaneous gaze posture is also displaced following such unilateral lesions. For example, cats with unilateral collicular lesion may show asymmetrical gaze posture at rest in a lighted environment (Flandrin & Jeannerod, 1981), the gaze being directed toward the lesion side.

In the monkey, unilateral excision of associative frontal cortex produces strong ipsilesional forced circling (Kennard & Ectors, 1938). Similarly unilateral lesion of posterior parietal cortex (particularly area 7) produces an ipsilesional bias of reaching movements (Faugier-Grimaud, Frénois & Stein, 1978).

In man, ipsilesional deviation of gaze posture is a common clinical finding during the acute stage following hemispheric lesion. Lesions restricted to the parietal lobe on one side often produce a systematic pointing or reaching bias toward the lesion side (Ratcliff & Davies-Jones, 1972; Perenin & Vighetto, 1983). Patients with unilateral neglect resulting from parietal lesion also make large errors in pointing at an imaginery point in space directly in front of the middle of their chest. Instead of pointing roughly at the objective midline (as normal subjects would do), they err toward the non-neglected side, that is toward the lesion (Heilman, Bowers & Watson, 1983).

According to Kinsbourne (1970), this abnormal behavior suggests "an imbalance between what are normally roughly equal and opposing orientational tendencies". Kinsbourne proposed that each hemisphere subserves contralateral orientation by competing with the other for the control of brainstem output mechanisms. This competition would be mediated by mutual inhibition across transverse commissures (Kinsbourne, 1970). The well-known observation by Sprague (1966) supports this theory. Cats with unilateral lesion of the occipital lobe tend to neglect stimuli appearing contralaterally. This neglect is decreased by excision of the superior colliculus opposite to the cortical lesion, or simply by section of the intercollicular commissure. Sprague's interpretation of this phenomenon implied that the activity in the two superior colliculi became asymmetric after the cortical lesion due to suppression of the excitatory cortico-tectal input on one side. As a consequence, the colliculus on the intact side exerted an exaggerated inhibitory influence on the other colliculus, and produced the neglect. Suppression of this inhibitory influence by section of the intercollicular commissure reestablished some balance in activity between the two sides, and accounted for disappearance of the neglect. A similar reasonning might apply to neglect syndromes produced by cortical lesions in primates, and to the possible role of the corpus callosum in mediating cortico-subcortical inhibitory influences (see Watson, Valenstein, Day & Heilman, 1984).

One can only speculate on the nature of the orienting bias following unilateral lesions. One possible interpretation is that orienting bias occurs as one of several consequences of a higher order deficit, affecting central representation of the body reference system. If this interpretation were correct, one should be able to observe at lower levels of the nervous system, symptoms which would directly reflect compensatory "reactions" to the higher level dysfunction. The vestibular symptoms described following

the same lesions as those that produce orienting bias might be explained
along this line.

It has recently been demonstrated that animals with such unilateral
lesion present a spontaneous nystagmus in the dark, with the fast phase
directed toward the lesion side. Vestibular stimulation in these animals
induces asymmetrical responses, the gain being increased during rotation
toward the lesion side and decreased during rotation toward the opposite.
This fact has been documented in the cat following unilateral lesion of the
superior colliculus (Flandrin & Jeannerod, 1981) and associative parietal
cortex (Ventre, 1985), and in the monkey following unilateral lesion of area
7 (Ventre & Faugier-Grimaud, 1986). In man, several authors have reported
asymmetrical vestibular responses following unilateral frontal or parietal
lobe lesions (Hécaen, Ajuriaguerra & Massonnet, 1951). As a rule, responses
have been found to be stronger during rotation toward the lesion (e.g.,
Takemori, Uchigata and Ishikawa, 1979).

These effects thus demonstrate the existence of a vestibulo-ocular
bias in the direction opposite to the lesion side. In order to reconcile this
phenomenon with the orienting bias following the same lesions, one might
speculate that these unilateral lesions produce an illusory "rotation" of
the egocentric reference, somewhat as if the subject felt being constantly
rotated toward the lesion side. In the absence of a visual reference (e.g.,
in the dark), this illusory "rotation" would induce a compensatory
vestibulo-ocular response toward the opposite (Ventre, Flandrin &
Jeannerod, 1984). The notion of a compensatory vestibular "response" to
explain the vestibulo-ocular asymmetry following unilateral lesions, seems
indirectly supported by the finding that vestibular stimulation in patients
presenting unilateral neglect transiently reduces both their orienting
bias and the extent of the neglected area (Rubens, 1985; see also
Silberpfennig, 1941). In order to obtain the effect, it is necessary to
stimulate the labyrinth on the same side as the cortical lesion, that is, to
reinforce the already existing vestibulo-ocular bias. This result
therefore suggests that the vestibulo-ocular asymmetry observed following
unilateral lesions is in fact a mechanism that opposes the dysfunction of
the body reference system produced by the same lesions.

4. Conclusion

The above review has examined some of the neurophysiological
mechanisms that operate at the junction between processing of incoming
sensory signals and generation of corresponding motor outputs. This
junction implies the delicate operation of transferring the position of
object images on the sensory maps into a body-centered system of
coordinates.

Neural signals for this transformation can be perturbed at several
levels, with the common consequence of producing orienting bias, a
systematic disorientation in one direction. In invertebrate and lower
vertebrate species, where the sensorimotor transformation seems to be
relatively direct, orienting bias may occur as a result of unilateral lesion
or asymmetrical functionning at the receptor level. In higher vertebrates
this type of orienting bias can still be observed following unilateral
labyrinthine lesion. Indeed, it remains to be demonstrated whether it would
not occur also following unilateral sensory dysfunction in the visual or
auditory modalities, for example.

Orienting bias produced by dysfunction or lesion at the central level
is a more common finding in higher vertebrates. Direct alteration of the
representation of body-centered space, or partial dysconnection of this
representation from its inputs (eye and/or head position signals for

instance) can be a cause of asymmetrical spatial behavior. The region of space where position of objects cannot be encoded and represented in the proper system of coordinates, and where orienting movements can no longer be generated, is disregarded and neglected.

This interpretation therefore relates spatial neglect to the orienting bias. In essence, this is another version of theories like those presented by Kinsbourne and by Heilman and his coworkers in this volume. It has the additional feature, however, of specifically predicting "inattention" for part of space in conditions where an orienting bias can be experimentally created. Experiments for testing this prediction are under way.

References

Adler, F.M. Pathologic physiology of convergent strabismus. Archives of Ophthalmology, 1943, 33, 362–377.
Allik, J., Rauk, M. & Luuk, A. Control and sense of eye movements behind closed eyelids. Perception, 1981, 10, 39–51.
Baker, R., Precht, W. & Llinas, R. Mossy and climbing fiber projections of extraocular muscle afferents to the cerebellum. Brain Research, 1972, 38, 440–445.
Batini, C. & Buisseret, P. Sensory peripheral pathway from extrinsic eye muscles. Archives Italiennes de Biologie, 1974, 112, 18–32.
Biguer, B., Donaldson, I.M.L., Hein, A. & Jeannerod, M. La vibration des muscles de la nuque modifie la position apparente d'une cible visuelle. Comptes Rendus de 1 'Académie des Sciences (Paris), 1986., 303, 43–48.
Biguer, B., Jeannerod, M. & Prablanc, C. The coordination of eye, head and arm movements during reaching at a single visual target. Experimental Brain Research, 1982, 46, 301–304.
Biguer, B., Prablanc, C. & Jeannerod, M. The contribution of coordinated eye and head movements in hand pointing accuracy. Experimental Brain Research, 1984, 55, 462–469.
Boussaoud, D. & Joseph, J.P. Role of cat substantia nigra pars reticulata in eye and head movements. II. Effects of local pharmacological injections. Experimental Brain Research, 1985, 57, 297–304.
Bowers, D. & Heilman, K.M. Pseudoneglect: effect of hemispace on a tactile line bisection task. Neuropsychologia, 1980, 18, 491–498.
Bradshaw, J.L., Nettelton, N.C., Nathan, G. & Wilson, L. Head and body space to left and right, front and rear. II. Visuotactual and kinesthetic studies and left-side underestimation. Neuropsychologia, 1983,
Brindley, G. & Merton, P.A. The absence of position sense in the human eye. Journal of Physiology (Lond), 1960, 153, 127–130.
Brindley, G.S., Goodwin, G.M., Kulikowski, J.J. & Leighton, D. Stability of vision with paralyzed eye. Journal of Physiology (Lond), 1976, 258, 65–66P.
Buisseret, P. & Maffei, L. Extraocular proprioceptive projections to the visual cortex. Experimental Brain Research, 1977, 28, 421–425.
Cohen, L.A. Role of eye and neck proprioceptive mechanisms in body orientation and motor coordination. Journal of Neurophysiology, 1961, 24, 1–11.
Donaldson, I.M.L. & Long, A.C. Interaction between extraocular proprioceptive and visual signals in the superior colliculus of the cat. Journal of Physiology (Lond) , 1980, 298, 85–110.
Faugier-Grimaud, S., Frenois, C. & Stein, D.G. Effects of posterior parietal lesions on visually guided behavior in monkeys. Neuropsychologia, 1978, 16, 151–168.

Festinger, M.L. & Canon, L.K. Information about spatial location based on knowledge about efference. Psychological Review, 1965, 72, 373-384.

Fiorentini, A. & Ercoles, A.M. Visual direction of a point source in the dark. Atti. della Fondazione B. Ronchi., 1966, 23, 405-428.

Fiorentini, A., Berardi, N. & Maffei, L. Role of extraocular proprioception in the orienting behavior of cats. Experimental Brain Research, 1982, 48, 113-120.

Flandrin, J.M. & Jeannerod, M. Effects of unilateral superior colliculus ablation on oculomotor and vestibulo-ocular responses in the cat. Experimental Brain Research, 1981, 42, 73-80.

Fuchs, A. & Kornhuber, H.H. Extra-ocular muscle afferents to the cerebellum of the cat. Journal of Physiology (Lond), 1969, 200, 713-723.

Gesell, A. The tonic neck reflex in the human infant. Journal of Pediatrics, 1938, 13, 455-464.

Goodwin, G.M., McCloskey, D.I. & Matthews, P.B.C. A systematic distortion of position sense produced by muscle vibration. Proceedings of the Physiological Society, nov. 1971.

Graefe, A. von. Les paralysies des muscles moteurs de l'oeil, translated from german by A. Sichel, Delahaye, Paris, 1870.

Guitton, D., Douglas, R.M. & Volle, M. Eye-head coordination in the cat. Journal of Neurophysiology, 1984, 52, 1030-1050.

Hallett, P.E. & Lightstone, A.D. Saccadic eye movement towards stimuli triggered by prior saccades. Vision Research, 1976, 16, 99-106.

Harris, L.R., Blakemore, C. & Donaghy, M. Integration of visual and auditory space in the mammalian superior colliculus. Nature, 1980, 288, 56-59.

Hécaen, H., Ajuriaguerra, J. de & Massonnet, J. Les troubles visuo-constructifs par lésion parieto-occipitale droite. Role des perturbations vestibulaires. L'Encéphale, 1951, 40, 122-179.

Heilman, K.M., Bowers, D. & Watson, R.T. Performance on hemispatial pointing task by patients with neglect syndrome. Neurology, 1983, 33, 661-664.

Hein, A., Vital-Durand, F., Salinger, W. & Diamond, R. Eye movement initiate visual-motor development in the cat. Science, 1979, 204, 1221-1222.

Hein, A. & Diamond, R. Contribution of eye movement to the representation of space. In A. Hein and M. Jeannerod (Eds.), Spatially oriented behavior. New York: Springer-Verlag, 1983, pp. 119-133.

Helmholtz, H. von. Handbuch des physiologischen Optik, VOS, Leipzig, 1866. French translation, Masson, Paris, 1867; English translation, Optical Society of America, 1925.

Hill, A.L. Direction constancy. Perception and Psychophysics, 1972, 11, 175-178.

Holst, E. von & Mittelstaedt, H. Das Reafferenzprinzip. Wechselwirkungen zwischen Zentralnervensystem und Peripherie. Naturwissenschaften, 1950, 37, 464-476.

Honda, H. Eye position signals in successive saccades. Perception and Psychophysics, 1984, 36, 15-20.

Howard, I.P. Human visual orientation. J. Wiley Sons, Toronto, 1982.

Jackson, J.H. & Paton, L. On some abnormalities of ocular movements. Lancet, 1909, March. 27, pp. 900-905.

James, W. The principles of Psychology. London: MacMillan, 1890.

Jay, M.F. & Sparks, D.L. Auditory receptive fields in primate superior colliculus shift with changes in eye position. Nature, 1984, 309, 345-347.

Jeannerod, M., Gerin, P. & Mouret, J. Influence de l'obscurité et de l'occlusion des paupières sur le contrôle des mouvements oculaires. L'Année Psychologique, 1965, 65, 309-324.

Keller, E.L. & Robinson, D.A. Absence of stretch reflex in extraocular muscles of the monkey. Journal of Neurophysiology, 1971, 34, 908–919.

Kelso, J.A.S., Holt, K.G., Kugler, P.N. & Turvey, M.T. On the concept of coordinative structures as dissipative structures. II. Empirical lines of convergence. In G.E. Stelmach and J. Requin (Eds.), Tutorials in motor behavior. Amsterdam: North–Holland, 1980, pp. 49–70.

Kennard, M.A. & Ectors, L. Forced circling in monkeys following lesions of the frontal lobes. Journal of Neurophysiology, 1938, 1, 45–54.

Kinsbourne, M. A model for the mechanism of unilateral neglect of space. Transactions of the American Neurological Assocation, 1970, 95, 143–146.

Kornmüller, A.E. Eine Experimentelle Anästhesie der aüsseren Augenmuskeln am Meschen und ihre Auswirkungen. J. f. Psychologie und Neurologie, 1931, 41, 351–366.

Laverne Morgan, C. Constancy of egocentric visual direction. Perception and Psychophysics, 1978, 23, 61–68.

Liederman, J. & Kinsbourne, M. The mechanism of neonatal rightward turning bias. A sensory or motor asymmetry? Infant. behavior and Development, 1980, 3, 223–238.

Mann, V.A., Hein, A. & Diamond, R. Localization of targets by strabismic subjects: contrasting patterns in constant and alternating suppressors. Perception and Psychophysics, 1979, 25, 29–34.

Marteniuk, R.G. The role of eye and head positions in slow movement execution. In G.E. Stelmach (Ed.), Information Processing in motor learning and control. New York: Academic Press, 1978, pp. 267–288.

Matin, M. & Kibler, G. Acuity of visual perception of direction in the dark for various positions of the eye in the orbit. Perceptual and Motor Skills, 1966, 22, 407–420.

Matin, L., Pearce, D.G., Matin, E. & Kibler, G. Visual perception of direction. Roles of local sign, eye movements and ocular proprioception. Vision Research, 1966, 6, 453–469.

Matin, L., Stevens, J.K. & Picoult, E. Perceptual consequences of experimental extraocular muscle paralysis. In A. Hein and M. Jeannerod (Eds.), Spatially oriented behavior. New York: Springer–Verlag, 1983, pp. 243–262.

Mays, L.E. & Sparks, D.L. Saccades are spatially, not retinocentrically, coded. Science, 1980, 208, 1163–1165.

Meyer, D.L. & Bullock, T.H. The hypothesis of sense–organ–dependent tonus mechanisms: history of a concept. Annals of the New York Academy of Sciences, 1977, 290, 3–17.

Miles, F.A. & Evarts, E.V. Concepts of motor organization. Annual Review of Psychology, 1979, 30, 327–362.

Mittelstaedt, H. A new solution to the problem of the subjective vertical. Naturwissenschatfen, 1983, 70, 272–281.

Olson, C.R. Spatial localization in cats reared with strabisms. Journal of Neurophysiology, 1980, 43, 792–806.

Orem, J., Schlag–Rey, M. & Schlag, J. Unilateral visual neglect and thalamic intralaminar lesions in the cat. Experimental Neurology, 1973, 40, 784–797.

Paillard, J. & Brouchon, M. A proprioceptive contribution to the spatial encoding of position cues for ballistic movements. Brain Research, 1974, 71, 273–284.

Palka, J. Discrimination between movements of eye and object by visual interneurones of crickets. Journal of Experimental Biology, 1969, 50, 723–732.

Perenin, M.T., Jeannerod, M. & Prablanc, C. Spatial localization with paralysed eye muscles. Ophthalmologica, 1977, 175, 206–214.

Perenin, M.T. & Vighetto, A. Optic ataxia: a specific disorder in visuomotor coordination. In A. Hein and M. Jeannerod (Eds), Spatially oriented behavior. New York: Springer-Verlag, 1983, pp. 305–326.

Prablanc, C., Echallier, J.F., Komilis, E. & Jeannerod, M. Optimal response of eye and hand motor systems in pointing at a visual target. I. Spatio-temporal characteristics of eye and hand movements and their relationships when varying the amount of visual information. Biological Cybernetics, 1979, 35, 113–124.

Ratcliff, G., & Davies-Jones, G.A.E. Defective visual localization in focal brain wounds. Brain, 1972, 95, 46–60.

Robinson, D.A. Oculomotor control signals. In G. Lennerstrand and P. Bach-Y-Rita(Eds.), Basic mechanisms of ocular motility and their clinical implications. Oxford: Pergamon Press, 1975, pp. 337–374.

Robinson, D.L. & Wurtz, R.H. Use of an extra-retinal signal by monkey superior colliculus neurons to distinguish real from self-induced stimulus movement. Journal of Neurophysiology, 1976, 39, 852–870.

Rose, P.K. & Abrahams, V.C. The effect of passive eye movement on unit discharge in the superior colliculus of the cat. Brain Research, 1975, 97, 95–106.

Rubens, A.B. Caloric stimulation and unilateral visual neglect. Neurology, 1985, 35, 1019–1024.

Schaeffer, A.A. Spiral movement in man. Journal of Morphology and Physiology, 1928, 45, 293–398.

Schilder, P. The image and appearance of the human body. Routledge and P. Kegan, London, 1935.

Schwartz, D.W.F. & Tomlinson, R.D. Neuronal responses to eye muscle stretch in cerebellar lobule VI of the cat. Experimental Brain Research, 1977, 27, 101–111.

Sherrington, C.S. Further note on the sensory nerves of muscles. Proceedings of the Royal Society, 1897, 61, 247–249.

Sherrington, C.S. Further note on the sensory nerves of muscles. Proceedings of the Royal Society, 1898, 62, 120–121.

Siebeck, R. Wahrnehmungsstörung und Störungswahrnehmung bei Augenmuskellähmungen. Von Graefes Archiv für klinische experimentelle Ophthalmologie, 1954, 155, 26–34.

Silberpfennig J. Contributions to problem of eye-movements. III. Disturbances of ocular movements with pseudo hemianopsia in frontal lobes tumors. Confinia Neurologica, 1941, 4, 1–13.

Skavenski, A.A. Inflow as a source of extraretinal eye position information. Vision Research, 1972, 12, 221–229.

Skavenski, A.A. The nature and role of extraretinal eye-position information in visual localization. In R.A. Monty and J.W. Senders (Eds.), Eye movements and psychological processes. Erlbaum, Hillsdale, 1976, pp. 277–287.

Sparks, D.L. & Mays, L.E. Role of the monkey superior colliculus in the spatial localization of saccade targets. In A. Hein and M. Jeannerod (Eds.), Spatially oriented behavior. New York: Springer-Verlag, 1983, pp. 63–85.

Sperry, R.W. Effect of 180° rotation of the retinal field in visuomotor coordination. Journal of Experimental Zoology, 1943, 92, 263–279.

Sperry, R.W. Neural basis of the spontaneous optokinetic response produced by visual inversion. Journal of Comparative Physiology and Psychology, 1950, 43, 482–489.

Sprague, J.M. Interactions of cortex and superior colliculus in mediation of visually guided behaviour in the cat. Science, 1966, 152, 1544–1547.

Sprague, J.M. & Meikle, T.H. The role of superior colliculus in visually guided behavior. Experimental Neurolopgy, 1965, 11, 115-146.

Steinbach, M.J. & Smith, D.R. Spatial localization after strabismus surgery: evidence for inflow. Science, 1981, 213, 1407-1409.

Stevens, J.K., Emerson, R.C., Gerstein, G.L., Kallos, T., Neufeld, G.R., Nichols, C.W. & Rosenquist, A.C. Paralysis of the awake human: visual perceptions. Vision Research, 1976, 16, 93-98.

Takemori, S., Uchigata, M. & Ishikawa, M. Eye movements in cerebral lesions. Neuroscience letters, 1979, suppl. 2, S30.

Teuber, H.L. Perception. In J. Field, H.W. Magoun, and V.E. Hall (Eds.), Handbook of Physiology, Section I.: Neurophysiology. Washington: American Physiological Society, 1960, pp. 89-121.

Ventre, J. Cortical control of oculomotor functions. II. Vestibulo-ocular reflex and visual-vestibular interaction. Behavorial Brain Research, 1985, 1, 221-234.

Ventre, J. & Faugier-Grimaud, S. Effects of posterior parietal lesions (area 7) on VOR in monkeys. Experimental Brain Research, 1986, 62, 654-658.

Ventre, J., Flandrin, J.M. & Jeannerod, M. In search for the egocentric reference. A neurophysiological hypothesis. Neuropsychologia, 1984, 22, 797-806.

Von Noorden, G.K., Awaya, S. & Romano, P.E. Past-pointing in paralytic strabismus. American Journal of Ophthalmology, 1971, 71, 27-33.

Wade, N.J. Sir Charles Bell on visual direction. Perception, 1978, 7, 359-362.

Watson, R.T., Valenstein, E., Day, A.L. & Heilman, K.M. The effects of corpus callosum lesions on unilateral neglect in monkeys. Neurology, 1984, 34, 812-815.

Werner, H., Wapner, S. & Bruell, J.H. Experiments on sensory-tonic field theory of perception: VI. Effect of position of head, eyes and of object on position of the apparent mdian plane. Journal of Experimental Psychology, 1953, 46, 293-299.

Wiermsa, C.A.G. & Yamaguchi, T. Integration of visual stimuli by the crayfish central nervous system. Journal of Experimental Biology, 1967, 47, 409-431.

Young, L.R. & Stark, L. Variable feedback experiments testing a sampled-data model for eye tracking movement. IEEE Transactions. Human Factors in Electronics, 1963, HFE 4, 38-51.

Neurophysiological and Neuropsychological Aspects
of Spatial Neglect, M. Jeannerod (editor)
© Elsevier Science Publishers B.V. (North-Holland), 1987

HEMISPACE AND HEMISPATIAL NEGLECT

Kenneth M. Heilman, Dawn Bowers, Edward Valenstein
and
Robert T. Watson

A patient with hemispatial neglect may fail to report, respond, or
orient toward novel or meaningful stimuli presented in the
hemispace contralateral to a brain lesion. Hemispatial neglect
may be induced by a sensory-attentional, motor-intentional,
memory, or an exploratory disorder.
This chapter defines hemispatial neglect and describes how it may
be tested in patients. There is a review of hemispace studies in
normal subjects. The pathophysiology of the attentional,
intentional memory, and exploratory defects is discussed.
Finally, recovery of function and treatments are also discussed.

I. Introduction

Recently, we have written chapters about neglect and related disorders
(Heilman, Valenstein & Watson, 1985b; Heilman, Valenstein & Watson, in
press). Rather than write a third comprehensive chapter, we thought it best
in this chapter to focus on hemispace and hemispatial neglect. Although there
continues to be an overlap with prior chapters, portions of the neglect
syndrome such as extinction, motor (limb) neglect, neglect of body parts, and
neglect of hemiplegia are discussed in this chapter only insofar as they may
pertain to hemispatial neglect. We first define what we mean by hemispatial
neglect and discuss studies of hemispace in normal subjects. We describe how
to test for hemispatial neglect and discuss the mechanisms underlying it.
Last, we describe recovery and treatment.

II. Definition of Hemispace

Hemispace is a complex concept because it can be defined according to the
visual half field, head hemispace, or trunk hemispace. With the eyes and head
facing directly ahead, so that the midsagittal plane of all these structures
is parallel, all three hemispatial fields are congruent. If, however, the
eyes are directed to the far right, an object presented in the left visual
half field can be in the hemispatial field of the right side of the head and
body. If the head is also turned to the right, that object will be in the left
visual head hemifield but may be still in the right body hemispatial field.

Not only can stimuli be presented in either the right or left visual half
field or head or body hemispatial field, but each limb (right or left) can
also work in either the right or left body, head, or visual half field. For
example, the right hand can work on the right or left side of the body. If the
head is turned sharply to the right, the right hand can work in right body
hemispace but still be in left head hemispace. If the eyes are also deviated
to the right, the hand can work in right body space but also in left head
hemispace and in the left visual half field.

III. Definition of Hemispatial Neglect

A patient with sensory (attentional) neglect may fail to report, respond, or orient to novel or meaningful stimuli presented contralateral to a hemispheric lesion. We will not discuss tactile neglect because tactile neglect has not yet been shown to vary with hemispace (e.g., a patient does not respond better to stimuli applied to the left hand when the hand is moved into right hemispace) and the tactile (somatesthetic) modality does not sense spatial stimuli (stimuli presented in space rather than on the body). Hemispatial sensory neglect then refers to the failure to respond to stimuli (e.g., visual, auditory) that are presented in a visual half field or in head or body hemispace.

When patients do not report, respond, or orient to the stimuli and the defect cannot be attributed to a sensory or motor defect or to motor neglect, they are considered to have hemispatial sensory neglect.

An inability to move a limb, turn one's head or move one's eyes may be termed "plegia" (e.g., hemiplegia, ophthalmoplegia) and a weakness may be termed "paresis". Many of these movement abnormalities can be caused by injury to motor neurons; however, defective movement can also be associated with lesions that do not destroy or injure motor neurons but rather affect the activation of motor neurons. When absent or weak movements are caused by dysfunction of the systems that activate motor neurons, we term them "akinesia" or "motor (intentional) neglect". Motor (intentional) neglect may involve a limb (limb akinesia), but some forms of limb akinesia can vary with hemispatial field (hemispatial limb akinesia). There are also patients who have difficulty moving a limb, the head, or eyes toward the hemispace contralateral to a hemispheric lesion. The inability to move the eyes toward contralateral hemispace has been called a gaze paresis. However, it also can be seen in the limb and head, and because these disorders are not caused by lesions of the motor neurons, we call these "directional akinesis (or hypokinesis)".

Not all the behavioral abnormalities associated with the neglect syndrome can be subsumed under the attentional-intentional dichotomy. As will be discussed in the subsequent section, there also appear to be hemispatial memory defects, both anterograde and retrograde.

IV. Studies of Hemispace in Normal Subjects

Based on the profound hemispatial defects that are often observed in patients with right hemisphere lesions, the question arises as to the extent to which hemispatial-attentional factors are reflected and observed in the "normal" non-brain-damaged person. During the past several years, we and others have examined this possibility through a series of studies with normal subjects. These studies have generally relied on the use of various experimental laterality paradigms, including tachistoscopic and tactile procedures. As has been well documented in the literature, use of such tasks with normal adult right-handers has indicated that verbal stimuli are more readily responded to when presented to the right than left sensory channel (ear, visual half field, hand). In contrast, many nonverbal stimuli are better responded to when presented to the left ear, left visual half field, or left hand. Traditionally, the right-sided superiority for verbal stimuli and the left-sided superiority for nonverbal stimuli have been interpreted according to an anatomical pathway-transmission model. Briefly, this model states that stimuli are more readily processed when they have direct anatomical access to the hemisphere (left or right) that is most specialized for processing them.

However, this anatomical connectivity model has been challenged on both empirical and theoretical grounds. _First_, numerous studies have suggested that attentional factors modulate the extent to which these verbal and nonverbal asymmetries are observed (Kinsbourne, 1974; Klein et al., 1976). Although the precise mechanism by which attentional factors affect laterality phenomena remains unclear, what is clear is that a stringent version of the pathway-transmission model does not account for attentional variables. Second, studies have also indicated that "spatial" factors appear to influence laterality effects. Goldstein and Lackner (1974) reported that the right ear asymmetry for verbal stimuli on a dichotic listening task was significantly enhanced when their subjects wore prisms that laterally displaced their visual environment to the right. Prisms that displaced the visual environment to the left resulted in reduced right ear asymmetries.

A third and related problem for anatomical connectivity interpretations of laterality effects concerns a paradigmatic confounding that occurs in traditional laterality tasks. Namely, when one considers the experimental paradigms that are used in traditional laterality research with normal subjects, there is a perfect one-to-one relationship between the sensory channel to which a stimulus is presented (ear, visual half field, hand) and the side of hemispace in which this sensory channel is located. As previously discussed, hemispace is not the same as the visual half field but refers to the corporeal and extracorporeal space to the left and right of body (head) midline. In tactile studies, a stimulus to be felt is presented to the left hand located in left hemispace or to the right hand located in right hemispace. Similarly, in visual half-field studies, the subject fixates on a midline stimulus so that the right visual field falls within right hemispace and the left visual field falls within left hemispace. Because of this confounding between sensory channel and hemispace, one could logically attribute laterality effects to: (a) the anatomical relationship between each hemisphere and the contralateral sensory input-motor output apparatus; and/or (b) the specialization of each hemisphere for perceiving, attending and/or acting on stimuli in the contralateral hemispatial field.

In an initial attempt to disentangle the contribution of hemispace from that of sensory input channel, we gave a tactile line bisection task to normal right-handed adults (Bowers & Heilman, 1980). This task – which was a tactile analogue to visual line bisection given to patients with hemispatial neglect (Heilman & Valenstein, 1978) – involved presenting a straight horizontal wooden stick to blindfolded subjects. Their task was merely to find the midpoint of the wooden stick after running an index finger along the length of the stimulus.

It was reasoned that due to the intrinsic tactile-spatial demands, the processing of this task would be more strongly mediated by the right hemisphere. This assumption was based, in part, on previous tactile laterality studies finding a left hand superiority for various tactually guided spatial tasks, such as the discrimination of rods in different angular orientations (Benton et al., 1973; Oscar-Berman, Rehbein & Porfeit, 1969) and three-dimensional forms (Witelson, 1974).

To separate experimentally the effects of hemispace from the hand that felt the stimulus, the line stimuli were positioned at midline or in left or right hemispace. The left and right hands performed the task in each of these spatial conditions.

Three predictions were made. First, if the anatomical connections between the hand and the target right hemisphere were the sole critical factor for task performance, then the left hand would be more accurate than the right hand, regardless of the hemispatial position in which the task was executed. If, however, the hemispace contralateral to the target hemisphere was most critical, then line bisection would be more accurate when carried out in left than right hemispace, regardless of the hand used to feel the stimulus. Alternatively, if <u>both</u> the hemisphere-hand connections and the hemisphere-hemispace relationship were important, this would be reflected in an interaction between the hand used and the hemispatial position of the task.

The findings of this initial study supported the latter hypothesis. Bisection performance was significantly more accurate when carried out in left hemispace than at midline or in right hemispace. Furthermore, there was a significant interaction between hand and hemispace; the best bisection performance was made by the left hand positioned in left hemispace and the worst performance by the right hand in right hemispace.

Taken together, these results suggested, at least for the tactile modality and at least for right-handers, that laterality effects on line bisection stem from the combined effects of two factors – some hemispheric mechanism involved in attention to or mediation of activities in the contralateral hemispatial field, as well as the anatomical connections between the specialized hemisphere and the contralateral hand.

Such does not appear to be the case for left-handers, however. In a subsequent study (Bowers, Caffey & Heilman, unpublished observations) we found that left-handers performed the tactile bisection task equally well across the three hemispatial conditions. And, when compared with dextrals, the left-handed group generally performed the bisection task more accurately, a finding that argues against reports that the spatial abilities of sinistrals are inferior to those of right-handers. The failure of the left-handed group to show any hemispatial effect on this task is not clear, although these "nonresults" are consistent with findings from a massive body of literature in which sinistrals show either attenuated or absent laterality effects across visual half field and dichotic-listening studies. One possibility, however, is that left-handers have more variable and flexible attentional scanning strategies.

Like the dextrals, however, the left-handed subjects made systematic directional errors in their attempts to find the midpoint of the tactile stimulus. When the bisection task was carried out at midline or in right hemispace, both dextrals and sinistrals consistently and significantly erred to the left. That is, the phenomenological midpoint was estimated as occurring to the "left" of the actual midpoint. We have previously referred to these left-sided errors made by our normal subjects as "pseudoneglect". As mentioned, this "pseudoneglect" phenomenon was observed in both handedness groups, although the magnitude of the left-sided errors was greater for the right-handers.

What might be the basis for these consistent pseudoneglect errors? As has been well documented in the clinical literature, patients with hemispatial neglect visually bisect visually presented lines to the right of the actual midpoint (right-sided errors), thereby neglecting the left side of the line. Heilman and Valenstein (1979) proposed that these errors occurred because of the failure of these patients to direct attentional-intentional processes toward the left side of the line to be bisected. Instead, attention-intention is directed toward the right, the net effect being that the right side of the line is estimated as being larger than it really is.

A similar explanation might be forwarded to account for the left-sided pseudoneglect errors made by normal subjects on the tactile line-bisection task. It could be argued that the right hemisphere, which has a greater role in the processing of tactuospatial stimuli, becomes more activated than the left hemisphere when performing this task (Kinsbourne, 1970, 1974). Within a Kinsbournian framework, this would result in attention-intention being directed more to the left, so that the left side of the line was phenomenologically judged to be larger than it really was. If so, one might then predict that left-sided spatial stimuli would be judged larger than comparable right-sided spatial stimuli.

This possibility was examined in a subsequent study in which right-handed subjects felt sticks that were vertically arrayed in either left hemispace or right hemispace. The task was to feel the stimulus and to then estimate its size. Our findings were partially consistent with the activation-overestimation hypothesis. Namely, stimuli felt in left hemispace were judged to be larger than those felt in right hemispace. This was true, however, only for the right hand. There were no hemispatial differences in performance of the left hand.

Other laterality studies have also indirectly suggested that hemispace may share some functional relationship to contralateral hemispheric mechanisms in humans. Previous visual half-field studies, for example, have shown that stimuli directed to one hemisphere are responded to more quickly by the contralateral than the ipsilateral hand (Berlucchi, Heron, Hyman, Rizzolatti & Umilta, 1971). These findings presumably reflect the difference between intrahemispheric versus interhemispheric processing speed.

Such an interpretation has recently been challenged by findings from stimulus-response compatibility studies (Anzola, Bertolini, Buchtel & Rizzolatti, 1977; Berlucchi, Crea, DiStefano & Tassinari, 1977). In these studies, choice reaction times to lateralized neutral stimuli are found to be affected by changing the hemispatial position of the responding hand. If the hands are uncrossed (right hand in right hemispace and left hand in left hemispace), then reaction times to right visual field stimuli are faster with the right hand, and reaction times to left visual field stimuli are faster with the left hand. If, however, the hands are crossed, then reaction times to right visual field stimuli are faster with the left hand (in right hemispace), and reaction times to left visual field stimuli are faster with the right hand (in left hemispace). These findings question the integrity of the intrahemispheric versus interhemispheric processing model because moving one's hands from one side of space to the other should not alter the anatomical arrangements of hemisphere input-hemisphere output connection.

Cognitive theorists have attributed stimulus-response compatibility to a "natural tendency to respond toward a lateralized stimulus with the hand that is in a corresponding spatial position" (Craft & Simon, 1970, p. 419). Others have argued that stimulus-response compatibility effects occur because of a correspondence in the spatial coding of the stimulus and the responding hand (Wallace, 1971; Nicoletti, Anzola, Luppino, Rizzolatti & Umilta, 1982). An alternative explanation for stimulus-response compatibility, however, is that each hemisphere may be specialized for either or both attending to and acting on stimuli in the contralateral hemispatial field (Heilman & Valenstein, 1979; Bowers & Heilman, 1980).

Findings from a recent study in our laboratory (Verfaellie, Bowers & Heilman, 1985) are more consistent with the latter interpretation. A choice reaction time task was given to normal right-handers who manually responded to target stimuli (lights) located in either right or left hemispace. In an attentional condition a central warning cue was presented indicating the likely spatial (right, left) location of the subsequently occurring target. In the intentional condition, the central cue indicated which hand should most likely be used to respond. Stimulus-response compatibility effects were observed only in the condition when intentional cues were provided and were not present when attentional cues were given. This finding points to the role of intentional factors in obtaining compatibility effects and cannot be explained by spatial coding or cognitive models of stimulus-response effects.

Although previous stimulus-response studies have found a compatibility between the hemispatial position of the responding hand and the visual half field to which a stimulus is presented, the question arose whether there was a similar compatibility between the visual half-field to which the stimulus is presented and the side of hemispace in which the visual half field is aligned (i.e., hemispace/visual half-field compatibility). That is, are right visual field stimuli responded to more quickly when the right visual field falls within right than left hemispace? Conversely, are left visual field stimuli responded to more quickly when the left visual field falls within left than right hemispace. Evidence for such a hemispace—visual half field compatibility effect would be critical for the hypothesis that there is some functional relationship between each hemisphere and the contralateral hemispace.

To address this question, we gave a go/no-go reaction time task to normal dextrals who manually responded to neutral light stimuli presented to the left or right visual field. The visual half field in which the stimuli occurred was experimentally dissociated from the hemispace in which the visual half field aligned. This was done by having subjects deviate their eyes to a right fixation point (so that both the left and right visual fields fell within right hemispace) or by deviating their eyes to a left fixation point (so that both visual half fields fell within left hemispace).

As predicted, reaction times were more rapid when the visual half field to which a stimulus was presented was aligned in a compatible side of hemispace (right visual field-right hemispace, left visual field-left hemispace) than when the visual half field and side of hemispace were not so aligned (i.e., left visual field-right hemispace). This hemispace-visual half field compatibility effect was "elusive", however, and only present during the initial part of a session.

It is unclear why the hemispace—visual half field compatibility effect attenuated over trials. One possibility is that each hemisphere may be specialized for attending to and/or acting on stimuli in the contralateral hemispace only in a "free-field" situation – when there is high probability that stimuli will randomly occur in either hemispace. When the probability is high that stimuli will repeatedly occur in only one side of space (as with blocked presentation of unilateral visual half field trials in this study), both hemispheres may dynamically realign or refocus their attention to that side of space. In this case, the body midline no longer serves as a functional axis for dividing space into left and right sectors. The functional midline has shifted. To test the hypothesis that each hemisphere undergoes a process of refocusing and realignment of attention to the hemispace in which stimuli are presented, one would need to repeat the present paradigm using a randomized, rather than blocked presentation of visual half field trials across hemispace.

Nevertheless, the hemispace and visual half-field compatibility effect that was observed during the first half of each session is not predicted by the intrahemispheric versus interhemispheric model because varying the location of the visual half field in space should not alter the anatomical relationship between the visual half field and the contralateral hemisphere. Rather, these findings were interpreted as supporting the hypothesis that each hemisphere may be specialized for the perception and/or mediation of activities in the contralateral hemispatial field.

The next question we addressed was whether such a hemisphere—hemispace relationship might also contribute to laterality effects that are observed with tachistoscopically presented verbal and nonverbal stimuli. That is, are right visual field asymmetries for verbal stimuli greater when the right visual field falls within right than left hemispace? Conversely, are left visual field asymmetries for nonverbal stimuli greater when the left visual field falls within left than right hemispace? To determine this, Williams, Bowers & Heilman (1984) gave another group of normal subjects the basic hemispace/visual half field paradigm, as described, using either verbal (words) or nonverbal stimuli (line angles). Although the expected right visual field superiority for verbal stimuli and left visual field superiority for nonverbal stimuli were found, these verbal and nonverbal asymmetries were unaffected by the hemispace in which the visual half fields were aligned. That is, the right visual field asymmetry for verbal stimuli did not differ according to the hemispace in which the visual half field was aligned, and likewise for the left visual field nonverbal asymmetry. Thus, no support was found for the contribution of hemispatial factors on verbal and nonverbal visual half field tasks. This finding was clearly at odds with the salient role that hemispace appeared to have when hemispherically "neutral" stimuli had been used in the initial hemispace/visual half field study. Other studies also have not found hemispatial effects on tactile laterality trials (Bradshaw, Nettleton, Nathan & Wilson, 1983; Cimino & Bowers, 1986).

One post-hoc explanation for these negative findings is that hemispatial effects are subtle. When verbal or nonverbal stimuli are used, it may be that strong potent hemispheric specialization overrides any subtle hemispatial attention-intentional effects.

Alternatively, hemispatial effects may be closely tied to the initial exploration and search of environmental stimuli. Consistent with this hypothesis are findings from recent studies by Levy and colleagues (Levy & Kueck, in press; Levy, Heller, Bainich & Barton, 1983). They gave free-field visual search tasks to normal right-handers who searched for targets that were scattered across a stimulus page. When verbal stimuli were used, subjects were more accurate at detecting targets in the right hemispatial field (Levy & Kueck, in press), and a left hemispace advantage was found when nonverbal (faces) stimuli were used.

V. Testing Patients for Hemispatial Disorders

A. Spatial Operations

Many clinical observations suggest the presence of hemispatial neglect. Patients with this disorder often fail to dress or groom the abnormal side. Although this failure may be considered a form of dressing apraxia, it may be pathophysiologically different from that accompanying other forms of apraxia or from that in patients with profound visuospatial disorders.

Patients with neglect may also fail to read part of a word or sentence (i.e., they may read the word "cowboy" as "boy"). This disorder has been termed paralexia (Benson & Geschwind, 1969). Patients may write on only one side of a page, or when using a typewriter may fail to type letters correctly on the side of the keyboard contralateral to their lesion. This has been termed neglect-induced paragraphia (Valenstein & Heilman, 1978).

The two tasks most commonly used to assess for hemispatial neglect are the cancellation task and the line-bisection task. In the simplest form of the cancellation task, many (10 to 20) small (approximately 2.5 cm) lines are randomly drawn on an 20.3 x 28 cm page and the patient is asked to cross out or cancel all the lines. Patients with hemispatial neglect from right hemisphere lesions fail to cancel lines on the left side of the page, and often omit more lines on the left lower portion of the page than on the left upper quadrant (Morris, Mickel, Brooks, Sinavely & Heilman, 1986). In the line-bisection task, a horizontal line is placed before the patient who is asked to bisect (find the middle of) the line. Patients with hemispatial neglect from right hemisphere lesions err by bisecting the line toward the right of the actual midpoint.

To demonstrate hemispatial effects, one can put the line to be bisected in either right or left hemibody hemispace. Patients with hemispatial neglect from right hemisphere lesions typically perform more poorly in left than in right hemispace (Heilman & Valenstein, 1979). Body hemispace may even affect complex spatial operations such as typing. For example, Valenstein and Heilman (1978) showed a reduction in neglect-induced paragraphia when the typewriter was moved to the right. Although body and head hemispace may affect neglect, a patient may also show hemispatial neglect within the normal hemispatial field. For example, even when a line is bisected in right head and body hemispace, a patient may err toward the right. This hemispatial defect appears to be related to an attentional spatial field rather than to head or body hemispace per se. When we used a task that required various levels of focused attention, we found that detecting the target from foils, which requires close scrutiny of details and therefore focused attention, led to an increase of hemispatial neglect (increased number of omission errors) (Rapcsak, Fleet & Heilman, 1986). Not only do tasks that require close scrutiny increase the symptoms of hemispatial neglect, but also if the cancellation task is given repeatedly, there appears to be a fatigue effect and patients' performance will progressively decline (Fleet & Heilman, 1986).

Spatial operation tasks, such as the line-bisection tasks or cancellation task, are complex. Failure on such tasks may be related to several factors: Patients with neglect may be inattentive to stimuli presented in left space (hemispatial inattention), they may have a directional or hemispatial akinesia, or they may have an exploratory defect. Exploration, either manually or visually, has both a motor-intentional component and a sensory-attentional component, and a defect in either of these systems may lead to an exploratory defect.

In a recent study, we attempted to determine whether the impaired line-bisection performance of patients with neglect was due to a directional-hemispatial akinesia or to inattention to stimuli in left hemispace (Coslett, Bowers, Fitzpatrick, Hans & Heilman, 1986). We used a video camera and a moveable TV monitor and tested patients with hemispatial neglect on a line-bisection task. During the task the patients were prevented from directly seeing the line and how their hand interacted with it. Instead, the hand and line were viewed by the camera and projected back to the patient by the TV monitor. The monitor and line could be placed in either the same or different hemispace. That is, a line to be bisected might be located in left hemispace but would be seen on the TV monitor that was located in right hemispace. Using this technique, we found that independent of the hemispace in which the line was actually bisected (i.e., hemispace of action), two patients performed better when the monitor was located in right than in left hemispace. These results suggested that hemispatial inattention was at least partly responsible for their hemispatial neglect. In two other patients, however, the hemispace of the monitor did not affect performance but the hemispace of action did. These results suggest that these patients had a hemispatial or directional hypokinesia.

B. Hemispatial Sensory Inattention

In addition to performing poorly on hemispatial tasks such as cancellation or line-bisection, patients with hemispatial neglect may also fail to detect stimuli. Although sensory disturbance may be the most common cause of a failure to report or respond to stimuli presented in contralateral hemispace, patients and animals with lesions in locations other than a primary sensory area or the sensory projection system may also fail to report or respond to stimuli presented in contralateral hemispace. This has been termed hemi-inattention or sensory neglect. Without knowing the site of the lesion, one may be unable to distinguish hemianopia from severe visual-field hemi-inattention. Unlike patients with hemianopia, however, patients with hemi-inattention may be able to detect the stimulus if their attention is directed to the abnormal side or if the attentional value of the stimulus is increased.

Although hemianopia is a common manifestation of central nervous system lesions, unilateral hearing loss is almost always caused by a disturbance in the peripheral hearing mechanisms or in the auditory nerve because the auditory pathways that ascend from the brainstem to the cortex are bilateral; thus, each ear projects to both hemispheres. A unilateral central nervous system lesion will not cause unilateral hearing loss. Consequently, patients without peripheral hearing loss who fail to report unilateral auditory stimulation usually do have hemi-inattention. Furthermore, because sound presented on one side of the body projects to both ears, patients with unilateral hearing loss from a peripheral lesion usually do not fail to respond to unilateral auditory stimulation, unless the stimulus is very close to the ear. Therefore, patients who fail to respond to unilateral auditory stimuli most often have unilateral sensory neglect.

Formal audiometry or tangent screens may be used when testing for auditory or visual hemi-inattention (sensory neglect), but we typically use bedside testing. We make sounds by rubbing or snapping our fingers and have our patients detect the movement of fingers. For visual testing, a modified Poppelreuter diagram, words, or sentences may also be used.

When testing for inattention, one can present novel stimuli to determine whether patients appropriately orient to a stimulus. One can also use a detection task, in which patients are forewarned that a stimulus will be presented and are instructed to indicate when they see (or hear) the stimulus or to tell where they see (hear) the stimulus. Normally, animals or humans presented with a novel stimulus stop performing whatever activity they are engaged in and deviate their eyes, head, and body toward the stimulus. Changes in the automatic nervous system also occur, including dilation of the pupils, increased sweating, and changes in heart rate. Somatic and automatic correlations of orienting can be tested when assessing for sensory neglect. However, when performing a clinical examination, it is easier to assess the somatic orienting response. Some patients with the neglect syndrome fail to orient to visual or auditory stimuli presented in contralateral hemispace, whereas others orient toward the incorrect (normal) side. For example, when a novel noise is made on a patient's left side, he or she may respond either not at all or inappropriately by orienting toward the incorrect ipsilateral side (i.e., allesthesia). Because hemisphere lesions induce neither contralateral deafness nor paralysis of the head or eyes, the failure to orient to the contralateral side cannot be explained by a sensory defect or weakness. The most parsimonious explanation for lack of response is inattention to the novel stimulus. If a reponse is inappropriate, directional akinesia may be present (i.e., inability to make directional movements toward the right), although one cannot rule out the possibility that the stimulus was in fact misperceived.

When using visual stimuli to dissociate visual field from body and head hemispatial neglect, it is best to use detection tasks. As mentioned, without knowledge of the lesion site, it may be impossible to distinguish between hemianopsia and visual neglect. If, however, patients have visual neglect while looking straight ahead, it may be useful to have them deviate their eyes or head, so that their "normal" visual field is in their abnormal head or body hemispace. If they continue to demonstrate detection failures, they have head or body (or both) hemispatial neglect. Head and body hemispatial neglect cannot be accounted for by hemianopsia.

C. Hemispatial and Directional Akinesia

Watson, Miller and Heilman (1978) recognized that in most animal-testing paradigms for neglect, the animal was required to respond to a stimulus contralateral to the lesion either by orienting to the stimulus or by moving the limbs on the side of the stimulus. Because animals with neglect from frontal lobe lesions were not weak on clinical testing, when they failed to make the appropriate response, it was assumed that they had sensory neglect. Although this neglect was usually assumed to result from inattention to the sensory stimuli, Watson et al. (1978) suggested that it could be equally attributable to unilateral akinesia. We therefore trained monkeys to use the left hand in responding to a tactile stimulus on the right leg, and the right hand in responding to a left-sided tactile stimulus. After a unilateral frontal arcuate lesion, the monkeys showed contralateral neglect, but when stimulated on their neglected side, they responded normally with the limb on the side of the lesion. When stimulated on the side ipsilateral to the lesion, however, they often failed to respond (with the limb on the neglected side), or responded by moving the limb ipsilateral to the lesion. These results cannot be explained by sensory inattention and are thought to reflect a defect in motor activation (motor neglect).

It has not been determined whether the monkey's motor neglect was limb akinesia or hemispatial akinesia or both. In the clinic, we may see patients who appear to be hemiparetic; however, when their "paretic" arm is moved to the opposite hemispace, they may show an abatement in the limb akinesia and the movements may have increased amplitude and strength (Meador, Watson, Bowers & Heilman, 1986). Patients with motor (hemispatial) neglect may have slower reaction times in contralateral (e.g., left) than ipsilateral (e.g., right) hemispace (Meador et al., 1986b).

Patients with hemispatial neglect may also have directional akinesia. When asked to perform directional reaction times with their normal (ipsilateral) limb, they may be slower initiating a response toward contralateral hemispace than toward ipsilateral hemispace (Heilman, Bowers, Coslett, Whelan & Watson, 1985a). When patients with hemispatial neglect are given a novel or significant stimulus in left hemispace or on the left portion of the body, they may orient their head and eyes toward the incorrect (ipsilateral) side. Although this defective behavior may be attributed to misperception of contralateral stimuli, if the task requires patients to turn their head and eyes toward the side opposite that touched, directional akinesia of the head or eyes or both can often be detected.

The inability to sustain a movement in or toward the contralateral hemispace may also be considered a form of hemispatial motor neglect. Fischer (1956) and more recently Kertesz, Nicholson, Cancelliere, Kassa & Black (1985) have demonstrated that patients with right hemisphere disease may show an ocular impersistence, in that they cannot persistently gaze toward the contralateral hemispace.

D. Exploratory Defects

Patients with hemispatial neglect may fail to explore in and toward the hemispace contralateral to the brain lesion (Chédru, Leblanc & Lhermitte, 1973). This failure to explore contralateral hemispace may not be limited to the visual modality but may also be present in the tactile modality (DeRenzi, Faglioni & Scotti, 1970). As discussed, their failure to explore may be related to either hemispatial inattention or hemispatial and directional akinesia. The hemispatial akinesia may include eye, head, or limb movements. To determine whether the exploratory defect is being caused by inattention or akinesia, it is important to observe the patient's eyes, head, and arms during exploration. If patients have an exploratory defect induced by inattention, they may fail to focus on the target image but will explore the contralateral hemispatial field. Patients with directional and hemispatial akinesia will fail to move their eyes, head, or hand into contralateral hemispace; or if they do move these body parts into contralateral hemispace, the movements will be inadequate to explore the entire spatial field (Chédru et al. 1973). For example, in asking patients to find an object placed in contralateral hemispace, if they fail to move their eyes and head or arm (depending whether the task is visual or nonvisual), the exploratory defect is induced by hemispatial akinesia. If they move their eyes into contralateral hemispace but fail to direct them to the target, the patient may be inattentive.

E. Memory Defects

1. **Anterograde.** In our laboratory we demonstrated that patients with neglect have a unilateral memory defect for auditory stimuli. We randomly presented consonants through earphones to patients on either the neglected or non-neglected side. We asked them to report the stimulus either immediately or after a distraction-filled interval. We found that distraction induced more of a defect in the neglected ear than in the normal ear (Heilman, Watson & Schulman, 1974).

Samuels, Butters and Goodglass (1971) tested patients with right parietal lesions and found a similar phenomenon in the visual modality. Unfortunately, they did not evaluate their subjects for neglect. Similar types of paradigms can be used at the bedside.

2. **Retrograde.** Bisiach and Luzzatti (1978) described patients with neglect who were unable to recall left-sided details when imagining they face toward a cathedral in a square in Milan. However, when asked to imagine that they were facing away from the cathedral, they could recall details that had been on the left side but now were on the right. In testing patients for a retrograde hemispatial memory defect, patients can be asked to recall what stores one may see when driving down a familiar street and then compare the number or items recalled for each side of the street. To verify that there is a hemispatial defect, one could ask the patient to imagine driving in the other direction.

VI. Pathophysiology of Hemispatial Neglect

In our discussion of the symptoms and signs of hemispatial neglect, we have distinguished several behavioral subtypes. These include hemispatial sensory inattention (sensory neglect), hemispatial and directional akinesia, and memory defects. Although these subtypes often coexist, they can occur in isolation, and therefore must have distinct, although probably related, mechanisms. Furthermore, not every patient with neglect manifests all of these subtypes, and in some there are dramatic dissociations.

A. Sensory Inattention

1. **Sensory and Perceptual Hypothesis.** Battersby, Bender and Pollack (1956) thought that neglect in humans resulted from decreased sensory input superimposed on a background of decreased mental function. Sprague, Chambers and Stellar (1961) concluded that neglect was caused by loss of patterned sensory input to the forebrain, particularly to the neocortex.

Brain (1941) believed that the parietal lobes contained the body schema and also mediated spatial perception. Parietal lesions therefore caused a patient to fail to recognize not only half of his body but also half of space. Denny-Brown and Banker (1954) proposed that the parietal lobes were important in cortical sensation and that the phenomenon of inattention belonged to the whole class of cortical disorders of sensation: "...a loss of fine discrimination...an inability to synthesize more than a few properties of a sensory stimulus and a disturbance of synthesis of multiple sensory stimuli". The neglect syndrome was ascribed to a defect in spatial summation that they called "amorphosynthesis".

2. **Attentional Hypothesis.** Attention is a complex psychological construct that includes arousal and selective attention. Poppelreuter (1917) introduced the word inattention, and Critchley (1966) was also a strong proponent of this view of neglect. However, Bender and Furlow (1944, 1945) challenged the attentional theory of neglect. They thought that inattention could not be important in the pathophysiology of the syndrome because neglect could not be overcome by having the patient "concentrate" on the neglected side.

Heilman and Valenstein (1972) and Watson, Heilman, Cauthen and King (1973) and Watson, Heilman, Miller and King (1974) again postulated an attention-arousal hypothesis. These authors argued that the sensory and perceptual hypothesis could not explain all cases of neglect, since neglect was often induced by lesions outside the traditional sensory pathways. Evoked potential studies in animals and humans with unilateral neglect have demonstrated a change in late waves (that are known to be influenced by changes in attention and stimulus significance) but no change in the early (sensory) waves (Watson, Miller & Heilman, 1977; Lhermitte, Turell, LeBrigand & Chain, 1985). Furthermore, sensory neglect is often multimodal and therefore cannot be explained by a defect in any one sensory modality.

Unilateral neglect in humans and monkeys can be induced by lesions in many different brain regions. These include cortical areas such as the temporoparietal-occipital junction (Critchley, 1966; Heilman, Pandya & Geschwind, 1970; Heilman, Bowers, Valenstein & Watson, 1983), limbic areas such as the cingulate gyrus (Heilman & Valenstein, 1972; Watson et al., 1973), and subcortical areas such as the thalamus (Watson & Heilman, 1979; Watson, Valenstein & Heilman, 1981) and mesencephalic reticular formation (Watson, Heilman, Miller & King, 1974). As we will discuss, these subcortical areas have been shown to be important in mediating arousal and attention, and the cortical areas are regions that are probably specifically involved in the analysis of the behavioral significance of stimuli. We have proposed that sensory neglect is an attentional-arousal disorder induced by dysfunction in a corticolimbic reticular formation loop (Heilman & Valenstein, 1972; Watson et al., 1973; Heilman, 1979; Watson et al., 1981). We will review the evidence for this view, and develop a model or schema to explain the neglect syndrome.

In monkeys and cats, discrete lesions of the mesencephalic reticular formation cause profound sensory neglect (Reeves & Hagaman, 1971; Watson et al., 1974). Stimulation of the MRF is associated with behavioral arousal and also with desynchronization of the electroencephalogram (EEG), a physiologic measure of arousal (Moruzzi & Magoun, 1949). Unilateral stimulation induces greater EEG desynchronization in the ipsilateral than in the contralateral hemisphere (Moruzzi & Magoun, 1949). Arousal is a physiologic state that increases neuronal excitability and thereby prepares the organism for sensory and motor processing. Bilateral MRF lesions result in coma. Unilateral lesions cause contralateral neglect, which is probably due to unilateral hemispheric hypoarousal (Watson et al., 1974).

During the last 30 years, there has been growing criticism of the mesencephalic reticular activating system-arousal theory (Vanderwolf & Robinson, 1981). Much of this criticism stemmed from the observation that under many circumstances EEG desynchronization correlates poorly with levels of arousal. For example, animals given drugs such as atropine may be behaviorally aroused but do not have a low-voltage fast (desynchronized) EEG activity. These observations do not disprove the hypothesis but only suggest that the EEG may not be a perfect correlate of arousal mediated by the mesencephalic reticular activating system. For example, increased neuronal excitability is seen in the responses of single neurons in the striate cortex when the reticular system is stimulated (Bartlett & Doty, 1974).

It is not clear how the mesencephalic reticular activating system mediates its effects on the cortex. The recently defined major neurotransmitter pathways have been considered obvious candidates for this function, but no one system is clearly associated with arousal.

Acetylcholine, however, appears to have a more promising role in the mediation of arousal. Shute and Lewis (1967) described an ascending cholinergic activating system. Stimulation of the midbrain mesencephalic reticular activating system not only induces the arousal response but also increases the rate of acetylcholine release from the neocortex (Kanai & Szerb, 1965). Cholinergic agonists induce neocortical desynchronization, whereas antagonists abolish desynchronization (Bradley, 1968). Unfortunately, however, although cholinergic blockers such as atropine interfere with EEG desynchronization, they do not dramatically affect behavioral arousal. Vanderwolf and Robinson (1981) suggested that there may be two types of cholinergic input to the neocortex from the reticular formation, only one of which is sensitive to atropine. Therefore, the other cholinergic input may be responsible for behavioral arousal.

The mesencephalic reticular activating system probably projects to the cortex in a diffuse polysynaptic fashion (Scheibel & Scheibel, 1967) and thereby influences cortical processing of sensory stimuli. Steriade and Glenn (1982) found that the centralis lateralis and paracentralis thalamic nuclei also project to widespread cortical regions. Other neurons from these thalamic areas project to the caudate. Thirteen percent of neurons with cortical or caudate projections could be activated by mesencephalic reticular activating system stimulation.

There is, however, an alternative means whereby the mesencephalic reticular activating system may affect cortical processing of sensory stimuli. Sensory information that reaches the cortex is relayed through specific thalamic nuclei: somatosensory information is transmitted from the ventralis posterolateralis to the postcentral gyrus (Brodmann's areas 3, 1, 2), auditory information is transmitted through the medial geniculate nucleus to the supratemporal plane (Heschl's gyrus), and visual information is transmitted through the lateral geniculate nucleus to the occipital lobe (area 17). The thin reticular nucleus enveloping the thalamus projects to the thalamic relay nuclei and appears to inhibit thalamic relay to the cortex (Scheibel & Scheibel, 1966). The mesencephalic reticular activating system also projects to the reticular nucleus of the thalamus. High frequency mesencephalic reticular activating system stimulation or behavioral arousal inhibits the reticular nucleus and is thereby associated with enhanced thalamic transmission to the cerebral cortex (Singer, 1977). Therefore, unilateral lesions of mesencephalic reticular formation may induce neglect not only because the cortex is not prepared for processing sensory stimuli in the absence of mesencephalic reticular formation-mediated arousal, but also because the thalamic sensory relay nuclei are being inhibited by the thalamic reticular nucleus. Modality-specific association areas may be detecting stimulus novelty (comparing incoming stimuli with neuronal models) (Sokolov, 1963). When a stimulus is neither novel nor significant, corticofugal projections to the reticular nucleus may allow habituation to occur by selectively influencing thalamic relay. When a stimulus is novel or significant, corticofugal projections might inhibit the reticular nucleus and thereby allow the thalamus to relay additional sensory input. This capacity for selective control of sensory input is supported by a study revealing that stimulation of specific areas within the thalamic reticular nucleus related to specific thalamic nuclei (e.g., reticular nucleus lateral geniculate, reticular nucleus medial geniculate, or reticular nucleus ventrobasal complex) results in abolition of corresponding (visual, auditory, tactile) cortically evoked responses (Yingling & Skinner, 1977).

Modality-specific association areas converge on polymodal association areas. In the monkey, these are the prefrontal cortex (periarcuate, prearcuate, orbitofrontal) and both banks of the superior temporal sulcus (Pandya & Kuypers, 1969). Unimodal association areas may also project directly to the caudal inferior parietal lobule or, alternatively, may reach the inferior parietal lobule after a synapse in polymodal convergence areas (e.g., prefrontal cortex and both banks of the superior temporal sulcus) (Mesulam, Van Hoesen, Pandya & Geschwind, 1977). Polymodal convergence areas may subserve cross-modal associations and polymodal sensory synthesis. Polymodal sensory synthesis may also be important in "modeling" (detecting stimulus novelty) and detecting significance. In contrast to the unimodal association cortex that projects to specific parts of the rerticular nucleus of the thalamus and thereby gates sensory input in one modality, these multimodal convergence areas may have a more general inhibitory action on the reticular nucleus and provide further arousal after cortical analysis. These convergence areas also may project directly to the mesencephalic reticular formation, which may either induce a general state of arousal because of diffuse multisynaptic connections to the cortex, or may increase thalamic transmission via connections with the reticular nucleus as discussed, or both. Evidence that polymodal areas of cortex are important in arousal comes from neurophysiologic studies showing that stimulation of select cortical sites induces a generalized arousal response. These sites include the prearcuate region and both banks of the superior temporal sulcus (Segundo, Naquet & Buser, 1955). When similar sites are ablated there is EEG evidence of ipsilateral hypoarousal (Watson et al., 1978).

Although determination of stimulus novelty may be mediated by sensory association cortex, stimulus significance is determined in part by the needs of the organism (motivational state). Limbic system input into brain regions important for determining stimulus significance might provide information about biological needs. The frontal lobes might provide input about needs related to goals that are neither directly stimulus-dependent nor motivated by an immediate biological need.

Polymodal (e.g., superior temporal sulcus) and supramodal (inferior parietal lobule) areas have prominent limbic and frontal connections. The polymodal cortices project to the cingulate gyrus (a portion of the limbic system), and the cingulate gyrus projects to the inferior parietal lobule. The prefrontal cortex, superior temporal sulcus, and inferior parietal lobule have strong reciprocal connections. The posterior cingulate cortex (Brodmann's area 23) has more extensive connections with pomymodal association areas (prefrontal cortex, and exclusively for superior temporal sulcus) and the inferior parietal lobule than does the anterior cingulate cortex (Brodmann's area 24) (Vogt, Rosene & Pandya, 1979; Baleydier & Mauguière, 1980). These connections may provide an anatomic substrate by which motivational states (e.g., biological needs, sets, and long-term goals) may influence stimulus processing (Heilman & Watson, 1977; Heilman, 1979; Mesulam, 1981; Watson et al., 1981).

In the past decade, investigators have been able to study the physiologic function of specific areas of the nervous system by recording from single neurons in awake animals. In this experimental situation, the firing characteristics of individual neurons can be measured in relation to specific sensory stimulation or motor behavior. For example, a single neuron in the visual cortex may respond maximally to a contrast border in a specific region of the visual field, sometimes in a specific orientation. By varying the nature of the stimulus and by training the animal to respond in specific ways, the characteristic patterns of firing of individual neurons can be defined in terms of the optimal stimulus or response, or both, parameters that cause a maximal change in firing rate. In this fashion, investigators have defined the properties of neurons in the inferior parietal lobule (area 7) of the monkey (Lynch, 1980; Motter & Mountcastle, 1981; Mountcastle, Lynch, Georgopoulos, Sakata & Acuna, 1975; Mountcastle, Anderson & Motter, 1981; Goldberg & Robinson, 1977; Robinson, Goldberg & Stanton, 1978; Bushnell & Robinson, 1981). Unlike single cells in the primary sensory cortex, the activity of many neurons in the inferior parietal lobule correlates best with stimuli or responses of importance to the animal, whereas similar stimuli or responses that are unimportant are associated with either no change or a lesser change in neuronal activity. Several types of neurons have been described. Projection neurons are active when an animal reaches toward an object of significance in immediate extrapersonal space, for example, food (when the animal is hungry). Visual fixation neurons are active when the animal fixates on an object of interest within arm's reach. If the animal fixates on a target that it must attend (in order to perform for a reward) these neurons remain active until the animal is rewarded. Visual fixation cells are also active during smooth pursuit of moving visual stimuli, independent of direction. Most fixation cells are active only when the biologically significant target is placed in one half or one quarter of the visual field contralateral to the active cells. Visual tracking neurons discharge only when the animal's eyes are smoothly pursuing an object of interest that is within arm's reach and is moving in a given direction.

Saccade neurons have little activity during fixation or slow pursuit, but become active just before (75 msec) a saccade. Like fixation and tracking neurons, these cells become active with biologically significant stimuli: spontaneous saccades do not induce activity in these cells. Some saccade neurons become active with saccades in all directions, whereas others appear to be directionally dependent. Of these direction-dependent saccade neurons, most are more active before saccades toward contralateral hemispace. Mountcastle and co-workers (1981) have identified light-sensitive neurons (formerly called "visual space" neurons) of the monkey inferior parietal lobule having large response areas that unlike the previously described neurons do not include the fovea. During an act of attentive fixation, these neurons have an enhanced response to peripheral visual stimuli. These parietal neurons may play a part in the residual visual function of destriate primates and may be the projection target of the "second" visual system of retinocollicular origin. The facilitation of this system during foveal attention presumably allows the subject to be prepared to shift attention to novel, threatening, or aversive stimuli appearing in the periphery.

The inattention to contralateral stimuli in humans and monkeys after lesions in the temporoparietal regions, however, is not limited to the visual modality. Meaningful somatesthetic and auditory stimuli are also neglected. Hyvarinen and Poranen (1974) noted that the inferior parietal lobule also contained cells that exhibited enhanced activity when animals manipulated biologically significant objects. Some inferior parietal lobule cells seem to be activated by stimuli in both the visual and the somatesthetic modalities.

Bushnell et al. (1981) have emphasized the importance of the inferior parietal lobule in directed attention. They saw no evidence that the parietal lobule contained cells that programmed responses. This area is not simply a sensory association region; it acts in parallel with the retinostriate system and functions as an interface between attention to, reception of, and response to significant events in extrapersonal space. The retinostriate system is important for discriminating shape, color, and size when a subject concentrates on foveal work. The light-sensitive neurons of the inferior parietal lobule provide continual updating of the neural image of extrapersonal space and therefore allow for the attraction of attention toward events in peripheral vision. Fixation neurons maintain attention on a significant fixated object. Oculomotor neurons, such as the saccade neurons described, subserve the motor events of shifting visual attention. Projection and manipulation neurons are active during limb movements directed toward an object in extrapersonal space. Neurons in the inferior parietal lobule are movement-independent (Bushnell et al., 1981). They are probably not only subserving attention to extrapersonal space but also processing information to determine its emotional or motivational significance.

Based on these electrophysiological studies it would appear that area 7 when ablated in monkeys would induce neglect. Although combined area 7 and superior temporal sulcus lesions induce neglect (Heilman et al., 1970) and superior temporal sulcus lesions alone induce neglect, lesions restricted to area 7 do not induce neglect (Watson, Valenstein, Day & Heilman, 1985). The reason for the discrepancy between the physiologic and ablation studies remains unknown.

B. Hemispatial and Directional Akinesia

Hemispatial and directional akinesia is the inability to initiate an action in or toward contralateral hemispace. To determine whether hemispatial neglect was being induced by a hemispatial or directional akinesia or by hemispatial visual inattention, a hemispatial memory defect, or a gaze defect, we performed a spatial task not requiring vision (Heilman et al., 1983). Hemispatial neglect has already been demonstrated in a nonvisual modality (De Renzi et al., 1970), but because hemispatial inattention, memory defects, and exploratory defects may be multimodal, we also wanted a task that did not require sensory input from the neglected hemispace. We asked control subjects and patients with left-sided hemispatial neglect to close their eyes, point their right index finger to their sternum, and then point to an imaginary spot in space that was midline with their chest (Heilman et al., 1983). The patients with neglect pointed approximately 9 cm to the right of midline, whereas the controls pointed slightly to the left of midline. Because this task did not require visual or somesthetic input from left hemispace, the defective performance could not be attributed to hemispatial inattention or to a defect in hemispatial visual or somesthetic memory. Similarly, because the patient did not need to explore left hemispace, this defect could not be explained by an exploratory or gaze defect. The findings of this study are most compatible with the hemispatial and directional hypokinesia or representational map hypothesis (Bisiach, Luzzatti & Perani, 1979). This, of course, does not mean that patients with hemispatial neglect cannot also have hemispatial inattention, memory defects, and exploratory defects.

To learn whether hemispatial akinesia and hypokinesia have a directional component, we tested the ability of patients with left-sided hemispatial neglect to move a lever toward or away from the side of their lesion. These subjects needed more time to initiate movement toward the neglected left hemispace than toward right hemispace, thus demonstrating a directional hypokinesia. These asymmetries were not found in brain-damaged controls without neglect (Heilman et al., 1985a). We concluded that each hemisphere may not only be important in mediating attention and intention in contralateral hemispace, but may also be important in mediating intention toward contralateral hemispace (directional intention). The directional hypokinesia demonstrated in this study cannot be explained by the representational map hypothesis. Support for the hemispatial and directional hypokinesia hypothesis comes from the work of Rubens (1985), who used caloric stimulation. Cold water caloric stimulation of the left ear induces gaze to the left and past pointing toward the left. When he stimulated patients with left hemispatial neglect by irrigating their left ear with cold water, he found a dramatic improvement in the left hemispatial neglect. Although the cortical lesion induced a directional and hemispatial akinesia, the caloric-induced brainstem activation may have helped the subjects compensate for the directional akinesia.

Although these studies provide support for a directional or hemispatial or both forms of akinesia, they neither refute the postulate that inattention may be associated with hemispatial neglect nor refute the representational map hypothesis of Bisiach et al. (1979) that will be discussed in a later section. However, the gaze defects reported by De Renzi, Colombo, Faglioni and Gibertoni (1982) may also be a manifestation of a directional intentional deficit (hemispatial directional akinesia).

1. **Pathophysiology of Akinesia.** Attention and intention are probably closely linked functions, but we have found evidence that these processes may be dissociable. A patient with intermittent right parieto-occipital seizures was monitored by an EEG while he received right, left, and bilateral stimuli (Heilman & Howell, 1980). Interictally, he did not have inattention or extinction; however, while the seizure focus was active, he had left-sided extinction. When asked to bisect lines immediately after a seizure, he tended to bisect the line to the right of midline, which was suggestive of left hemispatial neglect. However, when asked to bisect lines during two focal seizures, the patient attempted to make a mark to the left of the entire sheet of paper. This case illustrates that attention to contralateral stimuli and intention to perform in the contralateral hemispatial field may be dissociable. The seizure-induced hyperintention to contralateral hemispace followed by postictal hemispatial neglect cannot be completely explained by the representational map hypothesis. However, the parietal lobe in humans may contain attentional cells, similar to those described by Lynch (1980), that may be important in helping to select significant stimuli; after a stimulus is detected these cells may activate intentional systems to prepare the individual for action. During a seizure when these cells are functioning abnormally, they may be unable to respond normally to stimuli, which may account for inattention and extinction. At the same time, however, these cells may be activating hemispheric intentional systems, thereby inducing a hyperintentional state.

As discussed, monkeys with dorsolateral frontal lobe lesions placed in the region of the arcuate sulcus fail to respond to stimuli presented on the side contralateral to the lesion (Kennard & Ectors, 1938; Welch & Stuteville, 1958). Similar defects can be observed in humans with dorsolateral and medial frontal lesions (Heilman & Valenstein, 1972; Meador et al., 1986b).

Suzuki and Azuma (1977) recorded frontal unit activity from monkeys trained to make a rapid key release when a light dimmed. They found neurons in the prefrontal and periarcuate area that increased their activity during the gaze period when the monkeys were preparing to release the key. These neurons were not influenced by stimulus features but depended on the behavioral state of the animal so that if the animal was not prepared to release the key and the key release was delayed, these cells showed weak activation. The cells therefore appeared to have intentional activity. Their activation was related to the activation of the motor system in preparation to respond to a meaningful stimulus. Unfortunately, hemispace was not a critical variable in these studies. Perhaps there are also cells whose activity is related to the hemispace of the intended action.

As we discussed, hemispatial neglect may be induced by a gaze defect that may be associated with directional akinesia. Unlike limb movements, lateral eye movement has been studied using hemispace as a critical variable. Since the work of Ferrier (1874), the frontal lobes have been thought to have a critical function in oculomotor control. Robinson and Fuchs (1969) electrically stimulated the frontal eye fields and produced saccades. Goldberg and Bushnell (1981) and Bruce and Goldberg (1985) have made recordings from cells in the frontal eye fields in awake monkeys trained to perform oculomotor tasks; three types of presaccadic neurons were found – visual, movement, and visual movement. Forty percent of the cells had activity in response to a visual stimulus and one half of these cells showed an enhanced response if the animals were going to make an eye movement and fixate on the stimulus in the receptive field. However, if there is a purposeful saccade without a visual target, these cells would not discharge. Twenty percent of presaccadic neurons discharged before purposeful saccades in the absence of visual stimuli, and these cells had weak or absent responses to visual stimuli. When the monkeys had prior knowledge of what saccade had to be made, 20% of movement and visual–movement cells showed anticipatory activity and responded before the onset of signal stimulus. Purposeful or intentional behavior induced maximal activation of these cells.

The saccade-related enhanced cellular responses recorded in the frontal eye fields are similar to those recorded from neurons in the superficial layers of superior colliculus (Goldberg & Wurtz, 1972). Superior collicular lesions may be associated with neglect (Sprague, 1966; Sprague & Meikle, 1965).

The connections of the frontal eye field are important in understanding its possible role in attention and intention. The periarcuate region has reciprocal connections with auditory, visual, and somesthetic association cortex (Chavis & Pandya, 1976). Evoked potential studies have confirmed this as an area of sensory convergence (Bignall & Imbert, 1969). The periarcuate region is also reciprocally connected with the superior temporal sulcus, another site of multimodal sensory convergence, and with the intraparietal sulcus, area of somatosensory and visual convergence. There are also connections with the prearcuate cortex. The periarcuate cortex has reciprocal connections with subcortical areas – the paralamellar portion of the dorsomedial nucleus and the adjacent centromedian parafascicularis (CMPF) complex (Kievet & Kuypers, 1977; Akert & von Monakow, 1980). Just as the periarcuate region is transitional in architecture between the agranular motor cortex and granular prefrontal cortex, the paralamellar–CMPF complex is situated between the medial thalamus, which projects to the granular cortex, and the lateral thalamus, which projects to the agranular cortex. Projections to the mesencephalic reticular formation (Kuypers & Lawrence, 1967) as well as nonreciprocal projections to caudate also exist. Last, the periarcuate region also receives input from the limbic system, mainly from the anterior cingulate gyrus (Baleydier & Mauguière, 1980).

The neocortical sensory association and sensory convergence area connections may provide the frontal lobe with information about external stimuli that may call the individual to action. The limbic connections (anterior cingulate gyrus) may provide the frontal lobe with motivational information. Connections with the mesencephalic reticular formation may be important in arousal.

As mentioned, the dorsolateral frontal lobe has extensive connections with CMPF, one of the "nonspecific" intralaminar thalamic nuclei. Nonsensory neglect has also been reported to occur in monkeys after CMPF lesions (Watson et al., 1978), and an akinetic state (akinetic mutism) accompanies bilateral CMPF lesions in humans. We have postulated a role for CMPF in behavior (Watson et al., 1981). This role is based on behavioral, anatomic, and physiologic evidence that the CMPF and periarcuate cortex are involved in mediating the response of an individual to meaningful stimuli.

Low frequency stimulation of CMPF activates the inhibitory reticular nucleus of the thalamus through a CMPF-frontocortical thalamic reticular nucleus system (Yingling & Skinner, 1975). This thalamic reticular nucleus activation elicits inhibitory postsynaptic potentials in the ventrolateral thalamic nucleus (VL), and thus blocks VL transmission to motor cortex (Purpura, 1970). Transmission in VL has been shown to be inversely proportional to thalamic reticular nucleus activity (Filion, Lamarre & Cordeau, 1971). VL projects to motor cortex, and may be important in activation of motor neurons.

High-frequency stimulation of the CMPF or MRF induces inhibition of the thalamic reticular nucleus, EEG desynchronization, and behavioral arousal (Moruzzi & Magoun, 1949; Yingling & Skinner, 1975). These manifestations elicited by high-frequency CMPF stimulation are predominantly mediated through the MRF-thalamic reticular nucleus system, since they are blocked by a lesion between the CMPF and MRF (Weinberger, Velasco & Lindsley, 1965). A lesion of the CMPF-frontocortical-thalamic reticular nucleus system also prevents inhibition of the thalamic reticular nucleus response to rapid CMPF stimulation, whereas rapid MRF stimulation during this blockade will continue to inhibit the thalamic reticular nucleus (Yingling & Skinner, 1977). This indicates that the thalamic reticular nucleus can be inhibited by either an MRF-thalamic reticular nucleus system or CMPF frontocortical-NR system and suggests that different types of behavior may be mediated independently by these systems.

Novel or noxious stimuli, or anticipation of a response to a meaningful stimulus, produces inhibition of the NR and a negative surface potential over the frontal cortex (Yingling & Skinner, 1977). This surface-negative potential occurs if a stimulus has acquired behavioral significance (Walter, 1973). Specifically, when a warning stimulus precedes a second stimulus that requires a motor response, a negative waveform appears between stimuli and has been called the "contingent negative variation" and is thought to reflect motivation, attention, or expectancy.

Skinner and Yingling (1976) demonstrated that in a conditional tone/shock expectancy paradigm, both the frontal negative wave and inhibition of the thalamic reticular nucleus elicited by the tone were abolished by blockade of the CMPF-frontocortical-thalamic reticular nucleus system, although primitive orienting persisted. Novel or noxious stimuli or rapid MRF stimulation continued to inhibit the thalamic reticular nucleus. In an operant task involving alternate bar press for reward, cooling of the CMPF-frontocortical-thalamic reticular nucleus sufficient to block cortical recruitment induced incorrect responses to the previously reinforced bar press (i.e., perseveration) (Skinner & Yingling, 1977). Further cooling caused the subject to cease responding altogether. These behavioral observations demonstrated that an appropriate response to a meaningful stimulus in an aroused subject requires an intact CMPF-frontocortical-thalamic reticular nucleus system, whereas primitive behavioral orienting elicited by novel or noxious stimuli depends on an intact MRF-thalamic reticular nucleus system. Responding to basic survival stimuli (e.g., food when hungry) may also depend on this system.

Extensive connections exist from dorsolateral prefrontal cortex to anterior cingulate gyrus and through hippocampal mechanisms to lateral hypothalamus and the MRF (Nauta, 1958). Single-cell recordings from these hypothalamic neurons reveal cells firing before a monkey's response to food but not firing to objects other than food (Rolls, Sanghera & Roper-Hall, 1979).

Skinner and Yingling (1977) interpreted their data as supporting a role for the MRF-thalamic reticular nucleus system in tonic arousal and the CMPF-frontocortical-thalamic reticular nucleus system in preparing the aroused organism to respond to a meaningful stimulus. The demonstration that intralaminar neurons have activity time-locked to either sensory or motor events, depending on the experimental condition, supports the pivotal role of this structure in sensory-motor integration (Schlag-Rey & Schlag, 1980).

The periarcuate region and thalamic zone around the lateral aspect of the dorsomedial nucleus and intralaminar nucleus share common anatomic features. In addition to reciprocal connections, there is a complex arc from periarcuate cortex, motor cortex, and CMPF to the neostriatum (caudate and putamen), from the neostriatum to globus pallidus, from globus pallidus to CMPF and ventrolateral thalamic nucleus, and from CMPF and ventrolateral thalamic nucleus back to premotor and motor cortex. Not surprisingly, lesions of structures within this loop, including arcuate gyrus (Watson et al., 1978), basal ganglia (Valenstein & Heilman, 1981), ventrolateral thalamic nucleus (Velasco & Velasco, 1979), CMPF (Watson et al., 1978), and premotor cortex (supplementary motor area) (Meador et al., 1986b) have induced a deficit in responding to multimodal sensory stimuli.

Rizzolatti, Matelli and Pavesi (1983) ablated area 6 (premotor area) in monkeys and found a reluctance to use the hand and mouth in response to stimuli that were close to the animal. Lesions of area 8 (frontal eye field) were associated with more neglect of far hemispace. The studies by Rizzolatti and co-workers suggest that far and near space may have different neuronal representations within the frontal lobes.

2. **Neuropharmacology of Akinesia.** Much evidence points to the importance of dopaminergic neurons in the mediation of aspects of intention. Marked defects of intention have long been known to be prominent in patients with Parkinson's disease, which is characterized pathologically by degeneration of ascending dopaminergic neurons. Although limb akinesia may accompany Parkinson's disease, directional and hemispatial akinesia does not commonly occur. In animals, however, unilateral lesions in these pathways cause unilateral neglect, including an inability to orient to contralateral stimuli.

Three related dopaminergic pathways have been defined. The nigrostriatal pathway originates in the pars compacta of the substantia nigra and projects to the neostriatum (caudate and putamen). The mesolimbic and mesocortical pathways originate principally in the ventral tegmental area of the midbrain, just medial to the substantia nigra, and terminate in the limbic areas of the basal forebrain (nucleus accumbens septi and olfactory tubercle) and the cerebral cortex (frontal and cingulate cortex), respectively (Ungerstedt, 1971; Lindvall, Björklund, Moore & Stenevi, 1974).

These dopaminergic fibers course through the lateral hypothalamus in the medial forebrain bundle. Bilateral lesions in the lateral hypothalamus of rats induce an akinetic state (Teitelbaum & Epstein, 1962). Unilateral lateral hypothalamus lesions cause unilateral neglect, and the rats transiently circle toward the side of their lesion. After they recover to the point where spontaneous activity appears symmetrical, they still tend to turn toward the damaged side when stimulated (e.g., by pinching their tails), and they fail to respond to sensory stimuli delivered to the contralateral side (Marshall, Turner & Teitelbaum 1971). There is considerable evidence that lateral hypothalamic lesions cause neglect by damaging dopaminergic fibers passing through the hypothalamus. Neglect occurs with 6-hydroxydopamine lesions of the lateral hypothalamus which damage dopaminergic fibers relatively selectively (Marshall, Richardson & Teitelbaum, 1974), but not with kainic acid lesions, which damaged cell bodies but not fibers of passage (Grossman, Dacey, Hallaris, Collier & Routtenberg, 1978). Unilateral damage to the same dopaminergic fibers closer to their site of origin in the midbrain also cause unilateral neglect (Ljungberg & Ungerstedt, 1976; Marshall, 1979). Conversely, unilateral stimulation in the area of ascending dopaminergic fibers (Arbuthnott & Ungerstedt, 1975) or of the striatum (see Pycock, 1980) causes animals to turn away from the side of stimulation, as if they are orienting to the opposite side. Normal rats without brain lesions spontaneously turn more in one direction. They also have an asymmetry in striatal dopamine concentration, and their direction of turning is generally away from the side of the brain with more dopamine (Glick, Crane, Jerussi, Fleisher & Green, 1975).

Lesions of the ascending dopaminergic pathways affect the areas of termination of these pathways in at least two ways. First, degeneration of dopamine-containing axons depletes these areas of dopamine. Marshall (1979) has shown that the neglect induced in rats by ventral tegmental 6-hydroxydopamine lesions is proportional to the depletion of dopamine in the neostriatum and, to a lesser extent, in the olfactory tubercle and nucleus accumbens. Second, the target areas attempt to compensate for the depletion of dopaminergic afferents by increasing their responsiveness to dopamine. This is mediated, at least in part, by an increase in the number of dopaminergic receptors (Heikkila, Shapiro & Duvoisin, 1981), which correlates with behavioral recovery from neglect (Neve, Kozlowski & Marshall, 1982).

The frontal neocortex and cingulate cortex receive dopaminergic input from the ventral tegmental area (Brown, Crane & Goldman, 1979), and the entire neocortex projects strongly to the striatum. This corticostriatal projection is at least partly glutaminergic (Divac, Fonnum & Storm-Mathisen, 1977). Stimulation in the motor or visual areas of the cortex in cats causes a release of dopamine in the striatum and substantia nigra (Nieoullon, Cheramy & Glowinski, 1978).

In rats unilateral ablation of the shoulder cortex, which is anatomically similar to the dorsolateral frontal lobe of monkeys, induces a defect in orienting to contralateral stimuli. This neglect improved when the rats were given apomorpine, a dopamine receptor agonist, but failed to improve when a dopamine-receptor-blocking agent, spiroperidol, was given before the apomorphine (Kanter, Corwin, Hashimoto, Watson, Valenstein & Heilman, 1985). These results demonstrate that neglect induced by cortical (frontal) lesions is associated with dysfunction of the dopaminergic system.

C. Pathophysiology of Hemispatial Memory Defect
  1. **Anterograde.** As discussed in the testing section, we have demonstrated that patients with hemispatial neglect may have an anterograde hemispatial memory defect that may even be used to explain defects in performance on tasks such as line bisection. In the line-bisection task, although our subjects saw the full extent of the line, the part of the line in the left hemispatial field may not have formed a stable memory trace. As the subject explored the remainder of the line, he "forgot" the side of the line

in the left hemispatial field.

The hemispatial memory defect may be related to an attentional defect. William James (1890) noted that "an object once attended will remain in the memory whilst one inattentively allowed to pass will leave no trace behind". The concept of arousal and its relation to learning and retention has received considerable attention (for a review see Eysenck, 1976). For example, direct relationships have been found between phasic skin conductance response amplitude during learning and accuracy of immediate and delayed recall (Stelmack, Plouffe & Winogron, 1983). As discussed in an earlier section, neglect may be associated with an attention arousal defect. Stimuli presented in the hemisapce contralateral to a hemispheric lesion that induces neglect may be associated with less arousal than stimuli present in the ipsilateral hemispace. Because these stimuli are poorly attended to and do not induce arousal, they may be poorly encoded. The attentional arousal systems discussed earlier may, therefore, also be important in hemispatial memory.

2. **Retrograde.** As discussed in the testing section, Bisiach and Luzzatti (1978) asked two patients with right hemisphere damage to describe from memory a familiar scene (the main square in Milan) from two different spatial perspectives, one facing the cathedral and the other facing away from the cathedral. Regardless of the patients' orientation, left-sided details were omitted. On the basis of these findings and from a second study (Bisiach et al., 1979), these investigators postulated that the mental representation of the environment is structured topographically and is mapped across the brain. That is, the mental picture of the environment may be split between the two hemispheres (like the projection of a real scene). With right hemisphere damage there is a representational disorder for the left half of this image. The representational map postulated by Bisiach may be hemispatially organized so that left hemispace is represented in the right hemisphere and right hemispace is represented in the left hemisphere.

There are at least three reasons why the mental image could not be envisioned: 1. The representation may have been destroyed. 2. The representation may have been intact but could not be activated so that an image was formed. 3. The image was formed, but it was not correctly explored or attended to (e.g., hemispatial inattention to an internal representation). If the representation is destroyed, attentional manipulation should not affect retrieval, but if patients with neglect have an activational or attentional deficit, attentional manipulation may affect retrieval. Meador, Loring, Bowers and Heilman (1986a) replicated Bisiach and Luzzatti's observations and also provided evidence that behavior manipulations could affect performance. It has been shown that when normal subjects are asked to recall objects in space, they move their eyes to the position that object occupied in space (Kahneman, 1973). Although it is unclear why normal subjects move their eyes during this type of recall task, having patients move their eyes toward neglected hemispace may aid recall because the eye movement induces hemispheric activation or helps direct attention. Meador et al. (1986a) asked a patient with left hemispatial neglect and defective left hemispatial recall to move his eyes to either right or left hemispace while recalling. The patient's recall of left-side detail was better when he was looking toward the left than toward the right. Although this finding provides evidence that hemispatial retrograde amnesia may be induced by an exploratory-attentional deficit or an activation deficit, it does not differentiate between these possibilities.

D. Hemispheric Asymmetries of Hemispatial Neglect

Many early investigators noted that the neglect syndrome was more often associated with right than with left hemisphere lesions (Brain, 1941; McFie, Piercy & Zangwill, 1950; Critchley, 1966). Although Battersby et al. (1956) thought this preponderance of right hemisphere-damaged patients was the result of a sampling artifact caused by the exclusion of aphasic subjects, more recent studies confirm that lesions in the right hemisphere more often induce neglect and that the neglect induced by right hemisphere lesions is also more severe (Albert, 1973; Gainotti, Messerli & Tissot, 1972; Costa, Vaughan, Hornitz & Ritter, 1969).

In previous sections, we have reviewed evidence that the neglect syndrome may result from interference with normal brain mechanisms for attention and intention. The substantial asymmetry in hemispheric lesions causing neglect suggests that these brain mechanisms are asymmetrically distributed; specifically, that the right hemisphere is in some way more important for these functions than the left. There is evidence from work in both brain-damaged and normal persons that this is indeed the case.

The attentional cells (or comparator neurons) found in the parietal lobe of monkeys by Lynch (1980) and Robinson et al. (1978) usually have contralateral receptive fields, but some of these neurons have bilateral receptive fields. That is, some responded to stimuli presented in the right or the left visual half fields. To account for a hemispheric asymmetry of attention in humans, we suggest that the temporoparietal regions of the human brain also have attentional or comparator neurons, but that the cells in the right hemisphere are more likely than cells in the left hemisphere to have bilateral receptive fields. Thus, cells in the left hemisphere would be activated predominantly by novel or significant stimuli in the right hemispace or hemifield, but cells in the right hemisphere would be activated by novel or significant stimuli in either visual field or either side of hemispace (or both). If this were the case, right hemisphere lesions would more often cause inattention than left hemisphere lesions. When the left hemisphere is damaged, the right can attend to ipsilateral stimuli, but the left hemisphere cannot attend to ipsilateral stimuli after right-side damage. If activation of comparator neurons induces local EEG desynchronization (Sokolov, 1963) and if the right hemisphere is dominant for attention, the right hemisphere should desynchronize to stimuli presented in either field, whereas the left hemisphere should desynchronize only to right-side stimuli. We therefore gave lateralized visual stimuli to normal subjects while recording the EEG. We found that the right parietal lobe desynchronized equally to right- or left-side stimuli while the left parietal lobe desynchronized mainly to right-side stimuli. These observations are compatible with the hypothesis that the right hemisphere (parietal lobe) dominates the comparator, or attentional, processes (Heilman & Van Den Abell, 1980). A similar phenomenon was demonstrated using positron emission tomography (Rosen, Gur, Reivich, Alavi & Greenberg, 1981) and regional cerebral blood flow (Prohovnik, Risberg, Hagstadius & Maximilian, 1981). These electrophysiologic and isotope studies provide evidence for a special role of the right hemisphere in attention and may also help explain why inattention is more often caused by right hemisphere lesions.

Kinsbourne (1970) proposed that language-induced left hemisphere activation makes neglect more evident with right than with left hemisphere lesions. Behavioral and psychophysiologic studies have shown that language may induce left hemisphere activation (Kinsbourne, 1974; Bowers & Heilman, 1976). Patients are usually tested for hemispatial neglect using verbal instructions, and not being aphasic, they usually think and communicate verbally. To test Kinsbourne's hypothesis, we (Heilman & Watson, 1978) presented patients with left-side hemispatial neglect a crossing-out task in which the subject was asked either to cross out words or to cross out lines oriented in a specific direction (e.g., horizontal). In the verbal condition the target words were mixed with two others that were foils, and in the visuospatial condition the target lines were mixed with other lines (e.g., vertical and diagonal) that acted as foils. All the subjects who were tested crossed out more lines and went farther to the left on the paper in the nonverbal condition than in the verbal condition, thereby giving partial support to Kinsbourne's hypothesis. However, this study could not be replicated (Caplan, 1985). As discussed, performance on the cancellation task is a function of factors such as the degree to which one must focus attention (Rapcsak et al., 1986), and these visuospatial and verbal tasks were not balanced for all these factors.

As we discussed in earlier sections, one mechanism proposed to explain hemispatial neglect is that it could be induced by a hemispatial akinesia. Patients with right hemisphere lesions more often have contralateral limb akinesia than patients with left hemisphere lesions (Coslett & Heilman, 1984). Hypokinesia, however, is not always limited to the contralateral extremities. Although patients with neglect from cerebral lesions confined to a single hemisphere have slower reaction times with the hand contralateral to a lesion than with the hand ipsilateral to a lesion, they also have slower reaction times using the hand ipsilateral to the lesion than do non-brain-damaged controls using the right hand (Heilman et al., 1985a).

Pribram and McGuinness (1975) used the term "activation" to define the physiologic readiness to respond to environmental stimuli. Because patients with right hemisphere lesions have been shown to have reduced behavioral evidence of activation, we have postulated that in humans the right hemisphere may dominate in mediating the activation process. That is, the left hemisphere prepares the right extremities for action and the right hemisphere prepares both extremities for action. Therefore, with left-side lesions, left-side limb akinesia is minimal, but with right-side lesions there is severe left-side limb akinesia. In addition, because the right hemisphere is more involved than the left hemisphere in activating the right extremities with right hemisphere lesions, there will be more ispilateral hypokinesia than with left hemisphere lesions.

If the right hemisphere dominates mediation of activation or intention (physiologic readiness to respond), normal subjects may show more activation (measured behaviorally by the reaction time) with warning stimuli delivered to the right hemisphere than with warning stimuli delivered to the left hemisphere. We therefore gave normal subjects lateralized warning stimuli followed by central reaction time stimuli (Heilman & Van Den Abell, 1979). Warning stimuli projected to the right hemisphere reduced reaction times of the right hand more than warning stimuli projected to the left hemisphere reduced left-hand reaction times. Warning stimuli projected to the right hemisphere reduced reaction times of the right hand even more than did warning stimuli projected directly to the left hemisphere. These results support the hypothesis that the right hemisphere dominates activation.

That hemispatial neglect occurs more often after right hemisphere lesions may also be explained by a similar phenomenon. Namely, the right hemisphere can physiologically prepare the extremities to work in (or toward) either right or left hemispace, but the left hemisphere can activate only the extremities to work in (or toward) right hemispace. Therefore, with left hemisphere lesions the right hemisphere can activate the extremities to work in (or toward) either hemispace, and hemispatial neglect is not a prominent symptom; however, with right hemisphere lesions the left hemisphere can activate only the extremities to work in (or toward) right hemispace; therefore, profound neglect occurs.

DeRenzi et al. (1982) noted more frequent conjugate gaze paresis after right than after left hemisphere lesions. A gaze paresis may be at least partly responsible for the exploratory defects associated with neglect. De Renzi et al. (1982) postulated that the oculomotor centers are more focal on the right than on the left. This asymmetry of gaze paresis, however, could also be explained by a mechanism similar to that which we postulated to explain asymmetries of motor (limb) hemispatial neglect. Although the right hemisphere may be able to direct the eyes toward either right or left, the left hemisphere may be able to direct the eyes only toward the right.

E. Recovery of Function

Hier, Mondock and Caplan (1983) and Morris, Mickel, Brooks, Swavely and Heilman (1986) demonstrated that hemispatial neglect improves in most patients over a period of time. However, procedures that induce fatigue (Fleet & Heilman, 1986) or difficult tasks that require focused attention (Rapcsak et al., 1986) may still elicit neglect. The mechanism underlying recovery is not completely understood. One hypothesis is that the undamaged hemisphere is involved in recovery. It may receive sensory information from the side of the body opposite the lesion, either through ipsilateral sensory pathways or from the damaged hemisphere through the corpus callosum. The uninjured hemisphere might also enhance the ability of the injured hemisphere to attend to contralateral sensory information and to initiate contralateral and hemispatial limb movements. If the uninjured hemisphere is processing sensorimotor information delivered from the injured hemisphere or enhancing the injured hemisphere's capacity to process sensorimotor activity, a corpus callosum transection should worsen symptoms of neglect. Crowne, Yeo and Russell (1981) showed that neglect from frontal arcuate gyrus ablations was worse when the corpus callosum was simultaneously transected than when the callosum was intact. Watson, Valenstein and Heilman (1984) showed that monkeys receiving a frontal arcuate gyrus ablation several months after a corpus callosum transection also had worse neglect than did animals with intact callosa. These results suggest that the hemispheres are mutually excitatory or compensatory through the corpus callosum.

Although callosal section worsened the severity of neglect, both groups of investigators found that it did not influence the rate of recovery. Subjects with callosal transections recovered completely. This fact suggests that recovery is an intrahemispheric process. If the intact hemisphere is responsible for the recovery, a callosal transection after recovery should not reinstate neglect. Crowne et al. (1981) did reinstate neglect in three animals undergoing corpus callosum transections after recovery from neglect induced by frontal arcuate gyrus lesions. However, extracallosal damage might be responsible for reinstating neglect. We have followed this order of lesions in one animal without inducing neglect. Furthermore, if the intact hemisphere is responsible for recovery in an animal with divided hemispheres, this recovery would have to be mediated through ipsilateral pathways. We have made a unilateral spinal cord lesion to interrupt ipsilateral sensory pathways in one of our recovered animals without reinstating neglect. Our observations suggest that recovery occurs within the injured hemisphere.

Hughlings Jackson (Taylor, 1932) postulated that certain functions could be mediated at several levels of the nervous system. Lesions of higher areas (e.g., cortex) would release phylogenetically more primitive areas that may take over the function of the lesioned cortical areas. Perhaps after cortical lesions disrupt the corticolimbic-reticular loop, a subcortical area takes over function and is responsible for mediating responses. Ideally, the area that substitutes for the damaged area must have similar characteristics to the areas that when damaged cause neglect. It must have multimodal afferent input and must not only have reticular connections but also be capable of inducing activation with stimulation. Last, ablation of this area should induce the neglect syndrome, even if transient. The superior colliculus receives not only optic fibers but also somesthetic projections from the spinotectal tract (Sprague & Meikle, 1965) and fibers from the medial and lateral lemnisci and from the inferior colliculus (Truex & Carpenter, 1964). Sprague and Meikle believe that the colliculus is more than a reflex center controlling eye movements. They think it is a sensory integrative center. Tectoreticular fibers project to the mesencephalic reticular formation, and ipsilateral fibers are more abundant than are contralateral fibers (Truex & Carpenter, 1964). Stimulation of the colliculus (like stimulation of the arcuate gyrus or the inferior parietal lobe) induces an arousal response (Jefferson, 1958). Unilateral lesions of the superior colliculus induce a multimodal unilateral neglect syndrome, and combined cortical-collicular lesions induce a more profound disturbance, regardless of the order of removal (Sprague & Meikle, 1965). Therefore, in the absence of the corticoreticular loop, a collicular-reticular loop or a similar subcortical system might take over function.

Unlike cortical lesions in monkeys, some subcortical lesions of ascending dopamine projections in rats induce permanent neglect (Marshall, 1982). The severity and persistence of neglect induced by 6-hydroxydopamine injections into the ventral tegmental area of rats is correlated with the amount of striatal dopamine depletion: those with more than 95% loss of striatal dopamine have a permanent deficit. The extent of recovery of these animals is also directly related to the quantity of neostriatal dopamine present when the animal is killed. Nonrecovered rats show promounced contralateral turning after injections of apomorphine, a dopamine receptor stimulant. Recovered rats given methyl-p-tyrosine, a catecholamine synthesis inhibitor, or spiroperidol, a dopamine-receptor blocking agent, had their deficits reappear. These results suggest that restoration of dopaminergic activity in dopamine-depleted rats is sufficient to reinstate orientation (Marshall, 1979). Further investigation of these findings indicates that a proliferation of dopamine receptors may contribute to pharmacological supersensitivity and recovery of function (Neve et al., 1982). Implanting dopaminergic neurons from the ventral tegmental area of fetal rats adjacent to the striatum ipsilateral to the lesion will induce recovery in rats with unilateral neglect from a 6-hydroxydopamine lesion in the ascending dopamine tracts (Dunnett, Björklund, Stenevi & Iversen, 1981). This recovery is related to growth of dopamine-containing neurons into the partially denervated striatum.

(^{14}C)-2-deoxy-D-glucose (2-DG) incorporation permits a measure of metabolic activity. In rats with 6-OHDA lesions of the ventral tegmental areas that had shown no recovery from neglect, the uptake of (^{14}C)-2-DG into the neostriatum, nucleus accumbens septi, olfactory tubercle, and central amygdaloid nucleus was significantly less on the denervated side than on the normal side. Rats recovering by 6 weeks showed equivalent (^{14}C)-2-DG uptake in the neostriatum and central amygdaloid nucleus on the two sides. Recovery is therefore associated with normalization of neostriatal metabolic activity (Kozlowski & Marshall, 1981).

Similar results have been found in monkeys recovering from frontal arcuate gyrus-induced neglect (Deuel, Collins, Dunlop & Caston, 1979). Animals with neglect showed depression of (^{14}C)-2-DG in ipsilateral subcortical structures, including the thalamus and basal ganglia. Recovery from neglect occurred concomitantly with a   reappearance of symmetrical metabolic activity.

Cortical lesions in animals may induce only transient neglect because these lesions affect only a small portion of a critical neurotransmitter system. Critically placed small subcortical lesions, conversely, can virtually destroy all of a transmitter system, and can cause a permanent syndrome.

Recovery from cortically induced neglect might also depend on the influence of cortical lesions on subcortical structures. It is likely that just as certain homologous cortical structures are thought to be mutually inhibitory through the corpus callosum, certain pairs of subcortical structures may also be mutually inhibitory. For example, Watson et al. (1984) found that a prior corpus callosal lesion worsened neglect from a frontal arcuate lesion. Although this deterioration could be explained by loss of an excitatory or compensatory influence from the normal frontal arcuate region on the damaged hemisphere, it could also be interpreted as a loss of excitation from cortex on a subcortical structure, such as the basal ganglia, that in turn inhibits the contralateral basal ganglia. The latter thought is supported by a study showing that anterior callosal section in rats enhances the normal striatal dopamine asymmetry and increases amphetamine-induced turning (Glick et al., 1975). In addition, Sprague (1966) showed that the loss of visually guided behavior in the field contralateral to occipitotemporal lesions in cats could be restored by a contralateral superior colliculus removal or by transection of the collicular commissure. The only way to explain this observation is to assume that the superior colliculi are mutually inhibitory.

The two hemispheres are clearly cooperating in our daily activities. However, it seems that recovery from a central nervous system insult can occur within the injured hemisphere. For the neglect syndrome, this may be secondary to alteration in dopamine systems.

F. Treatment

Because alterations of the dopamine system may be partly responsible for the symptoms of neglect and recovery from neglect, we decided to learn whether we could improve frontal lesion-induced neglect in rats by using the dopamine agonist apomorphine (Kanter et al., 1985). Because the animals showed a dramatic improvement, we gave bromocriptine to a patient with hemispatial neglect. This patient improved with medication and had a relapse after the medication was withdrawn. The results suggest that improvement may have been related to the medicine and not to the natural history of the disease (Fleet, Watson, Valenstein & Heilman, 1986). Further trials are currently under way.

In addition, as previously discussed, Rubens (1985) improved neglect in man by stimulating the labyrinth. This finding suggests that although not practical for long-term care, labyrinthine or brainstem stimulation may be used in the future to treat these patients.

In addition to drug and physiologic treatments, several things can be done to manage the symptoms of the neglect syndrome. Patients with neglect should have their bed placed so that their "good" side faces the area where interpersonal actions are most likely to take place. When they must interact with people, these interactions should take place on the good side. When patients go home, the environment should be adjusted in a similar manner. Fleet and Heilman (1986) have demonstrated that hemispatial neglect may become worse with repeated trials. However, knowledge of results (i.e., feedback to the patient) that induces increased arousal and effort may reverse this fatigue effect. During the acute stages when patients have anosognosia, rehabilitation is difficult, but in most patients this symptom is transient. In addition, because patients with neglect remain inattentive to their left side and in general are poorly motivated, training extension and rehabilitation efforts are laborious and in many cases nonrewarding. Diller and Weinberg (1977) were however able to train patients with neglect to look to their neglected side, but unfortunately it has not been shown that the patients can generalize this training to non-task situations.

References

Akert, K. & von Monakow, K.H. Relationships of precentral, premotor, and prefrontal cortex to the mediodorsal and intralaminar nuclei of the monkey thalamus. Acta Neurobiologiae Experimentalis (Warszawa), 1980, 40, 7-25.

Albert, M.L. A simple test of visual neglect. Neurology, 1973, 23, 658-664.

Anzola, G.P., Bertoloni, G., Buchtel, H.A. & Rizzolatti, G. Spatial compatibility and anatomical factors in simple and choice reaction time. Neuropsychologia, 1977, 15, 295-302.

Arbuthnott, G.W. & Ungerstedt, U. Turning behavior induced by electrical stimulation of the nigro-striatal system of the rat. Experimental Neurology, 1975, 47, 162-172.

Baleydier, C. & Mauguière, F. The duality of the cingulate gyrus in monkey -neuroanatomical study and functional hypothesis. Brain, 1980, 103, 525-554.

Bartlett, J.R. & Doty, R.W. Influence of mesencephalic stimulation on unit activity in striate cortex of squirrel monkey. Journal of Neurophysiology, 1974, 37, 642-652.

Battersby, W.S., Bender, M.B. & Pollack, M. Unilateral "spatial agnosia" ("inattention") in patients with cerebral lesions. Brain, 1956, 79, 68-93.

Bender, M.B. & Furlow, C.T. Phenomenon of visual extinction and binocular rivalry mechanism. Transactions of the American Neurological Association, 1944, 70, 87-93.

Bender, M.B. & Furlow, C.T. Phenomenon of visual extinction on homonymous fields and psychological principles involved. Archives of Neurology and Psychiatry, 1945, 53, 29-33.

Benson, F. & Geschwind, N. The alexias . In P.J. Vinken & G.W. Bruyn (Eds.), Handbook of Clinical Neurology, Vol. 4. Amsterdam: North Holland, 1969, pp. 112-140.

Benton, A., Levin, H. & Varney, N. Tactile perception of directions in normal subjects. Neurology, 1973, 23, 1248-1250.

Berlucchi, G., Crea, F., DiStefano, M., Tassinari, G. Influence of spatial stimulus-response compatibility on reaction time of ipsilateral and contralateral hands to lateralized light stimuli. Journal of Experimental Psychology (Human Perception and Performance), 1977, 3, 505-517.

Berlucchi, G., Heron, W., Hyman, R. Rizzolatti, G. & Umilta, C. Simple reaction times of ipsilateral and contralateral hands to lateralized visual stimuli. Brain, 1971, 94, 419-430.

Bignall, K.E. & Imbert, M. Polysensory and cortico-cortical projections to frontal lobe of squirrel and rhesus monkey. Electroencephalography and Clinical Neurophysiology, 1969, 26, 206-215.

Bisiach, E. & Luzzatti, C. Unilateral neglect of representational space. Cortex, 1978, 14, 129-133.

Bisiach, E., Luzzatti, C. & Perani, D. Unilateral neglect, representational schema and consciousness. Brain, 1979, 102, 609-618.

Bowers, D. & Heilman, K.M. Material-specific hemispheric arousal.

Neuropsychologia, 1976, 14, 123-127.
Bowers, D. & Heilman, K.M. Pseudoneglect: effects of hemispace on tactile line bisection task. Neuropsychologia, 1980, 18, 491-498.
Bowers, D., Heilman, K.M. & Van Den Abell, T. Hemispace-VHF compatibility. Neuropsychologia, 1981, 19, 757-765.
Bradley, P.B. The effect of atropine and related drugs on the EEG and behavior. Progress in Brain Research, 1968, 28, 3-13.
Bradshaw, J., Nettleton, N., Nathan, G. & Wilson, L. Head and body space to left and right, front and rear. II. Visuotactile and kinesthetic studies and left-side underestimation. Neuropsychologia, 1983, 21, 475-486.
Brain, W.R. Visual disorientation with special reference to lesions of the right cerebral hemisphere. Brain, 1941, 64, 244-271.
Brown, R.M., Crane, A.M. & Goldman, P.S. Regional distribution of monoamines in the cerebral cortex and subcortical structures of the rhesus monkey: concentrations and in vivo synthesis rates. Brain Research, 1979, 168, 133-150.
Bruce, C.J. & Goldberg, M.E. Primate frontal eye fields. I. Single neurons discharging before saccades. Journal of Neurophysiology, 1985, 53, 603-635.
Bushnell, M.C., Goldberg, M.E. & Robinson, D.L. Behavioral enhancement of visual responses in monkey cerebral cortex: I. Modulation in posterior parietal cortex related to selected visual attention. Journal of Neurophysiology, 1981, 46, 755-772.
Caplan, B. Stimulus effects in unilateral neglect. Cortex, 1985, 21, 69-80.
Chavis, D.A. & Pandya, D.N. Further observations on corticofrontal connections in the rhesus monkey. Brain Research, 1976, 117, 369-386.
Chédru, F., Leblanc, M. & Lhermitte, F. Visual searching in normal and brain-damaged subjects. Cortex, 1973, 9, 94-111.
Cimino, C. & Bowers, D. Effects of hemispace on two tactile spatial tasks. Presented at meeting of International Neuropsychology Society, Denver, Colorado, February, 1986.
Coslett, H.B. & Heilman, K.M. Hemihypokinesia following right hemisphere stroke. Neurology, 1984, 34 (suppl 1), 190.
Coslett, H.B., Bowers, D., Fitzpatrick, E., Haws, B. & Heilman, K.M. Hemispatial hypokinesia and hemisensory inattention in neglect. (Abstract) Neurology, 1986, 36 (suppl 1), 344.
Costa, L.D., Vaughan, H.G., Horwitz, M. & Ritter, W. Patterns of behavior deficit associated with visual spatial neglect. Cortex, 1969, 5, 242-263.
Craft, J. & Simon, J. Processing symbolic information from a visual display: interference from an irrelevant directional clue. Journal of Experimental Psychology, 1970, 83, 415-420.
Critchley, M. The Parietal Lobes. New York: Hafner, 1966.
Crowne, D.P., Yeo, C.H. & Russell, I.S. The effects of unilateral frontal eye field lesions in the monkey: visual-motor guidance and avoidance behavior. Behavioral Brain Research, 1981, 2, 165-185.
Denny-Brown, D. & Banker, B.Q. Amorphosynthesis from left parietal lesions. Archives of Neurology and Psychiatry, 1954, 71, 302-313.
De Renzi, E., Colombo, A., Faglioni, P. & Gibertoni, M. Conjugate gaze paresis in stroke patients with unilateral damage. Archives of Neurology, 1982, 39, 482-486.
De Renzi, E., Faglioni, P. & Scotti, G. Hemispheric contribution to the exploration of space through the visual and tactile modality. Cortex, 1970, 6, 191-203.
Deuel, R.K., Collins, R.C., Dunlop, N. & Caston, T.V. Recovery from unilateral neglect: behavioral and functional anatomic correlations in

monkeys. Society of Neuroscience (Abstr), 1979, 5, 624.
Diller, L. & Weinberg, J. Hemi-inattention in rehabilitation: the evolution
    of a rational remediation program. In E.A. Weinstein and R.P. Friedland
    (Eds.), Advances in Neurology, vol. 18. New York: Raven Press, 1977, pp.
    63-80.
Divac, I., Fonnum, F. & Storm-Mathisen, J. High affinity uptake of glutamate
    in terminals of corticostriatal axons. Nature (Lond), 1977, 266,
    377-378.
Dunnett, S.B., Björklund, A., Stenevi, U. & Iversen, S.D. Behavioral
    recovery following transplantation of substantia nigra in rats
    subjected to 6-OHDA lesions of the nigrostriatal pathway. I. Unilateral
    lesions. Brain Research, 1981, 215, 147-161.
Eysenck, M.W. Arousal, learning and memory. Psychological Bulletin, 1976,
    83, 389-404.
Ferrier, D. The localization of function in the brain. Proceedings of the
    Royal Society (London), 1874, Ser B22, 229-232.
Filion, M., Lamarre, Y. & Cordeau, J.P. Neuronal discharges of the
    ventrolateral nucleus of the thalamus during sleep and wakefulness in
    the cat. II. Evoked activity. Experimental Brain Research, 1971, 12,
    499-508.
Fisher, M. Left hemiplegia and motor impersistance. Journal of Nervous and
    Mental Diseases, 1956, 123, 201-218.
Fleet, W.S. & Heilman, K.M. The fatigue effect in hemispatial neglect.
    (Abstract) Neurology, 1986, 36 (suppl 1), 258.
Fleet, W.S., Watson, R.T., Valenstein, E. & Heilman, K.M. Dopamine agonist
    therapy for neglect in humans. (Abstract) Neurology, 1986, 36 (suppl 1),
    347.
Gainotti, G., Messerli, P. & Tissot, R. Qualitative analysis of unilateral
    spatial neglect in relation to laterality of cerebral lesions. Journal
    of Neurology, Neurosurgery and Psychiatry, 1972, 35, 545-550.
Glick, S.D., Crane, A.M., Jerussi, T.P., Fleisher, L.N. & Green, J.P.
    Functional and neurochemical correlates of potentiation of striatal
    asymmetry by callosal section. Nature, 1975, 254, 616-617.
Goldberg, M.E. & Bushnell, M.C. Behavioral enchancement of visual responses
    in monkey cerebral cortex. II. Modulation in frontal eye fields
    specifically related to saccades. Journal of Neurophysiology, 1981, 46,
    773-787.
Golberg, M.E. & Robinson, D.C. Visual responses of neurons in monkey inferior
    parietal lobule. The physiologic substrate of attention and neglect.
    (Abstract) Neurology, 1977, 27, 350.
Goldberg, M.E. & Wurtz, R.H. Activity of superior colliculus in behaving
    monkey. I. Visual receptive fields of single neurons. Journal of
    Neurophysiology, 1972, 35, 542-559.
Goldstein, L. & Lackner, J. Sideways looking at dichotic listening. Journal
    of the Acoustical Society of America, 1974, 55 (suppl), S10.
Grossman, S.P., Dacey, D., Halaris, A.E., Collier, T. & Routtenberg, A.
    Aphagia and adipsia after preferential destruction of nerve cell bodies
    in hypothalamus. Science, 1978, 202, 537-539.
Heikkila, R.E., Shapiro, B.S. & Duvoisin, R.C. The relationship between loss
    of dopamine nerve terminals, striatal (^{3}H)spiroperidol binding and
    rotational behavior in unilaterally 6-hydroxydopamine-lesioned rats.
    Brain Research, 1981, 211, 285-292.
Heilman, K.M. Neglect and related disorders. In K.M. Heilman and E.
    Valenstein (Eds.), Clinical Neuropsychology. New York: Oxford
    University Press, 1979, pp. 268-307.
Heilman, K.M., Bowers, D., Coslett, H.B., Whelan, H. & Watson, R.T.

Directional hypokinesia: prolonged reaction times for leftward movements in patients with right hemisphere lesions and neglect. Neurology, 1985, 35, 855–859.

Heilman, K.M., Bowers, D., Valenstein, E. & Watson, R.T. Performance on hemispatial pointing task by patients with neglect syndrome. Neurology, 1983, 33, 661–664.

Heilman, K.M. & Howell, G.J. Seizure-induced neglect. Journal of Neurology Neurosurgery and Psychiatry, 1980, 43, 1035–1040.

Heilman, K.M., Pandya, D.N. & Geschwind, N. Trimodal inattention following parietal lobe ablations. Transactions of the American Neurological Association, 1970, 95, 259–261.

Heilman, K.M. & Valenstein, E. Fontal lobe neglect in man. Neurology, 1972, 22, 660–664.

Heilman, K.M. & Valenstein, E. Mechanisms underlying hemispatial neglect. Annals of Neurology, 1979, 5, 166–170.

Heilman, K.M., Valenstein, E. & Watson, R.T. The neglect syndrome. In P.J. Vinken and G.W. Bruyn (Eds.), Handbook of Clinical Neurology, Vol. I. Amsterdam: North Holland Publishing Company, 1985, pp. 153–183.

Heilman, K.M., Valenstein, E. & Watson, R.T. Neglect. In A.A. Asbury, G.M. McKhann & W.I. McDonald (Eds.), Diseases of the Nervous System. Philadelphia: Ardmore Books (W.B. Saunders Co) (in press).

Heilman, K.M. & Van Den Abell T. Right hemispheric dominance for mediating cerebral activation. Neuropsychologia, 1979, 17, 315–321.

Heilman, K.M. & Van Den Abell, T. Right hemisphere dominance for attention: the mechanism underlying hemispheric asymmetries of inattention (neglect). Neurology, 1980, 30, 327–330.

Heilman, K.M. & Watson, R.T. Mechanisms underlying the unilateral neglect syndrome. In E.A. Weinstein and R.P. Friedland (Eds.), Advances in Neurology, Vol. 18, 1977, pp. 93–106.

Heilman, K.M. & Watson, R.T. Changes in the symptoms of neglect induced by changing task strategy. Archives of Neurology, 1978, 35, 47–49.

Heilman, K.M., Watson, R.T. & Schulman, H.M. A unilateral memory defect. Journal of Neurology, Neurosurgery and Psychiatry, 1974, 37, 790–793.

Hier, D.B., Mondock, J. & Caplan, L.R. Recovery of behavioral abnormalities after right hemisphere stroke. Neurology, 1983, 33, 345–350.

Howes, D. & Boller, F. Simple reaction time: Evidence for focal impairment from lesions of the right hemisphere. Brain, 1975, 98, 317–332.

Hyvärinen, J. & Poranen, A. Function of the parietal associative area 7 as revealed from cellular discharge in alert monkeys. Brain, 1974, 97, 673–692.

James, W. The Principles of Psychology, vol. 2. New York; Holt, 1890.

Jefferson, G. Substrates for integrative patterns in the reticular core. In M.E. Scheibel and A.B. Scheibel (Eds.), Reticular Formation. Boston: Little Brown, 1958.

Kahneman, D. Eye Movement Attention and Effort. Englewood Cliffs, NJ: Prentice Hall, 1973.

Kanai, T. & Szerb, J.C. Mesencephalic reticular activating system and cortical acetylcholine output. Nature (Lond), 1965, 205, 80–82.

Kanter, S.L., Corwin, J.V., Hashimoto, A., Watson, R.T., Valenstein, E. & Heilman, K.M. Dopamine agonist treatment of cortical neglect in rats. (Abstract) Neurology, 1985, 35 (suppl 1), 179.

Kennard, M.A. & Ectors, L. Forced circling in monkeys following lesions of the frontal lobes. Journal of Neurophysiology, 1938, 1, 45–54.

Kertesz, A., Nicholson, I., Cancelliere, A., Kassa, K. & Black, S.E. Motor impersistance: a right-hemisphere syndrome. Neurology, 1985, 35, 662–666.

Kievit, J. & Kuypers, H.G.J.M. Organization of the thalamo-cortical connexions to the frontal lobe in the rhesus monkey. Experimental Brain Research, 1977, 29, 299-322.

Kinsbourne, M. A model for the mechanism of unilateral neglect of space. (Abstract) Transactions of the American Neurological Association, 1970, 95, 143.

Kinsbourne, M. Direction of gaze and distribution of cerebral thought processes. Neuropsychologia, 1974, 12, 270-281.

Klein, D., Moscovitch, M. & Vigno, C. Attentional mechanism and perceptual asymmetries in tachistocopic recognition of words and faces. Neuropsychologia, 1976, 14, 55-66.

Kozlowski, M.R. & Marshall, J.F. Plasticity of neostriatal metabolic activity and behavioral recovery from nigrostriatal injury. Experimental Neurology, 1981, 74, 313-323.

Kuypers, H.G.J.M. & Lawrence, D.G. Cortical projections to the red nucleus and the brain stem in the rhesus monkey. Brain Research, 1967, 4, 151-188.

Levy, J., Heller, W., Banich, M. & Barton, L. Asymmetry of perception in free viewing of chimeric faces. Brain and Cognition, 1983, 2, 404-419.

Levy, J. & Kuech, L. A right hemispatial field advantage on a verbal free-vision task. Brain and Cognition (in press).

Lhermitte, F., Turell, E., LeBrigand, D. & Chain, F. Unilateral visual neglect and wave P300. Archives of Neurology, 1985, 42, 567-573.

Lindvall, O., Björklund, A., Moore, R.Y. & Stenevi, U. Mesencephalic dopamine neurons projecting to neocortex. Brain Research, 1974, 81, 325-331.

Ljungberg, T. & Ungerstedt, U. Sensory inattention produced by 6-hydroxydopamine-induced degeneration of ascending dopamine neurons in the brain. Experimental Neurology, 1976, 53, 585-600.

Lynch, J.C. The functional organization of posterior parietal association cortex. Behavioral Brain Science, 1980, 3, 485-534.

Marshall, J.F. Somatosensory inattention after dopamine-deleting intracerebral 6-OHDA injections: spontaneous recovery and pharmacological control. Brain Research, 1979, 177, 311-324.

Marshall, J.F. Neurochemistry of attention and attentional disorders. Annual course 214, Behavioral Neurology. Presented at the American Academy of Neurology, April 27, 1982.

Marshall, J.F., Richardson, J.S. & Teitelbaum, P. Nigrostriatal bundle damage and the lateral hypothalamic syndrome. Journal of Comparative Physiological Psycholollgy, 1974, 87, 808-830.

Marshall, J.F., Turner, B.H. & Teitelbaum, P. Sensory neglect produced by lateral hypothalamic damage. Science, 1971, 174, 523-525.

McFie, J., Piercy, M.F. & Zangwill, O.L. Visual-spatial agnosia associated with lesions of the right cerebral hemisphere. Brain, 1950, 73, 167-190.

Meador, K.J., Loring, D.W., Bowers, D. & Heilman, K.M. Remote memory and neglect syndrome. (Abstract) Neurology, 1986a, 36 (Suppl 1), 170.

Meador, K.J., Watson, R.T., Bowers, D., Heilman, K.M. Hypometria with hemispatial and limb-motor neglect. Brain, 1986b, 109, 293-305.

Mesulam, M.M. A cortical network for directed attention and unilateral neglect. Annals of Neurology, 1981, 10, 309-325.

Mesulam, M., Van Hoesen, G.W., Pandya, D.N. & Geschwind, N. Limbic and sensory connections of the inferior parietal lobule (area PG) in the rhesus monkey: a study with a new method for horseradish peroxidase histochemistry. Brain Research, 1977, 136, 393-414.

Morris, R., Mickel, S., Brooks, M., Swavely, S. & Heilman, K. Recovery from neglect. (Abstract) Journal of Clinical and Experimental

Neuropsychology, 1986, 7, 618.
Moruzzi, G. & Magoun, H.W. Brainstem reticular formation and activation of the EEG. Electroencephalography and Clinical Neurophysiology, 1949, 1, 455-473.
Motter, B.C. & Mountcastle, V.B. The functional properties of the light sensitive neurons of the posterior parietal cortex studied in waking monkeys: foveal sparing and opponent vector organization. Journal of Neuroscience, 1981, 1, 3-26.
Mountcastle, V.B., Anderson, R.A. & Motter, B.C. The influence of attentive fixation upon the excitability of the light sensitive neurons of the posterior parietal cortex. Journal of Neuroscience, 1981, 1, 1218-1245.
Mountcastle, V.B., Lynch, J.C., Georgopoulos, A., Sakata, H. & Acuna, C. Posterior parietal association cortex of the monkey: command function for operations within extrapersonal space. Journal of Neurophysiology, 1975, 38, 871-908.
Nauta, W.J.H. Hippocampal projections and related neural pathways to the midbrain in cat. Brain, 1958, 81, 319-339.
Neve, K.A., Kozlowski, M.R. & Marshall, J.F. Plasticity of neostriatal dopamine receptors after nigrostriatal injury: relationship to recovery of sensorimotor functions and behavioral supersensitivity. Brain Research, 1982, 244, 33-44.
Nicoletti, R., Anzola, G., Luppino, G., Rizzolatti, G. & Umilta, C. Spatial compatibility effects on the same side of body midline. Journal of Experimental Psychology (Human Perception), 1982, 8, 664-673.
Nieoullon, A., Cheramy, A. & Glowinski, J. Release of dopamine evoked by electrical stimulation of the motor and visual areas of the cerebral cortex in both caudate nuclei and in the substantia nigra in the cat. Brain Research, 1978, 15, 69-83.
Oscar-Berman, M., Rehbein, M., Porfeit, A. & Goodglass, H. Dichaptic hand-order effects with verbal and nonverbal tactile stimuli. Brain and Language, 1978, 6, 323-333.
Pandya, D.M. & Kuypers, H.G.J.M. Cortico-cortical connections in the rhesus monkey. Brain Research, 1969, 13, 13-36.
Poppelreuter, W.L. Die psychischen Schadigungen durch Kopfschuss im Kriege 1914-1916: die Storungen der niederen und hoheren Leistungen durch Verletzungen des Oksipitalhirns, Vol. 1. Leipzig: Leopold Voss, 1917. Referred to by M. Critchley, Brain, 1949, 72, 540.
Pribram, K.H. & McGuinness, D. Arousal, activation and effort in the control of attention. Psychological Review, 1975, 182, 116-149.
Prohovnik, I., Risberg, J., Hagstadius, S. & Maximilian, V. Cortical activity during unilateral tactile stimulation: a regional cerebral blood flow study. Presented at the meeting of the International Neuropsychological Society, Atlanta, Georgia, February, 1981.
Purpura, D.P. Operations and processes in thalamic and synaptically related neural subsystems. In F.O. Schmitt (Ed.), The Neurosciences, Second Study Program. New York: Rockefeller University Press, 1970, pp. 458-470.
Pycock, C.J. Turning behavior in animals. Neuroscience, 1980, 5, 461-514.
Rapcsak, S.Z., Fleet, W.S. & Heilman, K.M. Selective attention in hemispatial neglect. (Abstract) Neurology, 1986, 36 (Suppl 1), 262.
Reeves A.G. & Hagamen, W.D. Behavioral and EEG asymmetry following unilateral lesions of the forebrain and midbrain of cats. Electroencephalography and Clinical Neurophysiology, 1971, 30, 83-86.
Rizzolatti, G., Matelli, M. & Pavesi, G. Deficits in attention and movement following removal of postarcuate (area 6) and prearcuate (area 8) cortex in Macaque monkeys. Brain, 1983, 106, 655-674.

Robinson, D.A. & Fuchs, A.F. Eye movements evoked by stimulation of frontal
    eye fields. Journal of Neurophysiology, 1969, 32, 637-648.
Robinson, D.L., Goldberg, M.E. & Stanton, G.B. Parietal association cortex
    in the primate: sensory mechanisms and behavioral modulations. Journal
    of Neurophysiology, 1978, 41, 910-932.
Rolls, E.T., Sanghera, M.K. & Roper-Hall, A. The latency of activation of
    neurons in the lateral hypothalamus and substantia innominata during
    feeding in the monkey. Brain Research, 1979, 164, 121-135.
Rosen, A.D., Gur, R.C., Reivich, M., Alavi, A. & Greenberg, J. Preliminary
    observation of stimulus-related arousal and glucose metabolism.
    Presented at the meetings of the International Neuropsychological
    Society, Atlanta, Georgia, February, 1981.
Rubens, A.B. Coloric stimulation and unilateral visual neglect. Neurology,
    1985, 35, 1019-1024.
Samuels, I., Butters, N. & Goodglass, H. Visual memory defects following
    cortical-limbic lesions: effect of field of presentation. Physiology
    and Behavior, 1971, 6, 447-452.
Scheibel, M.E. & Scheibel, A.B. The organization of the nucleus reticularis
    thalami: a Golgi study. Brain Research, 1966, 1, 43-62.
Scheibel, M.E. & Scheibel, A.B. Structural organization of nonspecific
    thalamic nuclei and their projection toward cortex. Brain, 1967, 6,
    60-94.
Schlag-Rey, M. & Schlag, J. Eye movement neurons in the thalamus of monkey.
    Investigative Ophtalmology and Visual Science (ARVO Suppl), 1980, 176.
Segundo, J.P., Naquet, R. & Buser, P. Effects of cortical stimulation on
    electrocortical activity in monkeys. Journal of Neurophysiology, 1955,
    18, 236-245.
Shute, C.C.D. & Lewis, P.R. The ascending cholinergic reticular system,
    neocortical, olfactory and subcortical projections. Brain, 1967, 90,
    497-520.
Singer, W. Control of thalamic transmission by corticofugal and ascending
    reticular pathways in the visual system. Physiological Reviews, 1977,
    57, 386-420.
Skinner, J.E. & Yingling, C.D. Regulation of slow potential shifts in nucleus
    reticularis thalami by the mesencephalic reticular formation and the
    frontal granular cortex. Electroencephalography and Clinical
    Neurophysiology, 1976, 40, 288-296.
Skinner, J.E. & Yingling, C.D. Central gating mechanisms that regulate
    event-related potentials and behavior-a neural model for attention. In
    J.E. Desmedt (Ed.), Progress in Clinical Neurophysiology. New York:
    Karger, 1977, vol. 1, pp. 30-69.
Sokolov, Y.N. Perception and the Conditioned Reflex. Oxford: Pergamon Press,
    1963.
Sprague, J.M. Interaction of cortex and superior colliculus in mediation of
    visually guided behavior in the cat. Science, 1966, 153, 1544-1547.
Sprague, J.M. & Meikle, T.H. The role of the superior colliculus in visually
    guided behavior. Experimental Neurology, 1965, 11, 115-146.
Sprague, J.M., Chambers, W.W. & Stellar, E. Attentive, affective and
    adaptive behavior in the cat. Sensory deprivation of the forebrain by
    lesions in the brain stem results in striking behavioral abnormalities.
    Science, 1961, 133, 165-173.
Stelmack, R.M., Plouffe, L.M. & Winogron, H.W. Recognition memory and the
    orienting response. An analysis of the encoding of pictures and words.
    Biological Psychology, 1983, 16, 49-63.
Steriade, M. & Glenn, L. Neocortical and caudate projections of intralaminar
    thalamic neurons and their synaptic excitation from the midbrain

reticular core. Journal of Neurophysiology, 1982, 48, 352-370.

Suzuki, H. & Azuma, M. Prefrontal neuronal activity during gazing at a light dot in the monkey. Brain Research, 1977, 126, 497-508.

Taylor, J. (Ed.) Selected Writings of John Hughlings Jackson. London: Hodder and Stoughton, 1932.

Teitelbaum, P. & Epstein, A.N. The lateral hypothalamic syndrome: recovery of feeding and drinking after lateral hypothalamic lesions. Psychological Review, 1962, 69, 74-90.

Truex, R.C. & Carpenter, M.B. Human Neuroanatomy. Baltimore: Williams and Wilkins, 1964.

Ungerstedt, U. Striatal dopamine relase after amphetamine or nerve degeneration revealed by rotational behavior. Acta Physiologica Scandinavica , 1971, 82 (Suppl 367), 49-68.

Valenstein, E. & Heilman, K.M. Apraxic agraphia with neglect-induced paragraphia. Archives of Neurology, 1979, 36, 506-508.

Valenstein, E. & Heilman, K.M. Unilateral hypokinesia and motor extinction. Neurology, 1981, 31, 445-448.

Vanderwolf, C.H. & Robinson, T.E. Reticulo-cortical activity and behavior: a critique of arousal theory and a new synthesis. Behavioral and Brain Science, 1981, 4, 459-514.

Velasco, F. & Velasco, M. A reticulothalamic system mediating proprioceptive attention and tremor in man. Neurosurgery, 1979, 4, 30-36.

Verfaellie, M. , Bowers, D. & Heilman, K.M. Effects of attention and intention on stimulus-response compatibility. Paper presented at Psychonomics Society Meeting, Boston Mass, November 1985.

Vogt, B.A., Rosene, D.L. & Pandya, D.N. Thalamic and cortical afferents differentiate anterior from posterior cingulate cortex in the monkey. Science, 1979, 204, 205-207.

Wallace, R. S-R compatibility and the idea of a response code. Journal of Experimental Psychology, 1971, 88, 354-360.

Walter, W.G. Human frontal lobe function in sensory-motor association. In K.H. Pribram and A.R. Luria (Eds.), Psychophysiology of the Frontal Lobes. New York: Academic Press, 1973, pp. 109-122.

Watson, R.T. & Heilman, K.M. Thalamic neglect. Neurology, 1979, 29, 690-694.

Watson, R.T., Heilman, K.M., Cauthen, J.C. & King, F.A. Neglect after cingulectomy. Neurology, 1973, 23, 1003-1007.

Watson, R.T., Heilman, K.M., Miller, B.D. & King, F.A. Neglect after mesencephalic reticular formation lesions. Neurology, 1974, 24, 294-298.

Watson, R.T., Miller, B. & Heilman, K.M. Evoked potential in neglect. Archives of Neurology, 1977, 34, 224-227.

Watson, R.T., Miller, B.D. & Heilman, K.M. Nonsensory neglect. Annals of Neurology, 1978, 3, 505-508.

Watson, R.T., Valenstein, E., Day, A. & Heilman, K.M. Ablation of area 7 or cortex around the superior temporal sulcus and neglect. (Abstract) Neurology, 1985, 35 (suppl 1), 179-180.

Watson, R.T., Valenstein, E. & Heilman, K.M. Thalamic neglect. Possible role of the medial thalamus and nucleus reticularis thalami in behavior. Archives of Neurology, 1981, 38, 501-506.

Watson, R.T., Valenstein, E., Day, A.L. & Heilman, K.M. The effects of corpus callosum lesions on unilateral neglect in monkeys. Neurology, 1984, 34, 812-815.

Weinberger, N.M., Velasco, M. & Lindsley, D.B. Effects of lesions upon thalamically induced electrocortical desynchronization and recruiting. Electroencephalography and Clinical Neurophysiology, 1965, 18, 369-377.

Welch, K. & Stuteville, P. Experimental production of neglect in monkeys. Brain, 1958, 81, 341-347.

Williams, S., Bowers, D. & Heilman, K.M. Effects of hemispace on verbal and nonverbal laterality effects. Presented at meeting of International Neuropsychology Society, Houston, TX, February, 1984.

Witelson, S. Hemispheric specialization for linguistic and nonlinguistic tactual perception using dichotomous stimulation techniques. Cortex, 1974, 10, 3-17.

Yingling, C.D. & Skinner, J.E. Regulation of unit activity in nucleus reticularis thalami by the mesencephalic reticular formation and the frontal granular cortex. Electroencephalography and Clinical Neurophysiology, 1975, 39, 635-642.

Yingling, C.D. & Skinner, J.E. Gating of thalamic input to cerebral cortex by nucleus reticularis thalami. In J.E. Desmedt (Ed.), Progress in Clinical Neurophysiology, vol. 1. New York: S. Karger, 1977, pp. 70-96.

Neurophysiological and Neuropsychological Aspects
of Spatial Neglect, M. Jeannerod (editor)
© Elsevier Science Publishers B.V. (North-Holland), 1987

PERCEPTUAL AND ACTION SYSTEMS IN UNILATERAL VISUAL NEGLECT

M. Jane Riddoch
and
Glyn W. Humphreys

In this chapter we review three different accounts of unilateral neglect: one maintaining that neglect is due to early visual processing deficits ; one maintaining that neglect is due to a disorder of an internal representation of space ; and one maintaining that neglect is due to a disorder of visual attention. An attentional view of neglect is elaborated in which neglect is attributed to a breakdown in the processes enabling stimuli on the contralateral side of space to a lesion to "capture" visual attention. This attentional account predicts that contralateral stimuli may vary according to the ease with which they "capture" the attention of neglect patients. Further, even when "attentional capture" does not occur, attention may nevertheless be consciously directed to the neglected side. Data supporting this position are reported from visual search tasks where targets are defined either by single feature differences relative to distractors or by some combination of local feature information, and where neglect patients are either free to adopt their own search strategy or they are cued to the neglected side. Neglect was more marked in the combined-feature searches than the single-feature searches, and it tended to be reduced by spatial cueing. Implications for understanding unilateral visual neglect and for understanding the operation of normal visual attention are discussed.

I. Introduction

Typically, theories of visual information processing distinguish two functionally independent processing levels (e.g., Duncan, 1980; Hoffman, 1979; Humphreys, 1985; Kahneman & Treisman, 1983; Neisser, 1967; Treisman & Gelade, 1980). At the first, pre-attentive level, processing is thought to be the fast and spatially parallel. Accounts of the information explicitly represented at this level differ. For instance, some theorists hold that only information about discrete feature attributes such as colour, shape and size (cf. Quinlan & Humphreys, 1984) are separately specified (e.g., Treisman, 1982; Treisman & Schmidt, 1982; Treisman, Sykes & Gelade, 1977) ; others hold that a full, integrated description of the stimulus is represented pre-attentively (e.g., Duncan, 1980; Humphreys, 1985). Whatever the case, it is generally thought that a conscious representation of an integrated stimulus is only made available at a second level of processing. The transition between the two processing levels can involve a limited-capacity, attentional mechanism, which operates serially on stimulus information (so that detriments are encountered when more than one stimulus must be attended at a time).

Unilateral visual neglect following brain damage may be defined as the failure to act to visual input on the side of space contralateral to the site of lesion (Friedland & Weinstein, 1977; Heilman & Valenstein, 1979). The failure to act to contralaterally presented stimuli can be found in a range of tasks, varying from everyday tasks such as eating the food from both sides of the plate to more specific tasks such as registering double simultaneous stimulation. Such a deficit suggests some fundamental impairment in information processing prior to the addressing of motor responses, such as an impaired ability to attend focally to stimuli in contralateral spatial regions.

In this chapter, we will consider various accounts of unilateral neglect and in particular, the idea that neglect patients are impaired at attending focally to information made available by early (pre-attentive) visual processes. New evidence consistent with the latter account will then be put forward and discussed in the light of current theories of visual attention in both normal subjects and in patients manifesting unilateral neglect. The relevance of the evidence for understanding normal visual perception will then be discussed.

II. Accounts of Unilateral Neglect

Historically there have been many attempts to explain the mechanisms underlying unilateral neglect, and they can be divided into three general classes : 1. those which attribute the phenomenon to early visual processing deficits ; 2. those which ascribe it to a disorder of representational schema ; and 3. those which ascribe it to disordered attentional or orienting systems.

1. Neglect as Due to Early Visual Processing Deficits

There are various forms of this argument. For instance, certain writers suggest that neglect is just one manifestation of the overall symptomatology produced by larger cerebral lesions. Indeed, Battersby, Bender, Pollack and Kahn (1965), in a study of 132 patients with space occupying lesions, found those with neglect to be hemianopic, to have marked deficits in general mental performance, and to show somato-sensory and motor defects. Zarit and Kahn (1974) also demonstrated that the degree of neglect in a sample of 89 patients correlated with the degree of other impairments. The highest neglect scores were obtained by patients who also had visual field defects and impaired intellectual capacities.

However, it is unlikely that neglect can be attributed to general mental deterioration. For example, Lawson (1962) found no degree of intellectual impairment in the two cases he studied ; Ettlinger, Warrington and Zangwill (1957) found intellectual impairment in only one of the nine cases they examined, and dementia was specifically excluded in at least two of the cases reported by McFie, Piercy and Zangwill (1950).

Given the equivocal data on the role played by gross organic impairment in the genesis of unilateral neglect, it seems reasonable to assume that the magnitude of cerebral damage is not causally related to neglect.

A rather different suggestion is that neglect is related to visual field defects in patients. Hecaen (1962) and Battersby et al. (1965) have both demonstrated that neglect is associated with a high incidence of hemianopia (with 76% and 100% of their respective samples of neglect patients having a hemianopia recorded). However, Albert (1973), in a study of 30 right hemisphere damaged patients, found that only 50% of those with visual field defects manifested neglect whilst only 55% of those showing neglect had visual field defects. It appears that there is no absolute relationship between neglect and visual field defects.

The above argument is further supported by the studies of Chedru (1976) and DeRenzi, Faglioni and Scotti (1970). Chedru presented 91 brain damaged patients with a teletype keyboard. Initially, patients were blindfolded and asked to tap keys all over the keyboard as quickly as possible. Patients then repeated the task without the blindfold. In the sighted condition, most keys were omitted by the right brain damaged patients with visual field defects and these omissions were on the left side of the keyboard (demonstrating neglect). Left hemisphere damaged patients with field defects made fewer omissions on the side contralateral to their lesions relative to the right hemisphere patients. Further, in the blindfolded condition, most neglect was produced by right hemisphere damaged patients without field defects.

DeRenzi et al. (1970) also attempted to demonstrate neglect in a task not dependent on visual cues. They asked patients to search with a forefinger for a marble placed at the end of one of four arms of a maze. The maze was hidden behind a curtain. They found that, overall, brain damaged patients were not worse on this task than non-brain damaged control subjects. However, within the brain damaged group, patients with visual field defects were reliably worse than those without, and patients took more time to find the marble when it was on the side of space contralateral to the lesion site. Differences between right and left hemisphere damaged patients may have been obscured in this study because of the use by DeRenzi et al. of a cut off search time, which meant that many patients performed at the floor level.

Both Chedru's (1976) and DeRenzi et al.'s (1970) results indicate that neglect can be found in tasks which do not require visual input : they therefore suggest that neglect cannot be attributed solely to visual field defects, and, rather, that patients neglect some internal representation of space. Both results also indicate differences between different classes of patients. Chedru's finding is particularly strong since differences were found between two patient groups with equal incidence of field defects (with neglect most manifest in the right hemisphere damaged group). This emphasises that field defects per se do not produce neglect, and it also rules out the idea that neglect was produced by poor motor responses on the side of space contralateral to the lesion site, since motor defects should be equal in the right and left hemisphere damaged groups.

A further account of neglect in terms of a failure in attaining appropriate stimulus information is the suggestion that patients with neglect have impaired visual scanning (Denny-Brown & Fischer, 1976). Support for this account is provided by Belluza, Rappaport, Kenneth and Hall (1979), who found that all the patients in their sample who manifested neglect on drawing tasks showed abnormal visual scanning patterns, as measured by eye movement recordings. Such patients had shorter fixation durations and spent significantly less fixation time on the informative parts of stimuli. Also, Albert (1973) found that 64% of his sample of patients with neglect had oculomotor defects. Similar results have been obtained by Chedru, LeBlanc and Lhermitte (1973). Again, however, this account has difficulty accounting for data such as those reported by Chedru (1976), since it is not clear why a scanning deficit should produce neglect under blindfold conditions. Also, neglect can be found in visual processing tasks where it is unlikely that eye movements mediate performance (e.g., Posner, Cohen & Rafal, 1982; Posner, Walker, Friedrich & Rafal, 1984). It does not seem that neglect is attributable to a scanning deficit ; indeed, it is quite possible that scanning deficits may themselves be caused by some other processing problem, such as an inability to orient to stimuli on the contralateral side of space to the lesion, which affects both overt and covert attentional mechanisms (see section III).

Two other proposals should also be mentioned in this section the perceptual rivalry hypothesis and the inter-hemispheric inhibition hypothesis. Both of the latter hypotheses hold that neglect occurs because patients do not receive appropriate stimulus information, though both suggest some central processing deficit as the cause (rather than a peripheral deficit such as a visual field defect). The perceptual rivalry hypothesis (Denny-Brown, Meyer & Horenstein, 1952) attributes neglect to an inability to synthesize multiple sensory input on the side of the body contralateral to the lesion. The suggestion is that this failure to synthesize sensory input prevents information from being passed on to higher-level recognition processes. The inter-hemispheric inhibition hypothesis holds that neglect occurs because stimuli on the non-neglected side of space inhibit the processing of neglect-side stimuli (e.g., Birch, Belmont & Karp, 1967), and that this disruption to processing prevents recognition from taking place.

In a detailed single case study of a patient with right hemisphere damage, Denny-Brown et al. (1952) found that elementary input properties such as the presence or absence of touch or a pin-prick on the neglected side could be perceived, but that the perception of double stimulation was deficient. Also, their patient was able to identify single objects presented on the left side of space but, when presented with pictures of several objects jumbled together, the patient correctly named only those on the right. When the picture was inverted, the patient then identified those items on the right (i.e., which had previously been on the left) but not those on the left (i.e., which had previously been on the right). Composite pictures with objects more widely spaced led to improved performance for left-side objects.

To account for the poor identification of left-side stimuli shown by their patient when presented with stimuli in both the left and the right visual fields, Denny-Brown et al. argue that the fixation of neglect patients is shifted to the right when the right and left side stimuli are both present, with a consequent reduction in visual perception to the left. However, neglect patients do not simply fail to recognise stimuli on the affected side, they typically react as if the stimuli do not exist. The argument that neglected stimuli are equivalent to stimuli presented in the visual periphery is not sufficient. Also, the proposal fails to accomodate the fact that neglect can be manifest in modalities other than vision (e.g., Chedru, 1976). Accordingly, Denny-Brown et al. further posit that perception results from the synthesis of stimulus properties via a summation process and that neglect patients effectively fail to synthesize more than a few stimulus properties. We may think of this as some form of central capacity limitation in processing multiple stimuli. The limitation is most manifest when stimuli are presented on both sides of space, since then capacity is devoted solely to the side ipsilateral to the lesion so producing neglect of the contralateral side.

The last suggestion is quite close to the inter-hemispheric inhibition argument that neglect is due to inhibition of the processing of stimuli presented on the affected side of space by non-neglected stimuli. For instance, Birch et al. (1967) suggest that the damaged nervous system is characterised by increased inertia, as shown by the increased time needed to process information and by increases in the time required to recover from the effects of preceeding stimulation. Thus, when the patient is given double simultaneous stimulation, there is interference from the more rapidly functioning intact divisions of the nervous system on the damaged portions. This interference can lead to an inability to register stimuli on the affected side under double simultaneous stimulation conditions.

Using a double simultaneous stimulation procedure, Birch et al. (1967) demonstrated in 19 patients with right hemisphere damage that 80% of responses showed extinction (i.e., the stimuli were not reported) on the affected side whilst only 8% of responses to stimuli on the intact side were so affected. Also, with successive increases in the time intervals between the paired stimuli, Birch et al. found decreases in the proportion of extinctions occurring on the neglected side and relative increases in the proportion of extinctions to stimuli on the intact side (although the overall numbers of extinctions decreased). They propose that the latter results occurred because extra time between inputs gives more opportunity for stimuli on the affected side to be processed, and because early processing of stimuli on the affected side can in turn inhibit information processing on the intact side.

Both the perceptual rivalry and the inter-hemispheric inhibition hypotheses presume that neglect patients fail to process stimuli on the affected side appropriately, so that later processes do not receive the correct input to enable recognition or even detection to occur. However, there are indications that this is not the case, or at least that the failure to report neglected stimuli does not accurately indicate the degree to which they are processed. One of the most drastic indications of a dissociation between the processing of neglected stimuli and the ability of patients to use the processed information for identification purposes comes from the work of Volpe, LeDoux and Gazzaniga (1979). Their patients were selected because they showed extinction to double simultaneous stimulation. Such patients were tachistoscopically presented with either single words or pictures to either the left or right visual field. All the patients named the stimuli with high accuracy (cf. Denny-Brown et al., 1952). Subsequently, words or pictures were presented simultaneously and bilaterally to the left and right of fixation for 150 msec. The patients had to judge whether or not the two stimuli were "same" or "different". For "same" matches the stimuli were identical ; for "different" trials, different items were displayed which shared no obvious relationship. Such matches were performed with high accuracy. The patients were then presented with the stimuli used in the matching task and they were asked to name them. On trials where the stimuli were identical, naming the item in the neglected field could be deduced from their naming in the non-neglected field. However, this was not possible on "different" trials. Over patients, very few of the neglect-side stimuli could be named in the simultaneous presentation condition, despite the high level of performance in the matching task. This suggests that the neglected stimuli were at least processed to levels supporting the "same-different" judgements used by Volpe et al. (1979), but that this does not ensure conscious identification. Indeed, two patients in the study reported that they could not even detect the presence of neglected stimuli. Now, whilst the reliability of such introspective reports may be questioned (e.g., Merikle, 1982), the data nevertheless indicate that neglected stimuli were processed to somewhat higher levels than would appear to be the case from the patients' identification responses. The result is difficult to accomodate if there is some early processing deficit for neglected stimuli.

A final point is that the perceptual rivalry and the inter-hemispheric inhibition hypotheses essentially attempt to explain extinction to double simultaneous stimulation. However, the relations between neglect and extinction remain far from clear. For instance, there is commonly some sensory loss on the side of the body contralateral to the site of a lesion, following brain damage ; consequently, many patients may exhibit some extinction to double simultaneous stimulation, not just those showing other signs of neglect, especially when sensory thresholds on the affected and the

unaffected sides have not been equated (cf. Birch et al., 1967: see also
Riddoch & Humphreys, 1983). Full accounts of neglect will need to explain
its occurrence in all circumstances.

2. Neglect as a Disorder of Representational Schema

If unilateral neglect cannot be accounted for in terms of low level
processing deficits, then consideration of higher-level processes becomes
necessary. Now, neglect is classically associated with lesions to the
parietal region of the right hemisphere in man (e.g., Brain, 1941;
Critchley, 1966; McFie et al., 1950; though see Mesulam, 1981). Bisiach and
his associates (e.g., Bisiach & Luzzati, 1978) have argued that the
posterior parietal cortex contains an elaborate spatial representation of
the external world (see also Lynch, 1980). It is argued that unilateral
damage to this area of the cortex causes a unilateral loss of this spatial
representation, and hence neglect of that area of space.

Evidence for this idea comes from two patients described by Bisiach and
Luzzati (1978). Both of these patients had suffered right cerebral damage
resulting in both neglect and left hemianopia. Both patients were asked to
describe the Piazza del Duomo in Milan, a place very familar to them. They
were asked to describe the square from different directions ; first, looking
at the cathedral, and then looking from the cathedral On each occasion, and
for both patients, left-side details were largely omitted from the
descriptions. Such data cannot be explained in terms of sensory input
deficits, as the descriptions did not depend on actual stimulation from the
scene.

This study was expanded by Bisiach, Capitani Luzzati and Perani
(1981). Three main groups of right hemisphere damaged patients were
studied: 12 patients without hemianopia or neglect (H-, N-) ; 10 patients
with hemianopia but without neglect (H[+], N-) ; and 13 patients with
hemianopia and neglect (judged from performance on a letter cancellation
task ; H[+], N[+]).

Following free verbal descriptions of the Piazza del Duomo all the
patients were asked to describe first the right and then the left side of the
square according to a first perspective, and the left and right sides from
another perspective. Group H[+], N[+] was found to differ significantly from the
other patients in that more detail was omitted from the left than the right,
for both perspectives. Further, the difference between the free and the cued
conditions of the task was only significant for this group, with performance
on left-side details being much improved in the cued condition. Bisiach et
al. (1981) suggest that their data confirm the observations made by Bisiach
and Luzzati (1978). They propose that imaginal space is topographically
structured across the hemispheres in an analogue of external space. If one
hemisphere is damaged, then that side of imaginal space will not be reported
in imagery tasks.

An alternative explanation of Bisiach's findings is that neglect
patients are impaired at scanning (covertly) one half of an internal spatial
representation. This scanning account neatly explains why cueing improved
the amount of detail recalled on the left side of both perspectives of the
imagined square in the H[+],N[+] group in Bisiach et al. (1981).

Two further experiments designed to explore the representation
argument are described by Bisiach, Luzzati and Perani (1979). Nineteen
patients with right cerebral damage took part. In a first experiment, the
patients were required to detect differences occurring within pairs of
successively presented patterns. The brain damaged group was reliably
impaired at detecting differences on the left side compared with the right

side of the patterns, and compared with non-brain damaged control subjects. In a second experiment the patterns moved behind a stationary vertical slit, with each pair of stimuli being shown in both a leftward and a rightward motion. Again subjects were asked to detect differences occurring within each pair of patterns. In order to perform this task, the patients must re-construct the forms by temporal integration of the successive episodes of the stimulus. In this instance, patients were impaired at detecting differences on the left side of the patterns, irrespective of whether the left side was the leading or the trailing edge.

Morgan, Findlay and Watt (1982) have discussed the processes involved in the visual perception of shapes moving behind narrow apertures with normal observers. When there is a relatively fast stimulus velocity (e.g., above 8°/sec), the observer may unconsciously follow the moving figure with his or her eyes so that successive impressions are formed on different parts of the retina during the motion of the shape. This is termed retinal painting. However, pursuit eye movements are not necessary for shape perception to occur. When observers fixate a stationary spot to the side of the aperture, relatively slowly moving shapes (e.g., less than 3°/sec) can be seen, due to the temporal integration of shape information (cf. Morgan et al., 1982). In Bisiach et al.'s study, the stimulus speed was relatively slow and the perception of shape by the patients was probably not taking place by retinal painting. Oculomotor disturbances should not therefore affect the task. Bisiach et al.'s finding that the effect of the direction of movement was negligible, is also consistent with the argument that oculomotor disturbances were not responsible for altered performance. However, it is not possible to conclude from the study that the patients had impaired representations of space or whether they were impaired at scanning the representation. To assess the latter possibility, patients should be cued to attend to either the left or right sides of the patterns ; such cueing may override (or at least ameliorate) an attentional deficit, whilst it should not affect performance if the representation of the neglected side of space is itself impaired (cf. Bisiach et al., 1981).

In summary, the representation hypothesis does not offer a ready explanation for why cueing should improve neglect ; indeed, the effects of cueing indicate some attentional component in unilateral neglect. However, the hypothesis does have some advantages over the sensory deficit notion, since it assumes that an internal representation of space is disrupted ; it can thus account for unilateral neglect in a variety of tasks which are subserved by the same spatial representation (e.g., in the tactile as well as the visual modality).

3. Neglect as a Disorder of Attention

Several different theories are subsumed under this heading. These are: Kinsbourne's attention hypothesis ; Heilman's unilateral akinesia hypothesis ; Posner's covert orienting hypothesis.

Kinsbourne's attentional hypothesis : Kinsbourne (1978) attempts to explain neglect in terms of his attentional account of inter-hemispheric activity (Kinsbourne, 1970). He argues that activation of one hemisphere causes inhibition of potentially homologous functions in the other. The consequence of within-hemisphere activation leads to a perceptual bias toward the contralateral side of space and transhemisphere inhibition. Further, there is thought to be an innate propensity to attend more to the right than to the left (Caplan & Kinsbourne, 1976; Turkewitz, Gordon & Birch, 1965). To account for this, Kinsbourne suggests that "in the left half of the brain are located not only the faculty that turns attention to the right but also the verbal processor. When the verbal processor is activated because a person is anticipating speaking, listening to speech or speaking, then that verbal activation overlaps the adjacent right turning control centre and the verbal activity biases attention to the right. The left turning centre, in the right hemisphere, is far removed from the site of activation and is overpowered by its activated opponent" (Kinsbourne, 1978, page 9).

While this notion gains support from the predominance of left sided neglect, it is open to criticism. If neglect is due to an imbalance of orienting tendencies resulting from increased (disinhibited) activity in the intact hemisphere, then the performance of the right hemisphere patients on right side stimuli should be at least normal, if not better than normal (Heilman & Watson, 1977). However, Heilman and Watson (1977) cite evidence where patients with left sided neglect made more errors on the non-neglected (ipsilateral) side than patients with left hemisphere lesions made on their left (ipsilateral) side. They also suggest that if Kinsbourne's hypothesis is correct, then bilateral lesions should ameliorate neglect. Against this, Segarra and Angelo (1970) demonstrate that bilateral cingulate or mesencephalic lesions produce bilateral neglect. Contrary to Heilman and Watson's suggestion, though, it remains possible for Kinsbourne's account to accommodate bilateral neglect. This is because a right hemisphere lesion would result in orienting to the right and neglect of the left, while a left hemisphere lesion would produce orienting to the left and neglect of the right. Either a bilateral lesion would cause bilateral neglect, or the opposite orienting tendencies will balance and mitigate any neglect.

Heilman's unilateral akinesia hypothesis : Heilman and his associates suggest that neglect is due to decreased activation of the arousal systems of the damaged hemisphere ; in particular (though not exclusively) as a result of lesions in the cortico-limbic reticular activating loop (Heilman & Valenstein, 1972; Watson, Heilman, Cauthen & King, 1973). The effect of such a unilateral decrease in arousal is thought to be the selective loss of the orienting response to the contralateral side of space, since it is assumed that orienting responses to the opposite side of space are represented in each cerebral hemisphere, so that the damaged hemisphere is rendered akinetic. To explain the predominance of neglect following right rather than left hemisphere lesions (see above, Chedru, 1976; also McFie & Zangwill, 1960; Brain, 1941; Critchley, 1966; Oxbury, Campbell & Oxbury, 1974; though Friedrich, Walker & Posner, 1985, and Riddoch, 1982, present some contrary evidence) Heilman and Van der Abel (1980) further assume that the left hemisphere only controls orienting to the right side of space while the right hemisphere controls orienting to both sides. The effect of a left hemisphere lesion on orienting can be compensated for by the right hemisphere ; however, a right hemisphere lesion may leave subjects with only a right-side (left-hemisphere mediated) orienting response.

If the arousal hypothesis is correct, it should be possible to demonstrate electrophysiological changes in subjects with neglect. Watson, Andriola and Heilman (1977) recorded electroencephalograms (EEGs) for 23 patients with unilateral neglect and compared them with 20 subjects with aphasia without neglect. Of the patients with neglect, 22 demonstrated diffuse ispilateral slow waves, while only 7 of the 20 aphasic patients showed ipsilateral EEG slowing. Such a result suggests a unilateral decrease in arousal in neglect patients.

The arousal hypothesis can be used to explain other data. For instance, consider Birch et al.'s (1967) finding that extinction to double simultaneous stimulation occurs in neglect patients and that it decreases as the interval between the presentation of stimuli to the neglected and the non-neglected sides lengthens (see above). Now, under conditions of double simultaneous stimulation, sensory information is transmitted to both cerebral hemispheres. If there is decreased arousal in one hemisphere, performance will come to be dominated by the reaction of the intact hemisphere, so causing extinction on the neglected side. Increasing the interval between the stimuli might also allow any stimuli projected to the impaired hemisphere to be processed against a lower level of background arousal (noise), so mitigating the effect of relative under-arousal in that hemisphere which is encountered under double simultaneous stimulation conditions.

One further consequence of Heilman's view that the damaged hemisphere in neglect patients is akinetic due to under-arousal is that the degree of neglect manifest should not be strongly affected by instructing subjects to attend to the neglected side, since, at least when there are competing stimuli present on the non-neglected side, the damaged hemisphere should still be under-aroused relative to the intact hemisphere. Heilman and Valenstein(1979) examined this possibility in a line bisection task. They presented neglect patients with a series of lines, with each line having a letter at either end. On half the trials, the patients were cued to look at the left end of the lines and to report the letter at that end ; on the other trials patients were cued to look to the right end of the lines and to report the letter there. Patients then had to draw a line bisecting the middle of the target line, and neglect was measured in terms of the magnitude of error (away from the neglected side). Heilman and Valenstein (1979) found that the cues had no effect on performance.

Heilman and Valenstein's failure to find an effect of cueing is contrary to the finding of reliable cueing effects in imagery tasks in neglect patients (Bisiach et al., 1981). Also Riddoch and Humphreys (1983), in a similar task to that used by Heilman and Valenstein, have reported an effect of cueing, with neglect being less when the patients were cued to report the left-side letter than when they were cued to report the right-side letter. Riddoch and Humphreys' result suggests that the damaged hemisphere in neglect patients should not be thought of as akinetic, since the degree of neglect can be influenced by instructing subjects to orient to the neglected side of space, keeping all other task constraints constant. One reason for the different results may be subject selection. Heilman and Valenstein's (1979) patients were selected on the basis of extinction to double simultaneous stimulation, which is a rather broad indicator of neglect ; Riddoch and Humphreys (1983) selected patients on the basis of their showing neglect in drawing tasks, which may only be manifest in patients with more severe neglect. Certainly, the degree of neglect in the line bisection task was more marked in Riddoch and Humphreys' patients than in those of Heilman and Valenstein, and it seems possible that the degree of neglect may be more labile in the former cases. Alternatively, it may be that different patients manifest neglect for different reasons.

Posner's covert orienting hypothesis : A third attentional explanation has recently been proposed by Posner and his associates (Posner & Rafal, in press; Posner et al., 1982; Posner et al., 1984). According to this hypothesis, neglect may be attributed to an inability to scan an internal spatial representation because of a defect in visual attention. This inability may exist independently of an impairment in sustaining the internal representation of the neglected side of space (see section 2 above; Bisiach & Luzzati, 1978).

Attempts to assess some of the properties of visual attention have been made by examining the effects of precues in simple reaction time (RT) tasks. Typically, the subjects has to fixate centrally and he or she is required to press a key if a target stimulus (a light, an asterisk etc.) is presented either to the right or to the left of fixation. Prior to the appearance of the target, a cue is presented ; this may be a central arrow indicating the likely location of the target on a given trial, or it can be a light briefly illuminated on the side of fixation where the target is likely to appear. On the majority of trials, the cue indicates the target location (i.e., it is valid) ; however, on a minority of trials, the cue is incorrect and it indicates a location on the opposite side of fixation to where the target appears (i.e., it is invalid). Performance with valid and with invalid cues can be compared with performance when the cue is neutral and conveys no information about the likely location of the target (i.e., when the cue is a central cross). RTs are faster (Jonides, 1981; Posner 1980) and discrimination is more accurate (Bashinski & Bacharach, 1980) when the cue is valid relative to when it is neutral (i.e., performance is facilitated) ; and RTs are slower and discrimination poorer (e.g., Bashinski & Bacharach, 1980; Posner, 1980; Posner, Snyder & Davison, 1980) with an invalid cue (i.e., performance is inhibited). The facilitated performance with a valid cue is attributed to the shifting of attention to the target's location.

Normally, attentional acts may be mediated either by shifts of the eyes (an overt mechanism) or by shifts in some form of internal attentional process (a covert mechanism); for instance, we might conceptualise that covert attention operates by a pre-activation of the processing pathways for stimuli falling at the attended location (e.g., Posner, 1978, 1980). The overt and covert attentional mechanisms can be separated, with simple RT performance being facilitated by a valid location cue even where trials on which eye movements are made are disgarded or where the stimuli are presented too briefly for eye movements to occur (e.g., Jonides, 1981; Posner, Nissen & Ogden, 1978). There is also a typical time course for processing facilitation, with RT decreasing (i.e., with there being more facilitation) as the interval between the cue and the appearance of the target increases, up to some optimal interval depending on the distance between the target and fixation (e.g., estimates indicate that attention may be shifted at a constant velocity of about 8 msec/deg. of visual angle ; Shulman, Remington & McLean, 1979; Tsal, 1983). Nevertheless, some facilitation generally occurs even when the target is presented less than 200 msec following the cue, which again emphasises that the benefits from covert shifts of attention can be separated from overt attentional processes such as eye movements (e.g., Remington, 1980).

Interestingly, the shifting of covert attention can itself be dependent on either of two separate mechanisms. This is best illustrated by an experiment reported by Posner et al. (1982). They presented a peripheral cue (signalled by the brightening of a box of 10 deg. to the left or right of fixation) prior to the presentation of a target light. However, the cue was only valid on 20% of the trials, so subjects were instructed to expect the target in the opposite visual field to where the cue appeared. The interval between the cue and the target was varied. With short intervals (less than 100 msec), RTs were quickest to targets appearing on the side of the cue. With longer intervals (over 150 msec), RTs were quickest to targets appearing on the opposite side to the cue. With the short interval then, the peripheral cue appeared to "capture" attention, so that attention was obligatorily drawn to this cue even though subjects were instructed to shift attention to the opposite side of fixation. With longer intervals, attention appears dependent on some more central control process (Posner & Cohen, 1984).

Posner et al. (1982) and Posner et al. (1984) have examined the performance of patients with unilateral neglect in the pre-cueing procedure. For instance, Posner et al. (1984) tested 13 patients with parietal lesions, 7 with left-side lesions and 6 with right-side lesions, 5 of whom showed some clinical signs of neglect (varying from extinction to double simultaneous stimulation to inattention to all stimuli on the neglected side). Such clinical symptoms of neglect were also present in 3 of the left parietal patients. Patients made a simple RT response to a peripheral target which was preceded by a peripheral cue. The cue was valid on 80% of the trials. They found that, when the cue was valid, there were relatively small differences in RTs to targets presented both contralaterally and ipsilaterally to the site of the lesion, for all patients. However, when the cue was invalid (i.e., when the target was presented on the opposite side of fixation to the cue), there were marked differences in performance for contralateral and for ispilateral targets, with RTs then being slow for contralateral stimuli. This difficulty in detecting contralateral stimuli given an invalid cue to the ipsilateral side was most pronounced with the right hemisphere damaged patients, and it was particularly severe for the patient with the most marked neglect. Posner et al's result is of interest, since it demonstrates that at least some patients with unilateral neglect can shift attention to the neglected side of space (contrary to Heilman's account; see above), and that such patients are primarily impaired only when attention has been drawn to the non-neglected side.

Posner et al. (1984) distinguish three component processes in covert visual attention : the ability to engage attention to a target ; the ability to disengage attention from a target ; and the ability to move attention from one target to another. Now, since there was little difference both in absolute RTs and in the time course of the responses to validly cued ipsilateral and contralateral targets for their parietal patients, it appears that such patients can move and engage attention to contralateral stimuli relatively normally. Posner et al. therefore suggest that the difficulty with invalidly cued contralateral stimuli occurs because such patients experience difficulty in disengaging attention from stimuli presented in the ispilateral field[1].

The suggestion, then, is that visual neglect can stem from a selective impairment to one component of covert attention. Since some impairments were found with both right and left hemisphere damaged patients, it appears that the processes involved in attending to visual stimuli are laterally organized, with each hemisphere controlling attention to the contralateral side of space. Thus, damage to those areas in the right and left cerebral hemispheres controlling attention will produce some difficulties in attending to the contralateral side (see also Friedrich, Walker and Posner, 1985). This is not to state, however, that there is complete symmetry of representation of attentional responses in the two hemispheres ; indeed, the evidence indicates that this is not so (e.g., see Posner et al., 1984). For instance, it may be that whilst the left hemisphere only controls attentional shifts to the contralateral (right) side of space, the right hemisphere may have some control over shifts to both sides ; accordingly, the difficulty in shifting attention to the right side of space following a left hemisphere lesion may be mitigated by ispilateral shifts made by the right hemisphere (see also Heilman & Van der Abel, 1980).

Posner et al.'s (1984) argument that neglect patients have particular problems in disengaging attention from stimuli presented to their non-neglected side can accommodate much of the data we have so far considered. For instance, extinction to double simultaneous stimulation is attributed to attention being held by the ispilateral stimulus, preventing its switching to the contralateral side. Also, for right hemisphere patients, increasing the time between the left and right side stimuli lessens extinction since there will then be less of a tendency to attend to the right side (cf. Birch et al., 1961). Similarly, in mental imagery tasks, attention may be engaged by stimuli on the right side of the internal spatial representation, with the result being that patients then find it difficult to shift attention to the neglected side (cf. Bisiach & Luzzati, 1978). Perhaps most importantly, the hypothesis also gives a ready explanation for why cueing can ameliorate neglect (Posner et al. 1982 ; Riddoch & Humphreys, 1983).

We have discussed proposals that neglect is due either to impaired sensory processes or to impaired input to higher-order recognition processes, that neglect is due to impaired representation of the side of space contralateral to the site of a lesion, and that neglect is due to some form of impairment to visual attention. Our suggestion is that, at least in some cases, neglect is caused by an attentional impairment. Perhaps the most convincing evidence for the latter suggestion is the finding, now shown in a number of laboratories, that instructing patients to attend to the neglected side of space lessons neglect (Bisiach et al., 1981; Posner et al., 1982, 1984 ; Riddoch & Humphreys, 1983; see also Diller & Weinberg, 1977; Weinberg, Diller, Gordon, Gerstman, Lieberman, Lakin, Hodges & Ezrachi, 1977, 1979). Without explicit instructions to shift attention contralaterally, however, patients with neglect are poor at disengaging attention from ispilateral stimuli. Since such effects are found predominantly following lesions to the right hemisphere, it appears that there may be some asymmetry in the organization of attentional mechanisms in the left and right cerebral hemispheres (Heilman & Van der Abel, 1980; Posner et al., 1984).

III. Some Further Questions

We have argued that visual neglect is caused by a problem in disengaging attention from stimuli presented on the side of space ipsilateral to the lesion site. It may also be possible to fractionate the difficulties in disengaging attention further. For instance, it could be that ipsilateral stimuli effect a stronger "hold" on attention in neglect patients than in normal subjects, or that contralateral stimuli fail to "capture" attention in neglect patients. If there is some breakdown in an obligatory attentional mechanism (i.e., in attentional capture), patients may be poor at detecting contralateral targets once attention is shifted to the ipsilateral side since attention may need to be captured by such targets for detection to occur. Nevertheless, such patients seem able to effect controlled shifts of attention ; thus there are only minor differences in responses to ipsilateral and contralateral stimuli with valid cueing and neglect is decreased by explicit instructions to shift attention (Posner et al., 1984 ; Riddoch & Humphreys, 1983).

Some evidence that neglect stems from a loss of attentional capture by contralateral stimuli rather than increased attentional hold by ipsilateral stimuli has been reported by Riddoch and Humphreys (1983). As noted earlier, Riddoch and Humphreys examined the effect of cueing on line bisection by neglect patients. In one experiment (Experiment 2), a group of 5 right hemisphere damaged patients with unilateral neglect were presented with lines which had letters at either end and, prior to line bisection, the patients were asked either to report only the left cue, only the right cue or both cues. Riddoch and Humphreys found marked neglect in the report right-cue condition relative to when no letter cues were provided, and reduced neglect in the report left-cue only and the report both-cues conditions. This result suggests that neglect can be reduced by cueing patients to the contralateral side (in this case, the left) even when they have first had to report a right-side cue (i.e., in the report both-cues condition). It did not seem to be the case that the right-side cue "held" attention, but simply that the patients failed to shift attention contralaterally unless explicitly instructed to do so, consistent with a breakdown in attentional capture.

If the latter hypothesis is correct, we may go on to ask whether some stimulus properties draw attention to the neglected side better than others. We may also question the fate of neglected stimuli.

We have already discussed one piece of evidence relevant to the question of the fate of neglected stimuli, namely Volpe et al.'s (1979) finding that neglect patients can use contralaterally presented stimuli to perform "same-different" visual matching tasks even when they are unable to identify, or perhaps even to detect, such stimuli. Thus the failure to identify neglected stimuli should not be taken to indicate their lack of processing.

Another finding which hints that there may be rather more processing of neglected stimuli than is apparent from their direct report is again contained in the data of Riddoch and Humphreys (1983). We have already noted that in this study neglect patients were given a line bisection task under a variety of cueing conditions. For our present purposes, the two relevant conditions were when the lines were flanked by two letters but the patients only had to report the right-side letter (dual cue, report right), and when only a right-side letter was present which patients had to report prior to bisecting the line. Neglect was slightly but reliably more severe in the right single-letter condition than in the dual cue, report right condition. That is, the presence of the left-side cue in the dual cue condition seemed to affect performance even though patients were not instructed to report it. This finding suggests that at least some processing of the left-side cue occurred, leading to a mild attenuation of neglect relative to when patients oriented to a single right-side cue.

The question is, what kinds of processing are neglected stimuli subject to ? It seems clear that this question can only be addressed indirectly, since, by definition, patients are poor at directly reporting stimuli on the neglected side. Recently, we have attempted to assess something about the kinds of processing carried out upon neglected stimuli by assessing visual search functions in the neglected and non-neglected fields of patients with unilateral neglect. In a visual search task, a subject is presented with a display comprising a varying number of items and he or she is asked to decide whether a pre-designated target item is present or absent. Measures are taken of the time taken and the number of errors made for each type of decision as a function of the number or distractor items present (the display size), and inferences about the nature of the underlying search process are made from the form of the search performance-display size function. For instance, if either the number of errors or the RTs to decide that a target is present increase linearly as a function of the display size, then there are grounds for suggesting that subjects are searching the display serially, with each item being treated as a separate perceptual object (e.g., Treisman & Gelade, 1980). When such a serial search is conducted, the rate of search is given by the slope of the RT-display size function. Search rate on the target-present trials should be about half that on the target-absent trials, since on average subjects will only need to search half the display items when the target is present, whereas they need to search all the display items when it is absent. In contrast, non-linear relationships between search performance and display size, and in particular, flat performance-display size functions, are indicative of a search process taking place in parallel across the display elements (Treisman & Gelade, 1980)[2].

One simple issue we might address, then, is whether neglect patients demonstrate similar search functions for stimuli presented in their neglected and their non-neglected fields. This issue is relevant for understanding the nature of neglect. If patients have deficient sensory processing of the neglected side of space, the search functions on the neglected and the non-neglected sides ought to differ quite drastically. In particular, there should be little evidence for the parallel processing of display elements in the neglected field, even when the discriminations in the non-neglected field are based on parallel processing. The predictions made by the theory that neglect patients have impaired representations of space are less clear. However, if we suppose that neglect patients are simply unable to represent the positions of display items on the side of space contralateral to the lesion site, then detections of neglect-side stimuli which require accurate spatial localization should be extremely difficult. Attentional theories assume that pre-attentive processing in neglect patients may be relatively intact. The effects of poor attentional-capture by neglect-side stimuli, then, will depend on the role of attention in vision. To formulate more detailed predictions, we need to consider more precise accounts of the function of visual attention.

IV. Accounts of Attention in Vision

Although there is a common distinction made between pre-attentional and attentional processing in vision, there are different views about the kinds of information which may be represented pre-attentively (see section I).

One position has been put forward by Treisman and her colleagues (Treisman, 1982, 1984; Treisman & Gelade, 1980; Treisman & Schmidt, 1982; Treisman et al., 1977), who have argued that pre-attentive vision is concerned with the parallel analysis of visual input in terms of independent maps for each separate visual feature (e.g., colour, local shape, size). Within each of these maps, there may be some grouping of the features so that areas of homogeneity and heterogeneity are made explicit. In the colour domain, such grouping processes will specify whether there is a homogeneous area of colour ; in the form domain, grouping may operate on the basis of simple inter-dependencies between local elements (such as their relative contrast and orientation) or on the coding of a few higher-order features (termed "textons" by Julesz, 1980, 1981), which code information about local display properties such as colinearity, closure, corner and the number of line ends or "terminators" (see Caelli, Julesz & Gilbert, 1978; Julesz, 1980, 1981; Julesz & Caelli, 1979). However, information about specific combinations of features is not available pre-attentively, and attention may be required to accurately combine the separate features of a given object. Thus, in visual search tasks where targets are defined on the basis of a single feature (such as being a particular colour, orientation or containing a particular local form element), responses may be determined by parallel pre-attentive processing. In contrast, responses in visual search tasks with targets defined by a particular combination of features will be dependent on the application of focal attention to each display item (in order to combine the separate feature coded at each location), so generating linear search functions (e.g., Treisman & Gelade, 1980). Now, according to this feature-integration position, patients who are unable to attend to one side of space may nevertheless be able to make discriminations to neglected stimuli based on the kinds of information made available by pre-attentive vision (i.e., single element codings or grouped information within a single feature domain). On the other hand, discriminations to neglect-side stimuli based on specific combinations of features will be extremely difficult[3, 4].

A rather different view is that information about the specific combinations of features is represented pre-attentively, but that attention must be engaged by this information for action to be directed to the stimulus (cf. Allport, Tipper & Chmiel, 1985) and even for the assignment of a unique discriminatory response to it (termed "perceptual identification" by Humphreys, 1985). According to this view, attention may need to be engaged even when single feature discriminations are required (see Duncan, 1985, for evidence on this point), though the ease with which attention is drawn to a given feature will depend on its discriminability. It follows that the efficiency of visual search will be determined by the relative discriminability of the target to its distractors and not by qualitative differences between single feature and combined-feature targets : parallel search functions will arise with relatively easy discriminations, serial search functions will arise with more difficult discriminations (Duncan, 1985).

We have suggested earlier that unilateral neglect may occur because stimuli on the neglected side of space fail to engage visual attention. Now, if attention is necessary for perceptual identification, neglect patients may often fail to detect both single and combined-feature targets presented to the neglected side of space, though some differences between the absolute numbers of correct detections may occur depending on the relative discriminability of targets and distractors. More importantly, when correct detections occur, the search functions for both single and combined-feature targets should be similar for neglect and for non-neglect side stimuli, since both single and combined-feature information is thought to be made available by pre-attentive vision.

V. Some Data

We have investigated the above predictions in a series of visual search tasks with neglect patients, which have examined search for targets defined by a variety of single feature differences relative to distractors (such as closure, colour, orientation and size) and for targets defined by combinations of features. We wish to highlight here the types of visual search functions found with one salient single feature target and with one combined-feature target, since it is the contrast between these two types of target which is critical to the different accounts of neglect. In the single feature condition, the target was a red circle and the distractors were all green circles ; in the combined-feature condition, the target was an inverted "T" and the distractors were all upright "T"s. In the latter condition, targets and distractors differ only in the spatial arrangement of their component lines, so that targets are defined only by the particular combination of component features.

General method

Three patients (one male, two female) participated in the experiments, H.C., I.J. and A.S. (ages 75, 68 and 76 years respectively). All the patients were right handed pre-morbidly, and each suffered damage to the parietal area of the right cerebral hemisphere consequent on a stroke. H.C. and I.J. had dense hemiplegias and A.S. had a more mild hemiparesis. All the patients were categorized as manifesting unilateral left-sided neglect in drawing tasks. I.J. and A.S. both had a homonymous left hemianopia ; H.C. had intact visual fields. Testing for each of the patients was commenced 4 months post lesion and continued for a further 4 months, during which time their condition remained relatively stable. Tests for the effects of practice on their visual search performance failed to reveal any strong improvements in any single condition over the test period.

In any one session, each patient performed at least two different visual search tasks drawn at random from the full range of searches examined. For any one condition within a session, the patient was presented with a series of 160 cards, 80 with the target present and 80 with the target absent. Of the target-present cards, 20 had the target in the left upper quadrant, 20 in the left lower quadrant, 20 in the right upper quadrant and 20 in the right lower quadrant. Within each quadrant, the target was positioned in the upper left region 4 times, the right upper region 4 times, the left lower region 4 times, the right lower region 4 times and the middle region 4 times. Distractor items were randomly arranged on the cards. The numbers of distractors was manipulated. Forty cards had 4 items per quadrant (16 per card), 40 had 6 items per quadrant (24 per card), 40 had 8 items per quadrant (32 per card) and 40 had 10 per quadrant (40 per card). The stimuli were presented on cards which were 12.6 cm (about 14 deg 24 min) wide and 10 cm (about 11 deg 26 min) in height.

The cards for each condition were presented randomly to the patient who was asked to decide whether the target was present or absent as quickly as possible without making errors. Each card was singly presented and positioned in the patient's midline, and each contained a central numeral which the patient was instructed to name aloud prior to commencing the search. RTs were recorded using a digital timer, and timing was started at the naming of the central numeral and it was completed by the patient giving a verbal "yes" (target present) or "no" (target absent) response. Within each condition, the numbers of trials carried out by each patient differed according to the numbers of errors each made, and a given condition was administered over a number of sessions until each patient contributed at least 7 RT data points at each display size to stimuli presented either contralaterally or ipsilaterally to the site of the lesion.

Experiment 1 : Colour search

In Experiment 1, subjects searched for a red circle against a background of green distractor circles. Each circle had a diameter of 8 mm. Each patient carried out a total of 320 trials, 40 target-absent trials at each display size and 20 target-present trials for each display-size and visual field combination.

Mean RTs and numbers of correct responses for each decision (target present and absent) at each display size (4,6,8 and 10 per quadrant) are given in Table 1.

Treating each patient as a single case study, there were no reliable effects of display size on either the RT or the error data for both H.C. and I.J.. There was a marginal effect of display size on A.S.'s RTs, though even in this case RTs did not increase linearly as a function of the display size. Thus, each patient appears to have been able to detect the colour-defined target on the basis of a parallel search of the display. Nevertheless, each patient also demonstrated neglect of the left side of the displays, since each made more errors to left than to right-side stimuli. For H.C. and A.S. there were no reliable differences between correct detection latencies for right and left side targets and both were faster than absent responses ; for I.J., correct detections were slower to left-side than to right-side targets, though absent responses were slower again.

These data indicate that neglect patients can manifest parallel processing of stimuli on the neglected side of space, at least when the task only requires the detection of a single disjunctive feature (such as a colour change relative to a homogeneous background). The result is consistent with the idea that such patients can have relatively intact pre-attentive visual processing; indeed, the latencies for correct target detections for H.C. and A.S. showed no effect of field of presentation. It is of interest, then, that despite demonstrating parallel processing in both visual fields, the patients also showed neglect in that they missed many left-side targets. The latter result is contrary to the argument that responses can be made directly on the basis of pre-attentive parallel processing (cf. Treisman & Gelade, 1980) ; rather, it appears that attention needs to be drawn to the information specified by pre-attentive vision for its detection to occur (cf. Duncan, 1985). In neglect patients, attention is not reliably captured by contralateral stimuli even when these stimuli are defined by a single, salient disjunctive feature which can be discriminated by means of a parallel search process ; consequently, targets are missed when they are presented contralaterally to the site of lesion. Patient I.J. also showed a latency increase on correct contralateral target detections, which further suggests that, at least in this patient, attention was first drawn to ipsilateral stimuli and it was only subsequently shifted to the contralateral side of space.

Experiment 2 : Inverted T search

In Experiment 2, subjects searched for an inverted T target against a background of upright T distractors. Each T was 8 mm high by 8 mm wide. H.C. performed a total of 640 trials, I.J. 480 trials and A.S. 320 trials.

The mean correct RTs and numbers of correct responses for each decision at each display size by each patient are presented in Table 2.

For all three patients, there were reliable effects on RTs of both the display size and the conditions (target-left, target-right and target absent). There were no reliable interactions. All the patients were slower to detect left than right-side targets, and, for H.C. and I.J., the RTs to left-side targets were as slow as those on target-absent trials. Also, for all the patients there were reliable linear increases in RTs as a function of the display size.

The error data tended to follow the same pattern as the RT data. All the patients made more errors to left than to right-side stimuli, and for H.C. and I.J., errors tended to increase as a function of the display size.

In this experiment, all the patients demonstrated serial visual search, with RTs increasing linearly as the display size increased. The search rates tended to be faster for right-field targets than for left-field targets, though the display size X condition interactions were all non-significant. The results suggest that a serial search is necessary to detect a target defined by the present combination of horizontal and vertical features (cf. Experiment 1)[5], and that the neglect patients here tended to search the right field prior to the left field. Absent responses were accurate and at least as slow as left-side target present responses. Now, given the large numbers of errors made to left-side targets, it would appear that patients often failed to search the left sides of the displays. On such trials, absent responses may be based on some internal deadline (which differed between patients ; compare H.C. with I.J.). Such a deadline may also come into play on the trials where subjects did search the left field, producing some fast absent responses close to some of the latencies for left-side target detections (particularly for H.C. and I.J.).

The contrast between the serial search functions found here and the parallel search functions for the colour-defined targets in Experiment 1 is

consistent with Treisman's argument that the combination of features needed
to distinguish an inverted T from upright T's demands the operation of a
serial attention-demanding process, whilst single feature targets can be
detected directly from parallel pre-attentive processing (e.g., Treisman &
Gelade, 1980; though see Experiment 1). The contrast is also consistent with
the idea that the colour-defined target captures attention more easily than
a target defined by a combination of features, so that steeper search
functions are obtained in the combined-feature condition (e.g., Duncan,
1985). Whichever position is adopted, the fact that the patients could
detect at least some left-side combined-feature targets here suggests that
the patients are able to represent detailed information about the spatial
positions of local form elements on the neglected side of space when the form
elements are attended (contrary to the representational schema account ;
see section II).

Experiment 3 : The effects of cueing

In a final experiment, we examined the effects of cueing on neglect for
single-feature (colour) and combined-feature (inverted T) targets. Prior
to commencing the search on each trial, the patients were cued to report a
letter positioned to the left side of the display. Now, if neglect patients
fail to attend to the side of space contralateral to the lesion because of
unilateral akinesia, or because of a failure to represent that side of space
internally, then cueing them to the neglected side whilst keeping other
display characteristics constant should not reduce neglect. However,
neglect should be reduced if patients neglect the contralateral side of
space because stimuli on that side fail to capture attention, even though
the processes involved in the conscious control of attention remain intact.

Experiment 3a : Cueing colour search. The same cards as used in Experiment 1
were employed, except that these cards were mounted on another card so that a
border 7.6 mm wide by 10 cm high occurred on the left side of each original
card. In the centre of this border was a capital letter. At the beginning of
each trial, the patient was instructed to read the letter on the left of the
card aloud prior to commencing the search. Timing began when the letter was
read aloud. All the patients undertook 320 trials.

Mean correct RTs and numbers of correct responses are presented in
Table 3.

For all the patients, there were reliable differences in RTs in the
three conditions, present-left, present-right and absent. Also, for H.C.
and for A.S. there were reliable main effects of display size, although in
both cases the linear component of the display size effect was not
significant. There were no interactions. Further analysis of the conditions
effect showed that for all patients absent responses were slower than
present responses, but that there were no differences in RTs to left and to
right-side targets. There was a similar lack of an effect of visual field in
the error data for each patient. It appears then that cueing the patients to
report a letter on the left side of the displays eliminated neglect.

When we compare the performance of each patient in the colour-search
task with and without cueing (Experiments 1 and 3a), we find that all the
patients were more likely to detect left-side targets under the cueing
conditions. However, RTs to left-side targets were not selectively
facilitated by cueing ; in fact, the only selective effect of cueing on
correct detection latencies was an increase in the right-side RTs for I.J..
The latter result suggests that cueing helped to override I.J.'s tendency to
attend first to the right sides of the displays.

The finding that cueing had a facilitatory effect on performance is contrary to both the unilateral akinesia account of unilateral neglect and to the representational schema account. Most interestingly, the contrast between the facilitation of target detections and the lack of facilitation in response latencies indicates that cueing benefitted a rather late detection process rather than target processing, since a processing benefit would presumably speed correct detections. It seems that the information specified by pre-attentive visual processing (e.g., the presence of a target against a homogeneous background) cannot be used directly for response purposes, and that attention needs to be drawn to the information before a discriminatory response can be based on it. For neglect patients, there is a breakdown in the processes which enable pre-attentive information to capture attention ; nevertheless, such patients remain able to shift attention consciously, and so they detect the information specified pre-attentively when cued to the contralateral side of space.

Experiment 3b : Cueing inverted T search

We have shown that cueing patients to the contralateral side of space can resolve neglect for single disjunctive feature targets. We have also investigated whether cueing can reduce neglect for combined-feature targets, such as an inverted T relative to a background of upright T's. The cueing procedure was the same as for Experiment 3a. H.C. performed 640 trials in total, I.J. and A.S. performed 320 trials.

Table 4 shows the mean correct RTs and the numbers of correct responses for each patient.

All the patients showed strong effects of both the condition and the display size on RTs, and there was a reliable condition X display size interaction for H.C.. Averaging over the conditions, I.J. and A.S. demonstrated reliable linear search functions. For I.J., absent responses were slower than present responses but there was no difference between left-side and right-side target present responses. For A.S., absent responses were also slower than present responses ; however, left-side present responses were also slower than right-side present responses. H.C. demonstrated reliable linear search functions on both the left-side present and on absent trials, but right-side present responses departed from linearity. Inspection of the error data reveals that the non-linear RT-display size search function shown by H.C. for right-side targets was probably due to a speed-accuracy trade-off, since he made more misses at the larger display sizes for right-side stimuli. All the patients missed more left than right-side stimuli.

Comparisons of performance here relative to when no cueing occurred (Experiment 2) indicate selectively faster and more accurate left-field target detections under the cueing condition for I.J. and A.S.. Thus, for these patients, cueing to the left side of the displays lessened neglect. In contrast, H.C.'s performance was not facilitated by cueing ; there were no reliable differences in either his response latencies or accuracy to left-side stimuli in Experiment 3a relative to Experiment 2. Our suggestion is that these different effects of cueing with different patients arose because of the strategies the patients adopted in the tasks. When cued to report the left-side letter prior to the search, H.C. tended to shift attention directly to the cue and then to revert to his normal strategy of searching the right-side of the displays. However, when cued to the left, I.J. and A.S. tended to conduct a serial search of the left hemifield. For H.C., then, left-side cues facilitate performance by allowing targets clearly specified by pre-attentive processing to be detected (e.g., with the colour-defined targets in Experiments 1 and 3a) ; however, since a left-side serial search is not induced, his detection of targets not easily

segmented from their background pre-attentively is not facilitated. I.J.
and A.S. do adopt a serial left-side search under the cueing conditions.
Their detection of inverted T targets is therefore facilitated, since the
detection of such targets is dependent on a serial search process.

VI. Conclusions and Speculations

In this chapter, we have attempted to outline some of the major accounts
of unilateral visual neglect, and we have presented data which we believe
throws further light on some of the processing difficulties encountered by
neglect patients. We have proposed that neglect may best be accounted for in
terms of a breakdown in the processes whereby visual stimuli capture visual
attention. The data we have presented support this account.

Three patients with right parietal damage have been shown to manifest
neglect in visual search tasks demanding the discrimination of targets
defined both by a single disjunctive feature and by a combination of
features. Neglect of single-feature targets is manifested in the accuracy
of response, while there is little difference in the search rates for those
stimuli in the neglected and the non-neglected fields which are correctly
detected. Also, the search in both fields appears to be spatially parallel.
From this evidence, it would appear that pre-attentive processing of the
neglected field may be relatively intact in such patients. It is important
to note that the findings suggest that discriminatory responses cannot be
formulated directly from pre-attentive information, otherwise no neglect
would occur ; rather, attention must be drawn to such information. Neglect
occurs because of a breakdown in the latter attentional-capture process.

In searches for combined-feature targets, neglect is manifest both in
response latencies and response accuracy. The detection of the
combined-feature targets here depended on a serial search process in both
hemifields. Slow and inaccurate responses to left-side targets would then
occur if neglect patients search the ipsilateral side of space prior to the
side contralateral to the side of lesion, and if they often fail to search
the contralateral side.

Interestingly, for two patients (I.J. and A.S.), neglect in both the
single and the combined-feature searches was reduced by cueing the patients
to attend to the left side of the displays. For a third patient, H.C., cueing
facilitated single-feature but not combined-feature search. The different
effects of cueing seem to depend on the strategy adopted by the patient when
instructed to shift attention in the combined-feature task. I.J. and A.S.
both conducted serial searches of the left hemifield when given the cueing
instruction ; H.C. appeared to shift attention directly to the left-side cue
without searching each individual left-side display member. Since
combined-feature information is not clearly specified pre-attentively (if
it is specified at all), the detection of such targets requires a serial
search process. Consequently, cueing only facilitated I.J. and A.S. in this
condition. Cueing reduced neglect for all patients in the single-feature
task, though, presumably because single-feature information is clearly
specified pre-attentively. The differential success of cueing for
different patients and different tasks may also go some way to explaining
some of the inconsistent effects of cueing on neglect which have been
previously reported. For instance, the results of cueing will depend on
whether patients are reliant on information specified pre-attentively or
whether they serially attend to the neglected hemifield, and on whether the
task can be performed on the basis of information made explicit
pre-attentively. The effects of the different processing strategies
adopted by patients under cueing conditions need to be examined more
thoroughly.

The present data have implications for understanding unilateral neglect and for understanding the role of attention in normal vision. First, consider the implications for understanding unilateral neglect. Our findings both support the kind of attentional argument we outlined above and they go against a number of other interpretations. For instance, the patients we have discussed all appear to have relatively intact pre-attentive processing, at least for colour. It is difficult to argue therefore that the patients had impaired early visual processes. Further, one patient (H.C.) had no visual field defects, so the results cannot be attributed to selective effects of hemianopia. In addition, whilst neglect tended to be more severe in the combined-feature than the single-feature condition (e.g , consider the proportions of correct detections made ; see Tables 1 and 2), it was by no means the case that the patients were unable to discriminate any combined-feature targets in the neglected hemifield. This suggests that such patients are able to represent the spatial locations of form elements presented contralaterally to the lesion site. Finally, the reliable effects of cueing which were found, with neglect even being eliminated in the single-feature condition, contradict the view that the damaged hemisphere of neglect patients is underaroused and akinetic. Since the display characteristics were kept constant under the cueing conditions, the damaged hemisphere should remain underaroused relative to the arousal level of the intact hemisphere, and neglect should still occur. The unilateral akinesia argument also has difficulty explaining why different effects of cueing should have been found in the single and the combined-feature tasks.

One implication for understanding the role of attention in normal vision is that attention does not seem to be required solely to combine local feature elements (cf. Treisman, 1982; Treisman & Gelade, 1980), since the patients manifested neglect with both single and combined-feature targets : attention needs to be engaged by all stimuli (even single features) for discriminatory responses to be made. The result is consistent with other data recently reported by Quinlan and Humphreys (1984). They investigated visual search in normal subjects for 2 single-feature targets, with responses contingent on the detection of both features in the display. They found that search rates in the both conditions were the same as those found when subjects had only to detect 1 single-feature target, but that there was a constant increment to the response latencies (i.e., there was an effect on the intercept but not the slopes of the RT-display size functions). The latter result suggests that subjects processed the 2 features in parallel, but that they needed to attend serially to the information specified by the parallel processing before responding ; the switching of attention between the 2 feature-defined targets produced the constant RT increment across the display sizes. Thus attention seems to be needed if we are to act on the basis of information specified by pre-attentional visual processes. Also, evidence for the operation of a parallel search process should not be taken as evidence that information may be made available for a response without attention (cf. Treisman & Kahneman, 1985).

Further work is needed if we are to understand in more detail the kinds of information specified by pre-attentive vision. The present contrast between the serial search functions for the combined-feature targets and the parallel functions for the single-feature targets is consistent with each of two rather different views of attention. It could be that the pre-attentional processes do not specify combined-feature information, so that a serial search is then demanded (Treisman & Gelade, 1980) ; alternatively, a full description of the stimulus may be specified pre-attentively but action may not be effected on the basis of the

description unless it is attended (cf. Duncan, 1980, 1985). According to the
latter account, combined-feature searches are relatively difficult not
because the information is unspecified pre-attentively but because it is
relatively difficult to discriminate (perhaps because location information
is not accurately coded or because it is rapidly lost). To separate the above
accounts, we need to examine whether neglect patients are sensitive to
higher-order properties of stimuli projected to the neglected hemifield,
such as their meaning. For the present, we are able to maintain that early
pre-attentive processing is relatively intact in at least some neglect
patients, and that neglect stems from an inability to translate the
information specified pre-attentively into a form which will support
action. Such a deficit could stem from a number of causes, such as damage to
cells mediating shifts of covert attention to stimuli (e.g., Wurtz,
Goldberg & Robinson, 1982), from damage to cells involved in the translation
of information specifying boundary regions in visual scenes into a visible
form suitable for the direction of action (e.g., Grossberg & Mingolla, 1985,
in press), or from cells mediating the translation of information about
"where" an object is to information about "what" the object is (cf.
Ungerleider & Mishkin, 1982). These possibilities are not mutually
exclusive, and it may be that translation from boundary information to
visible form information or from information about "where" objects are to
"what" they are, are mediated by covert visual attention.

References

Albert, M. A simple test of visual neglect. Neurology, 1973, 23, 658–665.
Allport, D.A., Tipper, S.P. & Chmiel, N.R.J. Perceptual integration and
    post-categorical filtering. In M.I. Posner & O.S.M. Marin (Eds.),
    Attention and Performance XI. Hillsdale, N.J.: Erlbaum, 1985.
Bashinski, H.S. & Bacharach, V R. Enhancement of perceptual sensitivity as
    the result of selectively attending to spatial locations. Perception
    and Psychophysics, 1980, 28, 241–248.
Battersby, W.S., Bender, M.B., Pollack, M. & Kahn, R.L. Unilateral spatial
    agnosia in patients with brain lesions. Brain, 1965, 79, 68–92.
Belluza, T., Rappaport, M., Hopkins, H.K. & Hall, K. Visual scanning and
    matching dysfunctions in brain damaged patients with drawing
    impairment. Cortex, 1979, 15, 19–36.
Birch, H.G., Belmont, I. & Karp, E. Delayed information processing
    following brain damage. Brain, 1967, 90, 113–130.
Bisiach, E. & Luzzati, C. Unilateral neglect of representational space.
    Cortex, 1978, 14, 129–133.
Bisiach, E., Capitani, E., Luzzati, C. & Perani, D. Brain and conscious
    representation of outside reality. Neuropsychologia, 1981, 19,
    543–551.
Bisiach, E., Luzzati, C. & Perani, D. Unilateral neglect, representational
    schema and consciousness. Brain, 1979, 102, 609–618.
Brain, W.R. Visual disorientation with special reference to lesions of the
    right hemisphere. Brain, 1941, 64, 244–272.
Caelli, T.M., Julesz, B. & Gilbert, E.N. On perceptual analyzers underlying
    visual texture discrimination : Part II. Biological Cybernetics,
    1978, 29, 201–214.
Caplan, P.J. & Kinsbourne, M. Baby drops the rattle : Asymmetry of duration
    of grasp by infants. Child Development, 1976, 47, 532–534.
Chedru, F. Space representation in unilateral spatial neglect. Journal of
    Neurology, Neurosurgery and Psychiatry, 1976, 39, 1057–1061.
Chedru, F., LeBlanc, M. & Lhermitte, F. Visual searching in normal and brain

damaged subjects. Cortex, 1973, 9, 94-111.

Critchley, M. The Parietal Lobes. New York : Hafner, 1966.

Denny-Brown, D. & Fisher, E.G. Physiological aspects of visuospatial perception. Archives of Neurology, 1976, 33, 228-242.

Denny-Brown, D., Meyer, J.S. & Horenstein, S. The significance of perceptual rivalry resulting from parietal lesion. Brain, 1952, 75, 434-471.

DeRenzi, E., Faglioni, P. & Scotti, G. Hemispheric contribution to the exploration of space through the visual and tactile modality. Cortex, 1970, 6, 191-203.

Diller, L. & Weinberg, J. Hemi-inattention in rehabilitation The evolution of a rational remediation programme. Advances in Neurology, 1977, 18, 63-82.

Duncan, J. The locus of interference in the perception of simultaneous stimuli. Psychological Review, 1980, 87, 272-300.

Duncan, J. Visual search and visual attention. In M.I. Posner & O.S.M. Marin (Eds.), Attention and Performance XI. Hillsdale, N.J. : Erlbaum, 1985.

Ettlinger, G., Warrington, E.K. & Zangwill, O.L. A further study of visuo-spatial agnosia. Brain, 1957, 80, 335-361.

Friedland, R. & Weinstein, E. Hemi-inattention and hemisphere specialisation : Introduction and historical review. Advances in Neurology, 1977, 18, 1-31.

Friedrich, F.J., Walker, J.A. & Posner, M.I. Effects of parietal lesions on visual matching : Implications for reading errors. Cognitive Neuropsychology, 1985, 2, 253-264.

Grossberg, S. & Mingolla, E. Neural dynamics of form perception : Boundary completion, illusory figures, and neon color spreading. Psychological Review, 1985, 92, 173-211.

Grossberg, S. & Mingolla, E. Neural dynamics of perceptual grouping : Textures, boundaries, and emergent features. Perception and Psychophysics, in press.

Hecaen, H. Clinical sympomatology in right and left hemisphere lesions. In V.B. Mountcastle (Ed.), Interhemispheric Relations and Cerebral Dominance. Baltimore : John Hopkins Press, 1962.

Heilman, K. & Valenstein, E. Frontal lobe neglect in man. Neurology, 1972, 22, 660-664.

Heilman, K. & Valenstein, E. Mechanisms underlying hemispatial neglect. Annals of Neurology, 1979, 5, 166-170.

Heilman, K. & Van der Abel, T. Right hemisphere dominance for attention. The mechanism underlying hemispheric asymmetries of attention (neglect). Neurology, 1980, 30, 327-330.

Heilman, K. & Watson, R.T. The neglect syndrome : A unilateral defect of the orienting response. In S. Harnad (Ed.), Lateralization in the Nervous System. New York : Academic Press, 1977.

Hoffman, J.E. A two-stage model of visual search. Perception & Psychophysics, 1979, 29, 319-327.

Humphreys, G.W. Attention, automaticity and autonomy in visual word processing. In D. Besner, T.G. Waller & G.E. Mackinnon (Eds.), Reading Research : Advances in Theory and in Practice. V.5. New York : Academic Press, 1985.

Humphreys, G.W., Riddoch, M.J. & Quinlan, P.T. Interactive processes in perceptual organization : Evidence from visual agnosia. In M.I. Posner & O.S.M Marin (Eds.), Attention & Performance XI. Hillsdale, N.J. : Erlbaum, 1985.

Jonides J Voluntary versus automatic control over the mind's eyes. In J.

Long & A.D. Baddeley (Eds.), <u>Attention and Performance IX</u>. Hillsdale, N.J. : Erlbaum, 1981.

Julesz B. Spatial nonlinearities in the instantaneous perception of textures with identical power spectra. <u>Philosophical Transactions of the Royal Society</u>, London, <u>B</u>, 1980, <u>290</u>, 83–94.

Julesz, B. Textons, the elements of texture perception and their interactions. <u>Nature</u>, 1981, <u>290</u>, 91–97.

Julesz, B. & Caell,; T.M. On the limits of Fourier decomposition in visual texture perception. <u>Perception</u>, 1979, <u>8</u>, 69–73.

Kahneman, D. & Treisman, A. Changing views of attention and automaticity. In R. Parasuraman, R. Davies & J; Beatty (Eds.), <u>Varieties of Attention</u>. New York : Academic Press, 1983.

Kinsbourne, M. Cerebral basis of lateral asymmetries in attention. In A.L. Sanders (Ed.), <u>Attention & Performance III</u> . Amsterdam : North Holland, 1970.

Kinsbourne, M. <u>Asymmetrical Function of the Brain</u>. Cambridge : Cambridge University Press, 1978.

Lawson, I.R. Visuospatial neglect in lesions of the right hemisphere : A study in recovery. <u>Neurology</u>, 1962, <u>12</u>, 23–33.

Lynch, J.C. The functional organization of posterior parietal association cortex. <u>The Behavioural and Brain Sciences</u>, 1980, <u>3</u>, 485–534.

McFie, J., Piercy, M.F. & Zangwill, O.L. Visuospatial agnosia associated with the lesions of the right cerebral hemisphere. <u>Brain</u>. 1950, <u>73</u>, 167–190.

McFie, J. & Zangwill, O.L. Visuo–constructive disabilities associated with lesions of the left cerebral hemisphere. <u>Brain</u>, 1960, <u>83</u>, 243–260.

Merikle, P.M. Unconscious perception revisited. <u>Perception and Psychophysics</u>, 1982, <u>31</u>, 298–301.

Mesulam, M.M. A cortical network for directed attention and unilateral neglect. <u>Annals of Neurology</u>, 1981, <u>10</u>, 309–325.

Morgan, M.J., Findlay, J.M. & Watt, R.J. Aperture viewing : A review and a synthesis. <u>Quarterly Journal of Experimental Psychology</u>, 1982, <u>34A</u>, 211–234.

Neisser, U. <u>Cognitive Psychology</u>. New York : Appleton–Century–Crofts, 1967.

Oxbury, J.M., Campbell, D.C. & Oxbury, S.M. Unilateral spatial neglect and impairments of spatial analysis and visual perception. <u>Brain</u>, 1974, <u>97</u>, 551–564.

Posner, M.I. <u>Chronometric Explorations of Mind. The Third Paul M. Fitts Lectures</u>. Hillsdale, N.J. : Lawrence Erlbaum Associates, 1978.

Posner, M.I. Orienting of attention. <u>Quarterly Journal of Experimental Psychology</u>, 1980, <u>32</u>, 3–25.

Posner, M.I. & Cohen, Y. Components of visual orienting. In H. Bouma & D. Bowhuis (Eds.), <u>Attention & Performance X</u>. Hillsdale, N.J. : Erlbaum, 1984.

Posner, M.I. & Rafal, R.D. Cognitive theories of attention and rehabilitation of attentional deficits. In R.J. Meier, L. Diller & A.C. Benton (Eds.), <u>Neuropsychological Rehabilitation</u>. London : Churchill Livingstone, in press.

Posner, M.I., Cohen, Y. & Rafal, R.D. Neural systems control of spatial orienting. <u>Philosophical Transactions of the Royal Society</u>, London, <u>B</u>, 1982, <u>298</u>, 60–70.

Posner, M.I., Nissen, M.J. & Ogden, W.C. Attended and unattended processing modes : The role of set for spatial location. In H.L. Pick & I.J. Saltzman (Eds.), <u>Modes of Perceiving and Processing Information</u>. Hillsdale, N.J. : Erlbaum. 1978.

Posner, M.I., Snyder, C.R.R. & Davison, B.J. Attention and the detection of signals. Journal of Experimental Psychology : General, 1980, 109, 160-174.

Posner, M.I., Walker, J.A., Friedrich, F.J. & Rafal, R.D. Effects of parietal injury on covert orienting of attention. The Journal of Neuroscience, 1984, 4, 1863-1874.

Quinlan, P.T. & Humphreys, G.W. Searching for features and searching for conjunctions. Paper presented to the Experimental Psychology Society, London, January, 1984.

Remington, R.W. Attention and saccadic eye movements. Journals of Experimental Psychology : Human Perception and Performance, 1980, 6, 726-744.

Riddoch, M.J. Unilateral neglect in the stroke patient : Implications for the physiotherapist. In Proceedings of the XIth World Congress of Physiotherapy, Stockholm, 1982.

Riddoch, M.J. & Humphreys, G.W. The effect of cueing on unilateral neglect. Neuropsychologia, 1983, 21, 589-599.

Segarra, J.M. & Angelo, J.N. Presentation I. In A.C. Benton (Ed.), Behavioural Changes in Cerebrovascular Disease. New York : Harper, 1970.

Shulman, G.L., Remington, R.W. & McLean, J.P. Moving attention through visual space. Journal of Experimental Psychology : Human Perception and Performance, 1979, 5, 522-526.

Treisman, A. Perceptual grouping and attention in visual search for features and for objects. Journal of Experimental Psychology : Human Perception and Performance, 1982, 8, 194-214.

Treisman, A. Properties, parts and objects. In K. Boff, L. Kaufman & J. Thomas (Eds.), Handbook of Perception and Human Performance. New York: Wiley, 1984.

Treisman, A. & Gelade, G. A feature-integration theory of attention. Cognitive Psychology, 1980, 12, 97-136.

Treisman, A. & Kahneman, D. Addendum : A reply to Duncan. In M.I. Posner and O.S.M. Marin (Eds.), Attention & Performance XI. Hillsdale, N.J. : Erlbaum, 1985.

Treisman, A. & Schmidt, H. Illusory conjunctions in the perception of objects. Cognitive Psychology, 1982, 14, 107-141.

Treisman, A., Sykes, M. & Gelade, G. Selective attention and stimulus integration. In S. Dornic (Ed.), Attention & Performance VI. Hillsdale, N.J. : Erlbaum, 1977.

Tsal, Y. Movements of attention across the visual field. Journal of Experimental Psychology : Human Perception and Performance, 1983, 9, 523-530.

Turkewitz, G., Gordon, E.W. & Birch, H.G. Head turning in the human neonate : Spontaneous patterns. Journal of Genetic Psychology, 1965, 107, 143.

Ungerleider, L.G. & Mishkin, M. Two cortical visual systems. In D.J. Ingle, M.A. Goodale & R.J.W. Mansfield (Eds.), Analysis of Visual Behaviour. Cambridge, Mass. : MIT Press.

Volpe, B.T., LeDoux, J.E. & Gazzaniga, M.S. Information processing in an "extinguished" visual field. Nature, 1979, 282, 722-724.

Watson, R.T., Andriola, M. & Heilman, K.M. The EEG in neglect. Journal of Neurological Science, 1977, 34, 343-348.

Watson, R.T., Heilman, K.M., Cauthen, J.C. & King, K.A. Neglect after cingulectomy. Neurology, 1973 23, 1003-1007.

Watson, R.T., Heilman, K.M., Miller, B.D. & King, F.A. Neglect after mesencephalic reticular formation lesions. Neurology, 1974, 24, 294-298.

Weinberg, J., Diller, L., Gordon, W.A., Gerstman, L.J., Lieberman, A., Lakin, P., Hodges, G. & Ezrachi, O. Visual scanning training effect on reading-related tasks in acquired right brain damage. Archives of Physical Medicine and Rehabilitation, 1977, 58, 479-486.
Weinberg; J., Diller, L., Gordon, W.A., Gerstman, L.J., Lieberman, A., Lakin, P., Hodges, G. & Ezrachi, O. Training sensory awareness and spatial organization in people with right brain damage. Archives of Physical Medicine and Rehabilitation, 1979, 60, 491-196.
Wurtz, R.H., Goldberg, M.E. & Robinson, D.L. Brain mechanisms of visual attention. Scientific American, 1982, 246, 124-135.
Zarit, S.H. & Kahn, R.L. Impairment and adaptation in chronic disabilities : spatial inattention. Journal of Nervous and Mental Disease, 1974, 159, 63-72.

Acknowledgements : The work reported in this chapter was supported by a grant from the Chest, Heart and Stroke Association to both authors. We wish to thank the Physiotherapy Department at Barnet General Hospital and Dr A. Wilson for facilitating the testing and for enabling our access to patients to occur, and Cathy Price and Philip Quinlan for carrying out the analyses of the data. We especially thank the patients for their kind co-operation.

Footnotes

1. Posner et al.'s (1984) argument that one component of covert attention is disrupted in neglect is supported by other evidence indicating the selective impairment of other component processes. For instance, mid-brain lesions appear to affect the time taken to shift attention between locations (Posner et al., 1982), suggesting a specific disruption to the "move" operation.

2. Non-linear effects of display size on search performance may be attributed to a parallel search process which either has some capacity limitations or which is constrained by lateral masking.

3. An analogy may be made here with the performance of normal subjects when focal attention to a visual display is prevented, where subjects may report incorrect combinations of separable features ("illusory conjunctions" ; see Treisman & Schmidt, 1982). Such reports can be interpreted as indicating that single feature information is made available pre-attentively but that, without focal attention, the features are combined at random.

4. Normally, discriminations requiring the combination of features in a visual search task are ensured by using distractors which contain some but not all of the critical features defining the target. The correct combination of such features will therefore demand their accurate localization, since otherwise illusory conjunctions may arise. The predictions of the feature-integration view, then, approximate those made by a representational account of neglect, and both predict that search for combined-feature targets on the neglected side of space will be very impaired.

5. Humphreys, Riddoch and Quinlan (1985) have recently reported that non-linear search functions can obtain in a task where subjects must discriminate an inverted T from a background of homogeneous upright T distractors. Whether or not linear search functions occur in this task seems to depend on the size of the local elements and on their relative positions in the visual field. Presumably, the position and size of the local elements did not enable parallel (non-linear) processing to obtain here.

TABLE 1

Mean correct RTs (secs) and numbers of correct responses for each patient in E1 : colour search.

	Target present, left field				Target present, right field				Target absent			
	4	6	8	10	4	6	8	10	4	6	8	10
H.C. RT	2.06	1.87	2.51	1.90	1.81	1.93	1.82	2.10	2.32	2.23	2.2	2.36
No correct	10/20	12/20	10/20	11/20	19/20	18/20	17/20	16/20	40/40	40/40	39/40	40/40
I.J. RT	2.81	3.16	3.01	3.15	2.39	2.45	2.54	2.62	3.85	3.93	4.02	4.37
No correct	14/20	11/20	9/20	13/20	20/20	20/20	20/20	20/20	40/40	40/40	40/40	40/40
A.S. RT	1.43	1.91	1.79	1.88	1.46	1.37	1.70	1.60	2.64	2.79	2.97	3.14
No correct	16/20	17/20	18/20	17/20	20/20	20/20	20/20	20/20	40/40	39/40	40/40	40/40

TABLE 2

Mean correct RTs (secs) and numbers of correct responses for each patient in E2 : inverted T search

	Target present, left field				Target present, right field				Target absent			
	4	6	8	10	4	6	8	10	4	6	8	10
H.C. RT	2.74	3.67	3.70	4.77	2.59	2.67	2.80	3.31	3.11	3.70	3.88	4.06
No correct	9/40	9/40	7/40	8/40	37/40	29/40	27/40	25/40	80/80	80/80	80/80	80/80
I.J. RT	5.96	8.04	7.46	8.63	3.19	4.37	4.43	4.07	6.92	7.81	8.73	9.22
No correct	15/30	16/30	10/30	7/30	30/30	30/30	28/30	28/30	60/60	60/60	60/60	60/60
A.S. RT	3.78	3.94	4.63	5.20	1.88	2.14	2.49	2.67	4.75	5.78	6.75	6.93
No correct	13/20	14/20	16/20	16/20	20/20	20/20	20/20	20/20	40/40	40/40	40/40	40/40

TABLE 3

Mean correct RTs (secs) and numbers of correct responses for each patient in Experiment 3a : Cued colour search.

	Target present, left field				Target present, right field				Target absent			
	4	6	8	10	4	6	8	10	4	6	8	10
H.C. RT	1.32	1.23	1.51	1.80	1.62	1.55	1.62	1.64	1.65	1.70	1.89	2.05
No correct	16/20	16/20	16/20	16/20	17/20	15/20	16/20	15/20	40/40	40/40	40/40	40/40
I.J. RT 2.81	3.50	3.41	3.57	3.34	2.90	2.91	3.06	3.38	4.82	5.09	6.16	5.65
No correct	20/20	18/20	20/20	20/20	20/20	20/20	20/20	20/20	40/40	40/40	40/40	40/40
A.S. RT	1.54	1.67	1.91	1.81	1.33	1.68	1.48	1.62	1.87	2.41	2.41	2.51
No correct	20/20	18/20	20/20	20/20	20/20	20/20	20/20	20/20	40/40	40/40	40/40	40/40

TABLE 4

Mean correct RTs (secs) and numbers of correct responses for each patient in Experiment 3b : Cued inverted T search.

	Target present, left field				Target present, right field				Target absent			
	4	6	8	10	4	6	8	10	4	6	8	10
H.C. RT	2.45	3.50	4.39	4.39	2.70	2.60	2.60	3.28	3.08	3.54	3.94	3.83
No correct	12/40	9/40	10/40	10/40	37/40	34/40	26/40	29/40	80/80	80/80	80/80	80/80
I.J. RT	5.01	5.39	4.17	5.43	4.09	5.92	5.04	6.19	7.73	8.27	9.59	8.86
No correct	15/20	13/20	11/20	11/20	11/20	20/20	17/20	18/20	40/40	40/40	40/40	40/40
A.S. RT	2.61	2.53	3.06	2.86	1.92	2.11	2.24	2.76	4.09	5.00	5.77	6.48
No correct	19/20	19/20	20/20	13/20	20/20	20/20	20/20	20/20	40/40	40/40	40/40	40/40

Neurophysiological and Neuropsychological Aspects
of Spatial Neglect, M. Jeannerod (editor)
© Elsevier Science Publishers B.V. (North-Holland), 1987

DYSCHIRIA. AN ATTEMPT AT ITS SYSTEMIC EXPLANATION

Edoardo Bisiach
and
Anna Berti

It is argued, in this chapter, that unilateral neglect is still in
need of a systemic explanation. The working hypothesis is then
suggested that unilateral neglect has remained conceptually
isolated within a syndrome of which it may constitute the most
common, but not the exclusive nor even the necessary component. A
theoretical neural model of an analog subserving both sensory and
mental representation in the visuo-spatial domain is outlined.
Depending on relatively minor changes in its location within the
same functional unit, a circumscribed failure of the analog may
involve neglect or misrepresentation of one side of space, thus
lending theoretical support to our working hypothesis. The term
dyschiria is proposed for the syndrome of hemispatial
neglect-misrepresentation as a late tribute to H. Zingerle, who
many years ago, in one of his papers which was a forerunner of this
subject, employed this term.

Introduction

Looking back over nearly one century of inquiry into the complex
condition which usually goes by the (arguably underinclusive) name of
unilateral neglect of space, it may be noticed that -- almost without
exception -- this condition has only been addressed under what might be
called a de-interpretative approach. The term de-interpretative is here
used, in hopeful but uncommitted correspondence with Haugeland (1978), to
denote the shift in scope which occurs when an operating system is not
explained as a whole but in terms of its single components, under the
assumption that the general pattern being carried out by the former is
opaque to the latter. Space-related behaviour may accordingly be
interpreted in terms of separate subroutines for sensory integration,
receptor orientation, attentional shift and steering of motor activity,
with little or no concern for the complexity and meaning of the total
program. Thus, local disfunctions may be held responsible for failure in the
execution of the latter, while the systemic disorder is lost to view. Such
having been the prevailing approach to unilateral neglect, the regrettable
consequences which have ensued are threefold: first, wrong interpretations
have been fostered; second, the cognitive aspects of this condition have
been obscured and, third, the contribution which the study of unilateral
neglect can give to the reappraisal of theories about the activity of the
brain as a whole has been delayed.

Sensory hypotheses as explanations of unilateral neglect are
well-known (see Heilman & Watson, 1977, for a review) and do not require
further assessment, since their validity against which undermining
arguments had already been anticipated by Zingerle (1913), has been

definitively refuted by the demonstration of neglect phenomena in the representational domain. These phenomena will presently be reviewed. This of course, does not mean that sensory disorders have no role to play in shaping the neglect syndrome. For example, it has been found that neglect patients with conventionally diagnosed hemianopia show more severe neglect of the affected hemispace under visual control, than in a condition in which the latter is prevented by a blindfold (Chedru, 1976).

Contrary to the sensory hypotheses, there has never been an unambiguous formulation of an oculomotor hypothesis. This sort of explanation, indeed, has been criticized by some writers although it has never been factually upheld. The paper by Schott, Jeannerod and Zahin (1966), to which such a hypothesis has been connected (e.g. De Renzi, 1982, p. 106), though laying special emphasis on oculomotor disorders in the description of the syndrome, is far from claiming their unique role in the causation of neglect; these authors, to the contrary, even suggest that it may be incorrect to talk of neglect or inattention with reference to a space which is lost in the subject's representation, thus hinting at the necessity of a much more sophisticated interpretation. It is, however, a well established fact that clear manifestations of unilateral neglect can be found, dissociated from clinically detectable oculomotor impairment (Hécaen, Penfield, Bertrand & Malmo, 1956; Hécaen, 1962; Gainotti, 1968; Bisiach, Luzzatti & Perani, 1979). Thus, the frequent association of the two disorders should either depend on the anatomical contiguity of the lesions respectively responsible for each of them, or on the disfunction of a common link, a disfunction which might express itself disproportionately on either versant. One point of interest, however, is the fact -- to which we shall return later -- that conjugate gaze defects toward the side contralateral to the lesion, occur more frequently after right-hemisphere injury (De Renzi, Colombo, Faglioni & Gibertoni, 1982), which is suggestive of a functional connection between these defects and unilateral neglect.

Attentional hypotheses are most prone to boil away as question-begging redescriptions of neglect phenomena and restatements of experimental results. In order for the explanations to be genuine, they must specify an underlying model of the mechanism which, under pathological conditions, may give rise to hemineglect. This requisite is met by the suggestions of Kinsbourne (1970, 1977) and of Heilman and his associates (Heilman & Van Den Abell, 1980; Heilman, Watson & Valenstein, 1985). According to Kinsbourne, in the nervous system there is a competition between two opposed vectors of lateral attention, each pointing to the side contralateral to the hemisphere of origin. Relative hyperactivation of one hemisphere, caused by selective engagement in processing information or resulting from impairment of the opposite hemisphere, enhances its own vector. The greater incidence and severity of left rather than right neglect might be due to the fact that, ceteris paribus, the left-hemisphere vector is physiologically dominant in right-handers, and that testing procedures often involve left-hemisphere activation. To account for hemispheric asymmetries in the occurrence of neglect, Heilman and associates have instead suggested that the right hemisphere controls attention over the entire space, whereas the control of the left is limited to the right hemispace.

We will not proceed to evaluate the attentional interpretation per se prior to considering a further conception, which sees unilateral neglect as a basically representational disorder. This is not intended as a tactic to create suspense; we wish to avoid arguing pro and con the same ideas defined with differing terms or metaphors. To prevent ambiguities, we shall hereafter employ the terms of "sensory" and "mental" representation to refer, respectively and without any further implication, to the pattern of constraints imposed upon neural activities by current sensory stimulation and to patterns of activity originating from within the nervous system itself, mimicking aspects of the former in any sensory domain and thereby recalling past (or simulating possible) states of affairs in the world. Whenever adjectivation is omitted, reference will be made to something shared by both kinds of representation.

A Neglected Classic on Neglect

The idea that unilateral neglect is a manifestation of a more general representational disorder is longstanding. It had been clearly expressed even before the full individuation of the syndrome had become, much to Babinski's credit, an established fact in clinical neurology.

In 1914 and 1918, Babinski submitted a partial outline of the syndrome under consideration, which was destined to remain famous, to the French Neurological Society. At a distance of many years, two aspects of those events may strike us as being singular. First, the bystanders (among whom were Souques, Déjerine, Pierre-Marie, Meige & Claude) reacted somewhat tepidly to Babinski's presentation of what was to become one of the major issues in neuropsychology. Second, notwithstanding the aura of novelty intimated by the records of the two sessions, the syndrome had in fact already been delineated. Even assuming that the recent, noteworthy contribution of Zingerle, published in the 1913 issue of Monatsschrift für Psychiatrie und Neurologie, could not have reached the French neurological community owing to the politico-military vicissitudes of the moment, it seems unlikely that earlier studies (quoted by Zingerle himself) had not enjoyed sufficiently wide circulation in France.

In that paper, Zingerle described two patients (Cases 2 and 3) who had completely lost "the notion of one side". Both patients had a right-hemisphere lesion: Case 2 a suspected hemorrage in the posterior limb of the internal capsule ; Case 3 an autoptically ascertained small abscess in the frontal lobe with diffuse meningeal phlogosis.

Case 2 had a left hemiplegia with hemianaesthesia and hemianopia. He would not talk about his paralysis. Whenever his attention was drawn to his left side, after a momentary glance at his left limbs, he would pay no further attention to them and would start to talk about another subject. Although acknowledging that all people have a right and a left side, he did not seem to apply that notion to himself. He would affirm that a woman was lying on his left side; he would utter witty remarks about this and sometimes caress his left arm. He would become perplexed and silent whenever the conversation touched upon the left half of his body; even attempts to evoke memories of it were unsuccessful. No other intellectual disorders were found during the course of the illness. About 14 days after the onset, delusional phenomena had dispersed; the patient remembered the impression of a strange woman at his side and wondered at it, but was only able to give a poor report of his earlier state. Commenting on this case, Zingerle acknowledged Anton's prior claims to having drawn attention to this peculiar syndrome and underlined that it was far from being a fixed concomitance of somatosensory disorders due to brain lesion, which could not, therefore, be ascribed any substantial causative role. On the other hand, Zingerle remarked that this patient, though having lost somatosensory information from the left side of his body, could still perceive it through other senses (sight and touch) of the unimpaired side; these percepts, however, had no bearing on his corporeal Ego. Moreover, the patient not only lacked sensations from the left side of his body and awareness of his paralysis: like Anton's patient he had also lost the memory of this side.

Case 3 never made use of his left limbs though they were not paralyzed.

Figure 1
Hermann Zingerle (1870-1935)

He was alert and co-operated in neurologic examinations except when reference was made to his left side, in which case he seemed suddenly deaf and would make no attempt to understand the examiner, whose request seemed rather to annoy him. About this case Zingerle remarked that since the patient was not paralyzed and his sensibility was retained at least in part on the left half of his body, one had to hypothesize a loss of representation of the latter or a disordered processing of sensory information needed for the spatial perception of the body. He also admitted that in this case the severe neglect of the left side might suggest a disorder of attention, a hypothesis he had not envisaged when discussing Case 2, presumably on account of the fact that patient 2 could give attention to his left limbs, though manifesting delusional ideas about them.

Zingerle's merit is not confined to the keenness of his clinical records. He offered an interpretation of the disorder which is still up-to-date and afforded a glimpse of the relevance it would have for the neurology of cognition.

The loss of sensory information may be placed alongside the impossibility of reproduction of earlier memories (from all sensory modalities) in the framework of a disordered awareness of the laterality of one's own body, ... It is particularly important, not only that the manifest recall cannot be awakened by corresponding sensory information, but also that the defect cannot be amended through sight and touch and the patient does not recognize the left half of his body, he does not see it as his property... . In his awareness, the body's representation is appearently confined to the right half ... (Zingerle's italics).

Thus, according to Zingerle, the basic explanation of the syndrome lies in disordered representation. He added that this explanation must be sufficiently flexible in order to account for the variability of the syndrome. Indeed, whereas some patients are totally oblivious of one side of the space, others, though unaware of their paralysis, do not ignore the left half of their body. As already remarked by Anton, sensory information in these patients could undergo faulty central processing, so that instead of neglect, they display delusional beliefs concerning the left half of their body.

It is not easy to find a satisfactory explanation for the singular state of oblivion which for so many years has deprived neuropsychology of such an important contribution and has left unchallenged the tendency whereby (stricto sensu considered) unilateral neglect has remained conceptually isolated within a syndrome of which it may indeed constitute the most common, but not the exclusive nor even the necessary component. Indeed, lesions which involve (in most instances) the right temporo-parieto-occipital carrefour or functionally related brain structures (see Vallar & Perani, this volume) do not always result in mere neglect: sometimes the patients do attend to the left half of space, though this reveals a pathological state of a generically negative kind. They may mourn over their paralyzed limbs while absurdly declaring themselves ready to engage in activities from which they are now obviously precluded. Well-known are the so-called somato-paraphrenic phenomena (Gerstmann, 1942), whereby a patient contends, e.g., that his left arm belongs to another person in spite of the fact that he can look at it, touch it and sometimes even move it deliberately, or can recognize a ring on one of the fingers of his left hand as his. Still more, the patients' attention appears in some instances invincibly attracted towards the alien limbs, for which they may show a spirited dislike and even persecutory impulses (Crtichley, 1953).

The pleomorphism of these manifestations could explain the delay, the slow course and the residual uncertainty of their framing into a unitary complex. Indeed, the lack in current literature of a term suitable for comprehensive denotation makes an during abeyance in the settlement of the disorders under consideration into a unitary syndrome evident. Yet, if under the working assumption of a single Grundstoerung it makes sense to collect the diverse phenomena at issue (whether defective — neglect — or productive — somato-paraphrenia and analogous disorders related to extrapersonal space) into a unitary cluster, it is also convenient to designate them collectively with a single term, which ought to be both

consistent at the descriptive level and uncommitted at the interpretative
level. There is indeed no need to coin a new word, since the term 'dyschiria'
(Greek chèir, cheiros: 'hand' and, by extension, 'side'), employed by
Zingerle (Note 1), meets both requirements and perfectly captures the
concept of alienation of one side of space which, however manifested, is the
essential feature of the syndrome.

It may be that on account of the heavy ideological conditioning due to
Behaviourism, and more precisely due to the aversion for postulated
entities such as representations, an even better circulation of Zingerle's
paper would not have exerted strong theoretical influence over several
decades. It is a fact (and perhaps a significant one) that the study of
dyschiria went through a long period of relative stagnation, until
Geschwind (1965), Kinsbourne (1970) and Heilman and associates (see Heilman
et al., 1985) reawakened interest in this area by demonstrating that it
could repay fresh and versatile inquiry.

Neglect Phenomena in the Representational Domain

In recent years a number of experimental contributions have resumed the
representational theory of dyschiria.

Patients with neglect for the left side of space can make correct
same-different judgments of pairs of visual stimuli whenever the difference
(e.g. in shape) lies in the unaffected right hemispace, whereas they commit
errors when the difference, as in Figure 2a, lies in the neglected left
hemispace. This is obvious enough. However the same outcome was obtained
(Bisiach et al., 1979) in a condition in which the patterns, instead of being
stationary and exposed to full vision, were moved from left to right or in
the opposite direction behind a central vertical slit (Figure 2b) so that

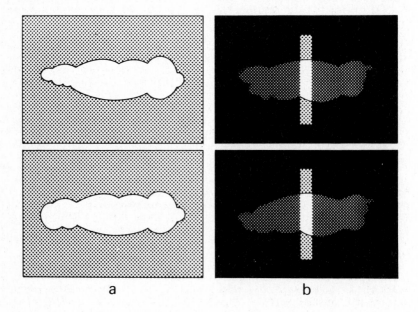

a   b

Figure 2
Patterns employed to demonstrate representational neglect.

the patients had the opportunity of focussing attention on all details in
succession but the apprehension of the whole shape required, as in
experiments such as those of Parks (1965) and Hochberg (1968), a process of
mental, representational reconstruction. Thus, the mental space in which
these visual representations were unfolded turned out itself to be
neglected in its left half exactly as the outer space. A similar experiment
with somewhat different patterns (Ogden, 1985) has recently confirmed these
results.

The same phenomenon was encountered with mental representations drawn
from long-term memory. Patients with left neglect were asked to give a
description of the cathedral square in Milan, with which they were quite
familiar, while imagining the cathedral to be in front of them (Bisiach &
Luzzatti, 1978; Bisiach, Capitani, Luzzatti & Perani, 1981). A variable
number of details, some of which fairly salient, were omitted from the left
half of the view. When a description of the same view was requested, but from
the opposite vantage point, previously omitted left-side details were
reported once transposed to the right, whereas right-side details which the
patient had reported a moment before, were omitted once transposed to the
left. Quite comparable records had previously been made by Messerli
(personal communication, February 1984) by asking neglect patients to give
a mental description of the Place Neuve in Geneva, during routine clinical
testing. A related and even more telling observation has more recently been
reported (Baxter & Warrington, 1983), relative to a patient with left
neglect who misspelled the left half of words, both forwards and backwards,
as if reading letter after letter from words written on an imaginary
display, of which the left half was hidden to the mind's eye. It is
especially significant (as it will be argued later) that this patient was
quite aware of his disorder and that he himself "described attempting to
spell like reading off an image in which the letters on the right side were
clearer than those on the left"! This singular phenomenon might in fact be
far from exceptional, since it has subsequently been observed in another
neglect patient (Gazzaniga & Barbut, personal communication, June 1985).

Implications Relative to the Structure and Levels of Neural Representation of Space

There seem to be two radically distinct ways in which the brain may
accomplish the task of preserving spatial properties of information
throughout perception, thought and action; that is performing the function
we consider when we talk of space representation. One way is that of some
mechanism operating as a spatial analog; the other is based upon a
propositional encoding of spatial relations. It would exceed the scope of
this chapter to dwell on and attempt a full elucidation of these two concepts
since the work of Shepard et al. (e.g. Shepard, 1975), Kosslyn et al. (e.g.
Kosslyn, 1980) and Pylyshin (e.g. Pylyshyn, 1980, 1981), along with a wealth
of corollary writings arguing pro and contra imaginal and imageless thought
-- or agnostic (e.g. Anderson, 1978) -- provides vast pabulum to whomever
were tempted by the enterprise.

What seems plain, anyhow, is that both modes exist and interplay in the
nervous system. This is obvious if, at one extreme of the dichotomy, one
thinks of the mapping of visual space on the surface of the retina and of the
more or less readjusted retinotopic arrangement of neural structures more
and more remote from the periphery up to the so-called association cortex,
and grants that anatomical contiguity corresponds, in these structures, to
functional contiguity. Consider for instance the projection of a
chess-board on the retina: spatial relations among different loci of the
chess-board are represented in a picture-like fashion by corresponding

relations among different loci of the retina; not, of course, by virtue of
the actual spatial position of the latter but through appropriate
connectivity which might preserve its function -- at the cost of
considerable wiring entanglement -- even if, owing to a whim of nature,
dioptric media were such as to scatter the images of external objects in a
disorderly way over the whole receptor surface. This not being the case, a
spatially circumscribed destruction of the retina or of a retinotopically
organized structure such as primary visual cortex, entails a spatially
circumscribed   sensory   scotoma   which   demonstrates   that   neural
representation of the external world, at these levels, depends on an analog
device, like a sun-dial (an exemplary analog) which if destroyed in one
quadrant can no longer represent the corresponding arc of time, while
regularly functioning for the remainder. At the other extreme, however, the
spatial   locations   of   individual   squares   of   the   chess-board   may   be
represented in a much more abstract way by means of symbols made up by one
letter and one digit; and the operations performed on such symbols rely upon
a neural mechanism, the properties of which are remote from those of the
above considered analog and more and more akin to the system subserving the
representation of spatial relations in any natural language, that is to the
propositional mode of representation par excellence. Any trace of analog
processing has here disappeared and no selective disorder of language would
entail a disordered representation of a circumscribed area of space.

    Now, if both modes of representation operate and co-operate in the
nervous system, why should there be any debate about them? The controversy
seems to relate to their comparative accessibility to the ill-defined
category of cognition. Needless to say that if such a category is simply
defined according to the propositional quality of representations active at
its level, then analogue processing is ope legis relegated to another (more
or less tacitly underrated) domain of nervous activity. What Kosslyn has
endeavoured to argue for a long time and what we ourselves have repeatedly
claimed (Bisiach et al., 1979; Bisiach, Berti & Vallar, 1985a; Bisiach,
1985; Bisiach , Meregalli & Berti, 1985c; Bisiach, Perani, Papagno, Vallar &
Berti, forthcoming) is that non-propositional modes of representation play
a central role in crucial aspects of cognition such as belief-fixation and
the complex of self-monitoring activities which constitute what we
ordinarily designate by the term 'awareness'. Further scrutiny of evidence
from investigation of unilateral neglect and related disorders and of
arguments advanced on its basis will elucidate the point.

    First of all, it needs be observed that the analog mode of processing of
spatial relations is not confined to perceptual activity: as stated in the
foregoing section, indeed, it is shared by representational activities such
as those involved in reconstituting the shape of an object moving behind a
slit, in imagining and describing a view and even, at least in some
occasions, in word-spelling. In fact, spatially circumscribed destruction
of brain structures may not only produce spatially circumscribed sensory
losses   but   also   spatially   circumscribed   scotomata   in   mental
representations. This suggests that the same analog may at a certain stage
subserve perception as well as mental repres   ,tion; which fits with the
anatomical argument suggesting that topologically organized cortex beyond
primary areas, given its considerable extent, is much more likely to be
implied both in perception and in mental representation (Merzenich & Kaas,
1980). To counter one of the arguments advanced against the thesis of
imaginal (i.e. analog) visuospatial mental representation (Pylyshyn,
1981), it is worth reaffirming (cf Bisiach et al., 1985a) that the
appearance of a mental scotoma in neglect patients cannot be interpreted as
construed by the patients themselves in the act of imagining how they would

perceive the represented object given their sensory loss. Indeed, unilateral neglect may be present in patients with frontal lesions which do not involve visual pathways, and when it is associated with true hemianopia the patients, as a rule, are quite unaware of the latter.

Thus, both perception and mental representation seem to require a common substratum on which information originating either from without (perception) of from within the nervous system itself (mental representation) is laid down by means of an analog procedure reinstating the spatial properties of sensory arrays. An oversimplified, two-dimensional model of this processing stage is presented in Figure 3 (see Bisiach et al., 1985c, for further details). In what follows, the terms 'cell assembly' will refer to long-term functional groupings of cross-connected neurons within a larger net (Hebb, 1949) as well as to very short-term groupings (Goddard, 1980; von der Malsburg, 1981; Crick, 1984) such as those which rapidly form and decay in consequence of current sensory stimulation.

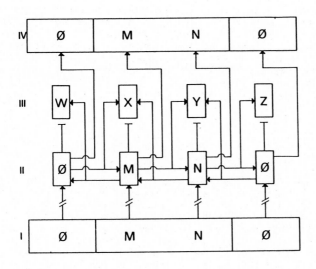

Figure 3
Model of 2-dimensional visuo-spatial processing.

Perception of the horizontally elongated pattern MN requires, in our model, transfer of information from a sensory transducer (layer I) to a spatial processor consisting of a neural net in which appropriate cell subassemblies (layer II) are directly recruited by single subpatterns (M,

N) and indirectly recruited by active subassemblies at the same level.
Indirect recruitment may contribute to the perception of a partially
occluded stimulus. Cell subassemblies unrelated to actual portions of the
incoming stimulation (layer III) but spatially corresponding to the
"veridical" subassemblies of layer II may also be recruited by the latter
and, through pathways omitted in the figure, by autochthonous,
self-organizing activity of the system. In normal perception cross-talk is
prevented by inhibition of parasitic layer III subassemblies from spatially
matching subassemblies of layer II, so that the output of the processor
(layer IV) constitutes the adequate codification of the perceived object,
ready for whatever further processing through higher order cell assemblies
and whatever mode of representation (analog or propositional) might be
required. Layer III, on the other hand, subserves mental representational
activities such as visual imagery, to which -- in normal conditions and by
virtue of the damping action from layer II -- no belief of reality is fixed.
Complete inactivation of one half of the analog (Figure 4) entails

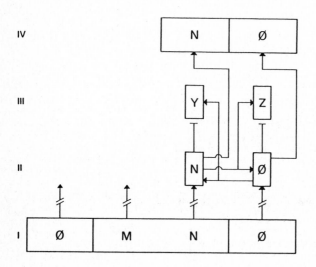

Figure 4
Disorder underlying unilateral neglect.

unilateral neglect of the corresponding half of space. Inactivation limited
to one half of layer II would uninhibit the activity in the corresponding
half of layer III (Figure 5) and release non-veridical representation of one
half of space resulting in phenomena of pathological completion and/or in
erroneous beliefs such as those exemplified by anosognosic and
somato-paraphrenic phenomena or by analogous delusions relative to one half
of extrapersonal space.

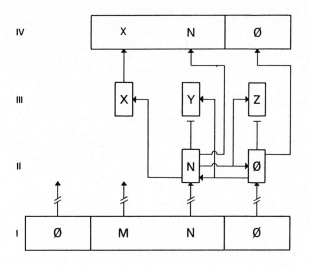

Figure 5
Disorder underlying pathological completion.

It is important to note that layer II is not directly accessed by the sensory transducer; taking visual modality as the most familiar paradigm, information carried by the sensory transducer is in fact assumed to undergo disjunct processing of separate features such as colour, shape and movement, carried out in parallel by specialized cortical areas before reaching layer II. Furthermore, the network of this layer acts as a retinoid (Trehub, 1977) on which overwritten images from temporo-spatially separate eye-fixations are disentangled and reassembled conforming to corollary information relative to exploratory eye- and head-movements. The same is true for the unfolding of images such as those generated by moving objects behind a stationary slit, which might imply computations over (not necessarily executed) oculomotor programs. A corresponding retinoid constituted by endogenously recruited cell assemblies, such as those artifically diagrammed as a separate layer of the same functional unit in our model (layer III) might achieve the synthesis of a composite mental representation. To what extent programs for eye- and head-moements are involved here is far from clear. The fact that, even in patients with severely depressed vigilance, ipsilesional eye deviation is more marked after right than after left acute brain damage (De Renzi et al., 1982) is suggestive of some implication of the oculomotor function, at its highest levels of organization, in the building of complex mental images which may

undergo the above mentioned local disarrangement in a syndrome -- dyschiria
-- which is itself mainly related to right hemishpere lesion. However, this
implication does not seem to be very close, since -- apart from the already
mentioned possibility of dissociation between neglect and oculomotor
disorders -- it has been argued that shiftings of attention may be quite
independent of eye-movements (Posner, Pea & Volpe, 1982).

It is also worth observing that the very concept of cell assembly
implies that the neural net of layers II and III is far from being a naive
structure. Even exclusively sensory-driven activity develops here through
synapses tuned by prior exposure to the environment. So, this neural net is
not a passive structure on which sensory and mental representations are
temporarily laid-down from a sensory buffer or from a separate long-term
store ; it is suggested to contain, besides the "surface" image currently
entertained and in the form of possible patterns of neural activity apt to be
triggered by appropriate input, all kinds of "deep" or "quiescent"
representations available to an individual nervous system depending on past
and present contingencies (see von der Malsburg, 1981, for a detailed model
of dynamic network structures such as the one envisaged here). The
combinatorial expanse of synaptic activity in this network is held to be
such as to make reasonable its suggested ability to subserve analog
representational processes in all their complexity.

Two other issues concerning the spatial processor outlined in our model
remain to be considered. The dynamics of the latter, indeed, must be such as
to account for two important data. One is the fact that in neglect patients a
left/right spatial anisotropy may also be observed in the hemispace
ipsilateral to the lesion. This phenomenon is known to clinical
neurologists in the guise of paradoxical extinction of the leftmost (nearer
to the fovea) of two simultaneous visual stimuli delivered in the right
field of right-parietal patients and has been demonstrated by various
experimental procedures both in animals (La Motte & Acuna, 1978) and in man
(Corin & Bender, 1972; Kinsbourne, 1977; Altman, Balonov & Deglin, 1979;
Bisiach, Cornacchia, Sterzi & Vallar, 1984; Gazzaniga & Ladavas, this
volume). The other is the fact that hemineglect seems to relate to at least
two distinct frames of spatial reference: one retinotopic and one possibly
connected with the mid-sagittal plane of the patient's body (Heilman &
Valenstein, 1979; Bisiach, Capitani & Porta, 1985b; Gazzaniga & Ladavas,
this volume). Perhaps, the best demonstration that the disorder is not only
framed in terms of retinotopic coordinates is the fact that in tasks
requiring the scanning of a visual array, e.g. in a cancellation task,
patients with left neglect almost always start from the rightmost item and
proceed leftwards until they stop, thus neglecting items located in the
same retinal position which, during foveation of the earlier scanned items,
was occupied by non-neglected items (a fact, incidentally, which seems to
provide the most elementary confutation of sensory explanations of
unilateral neglect).

An interpretation of the first phenomenon may be advanced in terms of
receptive fields of cells contributing to the constitution of neural nets
implementing analog spatial processors. Indeed, it has been found that in
the postarcuate cortex of monkeys, where one such analog might be located,
20% of the neurons have exclusively contralateral, 2% ipsilateral and 69%
bilateral fields (Rizzolatti, Scandolara, Matelli & Gentilucci, 1981).
Bilateral fields are always astride the midline, and vary in horizontal
extension, so that in its most lateral areas space representation relies
almost exclusively on the contralateral cortex, while proceeding towards
the midline it shows a progressive trend towards being equally shared
between the two hemispheres. "In the case of lesion of one hemisphere the

whole visual field will be affected but with a gradient of severity going from a maximum in the extreme contralateral hemifield to a minimum in the extreme ipsilateral hemifield" (Rizzolatti, Gentilucci & Matelli, 1985). In man, an asymmetrical ipsilateral contribution to space representation in analog processors might cause the disproportionate incidence of hemineglect following left and right hemisphere lesion. An alternative explanation of the same phenomenon might assume that sensory representation of a pattern of eccentric stimulation in the visual field, does not remain anchored to the retinal coordinates of the proximal stimulus, but its centroid, as it were, is foveated for further processing by the mind's eye through a translation over the surface of a retinoid structure; formal model of this process has been provided by Trehub (1977). In patients with left hemineglect, the left half of stimulus configuration, wherever located in the outer space, would thus fall into the disordered half of a structure supporting egocentric space representation so that its processing relative to that of the right half is to a variable extent impaired.

As for the second issue, it seems necessary to infer that each point of the analog for space representation -- whatever the relative contribution of each hemisphere to its implementation -- is double-indexed in terms of retinal and body coordinates, or that space representation articulates in a manifold of analogs with different frames of reference. It is worth noting here that the actual existence of more than one spatial analog is suggested by indications of double dissociation between neglect for personal or peripersonal space and neglect for extrapersonal space found in monkeys (Rizzolatti et al., 1985) as well as in man (Bisiach, Perani, Vallar & Berti, forthcoming).

Spatial Analogs and Cognitive Processes

In our model, representation by spatial analog is far from being a stupid picture-in-the-head critically surveyed and interpreted by an intelligent mind's eye. The firing of cell assemblies of layers II and III must be regarded as an intrinsecally cognitive activity, since no hierarchically higher form of sensory and mental representation seems to exist and, as will presently be argued, it shows direct involvement in consciousness. Whatever residues of ancestral aversion might be raised against the notion of an entity where cognitive properties merge with extensional properties, this is the crucial aspect of our model. Both lack of representation and contentful misrepresentation of one half of space such as conjointly or separately observable in dyschiria arise from intrinsic changes in the spatial analog, not from failure of a superimposed scanning device which we have no factual reason to hypothesize (Bisiach et al., 1985c; Bisiach & Berti, 1985) and which would imply an infinite regress of space representations.

It is worth stressing this point in order to dispel the belief that analog theories unavoidably share the "assumption that images are essentially inner objects at which the homunculus can look" (Neisser, 1978). Due to our natural disinclination to look critically beyond their face value, metaphors are often quite misleading and it is admonishing that under the very terms of "attentional searchlight" Crick (1984) has provided a neural model which nicely fits with our hypothesis identifying the mind's eye with the pattern of activities occurring in, not over, layers II and III. In Crick's model, "intensification" of part of a representation currently entertained in the brain may be self-operated by two positive feedback loops: one intrathalamic, involving relay and reticular neurons and basically sensory-driven; the other cortico-thalamic, grafted into the former and accepting top-down influences. Such a kind of autogenous,

selective modulation of information in an analog representational network
might constitute the neural implementation of non-propositional thought
processes.

In our model, shifts of focus in mental space reflect migration of
activity over the surface of spatial analogs; thus, to some extent,
interpretations of dyschiria may conveniently be phrased in terms of
attention as long as neglect phenomena are considered, even in the domain of
mental representation. This is however no longer true with reference to
misrepresentations which may sometimes be involved in foreground cognitive
activity. Furthermore, interpretations in terms of attention fail to
account for phenomena such as the introspective report of Baxter and
Warrington's patient and might miss the subtler point that what appears as a
shift of attention might mean a recoil from daunting representations.

Cognitive processes entering a way of propositional rather than of
analog processing, and therefore not primarily affected by the disorder
underlying dyschiria, may not only be totally unable to compensate the
latter but may themselves be entrapped and mislead, as we have argued on the
ground of clinical and of experimental evidence (Bisiach, Berti & Vallar,
1985; Bisiach, Meregalli & Berti, 1985); which is far from being an
indication of cognitive supremacy.

By far the most critical, there remain the implications of dyschiria
for theories of consciousness, meant as self-monitoring and the highest
form of self-control of nervous activities. In spite of its importance, or
rather because of it, this aspect will only be introduced here succintly
(see Bisiach, 1985, for ampler discussion and a tentative elucidation of the
term of consciousness as employed in this chapter).

Clinical and experimental evidence (e.g. Bisiach et al., 1985a, c;
Bisiach, Perani, Papagno, Vallar & Berti, forthcoming) shows that the
representational scotoma manifesting itself in the manifold traits of
unilateral neglect and the false beliefs which are fixed to representations
issued, in our model, from the disordered half of the spatial analog as a
consequence of some circumscribed brain lesions encroach uncontrolled on
cognitive processes. In severe cases, any effort to beset the patient and
force him to admit and critically evaluate his pathological condition is
doomed to failure: either the patient eludes the problem altogether, or he
cuts short and shelters his cognitive disorder by arguments of which a
confutation would be in vain. An illustrative instance of an unsuccessful
interview carried on longer than usual with a patient who had left neglect
and anosognosia for left hemiplegia, may be found in Bisiach et al. (1985c).
The consequences of this perturbation are however local and cognitive
activity outside the corrupted vein may remain totally unaffected. These
facts suggest that relatively peripheral levels of nervous activity such as
those of analog mechanisms of representation may play a crucial role in the
generation of those events whereby sensory and mental representations
acquire the property of being conscious. We know from blind-sight
(Weiskrantz, Warrington, Sanders & Marshall, 1974) that considerable
processing of information delivered by sensory transducers can take place
without any conscious correlate. We also know that interruption of the flow
of sensory information up to a certain stage beyond primary sensory areas is
monitored by the brain. On the other hand, we know (at least since Anton's
1899 celebrated paper) that failure of a more central structure (to which
the spatial analog of our model refers) not only cuts a definite amount of
information out of consciousness, but renders, as a rule, the defect itself
unconscious and may release uncriticized pathological representations.
This seems to entail that consciousness is inherent in the representational
activity of these analog structures, both as referring to the monitoring of

these activities and as referring to their control. Without taking into consideration the disordered apparatus which is responsible for anosognosia relative to some forms of dysphasia, and which is still too obscure to be discussed here, no further mechanisms for consciousness seem to exist, either in the form of a unitized, hierarchically superimposed component of the cognitive machinery or emerging from the whole of cognitive activities of the brain. As for the latter, what we have so far learnt from dyschiria challenges the hypothesis of an isotropic structure of thought, whereby at this level each process has free access to any other process, both in the sense of an unlimited range of information and in that of an unlimited field of control (Fodor, 1983). This hypothesis is undermined by phenomena such as those already pointed out by Zingerle with reference to his Case 2, who while knowing that all human bodies have a left and a right side, could not apply that notion to himself. Phenomena of this kind suggest that thought itself may have a texture imposed by processors organized in the form of analogs and may break along the lines of this texture, with consequences which cannot be amended by any kind of propositional activity.

Conclusions

We have tried to sketch a systemic analysis of disorders which have so far been relatively neglected notwithstanding the weight they may have in the advancement of our insight into cognition. We are still far from having an entirely connected story, however, and our representational explanation of these disorders, as well as our inferences about cognitive activities, largely rest on the assumption that neglect and misrepresentation of one side of space express disfunction of the same functional unit. We have outlined a model of a unit of this kind, where a circumscribed failure of the mechanism can indeed generate, according to relatively minor changes in its location, neglect or misrepresentation; yet, however plausible, this offers no proof that what really happens in the nervous system follows these lines.

Our suggestion has a notable antecedent in Zingerle's paper. To-day, a representational explanation of the disorders considered in this chapter also benefits from the fact that, unlike in Zingerle's times, 'representation' is no longer a merely psychological construct. Neurophysiologists have given this concept a physical foundation through discoveries concerning the activity of networks which are suggested to provide a neural model of egocentric space (e.g. Mountcastle, 1981). Indeed, it is in the light of recent neurophysiological and neuropsychological advances that Zingerle's contribution shows its full significance. Sent to press in the twilight of an epoch (whose dissolution, due to a curious coincidence, was delimited to time by the two speeches made by Babinski in France) the paper of the Graz neurologist would seem to have shared the destiny of the Austro-Hungarian empire. Its important theoretical message had no reverberation. In the present chapter, the restoration of the term 'dyschiria' has been proposed on two grounds. Its ability to cover the full range of phenomena of altered cognition of a half-space seems, at the very least, heuristically helpul in defining a field which still lacks the appropriate unity to be fully recognized as a crucial node in the investigation of cognitive brain-activities. Furthermore, readoption of this term would be a well-deserved tribute to the Austrian neurologist and would compensate for so many years of neglect. Although this proposal may encounter resistance ranging from personal theoretical stances to simple indifference, it is to be hoped that it will at least enjoy the serious consideration of those who attribute a certain value to our cultural inheritance.

References

Altman, J.A., Balonov, L.J. & Deglin, V.L. Effects of unilateral disorder of the brain hemisphere function in man on directional hearing. Neuropsychologia, 1979, 17, 295–301.

Anderson, J.R. Arguments concerning representations for mental imagery. Psychological Review, 1978, 85, 249–277.

Anton, G. Ueber die Selbstwahrnemung der Herderkrankungen des Gehirns durch den Kranken bei Rindenblindheit und Rindentaubheit. Archiv für Psychiatrie und Nervenkrankheiten 1899, 32, 86–127.

Babinski, M.J. Contribution à l'étude des troubles mentaux dans l'hémiplégie organique cérébrale (Anosognosie). Revue Neurologique, 1914, 27, 845–848.

Babinski, M.J. Anosognosie. Revue Neurologique, 1918, 31, 365–367.

Baxter, D.M. & Warrington, E.K. Neglect dysgraphia. Journal of Neurology, Neurosurgery and Psychiatry, 1983, 46, 1073–1078.

Bisiach, E. The (haunted) brain and consciousness. Paper presented at the meeting The Concept of Consciousness in Contemporary Science, Como, 16–19 April 1985.

Bisiach, E. & Berti, A. Representational impairment as a factor in neglect. Paper presented at the 13th Mondial Congress of Neurology, Hamburg, September 1985.

Bisiach, E., Berti, A. & Vallar, G. Analogical and logical disorders underlying unilateral neglect of space. In M.I. Posner and O.S.M. Marin (Eds.), Attention and Performance XI. Hillsdale, N.J.: Lawrence Erlbaum Ass., 1985a, pp 239–249.

Bisiach, E., Capitani, E., Luzzatti, C. & Perani, D. Brain and conscious representation of outside reality. Neuropsychologia, 1981, 19, 543–551.

Bisiach, E., Capitani, E. & Porta, E. Two basic properties of space representation in the brain. Journal of Neurology, Neurosurgery and Psychiatry, 1985b, 48, 141–144.

Bisiach, E., Cornacchia, L., Sterzi, R. & Vallar, G. Disorders of perceived auditory lateralization after lesions of the right hemisphere. Brain, 1984, 107, 37–52.

Bisiach, E. & Luzzatti, C. Unilateral neglect of representational space. Cortex, 1978, 14, 129–133.

Bisiach, E., Luzzatti, C. & Perani, D. Unilateral neglect, representational schema and consciousness. Brain, 1979, 102, 609–618.

Bisiach, E., Meregalli, S. & Berti, A. Mechanisms of production-control and belief-fixation in human visuospatial processing. Clinical evidence from hemispatial neglect. Paper presented at the Eight Symposium on Quantitative Analyses of Behavior, at Harvard University: Pattern Recognition and Concepts in Animals, People, and Machines. June 7 and 8 1985c.

Bisiach, E., Perani, D., Vallar, G. & Berti, A. (submitted) Unilateral neglect: Personal and extra-personal.

Bisiach, E., Vallar, G., Perani, D., Papagno, C. & Berti, A. Unawareness of disease following lesions of the right hemisphere: Anosognosia for hemiplegia and anosognosia for hemianopia. Neuropsychologia (in press).

Chedru, F. Space representation in unilateral spatial neglect. Journal of Neurology, Neurosurgery and Psychiatry, 1976, 39, 1057–1061.

Corin, M.S. & Bender, M.B. Mislocalization in visual space with reference to the midline at the boundary of a homonymous hemianopia. Archives of Neurology, 1972, 27, 252–262.

Crick, F. Function of the thalamic reticular complex: The searchlight hypothesis. Proceedings of the National Academy of Sciences, 1984, 81, 4585-4590.

Critchley, M. The Parietal Lobes. London: Hafner Press, 1953.

De Renzi, E. Disorders of Space Exploration and Cognition. New York: Wiley, 1982.

De Renzi, E., Colombo, A., Faglioni, P. & Gibertoni, M. Conjugate gaze paralysis in stroke patients with unilateral damage. Archives of Neurology, 1982, 39, 482-486.

Fodor, J.A. The Modularity of Mind. Cambridge, Mass. : MIT Press, 1983.

Gainotti, G. Les manifestations de négligence et d'inattention pour l'hémispace. Cortex, 1968, 4, 64-91.

Gerstmann, J. Problem of imperception of disease and of impaired body territories with organic lesions. Relation to body scheme and its disorders. Archives of Neurology and Psychiatry, 1942, 48, 890-913.

Geschwind, N. Disconnexion syndromes in animals and man. Brain, 1965, 88, 237-294 and 585-644.

Goddard, G.V. Component properties of the memory machine: Hebb revisited. In P.W. Jusczyk and R.M. Klein (Eds.). The Nature of Thought. Essays in Honor of D.O. Hebb. Hillsdale, N.J.: Lawrence Erlbaum Ass., 1980, pp 231-247.

Haugeland, J. The nature and plausibility of cognitivism. The Behavioral and Brain Sciences, 1978, 1, 215-260.

Hebb, D.O. Organization of Behavior. New York: Wiley, 1949.

Hécaen, H. Clinical symptomatology of right and left hemisphere lesions. In V.B. Mountcastle (Ed.), Interhemispheric Relations and Cerebral Dominance. Baltimore: Johns Hopkins Press, 1962, pp 215-243.

Hécaen, E., Penfield, W., Bertrand, C. & Malmo, R. The syndrome of apractognosia due to lesions of the minor hemisphere. Archives of Neurology and Psychiatry, 1956, 75, 400-434.

Heilman, K.M. & Valenstein, E. Mechanisms underlying hemispatial neglect. Annals of Neurology, 1979, 5, 166-170.

Heilman, K.M. & Van den Abell, T. Right hemisphere dominance for attention: The mechanism underlying hemispheric asymmetries of inattention (neglect). Neurology, 1980, 30, 327-330.

Heilman, K.M. & Watson, R.T. Mechanisms underlying the unilateral neglect syndrome. In E.A. Weinstein and R.P. Friedland (Eds.), Advances in Neurology, vol. 18: Hemi-Inattention and Hemisphere Specialization. New York: Raven Press, 1977, pp 93-106.

Heilman, K.M., Watson, R.T. & Valenstein, E. Neglect and related disorders. In K.M. Heilman & E. Valenstein (Eds.), Clinical Neuropsychology. New York: Oxford University Press, 1985, pp 243-293.

Hochberg, J. In the mind's eye. In R.N. Haber (Ed.), Contemporary Theory and Research in Visual Perception. New York: Holt, Rinehart and Winston, 1968, pp 309-331.

Jones, E. Die Pathologie der Dyschirie. Journal für Psychologie und Neurologie, 1910, 15, 145-183.

Kinsbourne, M. A model for the mechanism of unilateral neglect of space. Transactions of the American Neurological Association, 1970, 95, 143-146.

Kinsbourne, M. Hemi-neglect and hemisphere rivalry. In E.A. Weinstein and R.P. Friedland (Eds.), Advances in Neurology, vol. 18: Hemi-Inattention and Hemisphere Specialization. New York: Raven Press, 1977, pp 41-49.

Kosslyn, S.M. Image and Mind. Cambridge, Mass.: Harvard University Press, 1980.

LaMotte, R.H. & Acuna, C. Defects in accuracy of reaching after removal of posterior parietal cortex in monkeys. Brain Research, 1978, 139, 309-326.

Merzenich, M.M. & Kaas, J.H. Principles of organization of sensory-perceptual systems in mammals. Progress in Psychobiology and Physiological Psychology, 1980, 9, 1-41.

Mountcastle, V.B. Functional properties of the posterior parietal cortex and their regulation by state controls : influence on excitability of interested fixation and the angle of gaze. In O. Pompeiano and C. Ajmone-Marsan (Eds.), Brain Mechanisms of Perceptual Awareness and Purposeful Behavior. New York: Raven Press, 1981, pp 67-99.

Neisser, U. Anticipations, images and introspection. Cognition, 1978, 6, 169-174.

Ogden, J.A. Contralesional neglect of constructed visual images in right and left brain-damaged patients. Neuropsychologia, 1985, 23, 273-277.

Parks, T. Post-retinal visual storage. American Journal of Psychology, 1965, 78, 145-147.

Posner, M.I., Pea, R. & Volpe, B. Cognitive-neuroscience: developments toward a science of synthesis. In J. Mehler, E.C.T. Walker and M. Garrett (Eds.), Perspectives on Mental Representation. Hillsdale, N.J.: Lawrence Erlbaum Ass., 1982, pp 251-276.

Pylyshyn, Z.W. Computation and cognition: Issues in the foundations of cognitive science. The Behavioral and Brain Sciences, 1980, 3, 111-169.

Pylyshyn, Z.W. The imagery debate. Analog media versus tacit knowledge. In N. Block (Ed.), Imagery. Cambridge, Mass., MIT Press, 1981, pp 151-206.

Rizzolatti, G., Gentilucci, M. & Matelli, M. Selective spatial attention: One center, one circuit, or many circuits? In M.I. Posner and O.S.M. Marin (Eds.), Attention and Performance XI. Hillsdale, N.J.: Lawrence Erlbaum Ass., 1985, pp 251-165.

Rizzolatti, G., Scandolara, C., Matelli, M. & Gentilucci, M. Afferent properties of periarcuate neurons in macaque monkeys. II. Visual responses. Behavioural Brain Research, 1981, 2, 147-163.

Schott, B., Jeannerod, M. & Zahin, M.Z. L'agnosie spatiale unilatérale: perturbation en secteur des mécanismes d'exploration et de fixation du regard. Journal de Médecine de Lyon, 1966, 47, 169-195.

Shepard, R.N. Form, formation and transformation of internal representations. In R.L. Solso (Ed.), Information Processing and Cognition: The Loyola Symposium. Hillsdale, N.J.: Lawrence Erlbaum Ass., 1975, pp 87-122.

Trehub, A. Neuronal models for cognitive processes: Networks for learning, perception and imagination. Journal theoretical Biology, 1977, 65, 141-169.

von der Malsburg, C. The correlation theory of brain function. Internal Report 81-2, Department of Neurobiology, Max-Planck-Institute for Biophysical chemistry, D-3400 Goettingen, West-Germany, 1981.

Weiskrantz, L., Warrington, E.K., Sanders, M.D. & Marshall, J. Visual capacity in the hemianopic field following a restricted occipital ablation. Brain, 1974, 97, 709-728.

Zingerle, H. Ueber Stoerungen der Wahrnemung des eigenen Koerpers bei organischen Gehirnerkrankungen. Monatschrift für Psychiatrie und Neurologie, 1913, 34, 13-36.

Acknowledgements : The preparation of this chapter was supported by a grant from the Ministero della Pubblica Istruzione to the first author. We gratefully acknowledge the help of Frances Anolerson, who carefully reviewed the English.

Footnote
1. The term 'dyschiria' was taken from Jones, who is likely to have coined it. In 1910, under the title of "Die Pathologie der Dyschirie", E. Jones, a Toronto University professor, had described two patients suffering from "hysteria" and "hysteroneurastheny" respectively. Their symptoms were very complex but not without similarity to Zingerle's organic cases. The neurotic nature of such symptoms might however be questioned, since the first patient had developed them following a railway accident, possibly involving head trauma, whereas the second suffered from "hystero-epyleptic" seizures.

Neurophysiological and Neuropsychological Aspects
of Spatial Neglect, M. Jeannerod (editor)
© Elsevier Science Publishers B.V. (North-Holland), 1987

DISTURBANCES IN SPATIAL ATTENTION FOLLOWING LESION
OR DISCONNECTION OF THE RIGHT PARIETAL LOBE*

Michael S. Gazzaniga
and
Elisabetta Ladavas

A series of studies are reported that suggest the parietal lobe of
humans is involved in the establishment of spatial referents in
gravitational space. This function goes beyond the more
elementary function of processing retinotopic information and
most likely plays an important role in governing a wide range of
locomotor activities. It is also suggested that each parietal lobe
is active in this process.

Introduction

It has become increasingly clear over the past several years that
damage to the parietal lobe in primates produces disturbances in
attentional systems, particularly in man (for review, see De Renzi, 1982).
The dramatic clinical deficits seen following parietal lobe damage were
originally characterized in terms of an impairment in the processing of
basic sensory information (Denny-Brown, Meyer and Horenstein, 1952).
Recent observations suggest that the deficits are more closely related to
disturbances in the capacity to switch attention from one spatial location
to another (Posner, Cohen and Rafal, 1982; Riddoch and Humphrey, 1983).
Thus, in an initial observation by Posner and collegues (Posner, Walker,
Friedrich and Rafal, 1984), it was shown that patients with unilateral
parietal disease were delayed in shifting their attention from a point in
the intact visual field over to a point in the impaired visual field. This
kind of observation has now been confirmed and extended by others (Baynes,
Holtzman and Volpe, 1986).

These data were consistent with the view that the parietal lobe is
functional in establishing and maintaining spatial maps that appear to be
retinotopically organized. In other words, the coordinates of the
attentional spatial maps, as detected through priming studies, were in
register with the primary visual map as established through
retino-geniculo-striate projections. This interpretation is consistent
with a variety of neurophysiological analyses of parietal lobe function in
the monkey (Yin and Mountcastle, 1977). Results from animal studies
indicate that the facilitated responses detected in area 7 recordings was
part of a neural cell system that was retinotopically organized. The cells
responded most vigorously prior to eye and hand movements to particular
points in retinotopic coordinates. On the other hand, there have been other
reports suggesting some parietal cells respond only when the animal has
directed its gaze to a particular location in space (Lynn, 1966; Andersen,
Essick & Siegel, 1985). This would suggest that at least some of the cells
were organized in terms of referents in actual physical space.

Data from research on humans have also been accumulating in recent

*Dr. Jeffrey D. Holtzman was first invited to write this review. Upon his
death, we gladly prepared this chapter in his honor.

years and indicate that the parietal lobe is involved in establishing reference points in conceptual space. In an ingenious set of observations, Bisiach and Luzzati (1978) demonstrated that patients with right parietal disease were unable to describe information about the left half of an imagined scene when "viewed" from a particular vantage point. When subsequently asled to describe the same scene from the opposite vantage point, they were immediately able to describe the previously neglected aspect but failed to describe the view previously reported because it now fell into the left, internally neglected space. This observation suggests that the parietal lobe may be organized in such a way that it functions to establish and maintain reference points in both imagined and real physical space, independent of the retinotopic maps of primary sensory cortex. In this chapter we examine a series of quantitative studies in patients with right parietal disease as well as patients who have undergone callosal section. These studies are consistent with this interpretation of parietal lobe function. We will also suggest that the function of the parietal lobe to establish points of reference in physical space is not a specialized function of the right hemisphere. We will argue that, even if each hemisphere can attend to any position in the physical space, the right hemisphere is specialized in directing overt attention to left space, and the left hemisphere to right space.

Deficit on Distribution of Spatial Attention following Right Parietal Damage

There are two classic frames of reference for describing the position of visual stimuli related to an observer. There is a retinotopic frame of reference and a physical frame of reference. The retinotopic frame of reference if typically defined according to the retinotopic coordinates, e.g., the position of the stimulus on the retina. The physical or environmental frame of reference is defined according to gravitational coordinates.

The experiments described here attempt to ascertain which of these two frames of reference is disrupted following right parietal disease. We take as our point of departure the well-documented finding that patients with the extinction produced by right parietal disease are slower to respond to simple stimuli presented in the left as opposed to the right visual field.

When the head is in the normal upright position and the eyes are looking straight forward, these two frames of reference coincide, i.e., for the stimuli presented in this test condition, what is left and right in one frame of reference is left and right in the other (See Figure 1). However, when the head is tilted by 90 degrees, the two frames of reference no longer coincide. What are left and right in the physical frame of reference are left-down and left-up (head right-tilted) and right-up and right-down (head left-titled) in the retinal frame. As a consequence, with the head tilted one can use either the retinotopic or gravitational code for describing any position in visual space. When the head is tilted, if the attentional deficit associated with right parietal lobe damage is related to the retinotopic frame of reference, no differences in reaction time would be expected between the two stimuli since in retinotopic coordinates they both fall in the same visual field and one is above the other. In contrast, if the deficit is related strictly to the use of physical frame of reference, we would expect slower reaction times to the gravitational left than to the gravitational right stimulus.

Five patients with CT confirmed unilateral vascular lesions involving the right parietal lobe, who extinguished the left stimulus under double simultaneous visual stimulation, participated in this study (Ladavas,

RETINOTOPIC vs GRAVITATIONAL

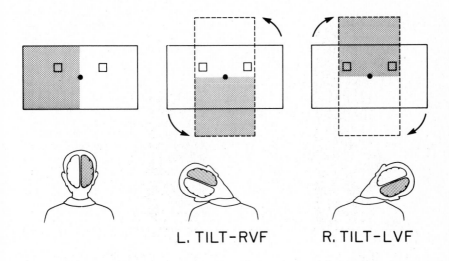

L. TILT-RVF   R. TILT-LVF

Figure 1
Shows experimental strategy for dissociating retinotopic factors from gravitational factors in assessing deficits in spatial orientation. With the head tilted to the left both stimulus locations fall into the right visual field and with the head tilted to the right, they both fall into the left visual field. In both conditions left in physical space remains constant.

1986). The visual display consisted of two square boxes located 10.0 degrees to either side of a fixation point, and 9 degrees above the plane of fixation. The patient was instructed to tilt the head to the left or the right by 90 degrees and to fixate at the central stimulus. They were then requested to push with the index finger of the right hand the response button when the stimulus ("x") appeared in one of the two boxes. The stimulus was displayed for 150 msec. The responsiveness in the two spatial positions was tested in four experimental sessions, two for each head-tilted condition. Each experimental session consisted of 30 practice trials and 100 experimental trials.

The results show that, independent of the visual field stimulated, the stimulus which occupied a relative left position yielded longer RTs than the one on the right (Figure 2). Thus, even when the two stimuli appeared in the right visual field (RVF), subjects responded more slowly to the target in the gravitational left visual field. Furthermore, the response latencies to LVF stimuli were longer than those to RVF stimuli.

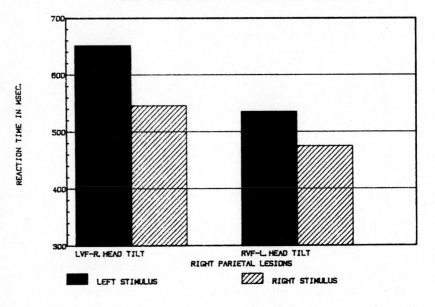

Figure 2
Right parietal lesioned patients are slower to respond to the leftward
most stimulus no matter which visual field is stimulated.

Taken together, the present findings suggest that the reduced ability
to shift attention from one spatial location to another is tied to
gravitational coordinates, in addition to retinotopic coordinates. In
short, these studies argue for interpreting parietal lobe function as
centered on directing attention in terms of actual physical space in
addition to retinotopic space.

Other studies have now been carried out to examine the gravitational
effect in a more natural head/body position, such as the upright position,
and to further characterize the nature of this deficit in the processing of
gravitational information. In a follow up study, Ladavas (1984), examined
whether or not the deficit was displayed on a continuum along a left–right
dimension in physical space. Furthermore, the experiment was designed to
investigate whether the deficit reflects an incapacity to disengage
attention from the rightmost stimulus in real space.

Visuomotor reaction times to three stimuli horizontally aligned above
the fixation mark were studied. The stimuli were located to the left, to the
right, and directly above the fixation mark. If the focus of attention is
caught by the stimulus ipsilateral to the lesion, and the attentional
deficit is associated with the gravitational coordinates, a facilitation of

processing efficiency at the rightmost location plus a gradual increase of RTs to the two stimuli located to the left of the ipsilateral stimulus would be expected. If, on the other hand, the deficit is only related to the retinotopic coordinates, we would expect a facilitation of processing efficiency at the midline position in comparison to the other locations, since central stimuli occupy a less eccentric position on the retina. We would also expect a decrease of RTs to LVF stimuli.

Six neurological subjects selected according to the same criteria as in the first experiments, and six patients without neurological or psychiatric disorders, matched according to age, participated in this experiment. The visual display consisted of three square boxes located 21.5 degrees to the left, 15.8 degrees above, and 21.5 degrees to the right of the fixation point, all 15.8 degrees above the plane of fixation. The patient was instructed to look at the central fixation point and to push the response button with the index finger of the right hand when the stimulus ("x") appeared in one of the three boxes. The stimulus was displyaed for 150 msec. The responsiveness in the three spatial positions was tested in three sessions. Each session consisted of 30 practice trials and 90 experimental trials.

The results obtained for both patients with extinction syndrome and those in the control group are depicted in Figure 3. All patients with right parietal lobe injury showed a gradual increase of RTs to those stimuli located to the left of the rightmost stimulus. They responded significantly more quickly to the right stimulus than to the central and left stimuli. Moreover, their response latencies to the central stimulus were significantly faster than response latencies to the left stimulus ($p<.01$) and significantly slower than to the right stimulus ($p<.05$). On the contrary, the control group was significantly faster to respond to the central stimulus ($p<.01$) than to left and right stimulus ($p<.01$), whereas no significant difference between RTs to left and right stimuli was obtained. In other words, the control group showed only the effect due to the different eccentricity of the three stimuli positions on the retina, whereas the patients with extinction showed that the attentional deficit is displayed along a left–right dimension in physical space. This suggests that right parietal injury may specifically affect the ability to shift attention from the rightmost stimulus to any stimulus located in a relative left position and that the deficit is not strictly confined to the field contralateral to the lesion.

Spatial Distribution of Attention and Hemispheric Specialization

It is commonly stated that attentional deficits of the kind observed in the foregoing more frequently accompany lesions in the right hemisphere than lesions in the left hemisphere. This assertion supports the model that the intact right hemisphere may contain the neural apparatus for attending to both sides of space, even though its preponderant tendency is to attend to the contralateral (left) hemispace, and that the left hemisphere is almost exclusively concerned with attending to the contralateral (right) hemispace (Mesulam, 1981). These claims have always been plagued by the fact that left lesions can disrupt other cognitive systems crucial to the proper comprehension of the task being examined. In addition, there is the persistent problem of variations in lesion size and place that make left and right lesion comparisons difficult to make. Accordingly, ascertaining whether or not the right hemisphere is specialized in some way for the processing of spatial information of the kind being examined here is more easily accomplished by examining patients who have undergone callosal

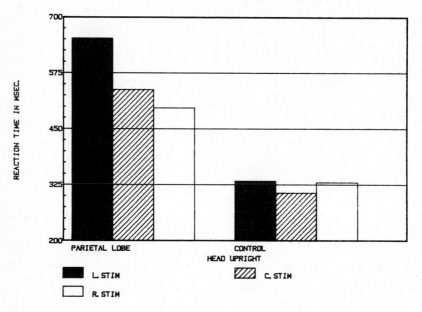

Figure 3
Studies examining further the nature of the spatial deficit in right
parietal cases. With head upright, reaction times are slowest to the
left most stimulus in a horizontal array of three and next slowest to
the middle stimulus, thereby suggesting there is a biasing of attention
to the right.

section. In these patients, disconnection of the left and right parietal
lobe ought to produce systematic deficits. If each hemisphere contributes
equally to the management of gravitational information in the contralateral
space, information presented to the left hemisphere should be processed as
if the right parietal lobe were damaged. Conversely, information presented
to the right hemisphere should show symmetrically opposite results, thereby
allowing one to conclude that the left parietal cortex also normally
contributes this function to information initially presented to the right
hemisphere.

   These questions were addressed by examining three patients who had
undergone surgical transection of the corpus callosum for the control of
intractable epilepsy, (Ladavas, Holtzman and Gazzaniga, in preparation).
These patients are of interest because, following callosal surgery, each
hemisphere perceives only stimuli presented in the contralateral visual
field. Thus, by restricting visual stimulation to a single hemifield, the
specialized capacities of each hemisphere can be evaluated independently.

The experimental situation was the same as reported in the first experiment : two stimuli were displayed above, and on either side of a fixation point and the patient's head was tilted 90 degrees to the left or to the right so that both stimuli fell in the RVF or LVF respectively, but could still be coded as "left" and "right" according to the gravitational coordinates. The patients pushed the response button with the index finger of the hand ipsilateral to the visual field stimulated (L-hand/LVF, R-hand/RVF).

In this context if the attentional control of each hemisphere is related strictly to the use of gravitational coordinates, when the two stimuli fall in the RVF-Left hemisphere we would expect slower RTs to the right than to the left, whereas when the two stimuli fall in the LVF-Right hemisphere we would expect slower RTs to the left than to the right stimulus. If this were not the case, we would expect only the small difference in RTs due to the positions of the two stimuli on the lower and upper retina.

The pattern of results, depicted graphically in Figure 4, supports the hypothesis that each hemisphere can attend to both sides of space, even though the preponderant tendency is to attend to the contralateral side, defined according to the gravitational rather than the retinal coordinates. When the two stimuli fall on the RVF, all patients were significantly faster to respond to the right than to the left stimulus (p<.05). This effect mimics the one seen in patients with right parietal lobe damage. However, in the condition where the two stimuli fall in the LVF, the subjects reverse the relationship and respond faster to the left than to the right stimuli (p<.05). This leads to the conclusion that the right hemisphere's visual system demonstrates the same "neglect" of the contralateral field usually associated with the left hemisphere.

Discussion

Determining the brain mechanisms contributing to the establishment and maintenance of spatial orientation in the human is a difficult task. There are, most likely, separate systems for the initial cueing of spatial location as opposed to the systems active in maintaining these spatial referents during subsequent processing of external sensory information. The set of studies described in this chapter address the latter problem and suggest a number of features about the nature of spatial orientation.

The studies on patients with right parietal lobe damage demonstrate how gravitational (i.e. physical) coordinates can be distinguished from retinotopic coordinates. In all other studies using attentional priming tasks as a method for assessing disturbances in spatial orientation of directed attention, the two kinds of frame of reference were confounded. By the simple turning of the head 90 degrees the two different frames are dissociated and it becomes possible to determine which of two systems is disturbed following parietal lobe damage. The results reported here suggest that right parietal damage produces deficits in the gravitational system of coordinates, in addition to the retinal system of coordinates. Moreover, the deficits in gravitational space appear to be relational in character. That is, the impairment in processing times is detected between two stimuli when one is left of the other no matter where they occur in the left or right visual fields.

The observed deficit in these patients appears to be due to an attentional bias for the right gravitational stimulus. The right stimulus seems to catch the attention to such an extent that the disengagement of attention from that position delays any response to left visual targets. The further away the left stimulus is from the right, the longer the reaction

ATTENTIONAL BIAS IN SPLITS

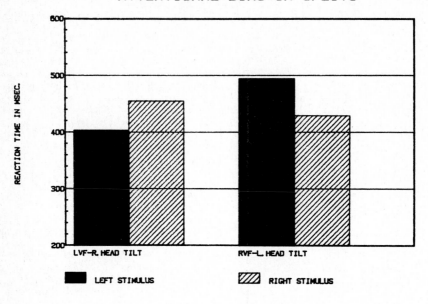

Figure 4
Results on patients with callosal section. As a result of the cortical
disconnection, the left hemisphere behaves as if the right parietal
cortex was damaged while the right hemisphere behaves as if the left was
damaged.

time to the target. One possible explanation for the right attentional bias
is that patients with right parietal lesion are forced by their intact left
hemisphere to attend to the right stimulus. This could occur because the
left hemisphere is more specialized for attending to the gravitational
right stimulus, and the right hemisphere for the gravitational left
stimulus. With brain damage present in the right hemisphere, the
attentional system allocates the majority of its resources to the intact
hemisphere, which is then reflected in faster reaction times to stimuli
which occupy a right position.

This hypothesis was tested in a group of patients who have undergone
brain bisection. Studying these patients would allow for insights into
whether or not each hemisphere is more efficient in manipulating attention
within the contralateral hemispace. Using the same testing procedures,
three patients who had undergone callosal section were tested. If the effect
of a right parietal lobe lesion on the information processing capacities of
the left hemisphere is mediated by the corpus callosum as opposed to
sub-cortical pathways, tilting the head to the left should produce deficits
mimicking those of pure right parietal damage. If the left parietal lobe has
similar influence on how the right hemisphere establishes spatial referents
in left hemispace, then tilting the head to the right should produce a

decrease in RTs for responses to the gravitational right stimulus. The data from all three patients corroborated these two pedictions.

Taken together, our studies suggest that the parietal lobe is involved in the establishment of spatial referents in the physical world. In the past these reference points were thought to be only retinotopically organized because of the way in which most assessment tests were administered, but infact they are not. Upon further consideration, however, it now seems clear that establishing reference points in real physical space is a sensible way to order one's relation with the environment. A quarterback, for example, falling back from the line of scrimmage to pass the ball down field spots an open receiver in his left visual field. The quarterback is chased and is hit. As he falls to the ground, he is able to pass the ball to the exact point in real space, even though his retinotopic coordinates may be looking at a small patch of green grass beneath him.

This interpretation of the deficit is consistent with other behavioral abnormalities that are sometimes reported following right parietal disease. Topographic amnesia is a disturbance in the ability to find spatial locations even though the patients know how to describe how to get to a particular point in space, such as the neighborhood market from their own home. It could well be this failure at a behavioral level reflects an inability to automatically place a referent in real space from which one can orient oneself for subsequent navigatory responses.

It is presumed that coordinates in real space are established through proprioceptive systems sensitive to the earth's gravitational field. Once a reference point is established in either a novel or practiced environment, it is potentially possible that the environment in question can be learned by rote, and recognition can become dependent on the visual cues of that environment. Yet, this would suggest that people subjected to non-gravitational fields would be affected in their spatial orientation, since it would be difficult to place referents in the environment in the absence of proprioceptive cues. In a series of fascinating studies, Lackner and his associates have described related phenomena in astronauts and in other observers experiencing the free-fall phase of parabolic plane flights (Lackner and Graybiel, 1984). In both instances there is sense of being in an inverted position in relation to the aircraft or space craft. He reports of several astronauts who said they could influence the feeling of being upside-down by changing their position within the space capsule in such a way that the rehearsed visual cues learned on earth were in register. If they did not do this, they sometimes felt that "walls turn into ceilings and ceilings turn into floors in a very arbitrary way".

Finally, it is worth noting our feeling about trying to tie this mechanism too closely to the parietal lobe per se. While the split-brain data allow one to be cautious about over-interpreting the function of the right parietal lobe, it begs the question of how specific one can be about the actual brain sites active in particular functional tasks. Even determining the structure-function relationships of the primary sensory cortex has become a difficult task. Over the past fifteen years, anatomical advances have dramatically undercut the once prevalent view that the primary sensory cortex is the initial processing site for visual information of all kinds. Instead, it is now recognized that a multiplicity of initial projections exists for each sensory system, thereby raising a host of new questions about the possible anatomical sites involved with spared function following lesions to primary cortical zones (Berkely, 1978).

Understanding the structure-function relationships of the association cortex is still more difficult. The number of recognized inputs and outputs

to various cortical and sub-cortical regions is several times greater than
for primary sensory cortex. In that light it is not surprising that damage to
these regions produces a variety of cognitive disturbances that intrigue
the student of cognitive processes. The careful study of frontal-,
temporal-, and parietal-lobe damaged patients with unilateral or bilateral
lesions has revealed a number or cognitive disturbances that suggest such
patients are rich sources of insights for viewing the kind of cognitive
dissociations of function that are possible. Yet, these same detailed
studies of cognitive disturbances rarely offer the student of structure
precise information about underlying neural mechanisms because of the rich
network of interconnections that exist in these cognitively oriented
cortical regions. Accordingly, it is frequently valuable to focus on the
exact nature of the cognitive disturbances in an effort to define properties
of the normal cognitive processes and to offer guidance to the structuralist
as to the kind of question he should be investigating about the nature of
neural action. Nowhere is this task more challenging then in attempting to
understand the cognitive disturbances accompanying right parietal damage
in the human brain. We hope we have thrown some light on that task.

References

Andersen, R.A., Essics, G.K. & Siegel, R.M. Encoding of spatial location by
    posterior parietal neurons. Science, 1985, 230. 456-458.
Attneave, R. & Reid, F.W. Voluntary control of frame of reference and slope
    equivalence under head rotation. Journal of Experimental Psychology,
    1968, 78, 153-159.
Baynes, K., Holtzman, J.D. & Volpe, B.T. Components of visual attention:
    Alterations in response pattern to visual stimuli following parietal
    lobe infarction. Brain, in press.
Berkley, M.A. Vision: The geniculo cortical system. In R.B. Masterson
    (Ed.), Handbook of Behavioral Neurobiology: Sensory Integration. New
    York: Plenum Press, 1978.
Bisiach, E. & Luzzati, C. Unilateral neglect of representational space.
    Cortex, 1978, 14, 129-133.
DeRenzi, E. Disorders of space exploration and cognition. New York: Wiley,
    1982.
Denny-Brown, C., Meyer, J.S. & Horenstein, S. The significance of
    perceptual rivalry resulting from parietal lesion. Brain, 1952, 75,
    433-471.
Holtzman, J.D., Volpe, B.T. & Gazzaniga, M.S. Spatial orientation following
    commissural section. In R. Parasuraman and D.R. Davies (Eds.),
    Varieties of Attention. London: Academic Press, 1984, pp. 375-394.
Ladavas, E. Is the hemispatial deficit produced by right parietal lobe
    damage associated with retinal or gravitational coordinates ? Brain,
    in press.
Lakner, J.R. & Graybiel, A. Perceived orientation in free-fall depends on
    visual, postural, and architectural factors. Aviat. Space environ
    Med., 1984, 54, 47-51.
Lynn, R. Attention arousal and the orientation reaction. Oxford: Pergamon
    Press, 1966.
Mesulam, M.M. A cortical network for directed attention and unilateral
    neglect. Annals of Neurology, 1981, 10, 309-325.
Posner, M.I., Cohen, Y. & Rafal, R.D. Neural systems control of spatial
    orientation. Philosophical Transection of the Royal Society of London,
    1982, B298, 187-198.

Posner, M.I., Walker, J.A., Friedrich, F.J. & Rafal, R.D. Effects of parietal injury on covert orienting of visual attention. Journal of Neuroscience, 1984, 4, 1863–1874.

Riddoch, M.J. & Humphrey, G.W. The effect of cueing on unilateral neglect. Neuropsychologia, 1983, 21, 589–599.

Yin, T.C.T. & Mountcastle, V.B. Visual input to the visuomotor mechanisms of monkey's parietal lobe. Science, 1977, 197, 1381–1383.

Acknowledgments: Aided by NIH Grants 2P01 NS17778 and 1R01 NS22626, and the Alfred P. Sloan foundation.

Neurophysiological and Neuropsychological Aspects
of Spatial Neglect, M. Jeannerod (editor)
© Elsevier Science Publishers B.V. (North-Holland), 1987

THE 'NEGLECTED' LEFT HEMISPHERE AND ITS CONTRIBUTION TO VISUOSPATIAL NEGLECT

Jenni A. Ogden

This chapter examines a range of studies on unilateral
spatial neglect in humans, with the emphasis on visuospatial
neglect and with the aim of discovering what role, if any, the
left hemisphere plays in the disorder. Evidence from
split-brain studies and studies on other spatial abilities
such as spatial imagery will be brought to bear on the
problem, and theories of neglect will be discussed in the
light of the contributions the left hemisphere may make to
spatial awareness.

Unilateral spatial neglect can occur in any modality, and in one or more
modalities in the same patient. Whether or not there is a single, underlying
cause for the different forms of neglect (i.e. neglect in different
modalities) is not clear. Human neglect is most often observed in the visual
modality, although this may be a function of the variety and sensitivity of
the tests used to assess visuospatial neglect relative to neglect in other
modalities. Visuospatial neglect can be very dramatic, and while most
patients with the disorder will demonstrate it by missing visual stimuli in
the contralesional half of space, or by drawing or copying only the
ipsilesional side of a picture, a few patients display bizarre behaviors
such as eating the food on only one half of their plates and then complaining
that they are hungry !

As patients with unilateral visual neglect may or may not have a visual
field defect, it is important to distinguish the two disorders. A visual
field defect is a sensory deficit, resulting from damage to the optic
pathways or visual cortex. Visual neglect refers to the patient's apparent
unawareness of visual stimuli impinging in the contralesional hemispace,
even in the absence of a visual field defect. The term 'hemispace' refers to
the extracorporeal space to the left or right of the body and head midline,
and it is distinct from the visual field. Only in the situation where a
person aligns body and head and visually fixates straight ahead, will the
left and right visual fields and left and right hemispaces coincide. If the
head or eyes are moved to the left or right, the visual fields are displaced
accordingly. The hemispaces are not, however, tied to eye movements and
therefore will no longer coincide with the visual fields. There is some
evidence to suggest that in patients with left-sided neglect, both head and
body orientation contribute to the perception of hemispace (Bisiach,
Capitani & Porta, 1985) and when the two are not aligned, the right and left
hemispaces are not clearly separated.

The Evidence for a Right-Left Hemispheric Difference in Incidence of Spatial Neglect

The single, most important claim relating to the neuropathology of human spatial neglect is that it is more frequent and more severe following right-hemispheric than following left-hemispheric lesions (Arrigoni & De Renzi, 1964; Benton, 1969; Brain, 1941, 1945; Chedru, 1976; Colombo, De Renzi & Faglioni, 1976; De Renzi, Faglioni & Scotti, 1970; Hecaen, 1962, 1969; McFie & Zangwill, 1960; Oxbury, Campbell & Oxbury, 1974; Piercy, Hecaen & Ajuriaguerra, 1960; Schenkenberg, Bradford & Ajax, 1980). If this is true then spatial neglect is of special interest because it does not belong exclusively to either of the two main categories of effects related to unilateral lesions. One category consists of deficits reflecting hemispheric specialization but unrelated to one or other side of space ; thus lesions to the left hemisphere typically produce aphasia or apraxia, and lesions to the right hemisphere may result in deficits of spatial cognition. The other category reflects hemispheric representation of the contralateral side of the body, but typically does not involve differential hemispheric specialization. For example, damage to the right motor cortex disrupts activities of the left limbs and damage to the left motor cortex disrupts the right limbs. Human spatial neglect, according to the claim, is a hybrid ; it is more frequent and severe following right than following left-hemispheric lesions, implying right-hemispheric specialization, yet it affects only the contralateral side of space.

However, a review of the many studies of spatial neglect reveals a lack of consistency in the incidence figures following right- and left-hemispheric lesions. Studies that have found a significantly higher incidence of neglect following right brain damage include those by Hecaen and Angelergues (1963) who found hemineglect in 34% of right brain-damaged patients and in only 2% of left brain-damaged patients, and Gloning, Gloning and Hoff (1968) who found hemineglect in 31% of right brain-damaged patients and 2% of left brain-damaged patients. Both of these studies were carried out on very large groups of patients with unilateral brain damage. Weinstein and Cole (1963) found that right-hemispheric hemineglect outnumbered left-hemispheric hemineglect by 22 to 3, Cohn (1961) found a right-left ratio of 3 to 1, Zarit and Kahn (1974) found a right-left ratio of 2 to 1, but Albert (1973) found no significant difference in incidence of visual hemineglect between left and right brain-damaged patients.

Why should there be such a variation in incidence of right- and left-sided neglect in different studies? A methodological argument that has been put forward by a number of researchers is that some studies of hemineglect exclude many patients with left-hemispheric lesions because they are aphasic. If all such patients were included then the incidence of hemineglect after left-hemispheric lesions might well be higher (Brain, 1941 Battersby, Bender, Pollack & Kahn, 1956; Oxbury et al., 1974; Zarit & Kahn, 1974). Nevertheless, in many studies that assessed the incidence of hemineglect in unselected samples of unilaterally brain damaged patients and in which simple tests were used in order to reduce the problem of exclusion of aphasic patients, a higher incidence of hemineglect was still found after right-hemispheric lesions (Arrigoni & De Renzi, 1964 ; Benton, 1969; Chedru, 1976; Colombo et al., 1976; Gainotti, 1968; Gainotti, Messerli & Tissot, 1972; Oxbury et al., 1974).

Even the results of some of these studies are open to question. For example, Gainotti et al. (1972) claimed a significantly higher incidence of left visual neglect on copying tasks in two unselected groups of patients with unilateral lesions. Their definition of neglect was the omission of a

<u>large</u> figure on the contralateral half of the drawing. If, however, they defined neglect as including the omission of a <u>small</u> figure on the contralateral half of the drawing, or as a tendency to close contralateral figures in a rough and undifferentiated way, then there was no significant difference in incidence of neglect between the left and right brain-damaged groups. Added to this, in one of their studies, their 'unselected' group excluded all patients with evidence of focal damage limited to the frontal lobes, and as will become apparent later in this chapter, patients with left frontal lesions are more likely to demonstrate neglect on a copying task than patients with left posterior lesions, although the reverse is true for patients with right-hemispheric lesions (Ogden, 1985a).

This highlights one of the problems that makes comparisons across human neglect studies so difficult. How should neglect be defined ? As it does not appear to be an all-or-nothing phenomenon, at what point on the continuum of deficit should we say one patient has neglect and another patient does not ? This is particularly important when considering the role of the left hemisphere in neglect, given that neglect is often much less dramatic in patients with left-hemispheric lesions.

One way of dealing with the problem is to consider all patients who demonstrate even mild neglect symptoms as having the disorder, but to assess the severity of the disorder independently. There is a much greater consistency across studies when the severity of neglect is considered, and I could find only one exception (Costa, Vaughn, Horwitz & Ritter, 1969) to the otherwise universal finding that neglect is more severe following right-than following left-hemispheric lesions. Even Costa et al. (1969) found an <u>equal</u> severity of neglect in their two hemispheric groups.

The incidence figures also reflect the sensitivities of the various tests used to elicit neglect. Added to this is the difference in the range of tests given to any patient. Some tests require the patient to search for or point to a visual stimulus in the contralesional side of space, some require spontaneous drawing, and others require copying drawings. Are all these measures of visuospatial neglect? Is one measure more sensitive than another? Some types of tests may be more or less sensitive to a neglect disorder following a left-hemispheric lesion, and some aspects of the neglect disorder may be more easily compensated for by left brain-damaged patients than by patients with right brain damage. For example, in a study of tactile neglect (De Renzi et al., 1970) patients explored a tactile finger maze in order to find a marble. Patients in both hemispheric groups took longer to find the marble when it was in one of the contralesional corners of the maze, but right brain-damaged patients sometimes failed to find the marble at all when it was in a contralesional corner.

Another possible reason why different frequencies of hemineglect are found in different studies is that the etiology of the lesions and the recency of the lesions may be different. Given that the more striking symptoms of hemineglect often diminish in the weeks directly following a brain lesion (Campbell & Oxbury, 1976; Gainotti, 1968) and assuming that neglect following left-hemispheric lesions tends to be less severe anyway than that following right-hemispheric lesions (Albert, 1973), then one might expect a greater right-left difference in incidence as the time interval between the sustaining of the lesion and the assessment of neglect increases.

Locus of Lesion Producing Spatial Neglect

In humans, spatial neglect has been reported most often following posterior parietal lesions of the right hemisphere (Bisiach, Capitani, Luzzatti & Perani, 1981; Bisiach, Luzzatti & Perani, 1979; Critchley, 1953;

Hecaen & Angelergues, 1963; Hecaen, Penfield, Bertrand & Malmo, 1956; Heilman & Watson, 1977). There have also been a number of reports of neglect following right-hemispheric frontal lesions and lesions of the cingulate gyrus (Damasio, Damasio & Chang Chui, 1980; Gloning, 1965; Heilman & Valenstein, 1972; Silberpfennig, 1961; Van der Linden, Seron, Gillet & Bredart, 1980), and the thalamus and basal ganglia (Damasio et al., 1980; Hier, Davis, Richardson & Mohr, 1977; Watson & Heilman, 1979). Spatial neglect has been reported following lesions to most of these areas in the left hemisphere as well, but such reports are relatively rare.

    In animals a similar lesion distribution emerges with the addition of superior collicular and mesencephalic reticular formation lesions, but the resulting disorder is usually extinction of the contralesional stimulus on double simultaneous stimulation rather than neglect. Unlike human neglect, extinction in animals follows lesions to either hemisphere with equal frequency and severity (Mountcastle, Lynch, Georgopoulos, Sakata & Acuna, 1975) and the disorder is transient (Orem, Schlag-Rey & Schlag, 1973). Extinction on double simultaneous stimulation in humans also differs from neglect in humans in that it follows right- and left-hemispheric lesions with equal frequency and severity (Weinstein & Friedland, 1977), suggesting that the deficit underlying extinction may be different from the deficit underlying unilateral spatial neglect.

Theories of Spatial Neglect

    A major difficulty faced by researchers when theorizing about the underlying cause of spatial neglect in humans, is to account for the apparently higher incidence of neglect following right-hemispheric lesions than following left-hemispheric lesions.

    Schott, Jeannerod, and Zahin (1966) and Kinsbourne (1970, 1977) postulated that neglect was the consequence of an imbalance between the control centers for head and eye turning that are present in both hemispheres. When one of these centers is suddenly inactivated it results in the disinhibition of the healthy hemisphere and an involuntary turning of the head and eyes to the opposite side. While this phenomenon only lasts a few days or weeks, the patient still displays a preference for looking towards the ipsilesional side, particularly when confronted with multiple displays.

    Kinsbourne (1974) extended this hypothesis to include a non-motor imbalance of attention in the absence of any gaze shift. That is, unilateral cerebral damage would drive attention to the normal hemisphere (i.e. to the side of space contralateral to it) even in situations when no oculomotor activity was involved (e.g. dichotic listening tasks). Kinsbourne attempted to explain the prevalence of left-sided neglect by suggesting that tests for neglect activated the left hemisphere because of the verbal set adopted by the patient when interacting with the tester or doctor. This activation of the left hemisphere would cause the patient's gaze to turn to the contralateral right side. Conversely, if the patient were engaged in non-verbal visuospatial tasks, the right hemisphere would be activated resulting in a shift of attention to the left. That is, left-sided neglect is more frequently observed because the patient is normally engaged in some verbal activity that will enhance a right shift of attention in patients with right-hemispheric damage, and counteract any left shift of attention caused by left-hemispheric damage. However, this theory is at best incomplete, as in many studies patients have been tested for neglect with visuospatial non-verbal tasks, yet the deficit is still apparent (De Renzi, 1982).

    A deficit of attention has long been implicated in the hemineglect disorders (Brain, 1941; Critchley, 1949; Poppelreuter, 1917). More recently, Heilman and his colleagues have expanded and strengthened this hypothesis by supporting it with anatomical and physiological data from both animal and human studies. They propose that hemineglect results from a disruption of a corticolimbic-reticular loop (similar to that proposed by Sokolov, 1963) that when intact activates the orienting reflex in response to novel or meaningful stimuli (Heilman and Watson, 1977). This results in hypoarousal and the animal or human is unable to deal with sensory events occurring in the contralateral half of space. The main support for this hypothesis derives from neuroanatomical and neurophysiological animal studies that show that the cortical and subcortical lesions associated with extinction and hemineglect are interconnected in a functional network (Mesulam, 1981, 1983) and that neurons in the inferior parietal lobule are specialized for encoding the psychological impact of sensory events occurring in the contralateral part of extrapersonal space (Lynch, 1980; Mountcastle et al., 1975; Robinson, Goldberg & Stanton 1978).

Mesulam (1981, 1983) collated these data and the evidence from animal and human studies of extinction and hemineglect into a comprehensive and persuasive "cortical network for directed attention and unilateral neglect". He postulated that the three major cerebral areas in this cortical network each had a particular role to play in unilateral neglect. The inferior parietal cortex may contain a <u>sensory</u> template of the extrapersonal world ; the frontal cortex, including the frontal eye fields may contain a <u>motor</u> map for the distribution of scanning, orienting and exploration within the extrapersonal world, and the cingulate cortex and surrounding areas may contain a <u>motivational</u> map for the distribution of interest and expectancy. The arousal level of each of these areas is regulated by input from the reticular formation. While each of these three representations (sensory, motor and limbic) is mostly responsive to the contralateral hemispace, ipsilateral representation is also present. For the effective distribution of directed attention in extrapersonal space, all three cortical areas and the reticular formation must be intact. If one area is damaged, or the connections between the areas are disrupted, contralateral neglect may result. Damage to a particular area may result in a particular clinical form of hemineglect. Damage to more than one area might result in a more severe clinical form of hemineglect (Mesulam, 1983).

In order to explain the more severe, and possibly more frequent occurrence of hemineglect after right- than after left-hemispheric lesions in humans, Heilman and Van Den Abell (1980) and Mesulam (1983) have postulated that the right hemisphere is dominant for attention. Data from EEG and evoked potential studies of normal humans (Desmedt, 1977; Heilman and Van Den Abell, 1980) and reaction times of patients with unilateral lesions (Howes & Boller, 1975) have suggested that the right hemisphere directs attention to both sides of space although the dominant tendency is to direct attention to the contralateral hemispace, whereas the left hemisphere directs attention almost exclusively to the right side of space. Therefore, lesions confined to the left hemisphere are less likely to result in contralateral neglect because the intact right hemisphere can utilize the neural mechanisms for directing attention to the right side. However, as the left hemisphere does not have the ability to direct attention to the left side, when the right hemisphere is lesioned a severe left-sided neglect results.

An alternative theory of neglect first suggested by De Renzi et al. (1970), was that neglect may be the result of a "mutilated representation of space". They suggested that patients with right-hemispheric lesions who could not find a marble when it was in the contralateral corner of a tactile finger maze, appeared to be unaware that the left side of space existed. This idea has been supported by Bisiach and his colleagues (see also Baxter &

Warrington, 1983) who found that patients with right-hemispheric lesions and left visuospatial neglect neglected the left sides of images retrieved from long-term memory (Bisiach et al., 1981; Bisiach & Luzzatti, 1978) and the left sides of images mentally constructed from immediate external input (Bisiach et al., 1979). The notion that contralateral neglect also occurs in internally generated representations, implies that at some level of processing in the intact brain images are represented analogically in the two hemispheres, at least with respect to their left and right sides.

This surely suggests that the right sides of images should also be disrupted in a patient with a lesion of the left parietal association cortex. However, Bisiach and his colleagues did not assess patients with left-hemispheric lesions, and did not comment on how their hypothesis might account for the apparently higher incidence of visual neglect following right-hemispheric lesions.

Two Experiments Implicating the Left Hemisphere in Visual Neglect

I have recently carried out two experiments on patients with unilateral focal lesions in an attempt to clarify the extent to which the left hemisphere is involved in visuospatial neglect. In the first experiment (Ogden, 1985a) an unselected group of 101 patients with acute unilateral focal lesions confirmed by computerized tomography were given a battery of five paper-and-pencil tests in order to assess the incidence of visual neglect following right- and left-hemispheric lesions. Lesions included meningiomas, gliomas, intracerebral hemorrhages and infarcts. Each lesion was categorized as anterior (A), that is wholly anterior to the central sulcus ; anterior/posterior (A/P), that is on both sides of the central sulcus ; or posterior (P), that is wholly posterior to the central sulcus.

Patients were asked to copy a 5-pointed star, a Necker cube and a simple line drawing of a tree, house, fence and tree. They were also asked to fill in the numbers on a clock face, the '12' already being in position, and cross out 40 lines dispersed apparently randomly over a page (Albert, 1973). Patients were permitted to move the paper horizontally, but were not permitted to tilt the page. A patient was designated to have neglect if he or she demonstrated contralateral neglect on at least one of the five tests. Severity of neglect scores for each test were given, and patients were also given a severity score based on the number of the five tests they demonstrated neglect on. Examples of neglect on four of the tests are shown in Figs. 1 and 2.

Visuospatial neglect was present in 28 out of a total of 56 left brain-damaged (LBD) patients and in 20 out of 45 right brain-damaged (RBD) patients. The incidence of neglect in these groups did not differ significantly. There were no significant differences in severity scores between the two hemispheric groups on four of the five tests. On Albert's (1973) crossing lines test there was a significant difference according to a one-tailed test only, with the RBD group demonstrating the most severe neglect. When the severity of neglect was assessed using the number of tests neglected out of five, the RBD group's scores were significantly greater than those of the LBD group.

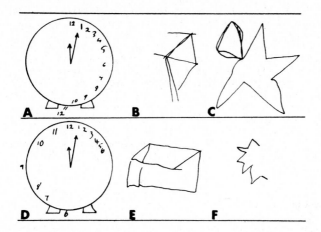

Figure 1
Drawings A–C are those of patients with posterior right-hemispheric
tumors, and D–F those of patients with tumors of the left hemisphere.
The patient who drew D had a posterior tumor, the patient who drew E an
anterior tumor, and the patient who drew F a basal ganglia tumor (From
Ogden, J.A., 1985a) (With permission of Academic Press, Inc.).

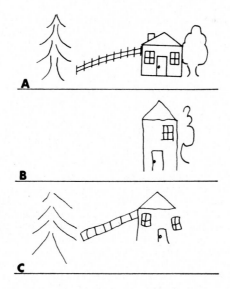

Figure 2
Drawing A is the test drawing copied by the patients. Drawing B was
drawn by a patient with a right basal ganglia tumor and drawing C by a
patient with a tumor of the left frontal lobe (From Ogden, J.A., 1985a)
(With permission of Academic Press, Inc.).

An interesting result emerged when the two groups were compared with respect to the loci of lesions resulting in neglect. Five patients with basal ganglia lesions and six patients with temporal lobe lesions were excluded from this analysis as their lesions could not readily be assigned to A, P, or A/P locations. In the LBD group most patients with neglect had <u>anterior</u> lesions, while in the RBD group most patients with neglect nad <u>posterior</u> lesions (See Table 1). This anterior-posterior interhemispheric difference was significant.

Table 1 : Numbers of patients in the different lesion locality groups with and without visual hemineglect.

Hemispheric group	Visual Hemineglect	Numbers of Patients		
		A	A/P	P
RBD	Present	2	4	12
	Absent	8	8	6
LBD	Present	12	4	9
	Absent	4	10	11

Note : Patients with basal ganglia lesions and lesions restricted to the temporal lobes are excluded from this table (From Ogden, J.A., 1985a) (With permission of Academic Press, Inc.).

The finding of an equal incidence of visuospatial neglect following right- and left-hemispheric lesions is perhaps not surprising when previous studies assessing incidence are reconsidered. If mild neglect were taken into account, such as neglecting to cross one or more lines on the contralesional half of a page (Albert, 1973) or neglecting to copy a small figure on the contralesional side of a drawing (Gainotti et al, 1972) a number of other studies may support the same conclusion.

The finding that individual RBD patients neglected on more tests than LBD patients means that a battery of five tests will be more effective in identifying LBD patients with neglect than using a single test. This may partially explain why more RBD than LBD patients are observed to have neglect in assessment programs where only one test is used. The method of testing nearly all patients with unilateral lesions also increases the chance of finding neglect in LBD patients, especially given that they are more likely to have anterior rather than posterior lesions. That is, some previous studies may have excluded patients with anterior lesions (e.g. Gainotti et al, 1972). Finally, the high proportion of patients with tumors in this study (66%) relative to most other studies, and the fact that most patients were assessed during the acute stage of their lesions (and therefore presumably before spontaneous recovery of neglect had begun) may have contributed to the higher incidence of visuospatial neglect in the LBD group.

The assessment of patients with acute lesions may also explain why on individual tests there was little indication that the neglect demonstrated by RBD patients was greater than that demonstrated by LBD patients. However, if the range of tests neglected is a measure of severity, then this study concurs with others; that is RBD patients tend to have a more severe neglect disorder than LBD patients.

In the second experiment (Ogden, 1985b) which was a version of Bisiach et al's (1979) experiment, nine RBD and nine LBD patients with well defined focal lesions categorized as A, A/P or P as in Experiment 1 comprised the experimental groups. All patients were right-handed. Twenty normal right-handed subjects acted as a control group. Experimental subjects were assessed for visuospatial neglect on the five paper-and-pencil tests described in Experiment 1. Seven LBD patients and three RBD patients demonstrated neglect on one or more of the five tests.

There were two conditions, a static condition and a dynamic condition. Whereas all patients completed the static condition, only four LBD patients and five RBD patients were able to complete the dynamic condition. Those who were unable to complete it said it made them dizzy or that they were unable to form images at all. In both conditions the subject's task was to make same/different judgements about 18 pairs of shapes that were presented according to a fixed random schedule. The shapes were displayed, one after the other, on a color video screen controlled by a microcomputer. In the static condition each shape appeared on the screen for 1 second and in the dynamic condition the shapes appeared to move behind a central vertical slit, 1.4 cm. wide, each shape taking 2 seconds to move past the slit. Because the subject could only see a section of each shape in the center of the screen at any one time, he/she had to construct a mental image of each shape in order to compare them. In each condition six pairs of shapes were identical, six pairs differed on the right only and six pairs differed on the left only. In the dynamic condition each pair was presented twice, once moving right to left, and once moving left to right.

Laterality quotients (LQ) were calculated using the correct responses for pairs that differed on the right and pairs that differed on the left so that a positive LQ indicated neglect of the left side and a negative LQ neglect on the right side. In both conditions the LBD group demonstrated neglect of the right sides of shapes relative to the RBD group, and the RBD group demonstrated neglect of the left sides of shapes, relative to the LBD group. The LQ scores of the RBD patients differed significantly from zero as did the scores of the LBD patients. The LQ scores of the control subjects did not differ significantly from zero. In the static condition only seven of the nine LBD patients demonstrated right-sided neglect and only four of the nine RBD patients demonstrated left-sided neglect. However, in the dynamic condition, all four LBD patients and all five RBD patients who completed the test demonstrated contralesional neglect. The mean number of correct responses for the RBD, LBD and control groups for the static and dynamic conditions are given in Table 2.

Table 2 : Group means for correct responses in the static and dynamic conditions.

Mean number of correct responses

| | Static condition* | | | | | | Dynamic condition[+] | | | | | |
	Same	S.D.	Different on left	S.D.	Different on right	S.D.	Same	S.D.	Different on left	S.D.	Different on right	S.D.
LBD	4.1	0.9	5.0	1.1	3.6	1.6	9.5	1.7	7.8	1.5	5.3	2.3
RBD	4.1	1.9	4.4	1.0	4.8	1.2	9.4	1.6	5.4	2.9	7.8	2.5
Controls	4.9	1.1	4.9	1.3	4.8	1.1	10.4	1.7	8.3	2.1	7.9	2.5

* Maximum possible correct for each pair type=6
+ Maximum possible correct for each pair type=12

(From Ogden, J.A., 1985b) (With permission of Pergamon Press Ltd).

These results confirm Bisiach et al's (1979) finding that patients with right-hemispheric lesions and left visuospatial neglect demonstrate neglect of the left sides of visuospatial images, and also show that patients with left-hemispheric lesions neglect the right sides of visuospatial images. An additional finding is that patients with acute unilateral lesions show contralesional neglect of visuospatial images, whether or not they demonstrate visuospatial neglect on drawing tasks. One possible conclusion that could be drawn from this is that unilateral cortical damage almost invariably results in some degree of contralesional visual neglect, at least when the lesion is acute, and that the imagery test is sensitive enough to pick up this subtle form of neglect.

Other Research Implicating the Left Hemisphere in Tasks Involving Visuospatial Abilities
    While it is generally accepted that visuospatial abilities are less lateralized than verbal abilities, there is ample evidence that the right hemisphere plays a major role in many spatial tasks (See De Renzi, 1982, for review). A number of lines of evidence point to the already mentioned possibility that the right hemisphere has the ability to attend to both sides of space, whereas the left hemisphere attends to the right side of space only (Desmedt, 1977 ; Heilman & Van Den Abell, 1980 ; Howes & Boller, 1975) and this is often given as the reason for the apparently higher

incidence and greater severity of unilateral spatial neglect following right-hemispheric lesions. Given the evidence just presented (Ogden, 1985a & b) it would seem that lesions to the left hemisphere result in mild visuospatial neglect as often as lesions to the right hemisphere. However, the greater severity of neglect following right-hemispheric lesions may well be explained by the right hemisphere's relatively greater ability to attend to both sides of space.

In the last few years a number of studies have been published that attest to a more extensive role being played by the left hemisphere than was previously thought in tasks involving visuospatial abilities. A commissurotomy study carried out by Plourde and Sperry (1984) was directed specifically at left spatial neglect and the assumption that the left hemisphere has only the ability to attend to the right side of space, and is lacking in awareness for the left half of the body and space. They found in three subjects that the disconnected left hemisphere could correctly carry out commands involving the left half of the body. In addition, the disconnected left hemispheres of the three subjects did not demonstrate any consistent right-sided neglect on a tactile line bisection task. This study therefore places in doubt the main explanation given for the greater incidence and severity of spatial neglect following right-hemispheric lesions ; that is, that the left hemisphere cannot attend to the left half of space.

Other recent studies have found a significant left hemisphere contribution in visuoperceptual, visuospatial, and visuomotor tasks. Kim, Morrow, Passafiume, and Boller (1984) assessed groups of patients with anterior and posterior unilateral lesions in five pairs of simple tasks ; one task of each pair being a visuoperceptual task with a motor component, and the other task being the same visuoperceptual task but without the motor component. Their aim was to see if deficits on visuoperceptual motor tasks were the consequence of the visuoperceptual component or the motor component of the task. They found that all brain-damaged groups were worse than controls, and that in both the right and left brain-damaged groups there was a significant positive correlation between the two types of tasks. That is, deficits on visuoperceptual motor tasks were due to the visuoperceptual component and not to the motor component.

The most interesting result was that while the patients with right posterior lesions were worse than those with right anterior lesions, in the left brain-damaged group patients with left anterior lesions were significantly worse than those with left posterior lesions. This finding is remarkably similar to the anterior-posterior interhemispheric difference in location of lesions producing visuospatial neglect in my study (Ogden, 1985a). These two studies in combination raise the possibility that the anterior region of the left hemisphere plays a major role in the execution of tasks involving visuoperceptual skills, and that this role is enhanced when the task includes a spatial component.

In another study involving visuospatial abilities, this time spontaneous drawing (Kimura & Faust, 1985), patients with left-hemispheric lesions made significantly poorer drawings than patients with right-hemispheric lesions, and patients with anterior left-hemispheric lesions were the worst of all. Kimura and Faust suggested that their results differed from previous results that found greater drawing impairment following right-hemispheric lesions (McFie, Piercy and Zangwill, 1950 ; Piercy et al, 1960 ; Hecaen, 1962 ; Binder, 1982) because most of these studies used copying tasks, and it has been postulated that left brain-damaged patients are assisted by having a model to copy, whereas right brain-damaged patients are not. However, this explanation does not account for my results (Ogden, 1985a) in that three of the five tasks I used to assess

visuospatial neglect were copying tasks, and in spite of this patients with
left lesions demonstrated a drawing neglect as often as those with right
lesions, and patients with left anterior lesions demonstrated a higher
incidence of neglect than those with left posterior lesions.

Kimura and Faust's (1985) patient population paralleled mine in that it
consisted of a series of unselected patients, and aphasic patients were not
excluded. The results of these two studies (Kimura & Faust, 1985 ; Ogden,
1985a) suggest that when unselected groups of patients with unilateral
brain lesions are assessed on drawing tasks involving spontaneous drawing
or copying, patients with left anterior lesions demonstrate greater
deficits than patients with left posterior lesions whether the deficit is
one of global drawing ability or neglect of the right side of the drawing.

Kimura and Faust also assessed their patient groups for neglect using a
visual search task. They found that moderate degrees of neglect on this task
were equally common following right- or left-hemispheric lesions, but that
severe neglect (i.e., a difference between fields of 5 items found out of 20
or a mean difference between fields of at least 5 seconds in locating
objects) was more common after right-hemispheric lesions. They comment that
severe neglect on visual searching is usually associated with extensive
rather than focal damage to the right hemisphere. On spontaneous drawings of
a house and a person 27% of their right brain-damaged patients demonstrated
clear contralateral neglect but none of their left brain-damaged patients
did. However, it should be noted that 31% of the left brain-damaged group
produced unrecognizable drawings that could not therefore be analyzed for
neglect, whereas only 12% of the right brain-damaged group produced
unrecognizable drawings. Added to this, most of the unrecognizable drawings
were those of patients with left anterior lesions, and according to my
study, this is just the group most likely to demonstrate neglect on drawing.

Other Research Implicating the Left Hemisphere in Tasks Involving Visual Imagery

If some forms of unilateral visuospatial neglect are the result of a
'mutilated representation of space' (Bisiach et al, 1979, 1981 ; Bisiach &
Luzzatti, 1978 ; Ogden, 1985b) then studies implicating the left hemisphere
in tasks involving visual imagery are relevant to theories of visuospatial
neglect. Erlichman and Barrett (1983) reviewed the visual imagery
literature and found little evidence to support the claim that the right
hemisphere is superior to the left in tasks involving visual imagery.

Farah (1984) reviewed reports in the neurological literature of a loss
of visual imagery following brain damage. By breaking down the imagery
process into its components and grouping together patients who were unable
to perform a particular component in the imagery process, she was able to
find some degree of consistency in the location of the lesions that result in
a particular pattern of deficits and preserved abilities in image
formation. She concluded that a loss of the ability to generate images was
most frequently a consequence of a posterior lesion in the left hemisphere.

In Farah's (1984) componential analysis of visual imagery, which she
based on Kosslyn's (1980) theory of visual imagery in normal adults, a
structure dubbed the 'visual buffer' was postulated. The visual buffer is
not a cognitive process and does not itself bear information, but rather it
is the medium in which images occur. For example, when we retrieve a visual
image from long-term memory, the generation process recreates it in a
spatial, pictorial form that we can consciously experience in the visual
buffer. By using an inspection process we can scan the picture in the visual
buffer and extract information.

The 'display screen' postulated by Bisiach et al (1979) is essentially
the equivalent of the 'visual buffer' postulated by Kosslyn (1980) and Farah

(1984). Farah did not analyse the experiments demonstrating the contralesional neglect of visuospatial images (Bisiach et al, 1979, 1981; Bisiach & Luzzatti, 1978; Ogden, 1985b) but in terms of her componential analysis it seems likely that acute lesions in either hemisphere can disrupt that part of the visual buffer on which the contralateral half of the represented visual stimulus is predominantly activated or displayed.

It is unclear whether a particular location within each hemisphere is associated with the disruption of the visual buffer. In both Bisiach et al's (1979) and my own (Ogden, 1985b) experiments all patients who neglected the left sides of images had lesions that included the right parietal cortex. However, in my experiment, two patients with right-hemispheric anterior lesions said they were unable to form images at all and therefore could not complete the task. The patients in my experiment who neglected the right sides of images included three with left posterior lesions and one with a solitary metastasis that appeared on CT to be restricted to the left frontal lobe. This patient demonstrated the most severe neglect in the LBD group. In the LBD group one patient with an anterior lesion and four with lesions including the posterior cortex could not complete the task, possibly because they were unable to form images at all (cf. Farah, 1984).

Further support for the involvement of the left hemisphere in image formation is furnished by an experiment carried out by Farah, Gazzaniga, Holtzman and Kosslyn (1985). They tested a commissurotomized patient with a letter classification task known to require imagery, and two control tasks requiring all the same processes except that of forming an image, and found that whereas both hemispheres could perform the control taks, only the left hemisphere could perform the imagery task.

These reviews and experiments, when viewed alongside the evidence for the neglect of the contralesional halves of visual images in unilaterally brain-damaged patients, point to a bilateral involvement in many visual imagery processes. Some simple imagery tasks and specific components of more complex imagery processes may be mediated by one or the other hemisphere, but the displaying of the image in analogue form so that it is available for conscious appraisal, would seem to require the collaboration of both hemispheres.

The Case for the Left Hemisphere's Involvement in Visuospatial Neglect

In summary, the following points would seem to be pertinent to the building of a theory that would explain contralateral visuospatial neglect after left- as well as right-hemispheric lesions.

(1) Mild neglect follows right- and left-hemispheric lesions with an equal frequency, at least in patients with acute lesions. This applies to visuospatial neglect when assessed using a line cancellation task (Albert, 1973; Ogden, 1985a), a visual search task (Kimura and Faust, 1985), a visual exploration task requiring patients to insert balls into each of 30 holes placed symmetrically in the lid of a box directly in from of them (Colombo et al, 1976), drawing tasks (Gainotti et al, 1972; Ogden, 1985a), and a visual imagery task (Ogden, 1985b).

(2) Given that right brain-damaged patients have more severe neglect than left brain-damaged patients when their lesions are acute, the neglect of left brain-damaged patients will resolve sooner than that of the right brain-damaged patients. This may partially explain the right-left difference in incidence of neglect that is found when patients are assessed weeks or months after sustaining their lesions. Another factor influencing the incidence figures is the sensitivity of the test or test battery used to assess neglect. That is, it may require a more sensitive test to identify neglect in left brain-damaged patients than in right brain-damaged patients.

(3) Visuospatial neglect may involve deficits in both visuoperceptual ability, that is the ability to perceive visuospatial objects per se, and in the awareness of egocentric space, that is how objects (or body parts) are distributed in space relative to the observer. There is evidence to suggest that both hemispheres are involved in visuoperceptual processes (Dee, 1970; Kim et al, 1984) as well as in the awareness of egocentric space (Plourde & Sperry, 1984). However, while lesions of the left hemisphere appear to be primarily responsible for some disorders of egocentric or body space, for example finger agnosia, (Kinsbourne & Warrington, 1962) left-right confusion (Benton 1959) and autotopoagnosia (Ogden, 1985c), on balance the right hemisphere would seem to take the more dominant role in a wide range of visuoperceptual/spatial abilities (De Renzi, 1982). This relatively greater involvement of the right hemisphere in these functions may underlie the finding that visuospatial deficits, including visuospatial neglect, are often more severe following right- than following left-hemispheric lesions, but are not necessarily more frequent.

(4) It is well documented that the posterior region of the right hemisphere is more specialized for visuoperceptual/spatial tasks than the anterior region of that hemisphere (De Renzi, 1982). However, recent evidence has pointed to the reverse situation in the left hemisphere. That is, the anterior region plays a greater role in visuoperceptual/spatial tasks that the posterior region (Kim et al. 1984; Kimura & Faust, 1985 ; Ogden, 1985a). This left anterior specialization does not appear to be related to motor components of tasks (Kim et al, 1984). Patients with left anterior lesions are also more likely to demonstrate right-sided visual neglect than patients with left posterior lesions (Ogden, 1985a). One possible explanation of this left anterior, right posterior difference in the mediation of visuoperceptual/spatial tasks is that as a consequence of language representation in the region of the parieto-temporal junction of the left hemisphere (Wernicke's area), the mediation of visuospatial abilities and representations has become more anterior in the left hemisphere.

(5) Visual imagery tasks appear to be particularly sensitive to neglect, and patients with acute lesions of either hemisphere demonstrate neglect of the contralesional sides of visual images even when they do not show any other symptoms of neglect (Ogden, 1985b). This may be a result of the additional complexity that must be involved in the constructing of visual images (whether from short- or long-term memory) over that of simply visually perceiving objects. It seems probable that a deficit of the awareness of space would disrupt the complex process more than the simpler process.

(6) Many patients with neglect continue to neglect the contralesional sides of objects even when the entire object is placed on the ispilesional side of their body and/or head (Bisiach, Capitani & Porta, 1985). Some patients when assessed on copying tasks demonstrate neglect of the contralesional side of one object while copying another object that is placed even further into the 'neglected' hemispace (Gainotti et al, 1972; see also Fig. 2B). One might speculate that for these patients the space neglected is representational, and not external to the patient. For example, when the patient is asked to attend to a display of two objects, he or she may represent the display as a whole so that only the external object on the side contralateral to the lesion is neglected. Alternatively, each object may be attended to and represented independently of the other. In this situation, the ipsilesional side of each external object will be represented in the non-neglected side of space (i.e. in the intact hemisphere) and the contralesional side of each external object will be represented in the neglected hemispace (i.e. in the lesioned hemisphere).

This latter strategy could explain the neglect disorder of the patient whose drawing can be seen in Fig. 2B.

Towards a Dual-Hemisphere Theory of Visuospatial Neglect

The term unilateral spatial neglect covers a number of neglect disorders, each of which conceivably results from one or more deficits at different levels of perceptual and cognitive processing. The clearest example of this is that while neglect has been observed in most modalities in humans, few if any patients demonstrate a generalized unilateral neglect that encompasses all modalities. Even within a single modality such as vision, a range of deficits may possibly underlie the neglect, and while a single deficit may result in a mild form of neglect, two or more deficits may result in a more severe or even a different form of neglect (cf. Mesulam, 1981, 1983).

While a unilateral attentional deficit could underlie some forms of neglect (Heilman & Watson, 1977) one form of visuospatial neglect would appear to be caused, at least in part, by a deficit at some level in the processing of visuospatial mental images (Bisiach et al, 1979, 1981; Bisiach & Luzzatti, 1978). The evidence that patients with lesions of either hemisphere neglect the contralesional sides of visuospatial images (Ogden, 1985b) implies that at some advanced level of processing, our mental images are represented in both hemispheres, perhaps in an analogue fashion, at least with respect to their left and right sides. That is, when we form mental visual images our interpretations or memories of the left side of the external world are represented predominantly by the right hemisphere, and those of the right side are represented predominantly by the left hemisphere. When there is unilateral damage to the cortical areas involved at this level of the imagery process (for example, the visual buffer), the image mediated by that hemisphere is disrupted and therefore neglected. Bisiach et al (1981) suggested that the parietal association cortex was the most likely location for a display screen (or visual buffer).

I (Ogden, 1985b) found that patients with acute left- or right-hemispheric lesions neglected the contralesional sides of their mental images even though some of them did not demonstrate neglect on a test battery for visual neglect. Given that this battery has proven to be very sensitive to visual neglect (i.e. it identified neglect in 50% of a group of 56 left brain-damaged patients and 44% of a group of 45 right brain-damaged patients, Ogden, 1985a), this raises the possibility that the majority of patients with acute unilateral lesions have some degree of visuospatial neglect, and this will become apparent if a sensitive enough test is used to assess it.

It could be that visuospatial neglect is in part a consequence of the general disorganization (physiological and/or functional) that occurs in the hemisphere immediately following a lesion to one part of it. This is similar to the concept of "diaschisis" proposed by von Monakow (1914). Acute focal brain damage and rapidly progressive lesions such as gliomas and metastases, even although apparently causing restricted neuronal damage, are likely to result in a widespread disturbance of higher cortical functions. In the case of non-progressive lesions such as infarcts, this general disturbance is transitory and in time the brain stabilizes around the lesion, resulting in some recovery of function. This could provide one explanation for the high incidence of visual neglect I found in groups of patients with acute left- or right-hemispheric lesions, especially given that a high proportion of these patients had lesions of tumoral etiology.

The display screen or visual buffer on which our images are displayed may be predominantly restricted to the posterior region of the right hemisphere, but may be more anteriorly placed in the left hemisphere, due to the presence of language functions in the posterior region of that hemisphere. This would explain the anterior-posterior interhemispheric difference in incidence of neglect. The finding that patients with acute lesions almost anywhere in the cortex or basal ganglia may demonstrate visual neglect on highly sensitive tests, suggests that in order for the visual buffer to function optimally, the hemisphere as a whole must be undisturbed. It does not seem too far fetched to suppose that a clear unbroken display-screen relies upon a disciplined, stable hemisphere.

Spontaneous recovery of neglect occurs in many patients (Campbell & Oxbury, 1976; Gainotti, 1968) as the lesioned hemisphere globally readapts allowing the visual buffer to regain its potency. Those patients whose lesions encroach upon and damage the area directly utilised by the visual buffer will demonstrate the most severe neglect and may continue to suffer from neglect even after the brain has stabilized. Patients with rapidly progressive lesions may also continue to demonstrate neglect even if the lesion has not damaged the visual buffer itself, because of the continuing instability of the hemisphere.

Patients with left-hemispheric lesions will, as a group, demonstrate less severe neglect than patients with right-hemispheric lesions because of the greater specialization of the right hemisphere for visuoperceptual /spatial functions in general. That is, the visual buffer in the right hemisphere has available to it all the specialized visuoperceptual resources of that hemisphere, and visual images mediated by it will predominate over those mediated by the left hemisphere.

Whether the deficit underlying visuospatial neglect is primarily one of unilateral hypoarousal, or an imbalance of attention, or a mutilated representation of space, the left hemisphere's role in neglect deserves to be carefully re-examined with the aid of up-to-date methods and technology, in the light of new evidence implicating it in mild neglect disorders at least, as well as in a number of other visuospatial and visual imagery functions.

References

Albert, M.L. A simple test of visual neglect. Neurology, 1973, 23, 658-664.

Arrigoni, G. & De Renzi, E. Constructional apraxia and hemispheric locus of lesions. Cortex, 1964, 1, 170-197.

Battersby, W.S., Bender, M.B., Pollack, M. & Kahn, R.L. Unilateral 'spatial agnosia' ('inattention') in patients with cerebral lesions. Brain, 1956, 79, 68-93.

Baxter, D.M. & Warrington, E.K. Neglect dysgraphia. Journal of Neurology, Neurosurgery and Psychiatry, 1983, 46, 1073-1078.

Benton, A.C. Right-left Discrimination and Finger Localization. New York: Hoeber-Harper, 1959.

Benton, A.L. Disorders of spatial disorientation. In P.J. Vinken and G.W. Bruyn (Eds.), Handbook of Clinical Neurology, Volume 3. Amsterdam: North Holland Publishing Company, 1969.

Binder, L.M. Constructional strategies on complex figure drawing after unilateral brain damage. Journal of Clinical Neuropsychology, 1982, 4, 51-58.

Bisiach, E., Capitani, E., Luzzatti, C. & Perani, D. Brain and conscious representation of outside reality. Neuropsychologia, 1981, 19, 543-551.

Bisiach, E., Capitani, E. & Porta, E. Two basic properties of space representation in the brain : evidence from unilateral neglect. Journal of Neurology, Neurosurgery and Psychiatry, 1985, 48, 141-144.

Bisiach, E. & Luzzatti, C. Unilateral neglect of representational space. Cortex, 1978, 14, 129–133.

Bisiach, E., Luzzatti, C. & Perani, D. Unilateral neglect, representational schema and consciousness. Brain, 1979, 102, 609–618.

Brain, W.R. Visual disorientation with special reference to lesions of the right cerebral hemisphere. Brain, 1941, 64, 244–272.

Brain, W.R. Speech and handedness. Lancet, 1945 2, 837–842.

Campbell, D.C. & Oxbury, J.M. Recovery from unilateral visual-spatial neglect. Cortex, 1976, 12, 303–312.

Chedru, F. Space representation in unilateral spatial neglect. Journal of Neurology, Neurosurgery and Psychiatry, 1976, 39, 1057–1061.

Cohn, R. The Person Symbol in Clinical Medicine. Charles C. Thomas, Springfield, Ill, 1961.

Colombo, A., De Renzi, E. & Faglioni, P. The occurrence of visual neglect in patients with unilateral cerebral disease. Cortex, 1976, 12, 221–231.

Costa, L.D., Vaughn, H.G., Horwitz, M. & Ritter, W. Patterns of behavioral deficit associated with visual spatial neglect. Cortex, 1969, 5, 242–263.

Critchley, M. The phenomenon of tactile inattention with special reference to parietal lesions. Brain, 1949, 72, 538–561.

Critchley, M. The Parietal Lobes. New York: Hafner, 1953.

Damasio, A.R., Damasio, H. & Chui, H.C. Neglect following damage to frontal lobe and basal ganglia. Neuropsychologia, 1980, 18, 123–132.

Dee, H.L. Visuoconstructive and visuoperceptive deficit in patients with unilateral cerebral lesions. Neuropsychologia, 1970, 8, 305–314.

De Renzi, E. Disorders of Space Exploration and Cognition. New York: John Wiley and Sons. 1982.

De Renzi, E., Faglioni, P. & Scotti, G. Hemispheric contribution to exploration of space through the visual and tactile modality. Cortex, 1970, 6, 191–203.

Desmedt, J.E. Active touch exploration of extrapersonal space elicits specific electrogenesis in the right cerebral hemisphere of intact right handed man. Proceedings of the National Academy of Science, U.S.A., 1977, 74, 4037–4040.

Erlichman, H. & Barrett, J. Right hemisphere specialization for mental imagery : a review of the evidence. Brain and Cognition, 1983, 2, 39–52.

Farah, M.J. The neurological basis of mental imagery : A componential analysis. Cognition, 1984, 18, 241–269.

Farah, M.J., Gazzaniga, M.S., Holtzman, J.D. & Kosslyn, S.M. A left hemisphere basis for visual mental imagery ? Neuropsychologia, 1985, 23, 115–118.

Gainotti, G. Les manifestations de négligence et d'inattention pour l'hemispace. Cortex, 1968, 4. 64–91.

Gainotti, G., Messerli, P. & Tissot, R. Qualitative analysis of unilateral spatial neglect in relation to laterality of cerebral lesions. Journal of Neurology, Neurosurgery and Psychiatry, 1972, 35, 545–550.

Gloning, K. Die Cerebral Bedingten Storungen des Raumlichen Sehen und des Raumerlebens. Wien: Maudrig, 1965.

Gloning, I., Gloning, K. and Hoff, H. Neuropsychological symptoms and syndromes in lesions of the occipital lobe and the adjacent areas. Paris: Gauthier-Villars, 1968.

Hecaen, H. Clinical symptomatology in right and left hemisphere lesions. In V.B. Mountcastle (Ed.), Interhemispheric Relations and Cerebral Dominance. Baltimore: The Johns Hopkins Press, 1962.

Hecaen, H. Aphasic, apraxic and agnosic syndrome in right and left hemisphere lesions. In P.J. Vinken and G.W. Bruyns (Eds.), Handbook of Clinical Neurology, Volume 4. Amsterdam: North-Holland Publishing

Company, 1969.

Hecaen, H. & Angelergues, R. La Cecité Psychique. Paris: Masson, 1963.

Hecaen, H., Penfield, W., Bertrand, C. & Malmo, R. The syndrome of apractognosia due to lesions of the minor hemisphere. Archives of Neurology and Psychiatry, 1956, 75, 400-434.

Heilman, K.M. & Valenstein, E. Frontal lobe neglect in man. Neurology, 1972, 22, 660-664.

Heilman, K.M. & Van Den Abell, T. Right hemisphere dominance for attention : The mechanism underlying hemispheric asymmetries of inattention (neglect). Neurology, 1980, 30, 327-330.

Heilman, K.M. & Watson, R.T. The neglect syndrome : A unilateral defect of the orienting response. In S. Harnad et al. (Eds.), Lateralization in the Nervous System. New York: Academic Press, 1977.

Heir, D.B., Davis, K.R., Richardson, E.P. & Mohr, J.P. Hypertensive putaminal hemorrhage. Annals of Neurology, 1977, 1, 152-159.

Howes, D. & Boller, F. Simple reaction time : Evidence for focal impairment from lesions of the right hemisphere. Brain, 1975, 98, 317-332.

Kim, Y., Morrow, L., Passafiume, D. & Boller, F. Visuoperceptual and visuomotor abilities and locus of lesion. Neuropsychologia, 1984, 22, 177-185.

Kimura, D. & Faust, R. Spontaneous drawing in an unselected sample of patients with unilateral cerebral damage. Research Bulletin N° 624, May, Department of Psychology, University of Western Ontario, Canada.

Kinsbourne, M. A model for the mechanism of unilateral neglect of space. Transactions of the American Neurological Association, 1970, 95, 143-146.

Kinsbourne, M. Direction of gaze and distribution of cerebral thought processes. Neuropsychologia, 1974, 12, 279-281.

Kinsbourne, M. Hemi-neglect and hemisphere rivalry. In E.A. Weinstein and R.P. Friedland (Eds.), Advances in Neurology, Volume 18. New York: Raven Press, 1977.

Kosslyn, S.M. Image and Mind. Cambridge, MA: Harvard University Press, 1980.

Lynch, J.C. The functional organization of posterior parietal association cortex. Behaviour and Brain Sciences, 1980, 3, 485-499.

McFie, J., Piercy, M.F. & Zangwill, O.L. Visual-spatial agnosia associated with lesions of the right cerebral hemisphere. Brain, 1950, 73, 167-190.

McFie, J. & Zangwill, O.L. Visual-constructive disabilities associated with lesions of the left cerebral hemisphere. Brain, 1960, 83, 243-260.

Mesulam, M.M. A cortical network for directed attention and unilateral neglect. Annals of Neurology, 1981, 10, 309-325.

Mesulam, M.M. The functional anatomy and hemispheric specialization for directed attention. Trends in Neurosciences, September 1983, 6, 384-387.

Mountcastle, V.B., Lynch, J.C., Georgopoulos, A., Sakata, H. & Acuna, C. Posterior parietal association cortex of the monkey : Command functions for operations within extrapersonal space. Journal of Neurophysiology, 1975, 38, 871-908.

Ogden, J.A. Anterior-posterior interhemispheric differences in the loci of lesions producing visual hemineglect. Brain and Cognition, 1985a, 4, 59-75.

Ogden, J.A. Contralesional neglect of constructed visual images in right and left brain-damaged patients. Neuropsychologia, 1985b, 23, 273-277.

Ogden, J.A. Autotopagnosia : Occurrence in a patient without nominal aphasia and with an intact ability to point to parts of animals and objects. Brain, 1985c, 108, 1009-1022.

Orem, J., Schlag-Rey, M. & Schlag, J. Unilateral visual neglect and thalamic intralaminar lesions in the cat. Experimental Neurology, 1973, 40, 784-797.

Oxbury, J.M., Campbell, D.C. and Oxbury, S.M. Unilateral spatial neglect and impairments of spatial analysis and visual perception. Brain, 1974, 97, 551-564.

Piercy, M., Hecaen, H. & Ajuriaguerra, J. De. Constructional apraxis associated with unilateral cerebral lesions - left and right sided cases compared. Brain, 1960, 83, 225-242.

Plourde, G. & Sperry, R.W. Left hemisphere involvement in left spatial neglect from right-sided lesions. A commissurotomy study. Brain, 1984, 107, 95-106.

Poppelreuter, W.K. Die psychischen Schadigungen durch Kopfschuss in Kreig 1914-1916 : Die Storungen der niederen und hoheren Leistungen durch Verletzungen des Okzipitalhirns. Volume 1. Leipzig: Leopold Voss, 1917.

Robinson, D.L., Goldberg, M.E. & Stanton, G.B. Parietal association cortex in the primate : Sensory mechanisms and behavioural modulations. Journal of Neurophysiology, 1978, 41, 910-932.

Schenkenberg, T., Bradford, D.C. & Ajax, E.T. Line bisection and unilateral visual neglect in patients with neurological impairment. Neurology, 1980, 30, 509-517.

Schott, B., Jeannerod, M. & Zahin, M.Z. L'agnosie spatiale unilatérale : Pertubation en secteur des mécanismes d'exploration et de fixation du regard. Journal de Médecine de Lyon, 1966, 47, 169-195.

Silberpfenning, J. Contribution to the problem of eye movements. III. Disturbances of ocular movements with pseudohemianopia in frontal lobe tumours. Confinia Neurologica, 1941, 4, 1-13.

Sokolov, Y.N. Perception and the conditional reflex. Oxford: Pergamon Press, 1963.

Van der Linden, M., Seron, X., Gillet, J. & Bredart, S. Heminegligence par lésion frontale droite. A propos de trois observations. Acta Neurologica Belgica, 1980, 80, 298-310.

Von Monakow, C. Die Lokalisation im Grosshirn und der Abbau der Funktion durch Cortikale. Wiesbaden: Herde, 1914.

Watson, R.T. & Heilman, K.M. Thalamic neglect. Neurology, 1979, 29, 690-694.

Weinstein, E.A. & Cole, M. Concepts of anosognosia. In L. Halpern (Ed.), Problems of Dynamic Neurology. Jerusalem: Jerusalem Post Press, 1963.

Weinstein, E.A. & Friedland, R.P. Behavioural disorders associated with hemi-inattention. In E.A. Weinstein and R.P. Friedland (Eds.), Advances in Neurology, Volume 18. New York: Raven Press, 1977.

Zarit, S.H. & Kahn, R.L. Impairment and adaptation in chronic disabilities : Spatial inattention. Journal of Nervous and Mental Diseases, 1974, 159, 63-72.

Acknowledgments : This chapter was prepared during my tenure as a Postdoctoral Associate in the Department of Psychology, Massachusetts Institute of Technology, Cambridge, Massachusetts, USA with support from a partial Overseas Research Fellowship from the Medical Research Council of New Zealand and from NIMH 24433. Many of the ideas expressed in this chapter were developed as a result of discussions with my colleagues, not all of whom agreed with me ! In particular I thank Professor Michael Corballis for stimulating discussions and for his comments on the chapter.

Neurophysiological and Neuropsychological Aspects
of Spatial Neglect, M. Jeannerod (editor)
© Elsevier Science Publishers B.V. (North-Holland), 1987

THE ANATOMY OF SPATIAL NEGLECT IN HUMANS

Giuseppe Vallar
and
Daniela Perani

A wide range of both cortical and subcortical lesions may be associated with contralateral neglect in humans. The most frequent <u>cortical</u> correlate of human neglect is a retro-rolandic damage involving the right infero-posterior parietal regions, while frontal neglect is comparatively rare. As for right <u>subcortical</u> lesions, both thalamic and lenticular lesions may be associated with neglect, which is unlikely to occur when the brain damage is confined to the right subcortical white matter. However, a remarkable number of thalamic or lenticular lesions without signs of contralateral neglect has been recently reported. The relevance of these anatomical data to neurophysiological models of directed attention (and neglect) is discussed. Finally, the limited available anatomical evidence concerning neglect after left hemisphere damage is reviewed.

I. Anatomical Correlates of Spatial Neglect from Right Hemisphere Damage
Although spatial neglect may occur after both right and left-sided lesions, most investigators agree that neglect is more frequent and/or more severe after right brain damage (see Gainotti, 1968; Costa, Vaughan, Horwitz & Ritter, 1969; DeRenzi, Faglioni & Scotti, 1970; Hécaen, 1972; Albert, 1973; Oxbury, Campbell & Oxbury, 1974; Colombo, DeRenzi & Faglioni, 1976; Ogden, 1985; but cf. Battersby, Bender, Pollack & Kahn, 1956; Zarit & Kahn, 1974). Most anatomical data concern patients suffering from damage of the right side of the brain, while limited evidence is available for the anatomical correlates of spatial neglect from left-sided lesions.

Early Localization Studies
The traditional anatomical correlation of spatial neglect is with lesions involving the retro-rolandic regions and a crucial role of right parietal damage is usually maintained (e.g., Brain, 1941; McFie, Piercy & Zangwill, 1950; Critchley, 1953). Such a view was supported by anatomo-clinical correlation studies, comprising both positive and negative cases. Battersby et al. (1956) investigated a large series of patients with unilateral space-occupying lesions (mainly tumors), localized by radiographic (angiography, pneumoencephalography) and neurosurgical evidence. Spatial neglect was assessed by a number of tests including figure-ground discrimination, constructional, copying, drawing from memory, geographical location, reading and visuo-spatial tasks. Battersby et al. (1956) found that 10 out of 22 patients with parieto-occipital and temporo-occipital damage had definite signs of neglect. Conversely, of 19 patients with frontal and fronto-parietal lesions only 2 showed neglect.

Hécaen (1972), who investigated spatial neglect in 179 patients suffering from a neurosurgically or postmortem assessed right hemisphere lesion, reports an association of neglect with parietal and occipital lesions, but not with frontal damage.

More recently, the availability of noninvasive neuroradiological techniques such as brain scan and, later, CT scan, has allowed relatively precise anatomo-clinical correlations in patients suffering from brain damage. Since the early seventies a wealth of cases has been reported, showing that neglect may be associated not only with retro-rolandic lesions, but also with frontal damage and with lesions confined to subcortical structures, such as the thalamus and the basal ganglia. This state of affairs parallels, in a way, the recent advances of anatomo-clinical CT correlation studies in aphasia. In this area, while the traditional associations have been by and large confirmed, clear evidence has been provided that lesions outside the cortical language areas, involving subcortical structures (i.e., thalamus, basal ganglia) may be associated with aphasic disorders (see Cappa & Vignolo, 1983, for a recent review of anatomo-clinical CT correlation studies in aphasia).

Some Methodological Issues in Anatomo-Clinical Correlation Studies in Neglect

When a correlation study is performed, to investigate the relationships between focal cerebral lesions and a neuropsychological deficit (e.g., spatial neglect) the following points appear to be relevant.

1. Etiology of brain damage and duration of disease. Neurological disorders (e.g., a tumor, a stroke) differ with respect to factors such as mode of onset and course, which may affect the anatomo-clinical correlation. Cerebrovascular diseases, such as infarction or haemorrhage, frequently have sudden onset. Conversely, in the case of brain tumors, the neurological and neuropsychological symptoms and signs tend to develop progressively, in a sub-acute or even chronic fashion.

Duration of disease is a factor closely connected with etiology. Clinical experience suggests that in stroke patients neglect is an ephemeral phenomenon, at least in its more dramatic manifestations, which vanishes fairly rapidly (days, weeks), though experimental assessment may show a long-lasting persistence of this deficit (Campbell & Oxbury, 1976; Colombo, DeRenzi & Gentilini, 1982). Conversely, in patients suffering from a brain tumor the neurological defects, including neglect, usually run a progressive course and, at variance with stroke patients, the onset of the disease cannot be easily determined. Strokes and tumors may also differ as to the extent of perifocal edema.

Different patterns of diaschisis (von Monakow, 1914), a type of functional impairment of anatomically undamaged brain structures, and of compensatory mechanisms by undamaged brain regions, may occur in patients with focal lesions of diverse etiology. In patients suffering from a cerebrovascular attack, diaschisis is presumably maximal at onset and gradually diminishes over time, while compensation runs an opposite course. Diaschisis and compensation are poorly understood phenomena and their differential features, in function of the etiology and duration of the cerebral disease, are largely unclear. For the purpose of correlation studies, it seems however safer to collect data from patients with homogeneous etiology and comparable length of illness, to avoid as much as possible biases from differences in diaschisis and compensation.

These factors, as obvious as they are, have seldom been taken into account in studies of anatomical correlates of neglect. The recent study by Ogden (1985) comprises patients with heterogeneous etiology: tumors (meningiomas, gliomas, metastases), strokes, abscesses and artero-venous malformations. In addition, no data about duration of disease are provided.

2. Group studies and individual case reports. Correlation studies require a relatively large sample of cases, including patients both affected and unaffected by the behavioral deficit under investigation. Unfortunately, a limited number of group studies investigating the effects of lesions involving cortical areas is available (e.g., Battersby et al., 1956; Ogden, 1985). As to subcortical lesions, their relationships with neglect rest on reports of individual positive cases, no group studies comprising negative cases being available.

3. Varieties of neglect. Neglect is often considered a clinical syndrome comprising a number of different symptoms. Heilman, Watson & Valenstein (1985) list the following: hemi-inattention, a failure to report or respond to stimuli presented contralateral to the hemispheric lesion (such a deficit, however, may often be explained in terms of sensory loss); sensory extinction to double simultaneous stimulation; hemiakinesia of the contralateral limbs (with no or minimal associated primary motor deficits), motor extinction (increased contralateral limb hypokinesia, when the simultaneous use of the ipsilateral extremity is required) and motor impersistence (a difficulty in sustaining postures); allesthesia (a stimulation contralateral to the lesion is reported by the patient as ipsilateral); neglect of the contralateral half-space ("hemispatial neglect"), as assessed by tasks such as drawing, reading, line bisection, crossing out of lines or circles, blind exploration of a tactile maze. Anosognosia may be an associated disorder.

These symptoms do not necessarily cooccur. While most patients show "hemi-inattention" and "hemispatial neglect", dissociated cases have been found. Hécaen (1962) found "exceptional" cases of neglect without hemianopia. Albert (1973) reports a double dissociation between the two disorders: seven out of 14 right brain-damaged patients with a visual field defect showed no signs of neglect on a crossing out lines task; five out of 11 neglect patients had no visual field deficits. Similarly, patients showing visual extinction without neglect have been found (Ogden, 1985). Finally, hemiakinesia and motor extinction may occur without evidence of spatial neglect (Valenstein & Heilman, 1981; Viader, Cambier & Pariser, 1982). These scattered data suggest a possible fractionation of Heilman et al. (1985)'s symptom complex "neglect": different patterns of impairment could be interpreted in terms of the deficit of discrete components of an information processing system.

The vast majority of studies relevant to the anatomo-clinical correlation issue considered here investigate what Heilman et al. (1985) define as "hemispatial neglect": accordingly, the anatomo-clinical correlates discussed in this chapter are by and large confined to such a disorder, even though individual patients may show associated symptoms such as extinction, hemiakinesia, anosognosia.

4. Assessment of neglect. A final issue concerns the task used to assess spatial neglect. A wide range of tests, including drawing from memory, copying, reading and exploratory (e.g., cancellation of lines and circles) tasks have been employed by different investigators. Most studies have been performed in the visual modality, even though contralateral neglect has also been shown by tactile exploratory tasks (DeRenzi et al., 1970). There is evidence to show that tests may differ in their sensitivity to detect neglect phenomena (e.g., Colombo et al., 1976; Colombo et al., 1982). Finally, the operational definitions of neglect may differ from one investigator to another. Costa et al. (1969) equate position preference, in tests such as Raven Progressive Matrices, with neglect. Heilman & Valenstein (1972a) consider auditory, visual and tactile extinction as an index of neglect.

Cortico-Subcortical Lesions: "frontal" vs "parietal" Neglect

There is clear evidence from individual case reports that neglect phenomena may be associated with frontal damage. Zingerle (1913, case 3) reported anosognosia and akinesia of the left arm without paresis in a patient with a small abscess in the right frontal lobe, ascertained by autopsy. Silberpfenning (1941) found visual neglect in two frontal patients who, on postmortem examination, showed respectively a supero-medial glioma and a dorso-lateral meningioma. It is worth noticing that case 1 of Silberpfenning showed some evidence to suggest a representational deficit in neglect (see Bisiach, Capitani, Luzzatti & Perani, 1981): this patient had a brief attack of delirium and her visual hallucinations appeared on the right side of the room. A strikingly similar case has been recently reported by Mesulam (1981): his patient, a chronic alcohol abuser who suffered an infarction which included the posterior parts of the right hemisphere, had severe contralateral spatial neglect and developed hallucinations appearing only on his right.

In recent years, further cases have been reported. Heilman & Valenstein (1972b) found visual neglect and anosognosia in 6 patients, three with dorso-lateral and three with medial right frontal lesions (infarctions and tumors), assessed by brain scan in five patients and by pathological examination in one case; in this latter case the lesion involved the cingulate gyrus, the adjacent white matter and portions of the superior frontal region. Additional cases of visual neglect associated with neoplastic frontal lesions were described by Castaigne, Laplane & Degos (1972, case 2) and by Van Der Linden, Seron, Gillet & Bredaert (1980, three cases). In the three cases reported by Stein & Volpe (1983) CT-assessed infarcts of the subcortical frontal white matter were shown; the lesions also involved the caudate and lenticular nuclei (cases 1 and 2) and the anterior temporal and insular region (case 1).

While frontal lesions may be associated with neglect phenomena, group studies appear to show that neglect occurs much more frequently when the retro-rolandic regions are damaged. In nine right brain-damaged patients with mixed etiology Heilman & Valenstein (1972a) reported visual and auditory neglect, assessed by double simultaneous stimulation : in all patients the lesion, as determined by brain scan, involved the inferior parietal lobule. Bisiach, Luzzatti & Perani (1979) and Bisiach et al. (1981) found that the temporo-parieto-occipital carrefour was the region most frequently involved in patients showing neglect, assessed by a task requiring the crossing out of circles symmetrically arranged around a central one in both half-spaces. Ogden (1985), in a study involving both positive and negative cases, found neglect in 12 out of 18 patients with posterior lesions (60%), while only 2 out of 10 patients with anterior lesions (20%) displayed visual neglect, as assessed by crossing lines and drawing tests.

We investigated the presence/absence of neglect (see Table 1) in a series of 59 right-handed stroke patients, with CT-assessed focal lesions of the right hemisphere. The vast majority of patients (16/20) with antero-posterior damage (usually large perisylvian lesions) showed signs of neglect (see Figure 1). In patients with lesions confined to either the pre- or the post-rolandic region, neglect was much more frequently associated with posterior damage: only 1 out of 12 patients with anterior lesions had neglect, which was revealed by the aforementioned cancellation task in 17 out of 27 patients with posterior damage (chi2= 9.98, p < .005, with 1 df). The dorso-lateral lesion of the frontal neglect patient is shown in Figure 2.

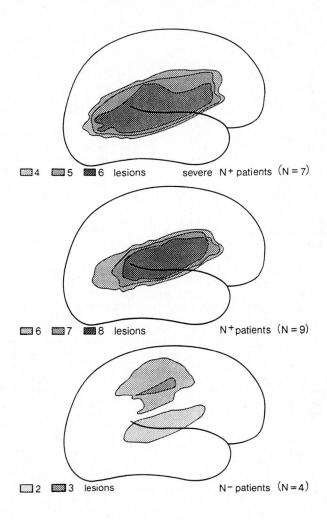

Figure 1
Composite contour maps (Howes and Boller, 1975) of the superficial and
deep lesions in stroke patients with antero-posterior damage. The
contours drawn on the standard lateral diagram of the brain represent
the degree of overlap of the lesions. From the top: (1) 7 patients with a
severe visuo-spatial neglect (N+), i.e., who did not cross out any
left-sided circle in a cancellation task; (2) 9 N+ patients, who
partially explored the left half-space, as seen from their crossing out
of some left-sided circles; (3) 4 patients without signs of neglect
(N−), as assessed by the cancellation task.

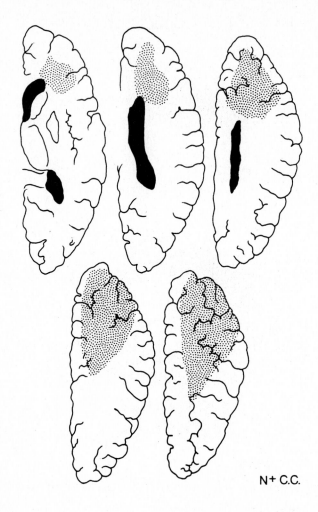

Figure 2
Frontal haemorrhagic lesion of a neglect patient on zero-degree
sections from Matsui & Hirano (1978). The dorso-lateral regions and the
underlying subcortical white matter are involved; the caudate and
lenticular nuclei appear spared.

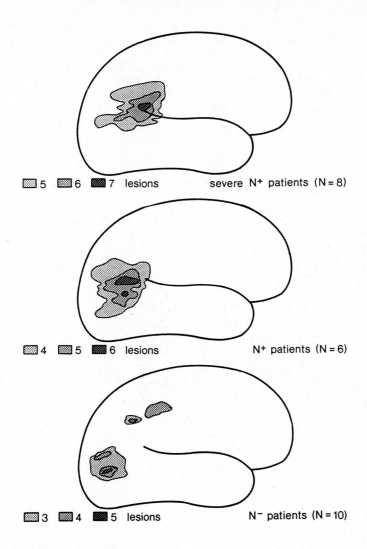

5 6 7 lesions   severe N+ patients (N = 8)

4 5 6 lesions   N+ patients (N = 6)

3 4 5 lesions   N− patients (N = 10)

Figure 3
Composite contour maps of the lesions of right brain-damaged stroke
patients with retro-rolandic damage. From the top: (1) 8 severe N+
patients; (2) 6 N+ patients; (3) 10 N− patients. See also caption to
Fig. 1.

In neglect patients with posterior lesions the inferior parietal region was the most frequently involved area. Conversely, in patients with retro-rolandic lesions who did not display signs of unilateral neglect, more superior or more postero-inferior regions were frequently damaged (see Figure 3). Three neglect patients had occipito-temporal medial lesions, which are shown in Figure 4.

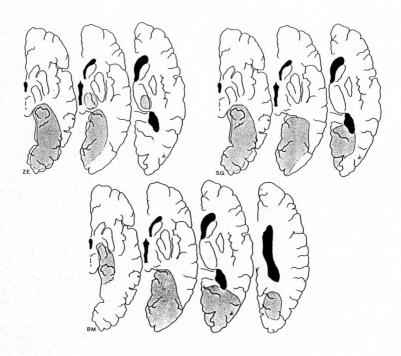

Figure 4
Occipito-temporal mesial vascular lesions of 3 severe N+ patients mapped on zero-degree sections from Matsui & Hirano (1978). In case Z.E. the thalamus was also damaged.

Within the posterior lesion group, the composite contour maps suggest a correlation between inferior parietal lobule damage (supramarginal gyrus) and neglect. Previously reported evidence is consistent with these findings (Hécaen, Penfield, Bertrand & Malmo, 1956; Heilman & Valenstein, 1972a). The study of Hécaen et al. (1956) is extremely relevant to the localization issue discussed here: they investigated patients who underwent precisely localized corticectomies for the relief of epilepsy and found an association between an apractognosic syndrome, including neglect, and lesions of the parieto-occipito-temporal junction, of which   the

Table I : Localization of CT-assessed lesions in 59 right brain-damaged stroke patients with superficial and deep lesions, subdivided according to the presence (N+) and absence (N-) of contralateral neglect, as assessed by a cancellation task, and to the locus of the hemispheric lesion, checked on the atlas by Matsui & Hirano (1978). Duration of disease: 8.39 days (range 1-29 days). Lesions are subdivided into three groups: anterior and posterior to the rolandic fissure; anteroposterior, involving both pre- and post-rolandic regions.

	ANTERIOR	POSTERIOR	ANTERO-POSTERIOR	TOTAL
N+	1	17	16	34
N-	11	10	4	25

supramarginal gyrus forms the center. Kertesz & Dobrowolski (1981) have shown that vascular lesions clustering in the superior parietal areas yield minimal signs of neglect; the deficit is much more severe when the fronto-temporo-parietal junction, which includes the inferior parietal lobule, is involved.

We have found a broadly similar localization pattern in right-handed patients suffering from CT-assessed cerebral tumors in the right hemisphere. Figure 5 shows the lesion maps of 19 patients with and without signs of neglect, as assessed by the cancellation task. Again, frontal lesions do not produce neglect phenomena, which occur much more frequently when the inferior parietal regions are affected. We have observed neglect in patients with rapidly growing malignant tumors, such as glioblastomas, but not in cases of more slowly developing tumors. Heilman et al. (1985) report similar clinical findings, even though neglect has also been observed in patients with slowly growing tumors, such as meningiomas (e.g., McFie et al., 1950; Heilman & Valenstein, 1972b). This clinical observation could possibly be interpreted in terms of differential degrees of compensation by undamaged brain regions: a rapidly developing neoplastic lesion, which sometimes may mimic a stroke, may interfere with compensatory mechanisms more substantially than a slowly growing tumor.

The functional dissociation between superior and inferior parietal lobule damage is consistent with some data concerning the anatomical correlates of reaching disorders. Ratcliff & Davies-Jones (1972) found that non-hemianopic patients with gross impairment in visual localization in the contralateral half-field had lesions clustering in the upper part of the parietal lobe. Levine, Kaufman & Mohr (1978) reported the case of a patient with a tumor involving the right superior parietal lobule, who had misreaching for visual objects without any sign of visual extinction or neglect. Taken together, these findings appear to suggest a possible difference within the posterior parietal region: while damage to the inferior parietal lobule is associated with contralateral neglect, misreaching without neglect may occur when the superior parietal lobule is selectively involved.

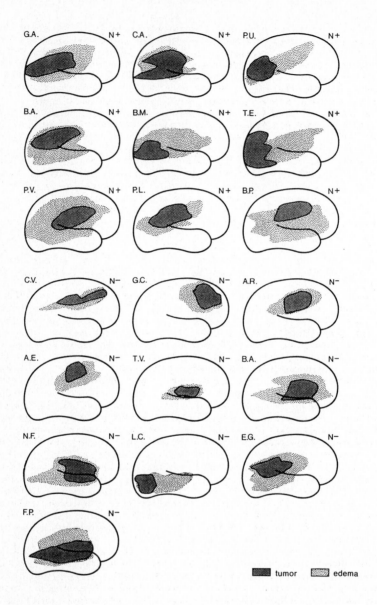

Figure 5

Lesion maps (Mazzocchi & Vignolo, 1978) of 9 patients with (N+) and 10 patients without (N−) signs of neglect, as assessed by the cancellation task. The maps show both the <u>tumor</u> and the surrounding peri-focal <u>edema</u>. In the <u>N+ group</u> the inferior parietal area appears involved in 8 patients and relatively spared in one (case B.P.). In the N− group, 7 patients showed anterior lesions; case L.C. had an occipital lesion; in cases E.G. and F.P. the inferior parietal region was involved.

A possible parietal anatomical correlate of the left/right asymmetry in the frequency and/or severity of spatial neglect has been recently provided by Eidelberg & Galaburda (1984), who performed architectonic parcellation of the inferior parietal lobule of 8 human brains. Volume measurements in the fields related to the angular gyrus showed in area PEG an asymmetry towards the right, which appeared not to be linked to the asymmetries present in the language areas. A differential role of the left and right inferior parietal regions is also suggested by the CT-clinical correlation study of Bisiach, Cornacchia, Sterzi & Vallar (1984): contralateral spatial neglect, as assessed by the aforementioned cancellation task, was found in 10 right brain-damaged patients with visual field defect, who had lesions clustering in the inferior parietal lobule. Conversely, no signs of neglect were present in 9 left brain-damaged hemianopic patients, who showed a comparable involvement of the inferior parietal regions. However, while anatomo-clinical correlation studies suggest a damage of the right supramarginal gyrus as the most frequent cortical correlate of left-sided spatial neglect, the asymmetry found by Eidelberg & Galaburda (1984) concerns a small portion of the angular gyrus (area PEG). A definite association between damage of right area PEG and left neglect is difficult, as rightly pointed out by Eidelberg & Galaburda themselves, since this small area amounts to at most one quarter of the total angular gyrus volume: acquired vascular or neoplastic cerebral lesions confined to this area, sparing the remaining inferior parietal regions, are most unlikely to occur.

Deep Lesions and Neglect

The association between lesions confined to subcortical structures and neglect is not a recent finding. Pick (1898) described a patient with a left hemiparesis and hemianopia, who in reading tasks systematically omitted the first (left-sided) word of each line and was anosognosic for his motor deficit. A postmortem examination showed encephalomalacia in the left temporal lobe and in the right thalamus. Oxbury et al. (1974) report neglect in a patient with an infarction of the right thalamus, optic tract and parts of the internal capsule, ascertained by autopsy. More recently, a number of individual cases have been reported with neglect phenomena and vascular CT-assessed lesions confined to subcortical structures.

Thalamus. A thalamic lesion appears to be the most frequent subcortical correlate of neglect (Watson & Heilman, 1979: three cases; Cambier, Elghozi & Strube, 1980: three cases; Watson, Valenstein & Heilman, 1981: one case; Schott, Laurent, Mauguière & Chazot, 1981: one case). In two cases (Watson & Heilman, 1979: case 3; Cambier et al., 1980: case 1) the thalamic lesion was confirmed by postmortem examination.

Additional support for a role of thalamic damage comes from the observation that stereotactic lesions, also including subthalamic and pallidal structures, performed for the relief of Parkinson disease, may produce hypokinesia of the contralateral hand (Velasco & Velasco, 1979) and a temporary contralateral neglect (Hassler, 1979). A patient of Perani, Nardocci & Broggi (1982), who underwent a right thalamotomy, still showed neglect three months after the operation.

In a number of cases, an intrathalamic localization of the lesion has been attempted. In the patient of Watson et al. (1981) the CT-assessed thalamic infarction is reported to involve the postero-ventral and the medial thalamic nuclei, and possibly the antero-inferior pulvinar. In case 1 of Cambier et al. (1980) ischemic damage of the pulvinar, ventro-postero-lateral and dorso-medial nuclei was found on pathologic examination. An hematoma presumably confined to the pulvinar was shown in

the patient of Schott et al. (1981). In Graff-Radford, Damasio, Yamada,
Eslinger & Damasio (1985)'s CT-clinical correlation study, 1 out of 3
patients with postero-lateral right thalamic ischemic lesions associated
with a posterior cerebral infarction showed left neglect. Duration of
disease of these three patients is unfortunately not homogeneous: while the
neglect patient was examined seven days after stroke, the time interval
between stroke onset and neuropsychological examination was respectively
unknown and 4 years in the two negative cases. The lesion site of these
patients is presumably similar to that of the neglect case Z.E. of the
present series (see Fig. 4). In Graff-Radford et al. (1985)'s series, the
one patient with a medial right thalamic infarction had contralateral
neglect, five months after stroke. The negative cases of Graff-Radford et
al. comprise 4 postero-lateral, 2 antero-lateral and 2 lateral
thalamic/posterior limb of internal capsule infarctions; all these
patients were tested in a recent phase, within one month after stroke.
Finally, Hirose, Kosoegawa, Saeki, Kitagawa, Oda, Kanda & Matsuhira (1985)
report left spatial neglect in 14 patients suffering from a right posterior
thalamic haemorrhage. To summarize, convincing evidence for an association
between thalamic lesions and neglect has been provided so far. However,
further research is needed to elucidate the possible differential roles of
the various thalamic nuclei, even though in a few neglect patients lesions
confined to the posterior or medial thalamic regions have been found.

    Basal ganglia. Hier, Davis, Richardson & Mohr (1977) reported a
"nondominant hemisphere syndrome", including neglect, in 7 out of 9 alert
patients with a CT-assessed right putaminal haemorrhage, but infortunately
did not provide any further neuropsychological detail. Damasio, Damasio &
Chang Chui (1980) found visual neglect in a patient with a CT-assessed
lesion involving the right putamen, the body of the caudate nucleus and
portions of the internal capsule. In Healton, Navarro, Bressman & Brust
(1982)'s case a neuropathologic examination showed an infarction of the
head of the right caudate nucleus, putamen, internal and external capsule.

    White matter. Visual neglect has been recently associated with
CT-assessed lesions confined to the posterior limb of the right internal
capsule (Masson, Decroix, Henin, Graveleau & Cambier, 1983 and Cambier,
Graveleau, Decroix, Elghozi & Masson, 1983: three cases; Ferro & Kertesz,
1984: one case). Stein & Volpe's (1983) case 3 had a subcortical infarction
in the right frontal lobe.

    To summarize, evidence from reports of positive individual cases
appears to suggest an association between lesions involving the subcortical
grey nuclei (the thalamus and the basal ganglia) and neglect, even though a
few patients with lesions confined to the white matter have been reported.

    To collect anatomo-clinical correlation data from both positive and
negative cases we have studied 51 right-handed patients with deep vascular
lesions in the right hemisphere. Only one out of 19 patients with lesions
confined to the white matter showed neglect, as assessed by the cancellation
task. Conversely, 12 out of 32 patients with lesions involving both the grey
nuclei and the white matter displayed signs of spatial neglect (see Table
II). Two findings of Table II are relevant here: (1) neglect tends to occur
much more frequently when the grey nuclei are involved, as opposed to
lesions confined to the subcortical white matter ($chi2=6.93$, $p<.01$, with
one df); (2) a remarkable number of negative cases was found: 2 out of 4
patients with thalamic lesions and 18 out of 25 (72%) patients with basal
ganglia lesions did not show signs of neglect, as assessed by the
cancellation task. The detailed localization of the deep lesions of the 13
neglect patients as well as of the 20 patients without neglect, who showed
lesions involving the grey nuclei, is shown in Table III.

Fromm, Holland, Swindell & Reinmuth (1985) have recently reported 9 patients, all examined within a few days after stroke, with a CT-assessed subcortical ischemic or heamorrhagic lesion. Left spatial neglect was found in 1 out of 3 patients with right thalamic lesions and in 3 out of 4 patients with right basal ganglia lesions, while two cases with a lacunar stroke confined to the right internal capsule showed no signs of contralateral spatial neglect. By and large in line with the present data, Fromm et al. (1985)'s study shows that while neglect is more likely to occur when the subcortical grey nuclei are damaged, a number of negative cases can be found.

Table II : Localization of deep vascular CT-assessed right-sided lesions in 51 patients with (N+) and without (N-) signs of contralateral neglect, revealed by a cancellation task. Duration of disease was 6.88 days (range: 1-24 days). The lesions sites were checked on the atlas by Matsui & Hirano (1978). "Extensive" lesions include both the thalamus and the basal ganglia.

	BASAL GANGLIA	THALAMUS	SUBCORTICAL WHITE MATTER	EXTENSIVE	TOTAL
N+	7	2	1	3	13
N-	18	2	18	0	38

The Problem with Deep Lesions: The Negative Cases

Neglect appears to be more likely to occur when the thalamus and/or the lenticular nucleus are damaged. However, whereas in the case of cortical damage neglect is associated with lesions involving the inferior parietal lobule and tends not to occur when this area is spared, a remarkable number of patients with thalamic or lenticular lesions without signs of neglect was found (see Table II and III). This parallels, in a way, the difficulty of predicting both the presence/absence and the type of aphasic syndrome in patients with deep left-sided lesions (Puel, Demonet, Cardebat, Bonafé, Gazounaud, Guiraud-Chaumeil & Rascol, 1984; Basso, Lecours, Moraschini & Vanier, 1985; Cappa, Papagno, Vallar & Vignolo, in press).

Noninvasive imaging techniques for measuring regional cerebral blood flow and metabolism could be a useful tool to investigate this issue. Studies using Positron Emission Tomography have revealed metabolic depression in cerebral areas, which appeared undamaged at the CT examination (Metter, Wasterlain, Kuhl, Hanson & Phelps, 1981). Patients with subcortical infarction without any cortical involvement, as assessed in CT scans, may, within 72 hours after stroke, show a massive blood flow reduction in the ipsilateral cortex (Olsen, Larsen, Hernig, Skriver & Lassen, 1983). Recently, remote ipsilateral functional abnormalities involving the fronto-temporo-parietal cortex have been discovered, two months to one year after stroke, in the ipsilateral hemisphere of patients with CT-assessed ischemic lesions confined to subcortical structures

(Perani, Gerundini, DiPiero et al., 1985). Finally, Olsen, Bruhn & Oberg (1984) have shown differential patterns of cortical blood flow in patients with CT-assessed subcortical lesions: while aphasics have a low cortical blood flow, nonaphasic patients do not display blood flow abnormalities. Taken together, these results appear to suggest a possible relation between the extent of cortical functional impairment and the presence/absence of neuropsychological deficits such as aphasia or neglect in patients with subcortical CT-assessed lesions.

Table III : Detailed localization of deep vascular lesions in 13 patients with (N+) and in 20 patients without (N-) signs of contralateral neglect.

N+ Lesion site	1	2	3	4	5	6	7	8	9	10	11	12	13
Caudate n.	x						x	x					
Lenticular n.	x	x	x	x	x		x	x	x		x	x	
Insula		x		x			x						
Thalamus		x	x		x			x		x			
Int. capsule													
−ant. limb	x		x			x	x	x			x		
−genu	x		x	x		x	x	x	x		x		
−post. limb	x		x	x		x	x	x			x	x	
Corona radiata													
−anterior	x				x	x	x	x		x		x	
−posterior				x					x		x		

N− Lesion site	1	2	3	4	5	6	7	8	9	10	11	12	13	14	15	16	17	18	19	20
Caudate n.		x						x							x					x
Lenticular n.	x	x	x	x	x		x		x	x	x	x	x	x	x	x	x		x	
Insula		x		x								x			x					
Thalamus						x												x		
Int. capsule																				
−ant. limb		x	x	x											x		x		x	
−genu		x	x	x	x											x	x		x	
−post limb		x	x	x				x						x		x	x	x	x	
Corona radiata																				
−anterior			x	x	x				x				x	x		x	x	x	x	x
−posterior																				

Neglect in Children

A localization pattern similar to that shown in adult patients has recently been documented in 5-9 year-old children. Ferro, Martins & Tavora (1984) reported spatial neglect in three children with right-sided CT-assessed lesions: an infarction involving the lenticular nucleus, the insula, the internal capsule and some adjacent white matter; posterior parietal and occipital haemorrhages; a large antero-posterior meningioma.

As to hemispheric asymmetries in neglect in children suffering from acquired brain lesions, the study by Hécaen (1976) appears to suggest a laterality pattern broadly similar to the usual findings in adult brain-damaged patients: in a series of 23 children with unilateral lesions, one out of six patients with right-sided lesions was reported to show signs of neglect, which was not found in the 17 patients with a left-sided lesion.

II. Anatomoclinical Correlation Studies and Neurophysiological Models of Directed Attention and Neglect in Man

In recent years a number or anatomophysiological models of directed attention (and neglect), drawing on both human and animal data, have been proposed. Three features of such models are relevant here. First, they incorporate the notion that spatial neglect, far from being uniquely associated with parietal damage, may be produced by lesions of a number of cortical and subcortical structures. Second, these models associate different brain regions with discrete functional components of spatial behavior. Finally, they draw on both human and animal data.

"Sensory" and "motor" Components in Human Neglect

Mesulam (1981) suggested a multiple-component model of directed attention and neglect. A posterior parietal component provides an internal sensory map of extrapersonal space. A frontal component coordinates the motor programs for exploration, scanning, reaching and fixating within extrapersonal space. A limbic component in the cingulate gyrus regulates the spatial distribution of motivational valence and a reticular component provides the underlying level of arousal and vigilance (see Mesulam, 1981, for further details).

Heilman et al. (1985) distinguish sensory neglect from intentional neglect and akinesia. Sensory neglect may occur when components of a loop comprising cortical (the temporo-parieto-occipital junction) and limbic (the posterior cingulate gyrus) areas are damaged. Structures such as the pre-frontal cortex, the anterior cingulate gyrus and the basal ganglia are involved in motor activation and preparation to respond: intentional neglect and akinesia would be associated with damage to these structures. As to the thalamus, different nuclei would be involved in sensory attention (i.e., ventralis postero-lateralis, medial and lateral geniculate) and motor activation (centromedian parafascicularis, ventral anterior and ventro-lateral). Finally, the mesencephalic reticular formation and the nucleus reticularis thalami would be components of both neural systems.

The distinction between "sensory" and "motor" components appears consistent with data from individual case studies. Zingerle (1913)'s frontal patient had akinesia of the contralateral limb. Castaigne et al. (1972) report akinesia of the contralateral limbs in one left and two right brain-damaged patients with frontal medial neoplastic lesions; one case with a right frontal damage also displayed signs of visual neglect.

For subcortical lesions, in two patients with lesions involving the head of the right caudate nucleus (Valenstein & Heilman, 1981) and the anterior limb of the right internal capsule (Viader et al., 1982) contralateral limb hypokinesia without neglect has been shown.

Contralateral hypokinesia associated with spatial neglect has been reported in patients with right thalamic damage (e.g., Watson & Heilman, 1979; Schott et al., 1981).

Hypokinesia of the contralateral limb, associated with visuo-spatial neglect, has also been reported in patients with lesions involving the right retro-rolandic regions (Critchley, 1953). Castaigne, Laplane & Degos (1970) have however found contralateral hypokinesia in two patients with left posterior (temporal and temporo-parietal) damage, without any sign of spatial neglect.

Bisiach, Berti & Vallar (1985) reported the case of a neglect patient, F.S., who had a right subcortical lesion involving the caudate and lenticular nucleus, the internal capsule and the frontal subcortical white matter: this patient showed a gross deficit in responding to right-sided visual stimuli with the right hand, when a motor response was required in the left half-space.

Laplane, Talairach, Meininger et al. (1977) found akinesia, more prominent contralaterally, in 3 patients who underwent unilateral corticectomies (one left and 2 right) of the medial part of the frontal lobe. No sensory disorders or visuo-spatial neglect are reported, but gaze towards the contralateral side was sluggish. However, Guitton, Buchtel & Douglas (quoted by Milner, 1982) have recently found that, in patients tested 14 days post-operatively, unilateral frontal lobe excisions, including the frontal eye fields (area 8), do not affect accuracy and latency of saccades to cues appearing in the visual half field contralateral to the lesion. Frontal patients have difficulty in inhibiting an initial response towards the cue in an "antisaccade task": in this test subjects are required to look away from the cue, towards the corresponding position in the opposite visual half field; patients with temporal lesions do not show such a deficit. This loss of inhibition, particularly marked in patients with excisions encroaching upon the frontal eye fields, is in these cases equally apparent in both visual fields. In addition to this lack of suppression of an inappropriate response - a deficit which in frontal patients is not confined to eye movements (see Milner, 1964) - patients with frontal eye fields lesions are also impaired in executing corrective responses generated by the damaged hemisphere, namely a saccade towards a target in the contralateral visual field, after an initial not inhibited saccade to a cue in the visual field ipsilateral to the lesion. While these data argue for a role of the human frontal eye fields in some aspects of oculomotor control (Milner, 1982), it is worth noticing here that eye movement deficits are frequently but not invariably found in patients with spatial neglect (see Hécaen, 1962; Albert, 1973), suggesting a dissociation between the two disorders.

Finally, a study performed by DeRenzi, Colombo, Faglioni & Gibertoni (1982) on a large number of patients with unilateral hemispheric lesions, has shown that conjugate paresis of gaze towards the side contralateral to the lesion is more likely to occur when the retrorolandic regions of the right hemisphere are damaged; neuroradiological information, unfortunately only available in a limited number or patients, seem to suggest a main role of parietal damage.

To summarize, these data seem to suggest the possibility of an association of frontal and anterior subcortical lesions with some deficit of a motor programming component, which most often shows as akinesia of the contralateral limbs. The precise nature of such a disorder, which may occur without contralateral spatial neglect and has been also associated with posterior and thalamic lesions, remains however unclear and further research is needed. The difficulty of providing a motor response in the neglected half-space using the ipsilateral unaffected hand, found in case F.S. of Bisiach et al. (1985), appears to be a different type of disorder, which resembles the "nonsensory neglect" shown in the monkey by Watson, Miller & Heilman (1978).

As for oculomotor disorders, the limited available evidence does not conjure up a definite pattern of impairment associated with frontal lesions. Furthermore, such deficits appear to be relatively independent from spatial neglect.

Frontal and Parietal Components in Human Neglect

Rizzolatti and Coworkers, drawing mainly on animal data, have recently proposed that a "constellation of centers", and not a single "master centre" (i.e., the posterior parietal lobe) would be responsible for directed attention (see Rizzolatti, Gentilucci & Matelli, 1985; Rizzolatti & Camarda, this volume, for further details). According to this model, each center is assumed to control orienting of attention towards different parts of visual space. A direct prediction from this hypothesis is that lesions of different centers may be associated with different types of neglect (Rizzolatti, Matelli & Pavesi, 1983; Rizzolatti et al., 1985). Consistent with this view, Rizzolatti et al. (1983; 1985) have recently fractionated neglect in the monkey, showing that neglect for "far" space is associated with lesions of the frontal eye fields (area 8), whereas ablation of the post-arcuate frontal cortex (area 6) or of the rostral part of the inferior parietal lobule (area 7b) produces a neglect syndrome confined to the "peripersonal" space.

A comparative discussion of human and animal data is not easy to carry out here: we are considering the effects of precisely localized and relatively small experimental lesions in the monkey, as opposed to those of often massive and imprecisely localized lesions in man. An interpretation of human neglect within a multiple center hypothesis, however, has to consider a possible anatomical difference between man and monkey, as far as the neurological basis of neglect is concerned. In humans, the more frequent association of neglect is with parietal damage. In monkeys, visual neglect is readily produced by frontal lesions, parietal neglect being considered somewhat less profound (Lynch, 1980; Hyvarinen, 1982) and more controversial (Ettlinger, 1984). The origin of this possible "discontinuity" between brain organization of spatial perception in man and monkey remains an unsolved issue (Ettlinger, 1984; Passingham & Ettlinger, 1974). Secondly, while a dissociation between personal and extrapersonal neglect in man, resembling Rizzolatti et al.'s (1983, 1985) observation in the monkey, has been shown by Bisiach, Perani, Vallar & Berti (in press), no anatomical counterpart was found: in both neglect syndromes the superficial and deep lesions superimposed in the inferior parietal regions of the right hemisphere, deep lesions involved the grey nuclei and in none of the patients a frontal lesion was found.

Within the "constellation of centers hypothesis", the greater frequency of parietal neglect, as compared with neglect associated with frontal lesions, has been explained assuming that post-rolandic and pre-rolandic lesions would have differential disruptive effects on cortical function (Rizzolatti & Camarda, this volume). Large lesions involving the parietal lobe would have a two-fold effect: in addition to the derangement of parietal function, such lesions would impair frontal activity, preventing the flow of sensory information from the pre-rolandic to the post-rolandic areas. On the contrary, large frontal lesions would of course impair frontal neural mechanisms, but parietal function would be spared. On this hypothesis, both pre- and post-rolandic regions are

substantially involved in selective spatial attention in humans, but
neglect is more frequent and more severe after lesions involving the
parietal areas, since retro-rolandic damage would cause an additional
frontal dysfunction, while the reverse would not occur in the case of
frontal lesions of comparable size. However, the assumption that posterior
lesions disrupt both parietal and frontal function predicts the occurrence
of the wide range of neuropsychological abnormalities often collected
under the rubric of "frontal lobe syndrome" after both anterior and
posterior lesions, unless one makes the additional assumption that the
frontal dysfunction produced by posterior lesions is confined to spatial
attention processes. On the contrary, frontal damage is associated with a
wide range of deficits (see Damasio, 1985, for a recent review), including
perseverative behavior (Milner, 1963), defective compliance with test
instructions (Milner, 1964), impairment in cognitive estimation (Shallice
& Evans, 1978) and in problem solving (Shallice, 1982), which do not occur -
or are much less severe - after posterior lesions.

Finally, in addition to the aforementioned general difficulty of the
hypothesis that posterior lesions disrupt both parietal and frontal
function, it must be reminded that the empirical evidence pointing to some
role for the frontal regions in directed spatial attention processes in
humans is rather scarce (see Damasio, 1985 for a recent review). A
remarkable exception is Teuber's (1964) finding that patients with
unilateral frontal lesions, when they are requested to look for objects by
means of active eye and head movements, show abnormally long visual
searching times in the half-space contralateral to the lesion.

A recent finding by Posner, Walker, Friedrich & Rafal (1984) is
relevant here: patients with unilateral parietal lesions show a deficit of
covert orienting of attention towards targets located in the half space
contralateral to the lesion. Such an impairment does not occur when the
damage is confined to the frontal or temporal regions. Posner et al. (1984)
argue that parietal lesions produce a major deficit of the disengagement and
some impairment of the engagement components of attention, when the target
is contralateral to the lesion. They suggest the superior parietal lobe as
the best anatomical correlate of the orienting of attention deficit, at
variance with the present conclusion of a major role of the inferior
parietal lobule. However, Posner et al.'s (1984) 12 patients with
CT-assessed lesions involving the parietal lobe differ from our series in a
number of important features. First, all patients had no or "minimal" to
"mild" signs of neglect (i.e., extinction on double simultaneous visual
stimulation, inconsistently found). Secondly, duration of disease was not
homogeneous, ranging from two weeks to ten years. Finally, both stroke and
tumors were included. These differences between the two series make a
comparative discussion difficult. However, on the clinical features of
Posner et al.'s (1984) cases, it seems reasonable to conclude that all 12
patients would have been classified by the cancellation task as patients
without neglect. In our series, the lesions of such patients superimpose in
the superior parietal areas, as well as in the occipital regions (see Fig.
3).

While the most frequent anatomical correlate of left-sided spatial
neglect is a lesion involving the inferior parietal regions, the occurrence
of this disorder after right frontal lesions remains an open issue, which
calls for further research. Frontal neglect could, at least at some extent,
reflect individual variability (see Eidelberg & Galaburda, 1984) in the
organization of brain structures involved in spatial directed attention. In
addition, in frontal patients with and without signs of contralateral
neglect standard CT assessment should be supplemented by imaging techniques

for measuring cerebral blood flow and metabolism, since metabolic depression in cerebral areas which appeared undamaged at the CT examination has been shown by Positron Emission Tomography (Metter et al., 1981). Accordingly, anatomo-clinical correlations relying only on CT information may be misleading.

III. Neglect from Left Hemisphere Damage

Little information is available as to the anatomical correlates of spatial neglect in patients with lesions involving left hemisphere structures. Only a few studies provide relevant data, possibly due to the relatively low frequency and/or minor severity of neglect phenomena in left-brain damaged patients, as compared with patients suffering from right brain damage.

Battersby et al. (1956) report neglect in two out of eight patients with left retro-rolandic lesions, while patients with left frontal lesions did not display signs of neglect. Albert (1973), who assessed visual neglect by a cancellation task, found neglect in 4 out of 14 patients with left anterior (29%) and in 4 out of 17 patients with left posterior (24%) surgically verified lesions.

A significant association between neglect and anterior left-sided lesions has been recently reported by Ogden (1985; this volume): 12 out of 16 (75%) patients with pre-rolandic lesions showed neglect, which was found only in 9/20 (45%) patients with post-rolandic lesions. On the face of it, this finding suggests a possible interhemispheric difference in the neural organization of cerebral structures involved in spatial behavior. However, a possible source of bias is to be considered. The incidence of aphasic patients with comprehension deficits severe enough to prevent them from entering the study could be different in the post-rolandic vs pre-rolandic group. Unfortunately, this issue is not considered by Ogden (1985), who does not provide any information concerning the exclusion of aphasic patients with anterior or posterior lesions.

The hypothesis of an association between left frontal damage and contralateral spatial neglect is consistent with data from individual case reports. Damasio et al. (1980) found visuo-spatial contralateral neglect, as assessed by a crossing lines task, in 3 right-handed patients, with dorso-lateral (case 1) and mesial (cases 2 and 3) frontal lesions, as assessed in CT scans. All patients were also inattentive to auditory stimuli presented from the right and case 1 showed paucity of visual saccades towards the right side. Heilman & Valenstein (1972a) reported auditory, visual and tactile contralateral neglect, as assessed by bilateral simultaneous stimulation, in a patient with a left frontal infarction, shown by brain scan.

For left thalamic or basal ganglia lesions, no signs of contralateral spatial neglect were shown in the patients reported by Graff-Radford et al. (1985) and Fromm et al. (1985). In Ogden (1985)'s series all 3 patients with left basal ganglia lesions had contralateral neglect.

IV. Conclusions

The present available evidence concerning the anatomical correlates of unilateral neglect in man may be summarized as follows :

(1) A wide range of right-sided lesions may be associated with neglect, including frontal and parietal damage, as well as lesions confined to structures such as the thalamus and the basal ganglia.

(2) However, the most frequent cortical correlate of spatial neglect is a retro-rolandic lesion involving the temporo-parieto-occipital-carrefour. The inferior parietal lobule appears to be a crucial area, while

the present evidence for a major role of the frontal areas appears rather
scanty, even though individual neglect patients with lesions confined to
the pre-rolandic regions have been reported. While it is conceivable that a
number of different brain structures (see Rizzolatti et al., 1983; 1985) may
be involved in the complex process of orienting of spatial attention (see
Posner et al., 1984), the inferior parietal region appears to be a most
important neural component, so that a lesion including this area would cause
a major disruption of the function of the whole system. From individual case
reports there is some evidence which supports the view that frontal lesions
and anterior subcortical damage of structures such as the caudate nucleus
and the anterior limb of the internal capsule may be associated with a
deficit of a motor component (contralateral akinesia). Such a disorder has
been reported after both left- and right-sided lesions.

(3) In the case of subcortical lesions, neglect tends to occur when the
thalamus and, possibly less frequently, the lenticular nuclei are damaged.
Lesions confined to the subcortical white matter are rarely associated with
neglect. The remarkable number of negative cases, i.e., thalamic or
lenticular patients without signs of neglect, is an unsolved issue, which
requires further research.

(4) Anatomical data concerning neglect in right-handed patients with
lesions of the left-hemisphere are too sparse to allow any definite
conclusion. The possibility of a main role of frontal lesions (see Ogden,
1985) is to be considered and further investigated.

References

Albert, M.L. A simple test of visual neglect. Neurology, 1973, 23, 658-664.
Basso, A., Lecours, A.R., Moraschini, S. & Vanier, M. Anatomoclinical
    correlations of the aphasias as defined through computerized
    tomography: exceptions. Brain & Language, 1985, 26, 201-229.
Battersby, W.S., Bender, M.B., Pollack, M. & Kahn, R.L. Unilateral "spatial
    agnosia" ("inattention") in patients with cerebral lesions. Brain,
    1956, 79, 68-93.
Bisiach, E., Berti, A. & Vallar, G. Analogical and logical disorders
    underlying unilateral neglect of space. In : M.I. Posner & O.S.M. Marin
    (Eds.), Mechanisms of attention. Attention and Performance XI.
    Hillsdale, N.J.: Lawrence Erlbaum, 1985, pp. 239-249.
Bisiach, E., Capitani, E., Luzzatti, C. & Perani, D. Brain and conscious
    representation of outside reality. Neuropsychologia, 1981, 19,
    543-551.
Bisiach, E., Cornacchia, L., Sterzi, R. & Vallar, G. Disorders of perceived
    auditory lateralization after lesions of the right hemisphere. Brain,
    1984, 107, 37-52.
Bisiach, E., Luzzatti, C. & Perani, D. Unilateral neglect, representational
    schema and consciousness. Brain, 1979, 102, 609-618.
Bisiach, E., Perani, D., Vallar, G. & Berti, A. Unilateral neglect :
    personal and extrapersonal. Neuropsychologia, in press.
Brain, W.R. (1941) Visual disorientation with special reference to lesions
    of the right hemisphere. Brain, 1941, 64, 244-272.
Cappa, S.F., Papagno, C., Vallar, G. & Vignolo, L.A. Aphasia does not always
    follow left thalamic hemorrhage: a study of five negative cases.
    Cortex, in press.
Cappa, S.F. & Vignolo, L.A. CT scan studies of aphasia. Human Neurobiology,
    1983, 2, 129-134.
Cambier, J., Elghozi, D. & Strube, E. Lésions du thalamus droit avec

syndrome de l'hemisphère mineur. Discussion du concept de négligence thalamique. Revue Neurologique, 1980, 136, 105–116.

Cambier, J., Graveleau, P.H., Decroix, J.P., Elghozi, D. & Masson, M. Le syndrome de l'artère choroidienne antérieure: étude neuropsychologique de 4 cas. Revue Neurologique, 1983, 139, 553–559.

Campbell, D.C. & Oxbury, J.M. Recovery from unilateral visuo-spatial neglect? Cortex, 1976, 12, 303–312.

Castaigne, P., Laplane, D. & Degos, J.D. Trois cas de négligence motrice par lésion retro-rolandique. Revue Neurologique, 1970, 122, 233–242.

Castaigne, P., Laplane, D. & Degos, J.D. Trois cas de négligence motrice par lésion frontale pre-rolandique. Revue Neurologique, 1972, 126, 5–15.

Colombo, A., DeRenzi, E., Faglioni, P. The occurrence of visual neglect in patients with unilateral cerebral disease. Cortex, 1976, 12, 221–231.

Colombo, A., DeRenzi, E. & Gentilini, M. The time course of visual hemi-inattention. Archiv für Psychiatrie und Nervenkrankheiten, 1982, 231, 539–546.

Costa, L.D., Vaughan, H.G., Horwitz, M. & Ritter, W. Patterns of behavioral deficit associated with visual spatial neglect. Cortex, 1969, 5, 242–263.

Critchley, M. The parietal lobes. London: Hafner Press, 1953, pp. 225–228..

Damasio, A.R. The frontal lobes. In : K.M. Heilman & E. Valenstein (Eds.) Clinical Neuropsychology, Second Edition. New York: Oxford University Press, 1985, pp. 339–375.

Damasio, A.R., Damasio, H. & Chang Chui, H. Neglect following damage to frontal lobe or basal ganglia. Neuropsychologia, 1980, 18, 123–132.

DeRenzi, E., Colombo, A., Faglioni, P. & Gibertoni, M. Conjugate gaze paresis in stroke patients with unilateral damage. Archives of Neurology, 1982, 39, 482–486.

DeRenzi, E., Faglioni, P. & Scotti, G. Hemispheric contribution to exploration of space through the visual and tactile modality. Cortex, 1970, 6, 191–203.

Eidelberg, D. & Galaburda, A.M. Inferior parietal lobule. Divergent architectonic asymmetries in the human brain. Archives of Neurology, 1984, 41, 843–852.

Ettlinger, G. Humans, apes and monkeys : the changing neuropsychological viewpoint. Neuropsychologia, 1984, 22, 685–696.

Ferro, J.M. & Kertesz, A. Posterior internal capsule infarction associated with neglect. Archives of Neurology, 1984, 41, 422–424.

Ferro, J.M., Martins, I.P. & Tavora, L. Neglect in children. Annals of Neurology, 1984, 15, 281–284.

Fromm, D., Holland, A.L., Swindell, C.S. & Reinmuth, O.M. Various consequences of subcortical stroke. Prospective study of 16 consecutive cases. Archives of Neurology, 1985, 42, 943–950.

Gainotti, G. Les manifestations de négligence et d'inattention pour l'hemispace. Cortex, 1968, 4, 64–91.

Graff-Radford, N.R., Damasio, H., Yamada, T., Eslinger, P.J. & Damasio, A.R. (1985) Nonhaemorrhagic thalamic infarction: clinical, neuropsychological and electrophysiological findings in four anatomical groups defined by computerized tomography. Brain, 1985, 108, 485–516.

Hassler, R. Striatal regulation of adverting and attention directing induced by pallidal stimulation. Applied Neurophysiology, 1979, 42, 98–102.

Healton, E.B., Navarro, C., Bressmann, S. & Brust, J.C.M. Subcortical neglect. Neurology, 1982, 32, 776–778.

Hécaen, H. Clinical symptomatology in right and left hemispheric lesions.

In : V.B. Mountcastle (Ed.), Interhemispheric relations and cerebral dominance. Baltimore: The Johns Hopkins Press, 1962, pp. 215-243.

Hécaen, H. Introduction à la neuropsychologie. Paris: Larousse, 1972, pp. 211-212.

Hécaen, H. Acquired aphasia in children and the ontogenesis of hemispheric functional specialization. Brain & Language, 1976, 3, 114-134.

Hécaen, H., Penfield, W., Bertrand, C. & Malmo, R. The syndrome of apractognosia due to lesions of the minor cerebral hemisphere. Archives of Neurology and Psychiatry, 1956, 75, 400-434.

Heilman, K.M. & Valenstein, E. Auditory neglect in man. Archives of Neurology, 1972a, 26, 32-35.

Heilman, K.M. & Valenstein, E. Frontal lobe neglect in man. Neurology, 1972b, 22, 660-664.

Heilman, K.M., Watson, R.T. & Valenstein, E. Neglect and related disorders. In : K.M. Heilman & E. Valenstein (Eds.) Clinical Neuropsychology, Second Edition. New York: Oxford University Press, 1985, pp. 243-293.

Hier, D.B., Davis, K.R., Richardson, E.P. & Mohr, J.P. Hypertensive putaminal hemorrhage. Annals of Neurology, 1977, 1, 152-159.

Hirose, G., Kosoegawa, H., Saeki, M., Kitagawa, Y., Oda, R., Kanda, S. & Matsuhira, T. The syndrome of posterior thalamic hemorrhage. Neurology, 1985, 35, 998-1002.

Howes, D. & Boller, F. Simple reaction time: evidence for focal impairment from lesions of the right hemisphere. Brain, 1975, 98, 317-332.

Hyvarinen, J. The parietal cortex of monkey and man. Berlin: Springer-Verlag, 1982, pp. 48-71.

Kertesz, A. & Dobrowolski, S. Right hemisphere deficits, lesion size and location. Journal of Clinical Neuropsychology, 1981, 3, 283-299.

Laplane, D., Talairach, J., Meininger, V., Bancaud, J. & Orgogozo, J.M. Clinical consequences of corticectomies involving the supplementary motor area in man. Journal of the Neurological Sciences, 1977, 34, 301-314.

Levine, D.N., Kaufman, K.J. & Mohr, J.P. Inaccurate reaching associated with a superior parietal lobe tumor. Neurology, 1978, 28, 556-561.

Lynch, J.C. The functional organization of posterior parietal association cortex. The Behavioral and Brain Sciences, 1980, 3, 485-534.

Mazzocchi, F. & Vignolo, L.A. Computer assisted tomography in neuropsychological research : a simple procedure for lesion mapping. Cortex, 1978, 14, 136-144.

Masson, M., Decroix, J.P., Henin, D., Graveleau, P. & Cambier, J. Syndrome de l'artère choroidienne antérieure: étude clinique et tomodensitométrique de 4 cas. Revue Neurologique, 1983, 139, 547-552.

Matsui, J. & Hirano, A. An atlas of the human brain for computerized tomography. Tokio: Igaku-Shoin, 1978.

McFie, J., Piercy, M.F. & Zangwill, O.L. Visual-spatial agnosia associated with lesions of the right cerebral hemisphere. Brain, 1950, 73, 167-190.

Mesulam, M.M. A cortical network for directed attention and unilateral neglect. Annals of Neurology, 1981, 10, 309-325.

Metter, E.J., Wasterlain, C.G., Kuhl, D.E., Hanson, W.R. & Phelps, M.E. 18FDG positron emission tomography in a study of aphasia. Annals of Neurology, 1981, 10, 173-183.

Milner, B. Effects of different brain lesions on card sorting. Archives of Neurology, 1963, 9, 100-110.

Milner, B. Some effects of frontal lobectomy in man. In : J.M. Warren & K. Akert (Eds.) The frontal granular cortex and behavior. New York: McGraw-Hill, 1964, pp. 313-331.

Milner, B. Some cognitive effects of frontal-lobe lesions in man. Philosophical Transactions, Royal Society London, 1982, B298, 211–226.

Monakow, C. Die lokalisation im Grosshirn. Wiesbaden: Bergmann, 1914.

Ogden, J.A. Antero-posterior interhemispheric differences in the loci of lesions producing visual hemineglect. Brain & Cognition, 1985, 4, 59–75.

Olsen, T.S., Bruhn, P. & Oberg, G. Cause of aphasia in stroke patients with subcortical lesions. Acta Neurologica Scandinavica, Suppl., 1984, 69, 311–312.

Olsen, T.S., Larsen, B., Hernig, M., Skriver, E.B. & Lassen, N.A. Blood flow and vascular reactivity in collaterally perfused brain tissue. Stroke, 1983, 14, 332–341.

Oxbury, J.M., Campbell, D.C. & Oxbury, S.M. Unilateral spatial neglect and impairments of spatial analysis and visual perception. Brain, 1974, 97, 551–564.

Passingham, R.E. & Ettlinger, G. A comparison of cortical functions in man and other primates. International Review of Neurobiology, 1974, 16, 233–299.

Perani, D., Gerundini, P., DiPiero, V., Savi, A., Carenzi, M., Vanzulli, A., Del Maschio, A., Lenzi, G.L. & Fazio, F. (1985) Remote cortical effects in patients with ischemic lesions of subcortical structures studied with 123HIPDM and SPECT. Journal of Nuclear Medicine and Allied Sciences, 1985, 29, 129–130.

Perani, D., Nardocci, N. & Broggi, G. Neglect after right unilateral thalamotomy. A case report. Italian Journal of Neurological Sciences, 1982, 3, 61–64.

Pick, A. Beitrage zur Pathologie und pathologischen Anatomie. Berlin: S. Karger, 1898, pp. 168–185.

Posner, M.I., Walker, J.A., Friedrich, F.J. & Rafal, R.D. Effects of parietal injury on covert orienting of attention. The Journal of Neuroscience, 1984, 4, 1863–1874.

Puel, M., Demonet, J.F., Cardebat, D., Bonafé, A., Gazounaud, Y., Guiraud-Chaumeil, B. & Rascol, A. Aphasies sous-corticales. Revue Neurologique, 1984, 140, 695–710.

Ratcliff, G. & Davies-Jones, G.A.B. Defective visual localization in focal brain wounds. Brain, 1972, 95, 49–60.

Rizzolatti, G., Gentilucci, M. & Matelli, M. Selective spatial attention: one center, one circuit or many circuits? In : M.I. Posner & O.S.M. Marin (Eds.) Mechanisms of attention. Attention and Performance XI. Hillsdale, N.J.: Lawrence Erlbaum, 1985, pp. 251–265.

Rizzolatti, G., Matelli, M. & Pavesi, G. Deficits in attention and movement following the removal of post-arcuate (area 6) and pre-arcuate (area 8) cortex in Macaque monkeys. Brain, 1983, 106, 655–673.

Schott, B., Laurent, B., Mauguière, F. & Chazot, G. Négligence motrice par hématome thalamique droit. Revue Neurologique, 1981, 137, 447–455.

Shallice, T. Specific impairments of planning. Philosophical Transactions, Royal Society, London, 1982, B298, 199–209.

Shallice, T. & Evans, M.E. The involvement of the frontal lobes in cognitive estimation. Cortex, 1978, 14, 294–303.

Silberpfenning, J. Contributions to the problem of eye movements. III. Disturbances of ocular movements with pseudohemianopsia in patients with frontal lobe tumors. Confinia Neurologica, 1941, 4, 1–13.

Stein, S. & Volpe, B.T. Classical "parietal" neglect syndrome after subcortical right frontal lobe infarction. Neurology, 1983, 33, 797–799.

Teuber, H.L. The riddle of frontal lobe function in man. In : J.M. Warren & K. Akert (Eds.) The frontal granular cortex and behavior. New York: McGraw-Hill, 1964, pp. 410-445.

Valenstein, E. & Heilman, K.M. Unilateral hypokinesia and motor extinction. Neurology, 1981, 31, 445-448.

Van Der Linden, M., Seron, X., Gillet, J. & Bredart, S. Heminégligence par lésion frontale droite. Acta Neurologica Belgica, 1980, 80, 298-310.

Velasco, F. & Velasco, M. A reticulothalamic system mediating proprioceptive attention and tremor in man. Neurosurgery, 1979, 4, 30-36.

Viader, F., Cambier, J. & Pariser, P. Phénomène d'extinction motrice gauche. Revue Neurologique, 1982, 138, 213-217.

Watson, R.T. & Heilman, K.M. Thalamic neglect. Neurology, 1979, 29, 690-694.

Watson, R.T., Miller, B.D. & Heilman, K.M. Nonsensory neglect. Annals of Neurology, 1978, 3, 505-508.

Watson, R.T., Valenstein, E. & Heilman, K.M. Thalamic neglect. Archives of Neurology, 1981, 38, 501-506.

Zarit, S.H. & Kahn, R.L. Impairment and adaptation in chronic disabilities: spatial inattention. The Journal of Nervous and Mental Disease, 1974, 159, 63-72.

Zingerle, H. Ueber Störungen der Wahrnehmung des eigenen Körpers bei organischen Gehirnerkrankungen. Monatsschrift für Psychiatrie und Neurologie, 1913, 34, 13-36.

Neurophysiological and Neuropsychological Aspects
of Spatial Neglect, M. Jeannerod (editor)
© Elsevier Science Publishers B.V. (North-Holland), 1987

ANIMAL MODELS FOR THE SYNDROME OF SPATIAL NEGLECT

A. David Milner

The effects of unilateral brain lesions in animals frequently
include a reduced responsiveness to contralaterally-presented
stimuli, although this reduction is typically mild and
transient in the case of cortical lesions. The term "neglect" is
often used by investigators in describing such observations,
apparently in the belief that the concept is a simple one. It is
suggested in the present chapter that the most appropriate
starting point for a discussion of putative animal models is the
clinical syndrome of unilateral neglect. There is at least
anecdotal evidence for partial fractionation within this
syndrome: consequently one should take seriously the separate
symptoms and attempt to characterise them psychologically. When
this has been done (and at present only a crude attempt can be
made) it should then be possible to design animal paradigms to
assay homologous psychological functions. The literature is
reviewed from such a standpoint, some of the problems are
outlined, and some suggestions for future research are offered.

1. Introduction

The term "neglect" has been used very imprecisely in the literature,
especially in regard to animal experiments. Some researchers, for
example, have taken contralateral behavioural "extinction" under
conditions of double simultaneous stimulation as sufficient to
demonstrate the presence of unilateral neglect (e.g., Watson, Heilman,
Cauthen & King, 1973). Others have used the phrase "visual neglect" to
refer to a lack of response to visual stimuli, despite arguing the case
that this lack of response might be explicable in purely sensory terms
(Dean & Redgrave, 1985a,b,c). Neither of these usages is fully consistent
with clinical conceptions of neglect (Friedland & Weinstein, 1977; De
Renzi, 1982). In particular, it is accepted clinically that there is a
group of partially-separable (though conceptually and clinically
related) components of the neglect syndrome (e.g., Damasio & Geschwind,
1985; De Renzi, Gentilini & Pattacini, 1984; Valenstein & Heilman, 1981).
It is unfortunately standard practice for animal researchers to assume
implicity that there is a single undifferentiated deficit. It is also
typical of such research that no precise operational definition of
'neglect' tends to be given.

Yet if research on animal behaviour is to be useful at all in this
context, it must be, from the beginning, consistent and clear in its
terminology and accurate in its claims. The first step in progressing
towards an animal model for a neurological condition should not
necessarily be to look for a close analogue to the human symptomatology.
Indeed such a search may necessarily be in vain in many instances,
particularly where, as in the present instance, the human disorder is

clearly contingent upon a marked processing asymmetry. Instead, the first step should be to attempt to identify the nature of the human impairment, and to specify what psychological processes or operations are defective. Neuropsychological studies over the past twenty years have greatly advanced our understanding of spatial neglect (see De Renzi 1982, for a review), and should allow at least a provisional taxonomy in psychological terms. This will be attempted in a preliminary fashion in the next section.

The second step should be to translate as closely as possible such psychological processes or operations into terms which can be given operational behavioural definitions applicable in animal experimentation. The behavioural tests thus arrived at may or may not closely resemble the tests suitable for human neurological patients; one might expect some similarity in the case of non-human primate research, but far less when the research is carried out with rats. In section 3 of the present chapter, some such translations into operational terms will be outlined. In the subsequent sections, animal experiments relevant to three distinguishable components of the neglect syndrome will be discussed.

It will become apparent that although evidence for deficits which in this present sense ´model´ features of clinical neglect does exist, by and large the picture is less clear than it is sometimes painted, and the deficits are generally mild, variable, and transient. But then, most aspects of human neglect are far more common, and more severe following right-hemisphere than left-hemisphere damage (De Renzi 1982; Heilman, Watson, Valenstein & Damasio, 1983a). Thus the syndrome could a priori quite conceivably have been peculiar to asymmetrical brains, and totally absent in (almost) symmetrical brains. (Although functional asymmetries have been observed in animals, no claim has yet been published that attentional processes, as disrupted in experimental ´neglect´, may be asymmetrically represented.)

For present purposes, it is necessary to distinguish animal research directed towards a fuller understanding of the brain mechanisms of attention, from animal research directed towards an understanding of the neglect syndrome. Of course the two efforts necessarily overlap, and profit from each other; but the present remarks are intended to apply only to the latter programme, and not to the former, which could proceed perfectly legitimately without the need to model neglect, which indeed might not exist in animals for all it would matter to the enterprise. The objective of the present chapter, then, is to examine critically the evidence for possible animal models, and to attempt to clarify what has become a rather confused picture. It is hoped that this exercise may open the way for more fruitful speculation about mechanisms in physiological, biochemical, and anatomical terms in the future, and lead to more tightly designed experiments to test them.

2. The Neglect Syndrome in Man

Although the terminology varies among different authors, it seems to be generally agreed that there are four major component clinical symptoms (or symptom groupings) which may be called hemispatial neglect, hemi-inattention, sensory extinction, and hemiakinesia, (Heilman, 1979; Heilman, Valenstein & Watson, 1985; Damasio & Geschwind, 1985). This constellation of deficits has a common thread of unilateral attentional deficiency, although the fact that they are conceptually different and are sometimes dissociable clinically attests to the broadness of the word "attentional". Less obviously "attentional" are other occasionally-associated deficits, chief among which are allaesthesia and anosognosia.

The latter (denial of symptoms such as hemiparesis) is not a disorder which lends itself easily to animal research, and will not be discussed further here. Nonetheless, the apparent association of the severest forms of the Neglect Syndrome with a general lack of insight and consequent lack of behavioural compensation, is undoubtedly of great importance in any full understanding of the nature of the human syndrome.

Hemispatial neglect: The most florid and striking features of the Neglect Syndrome tend to be grouped together, although they may not constitute a single processing deficit. Some evidence (e.g. Halsband, Gruhn & Ettlinger, 1986) suggests that they may be partly dissociable. The classic clinical picture is of failures to complete the following tests: draw or copy a picture (details are omitted on one side, generally the left); cross out all elements in a bilateral array (typically missing items on the left); bisect a line centrally (typically erring towards the right); and deal with people or objects (e.g. food) or even one's own limbs, on both sides (typically those on the left are ignored). In recent years it has been shown that neglect occurs in the tactile as well as the visual modality (De Renzi, Faglioni & Scotti, 1970; Chedru, 1976) in that manual search may be restricted in its lateral distribution; and in the elegant studies of Bisiach and his colleagues it has been shown that visual neglect extends to internal visuospatial representations. Thus Bisiach and Luzzatti (1978) and Bisiach, Capitani, Luzzatti and Perani (1981) demonstrated a failure to retrieve left-sided components of a reconstructed visual image of a familiar scene, and Bisiach, Luzzatti and Perani (1979) demonstrated a defect in matching visual patterns held in short-term memory, in respect of their left-side characteristics.

Most of these symptoms can be described as unilateral deficits of sampling, scanning, or exploration: reductions in sampling by eye or by hand of environmental arrays, or in sampling by an internal scanning process (cf. Sperling, 1960) of internal imagery; perhaps also in sampling of a visual array by use of covert attentional movements (Posner, 1980). But it would be implausible to attribute failure to use the left half of a page in writing, or rightward bisection of a line, to a sampling deficit; instead these could be seen as a distortion of the cerebral representation of external space (De Renzi, 1982). Likewise many patients with posterior right-hemisphere lesions systematically mislocalise auditory stimuli (in both halves of space) towards the right side (Bisiach, Cornacchia, Sterzi & Vallar, 1984), and this could be due to a similar distortion. (On the other hand, the fact that objects or words in either half of space may be only half-perceived: Kinsbourne, 1977; may be attributable to defective scanning of an 'iconic' image). In any event, it is clear that hemispatial neglect can not be reduced to a simple failure of stimuli on one side to reach awareness (hemi-inattention: see below) since that could not account for the findings of Bisiach and Luzzatti (1978) or Bisiach et al (1979) nor for tactile exploratory neglect (De Renzi et al, 1970). Furthermore it has been reported that cases exist where hemispatial neglect is present in the absence of hemi-inattention (Damasio and Geschwind, 1985, pp 16–17) or of extinction (De Renzi et al, 1984).

Hemi-inattention: This refers to a lack of awareness and responsiveness to unilateral sensory stimuli presented to the side contralateral to the lesion, which cannot be accounted for in terms of a sensory loss.   The latter can be excluded in all cases where a patient can be shown to be able to detect the stimulus when his attention has been drawn to it.

Hemi-inattention then may be characterised as a disorder in the ease with which a lateralised stimulus is able to attract selective attention. It can be exacerbated by drawing attention towards the unaffected side (e.g. Posner, Cohen & Rafal, 1982) or towards another location within the affected field (Baynes, Holtzman & Volpe, 1986).

Hemi-inattention also occurs in the somatosensory domain, but appears to be rare in audition (De Renzi, 1982; Heilman et al, 1985). A frequent observation however is that a patient may perceive auditory stimuli on the affected side but behave as if they arose from the ´good´ side (Heilman, 1979; De Renzi, 1982). Clearly this cannot be due to inattention to the stimulus: De Renzi (1982) suggests the name "alloacusis" for this phenomenon (see below). Conceivably it could be an extreme form of the auditory mislocalisation observed by Bisiach et al (1984), mentioned above.

Sensory extinction: This is regarded by some authors as a milder version of hemi-inattention, and certainly it is commonly observed in patients who have recovered from hemi-inattention. Extinction, like hemi-inattention, involves a failure to detect stimuli contralateral to the lesion, but in this case the failure is only manifest when there is bilateral simultaneous stimulation. Experimental studies of patients suffering from visual extinction following right-parietal lesions (Posner et al, 1982) confirm anecdotal reports that a similar detection failure tends to occur when the ipsilesional stimulus slightly precedes the contralateral. Furthermore, when instead of an ipsilateral visual stimulus, a different means of drawing attention to the ´good´ side (a brief centrally-presented directional cue) is used, a similar result is obtained. In addition, it has been long known that the bilateral stimuli can be of different sense modalities and in non-symmetrical loci (Denny-Brown, Meyer & Horenstein, 1952). Consequently usage of the term "extinction" might best be extended to include all such instances where attention drawn to one side prevents detection of stimuli on the other (unless of course future clinical experience indicates that dissociation among these sub-types can occur). It is also possible that a degree of extinction could occur, if that is not a contradiction in terms;   for example if binaural stimulation tends to result in an attenuated perception through the contralesional ear, it could be that the mislocalisation of sounds reported by Bisiach et al (1984) could be conceptualised in these terms.

Extinction may not be merely a less severe version of hemi-inattention, since it occurs equally frequently following left or right lesions (De Renzi, 1982; De Renzi et al, 1984), unlike hemi-inattention, which occurs predominantly after right-hemisphere lesions (Heilman et al, 1985; Damasio and Geschwind, 1985). The fact that extinction frequently becomes obvious only after hemi-inattention has recovered may be explicable by the fact that it is by definition untestable when the latter is present. Nonetheless the two phenomena are generally regarded as only quantitatively different;   and it has even been argued that apparent hemi-inattention following parietal lesions is actually always extinction brought about by ambient visual input on the ipsilesional side (Mesulam, 1981). That strong view can perhaps be rejected now, since it appears that hemi-inattention can be exaggerated by drawing attention away within the affected field, as well as towards the unaffected side (Baynes et al, 1985). However, both disorders seem to reflect a similar high threshold for attracting spatially-selective attention, and they will be discussed together in the body of this chapter.

<u>Hemiakinesia:</u>   This may be defined as a reluctance or failure to make a movement, or as a delay in initiating movement, in the absence of any clinical evidence for weakness or paralysis. The deficit appears to have an attentional component in that focusing attention on the extremity may permit the patient to use it (Heilman, 1979).   The notion has been extended, particularly in the writings of Heilman and his colleagues, to include a deficit in making movements of the head or eyes (Heilman, 1979) or of <u>either</u> limb (Heilman, Bowers, Coslett & Watson, 1983b) towards the half of space contralateral to the lesion.   [These workers have characterised hemiakinesia (or unilateral hypokinesia) as a "loss of intention" to perform a given act, to contrast it with sensory or perceptual aspects of attention. It is not clear however that use of this term lends any clarity to our understanding of hemiakinesia, and to the extent that in everyday usage the term "intention" is almost as problematic as "attention" (Anscombe, 1976) it perhaps intensifies rather than alleviates our conceptual problems to introduce it.]

Valenstein and Heilman (1981) describe a patient who suffered a haemorrhagic lesion in the region of the right caudate nucleus;   despite having neither left-sided hemi-inattention nor sensory extinction, he had a severe left-limb hypokinesia. His left hand was almost twice as slow in initiating key-press reactions as his right;   the reaction times of each hand doubled when bimanual reactions were elicited. There is no evidence, however, that differential effects would obtain for the left versus right halves of space. On the face of it this deficit is very different from one which affects visually-guided movements of either limb towards a contralateral target: however in the absence of a better term it may be acceptable to use "hemiakinesia" for both, providing the distinction is borne in mind.

The essential problem in all of these cases appears to be one of <u>initiating</u> movement, whether spontaneously, or in response to an instruction or to a lateralised sensory stimulus. It is possible that in some instances the deficit may be specific to one or other of these different instigating causes. However it appears normally to be a lateralised defect in what used to be called the ´will´.

<u>Allaesthesia:</u>   The tendency to mislocate a contralesional tactile stimulus as ipsilateral is not uncommon in neglect. Its auditory equivalent ("alloacusis") has also frequently been reported, but always in the presence of severe visual neglect. In may be significant that the visual equivalent ("optic allaesthesia" - Hecaen and Albert, 1978) has not (to my knowledge) been reported in the context of neglect. This would be consistent with a suggestion that tactile and auditory allaesthesic responses derive from a visual "capture" or "ventriloquism" effect. That is to say, a severe visual neglect and inattention might be sufficiently powerful to bias auditory and somatosensory perception of location from one side of visually-perceived space to the other. Even in normal subjects, auditory "laterality" differences can be obtained when the stimulation is nonlateralised but a dummy loudspeaker is present on the right or left side (Pierson, Bradshaw & Nettleton, 1983). It would be very interesting to know whether these tactile or auditory allaesthesic effects occur when the eyes are closed or blindfolded.

3. From Clinical Deficits to Experimental Paradigms

Not all aspects of attention are impaired in patients with unilateral neglect. For example, as Rizzolatti, Gentilucci and Matelli (1985) have pointed out, the work of Posner and his colleagues (Posner et al, 1982;

Posner, Walker, Friedrich & Rafal, 1984) shows that the visual orienting
of attention can be achieved such as to improve detection performance in
either of their visual hemifields. However, this improvement is of course
relative to a much lower baseline on the impaired side. On the other
hand, ´sustained´ attention to a source of signals probably does
constitute a specific problem in neglect, but it has not been specifically
investigated, perhaps because the initial orienting of attention is so
impaired.   The major problem in understanding neglect symptoms is to
delineate precisely which processes are (or can be) impaired, and which
are not. This problem is still far from being fully solved, and
consequently the following suggestions are necessarily tentative. It is
encouraging that some of the most ingenious studies in human experimental
psychology continue to be devoted to the study of various aspects of
normal attention (e.g. Kahneman and Treisman, 1984; Posner and Cohen,
1984).   It may be hoped that the present suggestions will be greatly
improved upon in the future as this burgeoning knowledge and theoretical
refinement come to be increasingly exploited by neuropsychological
researchers.

The present exercise is tentative even in its basic structure, in
that the classification of symptoms used is only provisional even for man;
it must be expected that data-driven developments will change our
framework in the future. It would be unrealistic to suppose that the
groupings are any less provisional for non-human animals.

Hemispatial neglect: As indicated in the previous section, there seem
to be two possibly separable disturbances in this category. The more
general one is of sampling or exploration, both of the external world and
of internal representations of it, in both the visual and the tactile
modalities (although it is possible that in some tactile tasks there is a
recoding into visuospatial co-ordinates and that the defect lies at a
stage following such recoding). Searching and sampling behaviour can be
tested in animals in a variety of ways, but thus far investigations have
been restricted to behaviour as such and have not extended to internal
sampling. Nonetheless techniques could in principle be devised for the
latter: e.g. Bisiach et al´s (1979) task of discriminating moving
patterns viewed in piecemeal fashion through an aperture could be adapted
for monkeys.

More conventional tests include visual search either for a particular
rewarded object or for food items; in the case of monkeys the task may be
accomplished primarily by use of head and eye movements, whilst in small
mammals locomotor exploration is generally employed. In both cases
paradigms may be specially designed such that the sought object is
embedded in an array of ´distractors´, or alternatively investigators may
examine behaviour in a standard simultaneous discrimination task, where
clearly there will be less premium (but not a negligible premium) on the
capacity to search. Similar tests can be used for tactile search or
exploration.

The second category of hemispatial neglect can be characterised as an
apparent distortion of subjective space, such that (typically) units of
size progressively further towards the left are increasingly under-scaled.
This gradient appears to be present in both halves of space, to judge from
line-bisection studies, but to be steeper in the left half, since the
effect is greater there (Heilman & Valenstein, 1979: Costello, 1985).
These same authors have shown that the effect is not attenuated by first
requiring the patient to fixate both ends of the line. Additional evidence
that the phenomenon is dissociable from an exploratory deficit has been

reported by Costello (1985): neglect as measured by a tactile ´search´ task was unaffected by spatial location of the stimulus array in the same patients who did show differential effects in visual line-bisection according to the spatial location of the lines.

If there is truly a scaling disorder in neglect, then one could look for systematic errors in simple reaching tasks in monkeys, or in eye or head-turning in various species. Monkeys, further, could be trained to set a movable collar on a horizontal rod into a central location for reward, and tested postoperatively in different portions of their personal space, and under different head-position conditions (cf Faugier-Grimaud, Frenois & Peronnet, 1985).

Hemi-inattention and extinction: In contrast to the active attentional scanning supposedly impaired in exploratory hemispatial neglect, a more passive, stimulus-driven type of attention-switching may be affected in hemi-inattention and extinction. A peripheral visual cue can draw the attention of a normal subject (with or without an associated eye-movement) towards that part of space in an automatic manner, but it can also elicit a voluntary movement of attention (even in the opposite direction in an appropriate experimental condition: Posner, 1980) with a longer latency. Presumably such a voluntary shift of attention is responsible for the improved detection of visual stimuli when their location is pre-cued by use of a centrally-presented arrow (Posner, 1980). At least the first of these types of pre-cueing can be used in animals ranging from frogs (Ingle, 1975) to monkeys (Robinson, Morris & Petersen, 1984), such that subsequent detection at the cued location improves despite the absence of overt orientation towards the cue. As noted earlier, extinction can perhaps be seen as the result of "invalid" pre-cueing (Posner et al., 1982; 1984) drawing attention away from the detection site. (Although the bilateral stimuli are traditionally presented simultaneously in the clinic, it may be that the stimulus on the ´good´ side is more rapidly processed and can therefore effectively act as an invalid prime). In general, however, hemi-inattention and extinction have been tested by the simple presentation of uncued food objects, or aversive or novel stimuli. Their presence has been inferred from a unilateral failure to orient, withdraw, or otherwise respond to such stimuli. Unfortunately, in most cases, especially where a single stimulus is used, such a failure is ambiguous; it could result from hemi-inattention, but might also result from sensory inefficiency or from a defect in initiating response. These problems of interpretation will be discussed later.

The procedures used to elicit extinction as demonstrated by bilateral sensory stimulation are very appealing to animal experimenters, since they have a built-in control for sensory defects. If an animal responds to a contralesional stimulus when presented alone but not when presented together with an ipsilateral stimulus, then clearly a deficiency of the sensory apparatus cannot explain the latter failure. However problems of interpretation may remain in normal testing as a result of a possibly strong response preference for the ipsilesional side of space. One solution is to require the animal to signal detection of ´both´ stimuli by use of a nonlateralised response (Schwartz and Eidelberg, 1968). Alternatively, it could be trained to do so by use of a response towards the contralesional (affected) side, providing the animal can be shown to respond reliably in the same way to unilateral stimuli given on that affected side (Watson et al, 1973).

Hemiakinesia: If this is conceptualised as a disorder of *initiating* movements (but not of executing them), its demonstration (in man or in animal) will require more than simply a slowed reaction time, which could result from a slowed <u>movement</u> (i.e. bradykinesia). One method to separate the two would be to measure in a spatial choice-reaction task the time taken for a human or monkey to release a ´start´ key following the onset of the lateralised stimulus (decision or initiation time) separately from the time then taken for the hand to move to the appropriate key (movement time). An analogous task for a rat is to respond to a lateralised light initially by withdrawing its snout from a hole, prior to executing a trained head-orienting response to the stimulus (Carli, Evenden & Robbins, 1985).

As indicated in the previous section, it is possible to distinguish at least 3 kinds of hemiakinesia within the above definition. The ´primary´ type of hemiakinesia refers to the contralesional limb, and makes no reference to one or other side of personal space. For example, the patient of Valenstein and Heilman (1981), who had a haemorrhage in the region of the right caudate nucleus, showed the classic symptom of initially only raising the ipsilesional arm when requested to raise both. He was able to use the affected limb, but only with long latency and with reduced spontaneity. In order to avoid multiplying technical terms, I will refer to this as hemiakinesia (i). The second kind which has been discussed extensively by Heilman and his colleagues (e.g. Heilman & Valenstein, 1979) refers again to voluntary limb movements, but not to the contralesional limb alone; rather it is a reduced readiness to act with either limb towards the contralesional half of space. This disorder, hemiakinesia (ii), was apparent in a paper by Heilman et al (1983b). Six patients with a left-sided neglect syndrome were reported to have significantly longer reaction times in initiating leftward movements of a lever than righthand movements of it, despite in all cases using the ipsilesional (right) arm. Finally a hemiakinesia (iii) can be distinguished: in this case, orienting movements of the eyes, head or body are affected, primarily in respect of movements towards the contralesional field. Many patients with a neglect syndrome show this disorder, particularly in relation to eye movements (De Renzi, 1982; Girotti, Casazza, Musicco & Avanzini, 1983).

It is rare for unambiguous demonstrations of hemiakinesia to be reported either in man or in animals; rather it exists as a <u>possible</u> explanation for a large number of findings which are candidates for other explanations (e.g. hemi-inattention).

4. Animal Models of Hemispatial Neglect

Most authors agree that hemispatial neglect in man is generally a parietal-lobe syndrome, although there are authenticated cases of exclusively frontal lesions (the evidence is discussed critically by De Renzi, 1982). For example, CT-scan analyses published in recent years point persuasively to the parieto-temporo-occipital junction (Bisiach et al, 1979, 1981).

In animal studies, however, the evidence for analogous deficits following lesions of the parietal cortex is minimal. It has been argued above that demonstrations of hemispatial neglect require a task in which the animal must ´search´ or ´explore´ within its extrapersonal space, such as to find, and respond appropriately to, relevant stimuli or stimulus features. Direct tests of visual search performance have revealed little or no impairment following bilateral lesions (Latto, 1978a) and no relevant visual tests have been carried out following unilateral lesions. However, Ettlinger and Kalsbeck (1962) did examine the errors made by their unilaterally-lesioned monkeys during performance of a tactile shape discrimination. Since successful performance requires tactual exploration, a comparison between response preference for the contralesional and the ipsilesional stimulus location (with the errors divided unevenly in favour of the latter) could reveal a hemispatial sampling deficit. This was indeed found, in that errors were committed by responding more frequently on the ipsilesional side of space both when the lesion was ipsilateral to the hand used (62% of errors) and also when it was contralateral (61% of errors). The effect over all animals is highly significant (chi-squared = 13.3, p<.001) despite the authors´ statement to the contrary. This demonstration is persuasive not only because the animals were their own controls (right and left lesions were performed successively): in addition, most of the errors analysed were made during performance with the contralesional hand. Under these circumstances, the monkeys were still making (significantly) more responses to the ipsilesional side of space, i.e. contralateral to the limb being used: this would oppose the monkey´s natural inclination to prefer to respond to the ´compatible´ side of space with a given hand.

Rather more evidence exists for a search deficit following lesions of the frontal cortex. Bilateral frontal eye-field damage results in inefficient visual searching in both a previously trained task (Latto, 1978a,b) and in a more natural food-seeking situation (Collin, Cowey, Latto & Marzi, 1982). In the latter study the deficit was found whether the search required visual discrimination between food and non-food items or simply efficient sampling of an array of locations. However, Collin et al found no deficit (unfortunately using only their discriminative task) in animals with unilateral lesions; consequently there has as yet been no published demonstration of unilateral visual neglect in monkeys following cortical lesions alone. It should be noted that these search tasks produced their deficits through inefficient head and eye movements, or an inefficient behavioural search strategy. It is not necessary to suppose that the movement of covert attention (Posner, 1980) was affected by the lesions. Indeed, there is evidence that it would not have been, from an experiment by Schiller, True & Conway (1980). Bilateral combined lesions of the frontal eye-field and superior colliculus resulted in a dramatic loss of saccadic eye movements in monkeys. This was demonstrated quantitatively in a task where the head was fixed and the monkey was faced with a board in which pieces of fruit were embedded in various locations. In contrast with preoperative behaviour, or behaviour following recovery from frontal eye-field or collicular lesions alone, the monkeys with combined lesions no longer fixated each of these locations in attempting to extricate the morsels. Nonetheless they succeeded in retrieving the food to a remarkable degree (although less rapidly), indicating that they were able to attend to different locations without fixating them.

It should be noted that a positive result was reported many years ago by Kennard (1939): lesions including the frontal eye field apparently caused transient contralateral neglect of food items laid out from left to right facing the monkey. However, interpretation is not perhaps unequivocal since the monkeys were tested in a locomotor apparatus, and similar animals had shown a tendency towards ´forced circling´ (Kennard & Ectors, 1938). It is possible that even a slight motor asymmetry might explain the results. The same argument may apply to the anecdotal report of similar effects occasionally reported following other lesions (e.g. Heilman, Pandya & Geschwind, 1970; Watson, Heilman, Miller & King, 1974).

Rats with unilateral frontal lesions (in the dorsomedial region of anterior cortex) have been found to show a spatial preference for the ipsilesional side in discrimination learning tasks (Cowey & Bozek, 1974; Steele Russell & Pereira, 1981). By analogy with the Ettlinger and Kalsbeck (1962) data, this could reflect a reduced tendency to sample the contralesional visual hemispace. However, in each case a running task was used, and such lesions generally cause at least a transient ipsiversive turning tendency. Consequently it is once again difficult to exclude entirely a mild motor bias as the primary deficit. No evidence for neglect was found after such lesions in a task requiring the sampling of a spatial array of holes using head movements only (Garcia, Charman, Sotsky & Sinnamon, 1985).

Lesions of the superior colliculus tend to result in broadly similar changes; bilaterally they impair visual search involving discrimination between targets and ´distractors´ in monkeys (Latto, 1978a; Collin et al, 1982), and unilaterally tend to cause biased choice responding in rats (Cooper, Bland, Gillespie & Whittaker, 1970). They did not, however, result in inefficient search strategies in Collin et al´s "non-visual" task requring systematic search of an array of identical foodwells by monkeys. On the other hand unilateral lesions in rats do cause an apparent contralateral neglect in Garcia et al´s (1985) task of sampling baited holes in a 3x3 array; this paradigm has not yet been described in full, but would seem to be analogous to Collin et al´s ´non-visual´ task for monkeys. Bilateral lesions are known to impair exploratory behaviour in the open field (Foreman, Goodale & Milner, 1978); stimulus sampling in discrimination tasks where there is discontiguity of the discriminanda from the response site (in both monkeys – Kurtz and Butter, 1980 – and rats – Milner, Goodale & Morton, 1979); and the retrieval of sunflower seeds in an open field following collicular undercutting in hamsters (Keselica & Rosinski, 1976). However, no unilateral studies have been carried out to test for a hemispatial deficit in any of these behaviours.

There have been no animal studies specifically directed at modelling the "distortion of space" apparent in the behaviour of patients with neglect, for example in their attempts to bisect a line. However, some authors have observed that the visual misreaching produced by unilateral posterior parietal lesions is nonrandom. Unfortunately there is a disagreement between them as to whether the errors tend to be towards the midline in both halves of vision (Hartje & Ettlinger, 1973; Faugier-Grimaud, Frenois & Stein, 1978), or whether throughout the visual field the errors tend to be towards the ipsilesional side of space (Lamotte & Acuna, 1978; Faugier-Grimaud et al, 1985). Only the latter type of result would provide evidence for a systematic distortion of the monkey´s visuomotor space. Even then, of course, since the disorder is limited to the contralateral hand, it would appear that the distortion could not be one of subjective visual space as such. [Although some authors have sought to explain the human line-bisection disorder in terms of a hemiakinesia type (ii) (Heilman & Valenstein, 1979) no patient to my knowledge has ever been described as having the impairment restricted to the contralesional hand.] It must be concluded therefore that neither in respect of distorted awareness of space nor in respect of the ´sampling´ type of visual hemi-neglect has any convincing evidence yet appeared for a model in non-human primates.

5. Animal Models of Hemi-inattention and Extinction

There is a vast number of publications in which unilateral or bilateral brain lesions have been found to reduce or abolish reactions to lateralised visual, auditory, or somaesthetic stimuli. For example, the literature on "visual neglect" following lesions of the superior colliculus in rats and hamsters alone has recently merited a three-part review paper (Dean & Redgrave, 1984a,b,c). No such exhaustive review will be attempted here. Instead, the effects of unilateral cortical lesions will be considered in some detail, since it is accepted that the neglect syndrome in man is generally (but not exclusively) consequent upon cortical damage (typically parietal, but also sometimes frontal).

Posterior Parietal Lobe and Superior Temporal Sulcus
     The common denominator of the majority of lesions in man producing hemi-inattention, like hemispatial neglect, lies close to the parieto-temporo-occipital junction. For example, a recent series of 10 such patients whose CT scans were studied by Heilman et al. (1983a) all had right hemisphere lesions which overlapped this region.
     In general, attempts to reproduce hemi-inattention in monkeys with posterior parietal cortical lesions have been somewhat disappointing. For example, large unilateral lesions of the area (extending back through the prelunate gyrus and including the depths and banks of the dorsal portion of the superior temporal sulcus) produced no evidence of visual, auditory or somatosensory inattention (Ettlinger & Kalsbeck, 1962). However, other relevant changes were observed (see sections 4 and 6). Similar negative results have been reported elsewhere (Lamotte & Acuna, 1978; Faugier-Grimaud et al, 1978,1985). Denny-Brown and Chambers (1958) did report unresponsiveness to contralateral visual sensory stimuli, but no details were given. Heilman and his colleagues (Heilman et al 1970,1971; Valenstein, Heilman, Watson & Van der Abell, 1982) made smaller lesions of parietal cortex (restricted to area 7) but included more of the cortex of the superior temporal sulcus (in the ventral direction) than previous authors. These authors, like Ettlinger and Kalsbeck, reported generally normal visual and somatosensory orienting responses to single stimuli; however there was anecdotal evidence of visual, auditory and somatosensory "extinction" (i.e. bilateral stimuli elicited orienting only to the ipsilateral side) and a reduction of blinking to a "threat" stimulus in the contralesional visual field (Heilman et al, 1970,1971). However, one of the four lesions in the more recent study caused no asymmetrical effects at all (Valenstein et al, 1982). A more systematic study of bilateral somatosensory stimulation by Schwartz and Eidelberg (1968) provides clear evidence for extinction following posterior parietal lesions. The monkeys tended to use a response lever which they associated with ipsilesional stimulation more often than a central lever they had learned to use with bilateral stimulation, relative to preoperative performance. In the auditory modality no evidence has been reported for inattention but Heilman and his colleagues did report an apparent "auditory allaesthesia" both in the 1970/1971 study and the 1982 study, finding that not only ipsilateral but sometimes also contralateral sounds would elicit turning to the ipsilateral side (see Section 7 below).
     Combined lesions of area 7 and the superior temporal sulcus were also made by Deuel and Regan (1985), though their lesions extended less far anterolaterally in area 7 than Heilman et al´s, largely sparing area 7b (see Hyvarinen, 1982). These authors, unlike previous workers, made quantitative estimates of the threshold eccentricity required for orienting to occur to food baits; this provided evidence for a small but reliable asymmetry in the visual hemifields favouring the ipsilesional side. Although this finding may resolve the discrepancy among the other reports, it would seem too mild to merit the label "hemi-inattention". A quantitative asymmetry in response to pin prick given to the extremities was also found, but this too was far from absolute (with contralateral

responses occurring on 28%, as opposed to 69% of ipsilateral occasions).
It is stated that in both visual and somatosensory testing bilateral
stimulation elicited fewer responses in the contralateral field than
unilateral stimuli.   These results are similar to those summarised by
Valenstein et al (1982), though in the latter report one of the four
lesions resulted in no noticeable asymmetries.   The mildness of any
tactile inattention in this study is indicated by the fact that in a
formal behavioural test, "misses" (as opposed to errors of commission) to
tactile stimuli on each leg were very rare, and were symmetrically
distributed.
      More recently, unilateral lesions restricted to both banks of
the superior temporal sulcus along most of its length have been made (Luh,
Butter & Buchtel, 1984), whilst sparing areas 5 and 7 of the traditional
parietal cortex.   A multi-modal inattention was reported, although details
had not yet been published at the time of writing (but see Butter, this
volume).   In a further new development, small unilateral lesions in the
anterior part of area 7 (area 7b) have been reported to produce a
transient hemi-inattention for food items placed close to the mouth
(Rizzolatti, Gentilucci & Matelli, 1985).   Since it is reported that
distant visual stimuli yielded normal orienting reactions, this
unresponsiveness to peribuccal stimuli cannot be attributed to sensory or
motor impairments.
      In summary, lesions in the posterior parietal/superior temporal
sulcus region have generally resulted in mild if any evidence for
hemi-inattention, though clear evidence for somato-sensory extinction has
been reported.   However, it may be that more careful testing at different
distances from the monkey (close to the face, within reach, and beyond
reach) may clarify the picture, as suggested by Rizzolatti et al (1985).
It is also clearly necessary to begin testing almost immediately
post-surgery since there is very rapid recovery in most cases.

Frontal cortex
      The evidence for hemi-inattention is generally clearer and
better-attested following lesions in the region of the monkey's frontal
arcuate sulcus than in posterior association cortex;   yet paradoxically
'frontal inattention' is considerably less common in man (De Renzi, 1982)
and the lesion locations appear to lack a focus in the human frontal lobe
(Heilman et al, 1983a).   Recent studies on monkeys began with that of
Welch and Stuteville (1958), who made small lesions largely restricted to
the anterior bank of the posterior half of the upper limb of the arcuate
sulcus.   Visual stimuli in the contralateral field were not responded to,
and variable inattention to contralateral tactile stimuli was reported.
"Auditory allaesthesia" but no auditory inattention, was observed.
[Similar results have been reported for rats subjected to anteromedial
cortical lesions (Crowne & Pathria, 1982), except that clear evidence for
reduced orienting to visual, tactile and auditory stimuli was found;   in
addition a failure of withdrawal from contralesional noxious stimuli was
noted,indicating that a contraversive hemiakinesia could not account for
all the data].
      It has recently been found that when the lesion is restricted
entirely to the anterior bank of the sulcus, i.e. within the frontal
eye-field proper, only visual effects are observed (Rizzolatti, Matelli &
Paresi, 1983), and that they are strongest for stimuli beyond the
immediate "peripersonal" space around the monkey's head.   Since most
previous experimenters have used more extensive lesions, which either
extended further anteriorly (Watson, Miller & Heilman, 1978) or further

posteriorly and medially (Welch and Stuteville, 1958) or both (Deuel and Collins, 1983,1984) it seems likely that their findings of contralateral somatosensory orienting impairment are attributable to the invasion of separate, perhaps modality-specific, areas around the arcuate sulcus. Tactile extinction-type effects are also seen following such lesions (Eidelberg and Schwartz, 1971). Rizzolatti et al (1983) have also discovered that small lesions of the posterior lip at the angle of the arcuate sulcus produce failures to respond to contralateral visual and tactual stimuli in the area of space close to the mouth (though there appear to be species differences in the severity of these effects, Rizzolatti et al, 1985). Yet the same animals showed no deficits in responding to more distant visual stimuli even in bilateral stimulation ("extinction") tests, which lesions in the anterior bank and adjacent cortex on the convexity (the "frontal eye-fields"/area 8) do regularly affect (e.g. Watson et al, 1978; Rizzolatti et al, 1983; Deuel and Collins, 1984; Latto and Cowey, 1971). In a detailed study of a single monkey trained to saccade towards a peripheral LED, Rizzolatti et al (1985) have demonstrated an impressive dissociation between near and far space. Following a right-sided lesion of postarcuate cortex, clear preferences for looking towards the rightmost of two stimuli were generally found at 10cm distance, but none at all at 150cm. This was even true when both stimuli were present in the right hemifield.

Evidence that damage to frontal eye-field cortex does not merely give the appearance of inattention by impairing the monkey's inclination to orient or make other forms of lateralised movement towards the contralesional field is reported by both Kennard and Ectors (1938) and Watson et al (1978). In both papers it is stated that the monkeys failed to blink to contralateral threat stimuli. It is impossible to account for this observation in terms of a hemiakinesia [although the finding of no response to unilateral contralesional threat is disputed by Crowne, Yeo & Russell (1981)], since blinking is a nonlateralised response. Additional evidence is provided by Latto and Cowey (1971). Using a perimetric technique in which detection was signalled by an appropriate lever-press, clear contralesional "field defects" were found, with worse performance towards the periphery and variable degrees of recovery over time. Yet further evidence is apparent in Rizzolatti et al's (1983,1985) work, in which a near/far dissociation has been achieved; pre- and post-arcuate lesioned monkeys respectively can orient at one but not the other distance, implying that neither a disorder in seeing nor in orienting per se can account for the respective failures.

Other cortical regions
     Unsurprisingly, tactile 'extinction' defined in the usual operational terms occurs also following damage to primary somatosensory cortex (Eidelberg and Schwartz, 1971); likewise, a unilateral lesion of primary visual cortex will produce failures to respond to contralateral visual stimuli (e.g. Weiskrantz and Cowey, 1970). However, the definitions of "inattention" and "extinction" given earlier demand that response failures should not be attributable to sensory deficiency. Consequently, it is likely that few investigators would regard such findings as these as compelling instances of hemi-inattention or extinction in the strict sense. Nonetheless, it may be dangerous to exclude too hastily the possibility that attentional failures are involved. An apparently dense hemianopia produced by visual cortex lesions can be alleviated following a lesion of the contralateral superior colliculus or of the tectal commissure (Sprague, 1966; Kirvel et al, 1974; Sherman, 1977). This

so-called ´Sprague effect´ would suggest that a cortical hemianopia is
normally a compounding of two deficits, one cortical and one collicular;
the former is doubtless sensory, but the latter might be attentional (see
next subsection). (Welch and Stuteville, 1958, tantalisingly hint at the
possibility that a contralateral frontal eye-field lesion may also
alleviate an occipital hemianopia; unfortunately no details are given).
In other words, damage to primary cortical areas may produce attentional
disorders of the type discussed here (in addition to sensory defects).

The only other major cortical area which it has been argued is
involved in these phenomena is the anterior part of the cingulate gyrus
(Watson et al, 1973). Monkeys were trained to respond to a touch on one
leg by pushing the ipsilateral one of two large doors; they were at the
same time trained to respond to bilateral stimulation by pushing the left
door. Behavioural evidence of extinction following right-cingulate damage
was reported, in that each animal pushed the right-side door in response
to bilateral stimulation; the results appeared not to be due to a
left-sided hemiakinesia since at least 2 of the 3 animals generally pushed
the left door in response to left-leg stimulation alone. The monkeys
showed no clear evidence of hemi-inattention; only one monkey failed to
respond to left-leg stimulation, and that one had a conjoint lesion of the
supplementary motor area, which caused a partial left hemiparesis. The
monkeys were described as having intact sensation in all modalities
tested.

Subcortical lesions
    Lesions of the nigrostriatal system (Marshall, Richardson &
Teitelbaum, 1974; Marshall, 1978; Dunnett, Lane & Winn, 1985), of the
mesencephalic reticular formation (Watson, et al, 1974), of the thalamus
(Watson et al, 1978; Orem, Schlag-Rey & Schlag, 1973), and of the superior
colliculus (e.g., Sprague and Meikle, 1965; Kirvel, 1975; Goodale and
Murison, 1975), all result in deficits in responding to contralateral
stimuli in the modalities of vision and touch, and in some cases hearing
or olfaction too. In man, also, rare cases of inattention and extinction
have been described (see Heilman et al, 1983b) following damage to the
basal ganglia of the right hemisphere (though not all such lesions do
cause similar effects: e.g. Valenstein & Heilman, 1981), or to the right
thalamus. In general terms it might seem unlikely that mesencephalic
lesions which cause more profound changes in animals than cortical lesions
will tell us much of relevance to hemi-inattention in man, most cases of
which follow telencephalic lesions. On the other hand, the lesions which
cause hemi-inattention in the clinic are probably never restricted to the
cortex, and frequently involve the basal ganglia either directly or by
severing corticostriatal projections. For this reason it would seem
inappropriate to restrict the present discussion to cortical lesions in
animals.

    Damage to the nigrostriatal bundle, which arises in the dopamine-
containing neurones of pars compacta of the substantia nigra, whether
produced incidentally through lateral-hypothalamic destruction (Marshall,
1978) or directly through injections of 6-hydroxydopamine (e.g.,
Schallert, Upchurch, Lobaugh, et al, 1982; Dunnett et al, 1985), causes
orienting failures to contralateral visual, tactile, and olfactory stimuli
in rats.

    The question as to whether the somatosensory deficit was due to
failures to make contralateral orienting movements rather than sensory or
attentional failures was addressed by Hoyman, Weese and Frommer (1979).
Rats were trained to make turning responses following lateralised

stimulation either towards the same side or in the opposite direction to the touch. It was found that nigrostriatal 6-hydroxydopamine lesions caused a failure to turn away from ipsilesional stimuli, just like the failure to turn towards contralesional stimuli. There was, however, normal turning away from contralesional stimulation, and towards ipsilesional stimuli. Thus the impairment is in turning towards the contralesional side, irrespective of the side stimulated.

A similar experiment has recently been reported by Carli et al (1985) who asked the same question about visual orienting. These authors found that rats with unilateral striatal dopamine depletion were impaired in a preoperatively-trained task that required turning the head towards contralesional visual stimuli, but an oppositely-trained group was unimpaired in turning the head away from such stimuli. Furthermore the initiation of response was slower only as a function of the responses to be made, not as a function of the side stimulated. Movement time itself was the same in both contralesional and ipsilesional directions. In a second experiment, Carli et al required similar rats to make a non-lateralised detection response (to a panel on the back wall), and found no asymmetry in performance between stimuli on either side. These observations strongly support an interpretation of the nigrostriatal and striatal-lesion deficits as predominantly hemiakinesic as presently defined (see section 6) rather than hemi-inattentional. [On the other hand, some observations do indicate that a unilateral hypokinesia cannot account for all the apparent hemi-inattention following such lesions. Thus Feeney and Wier (1979) reported failures of contralateral light stimuli to elicit a conditioned suppression of licking following unilateral lesions of either the lateral hypothalamus or internal capsule in cats. Yet suppression of the same response occurred normally to ipsilesional stimuli.]

Unilateral damage to the midbrain reticular formation (in the region of the mesencephalic reticular nucleus) results in a profound failure to respond towards contralateral visual, auditory, tactile or olfactory stimuli (Watson et al, 1974). However in performing the task described in the previous subsection (devised by Watson et al, 1973) the monkeys did not (in general) fail to respond on the contralesional tactile stimulation trials, but instead responded (incorrectly) by pushing the ipsilesional door (presumably with the ipsilesional hand). Consequently the unresponsiveness to informally presented contralesional stimuli can probably once more be attributed to hemiakinesia, and there cannot be said to be any convincing evidence for hemi-inattention.

Clearer evidence for inattention comes from studies of unilateral thalamic damage. Orem et al (1973) performed stereotaxic surgery upon a series of cats, in which unilateral ablations destroyed different portions of the thalamus. The most effective sites included the nuclei centralis lateralis and paracentralis, where damage caused deficits in visual orienting and following, and failures to blink to visual threat in the contralateral field. Watson et al (1978) report failures in monkeys to orient or make other responses to contralesional visual or tactile stimuli, including a failure to respond to a threatening visual stimulus, e.g. by blinking, following lesions which again included the nucleus paracentralis. The observation in both studies of nonresponse to contralateral visual threat is inexplicable in terms of a hemiakinesia, since blinking is in no sense a lateralised response. The tactile hemi-inattention in Watson et al's monkeys, however, must have been mild, since in their formal behavioural task, they recorded, if anything, fewer response omissions to the leg-touch stimulus on the contralesional side than on the ipsilesional side.

The superior colliculus has been studied in more behavioural settings than any of the other brain regions discussed here, but generally bilateral lesions have been used. Many studies have demonstrated reduced distractibility (Goodale & Murison, 1975; Milner, Foreman & Goodale, 1978; Albano, Mishkin, Westbrook & Wurtz, 1982), and absent or impaired orienting behaviour towards visual stimuli, especially when these occur outwith a broad central region of the visual field (Goodale & Milner, 1982; Butter, Kurtz, Leiby & Campbell, 1982; Dean & Redgrave, 1984a). Similar orienting deficits also occur in respect of auditory, tactile and olfactory stimuli (e.g. Kirvel, Greenfield & Meyer, 1974; Kirvel, 1975; Marshall, 1978). Because the superior colliculus, unlike any of the other candidate brain areas proposed for modelling neglect, receives "sensory" inputs -- in the case of vision directly from the retina -- more attention has been paid to the question whether the orienting deficits can be accounted for in purely sensory terms. Clearly if an animal is unable to detect a stimulus, it will be unable to orient towards it; at least if one uses a purely operational definition of ´detection´ which carries no implication of conscious registration.

Some direct evidence is available both for monkeys (Kurtz, Leiby & Butter, 1982) and for rats (Milner, Lines & Migdal, 1984) that following bilateral superior collicular lesions, any sensory loss which does exist is insufficient to account for the orienting defect. In Kurtz et al´s experiment, monkeys were trained to perform a colour discrimination in which a variable stimulus-response spatial separation was introduced. In different experimental conditions, the monkeys were required to respond to keys only 8° out from centre or 32° out; the stimuli could occur variously at 8° - 32° eccentricity. In all cases the monkeys began each trial with central fixation, so that the initial retinal eccentricity of the stimulus corresponded to its physical eccentricity. When responses were made at 8°, performance was impaired most in the lesioned monkeys with 32° stimuli; but when the responses had to be made peripherally there was a deficit only with the stimuli at 8° (if at all). It would seem then that the impairment with peripheral stimuli was dependent upon the response location, and could be abolished by shifting the response site to match the stimulus eccentricity. It follows that the impairment could not be attributed to perceptual failure; yet it went hand-in-hand with a loss of eye-movements to the stimuli (Kurtz & Butter, 1980). Confirmatory evidence comes from a study by Albano et al (1982). These authors were able to demonstrate good detection performance after the first postoperative week (using a key-release response) following unilateral collicular lesions even though the animals continued to make fewer eye movements towards the stimuli on the affected side, and to distracting stimuli in other tests.

The relevant data for rats come from experiments which examined orienting, and other behaviour, in response to unexpected visual (Milner et al 1984) or auditory (Milner & Taylor, 1985) stimuli presented during a running task. Following a 3-month recovery interval, rats with bilateral collicular lesions were found to show a profound loss of head-turning responses, just as occurs shortly post-operatively (Goodale & Murison, 1975). However their detection of the light or sound was apparent in that running times were clearly elevated on the test trials as compared with control running trials, and in that freezing and retreat responses to the test stimuli often occurred (indeed not significantly less frequently than in sham controls).

These data do not of course demonstrate the absence of sensory deficits following collicular lesions; indeed such impairments are highly probable (Latto, 1977; Overton, Dean & Redgrave, 1985), at least in the short term. However they do provide evidence for an additional impairment – namely one in initiating orienting head and/or eye movements towards important stimuli. Despite all the work which has been done in this field, however, it remains unclear whether this impairment is attentional or, in the present sense, akinesic, or indeed both.

Discussion

As indicated earlier, clinical "hemi-inattention" implies a non-sensory disturbance. The same applies to attentional interpretations of "extinction". In the latter case, it is possible that an impaired sensory threshold could produce apparent extinction, i.e. response to only the ipsilesional of two stimuli in the presence of intact responding to a contralesional stimulus alone. One can only respond to one stimulus at once, and the more salient will tend to be the one responded to; the other might then be ignored as no longer present or as no longer pressing. Investigations have rarely tested this by examining responses as a function of varying stimulus intensity in experimental animals.

There are several kinds of argument used to exclude sensory loss as a factor in allegedly inattentive animals. It is frequently argued that areas of association cortex (especially in frontal cortex) are too distant from afferent pathways to cause sensory impairment. This kind of argument can sometimes be strengthened by internal evidence: thus Deuel and Regan (1985) found that a contralateral visual abnormality was present equally in both upper and lower fields, although the parieto-temporal lesion would be likely to damage the optic radiations representing only the lower fields. Nonetheless it is not inconceivable that various areas not normally regarded as sensory could play a part in sensory detection; there are many visually-responsive neurones in area 7 (Robinson, Goldberg & Stanton, 1978), the superior temporal sulcus (Bruce, Desimone & Gross, 1981), and in the frontal eye-field (Mohler, Goldberg & Wurtz, 1973; Pigarev, Rizzolatti & Scandolara, 1979) as well as in the superior colliculus and other relevant areas.

Furthermore, as Heilman and his colleagues (e.g. Heilman et al, 1985) have argued, one major effect of several of the lesions discussed here may be to disinhibit the reticular nucleus of the thalamus, whose increased activity could globally suppress activity in thalamic relay nuclei (the lateral geniculate, medial geniculate, and ventro-postero-lateral nuclei). Such a suppression would result in a deficit in sensory detection.

Another argument, which applies to all the cortical areas considered above, is that the putative hemi-inattention effects recover rapidly (within 1-3 weeks). A sensory loss, it is assumed, would be more permanent. This argument is not entirely convincing; it does not follow that because detection deficits consequent upon lesions of primary sensory targets are generally long-lasting, therefore all detection deficits must be long-lasting. Nonetheless, this line of reasoning is intuitively plausible.

A third argument is based on the occurrence of multi-modal deficits: the more sense-modalities affected, the less plausible it becomes to invoke sensory losses. This argument too has appeal, though it is not compelling. In any case, on close examination, the case for multi-modal hemi-inattention or extinction is often weak; for example, restricted frontal eye-field and perhaps thalamic lesions cause a hemi-inattention only in vision. In the case of nigrostriatal and superior collicular lesions, stimuli are apparently disregarded in several modalities, but in

the former case recent experiments confirm suggestions that the disorder
is primarily hemiakinesic in the sense used here. Corresponding
experiments have not yet been performed on unilaterally colliculectomised
animals, but it is possible that for them too the ´multimodal´ deficit is
explicable as a hemiakinesia, and that the only truly attentional
impairment is visual.

Perhaps the most satisfactory approach is to use internal evidence
from within a single experiment, where inattention is present under some
conditions but not others. For example, Rizzolatti et al (1983 and 1985)
were able to demonstrate visual inattention and an extinction-like
stimulus preference which were associated not simply with one half of
visual space, but also with spatial location in the near/far dimension.
Such demonstrated dissociations between ´near´ and ´far´ space provide a
strong case against sensory defect as a cause for the lack of response;
in addition they exclude any explanation based on difficulties of response
initiation.

All of these arguments have some force, and in combination they may
be compelling. Nonetheless it is important that the fallibility of most
of them be recognised and that efforts be made to obtain independent data
on sensory detection, as has been done for superior collicular lesions.

The second major problem with modelling hemi-inattention in animals
is that the process of directing or switching attention can be covert
(Posner, 1980). That is, we can attend to a locus in the peripheral
visual field without moving ocular fixation to it (and indeed it is an
introspectively familiar experience for many people that conversely
fixations are not necessarily accompanied by attention). Monkeys can be
trained to attend to visual stimuli without looking at them (e.g. Wurtz &
Mohler, 1976) and it may be socially important that they have this
capacity (Wurtz, Goldberg & Robinson, 1980). The problem then in
demonstrating hemi-inattention or truly "attentional" extinction is that
an absence of overt orienting does not imply an absence of attending.

There are no good grounds for supposing that rats similarly cannot
attend to a stimulus without orienting towards it. Hence in the
experiments referred to in the previous sub-section by Milner et al (1984)
and Milner and Taylor (1985), the collicular-lesioned rats though failing
to turn towards a flashing light or intermittent tone may well have been
attending to the stimulus. The only certain way to determine this would
be by demonstrating knowledge of some feature of the stimulus on a
subsequent occasion: for example the occurrence of stimulus-selective
habituation on subsequent test trials.

Perhaps the most promising way of exploring whether the effects
described here as putative instances of hemi-inattention or attentional
extinction really are such, will be to develop animal procedures modelled
upon the techniques of Posner (1980). The basic paradigm is to pre-cue
one or other of two lateralised visual locations whilst the human subject
maintains fixation, and to follow this rapidly by a target stimulus in one
of the two places. If the cue is "valid" (ipsilateral to where the target
then appears) detection reaction-time is found to be faster than if the
cue is "invalid" (or neutral). Robinson and his colleagues (Robinson et
al, 1984; Petersen, Morris & Robinson, 1984) have recently succeeded in
teaching this task to monkeys, and obtain similar results. It seems
reasonable to argue that these monkeys ´covertly oriented´, or selectively
attended, to the cued location, such that there were ´benefits´ for
detection in the validly cued location and associated ´costs´ for
detection elsewhere (cf Posner, 1980).

Posner et al (1982, 1984) have successfully brought clinical hemi-inattention and extinction "into the laboratory" by use of such techniques. Patients with the neglect syndrome show a clear pattern of results. First, valid cueing improves detection performance in both contralesional and ipsilesional fields. This demonstrates that the contralesional deficit is attentional (in some sense) and not (wholly) sensory. Second, invalidly cueing the ipsilesional field (i.e. with the target stimulus then presented to the inattentive field) causes a severe deterioration of performance, and as the interstimulus interval approaches zero, this deterioration approaches absolute failure. In the limiting case this would be a formal demonstration of visual extinction. As mentioned in section 2 above, similar effects were obtained in these patients by use of a centrally-located arrowhead cue (pointing left or right) to direct attention. Thus extinction would seem to result from a movement of attention in such patients. These techniques are an important beginning in gaining an experimental "handle" upon aspects of the neglect syndrome in man. It should now be possible for animal researchers to examine similar processes in monkeys. The use of paradigms of this general type should permit a clarification of the role of different brain structures in hemi-inattention and extinction in animals.

6. Animal Models of Hemiakinesia

As already indicated in the last section, lesions in some brain areas produce a degree of movement-related impairment which could account for apparent hemi-inattention. However, in most cases there have been no direct attempts to specify the nature of such impairments.

All three types of hemiakinesia distinguished in section 3 as evident in the clinical literature can also be discerned in the animal literature, although in many cases they may be difficult to separate from hemi-inattentional or other deficits. A reluctance to use the contralesional limb is sometimes reported following posterior parietal removals (e.g. Faugier-Grimaud et al, 1978), and the well-researched reaching difficulty is restricted to that limb and is present in both halves of visual space (Ettlinger & Kalsbeck, 1962; Hartje & Ettlinger, 1973; Lamotte & Acuna, 1978). It has recently been shown that this reaching disorder is accompanied by a lengthened latency to initiate localisation movements of the contralateral arm (Faugier-Grimaud et al, 1985). The presence of a hemiakinesia following such posterior cortical lesions is further supported by recent research of Valenstein et al (1982), who used the apparatus of Watson et al (1973) mentioned earlier. However, in this instance the monkeys were pre-operatively trained to push the left door (with the left hand) in response to right-leg stimulation, and the right door (with the right hand) to left-leg stimulation. The parietotemporal lesion caused no deficit following one of 4 lesions (made successively in 2 monkeys), but in the others the result was clear: stimulation of the ipsilesional leg produced significantly more errors than the contralesional, i.e. the tendency was to make errors not in response to contralesional stimuli, but when the contralesional hand should have been used. In this experiment, the results might reflect either a hemiakinesia (i) or a hemiakinesia (ii), depending upon whether the crucial feature of the response was the hand used (i.e. type (i)) or the side of space responded in (i.e. type (ii)). In the light of the observations of Faugier-Grimaud et al (1985), it would be parsimonious to assume that the deficit was type (i); but of course reaching inaccuracy might be an additional deficit of sensorimotor guidance, on top of any disorder of response initiation. Finally, there is evidence for a slight increase in contralesional saccade latency in parietal monkeys (Lynch,

1980): this would indicate a mild hemiakinesia type (iii).

Paradoxically, a hemiakinesia (i) is not typically reported in patients with parietal neglect: rather it seems that types (ii) and (iii) (i.e. where side of space rather than side of limb defines the disorder) are more typical. Similarly, the spatial misreaching observed in parietal lesioned patients is usually (though not always) related to the contralateral half of space without regard to hand (Ratcliff & Davies-Jones, 1972; De Renzi, 1982).

Prefrontal lesions in monkeys also produce evidence for a possible hemiakinesia. An experiment by Watson et al (1978) similar to that described above by Valenstein et al (1982), gave a similar result (in the 2 out of 3 animals which were affected): errors were made to both ipsilesional and contralesional touch, but paradoxically more in the former case, i.e. more errors reflecting incorrect use of the contralesional hand instead of the ipsilesional one. Again this result could reflect either hemiakinesia (i) or (ii). Many investigators have also described ipsilesional turning tendencies of eyes, head, and body, following frontal eye-field lesions (see Crowne, 1983); these could be due to hemiakinesia (iii). On the other hand since the orienting disorder following more restricted frontal eye-field lesions seems to be purely visual, it may be possible that the turning behaviour is secondary to an inattention or neglect rather than reflecting a primary hemiakinesia. The larger lesions do, however, affect tactile-evoked behaviour as well as visual (Watson et al 1978; Deuel & Collins, 1983; Deuel & Regan, 1985). They also cause slowed and inaccurate visually-guided reaching (Crowne et al, 1981), which apparently does not follow lesions restricted to the frontal eye-field proper (Latto, 1982). This reaching disorder was not restricted to the contralesional hemifield, and since the monkeys used only their contralesional hand in performing the task, the deficit may not be greatly different from posterior-parietal misreaching: see, e.g., Lamotte and Acuna, (1978). Several investigators have reported a strong ipsilateral hand preference following lesions in the arcuate region (e.g. Welch & Stuteville, 1958; Deuel & Collins, 1984), which may be particularly pronounced with larger lesions. The parsimonious conclusion would then be that a hemi-akinesia type (i) (i.e. related to the contralesional hand) as well as possibly type (iii) (related to the initiation of orienting movements) is liable to result from these lesions, though it may range in severity according to the extent of the damage. It may be assumed that a caudal extension into area 6 is especially likely to produce a defect, whose precise nature may depend upon the portion of area 6 which is invaded (Rizzolatti et al, 1983). However some of the larger lesions also produce a contralesional loss of power, which makes the term "akinesia" inapplicable (Deuel & Collins, 1984).

Among subcortical areas, it has already been argued as likely that nigrostriatal damage results in a hypokinesia as defined here (see section 5). This appears to be primarily a deficit of type (iii), i.e. one of initiating turning responses, to judge from the work of Carli et al (1985) and Hoyman et al (1979). The independence of this deficit from lateralised sensory cues is indicated by the work of Dunnett and Bjorklund (1983): unilateral 6-hydroxydopamine lesions grossly reduced the incidence of contraversive turning (but not ipsiversive turning) in a preoperatively-trained task where the rats were rewarded for spontaneous turning in one direction or the other. In addition, in the experiment of Watson et al (1978) described above in which frontal lesions seemingly induced hypokinesia of either type (ii) or (iii), similar (though less severe) results were obtained following thalamic damage.

Unilateral damage to the superior colliculus also produces ipsiversive turning tendencies (e.g. Cooper et al, 1970; Sprague, 1972), especially with deeper lesions (e.g. Sprague and Meikle, 1965). In monkeys contralateral eye- and head-movements tend to be reduced in frequency and amplitude, both when spontaneous (Denny-Brown, 1962; Schiller et al, 1980; Albano et al, 1982) and in response to visual cues (Albano et al, 1982). Comparable deficits in eye-movements occur also in the cat (Flandrin & Jeannerod, 1981). Orienting to cues in various sense modalities is reduced in rats (e.g. Kirvel et al, 1974), whilst in cats unilateral lesions reduce contralateral visual orienting, but not auditory or somatosensory orienting, which tends instead to be misdirected (see section 7). The accuracy and incidence of visual reaching is impaired following collicular lesions, (Mackinnon, Gross & Bender, 1976; Butter, Weinstein, Bender & Gross, 1978; Latto, 1982) but evidently only when the stimuli are presented very briefly. Although these various findings could reflect in part a hemiakinesic disorder, there have been no convincing demonstrations of akinesia following collicular lesions. However, it is quite possible that it exists, perhaps to an extent depending on the depth of the lesion.

It will be apparent that the retrospective interpretation of reported deficits in terms of a possible hemiakinesia is difficult, and that special tests need to be employed (e.g. like those of Carli et al, 1985, or Watson et al, 1978).

7. Instances of "Allaesthesia" in Animals

Several authors have reported that contralesional auditory, and less frequently somatosensory, stimuli, are sometimes responded to by animals as if they were ipsilesional (e.g. Sprague & Meikle, 1965; Kirvel, 1975; Watson et al, 1973). Such auditory or somatosensory ´allaesthesia´ may be a ´ventriloquism´ effect caused by a more salient visual world on the ipsilesional side, and hence provide evidence for visual inattention or neglect. It is, however, difficult in most cases to exclude the alternative interpretation of hemiakinesia. Nonetheless the fact that it rarely occurs in vision (the only exception is following neonatal lesions: Schneider (1979)), tends to militate against this account. Allaesthesias are an interesting phenomenon; however they are under-researched, and it is perhaps logically impossible to determine whether a grossly misdirected response in an animal reflects a mislocalised perception in the way that this appears to occur in patients.

8. Discussion and Conclusions

It will be apparent from the survey of the literature that the evidence for animal analogues of the different components of the neglect syndrome is far from clear, although there are some interesting candidates. For an animal model to be fully satisfying, it ideally would need to occur following posterior cortical lesions, since that is the region in which most lesions that give rise to the human neglect syndrome are situated. Furthermore, this region in the monkey (particularly area 7a) contains many neurones whose activity is correlated with selective visual attention, such that their loss would be expected to lead to several aspects of the syndrome (e.g. Lynch, Mountcastle, Talbot & Yin, 1977; Bushnell, Goldberg & Robinson, 1981). Yet unilateral posterior parietal lesions in monkeys do not cause more than a mild hemi-inattention, a transient tendency for extinction to occur, a unilateral hypokinesia, and a degree of tactile hemispatial neglect. In short, they produce at most only a mild version of the neglect syndrome. Frontal pre-

and post-arcuate lesions do produce more convincing effects of "hemi-inattentive" behaviour, but there is no evidence for hemispatial neglect.

The evidence for "extinction" in most experiments with animals (as well as for hemi-inattention) is not unequivocal, as shown by the cautionary observations of Valenstein and Heilman (1981). Their patient with an apparent hemiakinesia type (i) appeared to have somatosensory extinction, in that he would raise the left or right arm when either was touched, yet only the right when both were. Yet when asked to respond verbally, he responded "left", "right", or "both" correctly without difficulty. Several of the published observations using an ´extinction´ paradigm suffer from this problem since they used lateralised responses (e.g. turning, following, or unimanual responding). It should be noted that extinction is certainly not a hemiakinesic phenomenon in man, since it can be demonstrated both verbally and by use of a detection response (Posner et al, 1982, 1984). Also there is no correlation between the incidence of visual and auditory extinction (De Renzi et al, 1984).

The dissociations observed in man between inattention or neglect in different sense-modalities (see also Chedru, 1976 and Halsband et al, 1986) suggest that the disorders cannot be regarded as intrinsically ´multimodal´. This would be consistent with our knowledge of normal attentional processes: one can attend selectively among as well as within different modalities, and there are well-known visual dominance (´ventriloquism´) effects, such that an auditory cue in one location can elicit a switch of visual attention towards an object elsewhere in space. Thus attention is not always multimodally targetted towards a given location. There are certainly truly multimodal neurones in the superior colliculus, which could serve, for example, to direct ocular fixation by use of auditory cues when the target is visually obscure (cf Meredith & Stein, 1983). However, in most other structures where lesions have been thought to cause inattention or neglect, multimodal interactions are probably more complex [for example the postarcuate neurones of Rizzolatti, Scandolara, Matelli and Gentilucci (1981), which seem to respond to both visual and tactile stimulation only when both arise from a food object being brought to the mouth.] In other areas multiple sense-modalities may be represented, but remain segregated from one another (e.g. in prearcuate lateral frontal cortex: Jones & Powell, 1970). Conversely, there is evidence now that the maintenance of spatially selective attention within vision may be controlled through cortical areas which are purely visual (Moran & Desimone, 1985). Perhaps one should not expect that different areas implicated in inattention or neglect will necessarily or even typically be multimodal (cf Mesulam, 1981); indeed, it seems more likely that there are many different attentional mechanisms with specialised functions, some of which may involve only one sense-modality, others more than one in differing ways.

As indicated in the Introduction, the explanation for the difficulty in modelling the neglect syndrome may be that it only exists in full form in man because of the evolution of a peculiar left hemisphere. Left hemisphere lesions, leaving an intact right hemisphere, rarely bring about neglect or severe or persistent hemi-inattention, probably even more rarely than do unilateral lesions in the monkey (though extinction may occur relatively commonly: De Renzi, 1982; Posner et al, 1984). However, right hemisphere lesions, presumably leaving the left-hemisphere to deal with spatial relationships, often precipitate the contralateral syndrome. Both hemispheres of the monkey contain neuronal systems which could organise attention to both sides of space in parietal and superior-temporal sulcal cortex (e.g. Yin & Mountcastle, 1977; Motter & Mountcastle, 1981) and both sides of the visual field are, of course, well-represented for pattern analysis in inferotemporal cortex (Desimone & Gross, 1979). It may be, as suggested by De Renzi (1982) that this is not so in the human left hemisphere, that although the analysis of objects may be bilateral, the control of one´s attention to them may not be; though why this should have come about, and what relation it may have to other specialised features of the left hemisphere, remain completely mysterious questions.

Animal investigators have in the past generally avoided using terms like "attention" or "inattention", because of the legacy of pre-war behaviourism which dubbed such language unscientific. On the other hand, it has been regarded as acceptable to use words like "extinction" and "neglect", in the belief that these can be defined in terms which avoid reference to concepts of attention. I consider that both of these assumptions are false, and that not only is attention a crucial concept for understanding the components of spatial neglect in both man and animals, but that it can be manipulated and measured in animals as well as in man. I would argue that attempts to model such components remain worthwhile, providing they are made carefully and systematically. Wherever a clear animal analogue of a human ´neglect´ symptom can be unequivocally devised, it will provide a potentially valuable vehicle for further behavioural and physiological analysis, regardless of its lesser severity. (One interesting development has already been to look at metabolic changes in other parts of the brain following unilateral frontal lesions and how these stabilise over time: Deuel & Collins, 1983.) The literature to date provides some grounds for optimism that research along these lines may be increasingly fruitful in the future.

References

Albano, J.E., Mishkin, M., Westbrook, L.E. & Wurtz, R.H.   Visuomotor deficits following ablation of monkey superior colliculus. Journal of Neurophysiology, 1982, 48, 338-351.

Anscombe, G.E.M.   Intention (2nd edition). Blackwell, Oxford, 1976.

Baynes, K., Holtzman, J.D., & Volpe B.T.   Components of visual attention: alterations in response pattern to visual stimuli following parietal lobe infarction.   Brain, 1985, 109, 99-114.

Bisiach, E. & Luzzatti, C.   Unilateral neglect of representational space. Cortex, 1978, 14, 129-133.

Bisiach, E., Luzzatti, C. & Perani, D.   Unilateral neglect, representational schema and consciousness. Brain, 1979, 102, 609-618.

Bisiach, E., Capitani, E., Luzzatti, C. & Perani, D.   Brain and conscious representation of outside reality.   Neuropsychologia, 1981, 19, 543-551.

Bisiach, E., Cornacchia, L., Sterzi, R. & Vallar, G.   Disorders of perceived auditory localization after lesions of the right hemisphere. Brain, 1984, 107, 37-52.

Bruce, C., Desimone, R. & Gross, C.G.   Visual properties of neurons in a polysensory area in superior temporal sulcus of the macaque.   Journal of Neurophysiology, 1981, 46, 369-384.

Bushnell, M.C., Goldberg, M.E. & Robinson, D.L.   Behavioral enhancement of visual responses in monkey cerebral cortex I.   Modulation in posterior parietal cortex related to selective visual attention.   Journal of Neurophysiology, 1981, 46, 755-772.

Butter, C.M., Kurtz, D., Leiby, C.C. & Campbell, A.   Contrasting behavioral methods in the analysis of vision in monkeys with lesions of the striate cortex or the superior colliculus.   In Analysis of Visual Behavior.   DJ Ingle, MA Goodale & RJW Mansfield (Eds.)   MIT Press, Cambridge MA, 1982, pp 301-334.

Butter, C.M., Weinstein, C., Bender, D.B. & Gross, C.G.   Localization and detection of visual stimuli following superior colliculus lesions in rhesus monkeys.   Brain Research, 1978, 156, 33-49.

Carli, M., Evenden, J.L. & Robbins, T.W.   Depletion of unilateral striatal dopamine impairs initiation of contralateral actions and not sensory attention.   Nature, 1985, 313, 679-682.

Chedru, F.   Space representation in unilateral spatial neglect.   Journal of Neurology, Neurosurgery & Psychiatry, 1976, 39, 1057-1061.

Collin, N.G., Cowey, A., Latto, R. & Marzi, C.   The role of frontal eye-fields and superior colliculi in visual search and non-visual search in rhesus monkeys.   Behavioural Brain Research, 1982, 4, 177-193.

Cooper, R.M., Bland, B.H., Gillespie, L.A. & Whittaker, R.H.   Unilateral posterior cortical and unilateral collicular lesions and visually guided behavior in the rat.   Journal of Comparative & Physiological Psychology, 1970, 72, 286-295.

Costello, A.   Investigation of neglect syndrome through the visual and tactile modalities.   Unpublished MSc Thesis, University of Manchester, 1985.

Cowey, A. & Bozek, T.   Contralateral ´neglect´ after unilateral dorsomedial prefrontal lesions in rats.   Brain Research, 1974, 72, 53-63.

Crowne, D.P.   The frontal eye field and attention.   Psychological Bulletin, 1983, 93, 232-260.

Crowne, D.P. & Pathria, M.N.   Some attentional effects of unilateral frontal lesions in the rat.   Behavioural Brain Research, 1982, 6, 25-39.

Crowne, D.P., Yeo, C.H. & Russell, I.S.   The effects of unilateral frontal eye field lesions in the monkey: visuo-motor guidance and avoidance behaviour.   Behavioural Brain Research, 1981, 7, 165-185.

Damasio, A.R. & Geschwind, N.   Anatomical localisation in clinical neuropsychology.   In: Handbook of Clinical Neurology I(45): Clinical Neuropsychology.   JAM Frederiks (Ed).   Elsevier, Amsterdam, 1985, pp 7-22.

Dean, P. & Redgrave, P.   The superior colliculus and visual neglect in rat and hamster: I. Behavioural evidence.   Brain Research Reviews, 1985a, 8, 129-141.

Dean, P. & Redgrave, P.   The superior colliculus and visual neglect in rat and hamster: II. Possible mechanisms.   Brain Research Reviews, 1985b, 8, 143-153.

Dean, P & Redgrave, P.   The superior colliculus and visual neglect in rat and hamster: III. Functional implications.   Brain Research Reviews, 1985c, 8, 155-163.

Denny-Brown, D.   The midbrain and motor integration.   Proceedings of The Royal Society of Medicine, 1962, 55, 527-538.

Denny-Brown, D. & Chambers, R.A. The parietal lobes and behavior. Research Publications of the Association for Research on Nervous and Mental Diseases, 1958, 36, 35-117.

Denny-Brown, D., Meyer, J.S. & Horenstein, S. The significance of perceptual rivalry resulting from parietal lesion. Brain, 1952, 75, 433-471.

De Renzi, E. Disorders of space exploration and cognition. Wiley:New York. 1982.

De Renzi, E., Faglioni, P. & Scotti, G. Hemispheric contribution to the exploration of space through the visual and tactile modality. Cortex, 1970, 6, 191-203.

De Renzi, E., Gentilini, M. & Pattacini, F. Auditory extinction following hemispheric damage. Neuropsychologia, 1984, 22, 733-44.

Desimone, R. & Gross, C.G. Visual areas in the temporal cortex of the macaque. Brain Research, 1979, 178, 363-380.

Deuel, R. & Collins, R. Recovery from unilateral neglect. Experimental Neurology 1983, 81, 733-748.

Deuel, R. & Collins, R. The functional anatomy of frontal lobe neglect in the monkey: behavioral and quantitative 2-deoxyglucose studies. Annals of Neurology, 1984, 15, 521-529.

Deuel, R.K. & Regan D.J. Parietal hemineglect and motor deficits in the monkey. Neuropsychologia, 1985, 23, 305-314.

Dunnett, S.B. & Bjorklund, A. Conditioned turning in rats: dopaminergic involvement in the initiation of movement rather than the movement itself. Neuroscience Letters, 1983, 41, 173-178.

Dunnett, S.B., Lane, D.M. & Winn, P. Ibotenic acid lesions of the lateral hypothalamus: comparison with 6-hydroxydopamine-induced sensorimotor deficits. Neuroscience, 1985, 14, 509-518.

Eidelberg, E. & Schwartz, A.S. Experimental analysis of the extinction phenomenon in monkeys. Brain, 1971, 94, 91-108.

Ettlinger, G. & Kalsbeck, J.E. Changes in tactile discrimination and in visual reaching after successive and simultaneous bilateral posterior parietal ablations in the monkey. Journal of Neurology, Neurosurgery & Psychiatry, 1962, 25, 256-268.

Faugier-Grimaud, S., Frenois, C. & Stein, D.G. Effects of posterior parietal lesions on visually guided behaviour in monkeys. Neuropsychologia, 1978, 16, 151-168.

Faugier-Grimaud, S., Frenois, C. & Peronnet, F. Effects of posterior parietal lesions on visually guided movements in monkeys. Experimental Brain Research, 1985, 59, 125-138.

Feeney, D.M. & Wier, C.S. Sensory neglect after lesions of substantia nigra or lateral hypothalamus: differential severity and recovery of function. Brain Research, 1979, 178, 329-346.

Flandrin, J.M. & Jeannerod, M. Effects of unilateral superior colliculus ablation on oculomotor and vestibulo-ocular responses in the cat. Experimental Brain Research, 1981, 42, 73-80

Foreman, N.P., Goodale, M.A. & Milner, A.D. Nature of postoperative hyperactivity following lesions of the superior colliculus in the rat. Physiology & Behavior, 1978, 21, 157-160.

Friedland, R.P. & Weinstein, E.A. Hemi-inattention and hemisphere specialization: introduction and historical review. In: EA Weinstein & RP Friedland (Eds), Hemi-inattention and Hemisphere Specialization. Raven Press:New York, 1977, pp 1-32.

Garcia, E., Charman, C., Sotsky, J. & Sinnamon, H.M.   Effects of lesions
    of the superior colliculus, striate cortex and anteromedial cortex on
    instrumental head movements in the rat.   Society for Neuroscience
    Abstracts, 1985, 11, 81.
Girotti, F., Casazza, M., Musicco, M. & Avanzini, G.   Oculomotor disorders
    in cortical lesions in man: the role of unilateral neglect.
    Neuropsychologia, 1983, 21, 543-553.
Goodale, M. & Milner, A.D.   Fractionating orientation behavior in rodents.
    In Analysis of Visual Behavior. DJ Ingle, MA Goodale & RJW Mansfield
    (Eds). MIT Press, Cambridge, MA, 1982, pp 267-299.
Goodale, M.A. & Murison, R.C.C.   The effects of lesions of the superior
    colliculus on locomotor orientation and the orienting reflex in the
    rat. Brain Research, 1975, 88, 243-261.
Halsband, U., Gruhn, S. & Ettlinger, G.   Unilateral spatial neglect and
    defective performance in one half of space. International Journal of
    Neuroscience, 1986, in press.
Hartje, W. & Ettlinger, G.   Reaching in light and dark after unilateral
    posterior parietal ablations in monkey. Cortex, 1973, 9, 346-354.
Hecaen, H. & Albert, M.L.   Human Neuropsychology. Wiley:New York. 1978
Heilman, K.M.   Neglect and related disorders. In: Clinical
    Neuropsychology. KM Heilman & E Valenstein (Eds). Oxford University
    Press:New York. 1979
Heilman, K.M. & Valenstein, E.   Mechanisms underlying hemispatial neglect.
    Annals of Neurology, 1979, 5, 166-170.
Heilman, K.M., Pandya, D.N. & Geschwind, N.   Trimodal inattention
    following parietal lobe ablations. Transactions of the American
    Neurological Association, 1970, 95, 259-261.
Heilman, K.M., Pandya, D.N., Karol, E.A. & Geschwind, N.   Auditory
    inattention. Archives of Neurology, 1971, 24, 323-325.
Heilman, K.M., Watson, R.T., Valenstein, E. & Damasio, A.T.   Localization
    of lesions in neglect. In: Localization in Neuropsychology. A
    Kertesz (Ed). Academic Press:New York, 1983a, pp 471-492.
Heilman, K.M., Bowers, D., Coslett, B. & Watson, R.T.   Directional
    hypokinesia in neglect. Neurology, 1983b, 33, Supp 2, 104.
Heilman, K.M., Valenstein, I.E. & Watson, R.T.   The Neglect Syndrome. In:
    Handbook of Clinical Neurology I (45):Clinical Neuropsychology.
    J.A.M. Frederiks (Ed). Elsevier:Amsterdam, 1985, pp 153-183.
Hoyman, L., Weese, G.D. & Frommer, G.P.   Tactile discrimination
    performance deficits following neglect-producing unilateral lateral
    hypothalamic lesions in the rat. Physiology and Behavior, 1979, 22,
    139-147.
Hyvarinen, J.   The Parietal Cortex of Monkey and Man. Berlin:Springer-
    Verlag, 1982
Ingle, D.J.   Focal attention in the frog: behavioral and physiological
    correlates. Science, 1975, 188, 1033-1035.
Jones, E.G. & Powell, T.P.S.   An anatomical study of converging sensory
    pathways within the cerebral cortex of the monkey. Brain, 1970, 93,
    793-820.
Kahneman, D. & Treisman A.   Changing views of attention and automaticity.
    In Varieties of Attention, R. Parasuraman & D.R. Davies (Eds.)
    Academic Press:Orlando, 1984, pp 29-61.

Kennard, M.A.   Alterations in response to visual stimuli following lesions of the frontal lobe in monkeys. Archives of Neurology and Psychiatry, 1939, 41, 1153–1165.

Kennard, M.A. & Ectors, L.   Forced circling in monkey following lesions of the frontal lobes. Journal of Neurophysiology, 1938, 1, 45–54.

Keselica, J.J. & Rosinski, R.R.   Spatial perception in colliculectomized and normal golden hamsters (Mesocricetus auratus).   Physiological Psychology, 1976, 4, 511–514.

Kinsbourne, M.   Hemi-neglect and hemisphere rivalry.   In E.A. Weinstein & P.P. Friedland (Eds) Hemi-inattention and Hemisphere Specialization. New York:Raven Press, 1977, 41–46.

Kirvel, R.D.   Sensorimotor responsiveness in rats with unilateral superior collicular and amygdaloid lesions.   Journal of Comparative & Physiological Psychology, 1975, 89, 882–891.

Kirvel, R.D., Greenfield, R.A. & Meyer, D.R.   Multimodal sensory neglect in rats with radical unilateral posterior isocortical and superior collicular ablations.   Journal of Comparative & Physiological Psychology, 1974, 87, 156–162.

Kurtz, D. & Butter, C.M.   Impairments in visual discrimination performance and gaze shifts in monkeys with superior colliculus lesions.   Brain Research, 1980, 196, 109–124.

Kurtz, D., Leiby, C.C. III & Butter, C.M.   Further analysis of S-R separation effects on visual discrimination performance of normal rhesus monkeys and monkeys with superior colliculus lesions.   Journal of Comparative & Physiological Psychology, 1982, 96, 35–46.

Lamotte, R.H. & Acuna, C.   Deficits in accuracy of reaching after removal of posterior parietal cortex in monkeys.   Brain Research, 1978, 139, 309–326.

Latto, R.   The effects of bilateral frontal eye-field, posterior parietal or superior collicular lesions on brightness thresholds in the rhesus monkey. Neuropsychologia, 1977, 15, 507–516.

Latto, R.   The effects of bilateral frontal eye-field, posterior parietal or superior collicular lesions on visual search in the rhesus monkey. Brain Research, 1978a, 146, 35–50.

Latto, R.   The effects of bilateral frontal eye-field lesions on the learning of a visual search task by rhesus monkeys.   Brain Research, 1978b, 147, 370–376.

Latto, R.   Visual perception and oculomotor areas in the primate brain. In: Analysis of Visual Behavior. D.J. Ingle, M.A. Goodale & R.J.W. Mansfield (Eds). M.I.T. Press:Cambridge, Mass., 1982, pp 671–691.

Latto, R. & Cowey, A.   Visual field defects after frontal eye-field lesions in monkeys. Brain Research, 1971, 30, 1–24.

Luh, K.E., Butter, C.M. & Buchtel, H.A.   Effects of unilateral superior temporal sulcus lesions on visual orientation in monkeys. Society for Neuroscience Abstracts, 1984, 10, 59.

Lynch, J.C.   The functional organization of posterior parietal association cortex. Behavioral and Brain Sciences, 1980, 3, 485–534.

Lynch, J.C., Mountcastle, V.B., Talbot, W.H. & Yin, T.C.T.   Parietal lobe mechanisms for directed visual attention. Journal of Neurophysiology, 1977, 40, 362–389.

Mackinnon, D.A., Gross, C.G. & Bender, D.B.   A visual deficit after superior colliculus lesions in monkeys.   Acta Neurobiologica Experimentalis, 1976, 36, 169–180.

Marshall, J.F.   Comparison of the sensorimotor dysfunctions produced by
    damage to lateral hypothalamus or superior colliculus in the rat.
    Experimental Neurology, 1978, 58, 203-217.
Marshall, J.F., Richardson, J.S. & Teitelbaum, P.   Nigrostriatal bundle
    damage and the lateral hypothalamic syndrome. Journal of Comparative
    & Physiological Psychology, 1974, 87, 808-830.
Meredith, M.A. & Stein, B.E.   Interactions among converging sensory
    inputs in the superior colliculus. Science, 1983, 221, 389-391.
Mesulam, M.-M.   A cortical network for directed attention and unilateral
    neglect. Annals of Neurology, 1981, 10, 309-325.
Milner, A.D. & Taylor, M.J.   A dissociation between hearing, and orienting
    towards, sounds, following lesions of the superior colliculus. Paper
    presented at EBBS Meeting, Oxford, September, 1985.
Milner, A.D., Foreman, N.P. & Goodale, M.A.   Go-left go-right
    discrimination performance and distractibility following lesions of
    prefrontal cortex or superior colliculus in stumptail monkeys.
    Neuropsychologia, 1978, 16, 381-390.
Milner, A.D., Goodale, M.A. & Morton, M.C.   Visual sampling following
    lesions of the superior colliculus in rats. Journal of Comparative &
    Physiological Psychology, 1979, 93, 1015-1023.
Milner, A.D., Lines, C.R. & Migdal, B.   Visual orientation and detection
    following lesions of the superior colliculus in rats. Experimental
    Brain Research, 1984, 56, 106-114.
Mohler, C.W. & Wurtz, R.H.   Role of striate cortex and superior colliculus
    in visual guidance of saccadic eye movements in monkeys. Journal of
    Neurophysiology, 1977, 40, 74-94.
Mohler, C.W., Goldberg, M.E. & Wurtz, R.H.   Visual receptive fields of
    frontal eye field neurons. Brain Research, 1973, 61, 385-389.
Moran, J. & Desimone, R.   Selective attention gates visual processing in
    the extrastriate cortex. Science, 1985, 229, 782-784.
Motter, B.C. & Mountcastle, V.B.   The functional properties of the
    light-sensitive neurons of the posterior parietal cortex studied in
    waking monkeys: foveal sparing and opponent vector organization.
    Journal of Neuroscience, 1981, 1, 3-26.
Orem, J., Schlag-Rey, M. & Schlag, J.   Unilateral visual neglect and
    thalamic intralaminar lesions in the cat. Experimental Neurology,
    1973, 40, 784-797.
Overton, P., Dean, P. & Redgrave, P.   Detection of visual stimuili in far
    periphery by rats: possible role of superior colliculus.
    Experimental Brain Research, 1985, 59, 559-569.
Petersen, S.E., Morris, J.D. & Robinson, D.L.   Modulation of attentional
    behavior by injection of GABA-related drugs into the pulvinar of
    macaque. Society for Neuroscience Abstracts, 1984, 10, 475.
Petrides, M. & Iversen, S.   Restricted posterior parietal lesions in the
    rhesus monkey and performance on visuospatial tasks. Brain Research,
    1979, 61, 63-77.
Pierson, J.M., Bradshaw, J.L. & Nettleton, N.C.   Head and body space to
    left and right front and rear - I. Unidirectional competitive auditory
    stimuli. Neuropsychologia, 1983 21, 463-473.
Pigarev, I.N., Rizzolatti, G. & Scandolara, C.   Neurons responding to
    visual stimuli in the frontal lobe of macaque monkeys. Neuroscience
    Letters, 1979, 12, 207-212.

Posner, M.I.   The orienting of attention.   Quarterly Journal of Experimental Psychology, 1980, 32, 3-25.

Posner, M.I. & Cohen, Y.A.   Components of visual orienting.   In Attention and Performance X.   H. Bouma & DG Bouwhuis (eds.)   Erlbaum:Hillsdale, N.J., 1984, pp 531-556.

Posner, M.I., Cohen, Y. & Rafal, R.D.   Neural systems control of spatial orienting.   Philosophical Transactions of the Royal Society of London, 1982, B298, 187-198.

Posner, M.I., Walker, J.A., Friedrich, F.J. & Rafal, R.D.   Effects of parietal injury on covert orienting of attention.   Journal of Neuroscience, 1984, 4, 1863-1874.

Ratcliff, G. & Davies-Jones, G.A.B.   Defective visual localization in focal brain wounds.   Brain, 1972, 95, 49-60.

Rizzolatti, G., Gentilucci, M. & Matelli, M.   Selective spatial attention:one center, one circuit, or many circuits?   In Attention and Performance XI   M.I. Posner & O.S.M. Marin (eds.)   Erlbaum:Hillsdale, N.J., 1985, pp 251-265.

Rizzolatti, G., Matelli, M. & Pavesi, G.   Deficits in attention and movement following the removal of postarcuate (area 6) and prearcuate (area 8) cortex in macaque monkeys.   Brain, 1983, 106, 655-673.

Rizzolatti, G., Scandolara, C., Matelli, M. & Gentilucci, M.   Afferent properties of periarcuate neurons in macaque monkeys. II   Visual responses.   Behavioural Brain Research, 1981, 2, 147-163.

Robinson, D.L., Goldberg, M.E. & Stanton, G.B.   Parietal association cortex in the primate: sensory mechanisms and behavioral modulations.   Journal of Neurophysiology, 1978, 41, 910-932.

Robinson, D.L., Morris, J.D. & Petersen, S.E.   Cued visual behavior and the pulvinar of the awake macaque.   Investigative Ophthalmology and Visual Science, 1984, 25, 33.

Schallert, T., Upchurch, M., Lobaugh, N., Farrar, S.B., Spirduso, W.W., Gilliam, P., Vaughn, D. & Wilcox, R.E.   Tactile extinction: distinguishing between sensorimotor and motor asymmetries in rats with unilateral nigrostriatal damage.   Pharmacology, Biochemistry and Behaviour, 1982, 16, 455-462.

Schiller, P.H., True, S.D. & Conway, J.L.   Deficits in eye movements following frontal eye-field and superior colliculus ablations.   Journal of Neurophysiology, 1980, 44, 1175-1189.

Schneider, G.E.   Is it really better to have your brain lesions early? A revision of the "Kennard principle".   Neuropsychologia, 1979, 17, 557-583.

Schwartz, A.S. & Eidelberg, E.   "Extinction" to bilateral simultaneous stimulation in the monkey.   Neurology, 1968, 18, 61-68.

Sherman, S.M.   The effect of superior colliculus lesions upon the visual fields of cats with cortical ablations.   Journal of Comparative Neurology, 1977, 172, 211-223.

Sperling, G.   The information available in brief visual presentations.   Psychological Monographs, 1960, 74 (11, whole No. 498).

Sprague, J.M.   Interaction of cortex and superior colliculus in mediation of visually guided behavior in the cat.   Science, 1966, 153, 1544-1547.

Sprague, J.M.   The superior colliculus and pretectum in visual behavior.   Investigative Ophthalmology, 1972, 11, 473-482.

Sprague, J.M. & Meikle, T.H., Jr.   The role of the superior colliculus in visual guided behavior. Experimental Neurology, 1965, 11, 115-146.

Steele Russell, I. & Pereira, S.C.   Visual neglect in rat and monkey: an experimental model for the study of recovery of function following brain damage. In: Functional Recovery from Brain Damage. MW van Hof & G Mohn (Eds). Elsevier:Amsterdam, 1981, pp 209-238.

Valenstein, E. & Heilman, K.M.   Unilateral hypokinesia and motor extinction. Neurology, 1981, 31, 445-448.

Valenstein, E., Heilman, K.M., Watson, R.T. & Van Den Abell, T. Nonsensory neglect from parietotemporal lesions in monkeys. Neurology, 1982, 32, 1198-1201.

Watson, R.T., Heilman, R.M., Cauthen, J.C. & King, F.A.   Neglect after cingulectomy. Neurology, 1973, 23, 1003-1007.

Watson, R.T., Heilman, K.M., Miller, B.D. & King, F.A.   Neglect after mesencephalic reticular formation lesions. Neurology, 1974, 24, 294-298.

Watson, R.T., Miller, B.D. & Heilman, K.M.   Nonsensory neglect. Annals of Neurology, 1978, 3, 505-508.

Weiskrantz, L. & Cowey, A.   Filling in the scotoma: a study of residual vision after striate cortex lesions in monkeys. In: Progress in Physiological Psychology, vol.3.   E Stellar & JM Sprague (Eds). Academic Press:New York, 1970.

Welch, K. & Stuteville, P.   Experimental production of unilateral neglect in monkeys. Brain, 1958, 81, 341-347.

Wurtz, R.H. & Mohler, C.W.   Organisation of monkey superior colliculus: enhanced visual response of superficial layer cells. Journal of Neurophysiology, 1976, 39, 745-765.

Wurtz, R.H., Goldberg, M.E. & Robinson, D.L.   Behavioral modulation of visual responses in the monkey: stimulus selection for attention and movement. Progress in Psychobiology and Physiological Psychology, 1980, 9, 43-83.

Yin, T.C.T. & Mountcastle, V.B.   Visual input to the visuomotor mechanisms of the monkey's parietal lobe. Science, 1977, 197, 1281-1383.

Acknowledgements: The author is grateful to Professor G Ettlinger and Drs D Perrett, M Rugg and P Winn for their helpful comments on the first draft of this chapter. However, they bear no responsibility for the views expressed.

Neurophysiological and Neuropsychological Aspects
of Spatial Neglect, M. Jeannerod (editor)
© Elsevier Science Publishers B.V. (North-Holland), 1987

NEURAL CIRCUITS FOR SPATIAL ATTENTION AND UNILATERAL NEGLECT

Giacomo Rizzolatti
and
Rosolino Camarda

What is the relationship between attention and unilateral neglect? In this article we review three theories that have been advanced to explain this neurological syndrome, discuss their limitations, and advance an alternative hypothesis. The theories are: the hemispheric hypoarousal hypothesis (Heilman & Watson, 1977), the hypothesis of an attentional master center (see De Renzi, 1982) and the hypothesis of a cortical circuit for directing attention (Mesulam, 1981). The analysis of these theories shows that none of them is able to accomodate three basic findings: a) the multiplicity of brain centers whose lesion produces neglect; b) the congruence between attentional and motor deficits after lesion of these centers; c) the anatomical independence of centers whose damage causes neglect.
A model of spatial attention is proposed based on a series of circuits largely independent one from another and formed by centers which program motor plans in a spatial framework. This conception is radically different from that of a single attentional center because it conceives spatial attention not as a supraordinate function controlling the activity of the brain as a whole, but as a property intrinsically linked to the premotor activity and distributed among various cerebral centers. In other words, spatial attention is a vertical modular function present in several independent circuits.

Introduction

Unilateral neglect is a rather common neurological syndrome observed in many species of animals and in man (see De Renzi, 1982; Friedland and Weinstein, 1977; Heilman and Watson, 1977; Heilman, Watson & Valenstein, 1985). The distinctive features of this syndrome are the following: 1) stimuli presented contralateral to the lesion are not responded to and, apparently, not perceived; 2) there is a marked decrease of exploratory movements towards the space contralateral to the lesion; 3) elementary sensory deficits or disturbances in execution of movements are insufficient, when present, to explain the symptomatology; 4) when the acute symptoms recede, a contralateral deficit can be demonstrated with a simultaneous presentation of two stimuli. Patients tested in this way may report of seeing only one stimulus, that ipsilateral to the lesion (extinction).

In the last decade there has been a growing consensus that hemineglect depends upon an attentional deficit. The ideas however on the precise attentional mechanisms impaired in the syndrome diverge considerably. Broadly speaking there are three possible ways of relating neglect to

attention and, accordingly, three possible versions of an attention theory
of this syndrome.

The first one is that the deficits concern the intensive aspects of
attention. According to this theory each side of the brain contains its own
activating system. When this system is destroyed half of the brain cannot
process properly the incoming   sensory information and organize the
appropriate motor activity. Hence the neglect syndrome (Heilman and Watson,
1977; Heilman, 1979).

The second theory proposes that responsible for the neglect is a lesion
of an attentional central mechanism which directs attention to various
portions of the space according to the internal needs of the individuals or
in response to relevant stimuli. The central attentional mechanisms can be
thought of either as localized in a particular brain area or as a network
formed by a chain of cortical areas and subcortical centers (see De Renzi,
1982; Mesulam, 1981). In both cases the lesion of a selective attention
mechanism is considered responsible for the neglect.

The third theory, as the previous one, maintains that neglect is due to
a deficit of selective attentional mechanisms. However it denies that there
is a single attentional circuit controlling spatial attention. It proposes
that attention to various parts of space results from the activity of
different circuits each of them having as its primary function that of
organizing movements toward a certain part of space (Rizzolatti, 1983).

One finding which any theory of neglect must accomodate is that neglect
results following lesions of a large variety of cortical areas and
subcortical centers. In primates, cortical areas whose lesion produce
neglect are the frontal eye field (see ref. in Crowne, 1983), the inferior
area 6 (Rizzolatti, Matelli & Pavesi, 1983), the inferior parietal lobe
(Denny-Brown and Chambers, 1958; Heilman, Pandya & Geschwind, 1970;
Rizzolatti, Gentilucci & Matelli, 1985; Stein, 1978; Valenstein, Heilman &
Watson, 1982), the polysensorial area of the superior temporal sulcus (Luh,
Butter & Buchtel, 1979; Petrides & Iversen, 1979) and the cingulate gyrus
(Watson, Heilman, Cauthen & King, 1973). Furthermore neglect can be
obtained after lesion of the superior colliculus (Albano, Mishkin,
Westbrook & Wurtz, 1982; Dean & Redgrave, 1984; Denny-Brown, 1962; Goodale &
Murison, 1975; Goodale, Foreman & Milner, 1978; Sprague & Meikle, 1965), the
lateral hypothalamus (Marshall, Turner & Teitelbaum, 1971; Marshall &
Teitelbaum, 1974), the substantia nigra, and the striatum (Dunnet &
Iversen, 1982; Ljungberg & Ungerstedt, 1976; Marshall, Berrios & Sawyer,
1980). Evidence exists also that lesions of intralaminar thalamic nuclei
(Orem, Schlag-Rey & Schlag, 1973) and of some parts of the brain stem may
produce neglect (Sprague, Chambers & Stellar, 1961; Watson, Heilman, Miller
& King, 1974).

In this chapter we will discuss the theoretical basis of these theories
and the neural circuits that according to the various theories subserve the
attentional functions.

Intensive Attention and Neglect

Figure 1 schematically represents the circuits which mediate the
attentional processes according to the intensive attention theory of
neglect. The diagram is based essentially on the ideas of Heilman and his
coworkers (Heilman & Watson, 1977; Heilman et al., 1985). In the upper part
of the figure two boxes represent the two cerebral hemispheres. Each of them
contains several areas. Squares indicate sensory areas, triangles motor
areas and circles associations areas. According to Heilman and his
coworkers (Heilman & Watson, 1977; Heilman et al., 1985) some of the
association areas like the frontal eye field, the inferior parietal lobule

and the cingulate gyrus evaluate the significance and the novelty of the stimuli. When the stimulus analysis performed in these areas meets certain requisites, the reticular formation ipsilateral to them is activated. This activation facilitates the ipsilateral hemisphere. A lesion of any of the association areas involved in the circuit or of the reticular formation produces neglect because the hemisphere ipsilateral to the lesion becomes hypoactive and unable to process properly sensory information.

The great asset of this theory is that it can easily explain the fact that lesions in many different areas produce apparently similar disturbances. The reticular formation acts as a link between cortical areas involved in attention and the rest of the cortex and therefore lesions of these areas as well as that of the reticular formation will produce the same deficits. There are however some difficulties with this theory.

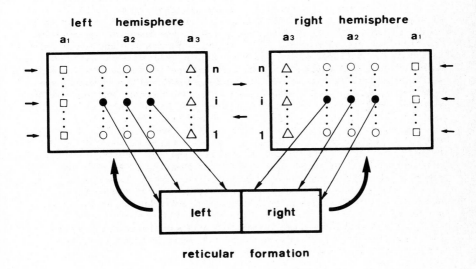

Figure 1
Schematic representation of the circuit which mediates spatial attention according to the intensive attention theory of neglect. Squares indicate sensory areas, triangles motor areas and circles association areas. Filled circles represent the areas involved in attentional processes. Their activation, due to novel or interesting stimuli contralaterally presented, triggers the reticular formation which in turn facilitates the ipsilateral hemisphere. For other explanations see text.

First, it is hard to believe that a lesion in one of many areas projecting to the reticular formation is sufficient to determine the inactivation of this structure and, as a consequence, the global hypoactivity of one hemisphere. The reticular formation receives so many afferents from subcortical pathways and centers that to assign to three cortical areas a crucial role in controlling its activity appears to be a post-hoc conceptual construction rather than an anatomical fact. Second, the intensive attention theory predicts (see Fig. 1) that neglect should be global, polymodal and that it should involve personal and extrapersonal space. We will show later that this claim is not supported by the experimental findings. Third, and most important, the intensive theory predicts that the most severe forms of neglect should be those consequent to a lesion of the reticular formation since the activity of this structure is responsible for the intensive aspects of attention. Although Watson and his coworkers (Watson, Heilman, Miller & King, 1974) have reported some data in this direction, a very detailed study performed by Sprague et al. (1961) on the effect of midbrain lesions on cats' behavior allows one to disprove this prediction.

Sprague and his associates placed well controlled lesion in the lateral part of the midbrain in correspondence to the lemniscal region, and in the central part of it in correspondence with midbrain reticular formation. Animals with lateral lesions sparing the reticular formation presented marked tactile, auditory, proprioceptive, gustatory as well as visual and olfactory deficits. They showed a generalized, but largely unadaptive and unlocalized arousal even to strong stimulation. They were mute, lacked facial expression and did not show any sign of affect. Much of their motor activity consisted of an aimless stereotyped wandering. In contrast, animals with large reticular lesion showed no spatial attention deficits. They were drowsy, presented a synchronized EEG and remained sluggish for over a month. The authors' conclusion was that "a large reticular lesion sparing the lemnisci results in an animal whose general behavior is much like that of a normal cat except for chronic hypokinesia or drowsiness". In other words a reticular formation lesion produces an arousal deficit, but not a deficit in the capacity of orienting attention.

The possibility of dissociate neglect from hypoactivity of one hemisphere has been recently demonstrated by Deuel, Collins & Caston (1980) using the deoxyglucose method. They found that monkeys showing hemineglect following a frontal lesion had a striking decrease in the deoxyglucose uptake in several subcortical structures but not in the cortical areas ipsilateral to the lesion. Furthermore, among the subcortical structures, some, as for example the sensory thalamus, were normal. It is obvious that these data are not compatible with any intensive attention theory of neglect. If indeed the brain stem facilitatory systems were crucially involved in the neglect syndrome one should expect a global decrease in the activity of the cerebral hemisphere ipsilateral to the lesion. This decrease was not found.

In conclusion, the intensive attention hypothesis has at present essentially a historical interest. It has had the enormous merit of stressing the importance of attention in the neglect syndromes when other hypotheses were more popular (see Heilman & Watson, 1977). The mechanisms however it proposes does not explain the deficits observed in hemineglect.

Selective Attention and Neglect: The Master Center Hypothesis

Once established that hemineglect cannot be explained by a reduced activity of one hemisphere the most likely hypothesis on its genesis is that it is related to a deficit of selective attention. Selective attention is usually thought of as a function above and beyond those related to the analysis of sensory information and the programming of motor acts. Thus it is not surprising that it is also usually postulated that the mechanisms responsible for spatial attention are located outside the circuits responsible for sensory and motor functions. In its simplest version the theory goes as follows: a) there is a cerebral center whose function is to render vivid certain parts of the extrapersonal or personal space; b) in man, this center is located in the right parietal lobe.

Although rather naïve and reminiscent of frenological localizations of functions, this interpretation is probably the most popular among clinical neurologists (cf. De Renzi, 1982; Vallar & Perani, 1986). There is one initial difficulty with this theory. Lesions of the right hemisphere, the putative attention master center, produce a neglect of the left hemispace, but leave the capacity to move attention in the right hemispace, within certain limits, normal. This obviously implies that movements of attention in the right hemispace can be controlled by a center different from that of the right parietal lobe. This difficulty however can be overcome. Bilateral parietal lesions produce very severe bilateral attentional deficits as in the case of the Balint syndrome (see De Renzi, 1982). It is therefore conceivable that the attentional center is formed by two moieties located respectively in the two parietal lobes. The right moiety is dominant and controls the attention movements bilaterally, the left one, possibly because of the expansion of language centers in this hemisphere, plays a minor role and can control the attention movements only in the contralateral space.

The large popularity of the master center idea stems from the fact that it seems to explain two very common neurological observations in a parsimonious way: a) the association in the vast majority of the cases of a severe clinical neglect with a right parietal lesion; b) the global, polysensory character of many cases of neglect. Taken together these two observations seem to indicate that an anatomical center for shifting attention does exist and that it is localized in the right parietal lobe.

The correctness of these observations is beyond any doubts, but their relevance for the understanding of neglect is not so obvious. In all animals in which experimental lesions have been made, neglect has been obtained also following damage to areas other than the inferior parietal lobule. The claim that, as far as spatial attention is concerned, man is radically different from all other animals including primates, is a very daring conclusion. Especially so if one considers that there are several case reports of neglect also in man following lesions of frontal lobe or subcortical structures (see references in Heilman et al., 1985). Any theory therefore that maintains that parietal lobe is the site of the central attentional mechanism should face the dilemma of either to discard all the reports of non-parietal neglect as artefacts or to admit that a certain portion of human population has a brain organization more similar to that of inferior primates than to the other human beings. Both solutions seem to be unacceptable.

While the frequent association of neglect with a parietal lesion is by no means a conclusive evidence in favor of a master center of attention, nevertheless this association deserves some comments. In general, the frequency with which a given cerebral area is hit by a pathological lesion has no relation with its functional properties but depends on factors intrinsic to the pathology itself. In the case of vascular injuries, for example, the frequency of lesions in certain cerebral districts will depend on the type of vascularization proper to the region, the richness of anastomoses present in it, and so on. Thus, if, let us say, the parietal lobe and the frontal eye field are equally important in shifting attention, but for vascular reasons, the parietal lobe is hit more frequently than the frontal lobe, there is no doubt that the parietal neglect will be much more frequent than frontal neglect. Any conclusion however about the importance of these two areas in attention will be completely arbitrary.

There is another aspect of the association between neglect and parietal lesions which requires comment. Although each cortical area, probably with no exception in the case of neocortex, receives a thalamic input, there is little doubt that the main stream of sensory information flows from the retrorolandic areas to the prerolandic areas. Given this, it should follow that large lesions of the parietal lobe, as those observed in neglect patients, have two effects. First, by destroying the neural circuits of the parietal lobe, they produce deficits due to the lack of the intrinsic activity of this lobe, second, by disconnecting the frontal lobe from the information coming from the posterior areas, they impair the function of this lobe. Frontal lesions of a comparable extent must have much less severe effects. They destroy the intrinsic frontal lobe circuits, but leave reasonably intact those of the parietal lobe. Thus it is not surprising that parietal lesions produce neglect more frequently and of greater severity than frontal lesions.

Selective Attention and Neglect: The Single Circuit Hypothesis

As shown above a theory of neglect which postulates an anatomical center controlling spatial attention is not supported by empirical facts. The tenet however that spatial attention is an independent, supramodal function can be reformulated by assuming that attention is controlled by a circuit including several brain areas. This idea has been recently developed with great ingenuity by Mesulam (1981).

Mesulam, in contrast with the anatomical single center theory admits that also in man hemineglect can occur after lesions outside parietal lobe. He surmises however that in primates cortical areas are particularly important in directing attention. As a consequence he does not include subcortical centers in the attentional circuit which is exclusively cortical. This circuit is formed by the frontal eye field, the posterior parietal lobe and the cingulate cortex. The reticular formation is thought of as an aspecific facilitatory system in line with the classical notion of Moruzzi and Magoun (1949). Figure 2, upper part, shows the circuit diagram of spatial attention according to this theory.

The lower part of the figure illustrates what Mesulam calls the network approach to the cortical localization of complex functions. According to this approach certain complex functions, like spatial attention, result from the interaction of several distinct regions, none of which is exclusively devoted to that function. As far as the spatial attention is concerned, the frontal eye field (Box 1), the parietal cortex (Box 2) and the cingulate cortex (Box 3) all contain cortical columns (indicated with a) involved in this function. Each of these areas has also other columns responsible for other complex functions (b, c, d). The presence of these additional columns explain why, besides hemineglect, other deficits may emerge after lesion of one of these areas. For example, anosognosia, dressing apraxia and constructional apraxia frequently occur after a right parietal lesion. These disturbances should be due to damage of columns of the parietal lobe physically adjacent to those mediating spatial attention but functionally independent of them.

The selective attention hypothesis as formulated by Mesulam seems to give a reasonable anatomical basis to the neglect phenomena. However it has two weak points: first, it is not clear how the attentional circuit interacts with the circuits which process sensory information and organize the movements. The intensive attention hypothesis overcame this difficulty by indicating in the reticular formation the center that controls the attentional state of the brain. Second, the Mesulam version of the selective attention hypothesis admits the existence of a single attentional circuit. In the next section we will show that there is strong evidence against this assumption.

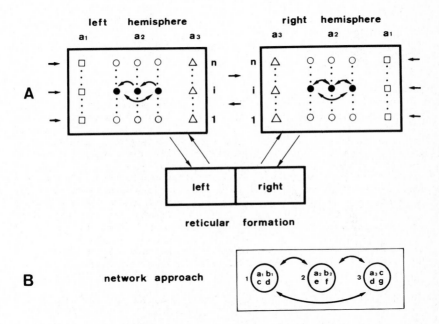

Figure 2
A: Schematic representation of the circuit which mediates spatial attention according to the attentional circuit theory of neglect (single circuit version). All conventions as in Figure 1. Filled circles represent frontal, parietal and limbic areas involved in selective attention. For other explanations see text.
B: Network approach to localization of selective attention. Circles represent the association areas involved in spatial attention. Each area contains independent columns (indicated by letters) responsible for complex psychological functions. Spatial attention (column a) is represented in all areas. Other complex functions are represented in one or two areas (columns b to g).

Selective Attention and Atypical Cases of Neglect
a) Vertical neglects

There are cases of neglect in which attentional deficits are present and yet their distribution in space is different from that observed in the classical neglect syndrome following right parietal lobe injury in the man or frontal eye field lesion in the monkey. we will refer to these cases as atypical neglect. A survey of some of them will show how the idea of a single attentional circuit is unsatisfactory and how spatial attention is closely linked with the organization of movement in space.

Atypical neglect is observed in cats after sagittal section of tectal commissures. Some years ago in a study of interocular transfer of visual information, Berlucchi, Buchtel & Leporé (1978) reported that animals with a lesion of the midbrain commissures have difficulty in detecting stimuli moved above their head. More recently the visual behavior of animals with such a lesion were reexamined by Matelli, Olivieri, Saccani & Rizzolatti (1983). The animals were neurologically tested and their visual field was mapped using a special perimeter which allowed the experimenters to test points located above and below the horizontal meridian.

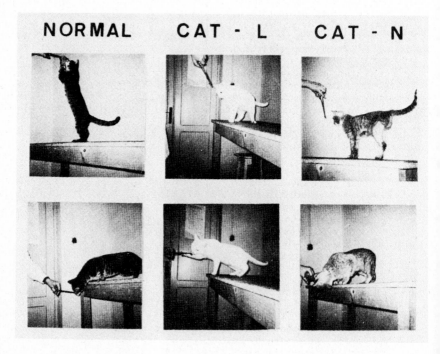

Figure 3
Responses of normal and commissurotomized animals to stimuli presented in the upper and lower visual space. Note the head posture of the operated animals and their lack of response to food in the upper space (from Matelli et al., 1983).

All animals with midbrain commissure lesions showed motor and attentional deficits. Motor deficits consisted in a marked reduction or even absence of vertical eye movements and in an abnormal posture of the head that was kept slightly ventroflexed (Figure 3, upper part, Cat L and Cat N). At variance with normal cats, commissurotomized animals never looked up and explored the space above their head. Visual stimuli presented in the upper visual space were neglected, whereas those in the lower space were responded to rapidly. This different reactivity to stimulus location is illustrated in Figure 3, where is also shown, for comparison, the behavior of a normal cat tested in the same way.

The capacity to follow objects along the vertical plane was also impaired. When a piece of food was moved in an upward direction starting from the lower field, the animal followed it until approximately the head midplane. Then the head movement stopped and the cat appeared to ignore where the food was. When the food was moved downwards starting from the upper visual field the animal had a startling reaction as soon as the food crossed the head midplane; until that moment the animal appeared to be completely unaware of the stimulus.

The results of a formal testing of upper and lower visual space in one cat with a complete section of tectal commissure is shown in Figure 4. The testing was done by conditioning the animal to fixate the center of a perimeter and by presenting a small piece of food either at this point (control trials) or at the periphery (test trials). The animal was rewarded when he walked straight to the center of the perimeter in case of control trials or towards the peripheral stimulus in case of test trials. The test showed a marked upper visual space deficit. The deficit was present both when the score was based on actual reaching of the food (A) or on the presence of an orienting response even if not followed by the approach to the stimulus (B). Similar results were obtained in all animals with a complete tectal lesion. The deficit was long lasting although some recovery was observed with time.

The animals in which the lesion of the tectal commissure was incomplete showed the same symptoms as those with a complete section but recovered rather rapidly, in about two weeks. In two animals the lesion was placed more rostrally and involved the posterior commissure and the rostral part of the intertectal commissure. These animals showed a behavior different from those with intertectal lesion. There was no ventral flexion of the head and no tendency to explore the lower space. In contrast the head was kept dorsiflexed and there was a preference for the stimuli presented in the upper space. Downwards tracking head movements were slow and less accurate than those upwards. When two stimuli were simultaneously moved in opposite directions the animals constantly followed that directed upwards. Formal testing of visual field performed in one animal showed a normal performance in the upper visual field and along the horizontal meridian. Correct responses in the lower field were less than 60%. Both animals recovered rather rapidly.

Modifications of the head posture after commissural lesions are in good agreement with the data of Hess and his coworkers (Hess, 1954; Hess, Burgi & Bucher, 1946). According to Hess (see also Hassler, 1972) there are two regions in the midbrain particularly involved in the control of head movements. The first, related to head elevation, has its center in correspondence to the nucleus praestitialis (rostral part of the nucleus interstitialis of Cajal) and comprises the system of fibers descending from it and the reticular neurons located along their course. Electrical stimulation of this system elicits raising of the head, whereas its destruction causes a head dorsiflexion. The second midbrain region

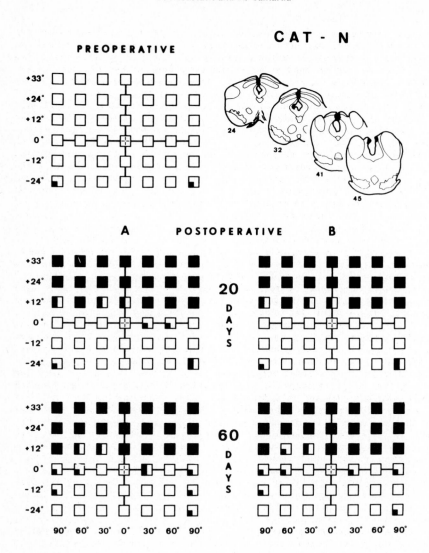

Figure 4
Visual field chart before and after the midbrain commissure section.
<u>Right upper side of the figure</u> : reconstruction of the midbrain lesion.
The dark area indicates the extent of the lesion. <u>Left upper side and
remainder of the figure</u> : preoperative and postoperative visual
fields. In each visual field chart a square indicates a visual field
point that has been tested; the square with the cross inside represents
the fixation point. Empty squares, percentage of correct responses
greater than 75%; filled squares, correct responses less than 25%;
half-filled squares, correct responses between 25% and 50%;
quarter-filled squares, correct responses between 50% and 75%. A,
orienting responses; B, reaching responses.

controlling head movements includes the nucleus of posterior commissure and its ascending and descending projections, most of which pass through the posterior commissure. Stimulation of the nuclei of the posterior commissure elicits lowering of head and foretrunk, whereas its destruction causes dorsiflexion of head, and a peculiar goose-like walking. If one accepts the notion that vertical head movements require bilateral activation of the midbrain centers analogous to that necessary for vertical eye movements (Bender, 1960; Pasik, Pasik & Bender, 1969), the data of Matelli et al. can be easily accounted for by admitting that the two systems of fibers which control vertical head movements cross midline in two different points. Precisely the system responsible for head lowering crosses midline rostrally in correspondence of the posterior commissure and possibly of the rostral part of the intertectal commissure, whereas the system responsible for head elevation crosses it more caudally in the tectal commissure. The two systems appear to be antagonist and a lesion of one of them determines the prevalence of the other.

The interest of these findings for neglect is twofold. First, it indicates that an attentional deficit can be obtained with a lesion of centers whose primary role is that of controlling head and eye movements; second, it shows that different types of motor deficits are associated with different types of attentional deficits and the latter are congruent with the former. Evidence obtained in patients affected by progressive supranuclear palsy points out that this association is not proper only of animals byt may occur also in man.

Patients with progressive supranuclear palsy show many neurological deficits among which a partial or total incapacity to move the eyes vertically, especially downwards, and a slight dorsiflexion of the head (see Steele, Richardson & Olszewski, 1964). These symptoms are accompanied by behavior abnormalities very likely caused by a difficulty of shifting attention toward lower space. Rafal and Grimm (1981), for example, reported that patients that are able to look down on command fumble with their meal looking straight again. They have problems with putting on their shoes or with tying shoe laces. Frequently they stumble over objects in their path. Recently Camarda (unpublished observations) studied a patient with progressive supranuclear palsy whose main deficits were a slight global akinesia, a gait disturbance, an abnormal posture of the head and a paralysis of downwards directed vertical eye movements. This patient, when tested with one stimulus at a time, did not show any obvious attentional defect. However when two stimuli were simultaneously presented one in his upper field, the other in his lower field, he reported of seeing only the upper one. CT scan showed, beside a zone of hypodensity in the pes pedunculi, a marked hypodensity in correspondence of the rostral pole of the superior colliculi at the level of their midline. The analogy between these data and the syndrome obtained in the cat following midbrain lesion, seems evident.

A formal proof that patients with progressive supranuclear palsy have attentional deficits has been provided by Posner and his coworkers (Posner, Cohen & Rafal, 1982). They used the following experimental procedure. The patients were instructed to respond as fast as possible (manual reaction time) to stimuli presented either on one side or on the other of a fixation point, without moving their eyes. A peripheral cue preceded the target stimulus and indicated a high probability (80%) of target occurence on that side. The trials in which the cue and the target were congruent were referred to as valid trials, those in which they were not congruent were referred to as invalid trials. The cue was presented for 300 msec followed by target occurring at different time intervals after the cue onset. Stimuli were presented in the vertical and horizontal dimension.

The results showed that patients with progressive supranuclear palsy
can orient rapidly in the horizontal direction. An advantage of the cued
side was present already at 50 msec and remained present over the entire
interval range. In contrast, in the vertical direction there was no
difference between the valid and invalid trials until 1000 sec after the
cue. So it was clear that the tested patients can orient in all directions.
However they needed a longer time when they had to shift attention "in the
direction in which saccades were most affected" (Posner et al., 1982).

b) Personal and peripersonal neglect

Another type of neglect in which the attentional deficit has a
different pattern from the one commonly observed following parietal lobe
lesion in man is that observed in the monkey after a lesion of inferior area 6
(Rizzolatti et al., 1983). Figure 5 (upper right corner) shows a lateral

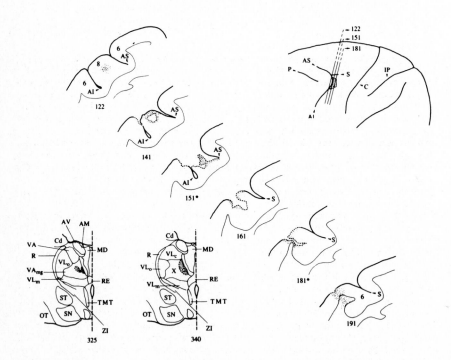

Figure 5

Reconstruction of the cortical lesion and of the thalamic degeneration
in one monkey with personal and peripersonal neglect. The histological
sections are coronal. They were progressively numbered and the
respective number is shown near each section. Dotted areas = denervated
cortex, white matter and thalamic degeneration. AS = arcuate superior.
AI = arcuate inferior. C = central. MD = nucleus medialis dorsalis. SP =
intraparietal. P = principalis. X = nucleus X of Olszewski (From
Rizzolatti et al., 1983).

view of a monkey brain. Inferior area 6 is the rostral part of agranular frontal cortex lying lateral to the spur of the arcuate sulcus. This part of area 6 can be distinguished from the upper part (medial to the spur) for its cytoarchitectonic, connectional and enzymatic properties (see Matelli, Camarda, Glickstein & Rizzolatti, 1986).

In a group of monkeys Rizzolatti et al. (1983) placed small lesions, like that illustred in Figure 5, to inferior area 6. The lesion did not invade the rostrally located frontal eye field as demonstrated by the reconstruction of the cortical damage and thalamic degeneration. The animal before and after lesion underwent a general neurological examination. In addition, the animal's responses to visual stimuli located outside its reach (far space), within the reach of its arm (distant peripersonal space) and around its mouth (pericutaneous buccal space) were studied with particular care. The testing was done: a) by moving a piece of food held by a pair of forceps at different distances from the animal; b) by moving simultaneously two pieces of food. The two pieces were kept initially close one to another, then, when the animal fixated them, they were moved laterally in opposite directions; c) by presenting abruptly a piece of food peripherally when the animal was fixating another one centrally located; d) by presenting frightening stimuli.

The first post-surgery testing was performed the first day after the operation. The monkey's behavior in its home cage was indistinguishable from its behavior before the operation except for a less frequent use of the right hand. When tested in a primate chair the animal did not show any obvious visual deficit for stimuli presented in the far space and in the distant peripersonal space. Stimuli on right or left sides were immediately detected and the presentation of two simultaneous stimuli, one ipsilateral, the other contralateral to the lesion did not produce any side preference. When food stimuli were introduced in distant peripersonal space the monkey consistently reached for them using the hand ipsilateral to the lesion. Only when this hand was blocked, the animal, although reluctantly, employed the contralateral arm. There was no misreaching, but movements of this arm were somewhat slower than those of the normal arm.

The most striking deficit was observed in the pericutaneous space around the mouth. When the animal was fixating a central stimulus, the introduction of a piece of food ipsilateral to the lesion produced, as in normal animals, an immediate mouth grasping response; the same stimulus shown contralaterally was ignored. Similarly, a rapid movement of a stimulus from the center of the mouth to the contralateral side did not elicit any reaction. When a stimulus was moved slowly from a central position near the mouth to the neglected side, the animal appeared to be aware of the stimulus and tended to follow it. However it had great difficulty in organizing the appropriate head and mouth movements necessary for grasping it. Most commonly the animal slowly opened its mouth and followed the stimulus with the mouth open but without trying to take the object. When lateral grasping occurred, it was executed in a stereotyped way without the richness of buccal and facial movements observed on the other side.

Deficits similar to those demonstrated with visual stimuli were present when the hemiface and especially the perioral region contralateral to the lesion was stimulated with tactile stimuli. Stimulation of the lips with food or other stimuli produced either no response or the opening of the mouth not accompanied by any attempt to bite. Similarly the raising of the corner of the lips as well as the other facial movements which normally accompany food grasping with the mouth were absent. Licking movements could not be elicited by wetting the contralateral lip with water or juice; a similar stimulation promptly evoked the response on the ipsilateral side. Blinking to threatening stimuli moved towards the contralateral hemiface was absent. Similarly there was no sign of fear or rage. In contrast, facial movements and a rich emotional response were easily elicited by threatening stimuli presented far from the animal. The eye movements which were hard to elicit with tactile or peribuccal stimuli, were easily triggered with stimuli presented far from the monkey.

There was a marked and rather fast recovery with time. Sixty days after the operation the only residual deficits were the preference in using the hand ipsilateral to the lesion and a constant turning, in the test with two peribuccal stimuli, towards the one ipsilateral to the lesion.

There are three aspects of these findings that are of particular interest. First, the presence of a dissociation between the capacity to shift attention in the far space and the capacity to do it in the personal and peripersonal space. The same monkey which reacted properly to a glove presented contralateral to the lesion at a distance of one meter, neglected a menacing stimulus near its face.

Second, as in the vertical neglect, there was a congruence between attentional ad motor deficits. In monkeys with area 6 lesions the attentional deficits did not include the far space and, on the motor side, there was no eye movement deficits. The attention deficit concerned the space within which stimuli can be reached, grasped and manipulated with hands and mouth. In accordance with the distribution of the attentional deficit the motor deficit comprised head-mouth movements and to a lower degree arm-hand movements. It is hard to say why the arm-hand movements were less impaired that one could expect from the electrophysiological data on this area (see Godschalk, Lemon, Nijs & Kuypers, 1981; Rizzolatti, Scandolara, Gentilucci & Camarda, 1981a; Rizzolatti, Scandolara, Matelli & Gentilucci, 1981b, c). Several interpretation can be offered on this point (see Rizzolatti et al., 1983). What is important here, however, is that in accordance with the greater severity of deficits of facial and mouth movements, there was also a greater deficit in attention to peribuccal space than to distant peripersonal space.

Third, the anatomical site of the lesion was outside the centers normally considered crucial for directing attention. The lesion was within a premotor area, that is in an area which organizes body movements and is strictly connected with area 4. We do not believe that this association between neglect and the lesion of a premotor area is an odd finding. On the contrary, this association may be a clue for a better understanding of the neglect syndrome.

c) Extrapersonal neglect

The observation that in the monkey a unilateral lobe excision rostral to the granular frontal cortex produces a contralateral neglect is very old. At the end of the last century Bianchi (1895) reported that following such a lesion monkeys presented rotatory movements to the side of the lesion and a visual disturbance that appeared as a contralateral hemianopia. Those findings were confirmed by Kennard (Kennard & Ectors, 1938; Kennard, 1939) who described in addition to visual disturbances a deficit in responding to cutaneous stimulation of the contralateral body. A similar observation was made by Welch and Stuteville (1958) after a lesion placed in the depth of the arcuate sulcus. More recently, Latto and Cowey (1971a, b) in a very careful study of monkey's deficits following lesions localized to the frontal eye field failed to confirm the somatosensory neglect, whereas they showed, in addition to the visual attention deficit, oculomotor disturbances.

Rizzolatti et al. (1983) tested two monkeys with a unilateral lesion of the frontal eye field employing the same testing procedure used in their area 6 study. In these monkeys spontaneous ocular saccades and head movements towards the side contralateral to the lesion were rare. Furthermore when a visual stimulus, presented in the neglected space, evoked a saccade, the fixation was short-lasting and the eyes returned immediately to the resting position. Stimuli presented in the far space contralateral to the lesion were neglected. This was particularly clear when the animal's attention was already engaged on another stimulus; in this case a stimulus in the ipsilateral field was responded to, while a contralateral one was neglected. When two stimuli were simultaneously moved from a central position towards right or left, the contralateral one was always preferred.

In sharp contrast with the behavior of monkeys with area 6 lesion, the tactile stimulation of the mouth with a piece of food produced a brisk grasping response. Similarly, the presentation of a stimulus in the peribuccal space evoked a precise mouth grasp movement also on the side contralateral to the lesion. The movement was accompanied by the normal pattern of facial muscle contractions. When two stimuli were moved in the space around the mouth, in one animal the ipsilateral stimulus was usually preferred, in the other no side preference was observed. Thus there is little doubt that after a frontal eye field lesion the animal can attend to the personal space. Furthermore it appears that the peripersonal space is only moderatly affected.

Prompted by these findings Gentilucci, Gentilini, Porro, Matelli & Rizzolatti (unpublished observations) tested two additional monkeys with frontal eye field lesions in a more formal situation. The animals were conditioned to perform two tasks originally devised by Wurtz (1969). In the first one – fixation task – the animal has to detect the dimming of a LED located in front of it and, in order to get a reward, to release a lever during the dimming. In the second one – saccade task – the central LED was turned off after a fixed time interval and, simultaneously, another light was turned on. The second light dimmed after a variable interval and, as in the fixation task, the animal had to release the bar during the dimming in order to be rewarded. Fixation trials and saccade trials were intermixed. Eye movements were recorded using the magnetic search coil technique.

The testing was done using three perimeters, located at the distance of 10, 30 and 150 cm from the monkey. Each perimeter carried rows of LEDs that permitted the testing of the upper, lower, right and left sectors of the visual field. In each perimeter the set of LEDs was located at the same angular distance from the center.

In both animals the frontal eye field lesion was unilateral and restricted to the lower (lateral) part of it. The purpose of a limited lesion was that of destroying the sector of frontal eye field that receives visual input, while sparing that related to the acoustical modality (Barbas & Mesulam, 1981). This was done in order to interfere as little as possible with the capacity of the animal to make saccades. One of the animals used in the experiment underwent, several months before the frontal eye field excision, an ablation of the rostral part of inferior parietal lobule (area 7b) and a very restricted lesion of postarcuate cortex. Both animals preoperatively performed quite well on all three perimeters.

The capacity to execute both the fixation and the saccade task was not impaired by the lesion. However, the latency of eye movements towards stimuli in the contralateral field increased in both animals. In the animal with a previous fronto-parietal lesion this increase concerned near and far stimuli, but the impairment was significantly greater for far stimuli. In the second animal only the latency to far stimuli increased.

Taken together these data indicate that even in the case of classical, "typical" neglect the attentional deficit is not global. The disturbance after frontal eye field lesion appears to concern essentially the far space.

Results congruent with this point of view can be also found in cases of human neglect. In a recent study Bisiach and his coworkers (Bisiach, Perani, Vallar & Berti, 1986) assessed the presence of personal and extrapersonal neglect in a large number of right brain-damaged patients. The extrapersonal neglect was tested by requiring the patients to cross circles on a sheet of paper. The personal neglect was assessed by pointing to the patient's right hand (that on the normal side) and by ordering him to touch with this hand the other one (that on the neglected side). As one can expect in most patients both extrapersonal and personal neglect was present. However out of 27 cases showing a very severe extrapersonal neglect, 9 had no deficit at all in the personal space. Similarly out of 6 cases with marked personal neglect one was free of any disturbance in the extrapersonal space. The dissociation between extrapersonal and personal space was confirmed by the fact that in a large number of patients the severity of the two deficits did not correlate. Thus, in good agreement with animal studies, also in man, the neural substrates controlling attention in the personal and extrapersonal space are not the same.

It is interesting to note here the frequent presence of oculomotor disturbances in human neglect (see Schott, Jeannerod & Zahin, 1966). These deficits cannot be a consequence of the attentional deficit since the conjugate gaze paralysis in stroke patients is much more frequent after right hemisphere injury (the side that produces more frequently neglect in humans) than after the left hemisphere injury (De Renzi, Colombo, Faglioni & Gibertoni, 1982). These findings indicate the close relations between the eye movement mechanisms and extrapersonal attention in the classical parietal lobe neglect.

Selective Attention: A Distributed System

In primary visual areas the location of stimuli in space is coded according to a retinotopic system of coordinates. There is little doubt however that the organization of movements in space requires a system of coordinates independent of the retina. Evidence for this comes from the common experience that movements of the eyes, head or arms towards a target can be executed without visual stimuli, for example in darkness to a remembered position or to auditory stimuli. Experimentally, the importance of spatial coordinates can be demonstrated by presenting tachistoscopically two lights in sequence and by instructing the subjects to make sequential saccades towards them (Hallet & Lightstone, 1976; Mays & Sparks, 1980). Suppose that the two lights are respectively 5° and 10° on the right of a fixation point and the instruction is to make the first saccade to the more peripheral light, the second saccade to the less peripheral light. If the duration of the lights is short they will stimulate the retina at the two eccentricities corresponding to the distance between their locations and the fixation point. If the motor commands were coded in retinal terms the subject after the first saccade to the 10° stimulus should execute another one 5° further to the right, since the retinal information indicates a point 5° on the right of the fixation point. Yet the experiment shows that subjects are able to execute the task. This in spite of the fact that the "go to left" order should be issued, according to the retinotopical rules, by the brain half that has never seen the light. It is obvious that even for such a simple task the visual information must be translated from retinal to spatial coordinates.

A stage therefore exists where visual stimuli are coded in spatial

terms and it is clear that those cortical areas and subcortical centers that
organize movements must use this code of reference. One might argue that all
systems involved in the organization of movements are under control of a

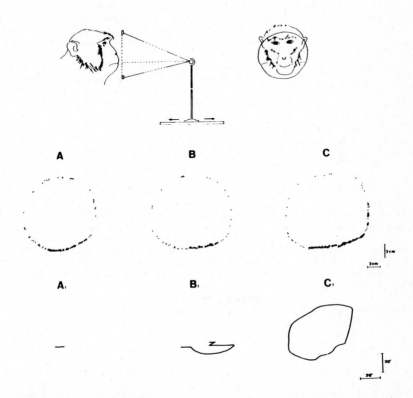

Figure 6
Study of a soma-related visually responsive neuron. <u>Upper row</u> (<u>left
side</u>): schematic drawing of the device used for stimulus presentation;
(<u>right side</u>): stimulus trajectory in respect to the animal's face.
<u>Middle row</u>: Neuron's responses in relation to the stimulus position.
the stimulus was moved circularly around the animal's face in a frontal
plane. The stimulus trajectory was recorded on a X-Y storage
oscilloscope and the brightness of the oscilloscope beam was
intensified in correspondence with the occurrence of action
potentials. Each dot represents one action potential. Note the
concentration of the dots in the lower part of the trajectory. Dots in
the upper part of it are due to the neuron's spontaneous activity. <u>Lower
row</u>: In A1, B1 and C1 are shown the X-Y records of the movements of the
right eye during the stimulus presentation A, B and C, respectively.
Given the non-linearity of the EOG when the eyes are in strongly
eccentric positions, the record indicates the eye excursion only
approximately. Note the lack of correlation between eye position and
the neuron's discharge (From Gentilucci et al., 1983).

single map which provides spatial information to the premotor system. This possibility is not supported by neurophysiological data. Neurons coding visual information in spatial terms have been described in inferior area 6 (Gentilucci, Scandolara, Pigarev & Rizzolatti, 1983), in area 7b (Leinonen & Nyman, 1979; Leinonen, Hyvarinen, Nyman & Linnankowski, 1979), in area 7a (Mountcastle, Lynch, Georgopoulos, Sakata & Acuna, 1975; Lynch, Mountcastle, Talbot & Yin, 1977; Sakata, 1980) and in the intralaminar thalamic nuclei (Schlag, Schlag-Rey, Peck and Joseph, 1980). It is very likely that the mechanisms by which the location in space is computed vary in different systems. In those primarily involved in extrapersonal space exploration and in programming eye movements the computation is based on information on position of the eyes in orbit and the part of the retina that is stimulated. Such a mechanism has been proposed for the fixation neurons described in the monkey's parietal lobe (Mountcastle et al., 1975; Lynch et al., 1977; Sakata, Shibutani & Kawano, 1980) and for some neurons of the cat's intralaminar thalamic nuclei (Schlag et al., 1980). A different mechanism is very likely to be responsible for the spatial properties of neurons involved in programming movements in the peripersonal space. In both area 6 and 7b, bimodal neurons have been found which respond to somatosensory and visual stimuli. In these neurons the somatosensory receptive field and the visually responsive spatial region are in register and the visually responsive region remains in the same, body-related, position irrespective of the eye location. Figure 6 shows one of these soma-related neurons recorded from inferior area 6 of the monkey. This neuron had a bilateral tactile receptive field extending from the lower lip to the chin. Visual responses were evoked by moving stimuli in the space around the tactile field. One can see that, regardless of eye position, the response (dots intensifying the stimulus trajectory) is always concentrated in the lower part of the visual space. Note that this occurred also when the animal tracked the stimulus and therefore when the stimulus position in respect to the retina remained relatively fixed. It is possible that soma-related neurons like that in Figure 6 signal the spatial location of the stimulus by comparing the position of visual stimulus with the vision of a body part or with the knowledge of its position based on proprioception. Regardless of the physiological mechanisms involved in the genesis of spatial neurons, the data reviewed in this section indicate that the organization of movement implies spatial maps and that neurons coding the position of stimuli in space are distributed in various independent centers. We propose that the capacity of shifting attention is due to the activity of those areas which program motor plans in a spatial framework. This conception is radically different from that of a single attentional circuit because it conceives spatial attention not as a supraordinate function controlling the activity of the brain as a whole, but as a property intrinsically linked to the premotor activity and distributed among various cerebral centers. In other words, spatial attention is a modular vertical function present in several independent circuits.

A Premotor Theory of Spatial Attention

It is generally accepted that attention may be attracted in a passive, effortless way by stimuli endowed with certain characteristics (passive attention) or it may be actively directed by the individuals (active attention). During neglect these two aspects of attention are impaired. A theory of spatial attention should therefore take into account both the active and passive attention phenomena.

According to the premotor theory of spatial attention (see for a former version Rizzolatti, 1983), when a stimulus endowed with attentional properties (Titchner, 1966; Berlyne, 1960, 1970) is presented, it triggers neurons which plan action in space. These neurons are present in various circuits and, according to stimulus location, several circuits controlling the same space sector are activated. Stimuli, for example, presented in the extrapersonal space may activate simultaneously cortical and midbrain circuits, controlling similar or congruent movements. In contrast, circuits whose function is to organize other types of movements, or movements of the same effectors in other directions will be not activated or even inhibited. The setting of a motor plan in a given circuit is accompanied by "taking possession by the mind, in a clear and vivid form" (James, 1950) of the space sector where the motor plan will be implemented, that is by an attention shift towards this space sector.

A crucial question, at this point, is why the increase of activity of premotor neurons should result in attention towards the space sector controlled by these neurons. One may argue that a new or interesting stimulus should simply elicit a motor reaction towards the stimulus. This type of close link between stimulus and response is present in lower vertebrates. The stereotyped response of a toad to a worm or a worm-like stimulus (see Ewert, 1979), is an example of such a rigid stimulus-response relationship. In higher mammals, however, the increase of encephalization has freed, to a large extent, the individuals from fixed reactions (see Jerison and his concept of representation, 1973; 1985). The motor plan elicited by the stimulus activates the representation of the space sector where the plan will be transformed into action. This representation allows the individuals to choose whether to respond or not and, in case of response, to select the response which is the most adequate.

The next question concerns the mechanisms by which activation of premotor neurons produces an increase of attention in a certain space region. The answer to this question can obviously be only hypothetical. Some solutions however can be advanced.

A possible way to solve the problem is to postulate that the world perception does not depend on the activity of one or few retrolandic areas, but on the activity of all areas where space is coded. As reviewed above, neurons with spatial properties are present not only in the inferior parietal lobe, but also in the frontal lobe, in the thalamus and possibly in other areas. Thus the activation of a given premotor area should give relevance to the space controlled by it and result therefore in a greater attention to that part of space.

Another, closely related solution of the problem, is that of postulating inhibitory interactions between premotor areas controlling different motor plans. Probably the best evidence in favor of the existence of these interactions is the so-called "Sprague effect" (Sprague, 1966). This effect consists in the recovery of visual responses to stimuli contralateral to the ablated posterior neocortex, when a second lesion is placed to the ipsilateral superior colliculus. The recovery occurs also when the cortical lesion is very large and the contralateral neglect permanent. Although the "Sprague effect" undoubtedly shows that inhibitory interactions do exist between areas controlling attention, it is difficult, at the present, to evaluate if inhibitory mechanisms control attention only in opposite directions like right-left or also play a role in distributing attention among personal, peripersonal and extrapersonal space sectors. Inhibition, however, certainly plays an important role within the centers controlling attentional shifts (Rizzolatti, Camarda, Grupp & Pisa, 1974; Buchtel, Camarda, Rizzolatti & Scandolara, 1979; Wurtz, Richmond & Judge, 1980).

Another way to explain the increase of attention to a given space sector

after a premotor activation is that of admitting a facilitatory influence of
the premotor areas on sensory centers connected with them. An example of
this is the facilitation that in an expectancy paradigm premotor neurons
located in the intermediate layers of the superior colliculus exert on
sensory neurons of the superficial layers of the same structure (Mohler &
Wurtz, 1976). The difference between this model and those presented above is
that here the attention is attributed to an increase of responsiveness of
sensory neurons caused by the activity of premotor neurons, whereas in the
other models it is attributed to the firing of premotor neurons per se.
Obviously these two possibilities are not mutually exclusive.

Besides being passively attracted by changes in the environment,
attention can be actively controlled by the subject. A shift of attention
can precede the appearance of a stimulus ("set" or " expectancy") and
accordingly influence the processing of input (Hebb, 1949; cf. also Posner,
1978). At a first glance actively directed attention seems to pose some
problems to the premotor theory of attention. If no central attentional
center of circuit exists, how can attention be actively shifted to different
space sectors ? The answer is rather simple. Since spatial attention is a
consequence of the organization of motor plans in a spatial framework, the
selection of a motor plan should automatically produce a shift of attention
toward the spatial sector where the action will be executed. It is beyond the
scope of this chapter to discuss how certain actions are selected and the
various motivational, hormonal and metabolic factors that may intervene in
this choice. A lesion however of areas selecting future actions should not
produce deficits of attention of the type discussed in this chapter. The
motivationally determined long-term goal are decided at a stage preceding
that where motor plans are organized. Lesions of these stages, should
produce   inability   to   organize   future   activity,   distractability,
vulnerability to interference, diminished exploratory drives and other
disturbances of this kind, but spatial attention should remain normal
during this poorly organized purposive behavior.

To conclude, a model of spatial attention based on a series of circuits
largely independent one from another is able to explain how the attention is
shifted actively or in response to external stimuli. In contrast, any single
attentional circuit theory has enormous explanatory difficulties when
examined   in   relation   to   real   brain   anatomy.   Neither   the
fronto-parietal-cingulate circuit (Mesulam, 1981), nor other cortical
circuits can easily account for the attentional deficit following lesions
of midbrain structures or the nigro-striatal system. What is more important
anatomical data on cortico-cortical connections also fail to support a
single circuit theory. In the monkey there are three main pathways which
connect the frontal and parietal lobes (see Petrides & Pandya , 1984). The
first links the superior parietal lobule (area 5) with the dorsal part of
areas 6 and with the supplementary motor area. The second leaves the rostral
part of the inferior parietal lobule (area 7b) and terminates in inferior
area 6, in area 46 below the sulcus principalis and in the frontal and
pericentral opercular cortex. The third pathway connects the caudal part of
the inferior parietal lobule (area 7a) with area 8, area 46, the most rostral
part of dorsal area 6 and the cingulate gyrus.

The first of these circuits conveys essentially proprioceptive
information (Mountcastle et al., 1975). The second circuit is mostly,
although not exclusively, involved in visually guided oculo-motor behavior
(Hyvarinen, 1982; Lynch, 1980). The third circuit is formed, at least in
part, by polysensory neurons that respond to somatosensory and visual
stimuli located in the animal's peripersonal space (Hyvarinen, 1982;
Rizzolatti et al., 1981, a, b, c). A lesion of these two last circuits

produces neglect, but the types of neglect are different according to which circuit is destroyed. The lesion of area 7b-area 6 circuit determines a "peripersonal space-reaching" neglect, the lesion of area 7a-area 8 circuit produce an "extrapersonal space – oculomotor neglect". This last type of neglect is not due to a lesion of the attentional circuit, but to a lesion of one of several premotor circuits involved in spatial attention.

In conclusion, the premotor theory of selective attention appears to be the only one able to accomodate the three basic findings which any theory of neglect must explain :

a) The multiplicity of brain centers whose lesion produces neglect.

b) The congruence between attentional and motor deficits after lesion of these centers.

c) The anatomical independence of the centers whose damage causes neglect.

References

Albano, J.E., Mishkin, M., Westbrook, L.E. & Wurtz, R.H. Visuomotor deficits following ablation of monkey superior colliculus. Journal of Neurophysiology, 1982, 48, 338-351.

Barbas, H. & Mesulam, M.M. Organization of afferent input to subdivisions of area 8 in the rhesus monkey. Journal of Comparative Neurology, 1981, 200, 407-431.

Bender, M.B. Comments on the physiology and pathology of eye movements in the vertical plane. Journal of nervous and mental Diseases, 1960, 130, 456-460.

Berlucchi, G., Buchtel, H.A. & Lepore, F. Successful interocular transfer of visual pattern discrimination in split-chiasm cats with section of the intertectal and posterior commissures. Physiology and Behavior, 1978, 20, 331-338.

Berlyne, D.E. Conflict, arousal and curiosity. New York: Mc Graw-Hill, 1960.

Berlyne, D.E. Attention as a problem in behavior theory. In D.I. Mostofsky (Ed.), Attention: Contemporary Theory and Analysis. Appleton Century Crofts, 1970, pp. 25-49.

Bianchi, L. The function of the frontal lobes. Brain, 1895, 18, 497-530.

Bisiach, E., Perani, D., Vallar, G. & Berti, A. Unilateral neglect: personal and extrapersonal. Forthcoming.

Buchtel, H.A., Camarda, R., Rizzolatti, G. & Scandolara, C. The effect of hemidecortication on the inhibitory interactions in the superior colliculus of the cat. Journal of Comparative Neurology, 1979, 184, 795-810.

Crowne, D.P. The frontal eye field and attention. Psychological Bulletin, 1983, 93, 232-260.

Dean, P. & Redgrave, P. The superior colliculus and visual neglect in rat and hamster. I. Behavioural evidence. Brain Research Review, 1984, 8, 129-141.

Denny-Brown, D. The midbrain and motor integration. Proceedings of the Royal Society of Medicine, 1962, 55, 527-538.

Denny-Brown, D. & Chambers, R.A. The parietal lobe and behavior. Proceeding of the Association for Research in Nervous and Mental Diseases, 1958, 36, 35-117.

De Renzi, E. Disorders of space exploration and cognition. London: J. Wiley, 1982.

De Renzi, E., Colombo, A., Faglioni, P. & Gibertoni, M. Conjugate gaze paresis in stroke patients with unilateral damage. Archives of Neurology, 1982, 39, 482-486.

Deuel, R.K., Collins, R.C. & Caston, T.W. The functional anatomy of neglect: behavioral and quantitative 2DG studies in the monkey. Neurology, 1980, 30, 390.

Dunnett, S.B. & Iversen, S.D. Sensorimotor impairments following localized kainic acid and 6-hydroxydopamine lesions of the neostriatum. Brain Research, 1982, 248, 121-127.

Ewert, J.P. Neuroethology. Berlin: Springer, 1980.

Friedland, R.P. & Weinstein, E.A. Hemi-inattention and hemisphere specialization: introduction and historical review. In E.A. Weinstein & R.P. Friedland (Eds.) Advances in Neurology, vol. 18. Raven press, 1977, pp 1-31.

Gentilucci, M., Scandolara, C., Pigarev, I.N. & Rizzolatti, G. Visual responses in the postarcuate cortex (area 6) of the monkey that are independent of eye position. Experimental Brain Research, 1983, 50, 464-468.

Gentilucci, M., Gentilini, M., Porro, C.A., Matelli, M. & Rizzolatti, G. Effects of unilateral frontal eye field lesions on saccadic eye movements to near and far targets. Forthcoming.

Godschalk, M., Lemon, R.M., Nijs, H.G.T. & Kuypers, H.G.J.M. Behaviour of neurons in monkey periarcuate and precentral cortex before and during visually guided arm and hand movements. Experimental Brain Research, 1981, 44, 113-116.

Goodale, M.A. & Morrison, R.C.C. The effects of lesions of the superior colliculus on locomotor orientation and the orienting reflex in the rat. Brain Research, 1975, 88, 243-261.

Goodale, M.A., Foreman, M.P. & Milner, A.D. Visual orientation in rats: a dissociation of deficits following cortical and collicular lesions. Experimental Brain Research, 1978, 31, 445-457.

Hallet, P.E. & Lightstone, A.D. Saccadic eye movements toward stimuli triggered by prior saccades. Vision Research, 1976, 16, 99-106.

Hassler, R. Supranuclear structures regulating binocular eye and head movements. In J. Dichgans & E. Bizzi (Eds.) Cerebral control of eye movements and motion perception. Basel: Karger, 1972, pp 207-219.

Hebb, D.O. The organization of behavior. New York: Wiley, 1949.

Heilman, K.M. Neglect and related disorders. In K.M. Heilman & E. Valenstein (Eds.) Clinical Neurophysiology. New York: Oxford University Press, 1979, pp. 268-307.

Heilman, K.M. & Watson, R.T. Mechanisms underlying the unilateral neglect syndrome. In E.A. Weinstein & R.F. Friedland (Eds.) Advances in Neurology. New York: Raven Press, 1977, pp. 93-105.

Heilman, K.M., Pandya, D.N. & Geschwind, N. Trimodal inattention following parietal lobe ablations. Transactions of the American Neurology Association, 1970, 95, 250-261.

Heilman, K.M., Watson, R.T. & Valenstein, E. Neglect and related disorders. In K.M. Heilman & E. Valenstein (Eds.) Clinical Neuropsychology, second edition. Oxford: Oxford University Press, 1985.

Hess, W.R. Das Zwischenhirn Syndrome, Lokalisationen, Funktionen. Basel: Benno Schwabe & Co, 1954, pp. 218.

Hess, W.R., Burgi, S. & Bucher, V. Motorische Funktion des Tektal- und Tegmental-Gebietes, Monatschrift für Psychiatrie und Neurologie, 1946, 112, 1-52.

Hyvärinen, J. The parietal cortex of monkey and man. Studies of Brain Function, vol. 8. Berlin: Springer, 1982.

James, W. The principles of psychology, vol. I. New York: Dover Publications, 1950.

Jerison, H.J. Evolution of brain and intelligence. New York: Academic

Press, 1973.

Jerison, H.J. Animal intelligence as encephalization. Philosophical Transactions of the Royal Society of London B, 1985, 308, 21-35.

Kennard, M.A. Alterations in response to visual stimuli following lesions of frontal lobe in monkeys. Archives of Neurology and Psychiatry, 1939, 41, 1153-1165.

Kennard, M. & Ectors, L. Forced circling in monkeys following lesions of frontal lobes. Journal of Neurophysiology, 1938, 1, 45-54.

Latto, R. & Cowey, A. Visual field defects after frontal eye-field lesions in monkeys. Brain Research, 1971a, 30, 1-24.

Latto, R. & Cowey, A. Fixation changes after eye-field lesions in monkeys. Brain Research, 1971b, 30, 25-36.

Leinonen, L. & Nyman, G. II. Functional properties of cells in anterolateral part of area 7 associative face area of awake monkey. Experimental Brain Research, 1979, 34, 321-333.

Leinonen, L., Hyvärinen, J., Nyman, G. & Linnankoski, I. I. Functional properties of neurons in lateral part of associative area 7 in awake monkeys. Experimental Brain Research, 1979, 34, 299-320.

Ljungberg, T. & Ungerstedt, U. Sensory inattention produced by 6-hydroxydopamine induced degeneration of ascending dopamine neurons in the brain. Experimental Neurology, 1976, 53, 585-600.

Luh, K.E., Butter, C.M. & Buchtel, M.A. Effects of unilateral superior temporal sulcus lesions on visual orientation in monkeys. Society for Neuroscience Abstracts, 1985, 677.

Lynch, J.C. The functional organization of posterior parietal association cortex. Behavioral and Brain Sciences, 1980, 3, 485-499.

Lynch, J.C., Mountcastle, V.B., Talbot, W.H. & Yin, T.C.T. Parietal lobe mechanisms for directed visual attention. Journal of Neurophysiology, 1977, 40, 362-389.

Marshall, J.F. & Teitelbaum, P. Further analysis of sensory inattention following lateral hypothalamic damage in rats. Journal of Comparative and Physiological Psychology, 1974, 86, 375-395.

Marshall, J.F., Berrios, N. & Sawyer, S. Neostriatal dopamine and sensory inattention. Journal of Comparative and Physiological Psychology, 1980, 94, 833-846.

Marshall, J.F., Turner, B.H. & Teitelbaum, P. Sensory neglect produced by lateral hypothalamic damage. Science, 1971, 174, 523-525.

Matelli, M., Camarda, R., Glickstein, M. & Rizzolatti, G. Afferent and efferent projections of the inferior area 6 in the macaque monkey. Journal of Comparative Neurology, 1986, (in press).

Matelli, M., Olivieri, M.F., Saccani, A. & Rizzolatti, G. Upper visual space neglect and motor deficits after section of the midbrain commissures in the cat. Behavioural and Brain Research, 1983, 10, 263-285.

Mays, L.E. & Sparks, D.L. Dissociation of visual and saccade-related response in superior colliculus neurons. Journal of Neurophysiology, 1980, 43, 207-232.

Mesulam, M.M. A cortical network for directed attention and unilateral neglect. Annals of Neurology, 1981, 10, 309-325.

Mohler, C.W. & Wurtz, R.H. Organization of monkey superior colliculus: Intermediate layer cells discharging before eye movements. Journal of Neurophysiology, 1976, 39, 722-744.

Moruzzi, G. & Magoun, M.W. Brain-stem reticular formation and activation of EEG. Electroencephalography and Clinical Neurophysiology, 1949, 1, 455-473.

Mountcastle, V.B., Lynch, J.C., Georgopoulos, A., Sakata, H. & Acuna, C. Posterior parietal association cortex of the monkey: command functions for operations within extrapersonal space. Journal of Neurophysiology, 1975, 38, 871–908.

Orem, J., Schlag-Rey, M., Schlag, J. Unilateral visual neglect and thalamic intralaminar lesions in the cat. Experimental Neurology, 1973, 40, 784–797.

Pasik, P., Pasik, T. & Bender, M.B. The pretectal syndrome in monkeys. I. Disturbances of gaze and body posture. Brain, 1969, 92, 521–534.

Petrides, M. & Iversen, S. Restricted posterior parietal lesions in the rhesus monkey and performance on visuospatial tasks. Brain Research, 1979, 161, 63–77.

Petrides, M. & Pandya, D.N. Projections to the frontal cortex from the posterior parietal region in the rhesus monkey. Journal of Comparative Neurology, 1984, 288, 105–116.

Posner, M.I. Chronometric exploration of mind. New York: Lawrence Erlbaum Associates, 1978.

Posner, M.I., Cohen, Y. & Rafal, R.D. Neural systems control of spatial orienting. In D.E. Broadbent & L. Weiskrantz (Eds.) The neuropsychology and cognitive function. London: The Royal Society, 1982, pp. 187–198.

Rafal, R.D. & Grimm, R.J. Progressive supranuclear palsy: functional analysis of the response to methysergide and anti-Parkinson agents. Neurology, 1981, 31, 1507–1518.

Rizzolatti, G. Mechanisms of selective attention in mammals. In J.P. Ewert, R.R. Capranica & D.J. Ingle (Eds.) Advances in Vertebrate Neuroethology. London: Plenum Press, 1983, pp. 261–297.

Rizzolatti, G., Gentilucci, M. & Matelli, M. Selective spatial attention: one center, one circuit or many circuits? In M.I. Posner & O. Marin (Eds.) Attention and Performance XI. Hillsdale, N.J.: Erlbaum, 1985, pp. 251–265.

Rizzolatti, G., Matelli, M. & Pavesi, G. Deficits in attention and movement following the removal of postarcuate (area 6) and prearcuate (area 8) cortex in macaque monkeys. Brain, 1983, 106, 655–673.

Rizzolatti, G., Camarda, R., Grupp, L.A. & Pisa, M. Inhibitory effect of remote visual stimuli on visual responses of cat superior colliculus: spatial and temporal factors. Journal of Neurophysiology, 1974, 37, 1262–1275.

Rizzolatti, G., Scandolara, C., Gentilucci, M. & Camarda, R. Response properties and behavioral modulation of "mouth" neurons of the postarcuate cortex (area 6) in macaque monkeys. Brain Research, 1981a, 255, 421–424.

Rizzolatti, G., Scandolara, C., Matelli, M. & Gentilucci, M. Afferent properties of periarcuate neurons in macaque monkeys. I. Somato-sensory responses. Behavioural Brain Research, 1981b, 2, 125–146.

Rizzolatti, G., Scandolara, C., Matelli, M. & Gentilucci, M. Afferent properties of periarcuate neurons in macaque monkeys. II. Visual responses. Behavioral Brain Research, 1981c, 2, 147–163.

Sakata, H., Shibutani, H. & Kawano, K. Spatial properties of visual fixation neurons in posterior parietal association cortex of the monkey. Journal of Neurophysiology, 1980, 43, 1654–1672.

Schlag, J., Schlag-Rey, M., Peck, C.K. & Joseph, J.P. Visual responses of thalamic neurons depending on the direction of gaze and the position of targets in space. Experimental Brain Research, 1980, 40, 170–184.

Schott, B., Jeannerod, M. & Zahin, M.Z. L'agnosie spatiale unilatérale: perturbation en secteur des mécanismes d'exploration et de fixation du regard. Journal de Médecine de Lyon, 1966, 47, 169–195.

Sprague, J.M. Interaction of cortex and superior colliculus in mediation of visually guided behavior in the cat. Science, 1966, 153, 1544–1547.

Sprague, J.M., Meikle, T.H. The role of the superior colliculus in visually guided behavior. Experimental Neurology, 1965, 11, 115–146.

Sprague, J.M., Chambers, W.W. & Stellar, E. Attentive, affective and adaptive behavior in the cat. Science, 1961, 133, 165–173.

Steele, J.C., Richardson, J.C. & Olszewski, J. Progressive supranuclear palsy. Archives of Neurology, 1964, 10, 333–359.

Stein, J. The effect of parietal lobe cooling on manipulative behaviour in the conscious monkey. In G. Gordon (Ed.) Active touch. Oxford: Pergamon, 1978, pp. 79–90.

Titchener, E.B. Attention as sensory clearness. In P. Bakan (Ed.) Attention: An enduring problem in psychology. Princeton: D. Van Nostrand, 1966.

Vallar, G. & Perani, D. The anatomy of spatial neglect in humans. In M. Jeannerod (Ed.) Neurophysiological and Neuropsychological aspects of spatial neglect, 1986.

Valenstein, E., Heilman, K.M., Watson, R.T. & Van Den Abell, T. Nonsensory neglect from parietotemporal lesions in monkeys. Neurology, 1982, 32, 1198–1201.

Watson, R.T., Heilman, K.M., Cauthen, J.C. & King, F.A. Neglect after cingulatectomy. Neurology, 1973, 23, 1003–1007.

Watson, R.T., Heilman, K.M., Miller, B.D. & King, F.A. Neglect after mesencephalic reticular formation lesions. Neurology, 1974, 24, 294–298.

Welch, K. & Stuteville, P. Experimental production of unilateral neglect in monkeys. Brain, 1958, 81, 341–347.

Wurtz, R.H. Visual receptive fields of striate cortex neurons in awake monkeys. Journal of Neurophysiology, 1969, 32, 727–742.

Wurtz, R.H., Richmond, B.J. & Judge, S.J. Vision during saccadic eye movements III: Visual interactions in monkey superior colliculus. Journal of Neurophysiology, 1980, 43, 1168–1181.

Acknowledgements : This work was supported in part by a N.I.H. grant 1 R01 NS 19206–01A1 and in part by a CNR grant.

Neurophysiological and Neuropsychological Aspects
of Spatial Neglect, M. Jeannerod (editor)
© Elsevier Science Publishers B.V. (North-Holland), 1987

NEURAL DYSFUNCTION DURING HEMINEGLECT AFTER
CORTICAL DAMAGE IN TWO MONKEY MODELS

Ruthmary K. Deuel

The neural pathological anatomy and pathophysiology of the
hemineglect syndrome was studied in 17 monkeys that underwent
circumscribed unilateral frontal or parietal association
cortical resections after a battery of laterally specific sensory
and motor tests. Postoperatively the (^{14}C)-2-DG autoradiographic
method showed that acute frontal hemineglect was accompanied by
deficient isotope uptake in anterior and medial thalamus, basal
ganglia, and deeper layers of the superior colliculus; parietal
hemineglect was accompanied by deficient uptake in the posterior
lateral thalamus, striate cortex and deeper layers of the superior
colliculus. In animals that recovered from neglect,
autoradiography defined recovery of the isotope uptake deficits.
The data thus suggest that neglect symptoms depend upon neural
dysfunction at multiple sites quite distant from the structural
damage, and that conventional anatomical representation of
function does not apply to neglect. Second, they suggest that a
complex set of interactions among damaged, dysfunctional, and
intact neural structures produces neglect as well as recovery from
neglect, and that such factors might eventually be manipulated to
enhance recovery in human stroke victims.

I. Introduction

The clinical syndromes of hemispatial neglect have been well described
elsewhere in this volume. From these and other descriptions (Friedland &
Weinstein, 1977; Bisiach, Luzatti & Perani, 1979; Stein & Volpe, 1983;
Heilman & Valenstein, 1972a, 1972b; Damasio, Damasio & Chang-Chi, 1979;
Critchley, 1953; Battersby, Bender & Pollack, 1956) it is clear that neglect
symptoms differ radically from primary sensory and motor symptoms that
similarly appear after cortical lesions. One clear difference, from which
the neglect syndrome derives its name, is that in neglect a patient may
verbally acknowledge an appendage or place, and yet completely fail to
incorporate the appendage or place in ongoing behavior - the appendage or
place is behaviorally "neglected". When a patient is more severely
affected, verbal acknowledgement may also be lacking - the neglected arm,
for instance, may be attributed to another person's body (Critchley, 1953;
Battersby et al., 1956; Friedland & Weinstein, 1977). The hemiparetic
patient, in contrast, is very much aware of the affected limb and its
deficits. Another point of difference from hemiparesis and hemisensory loss
is the inconstancy of neglect deficits. Weakness and spasticity are
relatively constant in the hemiparetic limb after a motor cortical lesion.
Movement deficits in neglect, however, are variable from moment to moment or
from test condition to test condition (Heilman & Watson, 1978). The sensory

symptoms of neglect also exhibit variability. A visual stimulus falling on a given retinal field may be consciously perceived at one moment and yet not perceived at the next moment (Critchley, 1953; Battersby et al., 1956; Heilman & Watson, 1978). These are important differences that set neglect apart from other types of symptoms that occur after cerebral damage.

Postmortem studies of gross and microscopic pathology have, over the years, provided a body of knowledge of the consequences, in terms of neglect symptoms, of structural damage to various sites in the nervous system. From these it is known that neglect symptoms appear only when there is damage beyond primary sensory and motor cortex. Neglect often occurs, however, in addition to primary sensory and motor loss when damage is in a hemisphere with extensive pathology. When neglect does appear by itself, lesions are most commonly found in inferior parietal and dorsolateral frontal association cortex (Critchley, 1953; Friedland & Weinstein, 1977; Heilman & Valenstein, 1972b; Battersby et al., 1956; Kertesz & Dobrowski, 1981) of the right hemisphere in right handed humans, although lesions in many other sites have been reported to be accompanied by hemispatial neglect (Damasio et al., 1979; Ferro & Kertesz, 1984; Cambier, Graveleau & Decroix, 1983; Watson, Valenstein & Heilman, 1981).

Conventional concepts of representation of functions by specific localized cortical and subcortical assemblies of cells connected by critical pathways do not seem to offer a complete explanation of neglect symptoms. For example, similar pathology may be found in cases with and without clinically documented neglect (Wallesch, Kornhuber, Kintz & Brunner, 1983; Watson et al., 1981), while clinically similar neglect syndromes appear with pathology in quite different cerebral loci (Stein & Volpe, 1983; Heilman & Valenstein, 1972; Damasio et al., 1979; Ferro & Kertesz, 1984; Cambier et al., 1983; Wallesch et al., 1983; Watson et al., 1981). The behavioral analysis of neglect symptoms has prompted several innovative topographical representational theories that apply to the supramodal qualities of attention and neglect. None of these concepts can yet fully explain the moment to moment changes in sensory and motor deficits observed in neglect patients. Thus, structural pathology and attendant very refined theories of topographic representation of function in the brain do not clarify a mechanism even for the gross clinical features of hemineglect in the monkey, let alone the more abstruse forms of the syndrome that have been documented from time to time in human patients. This inadequacy suggests that the neural mechanisms underlying spatially directed attention, as well as more readily measurable motor behaviors, that are impaired in neglect, may depend upon factors other than anatomic integrity of specific neuronal centers and their connecting pathways.

John Hughlings Jackson (Jackson, 1958) first postulated that after destruction of neural centers, interactions among surviving neural centers determined clinical symptomatology. Disabling one area or system of the brain, under this hypothesis, would alter the vectors of influence exerted by intact brain areas or systems upon the final product of their ongoing interactions. Extrapolating this "dynamic interaction" thesis to normal behavior as the product of an undamaged brain, responses to stimuli would depend on different sorts of cell assemblies and connections for different modalities, loci, and types of stimulus. Requirements for greater or less magnitude and complexity of responses would further modulate the types and quantity of synapses required to be active to produce a given response, as outlined in part by Hécaen & Albert (1978). In normal functioning, the brain must carry out multiple activities simultaneously. It is known that one such activity may impair or preclude simultaneous performance of another (Kimura, 1973), evidence that dynamic interactions of neural systems with

(Kimura, 1973), evidence that dynamic interactions of neural systems with each other may have a powerful effect upon behavior even in the undamaged brain (Kinsbourne, 1972).

Given a lesion and hemispatial neglect, symptoms could be influenced by what and how many simultaneous processes are required of the brain damaged subject, just as in the undamaged brain responses would be facilitated if simultaneous processes did not have to utilize the same neural systems. Responses requiring partially damaged systems could be blocked when systems that exert inhibitory actions are simultaneously activated. Such dynamic facilitory and inhibitory interactions among components of the nervous system can at least theoretically explain those features of neglect syndrome that cannot be explained by even the most detailed and refined topographic representation theories. Thus, a study that used a means of evaluation that could document changing functional connections and activations, rather than just static structural effects, could provide better understanding of the neural basis of neglect.

Evaluating the postulated and ever-changing relationships among neural systems and centers concomitant with behaviors makes heavy demands for resolution of small differences in time and space, however. Ideally, an anatomically precise, rapidly formed map of "activity" in all brain structures at once should be collected, together with behavioral observations on the same time course. Of course, these observations should not restrict the natural activities of the subject nor disrupt the integrity of the nervous system (Deuel, 1982).

II. Mapping Regional Brain Activity During Neglect

As a first approximation of the ideal means of mapping regional brain activity, we chose the (^{14}C)-2-deoxyglucose method (2-DG). The advantages of the 2-DG method for the type of study discussed above are that it has proven over a number of years to be reliable method for mapping regional brain metabolism in laboratory animals as described by Sokoloff and associates (Sokoloff, Reivich & Kennedy, 1977; Kennedy, Sakurada, Shinohara, Jehle & Sokoloff, 1978). It takes advantage of both the central nervous system's use of blood glucose as its primary and almost exclusive energy source under normal physiological conditions, and of the fact that 2-DG is extracted from blood and phosphorylated by tissues by the same mechanisms as glucose. Under most physiological conditions regional 2-DG extraction, oxygen consumption, and blood flow are proportionately increased when synaptic activity increases (Collins, Kennedy, Sokoloff & Plum, 1976). Thus, the 2-DG method is good for studying regional neural activity in a physiologically intact, awake behaving animal. Several general exceptions to this rule have been noted by others (Rapin, Lageron & Poncin-Lafitte, 1981; Ginsberg, Reivich, Giandomenico & Greenberg, 1977) and will not be further discussed.

The most important advantage of the 2-DG method is the availability of the entire neuraxis to high resolution anatomic and densitometric examination. Information about the location of enhanced or decreased glucose utilization even in small structures deep within the central nervous system may be obtained. Accompanying behaviors may be observed in the fully alert performing animal prior to sacrifice for the anatomic and densitometric analysis. In animals with lesions, 2-DG has revealed decreases in glucose utilization in interrupted synaptic pathways as shown by Schwartz & Evarts (1976) in rats, and by Jarvis, Mishkin, Shinohara, Sakurada, Miyaoka & Kennedy (1978) in monkeys. Dauth, Gilman, Frey, Penney & Agranoff (1979) studied motor cortex lesions while Deuel & Collins (1984) studied frontal association cortex lesions. Collins and others (Collins et al., 1976; Collins & Divac, 1983) have used increases in glucose utilization, caused by synaptic activation through kindled seizures, to demonstrate functional pathways as well. Thus, the 2-DG method has previously been used to outline functional systems of the type that could change with different pathological states and behaviors, as postulated by John Hughlings Jackson. One drawback of the 2-DG method is that the minute to minute changes in system activation that could take place within the 2-DG equilibration period of 45 minutes cannot be evaluated. Rather, all behavioral and neural activations that take place during the first 10 or 20 minutes after 2-DG injection are represented as the final regional 2-DG concentration values derived from densitometry of autoradiograms after sacrifice. The specific 2-DG techniques we used are described in detail in Deuel & Collins (1984). Of major importance, if a method is to be effective in directly relating behavior and neural activation, is that it does not interrupt nervous system integrity nor restrain a subject's psychological and behavioral freedom during the period of assessment in the behaving animal. This criterion also may be met for monkey subjects by the 2-DG method, if the conditions of the final 2-DG experiment are anticipated and the animal adapted to accept them (Kennedy, Miyaoka, Suda, Macko, Jarvis, Mishkin & Sokoloff, 1980).

III. Examination for Neglect in Monkeys

Patients may exhibit neglect in a single modality (e.g., visual hemineglect) (Heilman & Valenstein, 1972; Halstead, 1943), but quite often, they demonstrate it in several modalities (Friedland & Weinstein, 1977; Bisiach et al., 1979; Stein & Volpe, 1983; Heilman & Valenstein, 1972a and b; Damasio et al., 1979; Critchley, 1953; Battersby et al., 1956). To thoroughly analyze the neural substrates of neglect, thorough evaluation of neglect in each single modality, might be advantageous. To ascertain unimodal neglect in monkeys, where anatomically precise lesions are possible and confer a substantial advantage to the study, is a somewhat different matter than in patients, however, due to lack of verbal communication. When animals are highly trained to perform unimodal tasks, the possibility of mitigating lesion effects with training effects (Deuel & Dunlop, 1980; Petrides & Iversen, 1979) must be weighted heavily. To avoid these hazards we chose first to study the multimodal neglect syndrome that has frequently been described in monkeys in the past (Bianchi, 1895; Kennard, 1939; Denny-Brown & Chambers, 1958; Welsh & Stuteville, 1978; Latto & Cowey, 1972; Crowne, Yeo & Russell, 1981; Deuel & Collins, 1983). We adopted the following general definition of hemispatial neglect: "Diminished responses to sensory stimulation and disuse of limbs in half of personal and extrapersonal space under certain conditions or testing, with preservation of primary sensory and motor response on that side". We required the conditional response asymmetry to be present in at least the visual and somatosensory modalities.

Normal macaque monkeys can form habits that lend the appearance of lateral advantage of one hand over the other, but they do not exhibit lifelong lateral dominance of the same qualitative nature as that of humans (Deuel & Dunlop, 1980; Warren & Nonneman, 1976). This absence of handedness is an advantage to evaluation of response asymmetries due to cerebral lesions, as preexisting cerebral dominance factors do not confound lesion effects. To study spontaneously expressed lateral symmetry of responses to stimulation we constructed a brief battery of tests to survey neurological function in the monkey (Deuel, 1977; Deuel & Regan, 1985). A primary consideration was that the battery be brief and amenable to completion by any untrained monkey. A second important consideration in constructing this battery was the preservation, as far as possible, of the natural circumstances of orientation. For this reason we did not teach the animal to orient, nor force it into an involuntary orientation (e.g., by mechanically fixing the head). Instead, before each trial that had to start with midline fixation of the head and eyes (for instance, for a unilateral visual response trial) the animal was shown a bit of bait that it then voluntarily fixated, bringing its head and eyes into the desired position.

The battery first allowed evaluation of the animal's general alertness, response to specific emotional stimuli, posture and whole body movements. This was carried out during a three minute period when an examiner observed the animal moving freely about in its home cage. The animal's turning preferences, its responses to the examiner's threatening and then placating noises, and its use of limbs in spontaneous ambulation and reaching movements were noted. The animal was then placed in a primate chair that freed its upper extremities from postural support duties. It was then evaluated on 19 items that specifically tested manual preference and performance. The items included reaching for bait, tracking moving bait, traction against resistance, securing an unseen piece of bait, manual dexterity, reaching for bilateral simultaneously presented visual, auditory and somatosensory cues. Strength of upper extremities, walking gait, tactile placing of lower extremities, tone, muscle, bulk, coordination of upper extremities and lower extremities, tongue, eye, and facial movements and deep tendon reflexes were also assessed. Responses to visual cues presented from different quadrants, and to auditory cues from either side, and to pinprick (with vision occluded) in all four extremities were also tested during neurological examinations. The specific items are described in detail below.

Manual preferences was scored on items that required reaching and grasping. In several, one hand was restrained while the performance of the other was measured, allowing direct comparison of the performance of one hand with performance of the other, specifically in the reaching dexterity, tactile reaching, and traction-strength subtests. The saliency of left versus right stimuli in attracting directed attention was evaluated with bilateral simultaneously presented visual and somatosensory stimuli. In animals with acute neglect, responses to bilateral simultaneous stimulation were generally only to the stimulus ipsilateral to the lesion, i.e., complete extinction of the stimulus in the neglected field was usually demonstrated. Because of the absolute lack of response in one field under the bilateral simultaneous condition, the bilateral simultaneous condition could not be used to assess the degree of severity of neglect. To assess the degree of neglect we constructed a "symmetry index", a composite of six items that were separately presented in each lateral field.

While the six items, which are detailed below, were used for the symmetry index, it should be pointed out that there was considerable redundancy of items in the neurological examination, so that the other 14 items, not used in the index, did still test the same functions and served as intratest validations of the six index items. As none of the items on the neurological examination required learning, the neurological examination could be used to evaluate monkeys as soon as they arrived in the laboratory, before they were trained and of course at later intervals. All 20 items could be administered frequently, and no change in performance of any learned task was ever noted in any monkey after an administration of the neurological examination. However, the training of unimanual tasks did have a mild effect on hand preference in some animals (Deuel & Dunlop, 1980). Otherwise training did not affect performance on the 20 items. The reliability of the neurological examination in the hands of different observers was informally assessed, and interteam reliability was good.

The six symmetry index items will be described in some detail. They were all performed in the primate chair. No restraints other than the neck and waist piece were used. The chair was constructed so that the most comfortable position for the animal was facing forward with upper extremities resting on the waist piece and lower extremities supported by footbars. The examiner sat facing the monkey and ascertained that the monkey's head and eyes were fixed straight ahead at the beginning of each trial of each item where this was required.

Unilateral visual fields testing was carried out by two examiners. One examiner sat in front of the animal and ascertained forward head and eye fixation using a piece of bait. The other examiner brought stimuli from the periphery of each quadrant of a grid placed 10 inches in front of the animal's eyes, toward the animal's central gaze fixation point. The number of grid units between central fixation and the bait position where the animal shifted gaze (this shift was usually of both head and eyes simultaneously, but in a small portion of trials only the eyes moved) to fix directly upon the bait, were counted. At least four valid trials from each quadrant of the grid were required. A trial was counted as invalid if central fixation was broken before the saccade precisely to the moving stimulus.

Somatic sensation of the extremities was tested with the animal's vision of its extremities occluded by an extended neck piece. Again the examiner sat in front of the animal and found opportunities to randomly deliver pinpricks to the glabrous skin of each extremity. The reactive withdrawals from pinpicks were scored on a rating scale of 0 (no response) to 4 (rapid, large amplitude withdrawal plus vocalization). At least four trials were delivered to each hand and each foot. The upper and lower extremity scores of each side were added, so that the score of the left could be compared with that of the right. All of these tests including details of scoring are described in Deuel & Regan (1985).

Dexterity of one hand was tested by restraining the other hand and timing the active hand as it emptied 6 small food wells drilled in board that was held at the center of gaze slightly less than the animal's arms length in front of its face. The food wells were constructed so that efficient retrieval of bait demanded a finger–thumb pincher grasp. Four timed trials with the board were given to each hand. The test was scored in terms of the time required to empty 10 food wells.

For tactile reaching, a cup with 3 to 6 bits of bait was shown to the animal and then placed out of sight against the skin of the abdomen under the neck piece of the chair. A normal animal would reach into the cup, feel for the pieces, and pick up and eat as many as possible in a single reach. Four (with a total of 16 bits of bait) cups were presented to each hand. Scores were determined by the number of pieces per reach multiplied by the number of pieces taken relative to the number of piece offered.

Hand preference in reaching for bait was assessed by presenting the animal with bit of bait at its arms length. Twelve pieces of bait were delivered at the end of a thin stick to the center, 45 degrees to the left, or 45 degrees to the right of center in a non–repetitious order and then the series of 12 was repeated for a total of 24 trials per examination. A reaching trial was started when the animal's head and hands were correctly positioned. The hand used to reach into each position of presentation was noted, and hand, arm, and finger postures during the apprehension of food and placement of the food in the mouth were noted.

Strength of each hand and arm unit was measured as the number of grams exerted during a traction movement of the hand as it pulled against a spring that exerted a 2 kg force at maximum. Motivation was maintained by placing a piece of bait at the upper end of the spring.

The degree of lateral preference and lateral performance advantage exhibited on the occasion of a neurological examination was determined from the ratio of the right sided (ipsilateral to the damaged hemisphere, or preoperatively, to the hemisphere destined to be damaged) performance divided into the left sided performance (contralateral to the damaged hemisphere) for hand preference, dexterity, tactile reaching, strength, visual fields tested with unilateral stimuli and somatosensory responses tested with unilateral stimuli.

In summary, the 20 items of the neurological evaluation took only 45 minutes to perform (if two examiners were present), and allowed assessment of some basic neurologic functions including alertness and cooperativity, strength, tone, coordination, ability to detect visual, auditory, and somesthetic stimuli. Assessment of these primary functions was most important, because a deficit in strength, tone, coordination, vision, or somesthesis could easily result in a response asymmetry, but one that could not then be attributed to neglect. If the primary neurologic functions were present, then an absolute deficit on one side during bilateral simultaneous stimulation conditions signifed neglect, and the degree of neglect relative to other animals in the series, and to that exhibited by the same animal on the other neurological examinations could be quantified using the symmetry index.

IV. Neglect Following Frontal Lesions

Neglect of one-half of personal and extrapersonal space was clearly reported in the monkey by Bianchi (1895). The lesion was one in the frontal lobe. Hemispatial neglect has since been demonstrated repeatedly in the monkey after more circumscribed unilateral dorso-lateral frontal lesions (Kennard, 1939; Crowne et al., 1981; Latto & Cowey, 1972). When the lesion is small, confined to the posterior bank of the arcuate sulcus, neglect phenomena disappear rapidly, or within about 2 weeks after the lesion (Welsh & Stuteville, 1958). When the lesion is more extensive in dorsolateral frontal cortex, neglect is of longer duration (Deuel & Collins, 1983). Recovery generally does not even commence for two weeks after the lesion, and is not complete until 4 to 10 weeks after the lesion (Deuel & Collins, 1983, 1984).

Our first experiment was carried out using the frontal neglect model to determine regional (^{14}C)-2-DG uptake throughout the brains of animals with hemispatial neglect immediately after frontal cortex removal. In this experiment we examined regional neuronal activity, using the 2-DG autoradiographic method, in the brains of resting alert animals with documented hemineglect (as operationally defined in the section on the examination of neglect in monkeys above). We did not wish at first to study 2-DG uptake in the face of organized or prolonged sensory stimulation or motor activity. Rather, it seemed most important to document the resting activity of the brain, before specific external stimuli called for orientation and nonrandom shifts of attention and movement. The question we hoped to answer first was: "What is the baseline metabolic activity of various regions of a brain that when called upon to respond to bilateral simultaneous stimulation, cannot appropriately distribute attention and motor activity?"

The experimental protocol we used was simple. Macaca fascicularis monkeys weighting 1.9 to 2.5 kilos were used. They lived in individual cages. They were taken from the cage daily and fed one-half of the rations in the primate chair. When they had become accustomed to the chair, to the examiners, and to eating in the chair, they were given the battery of test items in one 45 minute session. Following completion of this initial standard neurological battery (that included determination of hand preference and symmetry index), animals were trained, generally with the hand contralateral to the contemplated lesion, to perform one or several discrimination and motor response tasks. After demonstration of adequate performance on these assigned tasks, the battery was again performed. The time from first to second neurological battery varied from 30 to 120 days, depending upon the animal's learning ability and number of tasks assigned. Hand preference and symmetry index were again calculated. Symmetry indices after training, just prior to operation, are shown in column 1 of Table 1.

Table 1 : The symmetry indices of the frontal and parietal groups before (postraining), and 3 to 5 days after (postoperative) unilateral cortical lesions, and in recovery (4 to 10 weeks after operation). The index was constructed from 6 items on the neurological examination. In each item, an independent value for the side contralateral to the lesion and the side ipsilateral to the lesion (or for preoperative exams, the side destined to be ipsilateral once the lesion was made) was obtained. Then the contralateral value was divided by the ipsilateral value, and this ratio weighted as 1/6 of the total index (i.e., multiplied by 16.6). The weighted numbers from the 6 items were added. If the animal's responses were absolutely symmetrical, this process would yield a symmetry index of 100. If an item had to be omitted, ratios of the other 5 items were weighted accordingly. Values markedly less than 100 indicated a decreased responsiveness contralateral to the lesion. Values greater than 100 (as noted for some animals preoperatively) indicated decreased responsiveness ipsilateral to the side of lesion.

	Animal Number	POST TRAINING Index	POST OPERATIVE Index	RECOVERY Index	Time after operation
PARIETAL	1	115	13		
	2	81	20		
	3	107	25	101	10 weeks
	4	93	31		
	5	101	32	84	8 weeks
	6	103	32		
	7	102	36	84	6 weeks
	8	147	39	98	6 weeks
	9	93	43		
	Group median =	102	32	91	
FRONTAL	10	116	42		
	11	89	27		
	12	81	36	71	5 weeks
	13	90	38	83	4 weeks
	14	110	18	86	6 weeks
	15	103	42		
	16	117	44	94	10 weeks
	17	NT	25		
	Group median =	103	37	85	

Two to 7 days after the second neurological exam, surgery was carried out. Continuous thiopenthol anesthesia and sterile conditions were used. The galea was incised, bone removed over the right frontal region and after dural incision the pia was coagulated and gray matter was aspirated under direct vision (Deuel & Collins, 1983, 1984). The intended lesion is shown in Fig. 1A. It includes both banks of the arcuate sulcus, a small amount of area 6 at the superior medial margin of the posterior bank of the arcuate sulcus and anterior and inferior to the precentral dimple, and the posterior one-third of both banks of the sulcus principalis. The dura and galea were closed in layers and the animal allowed to recover under supervision. Three to 5 days following operation, monkeys were evaluated with the 20 item neurological examination again, and hand preference and symmetry index calculated.

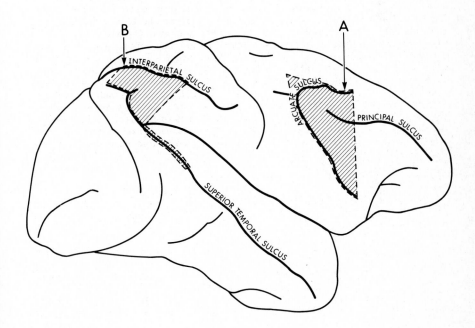

Figure 1
A lateral view of the macaque brain showing in cross hatching the intended extent of the two cortical lesions used to produce hemineglect. Animals were given unilateral lesions in the right hemisphere. They received either A – the <u>frontal</u> removal that included both banks of the arcuate sulcus, a small adjacent dorsolateral premotor region and the posterior third of the sulcus principalis, or B – the <u>parietal</u> removal that included the dorsolateral portion of area 7, including the anterior bank of the intraparietal sulcus, and both banks of the posterior superior temporal sulcus.

Analysis of the behavioral data from 8 frontal animals (the lesion maps
are displayed in Deuel & Collins, 1984) showed, both on the test of bilateral
simultaneous   visual   stimulation,   and   on   bilateral   simultaneous
somatosensory stimulation, that there was complete lack of response to the
stimulus presented in the field contralateral to the lesion, as long as the
stimulus in the field ispilateral was present. Despite these dramatic
changes in response to bilateral simultaneous stimulation, all primary
neurologic functions were present on both sides. Thus, the frontal animals
were characterized as demonstrating neglect. The preoperative neurological
examination of the 8 animals yielded a median symmetry index of 103.
Immediately after operation, however, their median symmetry index fell to
37 (see Table 1). Thus, neglect was quantitied as severe, as further
described in Deuel & Collins (1983, 1984).

Half of the 8 frontal animals were subjected to the 2-DG sacrifice
protocol the day after the first postoperative neurological examination.
The protocol is described by Sokoloff (Sokoloff et al., 1977), Kennedy
(Kennedy et al., 1978, 1980) and colleagues, and was modified by Collins and
previously described in full by Deuel & Collins (1984). In brief, on the
morning of the 2-DG experiment, right femoral arterial and venous catheters
were placed under Halothane anesthesia. The animal was allowed to recover
fully. Two to 3 hours after wakeful behavior resumed, the animal was placed
in the primary chair in the monkey laboratory, where all training and
testing had previously taken place. Thus, the animal was receiving all the
random stimuli of this particular setting, just as it had experienced daily
for at least six weeks. 2-DG was injected and arterial samples gathered via
the catheters. No specific or prolonged stimulus was given and no motor
activity was required. The animals' behaviors were, however, fully observed
and noted during the 50 minute interval between injection of 2-DG and
injection with nembutal. Following sacrifice with an overdose of nembutal,
brains were rapidly removed, frozen and sectioned at 30 microns.
Autoradiographs of the sections were made, and selected sections were
stained for histology.

V. Autoradiographic Findings in Frontal Neglect

For the 4 frontal animals sacrificed during acute neglect, evaluation
of histologic sections and quantitative densitometry was carried out using
the image analysis system described by Toga (Toga et al., 1984). While blood
curve measurements were carried out such that quantitative determination of
glucose utilization was available from the autoradiograms, in fact, left to
right ratios (damaged to intact ratios = D/I) of tissue concentrations of
^{14}C were used for the data analysis in this chapter. This management of the
data required fewer assumptions than use of quantitative glucose
utilization.

We found very clear deficits in (^{14}C)-2-DG uptake in the hemisphere
with the lesion. Deficits were most severe in lateral portions of nucleus
Medialis Dorsalis (nMD), pars multiformis and parvocellularis (mf-pc). The
ratio D/I in this part of Medialis Dorsalis was 0.59. This selective deficit
in 2-DG uptake is clearly shown in the right thalamus in Fig. 2 from UF15.
Less marked but still severe deficits were seen in the nucleus Ventralis
Anterior (nVA) - D/I = 0.67 -, and the caudate nucleus - D/I = 0.80. The
putamen - D/I = 0.84 - and the deeper layers of the superior colliculus (SC) -
D/I = 0.84 - as well as the nucleus Ventralis Lateralis (nVL) - D/I = 0.86 -
of thalamus and globus pallidus - D/I = 0.87. There were no significant
deficits in the motor, somesthetic, and auditory cortical areas sampled.
The striate (visual) cortex did show a mild laminar decrease that was not

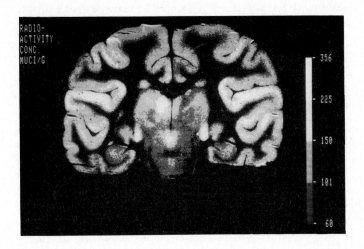

Figure 2
Autoradiograph of a section from a frontal animal (UF15), at
approximate stereotaxic level +4, showing a decreased tissue isotope
concentration in mid thalamus of the hemisphere with the lesion (right). The
scale at the right of the autoradiogram was produced by a computer from the
optical density reading of standards included with the autoradiograms of
the sections. White denotes greatest amount of (^{14}C)-2-DG uptake (the
highest isotope concentration) and black the lowest.

reflected in the value for the full thickness measurement represented in
Fig. 4 (see below).

Thus this first experiment reaffirmed that hemispatial neglect
symptoms existed in the context of dorsolateral frontal damage. In
addition, the 2-DG portion provided a new perspective on the metabolic
activity of forebrain structures, showing an unexpected and extensive
dysfunction in a network of cortical and subcortical structures. If in fact
the dysfunctional structures were basic to the behavioral abnormalities, as
both "motor" (caudate, putamen, globus pallidus, nVA, nVL) and "sensory"
(SC, deeper layers) structures were damaged or dysfunctional after the
frontal lesions, some sort of topographical localization explanation for
the sensory and motor symptoms seemed closer than before this experiment.
Perhaps all these neural structures together were involved in a system that
distributes spatially directed attention, although "localization" of that
function to any single one of these structures was not a priori ruled out.

VI. Autoradiographic Findings after Recovery from Frontal Neglect
Neglect in the frontal monkey almost always improves spontaneously
over time. Using this fact we carried out a second experiment to help define
the neural substrate of neglect. The method was straightforward. In 4
frontal monkeys we performed serial neurological examinations once every
two weeks until the symmetry indices had at least doubled from the first
postoperative examination. We then performed 2-DG sacrifice and evaluated

histological sections and autoradiograms from these recovered animals
(Deuel & Collins, 1983). The autoradiograms of these recovered animals
showed a marked improvement in right left ratios of (^{14}C)-2-DG
concentration. In fact, by this measure, complete recovery of 2-DG uptake
was evident in all structures with the exception of the lateral portions of
nMD. In nMD (mf-pc) and in nucleus "X" of Olszewski (Olszewski, 1952),
histological evaluation showed loss of neurons and glial proliferation,
while glial proliferation was not seen in other structures. As these
thalamic areas had suffered severe neuronal loss, it seemed unlikely that
the small residual neuronal population was capable of close to 90% of the
glucose utilization of the homologous structures noted in the
autoradiograms. We thus concluded that much of the 2-DG uptake noted in this
structure in behaviorally recovered animals was due to glial (i.e.,
non-neuronal) metabolism (Deuel & Collins, 1983). On the basis of this
consideration, when we correlated behavioral findings with neural
metabolism, we discounted neuronal metabolism in the nMD, mf-pc as relevant
to behavioral recovery. Since the region of frontal cortex we removed had of
course not regenerated, it too was discounted as a structure that is
unconditionally required to sustain bilaterally symmetrical spatial
directed attention and motor activities. Recovery of symmetrical 2-DG
uptake had occurred together with behavioral recovery in all the other
structures. In summary, this experiment showed that recovery to 75% or
better of normal spatially directed attention occurred within 4 to 10 weeks
after dorsolateral frontal removals (Deuel & Collins, 1983) and that brains
of animals sacrificed at recovery no longer exhibited clear deficits in
neuronal metabolism in the damaged hemisphere.

   This finding suggested that hemispatial neglect and diminished
neuronal activity in specific structures were indeed related, as both
recovered together. If that relationship was the case and neglect was
symptomatic of the dysfunction we observed, then we could begin to determine
which structures were relevant to the symptoms. While nMD mf-pc and the
frontal periarcuate could be components of a system of structures involved
in producing spatially directed attention in the normal animal, since nMD,
mf-pc and periarcuate frontal cortex remained missing or dysfunctional
following recovery of this behavioral function, either they were
nonessential in the first place, or their roles could be readily assumed by
other elements of the nervous system. We did not find any structure that had
perceptibly increased 2-DG uptake above controls among the recovered
animals, but reasoned that assumption of a new function by a structure need
not lead to increased metabolism of the marked degree that would render it
detectable by our method. After the second experiment then, a primarily
subcortical system for producing distribution of spatially directed
attention seemed likely, but with fewer essential structures than after the
first experiment. The recovery findings suggested that only Caudate, nVA,
nVL, Globus Pallidus, Putamen, and superficial and particularly deeper
layers of SC were relevant. The second experiment still did not, of course,
rule out the possibility that one or more selected structures, rather than
the whole system of structures, was critical for spatially directed
attention.

VII. Autoradiographic Findings in Parietal Neglect

   Hemineglect occurs in patients far more frequently after parietal than
after frontal lesions (Friedland & Weinstein, 1977; Battersby et al., 1956;
Hécaen & Albert, 1978). Monkeys, too, have been shown to demonstrate
hemineglect after parietal lesions (Denny-Brown & Chambers, 1958). In order

to continue the search for an essential neural substrate of hemineglect, we carried out a third experiment. Using the procedures employed in experiments 1 and 2 we made unilateral posterior parietal lesions in a new group of animals. Figure 1B shows the intended parietal lesion, with removal of all of the dorsolateral portion of area 7 of Brodmann, and the adjacent anterior bank of the interparietal sulcus (area 5), and removal of tissue of both banks of the superior temporal sulcus. Partial maps of the lesions have been previously published (Deuel & Regan, 1985). Preoperative neurological examination in this group showed no consistent response asymmetry in bilateral simultaneous stimulus conditions. The median preoperative symmetry index was 102 (See Table 1). In the examination given 3 to 5 days postoperative, however, responses to bilateral simultaneous stimulation were strictly lateralized despite the fact that primary neurological functions were intact. The median symmetry index, constructed from the six tests that evaluated each side equally and allowed strict side-to-side comparison, was only 32 in the parietal operates.

Acute parietal animals showed marked decrements of 2-DG uptake in the nucleus Lateralis Posterior (nLP) and its borders with pulvinar oralis and medialis – D/I = 0.52 – and pulvinar (particularly the lateral subnucleus – D/I = 0.62 – with relative preservation of 2-DG uptake in the inferior subnucleus) of thalamus. There were also substantial decrements in the nucleus Ventralis Lateralis (nVL) – D/I = 0.80 – and the deeper layers of SC – D/I = 0.76. The nucleus Ventralis Posterior Lateralis (nPVL), the superficial layers of SC, the lateral geniculate (LG) and the striate cortex all were mildly to moderately affected as were the globus pallidus and the putamen, with damaged to intact ratios ranging from 0.85 to 0.90. A tendency toward decrement was noted in primary sensory cortex. Figure 3 shows a pseudocolored monochrome autoradiograph of UP6, a parietal animal sacrificed after 2-DG infusion under resting conditions, 5 days after the lesion. As this image of the mid-posterior thalamus shows, the regional deficits found in parietal autoradiograms were in lateral and posterior thalamus and differed strikingly from those in the frontal autoradiograms that showed a distinct anterior and medial emphasis (compare Figs. 2 and 3).

IIX. Autoradiographic Findings after Recovery from Parietal Neglect

A fourth experiment was performed in order to compare the regional distribution of 2-DG uptake in recovery after parietal lesions with the distribution during neglect. The same criteria for recovery in each individual animal were applied as in the frontal recovery experiment. After recovery from parietal lesions autoradiography demonstrated that 2-DG uptake deficits disappeared in all cortical and subcortical regions but nucleus Lateralis Posterior of the thalamus. The nLP of the recovered animals, that were sacrificed between 3 and 10 weeks postoperatively, did not demonstrate histological neuronal degeneration, at least to the unequivocal extent noted in nMD in frontal animals. None of the other structures that had shown 2-DG uptake deficits in the acute parietal animals demonstrated neuronal degeneration either.

From the parietal recovery experiment we drew the conclusion that posterior parietal cortex (Brodmann area 7) is not unconditionally essential to symmetrical orientation responses in the visual and somesthetic modalities, nor is a fully functioning nucleus Lateralis Posterior. It should be noted that for the 2-DG portions of these experiments, the brains of sham operated animals sacrificed after DG infusion in exactly the same manner as the animals with the lesions were used as controls. As can be seen from Fig. 4, ratios of side-to-side tissue

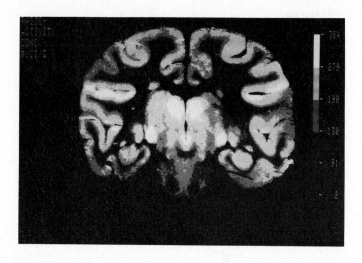

Figure 3
Autoradiograph of a section from a parietal animal (UP6) at approximate
stereotoxic level +4, sacrificed at 5 days after the lesion, showing
decreased isotope concentration in the lateral thalamus of the hemisphere
with the lesion. The picture was produced in the same way as Figure 2.

concentrations of (^{14}C) were always close to 100 in the control animals.

IX. Implications of Autoradiographic Findings for the Neural Basis of Hemineglect

The findings in the autoradiograms of parietal animals obviously
differ considerably from those in frontal animals. In general terms, the
parietal animals' 2-DG uptake was more deficient in posterior lateral
thalamus and striate cortex, while the frontal group displayed anterior and
medial thalamic deficits and marked caudate involvement. As affected
structures differ so widely in the two groups, it would be expected that the
quality of behavioral neglect in parietal operates would also differ
considerably from that in frontal operates. To determine, within the limits
of the examination given our animals, if this were the case, we compared the
results of 20 items examined in the immediate postoperative period between
frontal and parietal groups. Both groups of animals demonstrated a decrease
of responses to visual and somesthetic stimuli contralateral to the lesion,
and a preference for the hand ipsilateral to the lesion. As compared to the
preoperative findings this unilateral deficit was statistically
significant in both frontal and parietal groups. The symmetry indices that
we used as a means of assessing the severity of neglect (as explained in
detail above) were similar in the postoperative state in the two groups: 37
and 32, as can be seen from Table 1. They did not differ from each other on a
Mann-Whitney U test (U=28, Parietal N=9, Frontal N=8). Among the 6 items
used for the symmetry index, only the visual response asymmetry, as tested
on unilateral visual fields, was statistically significantly different.
The visual asymmetry was greater in the frontal than in the parietal group
(U=8.5, N=9,8).

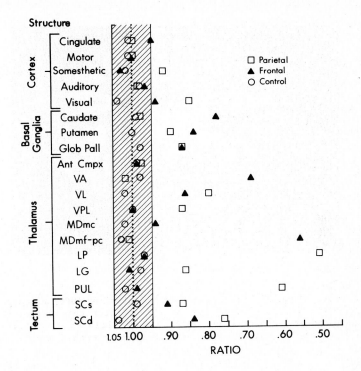

Figure 4

The diagram shows the extent of side to side differences in metabolic activity in acute neglect, expressed as the ratio of damaged to undamaged hemisphere isotope concentration in the structures named below. The values for each structure were derived by measuring isotope concentration (in microCurie per gramm of tissue) in as large a rectangular area as would fit into a structure. Coronal maps were prepared for each level and when structures appeared at multiple levels, values were averaged over the levels measured. For example, values for the right caudate, that appears less dense in both the frontal and parietal autoradiograms (Fig. 2 and 3) at level +4 averages to no deficit in parietals and considerable deficit in frontals when values from more anterior planes are considered. Autoradiograms from 4 acute frontal (shown by triangles), 4 acute parietal (shown by squares), and 4 sham operated animals (shown by circles) were used. Because of local tissue conditions some of the points were constructed from 3 values. Side to Side ratios in sham operated control animals all fell between 1.04 - 0.96, so this interval was shaded to demarcate a "normal" range.

The response asymmetries of the frontal and parietal groups, then, are similar in quality and quantity (except for response to unilateral visual stimuli) on the tasks presented. As far as these tasks are able to define hemispatial neglect, only one quantitative and no qualitative differences between "frontal neglect" and "parietal neglect" were found. Our data thus do not permit us to speak of separate neglect syndromes after the two lesions.

In the face of this finding, however, is the information from the 2-DG autoradiographic portion of the study: the structures involved in isotope concentration deficits differ widely between the two groups, as shown in Fig. 4. For frontals, the thalamic nuclei MDmf-pc, and VA were worst involved, but were not at all involved in the parietal group. For parietals, the thalamic nuclei LP and pulvinar were worst involved, but were not at all involved in the frontal group. Therefore, it seems that damage or dysfunction in nLP and pulvinar, nMD and nVA are not unconditionally required for neglect, although it is possible from these data that either pair must be dysfunctional, i.e., either Medialis Dorsalis mf-pc plus Ventralis Anterior must be dysfunctional, or Lateralis Posterior and pulvinar must be affected to result in neglect. Areas in the motor system where damage or dysfunction exist in both neglect groups include the nVL, globus pallidus and putamen. In the sensory system, the main convergence occurred in the deeper layers of the superior colliculus. If one wishes to think in representational terms then, one could say that orientation and spatially directed attention was represented by a four element network comprised of the deeper layers of the superior colliculus, the globus pallidus, the nVL and the putamen. The neural basis of neglect would then be damage or dysfunction in these four subcortical structures. The network hypothesis has recently been thoroughly discussed by Mesulam (1981), although these particular four structures are certainly not specifically discussed as the primary ones involved. In fact, it might be suggested that there are actually two networks - one centered in the di- and telencephalon, and including the putamen, GP and nVL, and the other centered in the deeper layers of the superior colliculus in the mesencephalon. On the basis of connectivity, it seems likely that they form parallel sensorimotor processing units rather than a single "in series" kind of network.

Another alternative, of course, is that neglect symptoms are due to, for instance, dysfunction in the deeper layers of the superior colliculus alone, or dysfunction in one of the other three structures. The deeper layers of the superior colliculus are perhaps the most attractive candidate for a single structure that controls laterally directed spatial orientation and attention, as in other species, this region of midbrain subserves both the sensory and motor aspects of orientation (Kirvel, Greenfield & Meyer, 1974; Meredith & Stein, 1983). While there is little evidence from monkey studies that multimodal neglect results from a unilateral colliculus lesion, neglect has not been systematically excluded by those studies either (Albano & Wurtz, 1982).

Despite our lack of behavioral evidence for separable "frontal" and "parietal" neglect, a third possibility is that response asymmetry is the sum product of the dysfunctions in all structures together for each lesion, i.e., the different structures that are dysfunctional in the two different preparations studied here form two different orientational attentional systems, the "parietal attentional system" and the "frontal attentional system". For that matter, if there are two separate neural substrates for this kind of attention, then one could just as well say that frontal neglect behavior is due to dysfunction in the nVA as it fulfills the criterion of being affected acutely and recovering when behavioral neglect occurs. Parietal neglect, on the same grounds, could be attributed to pulvinar dysfunction.

A fourth possibility is that the particular affected structures are less important to the production of neglect than the number of affected structures. Using this line of thinking, a sort of a mass action deficit could produce neglect. This notion could explain recovery as well in that as soon as any few structures of the originally affected group recover, behavioral recovery would also occur.

The findings we report here have obviously not solved the problem of the neural basis of hemispatial neglect. Only one finding is unambiguous, the finding that recovery of spatial attention and orientation abilities is possible in the face of absence of large amounts of contralateral frontal or parietal association cortex. The findings taken together do suggest that interactions among a group of subcortical structures is most likely required for symmetrical capabilities in orientation and spatially directed attention.

Our findings do not explain, nor do any current representation theories explain (Watson, Valenstein & Heilman, 1981; Rizzolatti, Gentilucci & Massimo, 1985), how in neglect responses may systematically vary from one test condition (unilateral stimulation) to the next (bilateral simultaneous stimulation). For explaining that particular facet of neglect, dynamic interactions among structures involved in producing a spatially directed movement of attention seems to be required. However, particularly in the case of the superior colliculus, our findings do suggest a possible mechanism. It is well known from the work of Sprague (1966) and Sprague & Meikle (1965) that the superior colliculi exert a mutually inhibitory influence upon each other's functioning. This mechanism, of an intact (both functionally and anatomically intact) structure inhibiting a functionally deficient (even though anatomically intact) structure on a moment to moment basis may underlie some of the surprising behavioral findings in neglect. Later Wurtz and Hikosaka (1983) demonstrated that simply by altering neurotransmitters directly in the superior colliculus, the laterality of saccades (and presumably laterally directed attention) can be markedly influenced. The hypothesis of interhemispheric interaction as described by Kinsbourne (Kinsbourne, 1970, 1973), could help explain it. In the stimulated animal there would be an increase in regional subcortical neural activity when a stimulus impinged only on structures contralateral to the damaged hemisphere, and then a marked decrease when a stimulus impinged upon structures that were contralateral to both the intact and the damaged hemisphere (the bilateral simultaneous stimulus condition), reasoned on the probability that the effects of processing in the intact hemisphere would lead to suppression of processing in structures of the vulnerable damaged hemisphere.

In summary, our studies of acute neglect (experiments 1 and 3) suggest that in the unoperated animal the neural substrate of orienting and laterally directed attention is quite extensive, involving several cortical and subcortical centers, and that after cortical damage dynamic interactions among intact and dysfunctional structures lead to neglect symptoms. Our studies of recovery (experiments 2 and 4) suggest in addition that frontal and parietal cortex need not be present bilaterally for normal orientation and spatially directed attention to occur, and that no strictly topographic representation theory is adequate to explain all behavioral neglect phenomena (Rizzolatti et al., 1985).

Many theories exist to explain the neglect syndrome. Of the many, the one that would most extensively explain both the well-known clinical facets, and in addition cover our recently obtained 2DG findings, is one that postulates dynamic interactions among task requirement and intact and damaged neural subsystems that lead to the behavioral responses we document. To further test this, a series of 2DG experiments are planned with acute neglect animals undergoing unilateral or bilateral simultaneous stimulation. If marked differences in neuronal activation (2DG uptake) are found between these two conditions, the dynamic interaction theory will be upheld.

Beyond the probable relevance of these data to hemineglect in human stroke patients, is the light they may shed upon the relationship of acute structural cerebral lesions to any neurological symptoms. We have demonstrated quite clearly that there is marked dysfunction of neural centers well out of the region of local tissue or vascular damage in both frontal and parietal animals sacrificed during the height of their neglect syndrome (Deuel & Collins, 1983, 1984). We postulate that the dysfunction occurs because of decreased synaptic excitation from cortex, consequent to its destruction. We further postulate, on the basis of the concomitant recovery of both the hemineglect syndrome and the structural dysfunction, that the symptoms are intimately related to the distant effects of the lesion. It would then seem reasonable that among the reasons for the puzzling variability of symptoms following anatomically similar strokes in humans is likely to be similar dysfunction of structurally intact well-perfused tissue distant from the lesion sites. Such dysfunction cannot be identified by structural assessments, such as computerized axial tomography, but could be evaluated by appropriate metabolic studies.

References

Albano, J.E. & Wurtz, R.H. Deficits in eye position following ablation of monkey superior colliculus, pretectum and posterior medial thalamus. Journal of Neurophysiology, 1982, 48, 318.

Battersby, W.S., Bender, M.B. & Pollack, M. Unilateral spatial agnosia (inattention) in patients with cerebral lesions. Brain, 1956, 79, 68.

Bianchi, L. The functions of the frontal lobes. Brain, 1895, 18, 497.

Bisiach, E., Luzatti, C. & Perani, D. Unilateral neglect, representational schema and consciousness. Brain, 1979, 102, 609.

Cambier, J., Graveleau, P. & Decroix, J. Le syndrome de l'artère choroidienne antérieure: Etude neuropsychologique de 4 cas. Revue Neurologique, 1983, 139, 553.

Collins, R. & Divac, I. Neostrial participation in prosencephalic systems: Evidence from deoxyglucose autoradiography. Advances in Neurology, 1983, 40, 117.

Collins, R., Kennedy, C., Sokoloff, L. & Plum, F. Metabolic anatomy of focal motor seizures. Archives of Neurology, 1976, 33, 536.

Critchley, M. The Parietal Lobes. London: Edward Arnold and Co, 1953.

Crowne, D., Yeo, C. & Russell, S. The effects of unilateral frontal eye field lesions in the monkey: Visual-motor guidance and avoidance behavior. Behavioral Brain Research, 1981, 2, 165.

Damasio, A., Damasio, H. & Chang Chi, H. Neglect following damage to frontal lobe or basal ganglia. Neuropsychologia, 1979, 18, 123.

Dauth, G., Gilman, S., Frey, K., Penney, J. & Agranoff, B. 14C-2-Deoxyglucose uptake in the monkeys with hypotonic hemiplegia after precentral cortical ablation. Neuroscience Abstracts, 1979, 5, 367.

Denny-Brown, D. & Banker, B. Amorphosynthesis from left parietal lesion.

Archives of Neurology and Psychiatry, 1954, 71, 302.

Denny-Brown, D. & Chambers, R. The parietal lobe and behavior. Chapter 3. In: The Brain and Human Behavior. Research Publications of the Association for Research in Nervous and Mental Diseases, 1958, 35-117.

Deuel, R.K. Determining sensory deficits in animals. In R.D. Myers (Ed.), Methods in Psychobiology III. Academic Press, 1977, pp. 99-125.

Deuel, R.K. Pathophysiology, Live. Pediatrics, 1982, 70, 650.

Deuel, R.K. & Collins, R.C. Recovery from unilateral neglect. Experimental Neurology, 1983, 81, 733.

Deuel, R.K. & Collins, R. Functional anatomy of frontal lobe neglect in the monkey: Behavioral and quantitative 2-deoxyglucose studies. Annals of Neurology, 1984, 15, 521.

Deuel, R.K. & Dunlop, N.A. Hand preference in the rhesus monkey: Implications for the study of cerebral dominance. Archives of Neurology, 1980, 37, 217.

Deuel, R. & Regan, D. Parietal hemineglect and motor deficits in the monkey. Neuropsychologia, 1985, 23, 305.

Ferro, J. & Kertesz, A. Posterior internal capsule infarction associated with neglect. Archives of Neurology, 1984, 41, 422.

Friedland, R.P. & Weinstein, E.A. Hemiattention and hemispheric specialization. Advances in Neurology, 1977, 18, 1.

Ginsberg, M., Reivich, M., Giandomenico, A. & Greenberg, J. Local glucose utilization in acute focal cerebral ischemia: Local dysmetabolism and diaschisis. Neurology, 1977, 27, 1042.

Halstead, W. Function of the frontal lobe in man: The dynamic visual field. Archives of Neurology and Psychiatry, 1943, 49, 633.

Hécaen, H. & Albert, H. Human Neuropsychology. New York: Wiley Interscience, 1978, pp. 415.

Heilman, K. & Valenstein, E. Auditory neglect in man. Archives of Neurology, 1972a, 26, 31.

Heilman, K. & Valenstein, E. Frontal lobe neglect in man. Neurology, 1972b, 22, 660.

Heilman, K. & Watson, R. Changes in the symptoms of neglect induced by changing task strategy. Archives of Neurology, 1978, 35, 47.

Heir, D., Mondlock, J. & Caplan, L. Behavioral abnormalities after right hemisphere stroke. Neurology, 1983, 33, 337.

Jackson, J.H. In J. Taylor (Ed.), Selected writings of John Hughlings Jackson. New York: Basic Books, 1958, pp. 171-173.

Jarvis, C.D., Mishkin, M., Shinohara, M., Sakurada, O., Miyaoka, M. & Kennedy, C. Mapping the primate visual system with the 14C-deoxyglucose technique. Neuroscience Abstracts, 1978, 4, 631.

Kennard, M.A. Alteration in response to visual stimuli following lesions of frontal lobe in monkeys. Archives of Neurology and Psyciatry (Chicago), 1939, 41, 1153.

Kennedy, C., Miyaoka, M., Suda, S., Macko, K., Javris, C., Mishkin, M. & Sokoloff, L. Local metabolic response in brain accompanying moor activity. Annals of Neurology, 1980, 8, 90.

Kennedy, C., Sakurada, O., Shinohara, M., Jehle, J. & Sokoloff, L. Local cerebral glucose utilization in the normal conscious macaque monkey. Annals of Neurology, 1978, 4, 293.

Kertesz, A. & Dobrowolski, S. Right hemisphere deficits, lesion size and location. Journal of Clinical Neuropsychology, 1981, 3, 283.

Kimura, D. Manual activity during speaking. I. Right handers. Neuropsychologia, 1973, 11, 45.

Kinsbourne, M. A model for the mechanism of unilateral neglect of space. Transactions of the American Neurological Association, 1970, 95, 143.

Kinsbourne, M. Eye and head turning indicate cerebral lateralization. Science, 1972, 179, 539.

Kinsbourne, M. Hemineglect and hemisphere rivalry. In E.A. Weinstein and E.L. Friedland (Eds.), Advances in Neurology. New York: Raven Press, 1973, pp. 41-52.

Kirvel, R., Greenfield, R. & Meyer, D. Multimodal sensory neglect in rats with radical unilateral posterior isocortical and superior collicular ablations. Journal of Comparative and Physiological Psychology, 1974, 87, 156.

Latto, R. & Cowey, A. Visual field defects after frontal eye-field lesions in monkeys. Brain Research, 1972, 30, 1.

Meredith, M. & Stein, B. Interactions among converging sensory inputs in the superior colliculus. Science, 1983, 221, 389.

Mesulam, M.M. A cortical network for directed attention and unilateral neglect. Annals of Neurology, 1981, 10, 309.

Olszewski, J. The Thalamus of Macaca Mulatta. Basel: Karger, 1952.

Petrides, M. & Iversen, S. Restricted posterior parietal lesions in the rhesus monkey and performance in visual spatial tasks. Brain Research, 1979, 161, 63.

Rapin, J., Lageron, A. & Poncin-Lafitte, M. Deoxyglucose uptake in pathological conditions. European Neurology, 1981, 20, 146.

Rizzolatti, G., Gentilucci, M. & Massimo, M. Selective spatial attention: one center, one circuit or many circuits. In M. Posner and O.S.M. Marin (Eds.), Attention and Performance XI. Hillsdale, N.J.: Erlbaum Assoc., 1985, pp. 251-264.

Schwartz, W., Sharp, G.M. & Evarts, E. Lesions of ascending dopaminergic pathways decrease forebrain glucose uptake. Nature, 1976, 261, 155.

Sprague, J. Interactions of the cortex and superior colliculus in visually guided behavior in the cat. Science, 1966, 153, 1544-1547.

Sprague, J. & Meikle, T. Role of the superior colliculus in visually guided behavior. Experimental Neurology, 1965, 11, 114-116.

Sokoloff, L., Reivich, M. & Kennedy, C. The 14C-deoxygloucose method for the measurement of local cerebral glucose utilization. Journal of Neurochemistry, 1977, 28, 897.

Stein, S. & Volpe, B. Classical "parietal" neglect syndrome after subcortical right frontal lobe infarction. Neurology, 1983, 33, 797.

Toga, A. et al. A neuroscience application of interactive image analysis. Optical Engineering, 1984, 23, 279.

Valenstein, E., Wallesch, C., Kornhuber, H., Kintz, T. & Brunner, R. Neuropsychological deficits associated with small unilateral thalamic lesions. Brain, 1983, 106, 141.

Warren, J. & Nonneman, A. Functional lateralization of the brain. Annals of the New York Academy of Sciences, 1976, 280, 732-734.

Watson, R., Valenstein, E. & Heilman, K. Thalamic neglect: possible role of the medial thalamus and nucleus reticularis thalami in behavior. Archives of Neurology, 1981, 38, 501.

Welsh, K. & Stuteville, P. Experimental production of unilateral neglect in monkeys. Brain, 1958, 81, 341.

Wurtz, R. & Hikosaka, O. Deficits in eye movements after injection of GABA related drugs in the monkey superior colliculus. Neuroscience Abstracts, 1983, 9, 750.

AUTHOR INDEX

Abrahams, V.C., 90
Acuna, C., 71, 129, 194, 218,
      268, 269, 277, 278,
      306
Adler, F.M., 93
Agranoff, B., 317
Ajax, E.T., 53, 216
Ajuriaguerra, J. de, 108, 216
Akert, K., 132
Alavi, A., 137
Albano, J.E., 274, 279, 290,
      330
Albert, M., 71, 137, 152, 153,
      216, 217, 220, 222,
      227, 235, 237, 250,
      253, 263, 316, 326
Allik, J., 92
Allport, D.A., 165
Altman, J.A., 72, 194
Andersen, R.A., 203
Anderson, R.A., 129
Andriola, M., 158
Angelergues, R., 216, 218
Angelo, J.N., 158
Anscombe, G.E.M., 263
Anton, G., 187, 196
Anzola, G., 119
Arbuthnott, G.W., 135
Arrigoni, G., 216
Ashton, R., 47
Assal, G., 59
Attneave, F., 60, 61
Aubert, 102
Avanzini, G., 266
Awaya, S., 93
Aymes, E.W., 73
Azuma, M., 131

Babinski, J., 69, 72, 185, 197
Bacharach, V.R., 160
Bach-Y-Rita, P.
Bainich, M., 121
Baker, R., 90

Baleydier, C., 9, 128, 132
Balonov, L.J., 72, 194
Banker, B.R., 72, 125
Barany, R., 71
Barbas, H., 9, 303
Barbut, 189
Bartlett, J.R., 127
Barton, L., 15, 121
Bashinski, H.S., 160
Basso, A., 15, 247
Bates, J.A.V., 11
Batini, C., 90
Battersby, W.S., 69, 125, 137, 152,
      216, 235, 237, 253, 315,
      316, 318, 326
Baxter, D.M., 189, 219
Baynes, K., 203, 262
Bear, D., 80
Beaumont, J.G., 72
Bell, Ch., 89
Belluza, T., 153
Belmont, I., 154
Bemporad, 73
Bender, M.B., 2, 69–71, 125, 126
      152, 194, 216, 235, 279
      299,315
Benson, B., 60, 61, 121
Benton, A.L., 117, 216, 228
Berardi, N., 90
Berkley, M.A., 211
Berlucchi, G., 26, 119, 296
Berlyne, D.E., 2, 307
Berrios, N., 290
Bertelson, P., 61
Berti, A., 2, 190, 195, 196, 250
      251, 304
Bertolini, G., 119
Bertrand, C., 184, 218, 242
Bianchi, L., 302, 318, 321
Bignall, K.E., 10, 132
Biguer, B., 97–101, 105
Binder, L.M. 225
Bingham, B.R., 78